Lecture Notes in Computer Science 12020

More information about this series at http://www.springer.com/series/7410

Zhe Liu · Moti Yung (Eds.)

Information Security and Cryptology

15th International Conference, Inscrypt 2019
Nanjing, China, December 6–8, 2019
Revised Selected Papers

 Springer

Editors
Zhe Liu
College of Computer Science
and Technology
Nanjing University of Aeronautics
and Astronautics
Nanjing, China

Moti Yung
Computer Science Department
Columbia University
New York, NY, USA

ISSN 0302-9743 ISSN 1611-3349 (electronic)
Lecture Notes in Computer Science
ISBN 978-3-030-42920-1 ISBN 978-3-030-42921-8 (eBook)
https://doi.org/10.1007/978-3-030-42921-8

LNCS Sublibrary: SL4 – Security and Cryptology

This Springer imprint is published by the registered company Springer Nature Switzerland AG
The registered company address is: Gewerbestrasse 11, 6330 Cham, Switzerland

Preface

The 15th International Conference on Information Security and Cryptology (Inscrypt 2019) was held during December 6–8, 2019, in Nanjing, China, with more than 250 attendees. Inscrypt is a well-recognized annual international forum for security researchers and cryptographers to exchange their ideas and present their research results, and is held every year in China. This volume contains all papers accepted by Inscrypt 2019. The program chairs also invited 6 distinguished researchers to deliver talks. The keynote speakers were Robert H. Deng from Singapore Management University, Singapore; Cetin Kaya Koc from University of California, Santa Barbara, USA; Marina Blanton from University at Buffalo (SUNY), USA; Willy Susilo from University of Wollongong, Australia; Joseph Liu from Monash University, Australia; and Pawel Szalachowski from Singapore University of Technology and Design, Singapore.

The conference received 95 submissions. Each submission was reviewed by at least three Program Committee (PC) members or external reviewers. The PC members accepted 24 full papers and 8 short papers to be included in the conference program. The PC members selected one best student paper and one best paper. The best student paper was "CAVAEva: An Engineering Platform for Evaluating Commercial Anti-Malware Applications on Smartphones" by Hao Jiang, Weizhi Meng, Chunhua Su, and Kim-Kwang Raymond Choo, and the best paper was "Invisible Poisoning: Highly Stealthy Targeted Poisoning Attack" by Jinyin Chen, Haibin Zheng, Mengmeng Su, Tianyu Du, Changting Lin, and Shouling Ji. The program chairs also invited one paper titled "Confidential Transactions in Blockchain" to be included in this volume. The proceedings therefore contain all 33 papers revised after the conference.

Inscrypt 2019 was held in cooperation with the International Association for Cryptologic Research (IACR), and was organized by the College of Computer Science and Technology, Nanjing University of Aeronautics and Astronautics, and the State Key Laboratory of Information Security (SKLOIS) of the Chinese Academy of Science. Inscrypt 2019 was co-organized by Jiangsu Software New Technology and Industrialization Collaborative Innovation Center, School of Computer Science/Software/Cyber Security, Nanjing University of Posts and Telecommunications.

Furthermore, we would like to thank all 362 authors who submitted their papers to Inscrypt 2019, and the conference attendees for their interest and support. We thank the PC members and external reviewers for their hard work in reviewing the submissions. We thank the Organizing Committee and all volunteers from Nanjing University of Aeronautics and Astronautics for their time and effort dedicated to arranging the conference. Finally, we thank the EasyChair system for making the entire process convenient.

December 2019

Zhe Liu
Moti Yung

Organization

Inscrypt 2019 was organized and sponsored by Nanjing University of Aeronautics and Astronautics and the State Key Laboratory of Information Security (SKLOIS) in cooperation with the International Association for Cryptologic Research (IACR).

Honorary Chairs

Zhiqiu Huang	Nanjing University of Aeronautics and Astronautics, China
Dongdai Lin	Chinese Academy of Sciences, China
Bing Chen	Nanjing University of Aeronautics and Astronautics, China
Sheng Zhong	Nanjing University, China

Technical Program Chairs

Zhe Liu	Nanjing University of Aeronautics and Astronautics, China
Moti Yung	Google and Columbia University, USA

Organizing Chairs

Liming Fang	Nanjing University of Aeronautics and Astronautics, China
Hao Han	Nanjing University of Aeronautics and Astronautics, China

Publicity Chairs

Debiao He	Wuhan University, China
Peng Xu	Huazhong University of Science and Technology, China
Jiangshan Yu	Monash University, Australia
Yushu Zhang	Nanjing University of Aeronautics and Astronautics, China

Publication Chair

Weizhi Meng	Technical University of Denmark, Denmark

Steering Committee

Feng Bao	Huawei International, Singapore
Kefei Chen	Hangzhou Normal University, China
Dawu Gu	Shanghai Jiao Tong University, China
Xinyi Huang	Fujian Normal University, China
Hui Li	Xidian University, China
Dongdai Lin	Chinese Academy of Sciences, China
Peng Liu	Pennsylvania State University, USA
Wenfeng Qi	National Digital Switching System Engineering and Technological Research Center, China
Willy Susilo	University of Wollongong, Australia
Meiqin Wang	Shandong University, China
Xiaofeng Wang	Indiana University at Bloomington, USA
Xiaoyun Wang	Tsinghua University, China
Jian Weng	Jinan University, China
Moti Yung	Snapchat Inc. and Columbia University, USA
Fangguo Zhang	Sun Yat-sen University, China
Huanguo Zhang	Wuhan University, China

Program Committee

Mauro Barni	University of Siena, Italy
Feng Bao	Huawei International, Singapore
Kai Chen	Chinese Academy of Sciences, China
Yu Chen	Chinese Academy of Sciences, China
Haibo Chen	Shanghai Jiao Tong University, China
Xiaofeng Chen	Xidian University, China
Kai Chen	Institute of Information Engineering, Chinese Academy of Sciences, China
Ting Chen	University of Electronic Science and Technology of China, China
Chang Choi	Chosun University, South Korea
Jérémie Decouchant	Grenoble University, France
Chunpeng Ge	Nanjing University of Aeronautics and Astronautics, China
Johann Großschädl	University of Luxembourg, Luxembourg
Dawu Gu	Shanghai Jiao Tong University, China
Jian Guo	Nanyang Technological University, Singapore
Feng Hao	University of Warwick, UK
Daojing He	East China Normal University, China
Xinyi Huang	Fujian Normal University, China
Shouling Ji	Zhejiang University, China
Yu Jiang	Tsinghua University, China
Howon Kim	Pusan National University, South Korea
Qi Li	Tsinghua University, China

Additional Reviewers

Veronica Becher
Biwen Chen
Hui Cui
Fei Chen
Chengyu Hu
Shen Hua
Sihuang Hu
Zhi Hu
Andrei Kelarev
Kassem Kallas
Mohammed Kaosar
Chao Lin
Fucai Luo
Guozhen Liu
Huimin Lao
Qiao Liu
Qinju Liu
Wenye Liu
Zengpeng Li
Guozhu Meng
Zhenhu Ning

Russell Paulet
Jing Pan
Alberto Pedrouzo-Ulloa
Jiangang Shu
Nasrin Sohrabi
Vladimir Soukharev
Aleksei Udovenko
Vesselin Velichkov
Dan Wang
Ge Wu
Haoyang Wang
Puwen Wei
Qizheng Wang
Shan Wang
Xuzi Wang
Yi Xie
Xuejing Yuan
Bowen Zhang
Fei Zhu
Yi Zhao
Yue Zhao

Contents

Side Channel Attacks

Identity-Based Cryptography

Signatures

Cryptanalysis

Authentication

Mathematical Foundations

Invited Paper

Revocable and Linkable Ring Signature

Xinyu Zhang, Joseph K. Liu$^{(\boxtimes)}$, Ron Steinfeld, Veronika Kuchta,
and Jiangshan Yu

Faculty of IT, Monash University, Melbourne, Australia
rayzhang.prc@gmail.com,
{Joseph.Liu,Ron.Steinfeld,Veronika.Kuchta,Jiangshan.Yu}@monash.edu

Abstract. In this paper, we construct a revocable and linkable ring signature (RLRS) scheme, which enables a revocation authority to revoke the anonymity of the real signer in linkable ring signature scheme under any circumstances. In other words, the revocability of RLRS is mandatory. The proposed RLRS scheme inherits the desired properties of group signature (anonymity revocation) and linkable ring signature (spontaneous group formation and linkability). In addition, we proved the security of our scheme in the random oracle model. We also provided a revocable ring confidential transaction protocol based on our RLRS scheme, which embedded the revocability in ring confidential transaction protocol.

Keywords: Ring signature · Ring confidential transaction ·
Revocability · Linkability

1 Introduction

1.1 Ring Signature and Variants

Ring Signature. Ring signature schemes (e.g., [1,6,13,28]) allow the user to sign a message on behalf of a spontaneous group in an anonymous way. Unlike group signature, ring signature scheme does not require the group manager to form the group or distribute keys to group members. In other words, the signer can build the group spontaneously (i.e., without the cooperation of other group members). Another special property of a ring signature scheme is *anonymity*. An honest signer can convince the verifier that the signature is signed by one of the group members, but the identity (i.e., public key) of the real signer remains to be hidden. According to different underlying public key systems, ring signature has enormous amount of different constructions, such as RSA based [28], discrete-logarithm based [13], mixture based [1], pairing based [6], and lattice based [8]. Ring signatures with different features are also proposed, such as forward security [15,22,24], threshold setting [20,23,30,35,36].

Linkable Ring Signature. The notion of linkable ring signature was first introduced in [19]. Linkable ring signature not only inherits the properties of ring

© Springer Nature Switzerland AG 2020
Z. Liu and M. Yung (Eds.): Inscrypt 2019, LNCS 12020, pp. 3–27, 2020.
https://doi.org/10.1007/978-3-030-42921-8_1

signature but also provides *linkability* for the verifier to verify if two signatures are generated by the same signer with respect to an event. *Linkability* is especially important for applications such as e-voting and e-cash. The motivation of [19] is that most of ring signature schemes achieved unconditional anonymity (e.g., [1,6,28]), which means the verifier has no way to determine if two signatures are signed using same private key. After the introduction of linkable ring signature, several schemes with different improvements were proposed (e.g., [2,4,11,12,18,21,31,32]). We summarise their contributions as follows:

- Constant size LRS: [2,31]
- LRS with unconditional anonymity: [18]
- LRS with traceability: [11,12]
- LRS with enhanced security: [21]
- Certificate-based LRS: [4]
- LRS with separability: [32]

Revocable (Traceable) Ring Signature. Another variant of ring signature is called traceable or revocable ring signature (e.g., [3,5,9,12,16,17,25]). The main objective of revocable (traceable) ring signature schemes is to provide a way to reduce the anonymity of ring signature. Revocable (traceable) ring signature is different from group signature since the signer still can form the group spontaneously. There are three categories of revocable (traceable) ring signature:

- Revocable Ring Signature (e.g., [17]): A set of pre-defined revocation authorities are able to open the anonymity of a ring signature at any time they want, [17] called this property a *Mandatory Revocability*.
- Traceable Ring Signature (e.g., [3,5,12]): The revocability (traceability) in traceable ring signature is not mandatory, that is, the signer's identity will be revealed universally if and only if he/she submits two signatures which are generated using the same private key based on an event.
- Convertible/Verifiable Ring Signature (e.g., [9,16,25]): The scheme is revocable if the signer wants to prove the ownership of a ring signature to the verifier. However, if the signer is reluctant to reveal his/her identity, the signature remains anonymous.

Nonetheless, ring signature schemes (and variants) we mentioned above do not provide the mandatory revocability as well as linkability. For example, traceable ring signature [12] can trace a signer only when the signer was double-signing. In other words, no one can determine the identity of an honest signer. In contrast, revocable ring signature [17] provides mandatory revocability, whereas the scheme cannot detect if two signatures are linked.

1.2   Ring Confidential Transaction

Monero, one of the largest cryptocurrencies, was introduced in 2014. Unlike Bit-Coin [26], Monero concentrates on protecting transaction privacy by applying ring signature techniques. Originally, Monero was based on CryptoNote protocol [33] which exploits properties of traceable ring signature [12] to enhance transaction anonymity as well as prevent the double-spending attack. Later in 2015, Noether [27] proposed *Ring Confidential Transaction* (Ring CT), which is based on linkable ring signature [19], to further advance the technique by solving several practical issues in CryptoNote. Specifically, Monero allows users to have multiple different accounts. Each account contains a "one-time" public key as account address and the coin. To authorise a transaction, the user has to use his/her corresponding private key. In order to construct an anonymous transaction, the user also needs to select several decoys (i.e., other users' account addresses) and generates a linkable ring signature.

Nevertheless, anonymity is not always good. According to the research [7], around US\$1.6 trillion was laundered in 2009. As claimed in [14], untraceability and lack of supervision of cryptocurrencies stimulate cyber-crimes like money laundering and terrorist financing. Authorities, such as FBI, found it is hard to "detect suspicious activities, identify users, and obtain the transaction" [10]. Therefore, it is critical to provide a method for the authority to supervise the transactions on blockchain, or at least, to revoke the anonymity of a suspicious spender.

1.3   Our Contributions

The contribution of the paper contains three parts:

- We present a ring signature scheme which achieves both **mandatory revocability** and **linkability**. Specifically, our scheme enables a revocation authority to revoke anonymity of a ring signature in any condition. Besides, our *Revocable and Linkable Ring Signature* (RLRS) scheme inherits the advantages of linkable ring signature schemes - an efficient way to prevent double-signing. We also construct a formal security proof of our RLRS scheme in random oracle model.
- The second contribution is that our scheme has more efficient revocation algorithm than [17] and [12]. The result shows that our scheme only needs one modular multiplication and one exponentiation in the revocation process while the computation time in [17] and [12] is linearly dependent on the group size. We present the comparison between our scheme and [12,17] in Sect. 6.
- The third contribution is that we extended our RLRS scheme to construct *Revocable Ring Confidential Transaction* protocol, which is presented in Appendix A.

Paper Organisation. The paper is organised in 6 parts, including the introduction. We compared our scheme with other revocable/traceable ring signature scheme and point out what are the advantages of our work in Sect. 2. Section 3 initialises the primitives of the scheme, which are utilised throughout the paper. In Sect. 4, we construct a security model and present our revocable and linkable ring signature protocol along with the security analysis of our scheme. Section 5 is an analysis of the efficiency of our scheme. The last section summarises our contributions and proposes several limitations which should be considered in future works.

2 Related Work

Revocable ring signature [17] was proposed in 2007, which shares similar idea with our construction. The scheme in [17] was based on bilinear pairing and proof-of-knowledge. The main advantage of [17] is that their protocol allows a set of revocation authorities to revoke anonymity of the real signer while our construction assumes the authority shares one public key. However, as we mentioned in the previous section, [17] did not introduce linkability to their scheme. The combination of mandatory revocability and linkability can especially benefit the construction of revocable e-cash systems (i.e., supervises users of the system as well as prevents double-spending). Another paper [34] applies revocable ring signature technique to build a bidder-anonymous English auction protocol. However, the scheme in [34] was similar to [17] except for that the revocation authority only has one public-private key pair, and the signer's public key is related to his/her identity in the initial phase.

Another type is called *Traceable ring signature* [12] which is comparable with *Revocable iff linked ring signature* [3,5]. Different from *Revocable ring signature* [17], a traceable ring signature scheme [12] does not enable mandatory signer revocation. Thus, only when the signer tries to generate multiple signatures with the same private key in one event (double-signing), his/her identity (i.e., public key) will be revealed. *Traceable ring signature* are closely related to linkable ring signature. Precisely, in [12], the linking tag in linkable ring signature schemes (e.g., [19,21]) is manipulated to trace the identity of the signer while the instantiation of zero-knowledge-proof in [12] is similar to [21]. We summarise the core function (i.e., signature signing) in [12] to two parts, the first part is to generate the linking tag which can be used to trace the signer, and the second part is based on (non-interactive) zero-knowledge-proof. Nonetheless, the construction in [12] was not very efficient since the signature size linearly depends on the group size. Therefore, in 2011, Fujisaki proposed [11] to enhance the security definition of [12] as well as reduce the signature size to $O(\sqrt{n})$.

The last type which is able to reduce the anonymity of ring signature is called *Convertible(Verifiable) Ring Signature* [9,16,25]. The convertible ring signature scheme [16] and verifiable ring signature scheme [25] achieve similar goals, that is, allow the signer to claim the ownership of the signature. However, if the signer refuses to do so, the signature is still anonymous. Their schemes are mostly based on RSA ring signature proposed in [28]. Nevertheless, as mentioned in [29], their original ring signature [28] is able to perform the function of verifiable ring signature, and they already described such a function in "Generalisations of Special Cases". Another deficiency is that the security model of verifiable and convertible ring signature is too simple. The researchers just explained the security model in [28], where they should build the security model based on their proposed scheme.

3 Preliminaries

3.1 Mathematical Assumptions

Definition 1 (Discrete Logarithm (DL) Assumption). *The Discrete Logarithm assumption in $\mathbb{G}$ is defined as follows: on input a tuple $(y, g) \in \mathbb{G}^2$ where $|\mathbb{G}| = q$ for some prime number q, outputs x such that $y = g^x \pmod{q}$. We say that $(t, \epsilon) - DL$ assumption holds in $\mathbb{G}$, if no t-time algorithm has advantage at lease ϵ in solving DL problem in $\mathbb{G}$.*

Definition 2 (Decisional Diffie-Hellman (DDH) Assumption). *The Decisional Diffie-Hellman Assumption in $\mathbb{G}$ is defined as follows: on input a quadruple $(g, g^a, g^b, g^c) \in \mathbb{G}^4$, where $|\mathbb{G}| = q$ for some prime number q, output 1 if $c = ab$. Otherwise 0. We say that $(t, \epsilon) - DDH$ assumption holds in $\mathbb{G}$, if no t-time algorithm has advantage at least ϵ over random guessing in solving DDH problem in $\mathbb{G}$.*

3.2 ElGamal Public Key Encryption

In our protocol, we apply ElGamal encryption scheme consisting of the following four algorithms:

1. $param \leftarrow \mathtt{Setup}(\lambda)$: On input a security parameter λ, returns public parameters $param = \{\mathbb{G}, q, g\}$, where $\mathbb{G}$ is a group with prime order q such that discrete logarithm is intractable, and g is the generator in $\mathbb{G}$.
2. $(sk, pk) \leftarrow \mathtt{KeyGen}(param)$: Takes the input $param = \{\mathbb{G}, q, g\}$, generates a pair of public key $(pk = y)$ and secret key $(sk = x)$ satisfying $y = g^x \pmod{q}$.
3. $c \leftarrow \mathtt{Encryption}(M, pk_r)$: On input a message M, and a receiver's public key $pk_r = y_r$, the sender randomly picks a number $k \in \mathbb{Z}_q$ and generates the first part of the ciphertext $c_1 = g^k \pmod{q}$. Then the signer takes y_r and generates the second part of the ciphertext $c_2 = y_r^k M \pmod{q}$. The final output of the algorithm is $c = \{c_1, c_2\}$.
4. $M \leftarrow \mathtt{Decryption}(c, sk_r)$: Takes the input $c = \{c_1, c_2\}$, and receiver's secret key $sk_r = x_r$, recovers the message by computing $M = c_2 \backslash c_1^{x_r} \pmod{q}$.

3.3 Signature of Knowledge

In our construction, we utilise Honest-Verifier Zero-Knowledge (HVZK) Proof of Knowledge Protocols (PoKs), which can be modified into a signature scheme by setting the challenge to a hash value of a commitment together with the message. The scheme is used in many (linkable) ring signature schemes such as [18, 19, 21]. A Signature of Knowledge (SoK) protocol contains following algorithms:

1. $param \leftarrow \mathtt{Setup}(\lambda)$: On input a security parameter λ, returns a public parameter $param$.
2. $\sigma \leftarrow \mathtt{Sign}(M, x, y)$: The algorithm takes a message M, a pair of (x, y), returns a SoK denoted as σ.
3. $0/1 \leftarrow \mathtt{Verify}(M, \sigma, y)$: On input a message M, a SoK σ, and a statement y, outputs $0/1$.

4 Revocable and Linkable Ring Signature

4.1 Technical Description

A revocable and linkable ring signature scheme (**RLRS**) is a tuple of six algorithms ($\texttt{Setup}, \texttt{KeyGen}, \texttt{Sign}, \texttt{Verify}, \texttt{Link}, \texttt{Revoke}$)

- $param \leftarrow \texttt{Setup}(\lambda)$ is a probabilistic polynomial time (PPT) algorithm which, on input a security parameter λ, outputs a set of public parameters $param$.
- $(sk_i, pk_i) \leftarrow \texttt{KeyGen}(param)$ is a PPT algorithm receives public parameters $param$ and returns a private/public key pair (sk_i, pk_i). We denote SK as the domain of possible private keys and PK as the domain of possible public keys.
- $\sigma \leftarrow \texttt{Sign}(event, n, \mathbb{Y}, sk, pk_{rev}, M)$ takes the input of an event description $event$, a group size n, a set $\mathbb{Y}$ contains n public keys $\{pk_1, \ldots, pk_n\}$ such that $pk_i \in PK$ for $i \in [1, n]$, a private key $sk \in SK$ which corresponds to one of the public keys in $\mathbb{Y}$, a public key of revocation authority $pk_{rev} \in PK$, and a message M, produces a signature σ.
- $accept/reject \leftarrow \texttt{Verify}(event, n, \mathbb{Y}, pk_{rev}, M, \sigma)$ accepts the input of an event description $event$, a group size n, a set $\mathbb{Y} = \{pk_1, \ldots, pk_n\}$ of n public keys, where $pk_i \in PK$ for $i \in [1, n]$, a revocation authority's public key $pk_{rev} \in PK$, and a message-signature pair (M, σ). If the message-signature pair is valid, the algorithm outputs $accept$. Otherwise, $reject$.
- $linked/unlinked \leftarrow \texttt{Link}(event, n_1, n_2, \mathbb{Y}_1, \mathbb{Y}_2, M_1, M_2, \sigma_1, \sigma_2)$ receives an event description $event$, two group sizes n_1 and n_2, two sets $\mathbb{Y}_1$ and $\mathbb{Y}_2$ of n_1 and n_2 public keys respectively, where all public keys in $\mathbb{Y}_1$ and $\mathbb{Y}_2$ are in PK, two valid message and signature pairs (M_1, σ_1) and (M_2, σ_2). The algorithm outputs $linked$ if two linking tags in σ_1 and σ_2 are the same. Otherwise $unlinked$.
- $pk \leftarrow \texttt{Revoke}(n, \mathbb{Y}, \sigma, sk_{rev})$ takes as input a group size n, a set of n public keys $\mathbb{Y} = \{pk_1, \ldots, pk_n\}$ such that $pk_i \in PK$ for $i \in [1, n]$, a valid signature σ, and revocation authority's secret key $sk_{rev} \in SK$ corresponding to pk_{rev}, returns a public key pk in $\mathbb{Y}$.

Correctness: A RLRS scheme should satisfy:

- *Verification Correctness*: A signature generated by an honest signer should be identified as a valid signature with overwhelming probability.
- *Linking Correctness*: If two signatures are determined as "linked", then they must have been signed using the same private key with respect to the same event description.
- *Revocation Correctness*: An honest signer's public key will be revealed by the revocation authority with overwhelming probability.

4.2 Security Definitions

Security of RLRS has five aspects, including unforgeability, anonymity, linkability, non-slanderability, and revocability. We define three oracles, which simulate abilities of the adversary:

1. *Joining Oracle* ($\mathcal{JO}$): on request, adds a new user to the system, then returns the public key $pk \in PK$ of the new user.
2. *Corruption Oracle* ($\mathcal{CO}$): on input a public key $pk_i \in PK$, returns the corresponding $sk_i \in SK$.
3. *Signing Oracle* ($\mathcal{SO}$): takes the input of an event description *event*, a group size n, a set $\mathbb{Y} = \{pk_1, \ldots, pk_n\}$ that contains n public keys, a signer's public key $pk_\pi \in \mathbb{Y}$, a revocation authority's public key $pk_{rev} \in PK$, and a message M, returns a valid signature denoted as $\sigma \leftarrow \texttt{Sign}(e, n, \mathbb{Y}, sk_\pi, pk_{rev}, M)$. Note that $\mathcal{SO}$ may query $\mathcal{CO}$ during its operation.

Unforgeability: The unforgeability game is defined between a simulator $\mathcal{S}$ and an adversary $\mathcal{A}$ with access to $\mathcal{JO}, \mathcal{CO}, \mathcal{SO}$:

a. $\mathcal{A}$ runs the $\texttt{Setup}$ algorithm on a security parameter λ and outputs *param*.
b. $\mathcal{A}$ can query $\mathcal{JO}, \mathcal{CO}, \mathcal{SO}$ adaptively.
c. $\mathcal{A}$ gives $\mathcal{S}$ an event description *event*, a group size n, a set $\mathbb{Y} = \{pk_1, \ldots, pk_n\}$ of n public keys, where $pk_i \in PK$ for $i \in [1, n]$, a message M, a revocation authority's public key $pk_{rev} \in PK$, and a signature σ.

$\mathcal{A}$ wins the game if:

1. $\texttt{Verify}(event, n, \mathbb{Y}, pk_{rev}, M, \sigma) = accept$;
2. all public keys in $\mathbb{Y}$ are query outputs of $\mathcal{JO}$;
3. no public keys in $\mathbb{Y}$ have been queried to $\mathcal{CO}$; and
4. σ is not a query output of $\mathcal{SO}$.

We denote by

$$\mathbf{Adv}_{\mathcal{A}}^{Unf}(\lambda) = Pr[\mathcal{A} \text{ wins the game}]$$

the success probability of adversary $\mathcal{A}$ in winning the unforgeability game.

Definition 3 (Unforgeability). *A RLRS scheme is existential unforgeable against adaptive chosen message and chosen public key attack if for all PPT adversary $\mathcal{A}$, $\mathbf{Adv}_{\mathcal{A}}^{Unf}(\lambda)$ is negligible.*

Anonymity: any verifier should not have a non-negligible probability greater than $1/n$ of correctly guessing the signer's identity in a valid ring signature when none of the ring members is known. Moreover, any party who has revocation authority's secret key can break anonymity due to the mandatory revocability of our scheme. Therefore, RLRS scheme is computationally anonymous if revocation authority has not been compromised. The anonymity game is defined between a simulator $\mathcal{S}$ and an adversary $\mathcal{A}$ who is given access to $\mathcal{JO}$:

a. $\mathcal{A}$ runs the Setup algorithm on a security parameter λ and outputs $param$.
b. $\mathcal{A}$ can make query to $\mathcal{JO}$ adaptively.
c. $\mathcal{A}$ gives $\mathcal{S}$ an event description $event$, a group size n, a set $\mathbb{Y}$ of n public keys such that all public keys in $\mathbb{Y}$ are generated by $\mathcal{JO}$, a revocation authority's public key $pk_{rev} \in PK$, a message M. $\mathcal{S}$ parses $\mathbb{Y}$ as $\{pk_1, \ldots, pk_n\}$ and randomly picks $\pi \in \{1, \ldots, n\}$. $\mathcal{S}$ computes a "Challenge Signature" σ_π using sk_π, where sk_π is a corresponding private key of pk_π. σ_π is given to $\mathcal{A}$.
d. $\mathcal{A}$ guesses $\pi' \in \{1, \ldots, n\}$.

We denote by

$$\mathbf{Adv}_{\mathcal{A}}^{Anon}(\lambda) = |Pr[\pi' = \pi] - \frac{1}{n}|$$

the success probability of adversary $\mathcal{A}$ in winning the anonymity game.

Definition 4 (Anonymity). *A RLRS scheme is computationally anonymous if for any adversary $\mathcal{A}$, $\mathbf{Adv}_{\mathcal{A}}^{Anon}(\lambda)$ is negligible.*

Linkability: linkability is a mandatory property of RLRS scheme, which means that the signer cannot generate two signatures using the same private key such that they are determined to be *unlinked* by Link algorithm. We adopt the linkability game defined by Liu et al. [19] to capture the scenario, where an adversary tries to generate two RLRS signatures (σ_1, σ_2) using the same private key yet $\mathrm{Link}(\cdot, \sigma_1, \sigma_2)$ algorithm outputs *unlinked*. Actually, if RLRS scheme is unforgeable, then the unlinked signatures can only be generated by different private keys with respect to the same event. The linkability game between a simulator $\mathcal{S}$ and an adversary $\mathcal{A}$ who is given access to $\mathcal{JO}, \mathcal{CO}, \mathcal{SO}$, is defined as follows:

a. $\mathcal{A}$ runs the Setup algorithm on a security parameter λ and outputs $param$.
b. $\mathcal{A}$ can query $\mathcal{JO}, \mathcal{CO}, \mathcal{SO}$ adaptively.
c. $\mathcal{A}$ gives $\mathcal{S}$ an event description $event$, two group size n_1, n_2 with assumption of $n_1 \leq n_2$ without loss of generality, two set $\mathbb{Y}_1, \mathbb{Y}_2$ with n_1, n_2 public keys respectively, two message-signature pairs $(M_1, \sigma_1), (M_2, \sigma_2)$, and a revocation authority's public key pk_{rev}.

$\mathcal{A}$ wins the game if:

1. All public keys in $\mathbb{Y}_1 \cup \mathbb{Y}_2$ are outputs of $\mathcal{JO}$;
2. $\mathrm{Verify}(event, n_i, \mathbb{Y}_i, pk_{rev}, M_i, \sigma_i) = accept$ for $i = 1, 2$ such that σ_i is not the output of $\mathcal{SO}$;
3. $\mathcal{CO}$ has been queried less than 2 times, that is, $\mathcal{A}$ can only have at most one user private key; and
4. $\mathrm{Link}(\cdot, \sigma_1, \sigma_2) = unlinked$.

We denote by

$$\mathbf{Adv}_{\mathcal{A}}^{Link}(\lambda) = Pr[\mathcal{A} \text{ wins the game}]$$

the success probability of adversary $\mathcal{A}$ in winning the linkability game.

Definition 5 (Linkability). *A RLRS is linkable if for all PPT adversary $\mathcal{A}$,* $\mathbf{Adv}_{\mathcal{A}}^{Link}(\lambda)$ *is negligible.*

Non-slanderability: the attacker should be unable to accuse an honest user for generating a signature which is determined to be *linked* with a malicious signature generated by attacker. The non-slanderability game is defined between a simulator $\mathcal{S}$ and an adversary $\mathcal{A}$ who is given access to $\mathcal{JO}, \mathcal{CO}, \mathcal{SO}$:

a. $\mathcal{A}$ runs the Setup algorithm on a security parameter λ and outputs *param*.
b. $\mathcal{A}$ can query $\mathcal{JO}, \mathcal{CO}, \mathcal{SO}$ adaptively.
c. $\mathcal{A}$ gives $\mathcal{S}$ an event description *event*, a group size n, a set $\mathbb{Y}$ of n public keys, a message m, a revocation authority's public key pk_{rev}, and a public key of an insider $pk_\pi \in \mathbb{Y}$ such that pk_π has not been queried to $\mathcal{CO}$ or has not been included as the insider public key of any query to $\mathcal{SO}$. $\mathcal{S}$ uses sk_π corresponding to pk_π to run $\mathtt{Sign}(event, n, \mathbb{Y}, sk_\pi, pk_{rev}, M)$ and produces σ to $\mathcal{A}$.
d. $\mathcal{A}$ queries oracles with arbitrary interleaving. Particularly, $\mathcal{A}$ can make query to $\mathcal{CO}$ of any public key except for pk_π.
e. $\mathcal{A}$ delivers group size n^*, $\mathbb{Y}^*$ with n^* public keys, a message M^*, a revocation authority's public key pk_{rev}, and a signature $\sigma^* \neq \sigma$.

$\mathcal{A}$ wins the game if

1. $\mathtt{Verify}(event, n^*, \mathbb{Y}^*, pk_{rev}, M^*, \sigma^*) = accept$;
2. σ^* is not an output of $\mathcal{SO}$;
3. All public keys in $\mathbb{Y}^*, \mathbb{Y}$ are query outputs of $\mathcal{JO}$;
4. pk_π has not been queried to $\mathcal{CO}$; and
5. $\mathtt{Link}(\sigma^*, \sigma) = linked$.

We denote by
$$\mathbf{Adv}_{\mathcal{A}}^{NS}(\lambda) = Pr[\mathcal{A} \text{ wins the game}]$$
the success probability of adversary $\mathcal{A}$ in winning the non-slanderability game.

Definition 6 (Non-slanderability). *A RLRS scheme is non-slanderable if for all PPT adversary $\mathcal{A}$,* $\mathbf{Adv}_{\mathcal{A}}^{NS}$ *is negligible.*

Revocability: revocability in RLRS scheme is compulsory, that is, the probability of a signer generates a signature without his/her identity gets revealed by revocation authority should be negligible. We define revocability game between a simulator $\mathcal{S}$ and an adversary $\mathcal{A}$ who is given access to $\mathcal{JO}, \mathcal{CO}, \mathcal{SO}$:

a. $\mathcal{A}$ runs the Setup algorithm on a security parameter λ and outputs *param*.
b. $\mathcal{A}$ can query $\mathcal{JO}, \mathcal{CO}, \mathcal{SO}$ adaptively.
c. $\mathcal{A}$ can only obtain at most one private key of ring member from $\mathcal{CO}$.
d. $\mathcal{A}$ gives $\mathcal{S}$ an event description *event*, a group size n, a set $\mathbb{Y}$ contains n public keys, a message M, a revocation authority's public key pk_{rev}, and a signature σ.

$\mathcal{A}$ wins the game if

1. $\text{Verify}(event, n, \mathbb{Y}, M, \sigma) = accept$;
2. all public keys in $\mathbb{Y}$ are query outputs of $\mathcal{JO}$;
3. σ is not an output of $\mathcal{SO}$;
4. $\mathcal{CO}$ has been queried less than two times ($\mathcal{A}$ can only obtain at most one private key denotes as x_π); and
5. $y_j = \text{Revoke }(n, \mathbb{Y}, \sigma, sk_{rev})$ where $j \neq \pi$.

We denote by
$$\mathbf{Adv}_{\mathcal{A}}^{Rev}(\lambda) = Pr[\mathcal{A} \text{ wins the game}]$$
the success probability of adversary $\mathcal{A}$ in winning the revocability game.

Definition 7 (Revocability). *A RLRS scheme is revocable if for any PPT adversary $\mathcal{A}$, $\mathbf{Adv}_{\mathcal{A}}^{Rev}(\lambda)$ is negligible.*

4.3   Scheme Description

$\text{Setup}(\lambda)$: Let $\mathbb{G}$ be a group with prime order q such that the underlying discrete logarithm problem is intractable, and g is the generator of $\mathbb{G}$. Define two hash functions: $H_1 : \{0,1\}^* \rightarrow \mathbb{Z}_q$ and $H_2 : \{0,1\}^* \rightarrow \mathbb{G}$. The public parameters are $param = \{\mathbb{G}, g, q, H_1, H_2\}$.

$\text{KeyGen}(param)$: Assume there are n users. User i, where $i \in [1, n]$, randomly chooses $x_i \in \mathbb{Z}_q$ and computes $y_i \leftarrow g^{x_i} \pmod{q}$. User i has secret key and public key pair $\{sk_i, pk_i\}$ such that $sk_i = x_i$ and $pk_i = y_i$.

$\text{Sign}(event, n, \mathbb{Y}, sk_\pi, pk_{rev}, M)$: Takes as input $(event, n, \mathbb{Y}, sk_\pi, pk_{rev}, M)$, where $event$ is the description of the event, n is the number of users in the ring, $\mathbb{Y} = \{pk_1, pk_2, \ldots, pk_n\}$ is a set of public keys of users in the ring, $sk_\pi = x_\pi$ is the secret key of user π and the corresponding public key is $pk_\pi = y_\pi$, note that $pk_\pi \in \mathbb{Y}$ with $\pi \in [1, n]$, $pk_{rev} = \tilde{y}$ is the public key of the revocation authority, and M is the message to be signed. Assume that the secret key $sk_{rev} = \tilde{x}$ of the authority and the corresponding public key $\tilde{y}$ are generated by KeyGen. User π with the knowledge of x_π computes a signature of knowledge as follows:

1. Compute the linking tag L by committing to x_π:
   (a) $h \leftarrow H_2(event)$,
   (b) $L \leftarrow h^{x_\pi}$.
2. Randomly pick $u \in \mathbb{Z}_q$, and compute the ciphertext by using ElGamal Encryption:
   (a) $C_1 \leftarrow g^u$,
   (b) $C_2 \leftarrow \tilde{y}^u y_\pi$,
   (c) $C \leftarrow \{C_1, C_2\}$.
3. Randomly pick $t_1, t_2 \in \mathbb{Z}_q$ and compute the following commitments:
   (a) $a_{1,\pi} \leftarrow g^{t_1}$ and $a_{2,\pi} \leftarrow \tilde{y}^{t_1}$,
   (b) $S'_{\pi+1} \leftarrow H_1(event, \mathbb{Y}, L, M, a_{1,\pi}, a_{2,\pi})$,
   (c) $\bar{a}_{1,\pi} \leftarrow g^{t_2}$ and $\bar{a}_{2,\pi} \leftarrow h^{t_2}$,

(d) $S''_{\pi+1} \leftarrow H_1(event, \mathbb{Y}, L, M, \bar{a}_{1,\pi}, \bar{a}_{2,\pi})$.

4. For $i = \pi + 1, \ldots, n, 1, \ldots, \pi - 1$, randomly pick $r_{1,i}, r_{2,i} \in \mathbb{Z}_q$, and compute:

   (a) $a_{1,i} \leftarrow g^{r_{1,i}} C_1^{S'_i}$ and $a_{2,i} \leftarrow \tilde{y}^{r_{1,i}} (\frac{C_2}{y_i})^{S'_i}$,

   (b) $S'_{i+1} \leftarrow H_1(event, \mathbb{Y}, L, M, a_{1,i}, a_{2,i})$,

   (c) $\bar{a}_{1,i} \leftarrow g^{r_{2,i}} y_i^{S''_i}$ and $\bar{a}_{2,i} \leftarrow h^{r_{2,i}} L^{S''_i}$,

   (d) $S''_{i+1} \leftarrow H_1(event, \mathbb{Y}, L, M, \bar{a}_{1,i}, \bar{a}_{2,i})$.

5. Compute $r_{1,\pi} \leftarrow t_1 u - S'_\pi u \pmod{q}$ and $r_{2,\pi} \leftarrow t_2 - S''_\pi x_\pi \pmod{q}$.

6. The signature is $\sigma = (S'_1, S''_1, r_{1,1}, \ldots, r_{1,n}, r_{2,1}, \ldots, r_{2,n}, L, C)$.

Verify$(event, n, \mathbb{Y}, pk_{rev}, M, \sigma)$: On input an event description $event$, a group $\mathbb{Y}$ of n public keys, a revocation authority's public key $pk_{rev} = \tilde{y}$, a message M, and a signature σ, verify the signature as follows:

1. On input σ, parse the ciphertext $C = \{C_1, C_2\}$.

2. For $i = 1, \ldots, n$, compute:

   (a) $Z'_{1,i} \leftarrow g^{r_{1,i}} C_1^{S'_i}$ and $Z'_{2,i} \leftarrow \tilde{y}^{r_{1,i}} (\frac{C_2}{y_i})^{S'_i}$,

   (b) $S'_{i+1} \leftarrow H_1(event, \mathbb{Y}, L, M, Z'_{1,i}, Z'_{2,i})$ if $i \neq n$,

   (c) $Z''_{1,i} \leftarrow g^{r_{2,i}} y_i^{S''_i}$ and $Z''_{2,i} \leftarrow h^{r_{2,i}} L^{S''_i}$,

   (d) $S''_{i+1} \leftarrow H_1(event, \mathbb{Y}, L, m, Z''_{1,i}, Z''_{2,i})$ if $i \neq n$.

3. Check

   (a) $S'_1 \overset{?}{=} H_1(event, \mathbb{Y}, L, m, Z'_{1,n}, Z'_{2,n})$,

   (b) $S''_1 \overset{?}{=} H_1(event, \mathbb{Y}, L, m, Z''_{1,n}, Z''_{2,n})$.

Link$(event, n_1, n_2, \mathbb{Y}_1, \mathbb{Y}_2, M_1, M_2, \sigma_1, \sigma_2)$: On input an event description $event$, two groups $\mathbb{Y}_1, \mathbb{Y}_2$ with group sizes n_1, n_2 respectively, and two valid message-signature pairs (M_1, σ_1), where $\sigma_1 = (\cdot, L_1)$; (M_2, σ_2), where $\sigma_2 = (\cdot, L_2)$, output $linked$ if $L_1 = L_2$. Otherwise, $reject$.

Revoke$(n, \mathbb{Y}, \sigma, sk_{rev})$: On input$(n, \mathbb{Y}, \sigma, sk_{rev})$, where n is the group size of ring group $\mathbb{Y}$, σ is the signature generated, $sk_{rev} = \tilde{x}$ is authority's secret key corresponds to $pk_{rev} = \tilde{y}$. The revocation authority first check whether the signature is valid. If yes, continue. Otherwise, abort. To revoke the anonymity of the real signer, the revocation authority computes as follows:

1. $C = \{C_1, C_2\}$.

2. $\exists y_\pi \in \mathbb{Y}(\pi \in [1, n])$ such that $y_\pi = C_2 \backslash C_1^{\tilde{x}}$.

y_π is the public key of the real signer.

4.4 Correctness Analysis

Verification Correctness. From the construction of revocable and linkable ring signature, we start with $S'_{\pi+1}, S''_{\pi+1}$, where π denotes the real signer's index such that $\pi \in [1, n]$ without loss of generality:

$$S'_{\pi+1} = H_1(event, \mathbb{Y}, L, m, g^{t_1}, (\tfrac{C_2}{y_\pi})^{t_1})$$
$$S'_{\pi+2} = H_1(event, \mathbb{Y}, L, m, g^{r_{1,\pi+1}} C_1^{S'_{\pi+1}}, \tilde{y}^{r_{1,\pi+1}} (\tfrac{C_2}{y_{\pi+1}})^{S'_{\pi+1}})$$

$$\vdots$$

$$S'_n = H_1(event, \mathbb{Y}, L, m, g^{r_{1,n-1}} C_1^{S'_{n-1}}, \tilde{y}^{r_{1,n-1}} (\tfrac{C_2}{y_{n-1}})^{S'_{n-1}})$$
$$S'_1 = H_1(event, \mathbb{Y}, L, m, g^{r_{1,n}} C_1^{S'_n}, \tilde{y}^{r_{1,n}} (\tfrac{C_2}{y_n})^{S'_n})$$
$$S'_2 = H_1(event, \mathbb{Y}, L, m, g^{r_{1,1}} C_1^{S'_1}, \tilde{y}^{r_{1,1}} (\tfrac{C_2}{y_1})^{S'_1})$$

$$\vdots$$

$$S'_{\pi-1} = H_1(event, \mathbb{Y}, L, m, g^{r_{1,\pi-2}} C_1^{S'_{\pi-2}}, \tilde{y}^{r_{1,\pi-2}} (\tfrac{C_2}{y_{\pi-2}})^{S'_{\pi-2}})$$

With the same sequence, we also start from computing $S''_{\pi+1}$ until $S''_{\pi-1}$.

$$S''_{\pi+1} = H_1(event, \mathbb{Y}, L, m, g^{t_2}, h^{t_2})$$
$$S''_{\pi+2} = H_1(event, \mathbb{Y}, L, m, g^{r_{2,\pi+1}} y_{\pi+1}^{S''_{\pi+1}}, h^{r_{2,\pi+1}} L^{S''_{\pi+1}})$$

$$\vdots$$

$$S''_n = H_1(event, \mathbb{Y}, L, m, g^{r_{2,n-1}} y_{n-1}^{S''_{n-1}}, h^{r_{2,n-1}} L^{S''_{n-1}})$$
$$S''_1 = H_1(event, \mathbb{Y}, L, m, g^{r_{2,n}} y_n^{S''_n}, h^{r_{2,n}} L^{S''_n})$$
$$S''_2 = H_1(event, \mathbb{Y}, L, m, g^{r_{2,1}} y_1^{S''_1}, h^{r_{2,1}} L^{S''_1})$$

$$\vdots$$

$$S''_{\pi-1} = H_1(event, \mathbb{Y}, L, m, g^{r_{2,\pi-2}} y_{\pi-2}^{S''_{\pi-2}}, h^{r_{2,\pi-2}} L^{S''_{\pi-2}})$$

For the verification, the verifier can simulate the process with the starting point S'_2 and S''_2, since S'_1 and S''_1 is given in the signature.

$$S'_2 = H_1(event, \mathbb{Y}, L, m, g^{r_{1,1}} C_1^{S'_1}, \tilde{y}^{r_{1,1}} (\tfrac{C_2}{y_1})^{S'_1})$$

$$\vdots$$

$$S'_\pi = H_1(event, \mathbb{Y}, L, m, g^{r_{1,\pi-1}} C_1^{S'_{\pi-1}}, \tilde{y}^{r_{1,\pi-1}} (\tfrac{C_2}{y_{\pi-1}})^{S'_{\pi-1}})$$
$$S'_{\pi+1} = H_1(event, \mathbb{Y}, L, m, g^{r_{1,\pi}} C_1^{S'_\pi}, \tilde{y}^{r_{1,\pi}} (\tfrac{C_2}{y_\pi})^{S'_\pi})$$
$$S'_{\pi+2} = H_1(event, \mathbb{Y}, L, m, g^{r_{1,\pi+1}} C_1^{S'_{\pi+1}}, \tilde{y}^{r_{1,\pi+1}} (\tfrac{C_2}{y_{\pi+1}})^{S'_{\pi+1}})$$

$$\vdots$$

$$S'_n = H_1(event, \mathbb{Y}, L, m, g^{r_{1,n-1}} C_1^{S'_{n-1}}, \tilde{y}^{r_{1,n-1}} (\tfrac{C_2}{y_{n-1}})^{S'_{n-1}})$$

We verify $S_1' \stackrel{?}{=} \bar{S}_1' = H_1(event, \mathbb{Y}, L, m, g^{r_{1,n}} C_1^{S_n'}, \tilde{y}^{r_{1,n}} (\frac{C_2}{y_n})^{S_n'})$.
Note that the verification of $S_{\pi+1}'$ holds because:

$$g^{r_{1,\pi}} C_1^{S_\pi'} = g^{t_1 - S_\pi' u} \cdot C_1^{S_\pi'} = g^{t_1 - S_\pi' u} \cdot g^{u S_\pi'} = g^{t_1}$$
$$\tilde{y}^{r_{1,\pi}} (\frac{C_2}{y_\pi})^{S_\pi'} = \tilde{y}^{t_1 - S_\pi' u} (\frac{\tilde{y}^u y_\pi}{y_\pi})^{S_\pi'} = \tilde{y}^{t_1 - S_\pi' u} \cdot \tilde{y}^{u S_\pi'} = \tilde{y}^{t_1}$$

Again, we start with verifying S_2'' in the same order.

$$S_2'' = H_1(event, \mathbb{Y}, L, m, g^{r_{2,1}} y_1^{S_1''}, h^{r_{2,1}} L^{S_1''})$$

$$\vdots$$

$$S_\pi'' = H_1(event, \mathbb{Y}, L, m, g^{r_{2,\pi-1}} y_{\pi-1}^{S_{\pi-1}''}, h^{r_{2,\pi-1}} L^{S_{\pi-1}''})$$
$$S_{\pi+1}'' = H_1(event, \mathbb{Y}, L, m, g^{r_{2,\pi}} y_\pi^{S_\pi''}, h^{r_{2,\pi}} L^{S_\pi''})$$
$$S_{\pi+2}'' = H_1(event, \mathbb{Y}, L, m, g^{r_{2,\pi+1}} y_{\pi+1}^{S_{\pi+1}''}, h^{r_{2,\pi+1}} L^{S_{\pi+1}''})$$

$$\vdots$$

$$S_n'' = H_1(event, \mathbb{Y}, L, m, g^{r_{2,n-1}} y_{n-1}^{S_{n-1}''}, h^{r_{2,n-1}} L^{S_{n-1}''})$$

We verify $S_1'' \stackrel{?}{=} \bar{S}_1'' = H_1(event, \mathbb{Y}, L, m, g^{r_{2,n}} y_n^{S_n''}, h^{r_{2,n}} L^{S_n''})$.
Similar to the verification of $S_{\pi+1}'$, we verify $S_{\pi+1}''$ by:

$$g^{r_{2,\pi}} y_\pi^{S_\pi''} = g^{t_2 - S_\pi'' x_\pi} \cdot g^{x_\pi S_\pi''} = g^{t_2}$$
$$h^{r_{2,\pi}} L^{S_\pi''} = h^{t_2 - S_\pi'' x_\pi} \cdot h^{x_\pi S_\pi''} = h^{t_2}$$

Linking Correctness. Linking correctness is guaranteed if the signer computes the linking tag as follows:

$$h = H_2(event) \text{ and } L = h^x.$$

Therefore, for the same event, the user can only compute the linking tag once.

Revoking Correctness. If the signer follows the protocol, the revocation can successfully recover signer's public with its secret by decrypting the cipher text in the following way:

$$y_\pi = \frac{C_2}{C_1^{\tilde{x}}},$$

where $\tilde{x}$ is revocation authority's private key and y_π is the real signer's public key.

4.5   Security Analysis

Theorem 1 (Existential Unforgeability).   *RLRS scheme is existential unforgeable in the random oracle model if DLP is hard.*

Proof. The simulator $\mathcal{S}$ simulates the oracles as follows:

- *Random Oracle H_1*: $\mathcal{S}$ randomly picks $\alpha \in \mathbb{Z}_q$ and returns the value which has not been assigned.
- *Random Oracle H_2*: $\mathcal{S}$ randomly picks $k \in \mathbb{Z}_q$ and returns g^k.
- *Joining Oracle $\mathcal{JO}$*: Assume $\mathcal{A}$ can query $\mathcal{JO}$ at most n' times, where $n' \geq n$. $\mathcal{S}$ randomly chooses a subset $\mathcal{I}_n$ which contains n indexes. We assign these n indexes with $1, \ldots, n$, note that $\mathcal{S}$ dose not know any secret key corresponding to public keys with index 1 to n. We denote $n' - n$ indexes as $n + 1, \ldots, n'$, and $\mathcal{S}$ generates the public/private key pairs according to the algorithm for these $n' - n$ indexes. On the ith query, $\mathcal{S}$ returns the corresponding public key.
- *Corruption Oracle $\mathcal{CO}$*: For query input the public key pk which is an output of $\mathcal{JO}$, $\mathcal{S}$ first checks if it is corresponding to the subset $\mathcal{I}_n$. If yes, $\mathcal{S}$ halts. Otherwise, $\mathcal{S}$ returns the corresponding private key.
- *Signing Oracle $\mathcal{SO}$*: On input a signing query with an event description *event*, a group size n, a public key set $\mathbb{Y} = \{y_1, \ldots, y_n\}$, a signer's public key pk_π, where $\pi \in [1, n]$, a revocation authority's public key pk_{rev}, and a message M, $\mathcal{S}$ simulates as follows:
  - If the query of $H(event)$ has not been made, $\mathcal{S}$ queries H_2 on *event* and sets $h = H_2(event)$. Note that $\mathcal{S}$ knows k of h to the base g such that $h = g^k$.
  - If y_π is not corresponding to any element in $\mathcal{I}_n$, $\mathcal{S}$ knows the private key and computes the signature according to the algorithm. Otherwise, we let y_π be the πth index from $\mathcal{JO}$. $\mathcal{S}$ sets the linking tag $L = y_\pi^k$.
  - $\mathcal{S}$ randomly pick $u \in \mathbb{Z}_q$ and compute cipher text $C_1 = g^u$, $C_2 = \tilde{y}^u y_\pi$, and $C = \{C_1, C_2\}$, where $\tilde{y}$ is the revocation authority's public key and y_π is signer's public key.
  - $\mathcal{S}$ randomly chooses $S'_{\pi'}$ and $S''_{\pi'} \in \mathbb{Z}_q$, For $i = \pi', \ldots, n, 1, \ldots, \pi' - 1$, randomly picks $r_{1,i}, r_{2,i} \in \mathbb{Z}_q$ and computes:

$$S'_{i+1} = H_1(event, \mathbb{Y}, L, M, g^{r_1, i} C_1^{S'_i}, \tilde{y}^{r_1, i} (\tfrac{C_2}{y_i})^{S'_i}),$$
$$S''_{i+1} = H_1(event, \mathbb{Y}, L, M, g^{r_2, i} y_i^{S''_i}, h^{r_2, i} L^{S''_i}).$$

  $\mathcal{S}$ sets the oracle outcome:

$$H_1(event, \mathbb{Y}, L, M, g^{r_1, \pi-1} C_1^{S'_{\pi-1}}, \tilde{y}^{r_1, i} (\tfrac{C_2}{y_{\pi-1}})^{S'_{\pi-1}}) = S'_\pi,$$
$$H_1(event, \mathbb{Y}, L, M, g^{r_2, \pi-1} y_i^{S''_{\pi-1}}, h^{r_2, \pi-1} L^{S''_{\pi-1}}) = S''_\pi.$$

  If collision occurs, repeat this step.
  - $\mathcal{S}$ returns the signature $\sigma = (S'_1, S''_1, r_{1,1}, \ldots, r_{1,n}, r_{2,1}, \ldots, r_{2,n}, L, C)$. $\mathcal{A}$ cannot distinguish between $\mathcal{S}$'s simulation from REAL scenario.

For one successful simulation, suppose $\mathcal{A}$ forged

$$\sigma^{(1)} = (S_1^{(1)\prime}, S_1^{(1)\prime\prime}, r_{1,1}^{(1)}, \ldots, r_{1,n}^{(1)}, r_{2,1}^{(1)}, \ldots, r_{2,n}^{(1)}, L^{(1)}, C^{(1)})$$

on an *event*, and a set $\mathbb{Y}^{(1)}$ of $n^{(1)}$ public keys such that it is a subset of public keys corresponding to the indexes in $\mathcal{I}_n$. We let $n^{(1)} = n$ without loss of generality. By the assumption of random oracle model, $\mathcal{A}$ queries $H_2(event)$ which is denoted as h and queries $H_1(event, \mathbb{Y}^{(1)}, L, M, a_{1,i}, a_{2,i})$, $H_1(event, \mathbb{Y}^{(1)}, L, M, \bar{a}_{1,i}, \bar{a}_{2,i})$ for $i \in \{1, n\}$ where

$$a_{1,i} = g^{r^{(1)}_{1,i}} C_1^{S^{(1)\prime}_i} \text{ and } a_{2,i} = \tilde{y}^{r^{(1)}_{1,i}} (\frac{C_2}{y_i})^{S^{(1)\prime}_i},$$
$$\bar{a}_{1,i} = g^{r^{(1)}_{2,i}} y_i^{S^{(1)\prime\prime}_i} \text{ and } \bar{a}_{2,i} = h^{r^{(1)}_{2,i}} L^{S^{(1)\prime\prime}_i}.$$

Suppose $\mathcal{A}$ forges the signature after kth query to the oracles and $\mathcal{S}$ returns $S_1^{(1)\prime}$ and $S_1^{(1)\prime\prime}$. In the rewind simulation, suppose $\mathcal{S}$ first invokes $\mathcal{A}$ to get its output and its Turing Transcript $\mathcal{T}$. Then $\mathcal{S}$ rewinds $\mathcal{T}$ to get $\mathcal{T}'$ while $\mathcal{S}$ consistently answers kth query. That is, kth query is common in transcript $\mathcal{T}$ and $\mathcal{T}'$, denoted as:

$$H_1(event, \mathbb{Y}^{(1)}, L, M, a_{1,\pi}, a_{2,\pi}),$$
$$H_1(event, \mathbb{Y}^{(1)}, L, M, \bar{a}_{1,\pi}, \bar{a}_{2,\pi}).$$

$\mathcal{S}$ knows the value of $a_{1,\pi}, a_{2,\pi}, \bar{a}_{1,\pi}, \bar{a}_{2,\pi}$ at the time of the rewind. After $\mathcal{A}$ returns its output from the rewind simulation, $\mathcal{S}$ can solve the discrete logarithm problem of pk_π and $\tilde{y}$ in $\mathbb{Y}^{(1)}$ by computing following steps:

$$g^{r^{(1)}_{1,\pi}} C_1^{S^{(1)\prime}_\pi} = g^{r^{(2)}_{1,\pi}} C_1^{S^{(2)\prime}_\pi}$$
$$\tilde{y}^{r^{(1)}_{1,\pi}} (\frac{C_2}{y_\pi})^{S^{(1)\prime}_\pi} = \tilde{y}^{r^{(2)}_{1,\pi}} (\frac{C_2}{y_\pi})^{S^{(2)\prime}_\pi}$$
$$g^{r^{(1)}_{2,\pi}} y_\pi^{S^{(1)\prime\prime}_\pi} = g^{r^{(2)}_{2,\pi}} y_\pi^{S^{(2)\prime\prime}_\pi}$$
$$h^{r^{(1)}_{2,\pi}} L^{S^{(1)\prime\prime}_\pi} = h^{r^{(2)}_{2,\pi}} L^{S^{(2)\prime\prime}_\pi}$$

That is

$$g^{r^{(1)}_{1,\pi}} g^{u S^{(1)\prime}_\pi} = g^{r^{(2)}_{1,\pi}} g^{u S^{(2)\prime}_\pi} \tag{1}$$

$$g^{\tilde{x} r^{(1)}_{1,\pi}} g^{\tilde{x} u S^{(1)\prime}_\pi} = g^{\tilde{x} r^{(2)}_{1,\pi}} g^{\tilde{x} u S^{(2)\prime}_\pi} \tag{2}$$

$$g^{r^{(1)}_{2,\pi}} g^{x_\pi S^{(1)\prime\prime}_\pi} = g^{r^{(2)}_{2,\pi}} g^{x_\pi S^{(2)\prime\prime}_\pi} \tag{3}$$

$$h^{r^{(1)}_{2,\pi}} h^{x_\pi S^{(1)\prime\prime}_\pi} = h^{r^{(2)}_{2,\pi}} h^{x_\pi S^{(2)\prime\prime}_\pi} \tag{4}$$

From Eq. (1), $\mathcal{S}$ derives $u = \frac{r^{(2)}_{1,\pi} - r^{(1)}_{1,\pi}}{S^{(1)\prime}_\pi - S^{(2)\prime}_\pi}$. Since $\mathcal{S}$ knows u, $\mathcal{S}$ can now derive $\tilde{x} = \frac{q-1}{r^{(1)}_{1,\pi} - r^{(2)}_{1,\pi} + u(S^{(1)\prime}_\pi - S^{(2)\prime}_\pi)}$. From Eqs. (3) and (4), $\mathcal{S}$ can derive $x_\pi = \frac{r^{(2)}_{2,\pi} - r^{(1)}_{2,\pi}}{S^{(1)\prime\prime}_\pi - S^{(2)\prime\prime}_\pi}$. $\mathcal{S}$ solves DLP, contradiction occurs. According to the forking lemma, the successful rewind simulation is at least $\epsilon/4$, where ϵ is the probability that $\mathcal{A}$ successfully forges a signature. Therefore, the successful chance of $\mathcal{S}$ breaks DLP is at least $\epsilon/4$. $\qquad\square$

Before we prove the anonymity of RLRS scheme, we provide a different definition of Decisional Diffie-Hellman (DDH) Assumption, which is used to derive the contradiction:

Definition 8 (A Different Decisional Diffie-Hellman (DDH) Assumption). *We define a different DDH assumption in $\mathbb{G}$ as follows: on input uniformly random $(l_0, l_1, l_2, l'_0, l'_1, l'_2) \in \mathbb{G}^6$, where the order of $|\mathbb{G}| = q$ for some prime number q. We set $\alpha_0 = g^{l_0}, \beta_0 = g^{l_1}, \gamma_0 = g^{l_2}, \alpha_1 = g^{l'_0}, \beta_1 = g^{l'_1}, \gamma_1 = g^{l'_0 l'_1}$. Any PPT adversary $\mathcal{A}$ takes a guess of $b \leftarrow \{0,1\}; (\alpha, \beta, \gamma) = (\alpha_b, \beta_b, \gamma_b)$. We say that $\Pr[(\alpha, \beta, \gamma) = b] = \frac{1}{2} + \frac{1}{Q_2(\lambda)}$ where Q_2 is some polynomial and λ is the security parameter.*

Theorem 2 (Anonymity). *RLRS scheme is computational anonymity in the random oracle model if DDHP (Definition 8) is hard.*

Proof. For each $\mathcal{JO}$ query, a DL instance $y = g^x$ is returned for some randomly generated value x. Assume $\mathcal{A}$ can query $\mathcal{JO}$ at most n' times where $n' \geq n$. The challenge signature is created using the randomly picked public key in $\mathbb{Y}$. We assume $H_2(\mathbb{Y}) = \beta$. Since β is randomly generated, H_2 remains random. In order to simulate the process, $\mathcal{S}$ generates a challenge signature σ_π with signer $\pi \in [1, n]$, where π is randomly picked by $\mathcal{S}$ on the request from $\mathcal{A}$:

- $\mathcal{S}$ randomly picks $u \in \mathbb{Z}_q$ and computes ciphertext $C_1 = g^u$, $C_2 = \tilde{y}^u y_\pi$, and $C = \{C_1, C_2\}$, where $\tilde{y}$ is the revocation authority's public key.
- $\mathcal{S}$ sets $y_\pi = \alpha$ and then randomly picks $t_1, t_2 \in \mathbb{Z}_q^*$. $\mathcal{S}$ computes $\tilde{S}'_\pi = g^{t_1}$ and $\tilde{S}''_\pi = g^{t_2}$.
- For $i = \pi, \ldots, n, 1, \ldots, \pi - 1$, $\mathcal{S}$ randomly picks $r_{1,i}, r_{2,i} \in \mathbb{Z}_q$ and computes:

$$S'_{i+1} = H_1(event, \mathbb{Y}, \gamma, M, g^{r_{1,i}} C_1^{S'_i}, \tilde{y}^{r_{1,i}} (\tfrac{C_2}{y_i})^{S'_i})$$
$$S''_{i+1} = H_1(event, \mathbb{Y}, \gamma, M, g^{r_{2,i}} y_i^{S''_i}, h^{r_{2,i}} \gamma^{S''_i})$$

- $\mathcal{S}$ sets the oracle outcome

$$H_1(event, \mathbb{Y}, \gamma, M, g^{r_{1,\pi-1}} C_1^{S'_{\pi-1}}, \tilde{y}^{r_{1,\pi-1}} (\tfrac{C_2}{y_{\pi-1}})^{S'_{\pi-1}}) = S'_\pi$$
$$H_1(event, \mathbb{Y}, \gamma, M, g^{r_{2,\pi-1}} y_i^{S''_{\pi-1}}, h^{r_{2,\pi-1}} \gamma^{S''_{\pi-1}}) = S''_\pi$$

- $\sigma_\pi = (S'_1, S''_1, r_{1,1}, \ldots, r_{1,n}, r_{2,1}, \ldots, r_{2,n}, \gamma, C)$

$\mathcal{S}$ outputs σ_π to $\mathcal{A}$. $\mathcal{A}$ can query H_1, H_2 adaptively. Note that $H_2(\mathbb{Y}) = \beta$ and the output of

$$H_1(event, \mathbb{Y}, \gamma, M, g^{r_{1,i}} C_1^{S'_i}, \tilde{y}^{r_{1,i}} (\tfrac{C_2}{y_i})^{S'_i})$$
$$H_1(event, \mathbb{Y}, \gamma, M, g^{r_{2,i}} y_i^{S''_i}, h^{r_{2,i}} \gamma^{S''_i})$$

for $i \in \{1, \ldots, n\}$ are predetermined since $\mathcal{S}$ has queried these values.

Suppose $\mathcal{A}$ guesses the signer's index is $j \in [1, n]$ and returns j to $\mathcal{S}$. By convention, $\mathcal{A}$ returns 0 if it cannot identify a signer. $\mathcal{S}$ returns 1 if $j = \pi$; returns 0 if $j = 0$; and returns $1/0$ with equal probability otherwise. Then

$$
\begin{aligned}
&\Pr[\mathcal{S}(\alpha, \beta, \gamma) = b | b = 1] \\
&= \Pr[\mathcal{S}(\alpha, \beta, \gamma) = b | b = 1, \mathcal{A}(\sigma_\pi) = \pi] \\
&+ \Pr[\mathcal{S}(\alpha, \beta, \gamma) = b | b = 1, \mathcal{A}(\sigma_\pi) \neq \pi, \neq 0] \\
&\geq 1 \cdot (\frac{1}{n} + \frac{1}{Q(\lambda)}) + \frac{1}{2}(1 - \frac{1}{n} - \frac{1}{Q(\lambda)}) \\
&\geq \frac{1}{2} + \frac{1}{2n} + \frac{1}{2Q(\lambda)}
\end{aligned}
$$

If $b = 0$, then all signers has equal probability to sign the signature from $\mathcal{A}$'s perspectives. Thus, $\mathcal{A}$ can do no better than random guessing.

$$
\begin{aligned}
&\Pr[\mathcal{S}(\alpha, \beta, \gamma) = b | b = 0] \\
&= \Pr[\mathcal{S}(\alpha, \beta, \gamma) = b | b = 0, \mathcal{A}(\sigma_\pi) = \pi] \\
&+ \Pr[\mathcal{S}(\alpha, \beta, \gamma) = b | b = 0, \mathcal{A}(\sigma_\pi) \neq \pi] \\
&\geq 0 \cdot \frac{1}{n} + \frac{1}{2}(1 - \frac{1}{n})
\end{aligned}
$$

Combining two probabilities, we have

$$
\begin{aligned}
&\Pr[\mathcal{S}(\alpha, \beta, \gamma) = b] \\
&\geq \frac{1}{2}(\Pr[\mathcal{S}(\alpha, \beta, \gamma) = b | b = 1] \\
&+ \Pr[\mathcal{S}(\alpha, \beta, \gamma) = b | b = 0]) \\
&= \frac{1}{2} + \frac{1}{4Q(\lambda)}
\end{aligned}
$$

Therefore, $\mathcal{S}$ solves DDHP with probability non-negligibly than $\frac{1}{2}$. Contradiction occurs. □

Theorem 3 (Linkability). *RLRS scheme is linkable in the random oracle model, if DLP is hard.*

Proof. In order to prove linkability of our RLRS scheme, we use the same oracle setting as the proof in Theorem 1 except we allow $\mathcal{S}$ to have at most one private key, say sk_π corresponding to two different public keys in ring group $\mathbb{Y}_i$ for $i = \{1, 2\}$. This private key is given to $\mathcal{A}$ during the query to the $\mathcal{CO}$, which is the only private key that $\mathcal{A}$ is allowed to have.

Suppose $\mathcal{A}$ produces two valid signature

$$
\begin{aligned}
\sigma^{(1)} &= (S_1^{(1)\prime}, S_1^{(1)\prime\prime}, r_{1,1}^{(1)}, \ldots, r_{1,n_1}^{(1)}, r_{2,1}^{(1)}, \ldots, r_{2,n_1}^{(1)}, L^{(1)}, C^{(1)}) \\
\sigma^{(2)} &= (S_1^{(2)\prime}, S_1^{(2)\prime\prime}, r_{1,1}^{(2)}, \ldots, r_{1,n_2}^{(2)}, r_{2,1}^{(2)}, \ldots, r_{2,n_2}^{(2)}, L^{(2)}, C^{(2)})
\end{aligned}
$$

where $L^{(1)} = H_2(event)^{x_\pi}$ and $L^{(2)} = H_2(event)^{x'_\pi}$ denote two linking tags of two signatures respectively. Note that the event description $event$ is fixed during both runs. For $\sigma^{(1)}$, S rewinds the tape with a different value for H_1 to obtain another valid signature $\bar{\sigma}^{(1)}$. We can derive

$$x_\pi = \frac{\bar{r}_{2,\pi}^{(1)} - r_{2,\pi}^{(1)}}{S_\pi^{(1)''} - \bar{S}_\pi^{(1)''}}$$

where $L^{(1)} = h^{x_\pi}$ and $y_\pi = g^{x_\pi}$.

For the second rewind simulation for $\sigma^{(2)}$, S obtains with non-negligible probability of $\bar{\sigma}^{(2)}$. The similar derivation shows that

$$x'_\pi = \frac{\bar{r}_{2,\pi}^{(2)} - r_{2,\pi}^{(2)}}{S_\pi^{(2)''} - \bar{S}_\pi^{(2)''}}.$$

Therefore, $x_\pi = x'_\pi$ and $L^{(1)} = L^{(2)}$. Two signatures $(\sigma^{(1)}, \sigma^{(2)})$ are linked. S can break DLP if the rewind simulation is successful.   □

Theorem 4 (Non-Slanderability). *RLRS scheme is non-slanderable in the random oracle model, if DLP is hard.*

Proof. The adversary $\mathcal{A}$ can query $\mathcal{CO}$ on any public key in $\mathbb{Y}$ except for signer's public key pk_π. $\mathcal{A}$ gives simulator S pk_π, an event description $event$, a message M, a set $\mathbb{Y}$ of n public keys, and a revocation authority's public key pk_{rev}, S generates a valid signature $\sigma = (\cdot, L)$ where L is the linking tag computed using sk_π. $\mathcal{A}$ can keep querying oracles with the restriction of submitting pk_π to $\mathcal{CO}$. Suppose $\mathcal{A}$ generates another valid signature $\sigma^* = (\cdot, L^*)$ which is not an output of $\mathcal{SO}$, and σ^* is linked to $\sigma = (\cdot, L)$. Therefore, $L^* = L$, which means:

$$L' = H_2(event)^{x_\pi^*} = L = H_2(event)^{x_\pi}$$

That is, $x_\pi = x_\pi^*$ which implies $\mathcal{A}$ knows the secret key sk_π corresponding to pk_π. This contradicts with the assumption that $\mathcal{A}$ cannot submit a query to $\mathcal{CO}$ to get the secret key of pk_π.   □

Theorem 5 (Revocability). *RLRS scheme is revocable in the random oracle model if the construction is unforgeable.*

Proof. We use the same setting as the proof in Theorem 1 but the adversary $\mathcal{A}$ is able to get one private key denoted as $sk_\pi = x_\pi$ corresponding to $pk_\pi = y_\pi$ in $\mathbb{Y}$ from $\mathcal{CO}$. Since $\{pk_1, \ldots, pk_{\pi-1}, pk_{\pi+1}, \ldots, pk_n\}$ are $n-1$ discrete logarithm instances generated from fresh coin flips, $\mathcal{A}$ cannot find the corresponding secret keys under our assumption. For contradiction, suppose $\mathcal{A}$ successfully generates one valid signature:

$$\sigma = (S_1', S_1'', r_{1,1}, \ldots, r_{1,n}, r_{2,1}, \ldots, r_{2,n}, L, C),$$

where $C = \{C_1, C_2\}$ and $C_1 = g^u, C_2 = \tilde{y}^u y_j$ for some randomly picked $u \in \mathbb{Z}_q$, and $\tilde{y}$ is revocation authority's public key. Since RLRS scheme is unforgeable, a valid signature is strictly generated by $sk_\pi = x_\pi$. There are two cases to break revocability of RLRS scheme:

- Case 1:
  1. $\mathcal{A}$ randomly picks $t_1, t_2 \in \mathbb{Z}_q$ and computes:
     (a) $S'_{j+1} = H_1(event, \mathbb{Y}, L, M, g^{t_1}, \tilde{y}^{t_1})$,
     (b) $S''_{j+1} = H_1(event, \mathbb{Y}, L, M, g^{t_2}, h^{t_2})$.
  2. For $i = j+1, \ldots, n, 1, \ldots, j-1$, $\mathcal{A}$ randomly picks $r_{1,i}, r_{2,i} \in \mathbb{Z}_q$ and computes:
     (a) $S'_{i+1} = H_1(event, \mathbb{Y}, L, M, g^{r_{1,i}} C_i^{S'_i}, \tilde{y}^{r_{1,i}} (\frac{C_2}{y_i})^{S'_i})$,
     (b) $S''_{i+1} = H_1(event, \mathbb{Y}, L, M, g^{r_{2,i}} y_i^{S''_i}, h^{r_{2,i}} L^{S''_i})$.

  Therefore, in order to close the ring, $\mathcal{A}$ has to know the secret key $x_j \neq x_\pi$ which contradicts with our assumption of $\mathcal{A}$ can only know one private key of ring member.

- Case 2:
  1. $\mathcal{A}$ randomly picks $t_1, t_2 \in \mathbb{Z}_q$ and computes:
     (a) $S'_{\pi+1} = H_1(event, \mathbb{Y}, L, M, g^{t_1}, \tilde{y}^{t_1})$,
     (b) $S''_{\pi+1} = H_1(event, \mathbb{Y}, L, M, g^{t_2}, h^{t_2})$.
  2. For $i = \pi+1, \ldots, n, 1, \ldots, \pi-1$, randomly picks $r_{1,i}, r_{2,i} \in \mathbb{Z}_q$ and computes:
     (a) $S'_{i+1} = H_1(event, \mathbb{Y}, L, M, g^{r_{1,i}} C_1^{S'_i}, \tilde{y}^{r_{1,i}} (\frac{C_2}{y_i})^{S'_i})$,
     (b) $S''_{i+1} = H_1(event, \mathbb{Y}, L, M, g^{r_{2,i}} y_i^{S''_i}, h^{r_{2,i}} L^{S''_i})$.
  3. $\mathcal{A}$ computes $r_{1,\pi} = t_1 - S'_\pi u$ and $r_{2_\pi} = t_2 - S''_\pi x_\pi$ to close the ring.

  However, The construction of σ will not pass the verification since an honest verifier will follow the protocol and computes as follows:

  $$S'_{\pi+1} = H_1(event, \mathbb{Y}, L, M, g^{r_{1,\pi}} C_1^{S'_\pi}, \tilde{y}^{r_{1,\pi}} (\frac{C_2}{y_\pi}) S'_\pi)$$
  $$\neq H_1(event, \mathbb{Y}, L, M, g^{t_1}, \tilde{y}^{t_1})$$

  This contradicts with our assumption that the signature σ is a valid signature.

The revocability of RLRS scheme is proved.   □

5   Efficiency Analysis

This section compares the efficiency (i.e., computational cost and signature size) between our proposed scheme and *Revocable Ring Signature* [17] and *Traceable Ring Signature* [12]. We start by addressing some computational notions as follows:

- T_{exp}: The time for one exponentiation computation
- T_{mul}: The time for one modular multiplication computation
- T_{add}: The time for one modular addition computation
- T_{pair}: The time for one pairing computation
- T_h: The time for executing the one-way hash function
- n: The number of public keys in the ring
- ℓ: The number of revocation authority's public key

- λ: The length of the elements in $\mathbb{Z}_q$

From the comparison (Table 1), we can see that our scheme is a lot efficient in revocation phase than [17] and [12]. Since [17] allows a group of authorities to revoke the anonymity of the signer, the signature size also depends on the amount of authority's public keys. Besides, our RLRS scheme highly depends on the computational time of hash functions which could be faster than bilinear pairing functions in practice. Another contribution of our scheme is that we introduce the first ring signature scheme which enables mandatory revocability and linkability.

Table 1. Comparison between RLRS and [17] and [12]

Scheme	Sign	Verify	Revoke	Signature size	Mandatory revocability	Linkability
[17]	$2\ell T_{pair} + T_h + (2n+2)T_{mul} + (n+2)T_{add}$	$\ell T_{pair} + T_h + (2n+\ell)T_{mul} + (\ell n + 2n)T_{add} + \ell T_{exp}$	T_{pair}(best case) nT_{pair}(worst case)	$(\ell + 2n + 2)\lambda$	✓	✗
[12]	$3T_h + (5n+1)T_{exp} + (3n-2)T_{mul} + (n+1)T_{add}$	$3T_h + 3nT_{mul} + 5nT_{exp} + nT_{add}$	$4T_h + 2nT_{mul} + 2nT_{exp}$	$(2n+1)\lambda$	✗	✓
RLRS	$(2n+1)T_h + (8n-1)T_{exp} + (5n-1)T_{mul} + 2T_{add}$	$8nT_{exp} + 5nT_{mul} + 2nT_h$	$T_{mul} + T_{exp}$	$(2n+5)\lambda$	✓	✓

6 Conclusion

In this paper, we extended [21] to construct a revocable and linkable ring signature (RLRS) scheme, which is the first ring signature scheme achieves mandatory revocability and linkability. In addition, our scheme is more efficient than [17] and [12] in terms of revocation time. We also provided a formal security proof of RLRS in random oracle model. In Appendix A, we further applied our RLRS scheme to design a revocable ring confidential transaction protocol.

There are several problems in our scheme that can be solved in future works such as:

1. Considering how to reduce signature size of RLRS scheme;
2. Considering how to construct a RLRS scheme with unconditional anonymity;
3. Providing a concrete security proof of *Revocable Ring Confidential Transaction*.

Appendix A. Revocable Ring Confidential Transaction

In Appendix A, we present a revocable ring confidential transaction protocol based on our RLRS scheme.

Setup(λ): Let $\mathbb{G}$ be a group of prime order q such that underlying discrete logarithm problem is intractable. Let $H_1 : \{0,1\}^* \to \mathbb{Z}_q$ and $H_2 : \{0,1\}^* \to \mathbb{G}$ be two hash functions, and g, h are two generators in $\mathbb{G}$. The public parameters are $param = \{\mathbb{G}, g, h, q, H_1, H_2\}$

KeyGen($param$): Randomly choose $x \in \mathbb{Z}_q$ and compute $y = g^x \pmod q$. The secret key is $sk = x$ and the corresponding public key is $pk = y$

Mint(a, pk): Given an amount a and a coin address pk, randomly choose $r \in \mathbb{Z}_q$ and compute $C = h^a g^r \pmod q$, where the coin in address pk is denoted as $cn_{pk} = C$ and the corresponding coin key $ck = r$. The public information of an account is $act = (y, C)$ and the secrete information is $ask = (x, r)$.

Spend($A_s, R, m, t, \mathbb{Y}, M, pk_{rev}$): On input the spender s's a set of m accounts A_s, a set of t output accounts R, a set of n group public keys $\mathbb{Y}$ such that $\mathbb{Y} = Y_1, \ldots, Y_n$, a transaction string M, and a revocation authority's public key $pk_{rev} = \tilde{y}$. The spender s can spend his/her m accounts to t output accounts by performing following steps:

1. The spender s parses $A_s = \{ack^{(k)}\}_{k \in [m]}$ into $\{(y_s^{(1)}, C_s^{(1)}), \ldots, (y_s^{(m)}, C_s^{(m)})\}$ and $K_s = \{ask^{(k)}\}_{k \in [m]}$ into $\{(x_s^{(1)}, r_s^{(1)}), \ldots, (x_s^{(m)}, r_s^{(m)})\}$ where $\{y_s^{(k)} = g^{x_s^{(k)}}\}_{k \in [m]}$ and $\{C_s^{(k)} = h^{a_s^{(k)}} g^{r_s^{(k)}}\}_{k \in [m]}$

2. Denote R as a set of output accounts where $R = \{pk_{out}^{(j)}\}_{j \in [t]}$, spender s randomly chooses $r_1, \ldots, r_t \in \mathbb{Z}_q$ and computes $C_{out}^j = h^{a_{out}^{(j)}} g^{r_j}$ for $j \in [t]$ where $a_{out}^{(1)} + \cdots + a_{out}^{(t)} = a_s^{(1)} + \cdots + a_s^{(m)}$

3. The spender s uses a public key encryption scheme $ENC_{pk}(\cdot)$ with public key pk to compute the cipher text $ctxt_j = ENC_{pk_{out}^{(j)}}(r_j)$ for $j \in [t]$ and send $\{ctxt_j\}_{j \in [t]}$ to the corresponding receiver's address.

4. In order to ensure that the amount of output coins equal to input coins, the spender s creates a new public key

$$y_s^{(m+1)} = \frac{\prod_{k=1}^m (y_s^{(k)} \cdot C_s^{(k)})}{\prod_{j=1}^t C_{out}^{(j)}}.$$

Since $a_{out}^{(1)} + \cdots + a_{out}^{(t)} = a_s^{(1)} + \cdots + a_s^{(m)}$, the $m + 1$ public key is

$$y_s^{(m+1)} = g^{\sum_{k=1}^m (x_s^{(k)} + r_s^{(k)}) - \sum_{j=1}^t r_j} = g^{x_s^{(m+1)}}$$

such that $x_s^{(m+1)} = \sum_{k=1}^m (x_s^{(k)} + r_s^{(k)}) - \sum_{j=1}^t r_j$.

5. The spender s randomly picks $n-1$ group public keys from the blockchain, where each group contains $m+1$ public keys. We denote these public keys as:

$$Y_1 = \{y_1^{(1)}, \ldots, y_1^{(m+1)}\}$$
$$\vdots$$
$$Y_{s-1} = \{y_{s-1}^{(1)}, \ldots, y_{s-1}^{(m+1)}\}$$
$$Y_{s+1} = \{y_{s+1}^{(1)}, \ldots, y_{s+1}^{(m+1)}\}$$
$$\vdots$$
$$Y_n = \{y_n^{(1)}, \ldots, y_n^{(m+1)}\}$$

The spender's public key is further denoted as $Y_s = \{y_s^{(1)}, \ldots, y_s^{(m+1)}\}$.

6. Compute $m+1$ linking base as $h_k = H_2(y_s^{(k)})$ for $k \in [m+1]$ and the linking tags are $L_k = h_k^{x_s^{(k)}}$ for $k \in [m+1]$. We denote $L = \{L_1, \ldots, L_{m+1}\}$.

7. Encrypt the spender's $m+1$ public keys by using revocation authority's public key $pk_{rev} = \tilde{y}$ as follows:
   For $k = 1, \ldots, m+1$, randomly pick $u_1, \ldots, u_{m+1} \in \mathbb{Z}_q$ and compute:
   (a) $CT_1^{(k)} = g^{u_k}$,
   (b) $CT_2^{(k)} = \tilde{y}^{u_k} y_s^{(k)}$,
   (c) Combine the cipher text $CX_k = (CT_1^{(k)}, CT_2^{(k)})$.

8. For $k = 1, \ldots, m+1$, randomly pick $t_1^{(k)}, t_2^{(k)} \in \mathbb{Z}_q$ and compute:
   (a) $a_{1,s}^{(k)} = g^{t_1^{(k)}}$ and $a_{2,s}^{(k)} = (\frac{CT_2^{(k)}}{y_s^{(k)}})^{t_1^{(k)}}$,
   (b) $c'_{s+1} = H_1(\mathbb{Y}, L, M, \{a_{1,s}^{(1)}, a_{2,s}^{(1)}\}, \ldots, \{a_{1,s}^{(m+1)}, a_{2,s}^{(m+1)}\})$,
   (c) $\bar{a}_{1,s}^{(k)} = g^{t_2^{(k)}}$ and $\bar{a}_{2,s}^{(k)} = h_k^{t_2^{(k)}}$,
   (d) $c''_{s+1} = H_1(\mathbb{Y}, L, M, \{\bar{a}_{1,s}^{(1)}, \bar{a}_{2,s}^{(1)}\}, \ldots, \{\bar{a}_{1,s}^{(m+1)}, \bar{a}_{2,s}^{(m+1)}\})$.

9. Generate a linkable ring signature with a group of n public key vectors $\mathbb{Y} = \{Y_1, \ldots, Y_n\}$ using spender's $m+1$ secret keys $\{x_s^{(1)}, \ldots, x_s^{(m+1)}\}$ with $m+1$ linking tags $\{L_1, \ldots, L_{m+1}\}$ and $m+1$ ciphertexts $\{CX_1, \ldots, CX_{m+1}\}$ on some transaction string M as follows:
   (a) For $i = s+1, \ldots, n, 1, \ldots, s-1$, randomly pick $v_{1,i}^{(1)}, \ldots, v_{1,i}^{(m+1)}$ and $v_{2,i}^{(1)}, \ldots, v_{2,i}^{(m+1)} \in \mathbb{Z}_q$ and compute:
   (b) $a_{1,i}^{(k)} = g^{v_{1,i}^{(k)}}(CT_1^{(k)})^{c'_i}$ and $a_{2,i}^{(k)} = \tilde{y}^{v_{(1,i)}^{(k)}}(\frac{CT_2^{(k)}}{y_i^{(k)}})^{c'_i}$ for $k \in [m+1]$,
   (c) $c'_{i+1} = H_1(\mathbb{Y}, L, M, \{a_{1,i}^{(1)}, a_{2,i}^{(1)}, \}, \ldots, \{a_{1,i}^{(m+1)}, a_{2,i}^{(m+1)}\})$,
   (d) $\bar{a}_{1,i}^{(k)} = g^{v_{2,i}^{(k)}}(y_i^{(k)})^{c''_i}$ and $\bar{a}_{2,i}^{(k)} = h_k^{v_{2,i}^{(k)}} L_k^{(c''_i)}$ for $k \in [m+1]$,
   (e) $c''_{i+1} = H_1(\mathbb{Y}, L, M, \{\bar{a}_{1,i}^{(1)}, \bar{a}_{2,i}^{(1)}\}, \ldots, \{\bar{a}_{1,i}^{(m+1)}, \bar{a}_{2,i}^{(m+1)}\})$.

10. For $k = 1, \ldots, m+1$, compute:
    (a) $v_{1,s}^{(k)} = t_1^{(k)} - c'_s u_k$,
    (b) $v_{2,s}^{(k)} = t_2^{(k)} - c''_s x_s^{(k)}$.

11. The signature is $\sigma = (c'_1, c''_1, \{v_{1,1}^{(1)}, \ldots, v_{1,1}^{(m+1)}\}, \ldots, \{v_{1,n}^{(1)}, \ldots, v_{1,n}^{(m+1)}\}, \{v_{2,1}^{(1)}, \ldots, v_{2,1}^{(m+1)}\}, \ldots, \{v_{2,n}^{(1)}, \ldots, v_{2,n}^{(m+1)}\}, \{L_1, \ldots, L_{m+1}\}, \{CX_1, \ldots, CX_{m+1}\})$.

Verify$(n, \mathbb{Y}, \sigma, M)$: The algorithm takes the input of a group $\mathbb{Y} = \{Y_1, \ldots, Y_2\}$ of n groups of public keys, a signature σ, and a transaction string M. To verify a transaction, the verifier computes follows:

1. First parse the $m + 1$ ciphertext $CX_k = \{CT_1^{(k)}, CT_2^{(k)}\}_{k \in [m+1]}$
2. For $i = 1, \ldots, n$, compute
   (a) $Z_{1,i}^{\prime(k)} = g^{v_{1,i}^{(k)}}(CT_1^{(k)})^{c'_i}$ and $Z_{2,i}^{\prime(k)} = \tilde{y}^{v_{1,i}^{(k)}}(\frac{CT_2^{(k)}}{y_i^{(k)}})^{c'_i}$ for $k \in [m + 1]$,
   (b) $c'_{i+1} = H_1(\mathbb{Y}, L, M, \{Z_{1,i}^{\prime(1)}, Z_{2,i}^{\prime(1)}\}, \ldots, \{Z_{1,i}^{\prime(m+1)}, Z_{2,i}^{\prime(m+1)}\})$ if $i \neq n$,
   (c) $Z_{1,i}^{\prime\prime(k)} = g^{v_{2,i}^{(k)}}(y_i^{(k)})^{c''_i}$ and $Z_{2,i}^{\prime\prime(k)} = h_k^{v_{2,i}^{(k)}}(L_k)^{c''_i}$ for $k \in [m + 1]$,
   (d) $c''_{i+1} = H_1(\mathbb{Y}, L, M, \{Z_{1,i}^{\prime\prime(1)}, Z_{2,i}^{\prime\prime(1)}\}, \ldots, \{Z_{1,i}^{\prime\prime(m+1)}, Z_{2,i}^{\prime\prime(m+1)}\})$ if $i \neq n$.
3. Check whether
   (a) $c'_1 \overset{?}{=} H_1(\mathbb{Y}, L, M, \{Z_{1,n}^{\prime(1)}, Z_{2,n}^{\prime(1)}\}, \ldots, \{Z_{1,n}^{\prime(m+1)}, Z_{2,n}^{\prime(m+1)}\})$,
   (b) $c''_1 \overset{?}{=} H_1(\mathbb{Y}, L, M, \{Z_{1,n}^{\prime\prime(1)}, Z_{2,n}^{\prime\prime(1)}\}, \ldots, \{Z_{1,n}^{\prime\prime(m+1)}, Z_{2,n}^{\prime\prime(m+1)}\})$.

Revoke$(n, \mathbb{Y}, sk_{rev}, \sigma)$: The algorithm receives a set $\mathbb{Y} = \{Y_1, \ldots, Y_n\}$ of n groups of public keys, a revocation authority's private key $sk_{rev} = \tilde{x}$, and a valid signature σ. The revocation authority with the knowledge of secret key $\tilde{x}$ corresponding to $\tilde{y}$ decrypts the $m + 1$ ciphertexts to get $m + 1$ public keys which belong to the real spender as follows

1. For $k = 1, \ldots, m + 1$, parse $CT_k = (CT_1^{(k)}, CT_2^{(k)})$.
2. Get the k-th public key $y_s^{\prime(k)} = CT_2^{(k)}/CT_1^{(k)^{\tilde{x}}}$ and output all public keys into a set of $Y'_s = \{y_s^{\prime(1)}, \ldots, y_s^{\prime(m+1)}\}$.
3. There exists a public key vector $Y_s \in \mathbb{Y}$ such that $Y_s = Y'_s$.

References

1. Abe, M., Ohkubo, M., Suzuki, K.: 1-out-of-n signatures from a variety of keys. In: Zheng, Y. (ed.) ASIACRYPT 2002. LNCS, vol. 2501, pp. 415–432. Springer, Heidelberg (2002). https://doi.org/10.1007/3-540-36178-2_26
2. Au, M.H., Chow, S.S.M., Susilo, W., Tsang, P.P.: Short linkable ring signatures revisited. In: Atzeni, A.S., Lioy, A. (eds.) EuroPKI 2006. LNCS, vol. 4043, pp. 101–115. Springer, Heidelberg (2006). https://doi.org/10.1007/11774716_9
3. Au, M.H., Liu, J.K., Susilo, W., Yuen, T.H.: Constant-size ID-based linkable and revocable-iff-linked ring signature. In: Barua, R., Lange, T. (eds.) INDOCRYPT 2006. LNCS, vol. 4329, pp. 364–378. Springer, Heidelberg (2006). https://doi.org/10.1007/11941378_26
4. Au, M.H., Liu, J.K., Susilo, W., Yuen, T.H.: Certificate based (linkable) ring signature. In: Dawson, E., Wong, D.S. (eds.) ISPEC 2007. LNCS, vol. 4464, pp. 79–92. Springer, Heidelberg (2007). https://doi.org/10.1007/978-3-540-72163-5_8

5. Au, M.H., Liu, J.K., Susilo, W., Yuen, T.H.: Secure ID-based linkable and revocable-iff-linked ring signature with constant-size construction. Theoret. Comput. Sci. **469**, 1–14 (2013)
6. Boneh, D., Gentry, C., Lynn, B., Shacham, H.: Aggregate and verifiably encrypted signatures from bilinear maps. In: Biham, E. (ed.) EUROCRYPT 2003. LNCS, vol. 2656, pp. 416–432. Springer, Heidelberg (2003). https://doi.org/10.1007/3-540-39200-9_26
7. Brenig, C., Accorsi, R., Müller, G.: Economic analysis of cryptocurrency backed money laundering. In: ECIS (2015)
8. Cayrel, P.-L., Lindner, R., Rückert, M., Silva, R.: A lattice-based threshold ring signature scheme. In: Abdalla, M., Barreto, P.S.L.M. (eds.) LATINCRYPT 2010. LNCS, vol. 6212, pp. 255–272. Springer, Heidelberg (2010). https://doi.org/10.1007/978-3-642-14712-8_16
9. Changlun, Z., Yun, L., Dequan, H.: A new verifiable ring signature scheme based on Nyberg-Rueppel scheme. In: 2006 8th International Conference on Signal Processing, vol. 4. IEEE (2006)
10. FBI: Bitcoin virtual currency: Unique features present distinct challenges for deterring illicit activity. Intelligence Assessment (2012)
11. Fujisaki, E.: Sub-linear size traceable ring signatures without random oracles. In: Kiayias, A. (ed.) CT-RSA 2011. LNCS, vol. 6558, pp. 393–415. Springer, Heidelberg (2011). https://doi.org/10.1007/978-3-642-19074-2_25
12. Fujisaki, E., Suzuki, K.: Traceable ring signature. In: Okamoto, T., Wang, X. (eds.) PKC 2007. LNCS, vol. 4450, pp. 181–200. Springer, Heidelberg (2007). https://doi.org/10.1007/978-3-540-71677-8_13
13. Herranz, J., Sáez, G.: Forking lemmas for ring signature schemes. In: Johansson, T., Maitra, S. (eds.) INDOCRYPT 2003. LNCS, vol. 2904, pp. 266–279. Springer, Heidelberg (2003). https://doi.org/10.1007/978-3-540-24582-7_20
14. Houben, R., Snyers, A.: Cryptocurrencies and blockchain: legal context and implications for financial crime, money laundering and tax evasion (2018)
15. Huang, X., et al.: Cost-effective authentic and anonymous data sharing with forward security. IEEE Trans. Comput. **64**(4), 971–983 (2015)
16. Lee, K.C., Wen, H.A., Hwang, T.: Convertible ring signature. IEE Proc.-Commun. **152**(4), 411–414 (2005)
17. Liu, D.Y., Liu, J.K., Mu, Y., Susilo, W., Wong, D.S.: Revocable ring signature. J. Comput. Sci. Technol. **22**(6), 785–794 (2007)
18. Liu, J.K., Au, M.H., Susilo, W., Zhou, J.: Linkable ring signature with unconditional anonymity. IEEE Trans. Knowl. Data Eng. **26**(1), 157–165 (2013)
19. Liu, J.K., Wei, V.K., Wong, D.S.: Linkable spontaneous anonymous group signature for ad hoc groups. In: Wang, H., Pieprzyk, J., Varadharajan, V. (eds.) ACISP 2004. LNCS, vol. 3108, pp. 325–335. Springer, Heidelberg (2004). https://doi.org/10.1007/978-3-540-27800-9_28
20. Liu, J.K., Wong, D.S.: On the security models of (threshold) ring signature schemes. In: Park, C., Chee, S. (eds.) ICISC 2004. LNCS, vol. 3506, pp. 204–217. Springer, Heidelberg (2005). https://doi.org/10.1007/11496618_16
21. Liu, J.K., Wong, D.S.: Linkable ring signatures: security models and new schemes. In: Gervasi, O., et al. (eds.) ICCSA 2005. LNCS, vol. 3481, pp. 614–623. Springer, Heidelberg (2005). https://doi.org/10.1007/11424826_65
22. Liu, J.K., Wong, D.S.: Solutions to key exposure problem in ring signature. IJ Netw. Secur. **6**(2), 170–180 (2008)

23. Liu, J.K., Yeo, S.L., Yap, W., Chow, S.S.M., Wong, D.S., Susilo, W.: Faulty instantiations of threshold ring signature from threshold proof-of-knowledge protocol. Comput. J. **59**(7), 945–954 (2016)

24. Liu, J.K., Yuen, T.H., Zhou, J.: Forward secure ring signature without random oracles. In: Qing, S., Susilo, W., Wang, G., Liu, D. (eds.) ICICS 2011. LNCS, vol. 7043, pp. 1–14. Springer, Heidelberg (2011). https://doi.org/10.1007/978-3-642-25243-3_1

25. Lv, J., Wang, X.: Verifiable ring signature. In: Proceedings of DMS 2003-The 9th International Conference on Distribted Multimedia Systems, pp. 663–667 (2003)

26. Nakamoto, S., et al.: Bitcoin: a peer-to-peer electronic cash system (2008)

27. Noether, S.: Ring signature confidential transactions for monero. IACR Cryptology ePrint Archive 2015, 1098 (2015)

28. Rivest, R.L., Shamir, A., Tauman, Y.: How to leak a secret. In: Boyd, C. (ed.) ASIACRYPT 2001. LNCS, vol. 2248, pp. 552–565. Springer, Heidelberg (2001). https://doi.org/10.1007/3-540-45682-1_32

29. Rivest, R.L., Shamir, A., Tauman, Y.: How to leak a secret: theory and applications of ring signatures. In: Goldreich, O., Rosenberg, A.L., Selman, A.L. (eds.) Theoretical Computer Science. LNCS, vol. 3895, pp. 164–186. Springer, Heidelberg (2006). https://doi.org/10.1007/11685654_7

30. Tsang, P.P., Au, M.H., Liu, J.K., Susilo, W., Wong, D.S.: A suite of non-pairing ID-based threshold ring signature schemes with different levels of anonymity (extended abstract). In: Heng, S.-H., Kurosawa, K. (eds.) ProvSec 2010. LNCS, vol. 6402, pp. 166–183. Springer, Heidelberg (2010). https://doi.org/10.1007/978-3-642-16280-0_11

31. Tsang, P.P., Wei, V.K.: Short linkable ring signatures for e-voting, e-cash and attestation. In: Deng, R.H., Bao, F., Pang, H.H., Zhou, J. (eds.) ISPEC 2005. LNCS, vol. 3439, pp. 48–60. Springer, Heidelberg (2005). https://doi.org/10.1007/978-3-540-31979-5_5

32. Tsang, P.P., Wei, V.K., Chan, T.K., Au, M.H., Liu, J.K., Wong, D.S.: Separable linkable threshold ring signatures. In: Canteaut, A., Viswanathan, K. (eds.) INDOCRYPT 2004. LNCS, vol. 3348, pp. 384–398. Springer, Heidelberg (2004). https://doi.org/10.1007/978-3-540-30556-9_30

33. Van Saberhagen, N.: Cryptonote v 2.0 (2013)

34. Xiong, H., Chen, Z., Li, F.: Bidder-anonymous english auction protocol based on revocable ring signature. Expert Syst. Appl. **39**(8), 7062–7066 (2012)

35. Yuen, T.H., Liu, J.K., Au, M.H., Susilo, W., Zhou, J.: Threshold ring signature without random oracles. In: ASIACCS 2011, pp. 261–267. ACM (2011)

36. Yuen, T.H., Liu, J.K., Au, M.H., Susilo, W., Zhou, J.: Efficient linkable and/or threshold ring signature without random oracles. Comput. J. **56**(4), 407–421 (2013). https://doi.org/10.1093/comjnl/bxs115

Post-Quantum Cryptography

Efficient Password-Authenticated Key Exchange from RLWE Based on Asymmetric Key Consensus

Yingshan Yang[1,2], Xiaozhuo Gu[1,2(✉)], Bin Wang[1,2], and Taizhong Xu[3]

[1] SKLOIS, Institute of Information Engineering, CAS, Beijing, China
{yangyingshan,guxiaozhuo}@iie.ac.cn
[2] School of Cyber Security, University of Chinese Academy of Sciences, Beijing, China
wangbin171@mails.ucas.edu.cn
[3] CNCERT/CC, Beijing, China

Abstract. A password-authenticated key exchange (PAKE) protocol allows two entities sharing a password to perform mutual authentication and establish a session key. Benefiting from the use of a low-entropy human-memorable password, PAKE avoids the use of PKI in the authentication process, making it more flexible and cheaper. However, with the development of quantum computing, protocols based on classical assumptions will no longer be secure, so designing a PAKE protocol capable of resisting quantum attacks has become an important research direction. In this work, we propose an efficient PAKE protocol using a new error reconciliation mechanism based on the ring learning with errors (RLWE) problem, which is considered to resist quantum attacks. Our protocol is proven security under the Bellare-Pointcheval-Rogaway (BPR) model. The protocol is implemented using the C language, which is highly portable, and is also optimized utilizing the Advanced Vector Extensions 2 (AVX2) instruction set. Compared with the C implementation of Ding's protocol, our reference C implementation is more than 12x faster, and the efficiency is doubled after AVX2 optimization. Moreover, by choosing the appropriate parameters, the security strength of our scheme is improved and the message size is reduced.

Keywords: RLWE · PAKE · Post-quantum

1 Introduction

PAKE allows participants to agree on a common session key to be used for protecting their subsequent communication on an insecure channel, and use low-entropy, human-memorable passwords for authentication, which provides

Supported by National Natural Science Foundation of China (Grant No. 61602475, No. 61802395), National Cryptographic Foundation of China (Grant No. MMJJ20170212), the National S&T Major Project of China (No. 2018ZX09201011).

Z. Liu and M. Yung (Eds.): Inscrypt 2019, LNCS 12020, pp. 31–49, 2020.
https://doi.org/10.1007/978-3-030-42921-8_2

stronger security against active adversaries. It does not require additional storage and hardware. This is very useful in an era when users are increasingly using mobile devices.

However, PAKE protocols face the problem of off-line and on-line dictionary attacks for the reason that passwords are drawn from a small space. We need to restrict the adversaries success to on-line guessing attacks and prevent off-line dictionary attacks when designing PAKE.

In addition, with the development of quantum computers, many cryptographic primitives may be threatened by quantum adversaries. This prompted researchers to design cryptographic protocols that would resist quantum computer attacks, called post-quantum cryptography. Lattice techniques are some of the most common mathematical techniques for building post-quantum cryptography. This paper focuses on building a PAKE protocol based on lattices.

1.1 Related Works

The first PAKE protocol called encrypted key exchange (EKE) protocol was suggested by Bellovin and Merritt [3]. After that, a lot of works in this area were put forward. In 2001, Katz et al. proposed an efficient PAKE protocol under the standard model using smooth projection hash functions [12]. In 2000, Boyko et al. presented new PAKE protocols called PAK, PPK and PAK-X [6], and gave security proofs in the random oracle model (ROM). Then more variants of PAK were proposed. But these protocols are based on classical assumptions and will no longer be secure in a quantum environment.

However, there is relatively little research on lattice-based PAKE protocols. In 2009, Katz and Vaikuntanathan proposed the first lattice-based PAKE protocol using common reference string (CRS) and gave the security proof in the standard model [13]. In 2017, Zhang et al. proposed a new CRS-based PAKE protocol and instantiated it on lattices [16]. Due to the CRS-based design, these protocols use complicated cryptographic tools to achieve security under the standard model and are therefore inefficient. In contrast, the ROM-based design is simpler and more elegant. In 2017, Ding et al. presented a more efficient PAKE protocol based on the RLWE problem and proved its security in ROM [8]. However, its analysis of the error reconciliation mechanism was not tight, resulting in a decline in performance and security. Therefore, it is attractive to design an efficient post-quantum PAKE protocol.

1.2 Our Contributions

Toward the goal of improving the efficiency and practicability of the PAKE protocol, we propose a new lattice-based PAKE protocol in this work, which is efficient in key exchange and can achieve post-quantum security. Our proposal has the following characteristics.

- A new PAKE protocol uses a ROM-based design based on the framework in [6] that circumvents the inefficiency of using complicated cryptographic tools in the CRS-based design. In addition, our proposal is based on the RLWE problem, which makes the protocol resistant to quantum attacks. Compared to other post-quantum hardness assumptions, the RLWE problem is more versatile and computationally efficient.

- By using a new error reconciliation mechanism, a portion of the intermediate results can be pre-calculated in idle time to reduce the load on the server, thereby increasing the response efficiency of the server.
- By regenerating the public parameter a in each connection, the backdoor placement and all-for-the-price-of-one attacks are prevented. At the same time, a can be generated more efficiently by reducing the sample rejection rate of a. Sampling noise with a central binomial distribution further increases efficiency and prevents timing attacks.
- In terms of parameter selection, we choose a smaller $q = 12289$ to reduce the sent message size while improving the scheme's efficiency and security. And this q allows us to use a faster polynomial multiplication algorithm.
- The protocol is analyzed by means of a formal security argument under the BPR model [2], and it can withstand dictionary attacks and loss of session keys, and has forward secrecy.
- We implement the proposed protocol through portable C and avoid some time-consuming operations in its implementation. At the same time, the implementation is optimized through the AVX2 instruction set, which significantly improves the efficiency. Our reference C implementation and AVX2 implementation are at least 12x and 24x faster than the implementation of Ding's scheme [8], respectively.

We briefly introduce the main points of this paper and related works in Sect. 1. In Sect. 2, we review the background knowledge and theory to be used later and recall the security model. Our protocol is described in detail in Sect. 3, and a security proof is given in Sect. 4. Next, the implementation details are given in Sect. 5, and the comparison and performance analysis are performed in Sect. 6. Finally, we conclude this paper in Sect. 7.

2 Preliminaries

2.1 Notation

$\mathbb{Z}$ denotes the ring of rational integers. For an integer $q \geq 1$, let $\mathbb{Z}_q$ be the quotient ring $\mathbb{Z}/q\mathbb{Z}$. $R = \mathbb{Z}[x]/(x^n + 1)$ denotes the ring of integer polynomials modulo $x^n + 1$. $R_q = \mathbb{Z}_q[x]/(x^n + 1)$ denotes the ring of integer polynomials modulo $x^n + 1$ where each coefficient is in $\{0, 1, \ldots, q - 1\}$.

If χ is a probability distribution over R, $x \xleftarrow{\$} \chi$ means the sampling of $x \in R$ according to χ. If S is a set, $x \xleftarrow{\$} S$ means the sampling of x uniformly at random from S. For any real number x, we define $\lfloor x \rfloor$ as the largest integer that less than or equal to x, and $\lfloor x \rceil = \lfloor x + 1/2 \rfloor$ represents the nearest integer to x.

2.2 Key Consensus

Jin and Zhao proposed the concepts of key consensus (KC) and asymmetric key consensus (AKC) [11], which allow two parties to reach consensus from approximations and are optimizations of the previous error reconciliation mechanism. Next, we recall the definition of AKC which will be used later.

Definition 1 (AKC). *The asymmetric key consensus scheme AKC = (params, Con, Rec) is defined as follows:*

- *params* $= (q, m, g, d)$ *denotes the system parameters, where* q, m, g, d *are positive integers,* $2 \leq m \leq q$, $2 \leq g \leq q$, $1 \leq d \leq \lfloor q/2 \rfloor$.
- $(k_1, v) \leftarrow Con(\sigma_1, params)$: *On input of* $(\sigma_1 \in \mathbb{Z}_q, params)$, *the probabilistic polynomial-time conciliation algorithm Con outputs* $k_1 \in \mathbb{Z}_m$ *and the public hints signal* $v \in \mathbb{Z}_g$. k_1 *is uniformly distributed on* $\mathbb{Z}_m$.
- $k_2 \leftarrow Rec(\sigma_2, v, params)$: *On input of* $(\sigma_2, v, params)$, *the deterministic polynomial-time algorithm Rec outputs* $k_2 \in \mathbb{Z}_m$.

If $k_1 = k_2$ *for any* $\sigma_1, \sigma_2 \in \mathbb{Z}_q$ *such that* $|\sigma_1 - \sigma_2|_q \leq d$, *then the scheme is correct. If* v *is independent of* k_1 *whenever* σ_1 *is uniformly distributed over* $\mathbb{Z}_q$, *then the scheme is secure. Specifically, for arbitrary* $\tilde{v} \in \mathbb{Z}_g$ *and* $\tilde{k}_1, \tilde{k}'_1 \in \mathbb{Z}_m$, *it holds that* $Pr[v = \tilde{v}|k_1 = \tilde{k}_1] = Pr[v = \tilde{v}|k_1 = \tilde{k}'_1]$, *where the probability is taken over* $\sigma_1 \leftarrow \mathbb{Z}_q$ *and the random coins used by Con.*

The specific construction of AKC is depicted in Algorithm 1. The *Con* and *Rec* functions can be extended to polynomials by applying them to each of the coefficients respectively.

Algorithm 1. AKC: Asymmetric Key Consensus

---
params$=(q, m, g, d)$
function CON$(\sigma_1, params)$ ▷ $\sigma_1 \in [0, q-1]$

  $k_1 \xleftarrow{\$} \mathbb{Z}_m$
  $v = \lfloor g(\sigma_1 + \lfloor k_1 q/m \rceil) \rfloor \bmod g$
  return (k_1, v)

function REC$(\sigma_2, v, params)$ ▷ $\sigma_2 \in [0, q-1]$
  $k_2 = \lfloor m(v/g - \sigma_2/q) \rceil \bmod m$
  return k_2

For the correctness and security of AKC, we will use the following theorem.

Theorem 1 (Correctness and security). *If the parameters of AKC satisfy* $(2d+1)m < q(1 - m/g)$, *then the AKCN scheme is correct and secure. Specifically,* v *is independent of* k_1 *when* $\sigma_1 \leftarrow \mathbb{Z}_q$.

2.3 Hard Problems

Lyubashevsky et al. introduced the RLWE problem [14], which is a quantum-resistant hard mathematical problem and is convenient and efficient when constructing a cryptosystem.

Definition 2 (Decision RLWE problem). *Let n and q be positive integers. Let χ be distributions on R_q and let $s \xleftarrow{\$} \chi$. The decision RLWE problem for (n, q, χ) is to distinguish the sample $(a, as + e)$, where $a \xleftarrow{\$} R_q$ and $e \xleftarrow{\$} \chi$, from the sample drawn from the uniform distribution on $R_q \times R_q$.*

For convenience in the proof, we define the pairing with errors (PWE) assumption according to [8].

Definition 3 (PWE problem). *Let n and q be positive integers. Let χ be distributions on R_q. Let $s, e, e' \xleftarrow{\$} \chi$, $a, X \xleftarrow{\$} R_q$, and $(\tau, v) \leftarrow Con(Xs + e')$, where v is the signal value. Given $(a, X, Y = as + e, v)$, the goal of the adversary $\mathcal{A}$ who runs in time t is to include τ in its output containing at most N elements. The advantage follows the form of $Adv_{R_q}^{PWE}(t, N) = max_{\mathcal{A}}\{Adv_{R_q}^{PWE}\}$.*

From [8], we have the following corollary.

Corollary 1. *The PWE problem is hard if the RLWE problem is hard.*

2.4 Security Model

Bellare et al. designed a model [2] for authenticated key exchange between two parties with a shared secret. In this model, the probabilistic, polynomial-time active adversary $\mathcal{A}$ can fully control the network.

P denotes a PAKE protocol. We set $ID \overset{def}{=} Clients \cup Servers$ to be a non-empty set of principals, where $Clients$ and $Servers$ are finite, disjoint, non-empty sets. Each principal $U \in ID$ is associated with an unlimited number of instances Π_U^i, where i is a positive integer.

Let D be a fixed, non-empty set of size L from which a password pw_C for client C is selected uniformly at random. And each server $S \in Servers$ holds $pw_S = (f(pw_C))_C$, where f is an efficiently computable one-way function.

Adversarial Capabilities. Adversary $\mathcal{A}$ is a probabilistic polynomial time algorithm. The allowed queries are as follows:

- $Send(U, i, M)$: Receiving the message M, Π_U^i computes and returns the response output to $\mathcal{A}$. If Π_U^i accepts or terminates, $\mathcal{A}$ will be notified.
- $Execute(C, i, S, j)$: Π_C^i and Π_S^i perform a complete execution of protocol P and return a transcript to $\mathcal{A}$.
- $Reveal(U, i)$: $\mathcal{A}$ will obtain the session key held by Π_U^i.
- $Test(U, i)$: The fresh instance Π_U^i is to flip a bit b. If $b = 1$, the actual session key held by Π_U^i is output to $\mathcal{A}$; otherwise, a string drawn uniformly from the space of session keys is output to $\mathcal{A}$. This query can only be asked once.

- $Corrupt(U)$: When $U \in Servers$, $\mathcal{A}$ will obtain $(f(pw_C))_C$; when $U \in Clients$, $\mathcal{A}$ will obtain pw_U.

Definition 4 (Partnering). *When an instance Π_U^i accepts, it holds a partner-id pid_U^i, a session-id sid_U^i and a session key sk_U^i. We say that Π_C^i and Π_S^j where $C \in Clients$ and $S \in Servers$ to be partnered if both accept with $pid_C^i = S$, $pid_S^j = C$, $sid_C^i = sid_S^j =: sid$, and no other instance accepts with sid.*

Definition 5 (Freshness). *We say that an instance Π_U^i is fresh with forward secrecy unless either (1) a $Reveal(U, i)$ is queried, (2) a $Reveal(V, j)$ is queried where Π_U^i and Π_V^i are partnered, or (3) a $Corrupt(V)$ is queried before the Test query and a $Send(U, i, M)$ is queried for some string M.*

Definition 6 (Security). *The adversary $\mathcal{A}$ needs to distinguish between the actual session key held by a fresh instance and a random string. Let $Succ_P^{ake}(\mathcal{A})$ to be the event that $\mathcal{A}$ makes a $Test(U, i)$ query to a fresh instance Π_U^i, that has terminated, and $b' = b$ where b is the bit selected in the Test query and b' is the bit that $\mathcal{A}$ outputs eventually. The advantage of $\mathcal{A}$ breaking P is defined to be*

$$Adv_P^{ake}(\mathcal{A}) = 2Pr[Succ_P^{ake}(\mathcal{A})] - 1.$$

We say the PAKE protocol is secure if the adversary $\mathcal{A}$ can't determine fresh instances' session keys with greater advantage than that of an on-line dictionary attack, i.e. $Adv_P^{ake}(\mathcal{A}) \leq Adv_P^{online}(\mathcal{A}) + \epsilon$.

3   Password-Authenticated Key Exchange

3.1   The Protocol

In this section, we present our proposal (see Fig. 1). Let Gen be a pseudo-random generator (PRG), which can generate $\boldsymbol{a} \in R_q$ from a small seed. Let κ be a bit-length of the final shared key. $H_1 : \{0,1\}^* \to R_q$ denotes a hash function. $H_l : \{0,1\}^* \to \{0,1\}^\kappa$ for $l \in \{2,3\}$ denote hash functions which are used for verification. $H_4 : \{0,1\}^* \to \{0,1\}^\kappa$ denotes a Key Derivation Function (KDF). We define ψ_b as a centered binomial distribution with a standard deviation of $\varsigma = \sqrt{b/2}$. The protocol process is as follows:

- The client C chooses $seed$ randomly and generates the public parameter $\boldsymbol{a}$. Next, C samples $\boldsymbol{s}_C$ and $\boldsymbol{e}_C$ from ψ_b^n, and computes $\boldsymbol{y}_C = \boldsymbol{a}\boldsymbol{s}_C + \boldsymbol{e}_C$, $\boldsymbol{\gamma} = H_1(pw_C)$ and $\boldsymbol{m} = \boldsymbol{y}_C + \boldsymbol{\gamma}$. Then C sends $<C, \boldsymbol{m}, seed>$ to S.
- Receiving $<C, \boldsymbol{m}, seed>$, the server S checks $\boldsymbol{m}$. If $\boldsymbol{m} \notin R_q$, it aborts; otherwise, it generates $\boldsymbol{a}$ using the small seed and computes $\boldsymbol{y}_C = \boldsymbol{m} + \boldsymbol{\gamma}'$ where $\boldsymbol{\gamma}' = -H_1(pw_C)$. Next, S samples $\boldsymbol{s}_S$, $\boldsymbol{e}_S$ and $\boldsymbol{e}_\sigma$ from ψ_b^n, and computes $\boldsymbol{y}_S = \boldsymbol{a}\boldsymbol{s}_S + \boldsymbol{e}_S$ and $\boldsymbol{\sigma}_S = \boldsymbol{y}_C\boldsymbol{s}_S + \boldsymbol{e}_\sigma$. Then S obtains $(k_\sigma, v) = Con(\boldsymbol{\sigma}_S)$, $k = H_2(C, S, \boldsymbol{m}, \boldsymbol{y}_S, k_\sigma, \boldsymbol{\gamma}')$ and $k'' = H_3(C, S, \boldsymbol{m}, \boldsymbol{y}_S, k_\sigma, \boldsymbol{\gamma}')$ and sends $<\boldsymbol{y}_S, v, k>$ to C.

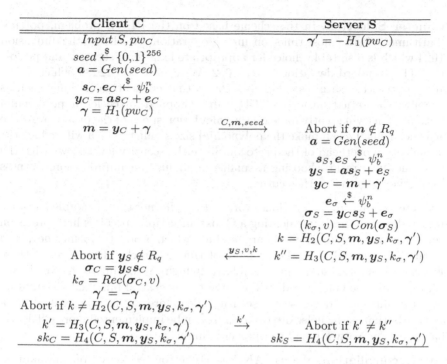

Fig. 1. Password-authenticated key exchange protocol

- Receiving $<y_S, v, k>$, the client C checks y_S. If $y_S \notin R_q$, it aborts; otherwise, it computes $\sigma_C = y_S s_C$ and $k_\sigma = Rec(\sigma_C, v)$. Next, it verifies whether k equals to $H_2(C, S, m, y_S, k_\sigma, \gamma')$ where $\gamma' = -\gamma$; if not, it aborts. Otherwise, it computes $k' = H_3(C, S, m, y_S, k_\sigma, \gamma')$ and $sk_C = H_4(C, S, m, y_S, k_\sigma, \gamma')$. Then it sends k' to C.
- Receiving k', the server S verifies whether k' equals to k''; if not, it aborts. Otherwise, S computes $sk_S = H_4(C, S, m, y_S, k_\sigma, \gamma')$.

ROM-Based. In some previous works, in order to achieve the security under the standard model, CRS is usually used to design PAKE. This approach often results in a more complicated scheme, which has an impact on the scheme's efficiency. Therefore, we choose to use a ROM-based design, which does not require complicated cryptographic tools and makes the scheme simpler and more efficient.

Authentication. The client holds the password pw_C. When sending a message, the client adds the hash value of the password to the original message, and the server can only get the correct original message if it holds the corresponding hash value. Once the original message calculated by the server is incorrect, the subsequent verification value k will be inconsistent with that of the client, and the protocol will be terminated.

Parameter Selection. In the scheme based on the RLWE problem, polynomial arithmetic is the most time-consuming operation. We choose the dimension n=1024 which is a suitable choice for appropriate long-term security and performance. The standard deviation $\varsigma = \sqrt{16/2}$. We choose $q = 12289$, which is the smallest prime that satisfies $q \equiv 1 \bmod 2n$ so that efficient algorithms, such as the number theoretic transform (NTT), can be applied to accelerate polynomial operations. This will greatly increase the calculation speed of the protocol. At the same time, a small q can make the polynomial size smaller, which will reduce the communication overhead of the protocol. Since the security level grows with the noise-to-modulus ratio, choosing a smaller modulus can improve compactness and efficiency together with security.

Noise Distribution. In previous works [4,8], the noise was sampled from a Gaussian distribution. Implementing a Gaussian sampler requires high-precision calculations or a pre-computed large table, which leads to inefficiency, and this sampling method faces the problem of timing attacks. Therefore, in these schemes, the cost of noise sampling is relatively high. According to the conclusion in [1], replacing the Gaussian distribution with the central binomial distribution does not significantly decrease the security. Therefore, we use the central binomial distribution as the noise distribution. It can be implemented more efficiently in hardware and software and can prevent timing attacks.

Error Reconciliation. We use AKC as the error reconciliation mechanism. It is a generalization and optimization of previous reconciliation mechanisms. According to Definition 1, when $|\sigma_C - \sigma_S|_q \leq d$, two participants can get the same k_σ, which guarantees the correctness of the protocol. At the same time, the signal value v and k_σ are independent. Even if the adversary knows v, the extracted value k_σ is uniformly random. By adjudging the parameter m, the length of reconciliation bits obtained in one calculation can be changed, whereas in some mechanisms [7,15], only one single bit can be extracted. Moreover, when using the previous error reconciliation mechanism [1,4,7,15], the server can calculate the session key only after receiving the ephemeral message from the client. However, for AKC, k_1 and $g\lfloor k_1 q/m \rfloor$ in Algorithm 1 can be sampled, stored and calculated off-line in actual usage, which can improve on-line performance and reduce the burden on the server. Especially when connecting with a large number of clients at the same time, it can improve the response speed of the server.

Public Parameter. In previous work such as [4,8], the public parameter a is fixed, which brings some drawbacks. From the worst case scenario, it is possible to put backdoors in a, making the subsequent communication unsafe. Even if there is no backdoor in a, it is risky to rely on a single instance of a lattice problem for all connections. It is possible for an adversary to perform large-scale calculations on this instance, compromising all communications. This type of attack is called all-for-the-price-of-one attack. To avoid those pitfalls, we take the approach of regenerating a fresh a every time the two parties connect. At each connection we randomly select a small seed and expand the seed to get a. This will have a slight performance impact. In order to minimize performance loss, we only transmit small seeds and assume that the generated a is directly in the NTT domain to reduce the times of using NTT. At the same time, we take measures to reduce the sample rejection rate of a and speed up its generation.

3.2 Correctness

From Definition 1 and Theorem 1, we know that the participants can get the same k_σ and the protocol is executed correctly when $|\sigma_C - \sigma_S|_q \leq d$ and $(2d + 1)m < q(1 - m/g)$. We choose $q = 12289$, $m = 2$ and $g = 2^6$, then we can conclude that the maximum d that satisfies the condition is 2975.

$$\sigma_C - \sigma_S = y_S s_C - y_C s_S - e_\sigma = e_S s_C - e_C s_S - e_\sigma$$

In order to get a concrete failure probability, we need to analyze the probability of $|e_S s_C - e_C s_S - e_\sigma|_q > 2975$. This distribution can be obtained directly by running the code of Jin and Zhao [11], so we get this probability of 2^{-41}. In other words, the protocol will fail only with a probability of 2^{-41} under these parameter settings. It is sufficient for most application scenarios of key exchange.

4 Security

We divide queries into client action (CA) and server action (SA). CA0 denotes a *Send* query to Π_C^i with input S. SA1 denotes a *Send* query to unused Π_S^j. CA1 denotes a *Send* query to Π_C^i that expects the second protocol message. SA2 denotes a *Send* query to Π_S^j that expects the last protocol message.

We define the following events that correspond to $\mathcal{A}$ making password guesses:

- *guess_client_1*(C, i, S, pw, l): $\mathcal{A}$ makes an $H_l(C, S, \boldsymbol{m}, \boldsymbol{y_S}, k_\sigma, \boldsymbol{\gamma}')$ query, a CA0 query to Π_C^i with input S and output $<C, \boldsymbol{m}, seed>$, a CA1 query to Π_C^i with input $<\boldsymbol{y_S}, v, k>$ and an $H_1(pw)$ query. The associated value is the output of the $H_l(\cdot)$ query, or k, k', sk_C^i.
- *guess_client_2*(C, i, S, pw): a CA1 query with input $<\boldsymbol{y_S}, v, k>$ causes *guess_client_1*$(C, i, S, pw, 2)$ to occur with associated value k.
- *guess_server_1*(S, j, C, pw, l): $\mathcal{A}$ makes an $H_l(C, S, \boldsymbol{m}, \boldsymbol{y_S}, k_\sigma, \boldsymbol{\gamma}')$ query and previously made a SA1 query to Π_S^j with input $<C, \boldsymbol{m}, seed>$ and output $<\boldsymbol{y_S}, v, k>$, and an $H_1(pw)$ query. The associated value is k, k', or sk_S^j.
- *guess_server_3*(S, j, C, pw): A SA2 query is made with k', where *guess_server_1*$(S, j, C, pw, 3)$ previously occurred with associated value k'.
- *guess_server*(S, j, C, pw): *guess_server_1*(S, j, C, pw, l) occurs.
- *guess_client_server*(C, i, S, j, pw): Both *guess_client_1*(C, i, S, pw, l) and *guess_server_1*(S, j, C, pw, l) occur where Π_C^i and Π_S^j are paired with each other after its SA1 query.
- *guess_exec*(C, i, S, j, pw): $\mathcal{A}$ makes an $H_l(C, S, \boldsymbol{m}, \boldsymbol{y_S}, k_\sigma, \boldsymbol{\gamma}')$ query, and previously made an *Execute*(C, i, S, j) query and an $H_1(pw)$ query.

- *correctpw*: Either $guess\_client\_2(C, i, S, pw_C)$ occurs, or $guess\_server(S, j, C, pw_C)$ occurs before *Corrupt* happens.
- *correctpwexec*: $guess\_exec(C, i, S, j, pw_C)$ occurs.
- *guess_double_server*: Both $guess\_server(S, j, C, pw)$ and $guess\_server(S, j, C, pw')$ occur before *Corrupt* happens where $pw \neq pw'$.
- *guess_paired*: $guess\_client\_server(C, i, S, j, pw_C)$ occurs.

Theorem 2. *P denotes our protocol shown in Fig. 1. Let n and q be positive integers. R_q is defined as above. The size of the password dictionary is N. For an adversary $\mathcal{A}$ that runs in time t, let $q_{se}, q_{ex}, q_{re}, q_{co}, q_{ro}$ be the maximum number of Send, Execute, Reveal, Corrupt, random oracle queries, respectively, $t' = O(t + (q_{ro} + q_{se} + q_{ex})t_{exp})$, and $t'' = O(t + (q_{ro}^2 + q_{se} + q_{ex})t_{exp})$. We assume that q_{ro} and $q_{se} + q_{ex}$ are both at least 1. Then the advantage of $\mathcal{A}$ breaking P is*

$$Adv_P^{ake}(\mathcal{A}) = O(q_{se} Adv_{R_q}^{PWE}(t'', q_{ro}^2) + Adv_{R_q}^{DRLWE}(t', q_{ro})$$
$$+ \frac{q_{se}}{2^\kappa} + \frac{(q_{se} + q_{ex})(q_{ro} + q_{se} + q_{ex})}{q^n}) + \frac{q_{se}}{N}.$$

Proof. We set up a sequence of protocols, where $P_0 = P$, and P_7 is designed to use only natural on-line guessing attack. We will prove that the advantage of $\mathcal{A}$ attacking P_{i-1} is at most negligibly more than the advantage of $\mathcal{A}$ attacking P_i for i from 1 to 7, i.e., $Adv_{P_0}^{ake}(\mathcal{A}) \leq Adv_{P_1}^{ake}(\mathcal{A}) + \epsilon_1 \leq \ldots \leq Adv_{P_7}^{ake}(\mathcal{A}) + \epsilon_7$.

Protocol P_0. $P_0 = P$.

Protocol P_1. $P_1 = P_0$, except that P_1 is halted and $\mathcal{A}$ fails when m and y_S chosen by the honest party have appeared in the previous execution.

Claim. For any adversary $\mathcal{A}$, $Adv_{P_0}^{ake}(\mathcal{A}) \leq Adv_{P_1}^{ake}(\mathcal{A}) + \frac{O((q_{se}+q_{ex})(q_{ro}+q_{se}+q_{ex}))}{q^n}$.

Proof. The probability that the latest m or y_S has previously appeared is $\frac{q_{ro}+q_{se}+q_{ex}}{q^n}$. Let E denote that the m and y_S generated in *Send* or *Execute* has appeared in the previous *Send*, *Execute* or $H_l(\cdot)$. If E does not occur, $q_{se} + q_{ex}$ values need to be unique. The probability of event E occurring is $\frac{O((q_{se}+q_{ex})(q_{ro}+q_{se}+q_{ex}))}{q^n}$.

Protocol P_2. $P_2 = P_1$, except that P_2 answers *Send* and *Execute* in the following way, and subsequent random oracle queries are consistent with the results of these *Send* and *Execute* queries.

- In an $Execute(C, i, S, j)$ query, $seed \xleftarrow{\$} \{0,1\}^{256}$, $a = Gen(seed)$, $m = as_m + e_m$, $y_S = as_S + e_S$, where $s_m, e_m, s_S, e_S \xleftarrow{\$} \chi$, $k, k', sk_C^i, sk_S^j \xleftarrow{\$} \{0,1\}^\kappa$, $v \xleftarrow{\$} \{0, 1, \ldots, g-1\}^n$.
- In a CA0 query to Π_C^i, $seed \xleftarrow{\$} \{0,1\}^{256}$, $a = Gen(seed)$, $m = as_m + e_m$, where $s_m, e_m \xleftarrow{\$} \chi$.

- In a SA1 query to Π_S^j, $\boldsymbol{a} = Gen(seed)$, $\boldsymbol{y}_S = \boldsymbol{a}\boldsymbol{s}_S + \boldsymbol{e}_S$, where $\boldsymbol{s}_S, \boldsymbol{e}_S \xleftarrow{\$} \chi$, $k, k'', sk_S^j \xleftarrow{\$} \{0,1\}^\kappa$, $v \xleftarrow{\$} \{0, 1, \ldots, g-1\}^n$.
- In a CA1 query to Π_C^i, if this query causes $guess\_client\_2(C, i, S, pw_C)$ to occur, then set k' to associated value of $guess\_client\_1(C, i, S, pw_C, 3)$, and set sk_C^i to the associated value of $guess\_client\_1(C, i, S, pw_C, 4)$; else if Π_C^i is paired with Π_S^j, $sk_C^i \leftarrow sk_S^j$, $k' \xleftarrow{\$} \{0,1\}^\kappa$; otherwise, Π_C^i aborts.
- In a SA2 query to Π_S^j, if this query causes $guess\_server\_3(S, j, C, pw_C)$ to occur, or if Π_S^j is paired with Π_C^i, terminate; otherwise, Π_S^j aborts.
- In a $H_l(C, S, \boldsymbol{m}, \boldsymbol{y}_S, k_\sigma, \gamma')$ query, if this query causes $guess\_server\_1(S, j, C, pw_C, l)$ or $guess\_exec(C, i, S, j, pw_C)$ to occur, then output the associated value of this event; otherwise, output a random value from $\{0,1\}^\kappa$.

Claim. For any adversary $\mathcal{A}$, $Adv_{P_1}^{ake}(\mathcal{A}) = Adv_{P_2}^{ake}(\mathcal{A}) + \frac{O(q_{ro})}{q^n} + \frac{O(q_{se})}{2^\kappa}$

Proof. In P_1, the following cases may occur. (1) An unpaired client instance Π_C^i may terminate without $guess\_client\_2(C, i, S, pw_C)$. The probability of this case is at most $\frac{q_{se}}{2^\kappa}$. (2) An unpaired server instance Π_S^j may terminate without $guess\_server\_3(S, i, C, pw_S)$. The probability of this case is at most $\frac{q_{se}}{2^\kappa}$. (3) For any $H_l(\cdot)$ query, $l \in \{2,3,4\}$, $\gamma' = H_1(pw_C)$ but the adversary has not made an $H_1(pw_C)$ query. The probability of this case is bounded by $\frac{q_{ro}}{q^n}$. If these cases do not occur, P_2 is consistent with P_1.

Protocol P_3. $P_3 = P_2$, except that P_3 uses the random output to answer $H_l(\cdot)$ for $l \in \{2,3,4\}$ without checking the consistency with *Execute*. $guess\_exec(C, i, S, j, pw_C)$ is not checked.

Claim. For any adversary $\mathcal{A}$, $Adv_{P_2}^{ake}(\mathcal{A}) \leq Adv_{P_3}^{ake}(\mathcal{A}) + Adv_{R_q}^{DRLWE}(t', q_{ro}) + 2Adv_{R_q}^{PWE}(t', q_{ro})$.

Proof. If *correctpwexec* does not occur, then P_2 and P_3 are indistinguishable. We set E as the event that *correctpwexec* occurs, and the probability that E occurs is ϵ. Then we have $Adv_{P_2}^{ake}(\mathcal{A}) \leq Adv_{P_3}^{ake}(\mathcal{A}) + 2\epsilon$.

We construct an algorithm $\mathcal{D}$ to solve PWE by running $\mathcal{A}$. Given $(\boldsymbol{a}, \boldsymbol{X}, \boldsymbol{Y}, v)$, $\mathcal{D}$ simulates P_2 for $\mathcal{A}$ with these changes:

- In an $Execute(C, i, S, j)$ query, set $seed \xleftarrow{\$} \{0,1\}^{256}$, $\boldsymbol{m} = \boldsymbol{X} + \boldsymbol{a}\boldsymbol{s}_f + \boldsymbol{e}_f$, $\boldsymbol{y}_S = \boldsymbol{Y} + \boldsymbol{a}\boldsymbol{s}_{ff} + \boldsymbol{e}_{ff}$, and $v \xleftarrow{\$} \{0, 1, \ldots, g-1\}^n$, where $\boldsymbol{s}_f, \boldsymbol{e}_f, \boldsymbol{s}_{ff}, \boldsymbol{e}_{ff} \xleftarrow{\$} \chi$.
- When $\mathcal{A}$ finishes, for every $H_l(C, S, \boldsymbol{m}, \boldsymbol{y}_S, k_\sigma, \gamma')$ query, where $\boldsymbol{m}$ and $\boldsymbol{y}_S$ were generated in *Execute*, and H_1 returned $-\gamma' = \boldsymbol{a}\boldsymbol{s}_h + \boldsymbol{e}_h$, then the simulator can compute $\boldsymbol{X} \cdot \boldsymbol{s}_y + \boldsymbol{e} = \boldsymbol{\sigma}_S - \boldsymbol{Y}(\boldsymbol{s}_f - \boldsymbol{s}_h) - (\boldsymbol{X} + \gamma' + \boldsymbol{a}\boldsymbol{s}_f + \boldsymbol{e}_f) \cdot \boldsymbol{s}_{ff}$, and add $k'_\sigma = Rec(\boldsymbol{\sigma}_S - \boldsymbol{Y}(\boldsymbol{s}_f - \boldsymbol{s}_h) - (\boldsymbol{X} + \gamma' + \boldsymbol{a}\boldsymbol{s}_f + \boldsymbol{e}_f) \cdot \boldsymbol{s}_{ff}, v)$ to the list of possible values for τ.

Since $y_S = Y + as_{ff} + e_{ff}$ instead of $y_S = as_S + e_S$ in the simulation, this can be distinguishable if the decision RLWE problem can be solved. And if E occurs, the correct τ is added to the list. Therefore, if E occurs or DRLWE problem is solved with non-negligible advantage, the simulation is distinguishable from P_2. $\mathcal{D}$ creates a list of size q_{ro} with advantage ϵ. We set $t' = O(t + (q_{ro} + q_{se} + q_{ex})t_{exp})$ as the running time of $\mathcal{D}$. The claim follows from the fact $Adv_{R_q}^{PWE}(\mathcal{D}) \leq Adv_{R_q}^{PWE}(t', q_{ro})$.

Protocol P_4. $P_4 = P_3$, except that if a correct password guess is made before *Corrupt*, i.e. if *correctpw* occurs, then the protocol halts and the adversary automatically succeeds. The changes are as follows:

- In a CA1 query to Π_C^i, if *guess_client_2*(C, i, S, pw_C) occurs before *Corrupt*, the protocol halts and the adversary succeeds.
- In an $H_l(\cdot)$ query for $l \in \{2, 3, 4\}$, if a *guess_server*(S, j, C, pw_C) event occurs before *Corrupt*, the protocol halts and the adversary succeeds.

Claim. For any adversary $\mathcal{A}$, $Adv_{P_3}^{ake}(\mathcal{A}) \leq Adv_{P_4}^{ake}(\mathcal{A})$.

Proof. Obviously, the changes will increase the chances of the adversary winning.

Protocol P_5. $P_5 = P_4$, except that if a password guess against partnered instances is made, i.e. if a *guess_paired* event occurs, the protocol halts and the adversary fails. We assume that the test for *correctpw* occurs after the test for *guess_paired*.

Claim. For any adversary $\mathcal{A}$, $Adv_{P_4}^{ake}(\mathcal{A}) \leq Adv_{P_5}^{ake}(\mathcal{A}) + 2q_{se} Adv_{R_q}^{PWE}(t', q_{ro})$.

Proof. If *guess_paired* does not occur, then P_4 and P_5 are indistinguishable. We set E as the event that *guess_paired* occurs, and the probability that E occurs is ϵ. Then we have $Adv_{P_4}^{ake}(\mathcal{A}) \leq Adv_{P_5}^{ake}(\mathcal{A}) + 2\epsilon$.

We construct an algorithm $\mathcal{D}$ to solve PWE by running $\mathcal{A}$. Given (a, X, Y, v), $\mathcal{D}$ chooses $d \in \{1, \ldots, q_{se}\}$ and simulates P_4 for $\mathcal{A}$ with these changes:

- In the dth CA0 query to $\Pi_C^{i'}$ with input S, let *seed* $\xleftarrow{\$} \{0,1\}^{256}$, $m = X$.
- In a SA1 query to Π_S^j with input $<C, m, seed>$ generated by a CA0 query to $\Pi_C^{i'}$ with input S, set $y_S = Y + as_{ff} + e_{ff}$, where $s_{ff}, e_{ff} \xleftarrow{\$} \chi$.
- In a CA1 query to $\Pi_C^{i'}$, if $\Pi_C^{i'}$ is unpaired, $\mathcal{D}$ outputs 0 and halts.
- In a SA2 query to Π_S^j, if Π_S^j was paired with $\Pi_C^{i'}$ after its SA1 query, but is not now paired with $\Pi_C^{i'}$, no test *correctpw* is made and Π_S^j aborts.
- When $\mathcal{A}$ finishes, for every $H_l(C, S, m, y_S, k_\sigma, \gamma')$ query, where m and y_S were generated by $\Pi_C^{i'}$ and Π_S^j, where Π_S^j was paired with $\Pi_C^{i'}$ after its SA1 query, and H_1 returned $-\gamma' = as_h + e_h$, then the simulator can compute $X \cdot s_y + e = \sigma_S + Y \cdot s_h - (X + \gamma') \cdot s_{ff}$, and add $k'_\sigma = Rec(\sigma_S + Y \cdot s_h - (X + \gamma') \cdot s_{ff}, v)$ to the list of possible values for τ.

The probability that *guess_paired* occurs for $\Pi_C^{i'}$ is at least $\frac{\epsilon}{q_{se}}$. The simulation is perfectly indistinguishable from P_4 unless (1) *guess_server*(S, j, C, pw) occurs, where Π_S^j was paired with $\Pi_C^{i'}$ after its SA1 query, or (2) $\Pi_C^{i'}$ is unpaired with a server instance when the CA1 query is made. Since case 2 implies that *guess_paired* will not occur for $\Pi_C^{i'}$, the probability of case 1 is at most $\frac{\epsilon}{q_{se}}$. If case 1 occurs, the correct τ is added to the list. $\mathcal{D}$ creates a list of size q_{ro} with advantage $\frac{\epsilon}{q_{se}}$. We set $t' = O(t + (q_{ro} + q_{se} + q_{ex})t_{exp})$ as the running time of $\mathcal{D}$. The claim follows from the fact $Adv_{R_q}^{PWE}(\mathcal{D}) \leq AdvR_q^{PWE}(t', q_{ro})$.

Protocol P_6. $P_6 = P_5$, except that if two password guesses against the same server instance are made, i.e. if *guess_double_server* occurs, the protocol halts and the adversary fails. We assume that the test for *guess_paired* or *correctpw* occurs after the test for *guess_double_server*.

Claim. For any adversary $\mathcal{A}$, $Adv_{P_5}^{ake}(\mathcal{A}) \leq Adv_{P_6}^{ake}(\mathcal{A}) + 4Adv_{R_q}^{PWE}(t'', q_{ro}^2)$.

Proof. We set E as the event that *guess_double_server* occurs, and the probability that E occurs is ϵ. Then we have $Adv_{P_4}^{ake}(\mathcal{A}) \leq Adv_{P_5}^{ake}(\mathcal{A}) + 2\epsilon$.

We construct an algorithm $\mathcal{D}$ to solve PWE by running $\mathcal{A}$. Given (a, X, Y, v), $\mathcal{D}$ simulates P_5 for $\mathcal{A}$ with these changes:

– In an $H_1(pw)$ query, output $X \cdot s_h + (as_f + e_f)$, where $s_f, e_f, s_h \xleftarrow{\$} \chi$.
– In a SA1 query to Π_S^j with input $<C, m, seed>$ where $m \in R_q$, $seed \xleftarrow{\$} \{0, 1\}^{256}$, set $y_S = Y + as_{ff} + e_{ff}$, where $s_{ff}, e_{ff} \xleftarrow{\$} \chi$.
– There is no test for *correctpw* and *guess_paired*. The client or server instances that are unpaired but receive a CA1 or SA2 query abort. And H_l queries return random values from $\{0, 1\}^\kappa$.
– When $\mathcal{A}$ finishes, for every pair of $H_l(C, S, m, y_S, k_\sigma, \gamma')$ and $H_l(C, S, m, y_S, \hat{k}_\sigma, \hat{\gamma}')$, there is a SA1 query to Π_S^j with input $<C, m, seed>$ and output $<y_S, k, v'>$, an $H_1(pw)$ query returned $-\gamma' = X \cdot s_h + (as_f + e_f)$, an $H_1(\hat{pw})$ query returned $-\hat{\gamma}' = X \cdot s_{\hat{h}} + (as_{\hat{f}} + e_{\hat{f}})$ and $s_h \neq s_{\hat{h}}$, then the simulator can compute $X \cdot s_y = (\sigma_S - \hat{\sigma}_S - Y(s_f - s_{\hat{f}}) - (\hat{\gamma}' - \gamma') \cdot s_{ff}) \cdot (s_h - s_{\hat{h}})^{-1}$, and add $k'_\sigma = Rec((\sigma_S - \hat{\sigma}_S - Y(s_f - s_{\hat{f}}) - (\hat{\gamma}' - \gamma') \cdot s_{ff}) \cdot (s_h - s_{\hat{h}})^{-1}, v)$ to the list of possible values for τ.

The simulation is perfectly indistinguishable from P_5 unless *guess_double_server*, *guess_paired* or *correctpw* occurs, or $\mathcal{A}$ makes a *Corrupt* query. If *Corrupt*, *correctpw* or *guess_paired* occurs, *doublepwserver* will not occur. if *guess_double_server* occurs, then with a probability of $\frac{1}{2}$ it occurs for two passwords pw and $\hat{pw}$ with $s_h \neq s_{\hat{h}}$, and the correct τ is added to the list. $\mathcal{D}$ creates a list of size q_{ro}^2 with advantage $\frac{\epsilon}{2}$. We set $t'' = O(t + (q_{ro}^2 + q_{se} + q_{ex})t_{exp})$ as the running time of $\mathcal{D}$. The claim follows from the fact $Adv_{R_q}^{PWE}(\mathcal{D}) \leq AdvR_q^{PWE}(t'', q_{ro}^2)$.

Protocol P_7. $P_7 = P_6$, except that there is an internal password oracle that is not available to the adversary and generates all passwords during initialization. It holds all passwords, accepts queries of the form $testpw(C, pw)$ that test the correctness of a given password and return 1 if $pw = pw_C$ and 0 otherwise. It also accepts $Corrupt(U)$ queries. To test if $correctpw$ occurs, whenever the first $guess\_client\_2(C, i, S, pw)$ event or the first $guess\_server(S, j, C, pw)$ event occurs, perform a $testpw(C, pw)$ query to see if $pw = pw_C$.

Claim. For any adversary $\mathcal{A}$, $Adv_{P_6}^{ake}(\mathcal{A}) = Adv_{P_7}^{ake}(\mathcal{A}) \leq \frac{q_{se}}{N}$.

Proof. It can be found that P_7 and P_6 are perfectly indistinguishable.

Since a $Corrupt$ query to the password oracle occurs after at most q_{se} queries, and the passwords are uniformly selected from a dictionary of size N, $Pr(correctpw) < \frac{q_{se}}{N}$. If $correctpw$ does not occur, then the only way for the adversary to succeed is to make a $Test$ query to a fresh instance Π_U^i and guessing the bit used in that $Test$ query. Since the view of the adversary is independent of sk_U^i, the success probability is $\frac{1}{2}$.

$$Pr(Succ_{P_7}^{ake}(\mathcal{A})) \leq Pr(correctpw) + Pr(Succ_{P_7}^{ake}(\mathcal{A})|\neg correctpw)(Pr(\neg correctpw))$$

$$\leq Pr(correctpw) + \frac{1}{2}(1 - Pr(correctpw)) \leq \frac{1}{2} + \frac{q_{se}}{2N}$$

Then we can obtain the advantage of the adversary against P_7 as $Adv_{P_7}^{ake}(\mathcal{A}) = 2Pr(Succ_{P_7}^{ake}(\mathcal{A})) - 1 \leq \frac{q_{se}}{N}$.

Combining above claims, we can get the result in Theorem 2.

5 Implementation

This section focuses on our implementation details, including the C reference implementation and the optimized implementation with the AVX2 instruction set. We choose SHA3-256 as our hash function, which is based on Keccak and standardized in FIPS-202. An extendable-output function (XOF) called SHAKE-128 is also provided by FIPS-202, which offers 128-bits of (post-quantum) security against collisions and preimage attacks. We have $H_1 = $ SHAKE-128() and $H_i = $ SHA3-256() for $i \in \{2, 3, 4\}$.

For the parameters set, we choose the dimension $n = 1024$, the modulus $q = 12289$, the standard deviation $\varsigma = \sqrt{16/2}$, and $(m, g, d) = (2, 2^6, 2975)$.

5.1 Portable C Implementation

Our C reference implementation does not rely on hardware and instruction sets, so it is portable. In implementation, we try to avoid time-consuming operations such as floating point arithmetic, divide operations, and modulo operations. We make full use of bitwise operations and various programming techniques to reduce unnecessary overhead and achieve better performance. Therefore, the reference implementation is also more efficient.

Small seeds are obtained from Linux pseudo-random number generators/dev/urandom. We instantiate *Gen* with SHAKE-128. It extends a small seed to a polynomial a. Each of the outputs of SHAKE-128 is a 16-bit integer and will be reduced modulo 2^{14} by setting two most-significant bits to zero. If it is smaller than q, it will be used as a coefficient of a, otherwise it will be rejected.

For the noise distribution, we sample from the central binomial distribution ψ_b by calculating $\sum_{i=0}^{b} x_i - x_i'$, where $x_i, x_i' \in \{0,1\}$ are uniform independent bits. And we obtain uniform random bits from seeds using ChaCha20 stream cipher that is standardized for TLS.

We use NTT, Montgomery reductions and short Barrett reductions to speed up operations on polynomials. NTT is widely used for ideal lattice-based cryptography and can accelerate polynomial multiplications. Montgomery reductions can implement fast modular multiplication without using division, and short Barrett reduction is used to perform modular reductions after addition. The combination of these three algorithms can improve the efficiency of polynomial operations. We refer to the code in [1], which uses an optimized NTT and stores all precomputed constants in Montgomery representation to speed up the modular-arithmetic.

In addition, we assume that a is generated directly in the NTT domain, which reduces two NTT operations, and the polynomials are also sent in the NTT domain to reduce inverse NTT operations.

5.2 AVX2 Implementation

AVX2 is also known as Haswell New Instructions that supports operations on 256-bit vectors of 8 single-precision or 4 double-precision floating-point numbers, or of integers of various sizes in parallel. We use those instructions to optimize our implementation.

Referring to the method in [9], we optimized the generation of a. In the reference implementation, the sample rejection rate is $1 - q/2^{14} \approx 25\%$. In this implementation, we reject values that are larger than $5q$ from the pseudorandom stream without ignoring two most-significant bits, and subtract q up to four times from the accepted values. By doing so, the rejection rate is reduced to $1 - 5q/2^{16} \approx 6\%$, and the number of values we generate and check is reduced. Then, we use AVX2 instructions to parallelize the rejection sampling step and replace the SHAKE-128 by a faster, parallel implementation of SHA-256. Through the above two ways, the generation efficiency of a is improved.

When sampling noise distribution, we use AES-256 to generate uniform noise by taking the advantage of AES instruction set provided by processors. Then we utilize AVX2 vector instructions to optimize the transformation from uniform noise to the centered binomial.

For polynomial arithmetic, AVX2 instruction set can also be used to speed up NTT. Güneysu et al. represent coefficients as double-precision integers and achieve a good performance [10]. We use a similar approach and represent polynomials as arrays of double-precision floating-point numbers. This vectorized double-precision floating point arithmetic is also used in [1,5].

6   Results and Comparison

In this section, we analyze the security strength and performance of the proposed protocol. For comparison, we implement our work and the currently relatively efficient lattice-based PAKE scheme [8] in C language. The results are obtained on a 1.80 GHz Intel Core i7-8550U CPU and 2 GB RAM computer with an Ubuntu 18.04.1 LTS 64 bit system.

To get concrete security strength analysis, we use the approach from [1] which provides the core-SVP hardness estimation under the primal and dual attacks. The smallest cost of attacks are shown in Table 1. In the analysis, since we are more optimistic about the ability of the adversary, the security of [8] is lower than they claimed. In [8], they choose a very large modulus $q = 2^{32} - 1$ due to a far from tight failure probability analysis, which results in a reduction in security strength. It can be seen that the security strength of our protocol is significantly higher than that of [8].

Table 1. Security strength

		Classical	Quantum	Best plausible
Ours	Primal	282	253	200
	Dual	229	206	165
Ding's [8]	Primal	86	77	61
	Dual	84	76	62

Table 2 lists the sizes of message to be transferred. In both protocols, the client needs to send a polynomial, a hash value and a client identity; the server needs to send a polynomial, a signal value and a hash value. The difference is that in our design the client needs to send a small seed. Due to the large q and polynomial size in [8], although we need to send one more seed, and our signal value is larger than [8], our total message size is still smaller than that of [8].

Table 2. Message size

	Client → Server (bytes)	Server → Client (bytes)
Ours	1,864	2,592
Ding's [8]	4,136	4,256

The cycle counts presented in Table 3 are the median and average of 1000 executions. In [8], since the chosen q prevents them from using NTT, they sample the noise from the Gaussian distribution and use Fast Fourier Transformation (FFT) to speed up the polynomial operations. By switching to the centered binomial noise distribution and utilizing NTT for acceleration, the performance of our scheme is greatly improved. It can be seen from Table 3 that our scheme is more than 12x faster than [8]. Moreover, the reconciliation mechanism used by [8] can only reconcile one single bit in one calculation, while the reconciliation mechanism we use can change the length of reconciliation bits by adjusting m. When m increases, the performance will not reduce significantly. Besides, after using AVX2 optimization in our scheme, the performance of sampling, generation of a, and NTT has increased significantly. The number of cycles required for protocol execution is only half that of the reference implementation, which means that the efficiency doubles. In general, our scheme is very efficient and practical.

Table 3. Cycle counts

		Client	Server	Generate a	Sample noise	NTT	inv-NTT
Ding's [8]	Median	3,374,046	3,435,200		↳		
	Average	3,574,888	3,666,014				
Our portable C implementation	Median	228,803	226,004	23,836	16,300	25,132	29,845
	Average	294,460	270,227	30,885	17,370	36,235	38,636
Our AVX2 implementation	Median	102,182	101,766	14,093	2,745	4,520	5,013
	Average	145,964	137,313	15,742	3,456	4,790	5,068

7   Conclusions

In this paper, we proposed an efficient PAKE protocol based on the RLWE problem for the post-quantum environment. By designing the protocol based on ROM instead of using a CRS, our scheme's construction is simpler and more practical. A new error reconciliation mechanism, namely asymmetric key consensus, was used in our protocol to allow the server to perform some pre-computation. In this way, the protocol could reduce the load on server and better adapt to the client-server scenario, especially the high concurrency situation.

We gave a formal security proof of our protocol under the BPR model, which implied that it had forward secrecy and was resistant to dictionary attacks and loss of session keys. Through regenerating the public parameter each time, the risks of backdoor placement and all-for-the-price-of-one attacks were reduced. And by choosing the central binomial distribution as the noise distribution, the efficiency of our scheme was improved and timing attacks could be prevented.

Benefiting from the selection of appropriate parameters, such as n and q, we further increased the security strength of the protocol while reducing the transmitted message size.

Finally, we implemented a portable C implementation of the protocol, in which we use efficient algorithms and programming techniques to achieve better performance. We used algorithms such as NTT to speed up polynomial operations, and tried to avoid the time-consuming operations like division and modulo operations. And by reducing the sample rejection rate and using parallelized algorithms, the performance loss caused by regenerating a was cut down. Furthermore, we also optimized the implementation using the AVX2 instruction set. Our reference C implementation and AVX2 implementation are more than 12x and 24x faster than the implementation of existing scheme, respectively.

References

1. Alkim, E., Ducas, L., Pöppelmann, T., Schwabe, P.: Post-quantum key exchange - a new hope. In: Holz, T., Savage, S. (eds.) 25th USENIX Security Symposium, USENIX Security 2016, Austin, TX, USA, 10–12 August 2016, pp. 327–343. USENIX Association (2016)
2. Bellare, M., Pointcheval, D., Rogaway, P.: Authenticated key exchange secure against dictionary attacks. In: Preneel, B. (ed.) EUROCRYPT 2000. LNCS, vol. 1807, pp. 139–155. Springer, Heidelberg (2000). https://doi.org/10.1007/3-540-45539-6_11
3. Bellovin, S.M., Merritt, M.: Encrypted key exchange: password-based protocols secure against dictionary attacks. In: 1992 IEEE Computer Society Symposium on Research in Security and Privacy, Oakland, CA, USA, 4–6 May 1992, pp. 72–84. IEEE Computer Society (1992). https://doi.org/10.1109/RISP.1992.213269
4. Bos, J.W., Costello, C., Naehrig, M., Stebila, D.: Post-quantum key exchange for the TLS protocol from the ring learning with errors problem. In: 2015 IEEE Symposium on Security and Privacy, SP 2015, San Jose, CA, USA, 17–21 May 2015, pp. 553–570. IEEE Computer Society (2015). https://doi.org/10.1109/SP.2015.40
5. Bos, J.W., et al.: CRYSTALS-Kyber: a CCA-secure module-lattice-based KEM. In: 2018 IEEE European Symposium on Security and Privacy, EuroS&P 2018, London, United Kingdom, 24–26 April 2018, pp. 353–367. IEEE (2018). https://doi.org/10.1109/EuroSP.2018.00032
6. Boyko, V., MacKenzie, P., Patel, S.: Provably secure password-authenticated key exchange using Diffie-Hellman. In: Preneel, B. (ed.) EUROCRYPT 2000. LNCS, vol. 1807, pp. 156–171. Springer, Heidelberg (2000). https://doi.org/10.1007/3-540-45539-6_12
7. Ding, J.: A simple provably secure key exchange scheme based on the learning with errors problem. IACR Cryptology ePrint Archive 2012/688 (2012)
8. Ding, J., Alsayigh, S., Lancrenon, J., RV, S., Snook, M.: Provably secure password authenticated key exchange based on RLWE for the post-quantum world. In: Handschuh, H. (ed.) CT-RSA 2017. LNCS, vol. 10159, pp. 183–204. Springer, Cham (2017). https://doi.org/10.1007/978-3-319-52153-4_11
9. Gueron, S., Schlieker, F.: Speeding up R-LWE post-quantum key exchange. In: Brumley, B.B., Röning, J. (eds.) NordSec 2016. LNCS, vol. 10014, pp. 187–198. Springer, Cham (2016). https://doi.org/10.1007/978-3-319-47560-8_12
10. Güneysu, T., Oder, T., Pöppelmann, T., Schwabe, P.: Software speed records for lattice-based signatures. In: Gaborit, P. (ed.) PQCrypto 2013. LNCS, vol. 7932, pp. 67–82. Springer, Heidelberg (2013). https://doi.org/10.1007/978-3-642-38616-9_5

11. Jin, Z., Zhao, Y.: Optimal key consensus in presence of noise. IACR Cryptology ePrint Archive 2017/1058 (2017)
12. Katz, J., Ostrovsky, R., Yung, M.: Efficient password-authenticated key exchange using human-memorable passwords. In: Pfitzmann, B. (ed.) EUROCRYPT 2001. LNCS, vol. 2045, pp. 475–494. Springer, Heidelberg (2001). https://doi.org/10.1007/3-540-44987-6_29
13. Katz, J., Vaikuntanathan, V.: Smooth projective hashing and password-based authenticated key exchange from lattices. In: Matsui, M. (ed.) ASIACRYPT 2009. LNCS, vol. 5912, pp. 636–652. Springer, Heidelberg (2009). https://doi.org/10.1007/978-3-642-10366-7_37
14. Lyubashevsky, V., Peikert, C., Regev, O.: On ideal lattices and learning with errors over rings. In: Gilbert, H. (ed.) EUROCRYPT 2010. LNCS, vol. 6110, pp. 1–23. Springer, Heidelberg (2010). https://doi.org/10.1007/978-3-642-13190-5_1
15. Peikert, C.: Lattice cryptography for the internet. In: Mosca, M. (ed.) PQCrypto 2014. LNCS, vol. 8772, pp. 197–219. Springer, Cham (2014). https://doi.org/10.1007/978-3-319-11659-4_12
16. Zhang, J., Yu, Y.: Two-round PAKE from approximate SPH and instantiations from lattices. In: Takagi, T., Peyrin, T. (eds.) ASIACRYPT 2017. LNCS, vol. 10626, pp. 37–67. Springer, Cham (2017). https://doi.org/10.1007/978-3-319-70700-6_2

A Lattice-Based Certificateless Public Key Encryption with Equality Test in Standard Model

Dung Hoang Duong[1(✉)], Willy Susilo[1], Minh Kim Bui[2], and Thanh Xuan Khuc[3]

[1] Institute of Cybersecurity and Cryptology, School of Computing and Information Technology, University of Wollongong, Northfields Avenue, Wollongong, NSW 2522, Australia
{hduong,wsusilo}@uow.edu.au
[2] Faculty of Mathematics and Computer Science, University of Science, Vietnam National University, Ho Chi Minh City, Vietnam
kmath93@gmail.com
[3] Institute of Cryptography Science and Technology, Government Information Security Committee, Hanoi, Vietnam
khucxuanthanh@gmail.com

Abstract. Certificateless public key encryption (CL-PKE) solves the problems of establishing public-key infrastructure for traditional public key encryption and resolving key escrow for identity-based encryption. Equality test is an extremely useful property that enables the ability of checking whether two ciphertexts encrypting the same message. Qu et al. (Information Science 2019) introduced the notion of certificateless public key encryption with equality test (CL-PKEET), together with four types of adversaries, that solves certificate manangement and key escrow problems of public key encryption with equality test (PKEET) and identity-based encryption with equality test (IBEET), and proposed a first CL-PKEET scheme based on Bilinear Diffie-Hellman assumption in random oracle model. In this paper, we propose the first lattice-based CL-PKEET in standard model whose security is reduced to the hardness of the learning with errors problem. In particular, we prove that our schemes are secure against two types of selective-identity adversaries introduced by Qu et al.

Keywords: CL-PKEET · Lattice-based cryptography · Learning with errors

1 Introduction

One of main difficulties today in developing secure systems based on public key cryptography is the deployment and management of infrastructures to support the authenticity of cryptographic keys: there is a need to provide an assurance

Z. Liu and M. Yung (Eds.): Inscrypt 2019, LNCS 12020, pp. 50–65, 2020.
https://doi.org/10.1007/978-3-030-42921-8_3

to the user about the relationship between a public key and the identity (or authority) of the holder of the corresponding private key. In the traditional Public Key Infrastructure (PKI), a trusted certificate authority (CA) composes certificates to ensure the authenticity of the users. It brings a vexing problem - certificate management problem. To deal with it, Shamir [14] introduced the notion of identity-based encryption (IBE). The public key of a user in IBE just is the user's identity (e.g., his email address), and the user's secret key is a product of the user's identity and the master secret key of a trusted private key generator (PKG). Although IBE no longer requires certificates, it suffers from the key escrow problem; namely, PKG knows all users' secret keys. In 2003, Al-Riyami and Paterson [4] proposed a new type of encryption scheme that avoids the drawbacks of both traditional public-key encryption and identity-based encryption. They termed this new type of encryption certificateless public-key encryption (CL-PKE) because their encryption scheme did not require a public key infrastructure. Roughly speaking, their idea was to combine the advantages of traditional PKI-based public-key encryption and identity-based encryption. In CL-PKE, the private key of a user includes two parts, namely, a secret value and a partial private key. The secret value is randomly selected by the user while the partial private key is generated with her/his identity by a key generation center (KGC). Hence, the KGC does not know a user's private key so that the key escrow problem occurred in IBE is avoided. In addition, the user independently generates and publishes the public key, so the need of certificates in conventional PKC is abolished.

In the cloud era, plenty of cloud services offer a broad set of global computation, analytics, storage, deployment, and application services to help organizations run faster and at lower cost. Encrypting data can also ensure that the cloud service providers do not get to access or accidentally expose users' data. Users may later need to access their encrypted data and information and hence they will be prompted to search for it. Boneh et al. [6] came up with the notion of incorporating searching using keywords with the public key encryption for an effective way for users to retrieve their information effectively, which is known as public key encryption with keyword search (PKEKS). Nonetheless, for this PKEKS scheme, the cloud server only compares keywords with trapdoors that have been encrypted with the same public keys and hence this scheme becomes unsuitable for searching the cloud. Public key encryption with equality test (PKEET), which was first introduced by Yang et al. [17], is a special kind of public key encryption that allows anyone with a given trapdoor to test whether two ciphertexts are generated by the same message. Compared to PKEKS, the equality test in PKEET can be performed between two ciphertexts encrypted in the same public key and different public keys. This property is of use in various practical applications, such as keyword search on encrypted data, encrypted data partitioning for efficient encrypted data management, personal health record systems, spam filtering in encrypted email systems and so on. However, anyone is able to verify the equality of ciphertexts without any authorization in Yang et al.'s scheme, which violates the data owners' privacy. Ma [11] proposed the concept of identity-based encryption with equality test (IBEET), which simplifies the certificate management problem of PKEET and supports user-level authorization. Recently, Qu et al. [12] proposed the concept of certificateless public key encryption with equality test (CL-PKEET), which integrates CL-PKE into PKEET to solve the key escrow problem of IBEET. However, the CL-PKEET scheme proposed by Qu et al. [12] is only proved secure in the random oracle model that does not guarantee the security in the real world.

The above encryption schemes are mainly based on bilinear pairing technique with the Bilinear Diffie-Hellman assumption. The main drawbacks of these schemes are vulnerable to quantum attacks. Currently, lattice-based cryptography is considered to be the most promising candidate for post-quantum cryptography, so far there is no viable quantum algorithm to solve difficulty lattice problems. Compared with bilinear pairing, lattice-based cryptography usually just involve simple vector-matrix multiplication and modular addition operations, thus huge of computational resources can be saved. Sepahi et al. [16] introduced a generic construction of a CL-PKE that makes use of a 2-level HIBE, an IBE, a MAC and an encapsulation scheme. And they yield the first instance of a lattice-based CL-PKE by utilizing HIBE and IBE from [1], an encapsulation scheme from [10] and a MAC using a universal hash function [8]. However, they have not actually provide a concrete scheme and how the schemes they used properly work together. Specially, we do not have a MAC in lattice settings.

Our Contribution. In this paper, we introduce a certificateless public key encryption with equality test (CL-PKEET) in standard model. We first revisit the generic construction of [16] and their instantiation on lattices. Instead of using an encapsulation scheme and a MAC, we utilize a strong unforgeable signature scheme based on the full IBE in [1]. In this way, we will force all HIBE, IBE and the signature scheme to have the same public key and make the instantiation in lattices simpler. In addition, we use the recent technique by Duong et al. [9] to add the equality test property for our instantiation, resulting to the first CL-PKEET based on lattices in standard model. We prove that our scheme is secure against two types of selective-identity chosen ciphertext attacks introduced in [12].

2   Preliminaries

2.1   Certificateless Public Key Encryption with Equality Test

In this section, we follow [12] to define certificateless public key encryption with equality test and its security model.

Definition 1 (CL-PKEET). *A certificateless public key encryption with equality test (CL-PKEET) scheme consists of nine algorithms:*

- Setup(λ): *This algorithm, run by the key generation center (KGC), takes the security parameter λ as input, and outputs the master public key MPK and the master secret key MSK.*

- ExtractPartialPrivateKey(MPK, MSK, ID): *This algorithm is run by the* KGC *once for each user when he requests for his partial private key. It takes the master public key* MPK, *the master secret key* MSK *and a receiver's identity* ID $\in \{0,1\}^*$ *as input, and outputs the receiver's partial private key* PSK_{ID}.
- SetSecretValue(MPK, ID): *This algorithm, run by a receiver, takes the master public key* MPK *and a receiver's identity* ID *as input, and outputs the receiver's secret value* SV_{ID}.
- SetPublicKey(MPK, SV_{ID}): *This algorithm, run by a receiver, takes the master public key* MPK *and the receiver's secret value* SV_{ID} *as input, and outputs the receiver's public key* PK_{ID}.
- SetPrivateKey(MPK, PSK_{ID}, SV_{ID}): *This algorithm, run by a receiver, takes the master public key* MPK, *the receiver's partial private key* PSK_{ID} *and the secret value* SV_{ID} *as input, and outputs the receiver's (full) private key* SK_{ID}.
- Encrypt($\mathbf{m}$, MPK, ID, PK_{ID}): *On input* MPK, *an identity* ID *with its public key* PK_{ID} *and a message* $\mathbf{m}$, *it outputs a ciphertext* CT.
- Dec(MPK, SK_{ID}, CT): *On input* MPK, *a user* ID*'s secret key* SK_{ID} *and a ciphertext* CT, *it outputs a message* $\mathbf{m}'$ *or* $\perp$.
- Trapdoor(SK_{ID}): *On input the secret key* SK_{ID} *for the user* ID, *it outputs a trapdoor* td_{ID}.
- Test(td_{ID_i}, td_{ID_j}, CT_{ID_i}, CT_{ID_j}): *On input two trapdoors* td_{ID_i}, td_{ID_j} *and two ciphertexts* CT_{ID_i}, CT_{ID_j} *for users* ID_i *and* ID_j *respectively, it outputs* 1 *or* 0.

For correctness, we require the following:

1. It holds that $\mathbf{m} =$ Decrypt(MPK, SK_{ID}, Encrypt($\mathbf{m}$, MPK, ID, PK_{ID})) where PK_{ID} and $SK_I D$ are the public key and private key of the identity ID respectively.
2. Let (CT_A, td_A) and (CT_B, td_B) are ciphertext and trapdoor of the identity ID_A and ID_B respectively, with $CT_A =$ Encrypt($\mathbf{m}_A$, MPK, ID_A, PK_{ID_A}) and $CT_B =$ Encrypt($\mathbf{m}_B$, MPK, ID_B, PK_{ID_B}). If $\mathbf{m}_A = \mathbf{m}_B$ then we must have Test(td_{ID_A}, td_{ID_B}, CT_{ID_A}, CT_{ID_B}) $= 1$; otherwise (in case $\mathbf{m}_A \neq \mathbf{m}_B$) $\Pr[$Test(td_{ID_A}, td_{ID_B}, CT_{ID_A}, CT_{ID_B}) $= 1]$ is negligible.

The security model of a CL-PKEET scheme against four types of adversaries above is described in the following.

- Type-1 adversary: The master key cannot be accessed by this type of adversary, but the adversary can replace the receiver's public key. Moreover, without the trapdoor, he cannot decide the ciphertext is computed on which message. We define the IND-CCA security model with respect to this type of adversary.
- Type-2 adversary: The master key can be accessed by this type of adversary, but the adversary cannot replace the receiver's public key. Moreover, without the trapdoor, he cannot decide the ciphertext is computed on which message. We define the IND-CCA security model with respect to this type of adversary.

- Type-3 adversary: The master key cannot be accessed by this type of adversary, but the adversary can replace the receiver's public key. Moreover, with the trapdoor, he cannot reveal the message from the challenge ciphertext. We define the OW-CCA security model with respect to this type of adversary.
- Type-4 adversary: The master key can be accessed by this type of adversary, but the adversary cannot replace the receiver's public key. Moreover, with the trapdoor, he cannot reveal the message from the challenge ciphertext. We define the OW-CCA security model with respect to this type of adversary.

In this paper, we propose a scheme that is secure against Type-1 and Type-3 adversaries. Hence, we only mention games in security model against those adversaries.

IND-CCA Security Against Type-1 Adversaries. We illustrate the game between a challenger $\mathcal{C}$ and a Type-1 adversary $\mathcal{A}_1$ as follows:

1. **Setup:** Suppose that the security parameter is λ. The master public key MPK and the master secret key MSK are generated by the challenger $\mathcal{C}$ by running the algorithm Setup. MSK and MPK are given to $\mathcal{A}_1$.
2. **Phase 1:** The adversary $\mathcal{A}$ may make queries polynomially many times adaptively and in any order to the following oracles:
   - Partial private key query (ID): Upon receiving a receiver's identity ID, $\mathcal{C}$ responds with the corresponding partial private key $\mathsf{PSK}_{\mathsf{ID}}$.
   - Private key query (ID): Upon receiving a receiver's identity ID, $\mathcal{C}$ responds with the corresponding private key $\mathsf{SK}_{\mathsf{ID}}$.
   - Public key query (ID): Upon receiving a receiver's identity $\mathsf{ID}_{\mathsf{ID}}$, $\mathcal{C}$ responds with the corresponding public key $\mathsf{PK}_{\mathsf{ID}}$.
   - Replace public key (ID, $\mathsf{PK}_{\mathsf{ID}}$): Upon receiving a receiver's identity ID and a public key $\mathsf{PK}_{\mathsf{ID}}$, $\mathcal{C}$ replaces the corresponding public key with $\mathsf{PK}_{\mathsf{ID}}$.
   - Decryption query (ID, CT): Upon receiving a receiver's identity ID and a ciphertext CT, $\mathcal{C}$ responds with the output of the algorithm Decryption $\mathsf{Decrypt}(\mathsf{MPK}, \mathsf{CT}, \mathsf{SK}_{\mathsf{ID}})$, where $\mathsf{SK}_{\mathsf{ID}}$ is the private key with respect to the identity ID.
   - Trapdoor query (ID): Upon receiving a receiver's identity ID, $\mathcal{C}$ responds with the corresponding trapdoor $\mathsf{td}_{\mathsf{ID}}$.
3. **Challenge:** $\mathcal{C}$ chooses a random message $\mathbf{m}$ in the message space and run $\mathsf{CT}^* \leftarrow \mathsf{Encrypt}(\mathbf{m}, \mathsf{MPK}, \mathsf{ID}^*, \mathsf{PK}_{\mathsf{ID}^*})$, and sends CT^* to $\mathcal{A}$.
4. **Phase 2:** $\mathcal{A}_1$ issues queries as done in Phase 1 with the following constraints:
   - ID^* should not appear in the Private key query, Partial private key query and Trapdoor query.
   - If a public key has been replaced, the corresponding identity ID should not appear in the Private key query.
   - $(\mathsf{ID}^*, \mathsf{CT}^*)$ should not appear in the Decryption query.
5. **Guess:** $\mathcal{A}_1$ outputs $\rho' \in \{0, 1\}$. If $\rho = \rho'$, $\mathcal{A}_1$ wins this game. The advantage of $\mathcal{A}_1$ is defined as

$$\mathsf{Adv}_{CLPKE, \mathcal{A}_1}^{\mathsf{IND\text{-}CCA}, \mathsf{Type\text{-}1}}(\lambda) = \left| \Pr\left[\rho = \rho'\right] - \frac{1}{2} \right|.$$

A CL-PKEET scheme is IND-CCA secure against Type-1 adversary if for any PPT adversary $\mathcal{A}_1$, its advantage $\mathsf{Adv}_{\mathsf{CL\text{-}PKEET},\mathcal{A}_1}^{\mathsf{IND\text{-}CCA,Type\text{-}1}}(\lambda)$ is negligible.

OW-CCA Security Against Type-3 Adversaries. We illustrate the game between a challenger $\mathcal{C}$ and a Type-3 adversary $\mathcal{A}_3$ as follows:

1. **Setup:** Suppose that the security parameter is λ. The master public key MPK and the master secret key MSK are generated by the challenger $\mathcal{C}$ by running the algorithm Setup. MSK is kept by $\mathcal{C}$ itself, and MPK is given to $\mathcal{A}_3$.
2. **Phase 1:** The following queries can be issued by $\mathcal{A}_3$ for polynomially many times.
   - Partial private key query (ID): Upon receiving a receiver's identity ID, $\mathcal{C}$ responds with the corresponding partial private key $\mathsf{PSK_{ID}}$.
   - Private key query (ID): Upon receiving a receiver's identity ID, $\mathcal{C}$ responds with the corresponding private key $\mathsf{SK_{ID}}$.
   - Public key query (ID): Upon receiving a receiver's identity ID, $\mathcal{C}$ responds with the corresponding public key $\mathsf{PK_{ID}}$.
   - Replace public key (ID,$\mathsf{PK_{ID}}$): Upon receiving a receiver's identity ID and a public key $\mathsf{PK_{ID}}$, $\mathcal{C}$ replaces the corresponding public key with $\mathsf{PK_{ID}}$.
   - Decryption query (ID, CT): Upon receiving a receiver's identity ID and a ciphertext CT, $\mathcal{C}$ responds with the output of the algorithm Decryption Decrypt(MPK, $\mathsf{SK_{ID}}$, CT), where $\mathsf{SK_{ID}}$ is the private key with respect to the identity ID.
   - Trapdoor query (ID): Upon receiving a receiver's identity ID, $\mathcal{C}$ responds with the corresponding trapdoor $\mathsf{td_{ID}}$.
3. **Challenge:** $\mathcal{A}_3$ submits an identity ID^* for challenge. $\mathcal{C}$ selects a message $\mathbf{m}^*$ randomly, and then sends the challenge ciphertext CT^* computed by $\mathsf{CT}^* = \mathsf{Encrypt}(\mathbf{m}^*, \mathsf{MPK}, \mathsf{ID}, \mathsf{PK_{ID^*}})$ to $\mathcal{A}_3$, where $\mathsf{PK_{ID^*}}$ is the public key with respect to ID^*.
4. **Phase 2:** $\mathcal{A}_3$ issues queries as done in Phase 1 with the following constraints:
   - ID^* should not appear in the Private key query and Partial private key query.
   - If a public key has been replaced, the corresponding identity ID should not appear in the Private key query.
   - $(\mathsf{ID}^*, \mathsf{CT}^*)$ should not appear in the Decryption query.
5. **Guess:** $\mathcal{A}_3$ output $\mathbf{m}'$. If $\mathbf{m}' = \mathbf{m}^*$, $\mathcal{A}_3$ wins this game. The advantage of $\mathcal{A}_3$ is defined as
$$\mathsf{Adv}_{\mathsf{CL\text{-}PKEET},\mathcal{A}_3}^{\mathsf{OW\text{-}CCA,Type\text{-}3}}(\lambda) = \Pr\left[\mathbf{m}' = \mathbf{m}^*\right].$$

A CL-PKEET scheme is OW-CCA secure against Type-3 adversary if for any PPT adversary $\mathcal{A}_3$, its advantage $\mathsf{Adv}_{\mathsf{CL\text{-}PKEET},\mathcal{A}_3}^{\mathsf{OW\text{-}CCA,Type\text{-}3}}(\lambda)$ is negligible.

2.2   Lattices

Throughout the paper, we will mainly focus on integer lattices, which are discrete subgroups of $\mathbb{Z}^m$. Specially, a lattice Λ in $\mathbb{Z}^m$ with basis $B = [\mathbf{b}_1, \cdots, \mathbf{b}_n] \in$

$\mathbb{Z}^{m \times n}$, where each $\mathbf{b}_i$ is written in column form, is defined as

$$\Lambda := \left\{ \sum_{i=1}^{n} \mathbf{b}_i x_i \,|\, x_i \in \mathbb{Z} \,\, \forall i = 1, \cdots, n \right\} \subseteq \mathbb{Z}^m.$$

We call n the rank of Λ and if $n = m$ we say that Λ is a full rank lattice. In this paper, we mainly consider full rank lattices containing $q\mathbb{Z}^m$, called q-ary lattices, defined as the following, for a given matrix $A \in \mathbb{Z}^{n \times m}$ and $\mathbf{u} \in \mathbb{Z}_q^n$

$$\Lambda_q(A) := \{\mathbf{e} \in \mathbb{Z}^m \text{ s.t. } \exists \mathbf{s} \in \mathbb{Z}_q^n \text{ where } A^{\mathrm{T}}\mathbf{s} = \mathbf{e} \mod q\}$$
$$\Lambda_q^\perp(A) := \{\mathbf{e} \in \mathbb{Z}^m \text{ s.t. } A\mathbf{e} = 0 \mod q\}$$
$$\Lambda_q^{\mathbf{u}}(A) := \{\mathbf{e} \in \mathbb{Z}^m \text{ s.t. } A\mathbf{e} = \mathbf{u} \mod q\}$$

Note that if $\mathbf{t} \in \Lambda_q^{\mathbf{u}}(A)$ then $\Lambda_q^{\mathbf{u}}(A) = \Lambda_q^\perp(A) + \mathbf{t}$.

Let $S = \{\mathbf{s}_1, \cdots, \mathbf{s}_k\}$ be a set of vectors in $\mathbb{R}^m$. We denote by $\|S\| := \max_i \|\mathbf{s}_i\|$ for $i = 1, \cdots, k$, the maximum l_2 length of the vectors in S. We also denote $\tilde{S} := \{\tilde{\mathbf{s}}_1, \cdots, \tilde{\mathbf{s}}_k\}$ the Gram-Schmidt orthogonalization of the vectors $\mathbf{s}_1, \cdots, \mathbf{s}_k$ in that order. We refer to $\|\tilde{S}\|$ the Gram-Schmidt norm of S.

Ajtai [2] first proposed how to sample a uniform matrix $A \in \mathbb{Z}_q^{n \times m}$ with an associated basis S_A of $\Lambda_q^\perp(A)$ with low Gram-Schmidt norm. It is improved later by Alwen and Peikert [3] in the following Theorem.

Theorem 1. *Let $q \geq 3$ be odd and $m := \lceil 6n \log q \rceil$. There is a probabilistic polynomial-time algorithm $\mathsf{TrapGen}(q, n)$ that outputs a pair $(A \in \mathbb{Z}_q^{n \times m}, S \in \mathbb{Z}^{m \times m})$ such that A is statistically close to a uniform matrix in $\mathbb{Z}_q^{n \times m}$ and S is a basis for $\Lambda_q^\perp(A)$ satisfying*

$$\|\tilde{S}\| \leq O(\sqrt{n \log q}) \quad and \quad \|S\| \leq O(n \log q)$$

with all but negligible probability in n.

Definition 1 (Gaussian distribution). *Let $\Lambda \subseteq \mathbb{Z}^m$ be a lattice. For a vector $\mathbf{c} \in \mathbb{R}^m$ and a positive parameter $\sigma \in \mathbb{R}$, define:*

$$\rho_{\sigma,\mathbf{c}}(\mathbf{x}) = \exp\left(\pi \frac{\|\mathbf{x} - \mathbf{c}\|^2}{\sigma^2}\right) \quad and \quad \rho_{\sigma,\mathbf{c}}(\Lambda) = \sum_{\mathbf{x} \in \Lambda} \rho_{\sigma,\mathbf{c}}(\mathbf{x}).$$

The discrete Gaussian distribution over Λ with center $\mathbf{c}$ and parameter σ is

$$\forall \mathbf{y} \in \Lambda, \quad \mathcal{D}_{\Lambda,\sigma,\mathbf{c}}(\mathbf{y}) = \frac{\rho_{\sigma,\mathbf{c}}(\mathbf{y})}{\rho_{\sigma,\mathbf{c}}(\Lambda)}.$$

For convenience, we will denote by ρ_σ and $\mathcal{D}_{\Lambda,\sigma}$ for $\rho_{0,\sigma}$ and $\mathcal{D}_{\Lambda,\sigma,0}$ respectively. When $\sigma = 1$ we will write ρ instead of ρ_1. We recall below in Theorem 2 some useful results. The first one is from [7] and formulated in [1, Theorem 17]. The second one is from [1, Theorem 19]. The third one is from [1, Corollary 30] and the last one is from [1, Corollary 31].

Theorem 2. *Let $q > 2$ and let A, B be a matrix in $\mathbb{Z}_q^{n \times m}$ with $m > n$ and B is rank n. Let T_A, T_B be a basis for $\Lambda_q^{\perp}(A)$ and $\Lambda_q^{\perp}(B)$ respectively. Then for $c \in \mathbb{R}^m$ and $U \in \mathbb{Z}_q^{n \times t}$:*

1. *Let M be a matrix in $\mathbb{Z}_q^{n \times m_1}$ and $\sigma \geq \|\widetilde{T_A}\| \omega(\sqrt{\log(m + m_1)})$. Then there exists a PPT algorithm $\mathsf{SampleLeft}(A, M, T_A, U, \sigma)$ that outputs a matrix $\mathbf{e} \in \mathbb{Z}^{(m+m_1) \times t}$ distributed statistically close to $\mathcal{D}_{\Lambda_q^{\mathbf{u}}(F_1), \sigma}$ where $F_1 := (A \mid M)$. In particular $\mathbf{e} \in \Lambda_q^U(F_1)$, i.e., $F_1 \cdot \mathbf{e} = U \mod q$.*

2. *Let R be a matrix in $\mathbb{Z}^{k \times m}$ and let $s_R := \sup_{\|\mathbf{x}\|=1} \|R\mathbf{x}\|$. Let $F_2 := (A \mid AR + B)$. Then for $\sigma \geq \|\widetilde{T_B}\| s_R \omega(\sqrt{\log m})$, there exists a PPT algorithm $\mathsf{SampleRight}(A, B, R, T_B, U, \sigma)$ that outputs a matrix $\mathbf{e} \in \mathbb{Z}^{(m+k) \times t}$ distributed statistically close to $\mathcal{D}_{\Lambda_q^U(F_2), \sigma}$. In particular $\mathbf{e} \in \Lambda_q^{\mathbf{u}}(F_2)$, i.e., $F_2 \cdot \mathbf{e} = U \mod q$.*
   Note that when R is a random matrix in $\{-1, 1\}^{m \times m}$ then $s_R < O(\sqrt{m})$ with overwhelming probability (cf. [1, Lemma 15]).

3. *There exists an algorithm $\mathsf{SampleBasisLeft}(A, M, T_A, \sigma)$ that outputs a short basis T of $\Lambda_q^{\perp}(F)$, where $F = (A|M) \in \mathbb{Z}_q^{n \times (l+1)m}$, satisfying that $\|\widetilde{T}\| \leq \|T\| \leq \sigma\sqrt{m}$ and every column of T is statistically closed to $\mathcal{D}_{\Lambda_q^{\perp}(F), \sigma}$, provided that A is rank n and $\sigma > \|\widetilde{T_A}\| \cdot \omega(\sqrt{\log(lm)})$.*

4. *There exisits an algorithm $\mathsf{SampleBasisRight}(A', B, R, T_B, \sigma)$ that outputs a basis T for $\Lambda_q^{\perp}(F)$, where $F = (A'|A'R + B) \in \mathbb{Z}_q^{n \times (l+1)m}$ with $A' \in \mathbb{Z}_q^{n \times lm}$, $R \in \mathbb{Z}_q^{m \times lm}$, satisfying $\|\widetilde{T}\| = \|\widetilde{T_B}\|$ and statistically closed to $\Lambda_q^{\perp}(F)$, provided that B is rank n and that $\sigma > \|\widetilde{T_B}\| \cdot \|R\| \omega(\sqrt{\log(m)})$.*

The security of our construction reduces to the LWE (Learning With Errors) problem introduced by Regev [13].

Definition 2 (LWE problem). *Consider publicly a prime q, a positive integer n, and a distribution χ over $\mathbb{Z}_q$. An $(\mathbb{Z}_q, n, \chi)$-LWE problem instance consists of access to an unspecified challenge oracle $\mathcal{O}$, being either a noisy pseudorandom sampler $\mathcal{O}_{\mathbf{s}}$ associated with a secret $\mathbf{s} \in \mathbb{Z}_q^n$, or a truly random sampler $\mathcal{O}_{\$}$ who behaviors are as follows:*

$\mathcal{O}_{\mathbf{s}}$: *samples of the form $(\mathbf{u}_i, v_i) = (\mathbf{u}_i, \mathbf{u}_i^T \mathbf{s} + x_i) \in \mathbb{Z}_q^n \times \mathbb{Z}_q$ where $\mathbf{s} \in \mathbb{Z}_q^n$ is a uniform secret key, $\mathbf{u}_i \in \mathbb{Z}_q^n$ is uniform and $x_i \in \mathbb{Z}_q$ is a noise withdrawn from χ.*

$\mathcal{O}_{\$}$: *samples are uniform pairs in $\mathbb{Z}_q^n \times \mathbb{Z}_q$.*

The $(\mathbb{Z}_q, n, \chi)$-LWE problem allows responds queries to the challenge oracle $\mathcal{O}$. We say that an algorithm $\mathcal{A}$ decides the $(\mathbb{Z}_q, n, \chi)$-LWE problem if

$$\mathsf{Adv}_{\mathcal{A}}^{\mathsf{LWE}} := \left| \Pr[\mathcal{A}^{\mathcal{O}_{\mathbf{s}}} = 1] - \Pr[\mathcal{A}^{\mathcal{O}_{\$}} = 1] \right|$$

is non-negligible for a random $\mathbf{s} \in \mathbb{Z}_q^n$.

Regev [13] showed that (see Theorem 3 below) when χ is the distribution $\overline{\Psi}_\alpha$ of the random variable $\lfloor qX \rceil \mod q$ where $\alpha \in (0,1)$ and X is a normal random variable with mean 0 and standard deviation $\alpha/\sqrt{2\pi}$ then the LWE problem is hard.

Theorem 3. *If there exists an efficient, possibly quantum, algorithm for deciding the $(\mathbb{Z}_q, n, \overline{\Psi}_\alpha)$-LWE problem for $q > 2\sqrt{n}/\alpha$ then there is an efficient quantum algorithm for approximating the SIVP and GapSVP problems, to within $\tilde{O}(n/\alpha)$ factors in the l_2 norm, in the worst case.*

Hence if we assume the hardness of approximating the SIVP and GapSVP problems in lattices of dimension n to within polynomial (in n) factors, then it follows from Theorem 3 that deciding the LWE problem is hard when n/α is a polynomial in n.

In our construction, we need a special encoding function $H : \mathbb{Z}_q^n \to \mathbb{Z}_q^{n \times n}$ that maps identities in $\mathbb{Z}_q^n$ to matrices in $\mathbb{Z}_q^{n \times n}$. The encoding H needs to satisfy the following:

1. for all distinct $u, v \in \mathbb{Z}_q^n$, the matrix $H(u) - H(v) \in \mathbb{Z}_q^{n \times n}$ is full rank; and
2. H is computable in polynomial time (in $n \log(q)$).

Such an H is called an **encoding with full-rank differences (FRD)**. An explicit FRD construction was introduced in [1, Section 5].

3   Proposed Construction: **CL-PKEET**

In this paper, we propose a CL-PKEET that is secure against Type-1 and Type-3 adversaries (cf. Sect. 2.1) under selective-identity chosen-ciphertext attacks. Hence we consider the IND-sID-CCA and OW-sID-CCA models in which the attacker should announce in advance the identity that he intends to attack.

3.1   Construction

Setup(λ): On input a security parameter λ, set the parameters q, n, m, σ, α as in Sect. 3.2, and do the following:
1. Use TrapGen(q, n) to generate uniformly random $n \times m$-matrices $A, A' \in \mathbb{Z}_q^{n \times m}$ together with trapdoors T_A and $T_{A'}$ respectively.
2. Select $l + 1$ uniformly random $n \times m$ matrices $A_1, \cdots, A_l, B \in \mathbb{Z}_q^{n \times m}$.
3. Select a uniformly random matrix $U \in \mathbb{Z}_q^{n \times t}$.
4. $H : \mathbb{Z}_q^n \to \mathbb{Z}_q^{n \times n}$ is an encoding with full-rank differences (FRD).
5. $H_1 : \{0,1\}^* \to \mathbb{Z}_q^{n \times n}$ is a composition of a hash function $\{0,1\}^* \to \mathbb{Z}_q^n$ and the encoding H above.
6. $H_2 : \{0,1\}^* \to \{0,1\}^t$ is a hash function.
7. $H_3 : \{0,1\}^* \to \{-1,1\}^l$ is a hash function.
8. Output the public key and the secret key

$$\mathsf{MPK} = (A, A', A_1, \cdots, A_l, B, U), \quad \mathsf{MSK} = (T_A, T_{A'}).$$

ExtractPartialPrivateKey(MPK, MSK, ID): On input the master public key MPK, the master secret key MSK $= (T_A, T_{A'})$ and an identity ID, extract the short basis $S_{\mathsf{ID}} \in \mathbb{Z}_q^{2m}$ for $\Lambda_q^{\perp}(F_{\mathsf{ID}})$ with $F_{\mathsf{ID}} := (A|A_1 + H(\mathsf{ID})B) \in \mathbb{Z}_q^{n \times 2m}$ by

$$S_{\mathsf{ID}} \leftarrow \mathsf{SampleBasisLeft}(A, A_1 + H(\mathsf{ID})B, T_A, \sigma).$$

Next, sample $S'_{\mathsf{ID}} \in \mathbb{Z}_q^{2m \times t}$ by

$$S'_{\mathsf{ID}} \leftarrow \mathsf{SampleLeft}(A', A_4 + H(\mathsf{ID})B, T_{A'}, U, \sigma).$$

Note that $F'_{\mathsf{ID}} \cdot S'_{\mathsf{ID}} = U \mod q$, with $F'_{\mathsf{ID}} := (A' \mid A_4 + H(\mathsf{ID})B) \in \mathbb{Z}_q^{n \times 2m}$. Output $\mathsf{PSK}_{\mathsf{ID}} := (S_{\mathsf{ID}}, S'_{\mathsf{ID}})$.

SetSecretValue(MPK, ID): On input the master public key MPK and an identity ID, generate $(A_{\mathsf{ID}}, T_{\mathsf{ID}}) \leftarrow \mathsf{TrapGen}(q, n)$ and set the secret value of ID as $\mathsf{SV}_{\mathsf{ID}} := (A_{\mathsf{ID}}, T_{\mathsf{ID}})$.

SetPublicKey(MPK, $\mathsf{SV}_{\mathsf{ID}}$): On input the master public key MPK and secret value $\mathsf{SV}_{\mathsf{ID}} = (A_{\mathsf{ID}}, T_{\mathsf{ID}})$ of the identity ID, return the public key of ID as $\mathsf{PK}_{\mathsf{ID}} = A_{\mathsf{ID}}$.

SetPrivateKey(MPK, $\mathsf{PSK}_{\mathsf{ID}}$, $\mathsf{SV}_{\mathsf{ID}}$): On input the master public key MSK, the partial secret key $\mathsf{PSK}_{\mathsf{ID}} = (S_{\mathsf{ID}}, S'_{\mathsf{ID}})$ and the secret value $\mathsf{SV}_{\mathsf{ID}} = (A_{\mathsf{ID}}, T_{\mathsf{ID}})$, return the private key of the identity ID as $\mathsf{SK}_{\mathsf{ID}} = (S_{\mathsf{ID}}, S'_{\mathsf{ID}}, T_{\mathsf{ID}})$.

Encrypt(m, MPK, ID, $\mathsf{PK}_{\mathsf{ID}}$): On input the master public key MPK, an identity ID with its public key $\mathsf{PK}_{\mathsf{ID}}$ and a message $\mathbf{m} \in \{0,1\}^t$, do the following:

1. Choose a random string $\mathbf{m}_1 \in \{0,1\}^t$ and compute $\mathbf{m}_2 = \mathbf{m}_1 \oplus \mathbf{m}$.
2. Choose randomly $\mathbf{s}_1, \mathbf{s}_2, \mathbf{s}_3 \in \mathbb{Z}_q^n$.
3. Set $F_1 = (A \mid A_1 + H(\mathsf{ID})B \mid A_2 + H_1(A_{\mathsf{ID}})B) \in \mathbb{Z}_q^{n \times 3m}$ and $F_2 = (A_{\mathsf{ID}} \mid A_3 + H_1(A_{\mathsf{ID}})B) \in \mathbb{Z}_q^{n \times 2m}$.
4. Choose uniformly random matrices $R_1, R_2, R_3 \in \{-1, 1\}^{m \times m}$ and set $R_{12} = [R_1 \| R_2] \in \{-1, 1\}^{m \times 2m}$.
5. Choose $\mathbf{y}_1, \mathbf{y}_2, \mathbf{y}_3 \in \overline{\Psi}_{\alpha}^m$ and set $\mathbf{z}_1 = R_{12}^T \mathbf{y}_1 \in \mathbb{Z}_q^{2m}, \mathbf{z}_2 = R_2^T \mathbf{y}_2, \mathbf{z}_3 = R_3^T \mathbf{y}_3 \in \mathbb{Z}_q^m$.
6. Compute

$$CT_1 = F_1^T \mathbf{s}_1 + \begin{bmatrix} \mathbf{y}_1 \\ \mathbf{z}_1 \end{bmatrix} \in \mathbb{Z}_q^{3m},$$

$$CT_2 = F_2^T \mathbf{s}_2 + \begin{bmatrix} \mathbf{y}_2 \\ \mathbf{z}_2 \end{bmatrix} \in \mathbb{Z}_q^{2m},$$

$$CT_3 = (F'_{\mathsf{ID}})^T \mathbf{s}_3 + \begin{bmatrix} \mathbf{y}_3 \\ \mathbf{z}_3 \end{bmatrix} \in \mathbb{Z}_q^{2m}.$$

7. Compute $\mathbf{k} = H_2(CT_1 \| CT_2 \| CT_3) \in \{0,1\}^t$.
8. Choose $\mathbf{x}_1, \mathbf{x}_2, \mathbf{x}_3 \in \overline{\Psi}_{\alpha}^t$ and compute

$$CT_4 = U^T \mathbf{s}_1 + \mathbf{x}_1 + (\mathbf{k} \oplus \mathbf{m}_1)\lfloor \tfrac{q}{2} \rfloor \in \mathbb{Z}_q^t,$$

$$CT_5 = U^T \mathbf{s}_2 + \mathbf{x}_2 + (\mathbf{k} \oplus \mathbf{m}_2)\lfloor \tfrac{q}{2} \rfloor \in \mathbb{Z}_q^t,$$

$$CT_6 = U^T \mathbf{s}_3 + \mathbf{x}_3 + H_2(\mathbf{m})\lfloor \tfrac{q}{2} \rfloor \in \mathbb{Z}_q^t.$$

9. Compute $\mathbf{x} = H_3(\mathsf{CT}_1\|\mathsf{CT}_2\|\mathsf{CT}_3\|\mathsf{CT}_4\|\mathsf{CT}_5\|\mathsf{CT}_6\|\mathbf{m}) \in \{-1, 1\}^l$.
10. Generate $(A_{\mathbf{m}}, T_{\mathbf{m}}) \leftarrow \mathsf{TrapGen}(q, n)$ and set

$$F_{\mathbf{m}} := (A_{\mathbf{m}} \mid A_{\mathsf{ID}} + \sum_{i=1}^{l} x_i A_i) \in \mathbb{Z}_q^{n \times 2m}.$$

11. Compute a signature $\sigma \in \mathbb{Z}_q^{2m}$ by

$$\sigma \leftarrow \mathsf{SampleLeft}(A_{\mathbf{m}}, A_{\mathsf{ID}} + \sum_{i=1}^{l} x_i A_i, T_{\mathbf{m}}, \mathbf{0}, \sigma).$$

Note that $F_{\mathbf{m}} \cdot \sigma = \mathbf{0} \mod q$.
Output the ciphertext $\mathsf{CT} = (\mathsf{CT}_1, \mathsf{CT}_2, \mathsf{CT}_3, \mathsf{CT}_4, \mathsf{CT}_5, \mathsf{C}_6, \sigma, A_{\mathbf{m}})$.

Decrypt$(\mathsf{MPK}, \mathsf{SK}_{\mathsf{ID}}, \mathsf{CT})$: On input the master public key MPK, a ciphertext $\mathsf{CT} = (\mathsf{CT}_1, \mathsf{CT}_2, \mathsf{CT}_3, \mathsf{CT}_4, \mathsf{CT}_5, \mathsf{CT}_6, \sigma, A_{\mathbf{m}})$ and the secret key $\mathsf{SK}_{\mathsf{ID}} = (S_{\mathsf{ID}}, T_{\mathsf{ID}})$ of the identity ID, do:

1. Sample $E_{\mathsf{ID}} \in \mathbb{Z}_q^{3m \times t}$ as

$$E_{\mathsf{ID}} \leftarrow \mathsf{SampleLeft}(F_{\mathsf{ID}}, A_2 + H_1(A_{\mathsf{ID}})B, S_{\mathsf{ID}}, U, \sigma).$$

Note that $F_1 \cdot E_{\mathsf{ID}} = U \mod q$.
2. Compute $\mathbf{w} \leftarrow \mathsf{CT}_4 - E_{\mathsf{ID}}^T \mathsf{CT}_1 \in \mathbb{Z}_q^t$.
3. For each $i = 1, \cdots, t$, compare w_i and $\lfloor \frac{q}{2} \rfloor$. If they are close, output $m_i = 1$ and otherwise output $m_i = 0$. We then obtain $\mathbf{k} \oplus \mathbf{m}_1$.
4. Sample $E'_{\mathsf{ID}} \in \mathbb{Z}_q^{2m \times t}$ as

$$E'_{\mathsf{ID}} \leftarrow \mathsf{SampleLeft}(A_{\mathsf{ID}}, A_1 + H(ID)B, T_{\mathsf{ID}}, U, \sigma).$$

Note that $F_2 \cdot E'_{\mathsf{ID}} = U \mod q$.
5. Compute $\mathbf{w}' \leftarrow \mathsf{CT}_5 - (E'_{\mathsf{ID}})^T \mathsf{CT}_2 \in \mathbb{Z}_q^t$.
6. For each $i = 1, \cdots, t$, compare w'_i and $\lfloor \frac{q}{2} \rfloor$. If they are close, output $m'_i = 1$ and otherwise output $m'_i = 0$. We then obtain $\mathbf{k} \oplus \mathbf{m}_2$.
7. Compute the message $\mathbf{m} := (\mathbf{k} \oplus \mathbf{m}_1) \oplus (\mathbf{k} \oplus \mathbf{m}_2)$.
8. Compute $\mathbf{x} = H_3(\mathsf{CT}_1\|\mathsf{CT}_2\|\mathsf{CT}_3\|\mathsf{CT}_4\|\mathsf{CT}_5\|\mathsf{CT}_6\|\mathbf{m}) \in \{-1, 1\}^l$.
9. Check whether $F_{\mathbf{m}} \cdot \sigma = \mathbf{0} \mod q$. If yes then output $\mathbf{m}$. Otherwise output $\perp$.

Trapdoor$(\mathsf{SK}_{\mathsf{ID}})$: On input an identity's secret key $\mathsf{SK}_{\mathsf{ID}} = (S_{\mathsf{ID}}, S'_{\mathsf{ID}})$, it outputs a trapdoor $\mathsf{td}_i = S'_{\mathsf{ID}}$.

Test$(\mathsf{td}_{\mathsf{ID}_i}, \mathsf{td}_{\mathsf{ID}_j}, \mathsf{CT}_{\mathsf{ID}_i}, \mathsf{CT}_{\mathsf{ID}_j})$: On input trapdoors $\mathsf{td}_{\mathsf{ID}_i}, \mathsf{td}_{\mathsf{ID}_j}$ and ciphertexts $\mathsf{CT}_{\mathsf{ID}_i}, \mathsf{CT}_{\mathsf{ID}_j}$ for identities $\mathsf{ID}_i, \mathsf{ID}_j$ respectively, computes

1. For each i (resp. j), compute $\mathbf{w}_i \leftarrow \mathsf{CT}_{i6} - (S'_{\mathsf{ID}_i})^T \mathsf{CT}_{i3} \in \mathbb{Z}_q^t$. For each $k = 1, \cdots, t$, compare each coordinate w_{ik} with $\lfloor \frac{q}{2} \rfloor$ and output $\mathbf{h}_{ik} = 1$ if they are close, and 0 otherwise. At the end, we obtain the vector $\mathbf{h}_i$ (resp. $\mathbf{h}_j$).
2. Output 1 if $\mathbf{h}_i = \mathbf{h}_j$ and 0 otherwise.

Theorem 4. *Proposed* CL-PKEET *construction above is correct if H_2 is a collision-resistant hash function.*

Proof. It is easy to see that if CT is a valid ciphertext of $\mathbf{m}$ then the decryption will always output $\mathbf{m}$. Moreover, if CT_{ID_i} and CT_{ID_j} are valid ciphertext of $\mathbf{m}$ and $\mathbf{m}'$ of identities ID_i and ID_j respectively. Then the **Test** process checks whether $H_2(\mathbf{m}) = H_2(\mathbf{m}')$. If so then it outputs 1, meaning that $\mathbf{m} = \mathbf{m}'$, which is always correct with overwhelming probability since H_2 is collision resistant. Hence, proposed CL-PKEET described above is correct.   □

3.2   Parameters

We follow [1, Section 7.3 & 8.3] for choosing parameters for our scheme. Now for the system to work correctly we need to ensure

- the error term in decryption is less than $q/5$ with high probability, i.e., $q = \Omega(\sigma m^{3/2})$ and $\alpha < [\sigma l m \omega(\sqrt{\log m})]^{-1}$,
- that the TrapGen can operate, i.e., $m > 6n \log q$,
- that σ is large enough for SampleLeft and SampleRight, i.e., $\sigma > l m \omega(\sqrt{\log m})$,
- that Regev's reduction applies, i.e., $q > 2\sqrt{n}/\alpha$,

Hence the following choice of parameters (q, m, σ, α) from [1] satisfies all of the above conditions, taking n to be the security parameter:

$$m = 6n^{1+\delta}, \quad q = m^{2.5} \cdot \omega(\sqrt{\log n})$$
$$\sigma = ml\omega(\sqrt{\log n}), \quad \alpha = [l^2 m^2 \omega(\sqrt{\log n})]^{-1} \tag{1}$$

and round up m to the nearest larger integer and q to the nearest larger prime. Here we assume that δ is such that $n^\delta > \lceil \log q \rceil = O(\log n)$.

3.3   Security Analysis

In this section, we claim that our proposed scheme is IND-sID-CCA secure against Type-1 adversaries (cf. Theorem 5) and OW-sID-CCA secure against Type-3 adversaries (cf. Theorem 6). The proofs are in the same manner to [9] and hence we just sketch here and omit all the details.

Theorem 5. *The* CL-PKEET *with parameters* $(q, n, m, \sigma, \alpha)$ *as in* (1) *is* IND-sID-CCA *secure against Type-1 adversaries provided that the* $(\mathbb{Z}_q, n, \bar{\Psi}_\alpha)$-*LWE assumption holds.*

Proof. Let ID^* be the identity that the adversary $\mathcal{A}$ intends to attack. The proof proceeds in a sequence of games as the following.

Game 0. This game is identical to the IND-CCA Type-1 game from Sect. 2.1 between an attacker $\mathcal{A}$ against the scheme and an IND-CCA challenger $\mathcal{C}$.
Game 1. This Game is similar to Game 0, except in the way the challenger generates A_1, A_2 in the master public key MPK. Let $R_1^*, R_2^*, R_3^* \in \{-1, 1\}^{m \times m}$

denote the matrices used in creating the challenge ciphertext CT^*. Now, the matrices A_1, A_2, A_3, A_4 are constructed as

$$A_1 \leftarrow AR_1^* - H(\mathsf{ID}^*)B, A_2 \leftarrow AR_2^* - H_1(A_{\mathsf{ID}^*})B,$$
$$A_3 \leftarrow A_{\mathsf{ID}^*} R_2^* - H_1(A_{\mathsf{ID}^*})B, A_4 \leftarrow A'R_3^* - H(\mathsf{ID}^*)B.$$

In the challenge phase, the challenger $\mathcal{C}$ uses those R_1^*, R_2^* in generating the challenge ciphertext CT^*. The remainder of the game is unchanged.

Observe that in Game 1, the matrices R_1^* and R_2^* are used only in the construction of A_1, A_2 and in the construction of the challenge ciphertext, where $\mathbf{z}_1 = (R_{12}^*)^T \mathbf{y}_1, \mathbf{z}_2 = (R_2^*)^T \mathbf{y}_1$. By leftover hash lemma [1, Lemma 13], one obtains that in the adversary's view, the matrices AR_i^* for $i = 1, 2$ are statistically close to uniform and therefore the constructed A_1 and A_2 above are close to uniform. Hence A_1, A_2 in Game 0 and Game 1 are indistinguishable. Hence, Game 0 and Game 1 are statistically indistinguishable.

Game 2. In this game, we change the way of generating A and B in the MPK. We choose A randomly and generate B by $(B, T_B) \leftarrow \mathsf{TrapGen}(q, n)$. The remainder is the same to Game 1. The challenger $\mathcal{C}$ answers the queries of $\mathcal{A}$ as in Game 1, in particular:

- Partial private key query (ID): when the adversary $\mathcal{A}$ requests the partial private key of an identity $\mathsf{ID} \neq \mathsf{ID}^*$. Now F_{ID} and F'_{ID} are written as

$$F_{\mathsf{ID}} = (A|A_1 + H(\mathsf{ID})B) = (A|AR_1^* + (H(\mathsf{ID}) - H(\mathsf{ID}^*))B)$$
$$F'_{\mathsf{ID}} = (A'|A_4 + H(\mathsf{ID})B) = (A'|A'R_1^* + (H(\mathsf{ID}) - H(\mathsf{ID}^*))B).$$

Now, $\mathcal{B}$ sample S_{ID} and S'_{ID} as follows:

$$S_{\mathsf{ID}} \leftarrow \mathsf{SampleRight}(A, (H(\mathsf{ID}) - H(\mathsf{ID}^*))B, R_1^*, T_B, U, \sigma),$$
$$S'_{\mathsf{ID}} \leftarrow \mathsf{SampleRight}(A', (H(\mathsf{ID}) - H(\mathsf{ID}^*))B, R_1^*, T_B, U, \sigma).$$

And then $\mathcal{B}$ sends $\mathsf{PSK}_{\mathsf{ID}} = (S_{\mathsf{ID}}, S'_{\mathsf{ID}})$ to $\mathcal{A}$.
- Decryption query (ID, CT): the adversary $\mathcal{A}$ provides an identity ID and a ciphertext CT, then $\mathcal{C}$ can use the $\mathsf{PSK}_{\mathsf{ID}}$ as above and the secret value of ID (generated previously or generated as in $\mathsf{SetSecretValue}(\mathsf{MPK}, \mathsf{ID})$) to answer $\mathcal{A}$ the decryption of CT.

Game 3. This game is similar to Game 2, except that the challenge ciphertext CT^* is uniformly random chosen.

We will show that Game 2 and Game 3 are computationally indistinguishable by giving a reduction from the LWE problem.

Reduction from LWE. Suppose that $\mathcal{A}$ has non-negligible advantage in distinguishing Game 2 and Game 3. We use $\mathcal{A}$ to construct an algorithm $\mathcal{B}$ solving the LWE problem.

Setup. First of all, $\mathcal{B}$ requests from $\mathcal{O}$ and receives, for each $j = 1, \cdots, t$ a fresh pair $(\mathbf{a}_i, d_i) \in \mathbb{Z}_q^n \times \mathbb{Z}_q$ and for each $i = 1, \cdots, m$, a fresh pair $(\mathbf{u}_i, v_i) \in \mathbb{Z}_q^n \times \mathbb{Z}_q$. $\mathcal{A}$ announces an identity ID^* that he intends to attack. Then $\mathcal{B}$ constructs $(\mathsf{MPK}, \mathsf{MSK})$ as follows:

1. Assemble the random matrix $A \in \mathbb{Z}_q^{n \times m}$ from m of previously given LWE samples by letting the i-th column of A to be the n-vector $\mathbf{u}_i$ for all $i = 1, \cdots, m$.
2. Assemble the first t unused LWE samples $\mathbf{a}_1, \cdots, \mathbf{a}_t$ to become a public random matrix $U \in \mathbb{Z}_q^{n \times t}$.
3. Run $\mathsf{TrapGen}(q, \sigma)$ to generate uniformly random matrices $A', B \in \mathbb{Z}_q^{n \times m}$ together with their trapdoor $T_{A'}$ and T_B respectively.
4. Choose random matrices $R_1^*, R_2^*, R_3^* \in \{-1, 1\}^{m \times m}$ and l construct the matrices A_1, A_2, A_3, A_4 as in Game 1 Note that it follows from the leftover hash lemma [15, Theorem 8.38] that A_1, A_2, A_3, A_4 are statistically close to uniform.
5. Choose $A_5, \cdots, A_l$ uniformly random from $\mathbb{Z}_q^{n \times m}$.
6. Send $\mathsf{MPK} := (A, A', A_1, \cdots, A_l, B, U)$ to $\mathcal{A}$.

Queries. $\mathcal{B}$ answers queries from $\mathcal{A}$ as in Game 2.

Challenge. After getting messages $\mathbf{m}_0$ or $\mathbf{m}_1$ from $\mathcal{A}$, $\mathcal{B}$ chooses a random bit $b \in \{0, 1\}$ and encrypt the message $\mathbf{m}_b$ as follows.

1. Choose a random $\mathbf{m}_{b1} \in \{0, 1\}^t$ and set $\mathbf{m}_{b2} = \mathbf{m}_{b1} \oplus \mathbf{m}$.
2. Assemble $d_1, \cdots, d_t, v_1, \cdots, v_m$ from the entries of LWE samples to form $\mathbf{d}^* = [d_1, \cdots, d_t]^T \in \mathbb{Z}_q^t$ and $\mathbf{v}^* = [v_1, \cdots, v_m]^T \in \mathbb{Z}_q^m$. Let $R_{12}^* = [R_1^* \| R_2^*]$ and set

$$\mathsf{CT}_1^* := \begin{bmatrix} \mathbf{v}^* \\ (R_{12}^*)^T \mathbf{v}^* \end{bmatrix} \in \mathbb{Z}_q^{3m}.$$

3. Choose $\mathbf{y}_2, \mathbf{y}_3 \leftarrow \overline{\Psi}_\alpha^m$ and set

$$\mathsf{CT}_2^* := \begin{bmatrix} (A_{\mathsf{ID}^*})^T \mathbf{s}_2 + \mathbf{y}_2 \\ (A_{\mathsf{ID}^*} R_2^*)^T \mathbf{s}_2 + (R_2^*)^T \mathbf{y}_2 \end{bmatrix} \in \mathbb{Z}_q^{2m},$$

$$\mathsf{CT}_3^* := \begin{bmatrix} (A')^T \mathbf{s}_3 + \mathbf{y}_3 \\ (A' R_3^*)^T \mathbf{s}_3 + (R_3^*)^T \mathbf{y}_3 \end{bmatrix} \in \mathbb{Z}_q^{2m}.$$

4. Compute $\mathbf{k} = H_2(\mathsf{CT}_1^* \| \mathsf{CT}_2^* \| \mathsf{CT}_3^*) \in \{0, 1\}^t$ and set

$$\mathsf{CT}_4^* \leftarrow \mathbf{d}^* + (\mathbf{k} \oplus \mathbf{m}_{b1}) \lfloor \tfrac{q}{2} \rfloor \in \mathbb{Z}_q^t.$$

5. Choose $\mathbf{s}_2, \mathbf{s}_3 \in \mathbb{Z}_q^n$, $\mathbf{x}_2, \mathbf{x}_3 \in \overline{\Psi}_\alpha^t$ and compute

$$\mathsf{CT}_2^* \leftarrow U^T \mathbf{s}_2 + \mathbf{x}_2 + (\mathbf{k} \oplus \mathbf{m}_{b2}) \lfloor \tfrac{q}{2} \rfloor \in \mathbb{Z}_q^t,$$

$$\mathsf{CT}_3^* \leftarrow U^T \mathbf{s}_3 + \mathbf{x}_3 + H_2(\mathbf{m}_b) \lfloor \tfrac{q}{2} \rfloor \in \mathbb{Z}_q^t.$$

Other parts of CT^* is computed as in Game 2.

When the LWE oracle is pseudorandom, i.e., $\mathcal{O} = \mathcal{O}_\mathbf{s}$ then $\mathbf{v}^* = A^T \mathbf{s} + \mathbf{y}$ for some random noise vector $\mathbf{y} \leftarrow \overline{\Psi}_\alpha^m$. Therefore

$$\mathsf{CT}_1^* := \begin{bmatrix} A^T \mathbf{s} + \mathbf{y} \\ (AR^*)^T \mathbf{s} + (R_{12}^*)^T \mathbf{y} \end{bmatrix} = (F_1)^T \mathbf{s} + \begin{bmatrix} \mathbf{y} \\ (R_{12}^*)^T \mathbf{y} \end{bmatrix}.$$

In addition, we have

$$\mathsf{CT}_2^* = (F_2)^T \mathbf{s}_2 + \begin{bmatrix} \mathbf{y}_2 \\ (R_2^*)^T \mathbf{y}_2 \end{bmatrix},$$

$$\mathsf{CT}_3^* = (F'_{\mathsf{ID}})^T \mathbf{s}_3 + \begin{bmatrix} \mathbf{y}_3 \\ (R_3^*)^T \mathbf{y}_3 \end{bmatrix}.$$

Therefore CT^* is a valid ciphertext.

When $\mathcal{O} = \mathcal{O}_\$$ we have that $\mathbf{d}^*$ is uniform in $\mathbb{Z}_q^t$ and $\mathbf{v}^*$ is uniform in $\mathbb{Z}_q^m$. Then obviously CT_4^* is uniform. It follows also from the leftover hash lemma (cf. [15, Theorem 8.38]) that CT_1^* is also uniform.

Guess. After Phase 2, $\mathcal{A}$ guesses if he is interacting with Game 2 or Game 3. The simulator $\mathcal{B}$ outputs the final guess as the answer for the LWE problem.

We have seen above that when $\mathcal{O} = \mathcal{O}_\mathbf{s}$ then the adversary's view is as in Game 1. When $\mathcal{O} = \mathcal{O}_\$$ then the view of adversary is as in Game 2. Because the $(\mathbb{Z}_q, n, \overline{\Psi}_\alpha)$-LWE assumption holds, Game 1 and Game 2 are then indistinguishable. This completes the proof. $\qquad\Box$

Theorem 6. *The* CL-PKEET *with parameters* $(q, n, m, \sigma, \alpha)$ *as in* (1) *is* OW-sID-CCA *secure against Type-3 adversaries provided that* H_2 *is a one-way hash function and the* $(\mathbb{Z}_q, n, \overline{\Psi}_\alpha)$-*LWE assumption holds.*

Proof. The proof is similar to that of Theorem 5. Notice that for this type of adversary, an attacker $\mathcal{A}$ can have the trapdoor of ID^*, and hence he can use it to obtain the hash value $H_2(\mathbf{m}^*)$ from the challenge ciphertext. If $\mathcal{A}$ can output $\mathbf{m}^*$ then $\mathcal{A}$ has broken the one-wayness of H_2. $\qquad\Box$

4 Conclusion

In this paper, we propose, for the first time, a certificateless public key encryption scheme with equality test from lattices in standard model. We prove that our scheme is secure against Type-1 and Type-3 attackers under selective-identity chosen ciphertext attacks. There is possibility to achieve IND-ID-CCA and OW-ID-CCA security by techniques from [1, Section 7],[5]. We leave as a future work to investigate and modify our scheme to obtai security against Type-2 and Type-4 attacks.

Acknowledgement. This work is supported by the Australian Research Council Discovery Project DP180100665.

References

1. Agrawal, S., Boneh, D., Boyen, X.: Efficient lattice (H)IBE in the standard model. In: Gilbert, H. (ed.) EUROCRYPT 2010. LNCS, vol. 6110, pp. 553–572. Springer, Heidelberg (2010). https://doi.org/10.1007/978-3-642-13190-5_28

2. Ajtai, M.: Generating hard instances of the short basis problem. In: Wiedermann, J., van Emde Boas, P., Nielsen, M. (eds.) ICALP 1999. LNCS, vol. 1644, pp. 1–9. Springer, Heidelberg (1999). https://doi.org/10.1007/3-540-48523-6_1

3. Alwen, J., Peikert, C.: Generating shorter bases for hard random lattices. Theory Comput. Syst. **48**(3), 535–553 (2011)

4. Al-Riyami, S.S., Paterson, K.G.: Certificateless public key cryptography. In: Laih, C.-S. (ed.) ASIACRYPT 2003. LNCS, vol. 2894, pp. 452–473. Springer, Heidelberg (2003). https://doi.org/10.1007/978-3-540-40061-5_29

5. Boneh, D., Boyen, X.: Efficient selective-ID secure identity-based encryption without random oracles. In: Cachin, C., Camenisch, J.L. (eds.) EUROCRYPT 2004. LNCS, vol. 3027, pp. 223–238. Springer, Heidelberg (2004). https://doi.org/10.1007/978-3-540-24676-3_14

6. Boneh, D., Di Crescenzo, G., Ostrovsky, R., Persiano, G.: Public key encryption with keyword search. In: Cachin, C., Camenisch, J.L. (eds.) EUROCRYPT 2004. LNCS, vol. 3027, pp. 506–522. Springer, Heidelberg (2004). https://doi.org/10.1007/978-3-540-24676-3_30

7. Cash, D., Hofheinz, D., Kiltz, E., Peikert, C.: Bonsai trees, or how to delegate a lattice basis. In: Gilbert, H. (ed.) EUROCRYPT 2010. LNCS, vol. 6110, pp. 523–552. Springer, Heidelberg (2010). https://doi.org/10.1007/978-3-642-13190-5_27

8. Carter, L., Wegman, M.N.: Universal classes of hash functions. J. Comput. Syst. Sci. **18**(2), 143–154 (1979)

9. Duong, D.H., Fukushima, K., Kiyomoto, S., Roy, P.S., Susilo, W.: A lattice-based public key encryption with equality test in standard model. In: Jang-Jaccard, J., Guo, F. (eds.) ACISP 2019. LNCS, vol. 11547, pp. 138–155. Springer, Cham (2019). https://doi.org/10.1007/978-3-030-21548-4_8

10. Kawachi, A., Tanaka, K., Xagawa, K.: Concurrently secure identification schemes based on the worst-case hardness of lattice problems. In: Pieprzyk, J. (ed.) ASIACRYPT 2008. LNCS, vol. 5350, pp. 372–389. Springer, Heidelberg (2008). https://doi.org/10.1007/978-3-540-89255-7_23

11. Ma, S.: Identity-based encryption with outsourced equality test in cloud computing. Inf. Sci. **328**, 389–402 (2016)

12. Qu, H., Yan, Z., Lin, X.J., Zhang, Q., Sun, L.: Certificateless public key encryption with equality test. Inf. Sci. **462**, 76–92 (2018)

13. Regev, O.: On lattices, learning with errors, random linear codes, and cryptography. J. ACM **56**(6), 1–40 (2009)

14. Shamir, A.: Identity-based cryptosystems and signature schemes. In: Blakley, G.R., Chaum, D. (eds.) CRYPTO 1984. LNCS, vol. 196, pp. 47–53. Springer, Heidelberg (1985). https://doi.org/10.1007/3-540-39568-7_5

15. Shoup, V.: A Computational Introduction to Number Theory and Algebra, 2nd edn. Cambridge University Press, Cambridge (2008)

16. Sepahi, R., Steinfeld, R., Pieprzyk, J.: Lattice-based certificateless public-key encryption in the standard model. Int. J. Inf. Sec. **13**(4), 315–333 (2014)

17. Yang, G., Tan, C.H., Huang, Q., Wong, D.S.: Probabilistic public key encryption with equality test. In: Pieprzyk, J. (ed.) CT-RSA 2010. LNCS, vol. 5985, pp. 119–131. Springer, Heidelberg (2010). https://doi.org/10.1007/978-3-642-11925-5_9

Attribute-Based Keyword Search from Lattices

Jie Li[1,2,3(✉)], Mimi Ma[3,4], Jiang Zhang[3], Shuqin Fan[3], and Shuaigang Li[1,2,3]

[1] State Key Laboratory of Information Security, Institute of Information Engineering, Chinese Academy of Sciences, Beijing, China
{lijie,lishuaigang}@iie.ac.cn
[2] School of Cyber Security, University of Chinese Academy of Sciences, Beijing, China
[3] State Key Laboratory of Cryptology, Beijing, China
mamimi421@126.com, jiangzhang09@gmail.com, shuqinfan78@163.com
[4] College of Information Science and Engineering, Henan University of Technology, Zhengzhou, China

Abstract. Attribute-based keyword search (ABKS) is a special case of public key encryption with keyword search (PEKS) which allows fine-grained control of the search ability and can be further categorized into key-policy ABKS (KP-ABKS) and ciphertext-policy ABKS (CP-ABKS). In a KP-ABKS (resp., CP-ABKS) scheme, a trapdoor that is associated with an access policy f (resp., an attributes string $\mathbf{x}$) can only be used to search over ciphertexts that is associated with an attributes string $\mathbf{x}$ (resp., an access policy f) if $f(\mathbf{x}) = 0$. As ABKS is very useful in the era of big data, many researchers have been devoted to design ABKS schemes with different features, but almost all the known schemes are based on the traditional number-theoretical assumptions such as Factoring or Discrete Logarithm, and thus are insecure against quantum adversaries.

In this paper, we propose a lattice-based KP-ABKS scheme supporting circuit policy of any predetermined polynomial depth. Our scheme is provably secure against chosen keyword attacks and keyword guessing attacks under the DLWE and ISIS assumptions in the random oracle model. By using a universal circuit, our scheme can also be converted into a CP-ABKS scheme.

Keywords: Attribute-based encryption · keyword search · Lattice · Post-quantum secure

1 Introduction

As the rapid growth of data volume, many users upload their (private) data to the cloud storage which is owned by the cloud service providers (CSP) such as OneDrive and Dropbox. However, the CSP is usually not fully trusted [44], which may poses serious threats on the security and privacy of users' data. Encryption

© Springer Nature Switzerland AG 2020
Z. Liu and M. Yung (Eds.): Inscrypt 2019, LNCS 12020, pp. 66–85, 2020.
https://doi.org/10.1007/978-3-030-42921-8_4

is an effective measure to provide confidentiality and privacy (i.e., users can encrypt the data before uploading it to the cloud server), but it also makes it difficult for users to search files over massive amounts of data. To solve this issue, the technology of searchable encryption (SE) is introduced [7,41,42,53]. SE is one of the cryptographic technologies that allows to efficiently search over encrypted data in a secure way and can be divided into two kinds, namely, searchable symmetric encryption (SSE) and public key encryption with keyword search (PEKS) [10].

Boneh et al. [7] introduced the notion of PEKS. In a PEKS scheme, there are three entities called data sender, data receiver and cloud server. The data sender first extracts some keywords from his/her own documents, and generates a set of PEKS ciphertexts of those keywords under the receiver's public key. Then, she/he attaches the encrypted keywords to the encryptions of his/her documents (which are encrypted by using traditional encryption schemes), and upload them together to the cloud server. Upon receiving the trapdoor, the cloud server will match it with the encrypted keywords and sends the correctly matched encrypted documents to the receiver. In the context of big data sharing, more and more data is expected to be shared by multiple users. However, in the traditional PEKS schemes, a user can only search over encrypted keywords which are encrypted by using his/her own public key. For multi-receiver scenarios, the data sender need to encrypt each keyword multiple times by using every receiver's public key, which brings large computation and storage overhead. The broadcast encryption [17,34] can be used to one-to-many scenarios, however, it is necessary to set up an authorized user group before encryption, which does not have flexible access control policy.

The attribute-based keyword search (ABKS) provides a new solution [52] for one-to-many scenarios with flexible access control. In a KP-ABKS (resp., CP-ABKS) scheme, the sender encrypts the keyword by using a public attribute vector $\mathbf{x}$ (resp., a policy f). For every receiver who holds the secret key sk associated with an access policy f (resp., an attribute vector $\mathbf{x}$) s.t. $f(\mathbf{x}) = 0$ can search the ciphertext. Therefore, ABKS allows the data sender to control the access for his own outsourced encrypted data without any interaction with receivers. In recent years, there has been many works [5,15,32,38,43,48] focusing on constructing ABKS schemes with different functionalities and security. Nevertheless, almost all previous works were based on the traditional cryptographic assumptions which will be insecure if quantum computers become realistic. Thus, it is very necessary to build an attribute-based keyword search (ABKS) scheme which can resist quantum attacks.

1.1 Our Contribution

In this paper, we propose a key-policy attribute-based keyword search (KP-ABKS) scheme based on the lattice assumptions. Our scheme supports circuit policy in polynomially bounded depth, and thus can support very flexible and fine-grained access control. We provide detailed correctness analysis of our proposed scheme, and show that our scheme is provable secure against chosen keyword attacks (under the DLWE assumption) and keyword guessing attacks (under the ISIS assumption). Our KP-ABKS scheme can also be transformed into a ciphertext-policy ABKS (CP-ABKS) scheme by encoding the access policy f in the ciphertext and generating the secret key for attribute $\mathbf{x}$ using a universal circuit $\mathcal{U}_{\mathbf{x}}(f) = f(\mathbf{x})$.

1.2   Overview of Our Construction

Our Construction. Let λ be the security parameter, set lattice parameters $n = n(\lambda), m = m(\lambda), q = q(\lambda)$ and let k be the dimension of the attribute vector $\mathbf{x} = (x_1, ..., x_k) \in \mathbb{Z}_q^k$. For random matrices $\mathbf{A}, \mathbf{A}_1, ..., \mathbf{A}_k, \mathbf{A}_{\mathbf{w}} \in \mathbb{Z}_q^{n \times m}$, the gadget matrix $\mathbf{G} \in \mathbb{Z}_q^{n \times m}$, and a random vector $\mathbf{u} \in \mathbb{Z}_q^n$ which is used to encrypt a binary string $\mathbf{a} \in \{0, 1\}^s$, the encryption lattice is defined as

$$\Lambda_{\mathbf{x},\mathbf{w}} = \Lambda_q(\mathbf{A}|\mathbf{A}_1 + x_1\mathbf{G}|...|\mathbf{A}_k + x_k\mathbf{G}|\mathbf{A}_{\mathbf{w}} + H_1(\mathbf{w})\mathbf{G})$$

The corresponding ciphertext is the matrices $CT = (\mathbf{C}_0, \{\mathbf{C}_i\}_{i \in \{1,...,k\}}, \mathbf{C}_{\mathbf{w}})$.

For a function $f : \mathbb{Z}_q^k \to \mathbb{Z}_q$, anyone with the knowledge of $\mathbf{x}$ can transform the ciphertext $CT = (\mathbf{C}_0, \{\mathbf{C}_i\}_{i \in \{1,...,k\}}, \mathbf{C}_{\mathbf{w}})$ into a ciphertext $CT_f = (\mathbf{C}_0, \mathbf{C}_f, \mathbf{C}_{\mathbf{w}})$ which closes to the lattice

$$\Lambda_{f,\mathbf{x},\mathbf{w}} = \Lambda_q(\mathbf{A}|\mathbf{A}_f + f(\mathbf{x})\mathbf{G}|\mathbf{A}_{\mathbf{w}} + H_1(\mathbf{w})\mathbf{G}),$$

where $\mathbf{A}_f$ is uniquely computed by f and $\mathbf{A}_1, ..., \mathbf{A}_k$. Note that the trapdoor $\mathbf{d}_{f,\mathbf{w}}$ of keyword $\mathbf{w}$ satisfies $\mathbf{F}_{\mathbf{w}} \cdot \mathbf{d}_{f,\mathbf{w}} = (\mathbf{A}|\mathbf{A}_f|\mathbf{A}_{\mathbf{w}} + H_1(\mathbf{w})\mathbf{G}) \cdot \mathbf{d}_{f,\mathbf{w}} = \mathbf{u}$. So if $f(\mathbf{x}) = 0$, the ciphertext CT and $\mathbf{d}_{f,\mathbf{w}}$ contain the same keyword $\mathbf{w}$, then the cloud server could decrypt to get $\mathbf{a}$ to finish the test algorithm.

Although the above construction satisfies chosen keyword attacks security, it can not resist keyword guessing attacks. That means an adversary who obtains the trapdoor of a keyword can encrypt any candidated keyword to generate a corresponding ciphertext. Then this adversary can run the test algorithm to check if the keyword been guessed is correct, if not, the adversary continues to guess. To prevent these attacks, we use the sender's private key to generate a signature θ such that $\mathbf{A}_s\theta = H_2(\mathbf{C}_{\mathbf{w}}, \mathbf{a})$, where $\mathbf{A}_s$ is the public key of the data sender. Thus we complete our construction.

1.3   Related Work

Searchable Encryption. SE is an encryption technology that can realize search on encrypted data according to keywords. In 2000, Song et al. [42] first proposed a SSE scheme. However, the search cost in their scheme is linear to the database size. To improve performance, Goh et al. [20] considered the method of constructing indexes for each file with a bloom filter, which greatly reduces the search cost. Following this work, lots of SSE schemes with distinct traits have been proposed [13,18,29,30,33,46]. SSE scheme is more efficient and has no limit on the length of encrypted data. However, there is only one key for encryption and decryption in SSE scheme, and the key distribution must be completed via a secure channel. Therefore, the security of the SSE scheme largely depends on the security of key management. Nevertheless, the key distribution and management are extremely complex.

To address this issue, Boneh et al. [7] proposed the first PEKS scheme, which can be well applied in multi-user model. Later, Golle et al. [21] designed a new PEKS scheme which supports conjunctive keyword search in the random oracle model. Boneh et al. [9] constructed a PEKS scheme that supports conjunctive, subset, and range queries. Recently, many works [14,25,26,35,47] have been done to construct PEKS schemes that meet different search patterns and security requirements. However, all these constructions will be insecure once the quantum computers become realistic [36]. To resist quantum attacks, Hou et al. [24] designed a novel PEKS scheme based on lattice. Zhang et al. [50] proposed a identity-based encryption with keyword search scheme from lattices. Behnia et al. [6] constructed two lattice-based PEKS schemes (IBEKS) based on NTRU and LWE assumption. Recently, Zhang et al. [51] proposed a lattice-based PEKS scheme which supports forward security. Zhang et al. [49] designed a proxy-oriented identity-based encryption with keyword search (PO-IBEKS) from lattices. In PO-IBEKS, a proxy is authorized to encrypt the keywords and uploads the ciphertexts to the cloud server. However, the proxy must be completely trusted.

Attribute-Based Encryption. Attribute-based encryption (ABE) [40] is a public-key encryption mechanism that supports fine-grained access control on encrypted data. The ABE schemes can be classified into key-policy ABE (KP-ABE) and ciphertext-policy ABE (CP-ABE) [23]. In KP-ABE, a user's secret key sk_f which is associated with access policy f can decrypt the ciphertext c which is associated with the attribute strings $\mathbf{x}$ if and only if $f(\mathbf{x}) = 0$. In CP-ABE, a user's secret key $sk_{\mathbf{x}}$ which is associated with the attribute strings $\mathbf{x}$ can decrypt the ciphertext c which is associated with access policy f if and only if $f(\mathbf{x}) = 0$. In the past few years, significant amount of effort has been made towards constructing ABE schemes from a variety of standard assumptions [8,11,22,23,27].

Attribute-Based Keyword Search. Applying the technology of ABE to searchable encryption can effectively realize multi-user management. Wang et al. [45] combined CP-ABE with PEKS and designed an attribute-based keyword search (ABKS) scheme. Zheng et al. [52] constructed a verifiable ABKS scheme. In Zheng et al.'s scheme [52], only the legitimate users can search the ciphertext and verify the correctness of the search results. Liu et al. [32] pointed out that Zheng et al.'s scheme requires secure channels for trapdoor transmission. To resolve this problem, an improved scheme was proposed in [32], which avoid the use of secure channels. Sun et al. [43] first designed a user-revocable ABKS scheme. After this work, several ABKS schemes with various features have been constructed [5,28,31,48]. However, almost all previous proposed ABKS schemes cannot resist the quantum attacks. In this paper, we propose a novel ABKS scheme from lattices that is secure against quantum attacks.

1.4 Organization

The rest of this paper is organized as follows. Section 2 reviews the related cryptographic primitives and lemmas. Section 3 defines the KP-ABKS scheme and security model in a formal way. Section 4 presents our KP-ABKS construction and gives the security proof. Finally, we conclude the paper in Sect. 5.

2 Preliminaries

Notations. Let λ be the security parameter and $\mathsf{negl}(\lambda)$ denote a negligible function.

For integer $q \geq 2$, $\mathbb{Z}_q$ denotes the quotient ring of integer modulo q. Let $\mathbb{N}$ denotes the set of positive integer. For integer n, let $[n] = \{1, ..., n\}$. We use bold capital letters to denote matrices, such as $\mathbf{A}, \mathbf{B}$, and bold lowercase letters to denote vectors, such as $\mathbf{x}, \mathbf{y}$. Let $\mathbf{A}^{\mathrm{T}}$ denote the transpose of the matrix $\mathbf{A}$, let $(\mathbf{A}|\mathbf{B})$ and $(\mathbf{A}||\mathbf{B})$ denote the matrix of horizontally and vertically concatenating $\mathbf{A}$ and $\mathbf{B}$, respectively. For a vector $\mathbf{u}$, let $||\mathbf{u}||$ denote the ℓ_2 norm and $||\mathbf{u}||_\infty$ denote the maximum element in $\mathbf{u}$.

2.1 Lattices

For positive integers n, m, q, and a matrix $\mathbf{A} \in \mathbb{Z}_q^{n \times m}$, the m-dimensional integer lattices are defined as: $\Lambda_q(\mathbf{A}) = \{\mathbf{y} : \mathbf{y} = \mathbf{A}^{\mathrm{T}}\mathbf{s} \text{ for some } \mathbf{s} \in \mathbb{Z}^n\}$ and $\Lambda_q^\perp(\mathbf{A}) = \{\mathbf{y} : \mathbf{A}\mathbf{y} = 0 \mod q\}$.

For $\mathbf{x} \in \Lambda$, define the Gaussian function $\rho_{s,\mathbf{c}}(\mathbf{x})$ over $\Lambda \subseteq \mathbb{Z}^m$ centered at $\mathbf{c} \in \mathbb{R}^m$ with parameter $s > 0$ as $\rho_{s,\mathbf{c}}(\mathbf{x}) = \exp(-\pi||\mathbf{x} - \mathbf{c}||/s^2)$. Let $\rho_{s,\mathbf{c}}(\Lambda) = \sum_{\mathbf{x} \in \Lambda} \rho_{s,\mathbf{c}}(\mathbf{x})$, and define the discrete Gaussian distribution over Λ as $\mathcal{D}_{\Lambda,s,\mathbf{c}}(\mathbf{x}) = \frac{\rho_{s,\mathbf{c}}(\mathbf{x})}{\rho_{s,\mathbf{c}}(\Lambda)}$, where $\mathbf{x} \in \Lambda$. For simplicity, $\rho_{s,\mathbf{0}}$ and $\mathcal{D}_{\Lambda,s,\mathbf{0}}$ are abbreviated as ρ_s and $\mathcal{D}_{\Lambda,s}$, respectively.

Matrix Norms. For a matrix $\mathbf{R} \in \mathbb{Z}^{k \times m}$, let $||\mathbf{R}||_\infty$ denote the maximum element in $\mathbf{R}$, let $\widetilde{\mathbf{R}}$ be the result of applying Gram-Schmidt (GS) orthogonalization to the columns of $\mathbf{R}$, let $||\mathbf{R}||$ denote the ℓ_2 length of the longest column of $\mathbf{R}$. $||\mathbf{R}||_2$ is the operator norm of $\mathbf{R}$ defined as $||\mathbf{R}||_2 = \sup_{||\mathbf{x}||=1}||\mathbf{R}\mathbf{x}||$.

B-Bounded. A distribution ensemble χ, supported over the integers, is called B-bounded if $\Pr_{a \leftarrow \chi}[|a| \leq B] = 1$.

Learning with Errors Problem. The learning with errors (LWE) problem, denoted by $\mathrm{LWE}_{q,n,m,\alpha}$, was first proposed by Regev [39]. For integer $n, m = m(n)$, a prime integer $q > 2$, a Gaussian parameter α, the decisional LWE problem $\mathrm{LWE}_{q,n,m,\alpha}$ is to distinguish the following pairs of distributions: $\{\mathbf{A}, \mathbf{A}^{\mathrm{T}}\mathbf{s} + \mathbf{e}\}$ and $\{\mathbf{A}, \mathbf{u}\}$, where $\mathbf{A} \leftarrow \mathbb{Z}_q^{n \times m}, \mathbf{s} \leftarrow \mathbb{Z}_q^n, \mathbf{u} \leftarrow \mathbb{Z}_q^m$ and $\mathbf{e} \leftarrow \mathcal{D}_{\mathbb{Z}^m,\alpha}$.

Regev [39] showed that solving decisional $\text{LWE}_{q,n,m,\alpha}$ (denoted by $\text{DLWE}_{q,n,m,\alpha}$) for $\alpha > 2\sqrt{2n}$ is (quantumly) as hard as approximating the SIVP and GapSVP problems to within $\widetilde{\mathcal{O}}(nq/\alpha)$ factors in the worst case.

Inhomogeneous Small Integer Solution. The inhomogeneous small integer solution (ISIS) problem was first introduced in [2]. For integer $n, m = m(n)$, a prime integer $q > 2$, with a matrix $\mathbf{U} \in \mathbb{Z}_q^{n \times m}$, a vector $\vartheta \in \mathbb{Z}_q^n$, a positive real number β, the goal is to solve a nonzero integer vector $\mathbf{z} \in \mathbb{Z}^m$ such that $\mathbf{Uz} = \vartheta$ mod q and $\|\mathbf{z}\| \leq \beta$.

As proved in [19], for any prime $q > \beta \cdot \omega(\sqrt{n \log n})$ and any poly-bounded $\beta = poly(n)$, the average hardness assumption of ISIS problem is as hard as approximating the problem SIVP in the worst case to within certain factor $\beta \cdot \widetilde{O}(\sqrt{n})$.

Gadget Matrix. As mentioned by [37], for $m > n\lceil \log q \rceil$, there exists a full-rank matrix $\mathbf{G} \in \mathbb{Z}_q^{n \times m}$ such that the lattice $\Lambda_q^\perp(\mathbf{G})$ has a public known basis $T_\mathbf{G} \in \mathbb{Z}_q^{m \times m}$ with $\|\widetilde{T_\mathbf{G}}\| \leq \sqrt{5}$. Moreover, there exists a deterministic PPT algorithm $\mathbf{G}^{-1}$ which takes the input $\mathbf{U} \in \mathbb{Z}_q^{n \times m}$ and outputs $\mathbf{V} = \mathbf{G}^{-1}(\mathbf{U})$ such that $\mathbf{V} \in \{0, 1\}^{m \times m}$ and $\mathbf{GV} = \mathbf{U}$.

Lemma 1. *Let p, q, n, m be positive integers with $q \geq p \geq 2$ with q prime. There exists PPT algorithms such that*

- *([3,4]): $\mathsf{TrapGen}(n, m, q)$, a randomized algorithm that, when $m \geq 6n\lceil \log q \rceil$, outputs a pair $(\mathbf{A}, \mathbf{T_A}) \in \mathbb{Z}_q^{n \times m} \times \mathbb{Z}^{m \times m}$ such that $\mathbf{A}$ is statistically close to uniform in $\mathbb{Z}_q^{n \times m}$ and $\mathbf{T_A}$ is a basis of $\Lambda_q^\perp(\mathbf{A})$, satisfying $\|\widetilde{\mathbf{T_A}}\| \leq \mathcal{O}(\sqrt{n \log q})$ with overwhelming probability.*
- *([19]): $\mathsf{SamplePre}(\mathbf{A}, \mathbf{T_A}, \mathbf{u}, \sigma) \rightarrow \mathbf{x}$, a randomized algorithm that, when $\sigma = \|\widetilde{T_A}\| \cdot \omega(\sqrt{\log m})$, outputs a random sample $\mathbf{x} \in \mathbb{Z}_q^m$ from a distribution that is statistically close to $\mathcal{D}_{\Lambda_q^\mathbf{u}(\mathbf{A}), \sigma}$.*
- *([12]): $\mathsf{RandBasis}(\mathbf{A}, \mathbf{T_A}, \sigma) \rightarrow \mathbf{T_{A'}}$, a randomized algorithm that, when $\sigma = \|\widetilde{\mathbf{T_A}}\| \cdot \omega(\sqrt{\log m})$, outputs a basis $\mathbf{T_{A'}}$ of $\Lambda_q^\perp(\mathbf{A})$ sampled from a distribution that is statistically close to $(\mathcal{D}_{\Lambda_q^\perp(\mathbf{A}), \sigma})^m$. Note that $\|\widetilde{\mathbf{T_{A'}}}\| < \sigma\sqrt{m}$ with all but negligible probability.*
- *([12]): $\mathsf{ExtendRight}(\mathbf{A}, \mathbf{T_A}, \mathbf{B}) \rightarrow \mathbf{T_{(A|B)}}$, a deterministic algorithm that given full-rank matrices $\mathbf{A} \in \mathbb{Z}_q^{n \times m_1}, \mathbf{B} \in \mathbb{Z}_q^{n \times m_2}$, and a basis of $\mathbf{T_A}$ of $\Lambda_q^\perp(\mathbf{A})$ outputs a basis $\mathbf{T_{(A|B)}}$ of $\Lambda_q^\perp(\mathbf{A}|\mathbf{B})$ such that $\|\widetilde{\mathbf{T_A}}\| = \|\widetilde{\mathbf{T_{(A|B)}}}\|$.*
- *([1]): $\mathsf{ExtendLeft}(\mathbf{A}, \mathbf{G}, \mathbf{T_G}, \mathbf{R}) \rightarrow \mathbf{T_H}$(where $\mathbf{H} = (\mathbf{A}|\mathbf{AR} + \mathbf{G})$), a deterministic algorithm that given full-rank matrices $\mathbf{A} \in \mathbb{Z}_q^{n \times m_1}, \mathbf{G} \in \mathbb{Z}_q^{n \times m_2}$, and a basis of $\mathbf{T_G}$ of $\Lambda_q^\perp(\mathbf{G})$ outputs a basis $\mathbf{T_H}$ of $\Lambda_q^\perp(\mathbf{H})$ such that $\|\widetilde{\mathbf{T_H}}\| \leq \|\widetilde{\mathbf{T_G}}\| \cdot (1 + \|\mathbf{R}\|_2)$.*
- *(Generalized Leftover Hash Lemma [1,16]): For $m > (n + 1) \log q + \omega(\log n)$ and prime $q > 2$, let $\mathbf{R} \leftarrow \{-1, 1\}^{m \times k}$ and $\mathbf{A} \leftarrow \mathbb{Z}_q^{n \times m}, \mathbf{B} \leftarrow \mathbb{Z}_q^{n \times k}$ be uniformly random matrices. Then the distribution $(\mathbf{A}, \mathbf{AR}, \mathbf{e}^\mathrm{T}\mathbf{R})$ is $\mathsf{negl}(n)$-close to the distribution $(\mathbf{A}, \mathbf{B}, \mathbf{e}^\mathrm{T}\mathbf{R})$ for all vector $\mathbf{e} \in \mathbb{Z}_q^m$. When $\mathbf{e}$ is always $\mathbf{0}$, this lemma is called Leftover Hash Lemma.*

3 Attribute-Based Keyword Search

In this section, we give the formal definition of key-policy attribute-based keyword search (KP-ABKS) as follows:

3.1 Definition of Key-Policy Attribute-Based Keyword Search

For a keyword space $\mathcal{W}$, attribute space $\mathcal{X}$ and policy space $\mathcal{F}$, a key-policy attribute-based keyword search (KP-ABKS) scheme $\Pi_{\mathsf{KP-ABKS}}$ consists five algorithms $\Pi_{\mathsf{KP-ABKS}} = (\mathsf{Setup}, \mathsf{KeyGen}, \mathsf{ABKS}, \mathsf{Trapdoor}, \mathsf{Test})$ which are PPT algorithms such that:

- $\mathsf{Setup}(1^\lambda, 1^k) \to (pp, msk)$: On input the security parameter λ, the number of attributes k, the setup algorithm outputs the public parameters pp and master secret key msk.
- $\mathsf{KeyGen}(pp, msk, f) \to sk_f$: On input the public parameters pp, the master secret key msk, a policy $f \in \mathcal{F}$, the key generation algorithm outputs the secret key sk_f.
- $\mathsf{ABKS}(pp, \mathbf{w}, \mathbf{x}) \to CT$: On input the public parameters pp and keyword $\mathbf{w} \in \mathcal{W}$, an attribute $\mathbf{x} \in \mathcal{X}$, this algorithm outputs a ciphertext CT related to the keyword $\mathbf{w}$ according to the attribute $\mathbf{x}$.
- $\mathsf{Trapdoor}(pp, sk_f, \mathbf{w}) \to \mathbf{d}_{f,\mathbf{w}}$: On input the public parameters pp and a secret key sk_f for the policy f, a keyword $\mathbf{w}$, the trapdoor algorithm outputs a trapdoor $\mathbf{d}_{f,\mathbf{w}}$ associated with the keyword $\mathbf{w}$ according to the secret key sk_f.
- $\mathsf{Test}(pp, CT, \mathbf{d}_{f,\mathbf{w}}) \to \{0,1\}$: On input the ciphertext CT related to the keyword $\mathbf{w}$ according to the attribute $\mathbf{x}$, and a trapdoor $\mathbf{d}_{f,\mathbf{w}}$ which is associated with a keyword $\mathbf{w}$ and a policy f, the deterministic test algorithm outputs 1 if $f(\mathbf{x}) = 0$, CT and $\mathbf{d}_{f,\mathbf{w}}$ contains the same keyword $\mathbf{w}$; otherwise, outputs 0.

The correctness and security of a KP-ABKS scheme are defined in Subsects. 3.2 and 3.3, respectively.

3.2 Correctness Consistence

For any honestly generated public parameters pp and a secret key sk_f for the policy f, and for any keyword $\mathbf{w}$, our KP-ABKS scheme requires that $\mathsf{Test}(pp, CT, \mathbf{d}_{f,\mathbf{w}}) = 1$, where $CT \leftarrow \mathsf{ABKS}(pp, \mathbf{w}, \mathbf{x})$, $\mathbf{d}_{f,\mathbf{w}} \leftarrow \mathsf{Trapdoor}(pp, sk_f, \mathbf{w})$ and $f(\mathbf{x}) = 0$.

3.3 Security

In this paper, we consider two kinds of security: ciphertext indistinguishability which can resist the chosen keyword attacks, and unforgeability which can resist the keyword guessing attacks even for the misbehaved cloud server. We first give the definition of ciphertext indistinguishability as follows:

Ciphertext Indistinguishability. Let $\Pi_{\mathsf{KP-ABKS}}$ = (Setup, KeyGen, ABKS, Trapdoor, Test) be a key-policy attribute-based keyword search (KP-ABKS) scheme for a keyword space $\mathcal{W}$, attribute space $\mathcal{X}$ and policy space $\mathcal{F}$. For all $\lambda \in \mathbb{N}$, the ABKS ciphertext indistinguishability security experiment $\mathsf{Expt}^{\mathsf{CI}}_{\Pi_{\mathsf{KP-ABKS}}}(\lambda, \mathcal{A})$ between an adversary $\mathcal{A}$ and the challenger $\mathcal{C}$ is defined as follows:

- Setup phase: The adversary sends the challenge attribute $\mathbf{x}^*$ to the challenger $\mathcal{C}$. The challenger then computes $(pp, msk) \leftarrow \mathsf{Setup}(1^\lambda, 1^k)$ and sends pp to the adversary $\mathcal{A}$.
- Query phase: The adversary $\mathcal{A}$ can make the following four types of queries adaptively:
  - Hash Queries: The adversary $\mathcal{A}$ can make a polynomial number of hash queries and obtain the corresponding hash values.
  - Key Queries: The adversary $\mathcal{A}$ can make a polynomial number of secret key queries on policy f, with the restriction that $f(\mathbf{x}^*) \neq 0$, the challenger generates the secret key sk_f and sends it to $\mathcal{A}$.
  - Trapdoor Queries: The adversary $\mathcal{A}$ can make a polynomial number of trapdoor queries for the keyword $\mathbf{w}$ and policy f to receive the trapdoor $\mathbf{d}_{f,\mathbf{w}}$ from the challenger.
  - Challenge Query: The adversary $\mathcal{A}$ chooses two keywords $(\mathbf{w}_0^*, \mathbf{w}_1^*)$ which have not been queried for the trapdoor query with some policy f such that $f(\mathbf{x}^*) = 0$, then $\mathcal{A}$ submits them to the challenger. The challenger chooses a bit $\beta \in \{0, 1\}$, computes $CT_\beta \leftarrow \mathsf{ABKS}(pp, \mathbf{w}_\beta^*, \mathbf{x}^*))$ and sends it to $\mathcal{A}$.
- Guess phase: At the end of the game, $\mathcal{A}$ outputs a bit $\beta' \in \{0, 1\}$. It wins the game if $\beta = \beta'$.

The advantage of the adversary in winning the above game is defined as $\mathsf{Adv}_\mathcal{A} = |\Pr[\beta = \beta'] - 1/2|$.

Now we give the security definition of unforgeability which can resist the keyword guessing attacks. In a KP-ABKS scheme, a malicious adversary (even for the malicious cloud server) may encrypt any candidate keyword to generate a corresponding ciphertext. If the adversary can obtain the trapdoor, then the adversary can use the trapdoor to run the test algorithm to identity the ciphertext of the keyword which matches the trapdoor. Once the test algorithm returns 1, the adversary can learn the keyword which is hidden in the trapdoor, and this manner violates the data privacy. Our KP-ABKS scheme can resist this kind of keyword guessing attacks even for the misbehaved cloud server. We give the formal security definition as follows:

Unforgeability. Let $\Pi_{\mathsf{KP-ABKS}}$ = (Setup, KeyGen, ABKS, Trapdoor, Test) be a key-policy attribute-based keyword search (KP-ABKS) scheme for a keyword space $\mathcal{W}$, attribute space $\mathcal{X}$ and policy space $\mathcal{F}$. For all $\lambda \in \mathbb{N}$, the KP-ABKS unforgeability security experiment $\mathsf{Expt}^{\mathsf{Unforgery}}_{\Pi_{\mathsf{KP-ABKS}}}(\lambda, \mathcal{A})$ between an adversary $\mathcal{A}$ and the challenger $\mathcal{C}$ is defined as follows:

- **Setup phase:** The challenger computes $(pp, msk) \leftarrow \mathsf{Setup}(1^\lambda, 1^k)$ and sends pp to the adversary $\mathcal{A}$.
- **Query phase:** The adversary $\mathcal{A}$ can make the following four types of queries adaptively:
  - **Hash Queries:** The adversary $\mathcal{A}$ can make a polynomial number of hash queries and obtain the corresponding hash values.
  - **Trapdoor Queries:** The adversary $\mathcal{A}$ can make a polynomial number of trapdoor queries for the keyword $\mathbf{w}$ and policy f to receive the trapdoor $\mathbf{d}_{f,\mathbf{w}}$ from the challenger.
  - **Key Queries:** The adversary $\mathcal{A}$ can make a polynomial number of key queries on policy f, the challenger generates the secret key sk_f and sends it to $\mathcal{A}$.
  - **Searchable Ciphertext Queries:** The adversary can make a polynomial number of ciphertext queries on keyword $\mathbf{w}$ under the attribute $\mathbf{x}$. The challenger generates the corresponding ciphertext and returns it to the adversary.
- **Forgery phase:** At the end of the game, $\mathcal{A}$ outputs a forged searchable ciphertext CT^* related to the keyword $\mathbf{w}^*$ according to the attribute $\mathbf{x}^*$. It wins the game if the ciphertext can pass the test process.

4   Our KP-ABKS Construction

In this section, we propose our KP-ABKS scheme. Let λ be the security parameter, $\mathbf{x} \in \mathbb{Z}_q^k$ and $\mathbf{w} \in \{0,1\}^s$. we construct our key-policy attribute-based keyword search (KP-ABKS) scheme $\Pi_{\mathsf{KP-ABKS}} = (\mathsf{Setup}, \mathsf{KeyGen}, \mathsf{ABKS}, \mathsf{Trapdoor}, \mathsf{Test})$ as follows:

Set lattice parameters $n = n(\lambda), m = m(\lambda), q = q(\lambda)$ and Gaussian parameters $\alpha = \alpha(\lambda), \sigma = \sigma(\lambda)$, set a family of circuits $\mathcal{F} = \{f : \mathbb{Z}_q^k \rightarrow \mathbb{Z}_q\}$ of depth $d = d(\lambda)$. We first assume the existence of the following deterministic algorithms as in [8].

- $\mathsf{Eval}_{\mathrm{pk}}(f \in \mathcal{F}, (\mathbf{A}_1, ..., \mathbf{A}_k)) \rightarrow \mathbf{A}_f \in \mathbb{Z}_q^{n \times m}$.
- $\mathsf{Eval}_{\mathrm{CT}}(f \in \mathcal{F}, \{(x_i, \mathbf{A}_i, \mathbf{C}_i)\}_{i=1}^k) \rightarrow \mathbf{C}_f$, where $\mathbf{C}_i := (\mathbf{A}_i + x_i \mathbf{G})^{\mathrm{T}} \mathbf{D} + \mathbf{E}_i$. It holds that:

$$\mathbf{c}_f := (\mathbf{A}_f + f(\mathbf{x})\mathbf{G})^{\mathrm{T}} \mathbf{D} + \mathbf{E}_f,$$

where $\mathbf{A}_f = \mathsf{Eval}_{\mathrm{pk}}(f, (\mathbf{A}_1, ..., \mathbf{A}_k))$, for $\mathbf{A}_1, ..., \mathbf{A}_k \in \mathbb{Z}_q^{n \times m}$, $\mathbf{D} \in \mathbb{Z}_q^{n \times s}$, $\mathbf{E}_1, ..., \mathbf{E}_k \in \mathbb{Z}_q^{m \times s}$. Note that if $||\mathbf{E}_i||_\infty \leq B$ for all $i \in [k]$, and p is the upper bound of all intermediate result of $f(\mathbf{x})$, we have $||\mathbf{E}_f||_\infty \leq B \cdot (m + p)^{O(d)}$.
- $\mathsf{Eval}_{\mathrm{sim}}(f \in \mathcal{F}, \{(x_i^*, \mathbf{R}_i)\}_{i=1}^k, \mathbf{A}) \rightarrow \mathbf{R}_f$, where $\mathbf{x}^* = (x_1^*, ..., x_k^*)$ is an attribute vector and $\mathbf{R}_i \in \{-1, 1\}^{m \times m}$, it holds that:

$$\mathbf{A}\mathbf{R}_f - f(\mathbf{x}^*)\mathbf{G} = \mathbf{A}_f,$$

where $\mathbf{A}_f = \mathsf{Eval}_{\mathrm{pk}}(f, (\mathbf{A}\mathbf{R}_1 - x_1^*\mathbf{G}, ..., \mathbf{A}\mathbf{R}_k - x_k^*\mathbf{G}))$. Note that if p is the upper bound of all intermediate result of $f(\mathbf{x})$, we have $||\mathbf{R}_f||_\infty \leq (m+p)^{O(d)}$.

Given the above algorithms, our KP-ABKS system works as follows:

- Setup($1^\lambda, 1^k, 1^d$) $\rightarrow$ (pp, msk): On input the security parameter λ, do:
  1. Invoke TrapGen(n, m, q) to generate a uniformly random matrix $\mathbf{A}$ together with the short basis $\mathbf{T_A}$ for $\Lambda_q^\perp(\mathbf{A})$.
  2. Invoke TrapGen(n, m, q) to generate a uniformly random matrix $\mathbf{A}_s \in \mathbb{Z}_q^{n \times m}$ together with the short basis $\mathbf{T_{A_s}}$ of $\Lambda_q^\perp(\mathbf{A}_s)$ for the data sender.
  3. Choose $k + 1$ uniformly random matrix $\mathbf{A_w} \in \mathbb{Z}_q^{n \times m}$ and $\mathbf{A}_i \in \mathbb{Z}_q^{n \times m}$ for $i = 1, \ldots, k$.
  4. Select a uniformly random vector $\mathbf{u} \in \mathbb{Z}_q^n$.
  5. Define two hash functions: $H_1 : \{0, 1\}^s \rightarrow \mathbb{Z}_q$ and $H_2 : \mathbb{Z}_q^{m \times s} \times \{0, 1\}^s \rightarrow \mathbb{Z}_q^n$.
  6. Output the public parameters pp and the master secret key msk given by,

$$pp = (\mathbf{A}, \mathbf{A}_s, \mathbf{A_w}, \{\mathbf{A}_i\}_{i \in \{1, \ldots, k\}}, \mathbf{u}, H_1, H_2) \qquad msk = (\mathbf{T_A})$$

- KeyGen(pp, msk, f): On input the public parameters pp and master secret key msk, and a access policy f, do:
  1. Set $\mathbf{A}_f = \mathsf{Eval}_{\mathrm{pk}}(f, (\mathbf{A}_1, \ldots, \mathbf{A}_k))$.
  2. Compute $\mathbf{T}_f \leftarrow \mathsf{RandBasis}(\mathbf{F}, \mathsf{ExtendRight}(\mathbf{A}, \mathbf{T_A}, \mathbf{A}_f), \sigma)$, where $\mathbf{T}_f$ is a trapdoor for $\mathbf{F} = (\mathbf{A}|\mathbf{A}_f) \in \mathbb{Z}_q^{n \times 2m}$.
  3. Output the secret key $sk_f = \mathbf{T}_f$.
- ABKS($pp, \mathbf{w}, \mathbf{x}$) $\rightarrow CT$: On input the public parameters pp and keyword $\mathbf{w}$, an attribute vector $\mathbf{x} = (x_1, \ldots, x_k) \in \mathbb{Z}_q^k$ of length k, do :
  1. Select a uniformly random matrix $\mathbf{D} \leftarrow \mathbb{Z}_q^{n \times s}$.
  2. Select noise vector $\mathbf{e} \leftarrow \mathcal{D}_{\mathbb{Z}_q^s, \alpha}$ and random noise matrix $\mathbf{E}_0 \leftarrow \mathcal{D}_{\mathbb{Z}_q^{m \times s}, \alpha}$.
  3. For $i = 1, \ldots, k$, choose these random matrices $\mathbf{R}_i \in \{-1, 1\}^{m \times m}$ and $\mathbf{R_w} \in \{-1, 1\}^{m \times m}$. Then define noise matrices $\mathbf{E}_i := \mathbf{R}_i^T \mathbf{E}_0$ and $\mathbf{E_w} := \mathbf{R_w}^T \mathbf{E}_0$.
  4. Select a random binary string $\mathbf{a} = (a_1, \ldots, a_s) \in \{0, 1\}^s$.
  5. For $i = 1, \ldots, k$, compute the ciphertext of keyword $\mathbf{w}$ as follows:
     (a) Compute the ciphertext,

$$\mathbf{c} := \mathbf{u}^T \mathbf{D} + \mathbf{e} + \mathbf{a} \lfloor \tfrac{q}{2} \rfloor, \mathbf{C}_0 := \mathbf{A}^T \mathbf{D} + \mathbf{E}_0,$$

$$\mathbf{C}_i := (\mathbf{A}_i + x_i \mathbf{G})^T \mathbf{D} + \mathbf{E}_i, \mathbf{C_w} := (\mathbf{A_w} + H_1(\mathbf{w})\mathbf{G})^T \mathbf{D} + \mathbf{E_w}$$

     (b) Compute $\mathbf{h} = H_2(\mathbf{C_w}, \mathbf{a})$, and evaluate $\theta \leftarrow \mathsf{SamplePre}(\mathbf{A}_s, \mathbf{T_{A_s}}, \mathbf{h}, \sigma)$.
     (c) Output the final ciphertext, $CT = (\mathbf{c}, \mathbf{C}_0, \{\mathbf{C}_i\}_{i \in \{1, \ldots k\}}, \mathbf{C_w}, \theta)$.
- Trapdoor($pp, sk_f, \mathbf{w}$) $\rightarrow \mathbf{d}_{f, \mathbf{w}}$: On input the public parameters pp, a secret key sk_f related to the access policy f, a keyword $\mathbf{w}$, do:
  1. Compute $\mathbf{A}_f = \mathsf{Eval}_{\mathrm{pk}}(f, (\mathbf{A}_1, \ldots, \mathbf{A}_k))$.
  2. Compute $\mathbf{T}_{f\mathbf{w}} \leftarrow \mathsf{RandBasis}(\mathbf{F_w}, \mathsf{ExtendRight}(\mathbf{F} = [\mathbf{A}|\mathbf{A}_f], \mathbf{T}_f, \mathbf{A_w} + H_1(\mathbf{w})\mathbf{G}), \sigma)$, where $\mathbf{T}_{f\mathbf{w}}$ is a trapdoor for $\mathbf{F_w} = (\mathbf{A}|\mathbf{A}_f|\mathbf{A_w} + H_1(\mathbf{w})\mathbf{G}) \in \mathbb{Z}_q^{n \times 3m}$.

3. Set $\mathbf{d}_{f,\mathbf{w}} \leftarrow \mathsf{SamplePre}(\mathbf{F}_{\mathbf{w}}, \mathbf{T}_{f_{\mathbf{w}}}, \mathbf{u}, \sigma)$. Note that $\mathbf{F}_{\mathbf{w}} \cdot \mathbf{d}_{f,\mathbf{w}} = \mathbf{u}$ in $\mathbb{Z}_q^n$.
4. Output the trapdoor $\mathbf{d}_{f,\mathbf{w}} \in \mathbb{Z}_q^{3m}$ of keyword $\mathbf{w}$.

- $\mathsf{Test}(pp, CT, \mathbf{d}_{f,\mathbf{w}}) \rightarrow \{0,1\}$: On input the searchable ciphertext $CT = (\mathbf{c}, \mathbf{C}_0, \{\mathbf{C}_i\}_{i\in\{1,...k\}}, \mathbf{C}_{\mathbf{w}}, \theta)$ associated with attribute $\mathbf{x}$, a trapdoor $\mathbf{d}_{f,\mathbf{w}}$ with policy f, do:
  1. If $f(\mathbf{x}) \neq 0$, return 0; otherwise, do:
     (a) Compute $\mathbf{C}_f = \mathsf{Eval}_{\mathrm{CT}}(f, \{(x_i, \mathbf{A}_i, \mathbf{C}_i)\}_{i=1}^k)$.
     (b) Let $\mathbf{C}_{f,\mathbf{w}} = (\mathbf{C}_0 || \mathbf{C}_f || \mathbf{C}_{\mathbf{w}}) \in \mathbb{Z}_q^{3m \times s}$
     (c) Compute $\mathbf{a} = (a_1, ..., a_s) \leftarrow \mathbf{c} - \mathbf{d}_{f,\mathbf{w}}^{\mathrm{T}} \mathbf{C}_{f,\mathbf{w}}$.
     (d) For $i = 1, ..., s$, compare each a_i and $\lfloor \frac{q}{2} \rfloor$, if $|a_i - \lfloor \frac{q}{2} \rfloor| < \lfloor \frac{q}{4} \rfloor$, set $a_i = 1$, otherwise set $a_i = 0$.
     (e) Compute $\mathbf{h} = H_2(\mathbf{C}_{\mathbf{w}}, \mathbf{a})$, and then check whether $\mathbf{A}_s \theta = \mathbf{h}$. If the equation holds, then the test algorithm returns 1, otherwise returns 0.

Remark 1. Note that our key-policy attribute-based keyword search (KP-ABKS) scheme can be transformed into a ciphertext-policy attribute-based keyword search (CP-ABKS) scheme. For access policy function $f : \{\mathbb{Z}_q^k \rightarrow \mathbb{Z}_q\}$, where $|f| = N$, we can set $\{\mathbf{C}_i := (\mathbf{A}_i + f_i \mathbf{G})^{\mathrm{T}} \mathbf{D} + \mathbf{E}_i\}_{i\in[N]}$, for public matrices $\mathbf{A}_1, ..., \mathbf{A}_N$. Now the secret key $sk_{\mathbf{x}}$ for attribute $\mathbf{x}$ is defined to be a trapdoor of $\mathbf{F} = [\mathbf{A}|\mathbf{A}_{\mathbf{x}}]$, where $\mathbf{A}_{\mathbf{x}} = \mathsf{Eval}_{\mathrm{pk}}(\mathcal{U}_{\mathbf{x}}, (\mathbf{A}_1, ..., \mathbf{A}_N))$ and $\mathcal{U}_{\mathbf{x}}$ is the universal circuit $\mathcal{U}_{\mathbf{x}}(f) = f(\mathbf{x})$. Other processes are identical to those described above.

Correctness Consistence. For any honestly generated public parameters pp and a secret key sk_f for the access policy f, and for any keyword $\mathbf{w}$, then $\mathsf{Test}(pp, CT, \mathbf{d}_{f,\mathbf{w}}) = 1$, where $CT \leftarrow \mathsf{ABKS}(pp, \mathbf{w}, \mathbf{x})$ and $\mathbf{d}_{f,\mathbf{w}} \leftarrow \mathsf{Trapdoor}(pp, sk_f, \mathbf{w})$ such that $f(\mathbf{x}) - 0$.

Proof. For $f(\mathbf{x}) = 0$, let $\mathbf{w}$ be the keyword contained in the chiphertext CT and $\mathbf{w}'$ be the keyword contained in trapdoor $\mathbf{d}_{f,\mathbf{w}'}$, we analysis the correctness in the following two cases:

1. If $\mathbf{w} = \mathbf{w}'$, for $\mathbf{C}_{f,\mathbf{w}} = (\mathbf{C}_0 || \mathbf{C}_f || \mathbf{C}_{\mathbf{w}}) = (\mathbf{A} || \mathbf{A}_f || \mathbf{A}_{\mathbf{w}} + H_1(\mathbf{w}) \mathbf{G})^{\mathrm{T}} \mathbf{D} + \mathbf{E}'$, with noise matrix $\mathbf{E}' = (\mathbf{E}_0 || \mathbf{E}_f || \mathbf{E}_{\mathbf{w}})$, we have $\mathbf{a}' = (a_1', ..., a_s') = \mathbf{c} - \mathbf{d}_{f,\mathbf{w}}^{\mathrm{T}} \mathbf{C}_{f,\mathbf{w}} = (a_0, ..., a_s) \lfloor \frac{q}{2} \rfloor + \underbrace{\mathbf{e} - \mathbf{d}_{f,\mathbf{w}}^{\mathrm{T}} \mathbf{E}'}_{\text{error-term:}\tilde{\mathbf{e}}}$.

   To decrypt correctly, for $\alpha = \sqrt{n}, \sigma = B \cdot (m + p)^{O(d)}$ ($\mathcal{D}_{\mathbb{Z}_q, \alpha}$ is B-bounded), the error term $||\tilde{\mathbf{e}}||_\infty \leq B^2 \cdot (m + p)^{O(d)}$ is guaranteed to less than $q/4$ as discussed in [8]. Thus we have $\mathbf{a} = \mathbf{a}'$ and $\mathbf{h} = H_2(\mathbf{C}_{\mathbf{w}}, \mathbf{a}) = H_2(\mathbf{C}_{\mathbf{w}}, \mathbf{a}')$, so the test algorithm returns 1.
2. If $\mathbf{w} \neq \mathbf{w}'$, we have $\mathbf{a}' = (a_1', ..., a_s') = \mathbf{c} - \mathbf{d}_{f,\mathbf{w}'}^{\mathrm{T}} \mathbf{C}_{f,\mathbf{w}} \in \mathbb{Z}_q^s$, the searchable ciphertext cannot be decrypted to $\mathbf{a} = (a_1, ..., a_s)$ with all but negligible probability. Thus we have $\mathbf{h} = H_2(\mathbf{C}_{\mathbf{w}}, \mathbf{a}) \neq H_2(\mathbf{C}_{\mathbf{w}}, \mathbf{a}')$, so the test algorithm returns 0.

Thus, as stated above, our KP-ABKS scheme satisfies correctness consistency. Once the test algorithm returns 1, the cloud server can make sure that the searchable ciphertext CT and the trapdoor $\mathbf{d}_{f,\mathbf{w}}$ contains the same keyword $\mathbf{w}$. Then the cloud server sends the corresponding encrypted files to the receiver. The receiver could use its own secret key to decrypt the encrypted files to learn the plaintext data.

Security. Now we will demonstrate that our $\Pi_{\mathsf{KP-ABKS}}$ scheme satisfies the ciphertext indistinguishability and unforgeability.

Theorem 1. *Suppose that an adversary can break the ciphertext indistinguishability of our $\Pi_{\mathsf{KP-ABKS}}$ scheme under the selective attribute security in the random oracle with non-negligible probability ϵ, then there exist an algorithm $\mathcal{B}$ that can solve the DLWE problem with non-negligible probability ϵ'*

Proof. Let $\Pi_{\mathsf{KP-ABKS}} = (\mathsf{Setup}, \mathsf{KeyGen}, \mathsf{ABKS}, \mathsf{Trapdoor}, \mathsf{Test})$ be a key-policy attribute-base keyword search (KP-ABKS) scheme. Let $\mathcal{A}$ be the adversary that breaks ciphertext indistinguishability, then we can construct an algorithm $\mathcal{B}$ to solve the DLWE problem. The algorithm $\mathcal{B}$ simulates the experiment as follows:

- Setup phase: At the start of the experiment, $\mathcal{A}$ submits the target attribute $\mathbf{x}^* = (x_1^*, ..., x_k^*)$. The algorithm $\mathcal{B}$ then requests from the DLWE oracle and receives pairs $(\mathbf{u}_k, v_{k1}, ..., v_{ks}) \in \mathbb{Z}_q^n \times \mathbb{Z}_q^s$, for $i = 0, ..., m$. It then sets two lists L_1, L_2. Set Q_{H_i} to be the maximum number of queries to H_i that the adversary makes, where $i = 1, 2$. The algorithm $\mathcal{B}$ prepares the setup algorithm as follows:
  1. Select the integer $I^* \in [Q_{H_1}]$.
  2. Sample $k + 1$ random matrices $\mathbf{R}_{\mathbf{w}}^*, \mathbf{R}_1^*, ..., \mathbf{R}_k^* \leftarrow \{-1, 1\}^{m \times m}$ and $p^* \leftarrow \mathbb{Z}_q$.
  3. Assemble a random matrix $\mathbf{A} \in \mathbb{Z}_q^{n \times m}$ from m of the LWE samples, by letting the ith column of $\mathbf{A}$ be the vector $\mathbf{u}_i$, where $i = 1, ..., m$.
  4. For $i = 1, ..., k$, set $\mathbf{A}_i = \mathbf{A}\mathbf{R}_i^* - x_i^*\mathbf{G}$ and $\mathbf{A}_{\mathbf{w}} = \mathbf{A}\mathbf{R}_{\mathbf{w}}^* - p^*\mathbf{G}$. (Note that $\mathbf{R}_i^*$ is used only in the construction of $\mathbf{A}_i$ and in the construction of the challenger ciphertext where $\mathbf{E}_i = (\mathbf{R}_i^*)^{\mathsf{T}}\mathbf{E}_0$, by the generalized Leftover Hash Lemma, $(\mathbf{A}_i, \mathbf{A}_i\mathbf{R}_i^*, \mathbf{E}_i)$ is statistically close to the distribution $(\mathbf{A}_i, \mathbf{A}_i', \mathbf{E}_i)$, where $\mathbf{A}_i'$ is a uniform $\mathbb{Z}_q^{n \times m}$ matrix. Thus $\mathbf{A}_1, ..., \mathbf{A}_k, \mathbf{A}_{\mathbf{w}}$ are statistically close to uniform.)
  5. Invoke $\mathsf{TrapGen}(n, m, q)$ to generate a uniformly random matrix $\mathbf{A}_s \in \mathbb{Z}_q^{n \times m}$ together with the short basis $\mathbf{T}_{\mathbf{A}_s}$ of $\Lambda_q^{\perp}(\mathbf{A}_s)$ for the data sender.
  6. Set the public parameters $pp = (\mathbf{A}, \mathbf{A}_s, \mathbf{A}_{\mathbf{w}}, \{\mathbf{A}_i\}_{i \in \{1, ..., k\}}, \mathbf{u}, H_1, H_2)$ and send pp to $\mathcal{A}$.
  We then assume that when $\mathcal{A}$ make the key queries and trapdoor queries, it has queried all relevant hash values.
- Query phase: The adversary $\mathcal{A}$ can make the following four types of queries adaptively:

- Hash Queries: The adversary $\mathcal{A}$ can make a polynomial number of hash queries, the algorithm $\mathcal{B}$ responds as follows:
  * H_1 query: For the Qth query, where $Q = 1, ..., Q_{H_1}$, the adversary queries on $\mathbf{w}$, then $\mathcal{B}$ answers:
    1. If $Q = I^*$ such that $\mathbf{w} = \mathbf{w}^*$, $\mathcal{B}$ sets $H_1(\mathbf{w}) \leftarrow p^*$ and returns it to the adversary. It adds $(\mathbf{w}^*, p^*)$ to L_1.
    2. Otherwise, $\mathcal{B}$ looks into list L_1 to check if the hash value was previously defined, if it was, the previous value is returned. If not, it randomly choose an element $h_1 \in \mathbb{Z}_q$. It adds $(\mathbf{w}, h_1)$ to L_1.
  * H_2 query: For the Qth query on $(\mathbf{C_w}, \mathbf{a})$, where $Q = 1, ..., Q_{H_2}$, $\mathcal{B}$ first checks if the value was previously defined. If it was, then $\mathcal{B}$ returns the defined value. If not, $\mathcal{B}$ randomly choose $\mathbf{h}_2 \leftarrow \mathbb{Z}_q^n$, adds $(\mathbf{C_w}, \mathbf{a}, \mathbf{h}_2)$ to L_2 and returns $\mathbf{h}_2$.
- Key Queries: The adversary $\mathcal{A}$ can make a polynomial number of key queries on f such that $f(\mathbf{x}^*) = y \neq 0$.
  1. $\mathbf{R}_f \leftarrow \mathsf{Eval}_{\mathrm{sim}}(f \in \mathcal{F}, \{(x_i^*, \mathbf{R}_i^*)\}_{i=1}^k)$, it holds that:

  $$\mathbf{AR}_f - y\mathbf{G} = \mathbf{A}_f,$$

  where $\mathbf{A}_f = \mathsf{Eval}_{\mathrm{pk}}(f, (\mathbf{AR}_1^* - x_1^*\mathbf{G}, ..., \mathbf{AR}_k^* - x_k^*\mathbf{G}))$.
  2. Run $\mathbf{T}_f \leftarrow \mathsf{RandBasis}(\mathbf{F}, \mathsf{ExtendLeft}(y\mathbf{G}, \mathbf{T_G}, \mathbf{A}, \mathbf{R}_f), \sigma)$, where $\mathbf{T}_f$ is a trapdoor for $\mathbf{F} = (\mathbf{A}|\mathbf{A}_f)$.
  3. Output the secret key $sk_f = \mathbf{T}_f$.
- Trapdoor Queries: The adversary $\mathcal{A}$ can adaptively query the trapdoor $\mathbf{d}_{f,\mathbf{w}}$ of keyword $\mathbf{w}$ associated with policy f, with the restriction that $f(\mathbf{x}^*) = y \neq 0$ or $f(\mathbf{x}^*) = 0$ but $\mathbf{w} \neq \mathbf{w}^*$.
  * If $f(\mathbf{x}^*) = y \neq 0$, do:
    1. $\mathbf{R}_f \leftarrow \mathsf{Eval}_{\mathrm{sim}}(f \in \mathcal{F}, \{(x_i^*, \mathbf{R}_i^*)\}_{i=1}^k)$, it holds that:

    $$\mathbf{AR}_f - y\mathbf{G} = \mathbf{A}_f,$$

    where $\mathbf{A}_f = \mathsf{Eval}_{\mathrm{pk}}(f, (\mathbf{AR}_1^* - x_1^*\mathbf{G}, ..., \mathbf{AR}_k^* - x_k^*\mathbf{G}))$.
    2. Run $\mathbf{T}_f \leftarrow \mathsf{RandBasis}(\mathbf{F}, \mathsf{ExtendLeft}(y\mathbf{G}, \mathbf{T_G}, \mathbf{A}, \mathbf{R}_f), \sigma)$, where $\mathbf{T}_f$ is a trapdoor for $\mathbf{F} = (\mathbf{A}|\mathbf{A}_f)$.
    3. Run $\mathbf{T}_{f_{\mathbf{w}}} \leftarrow \mathsf{RandBasis}(\mathbf{F_w}, \mathsf{ExtendRight}(\mathbf{F}, \mathbf{T}_f, \mathbf{A_w} + H_1(\mathbf{w})\mathbf{G}), \sigma)$, where $\mathbf{T}_{f_{\mathbf{w}}}$ is a trapdoor for $\mathbf{F_w} = (\mathbf{A}|\mathbf{A}_f|\mathbf{A_w} + H_1(\mathbf{w})\mathbf{G}) \in \mathbb{Z}_q^{n \times 3m}$.
    4. Set $\mathbf{d}_{f,\mathbf{w}} \leftarrow \mathsf{SamplePre}(\mathbf{F_w}, \mathbf{T}_{f_{\mathbf{w}}}, \mathbf{u}, \sigma)$.
    5. Output $\mathbf{d}_{f,\mathbf{w}}$ as the trapdoor of keyword $\mathbf{w}$.
  * Otherwise $f(\mathbf{x}^*) = 0 \wedge \mathbf{w} \neq \mathbf{w}^*$, do:
    1. Since $\mathbf{w} \neq \mathbf{w}^* \Rightarrow H_1(\mathbf{w}) - p^* \neq 0$, it holds that:

    $$\mathbf{AR}_f = \mathbf{A}_f,$$

    where $\mathbf{A}_f = \mathsf{Eval}_{\mathrm{pk}}(f, (\mathbf{AR}_1^* - x_1^*\mathbf{G}, ..., \mathbf{AR}_k^* - x_k^*\mathbf{G}))$.

2. Run $\mathbf{T}_{f_\mathbf{w}}$ $\leftarrow$ RandBasis($\mathbf{F}$, ExtendLeft(($H_1(\mathbf{w})$ $-$ p^*)$\mathbf{G}$, $\mathbf{T_G}$, $\mathbf{A}|\mathbf{A}_f$, $\mathbf{R}_\mathbf{w}^*$), σ), where $\mathbf{T}_{f_\mathbf{w}}$ is a trapdoor for $\mathbf{F_w} = (\mathbf{A}|\mathbf{A}_f|\mathbf{A_w} + H_1(\mathbf{w})G) \in \mathbb{Z}_q^{n \times 3m}$.

3. Set $\mathbf{d}_{f,\mathbf{w}} \leftarrow$ SamplePre($\mathbf{F_w}, \mathbf{T}_{f_\mathbf{w}}, \mathbf{u}, \sigma$).

4. Output $\mathbf{d}_{f,\mathbf{w}}$ as the trapdoor of keyword $\mathbf{w}$.

- Challenge Query: The adversary $\mathcal{A}$ sends two keywords $(\mathbf{w}_0^*, \mathbf{w}_1^*)$ which have not been queried for the trapdoor query with some policy f such that $f(\mathbf{x}^*) = 0$. Now $\mathcal{B}$ randomly chooses a bit $\beta \in \{0,1\}$. If $\beta = 0$, $\mathcal{B}$ returns a random KP-ABKS searchable ciphertext CT^* associated with the keyword $\mathbf{w}_0^*$. Otherwise, given that $\mathbf{AR}_i^* = \mathbf{A}_i + x_i^*\mathbf{G}$ and $\mathbf{AR}_\mathbf{w}^* = \mathbf{A_w} + H_1(\mathbf{w}^*)\mathbf{G}$, so $\mathcal{B}$ proceeds:
  1. For $k = 0, 1, ..., m$, retrieve $(v_{k1}, ..., v_{ks})$ from the LWE sample and set $\mathbf{v}_k = (v_{k1}, ..., v_{kl})$, let $\mathbf{V}^* = (\mathbf{v}_1, ..., \mathbf{v}_m) \in \mathbb{Z}_q^{m \times s}$.
  2. Randomly choose $\mathbf{a}^* = (a_1^*, ..., a_s^*) \in \{0,1\}^\ell$, set $\mathbf{c}^* = \mathbf{v}_0 + \mathbf{a}^*\lfloor q/2 \rfloor$.
  3. Set $\mathbf{C}_0^* = \mathbf{V}^* \in \mathbb{Z}_q^{m \times s}$.
  4. For $i = 1, ..., k$, set $\mathbf{C}_i^* = (\mathbf{R}_i^*)^\mathrm{T}\mathbf{C}_0^*$ and $\mathbf{C}_\mathbf{w}^* = (\mathbf{R}_\mathbf{w}^*)^\mathrm{T}\mathbf{C}_0^*$.
  5. Compute $\mathbf{h}^*$ $=$ $H_2(\mathbf{C}_\mathbf{w}^*, \mathbf{a}^*)$ $\in$ $\mathbb{Z}_q^n$,   then   run θ^* $\leftarrow$ SamplePre($\mathbf{A}_s, \mathbf{T}_{\mathbf{A}_s}, \mathbf{h}^*, \sigma$).
  6. $\mathcal{B}$ returns $CT^* = (\mathbf{c}^*, \mathbf{C}_0^*, \{\mathbf{C}_i^*\}_{i \in \{1,...k\}}, \mathbf{C_w}^*, \theta)$ as the ciphertext associated with keyword $\mathbf{w}_1^*$ to the adversary.

- Guessphase: At the end of the game, $\mathcal{A}$ outputs a bit $\beta' \in \{0,1\}$. It wins the game if $\beta = \beta'$.

Note that $\mathcal{B}$ simulates the challenge environment for the adversary. If the LWE samples are random, then $(\mathbf{c}^*, \mathbf{C}_0^*)$ are uniform random. So $(\{\mathbf{C}_i^*\}_{i \in \{1,...k\}}, \mathbf{C_w}^*)$ are uniform by a standard application of the Leftover Hash Lemma. We consider the case that $\mathcal{B}$ can successfully guess the keyword $\mathbf{w}_1^*$ with the non-negligible probability ϵ, where $\mathbf{w}_1^*$ is indeed the I^*th query in H_1 query, it means that $\mathbf{w}_1^* = \mathbf{w}^*$. This case occurs with probability $1/Q_{H_1}$. At the same time, $\mathcal{B}$ can return the ciphertext which really is associated with $\mathbf{w}_1^*$ with the probability $1/2$. If the adversary breaks the ciphertext indistinguishability with non-negligible probability ϵ, $\mathcal{B}$ has advantage at least $\epsilon' = \epsilon/(2Q_{H_1})$ in breaking the DLWE problem, thus we complete our proof.

Now we will demonstrate that our $\Pi_{\mathsf{KP-ABKS}}$ scheme satisfies the unforgeability security even for the misbehaved cloud server who can obtain the trapdoor.

Theorem 2. *Suppose an adversary $\mathcal{A}$ can break the unforgeability with non-negligible probability ϵ, then there exist an algorithm $\mathcal{B}$ that can solve the ISIS problem with non-negligible probability ϵ'.*

Proof. Let $\Pi_{\mathsf{KP-ABKS}} = (\mathsf{Setup}, \mathsf{KeyGen}, \mathsf{ABKS}, \mathsf{Trapdoor}, \mathsf{Test})$ be a key-policy attribute-base keyword search (KP-ABKS) scheme. Let $\mathcal{A}$ be the adversary that breaks unforgeability security, then we can construct an algorithm $\mathcal{B}$ to solve the ISIS problem. The algorithm $\mathcal{B}$ simulates the experiment as follows:

- **Setup phase:** At the start of the experiment, the algorithm $\mathcal{B}$ requests an instance of ISIS problem $(\mathbf{U}, \vartheta) \in \mathbb{Z}_q^{n \times m} \times \mathbb{Z}_q^n$, and it manages to solve the vector $\theta^* \in \mathbb{Z}_q^m$, such that $\mathbf{U}\theta^* = \vartheta$ and $0 < \|\theta^*\| \le \sigma\sqrt{m}$. To maintain the consistency, it then sets two lists L_1, L_2 and set Q_{H_i} to be the maximum number of queries to H_i that the adversary makes, where $i = 1, 2$. The algorithm $\mathcal{B}$ prepares the setup algorithm as follows:
  1. Select the integer $I^* \in [Q_{H_2}]$.
  2. Set $\mathbf{A}_s = \mathbf{U}$.
  3. Invoke $\mathsf{TrapGen}(n, m, q)$ to generate a uniformly random matrix $\mathbf{A}$ together with the short basis $\mathbf{T_A}$ for $\Lambda_q^\perp(\mathbf{A})$.
  4. Choose $k + 1$ uniformly random matrix $\mathbf{A_w} \in \mathbb{Z}_q^{n \times m}$ and $\mathbf{A}_i \in \mathbb{Z}_q^{n \times m}$ for $i = 1, \dots, k$.
  5. Select a uniformly random vector $\mathbf{u} \in \mathbb{Z}_q^n$.
  6. Set the public parameters $pp = (\mathbf{A}, \mathbf{A}_s, \mathbf{A_w}, \{\mathbf{A}_i\}_{i \in \{1, \dots, k\}}, \mathbf{u}, H_1, H_2)$ and send pp to $\mathcal{A}$.

  We then assume that when $\mathcal{A}$ make the key queries and trapdoor queries, it has queried all relevant hash values.
- **Query phase:** The adversary $\mathcal{A}$ can make the following four types of queries adaptively:

  - **Hash Queries:** The adversary $\mathcal{A}$ can make a polynomial number of hash queries, the algorithm $\mathcal{B}$ responds as follows:
    * H_1 query: For the Qth query, where $Q = 1, \dots, Q_{H_1}$, the adversary queries on $\mathbf{w}$, $\mathcal{B}$ first checks if the value was previously defined. If it was, then $\mathcal{B}$ returns the defined value. If not, $\mathcal{B}$ randomly choose $h_1 \leftarrow \mathbb{Z}_q$, adds $(\mathbf{w}, h_1)$ to L_1 and returns h_1.
    * H_2 query: For the Qth query on distinct $(\mathbf{C_w}, \mathbf{a})$, where $Q = 1, \dots, Q_{H_2}$, $\mathcal{B}$ first checks in L_2 if the value was previously defined. If it was, then $\mathcal{B}$ returns the defined value $\mathbf{h}_2$ to the adversary. If $Q = I^*$, such that $\mathbf{a} = \mathbf{a}^*$, and $\mathbf{C_w} = \mathbf{C_w^*}$ is just the ciphertext components of keyword $\mathbf{w}^*$, under the uniform matrix $\mathbf{D}^* \in \mathbb{Z}_q^{n \times s}$, the noise matrix $\mathbf{E_w^*} \in \mathbb{Z}_q^{m \times s}$, $\mathcal{B}$ adds $(\mathbf{C_w^*}, \mathbf{a}^*, \vartheta, \perp)$ to the list L_2, and returns ϑ to the adversary $\mathcal{A}$. Otherwise, $\mathcal{B}$ generates $\theta \leftarrow \mathcal{D}_{\mathbb{Z}^m, \sigma}$ and computes $\mathbf{h}_2 = \mathbf{U}\theta$, it then adds $(\mathbf{C_w}, \mathbf{a}, \mathbf{h}_2, \theta)$ to L_2 and returns $\mathbf{h}_2$.
  - **Key Queries:** The adversary $\mathcal{A}$ can make a polynomial number of key queries on f,
    1. Set $\mathbf{A}_f = \mathsf{Eval}_{\mathrm{pk}}(f, (\mathbf{A}_1, \dots, \mathbf{A}_k))$.
    2. Compute $\mathbf{T}_f \leftarrow \mathsf{RandBasis}(\mathbf{F}, \mathsf{ExtendRight}(\mathbf{A}, \mathbf{T_A}, \mathbf{A}_f), \sigma)$, where $\mathbf{T}_f$ is a trapdoor for $\mathbf{F} = (\mathbf{A}|\mathbf{A}_f) \in \mathbb{Z}_q^{n \times 2m}$.
    3. Output the secret key $sk_f = \mathbf{T}_f$.
  - **Trapdoor Queries:** The adversary $\mathcal{A}$ can adaptively query the trapdoor $\mathbf{d}_{f, \mathbf{w}}$ of keyword $\mathbf{w}$ associated with policy f.
    1. Set $\mathbf{A}_f = \mathsf{Eval}_{\mathrm{pk}}(f, (\mathbf{A}_1, \dots, \mathbf{A}_k))$.
    2. Compute $\mathbf{T}_f \leftarrow \mathsf{RandBasis}(\mathbf{F}, \mathsf{ExtendRight}(\mathbf{A}, \mathbf{T_A}, \mathbf{A}_f), \sigma)$, where $\mathbf{T}_f$ is a trapdoor for $\mathbf{F} = (\mathbf{A}|\mathbf{A}_f) \in \mathbb{Z}_q^{n \times 2m}$.

3. Compute $\mathbf{T}_{f_{\mathbf{w}}} \leftarrow \mathsf{RandBasis}(\mathbf{F}_{\mathbf{w}}, \mathsf{ExtendRight}(\mathbf{F}, \mathbf{T}_f, \mathbf{A}_{\mathbf{w}} + H_1(\mathbf{w})\mathbf{G}), \sigma)$, where $\mathbf{T}_{f_{\mathbf{w}}}$ is a trapdoor for $\mathbf{F}_{\mathbf{w}} = (\mathbf{A}|\mathbf{A}_f|\mathbf{A}_{\mathbf{w}} + H_1(\mathbf{w})\mathbf{G}) \in \mathbb{Z}_q^{n \times 3m}$.

4. Set $\mathbf{d}_{f,\mathbf{w}} \leftarrow \mathsf{SamplePre}(\mathbf{F}_{\mathbf{w}}, \mathbf{T}_{f_{\mathbf{w}}}, \mathbf{u}, \sigma)$. Note that $\mathbf{F}_{\mathbf{w}} \cdot \mathbf{d}_{f,\mathbf{w}} = \mathbf{u}$ in $\mathbb{Z}_q^n$.

5. Output the trapdoor $\mathbf{d}_{f,\mathbf{w}}$ of keyword $\mathbf{w}$.

- Searchable Ciphertext Queries: The adversary can make a polynomial number of ciphertext queries on keyword $\mathbf{w}$ under the attribute $\mathbf{x}$. The algorithm $\mathcal{B}$ chooses a binary string $\mathbf{a} \in \{0,1\}^s$, $\mathbf{D} \leftarrow \mathbb{Z}_q^{n \times s}$ and computes the noise matrices $\mathbf{E}_0, \mathbf{E}_1, ..., \mathbf{E}_k, \mathbf{E}_{\mathbf{w}} \in \mathbb{Z}_q^{m \times s}$. It then computes $(\mathbf{c}, \mathbf{C}_0, \{\mathbf{C}_i\}_{i \in \{1,...k\}}, \mathbf{C}_{\mathbf{w}})$ in a normal way. $\mathcal{B}$ generates $\theta \leftarrow \mathcal{D}_{\mathbb{Z}^m, \sigma}$ and returns $CT = (\mathbf{c}, \mathbf{C}_0, \{\mathbf{C}_i\}_{i \in \{1,...k\}}, \mathbf{C}_{\mathbf{w}}, \theta)$.

- Forgery phase: At the end of the game, $\mathcal{A}$ outputs a forged searchable ciphertext $CT^* = (\mathbf{c}^*, \mathbf{C}_0^*, \{\mathbf{C}_i^*\}_{i \in \{1,...k\}}, \mathbf{C}_{\mathbf{w}}^*, \theta^*)$ associated with $(\mathbf{w}^*, \mathbf{x}^*)$. With the restriction that $(\mathbf{w}^*, \mathbf{x}^*)$ can not be submitted to the searchable ciphertext oracle.

Note that $\mathcal{A}$ could query to $\mathcal{B}$ to get the trapdoor $\mathbf{d}_{f,\mathbf{w}^*}$ for policy f such that $f(\mathbf{x})^* = 0$. $\mathcal{B}$ recovers $\mathbf{a}^*$ by computing $\mathbf{a}^* = \mathbf{c} - \mathbf{d}_{f,\mathbf{w}^*}^T \mathbf{C}_{f,\mathbf{w}^*}$, where $\mathbf{C}_{f,\mathbf{w}^*} = (\mathbf{C}_0||\mathbf{C}_f||\mathbf{C}_{\mathbf{w}}^*) \in \mathbb{Z}_q^{3m \times s}$ for $\mathbf{C}_f = \mathsf{Eval}_{\mathsf{CT}}(f, \{(x_i, \mathbf{A}_i, \mathbf{C}_i)\}_{i=1}^k)$. $\mathcal{B}$ outputs θ^* as its answer to ISIS instance $(\mathbf{U}, \vartheta)$. If $\mathcal{A}$ wins the game, then we have $\mathbf{A}_s \theta^* = \mathbf{U}\theta^* = H_2(\mathbf{C}_{\mathbf{w}}^*, \mathbf{a}^*)$. Moreover, $\mathcal{B}$ could successfully guess that $H_2(\mathbf{C}_{\mathbf{w}}^*, \mathbf{a}^*) = \vartheta$ with probability $1/Q_{H_2}$. Thus, if the adversary can forge a valid searchable ciphertext with non-negligible probability ϵ, then $\mathcal{B}$ has advantage at least $\epsilon' = \epsilon/Q_{H_2}$ in finding a solution θ^* such that $\mathbf{U}\theta^* = \vartheta$ and $0 < ||\theta^*|| \leq \sigma\sqrt{m}$, which contradicts to the hardness of ISIS problem. Thus we complete our proof.

5   Conclusion

In this paper, we design a key-policy attribute-based keyword search (KP-ABKS) scheme based on the lattice assumptions. Our scheme support circuit policy in polynomially bounded depth, and thus can support very flexible and fine-grained access control. We provide detailed correctness analysis and provable security of our proposed scheme. The security analysis demonstrates that our KP-ABKS scheme can resist chosen keyword attacks and keyword guessing attacks. To check the correctness and completeness of the search result, in the future, we would like to design a verifiable attribute-based keyword search scheme based on lattices.

Acknowledgments. We thank the anonymous Inscrypt'2019 reviewers for their helpful comments. This work was supported by the National Natural Science Foundation of China (Grant Nos. 61902111, 61672030, 61602046, 61932019), the National Key Research and Development Program of China (Grant Nos. 2017YFB0802005, 2018YFB0804105), and the Young Elite Scientists Sponsorship Program by CAST (Grant No. 2016QNRC001).

References

1. Agrawal, S., Boneh, D., Boyen, X.: Efficient lattice (h)ibe in the standard model. In: Gilbert, H. (ed.) EUROCRYPT 2010. LNCS, vol. 6110, pp. 553–572. Springer, Heidelberg (2010). https://doi.org/10.1007/978-3-642-13190-5_28
2. Ajtai, M.: Generating hard instances of lattice problems. In: Proceedings of the Twenty-Eighth Annual ACM Symposium on Theory of Computing, pp. 99–108. ACM (1996)
3. Ajtai, M.: Generating hard instances of the short basis problem. In: Wiedermann, J., van Emde Boas, P., Nielsen, M. (eds.) ICALP 1999. LNCS, vol. 1644, pp. 1–9. Springer, Heidelberg (1999). https://doi.org/10.1007/3-540-48523-6_1
4. Alwen, J., Peikert, C.: Generating shorter bases for hard random lattices. Theory Comput. Syst. **48**(3), 535–553 (2011)
5. Ameri, M.H., Delavar, M., Mohajeri, J., Salmasizadeh, M.: A key-policy attribute-based temporary keyword search scheme for secure cloud storage. IEEE Trans. Cloud Comput. (2018)
6. Behnia, R., Ozmen, M.O., Yavuz, A.A.: Lattice-based public key searchable encryption from experimental perspectives. IEEE Trans. Dependable Secure Comput. (2018)
7. Boneh, D., Di Crescenzo, G., Ostrovsky, R., Persiano, G.: Public key encryption with keyword search. In: Cachin, C., Camenisch, J.L. (eds.) EUROCRYPT 2004. LNCS, vol. 3027, pp. 506–522. Springer, Heidelberg (2004). https://doi.org/10.1007/978-3-540-24676-3_30
8. Boneh, D., et al.: Fully key-homomorphic encryption, arithmetic circuit ABE and compact garbled circuits. In: Nguyen, P.Q., Oswald, E. (eds.) EUROCRYPT 2014. LNCS, vol. 8441, pp. 533–556. Springer, Heidelberg (2014). https://doi.org/10.1007/978-3-642-55220-5_30
9. Boneh, D., Waters, B.: Conjunctive, subset, and range queries on encrypted data. In: Vadhan, S.P. (ed.) TCC 2007. LNCS, vol. 4392, pp. 535–554. Springer, Heidelberg (2007). https://doi.org/10.1007/978-3-540-70936-7_29
10. Bösch, C., Hartel, P., Jonker, W., Peter, A.: A survey of provably secure searchable encryption. ACM Comput. Surv. (CSUR) **47**(2), 18 (2015)
11. Boyen, X.: Attribute-based functional encryption on lattices. In: Sahai, A. (ed.) TCC 2013. LNCS, vol. 7785, pp. 122–142. Springer, Heidelberg (2013). https://doi.org/10.1007/978-3-642-36594-2_8
12. Cash, D., Hofheinz, D., Kiltz, E., Peikert, C.: Bonsai trees, or how to delegate a lattice basis. In: Gilbert, H. (ed.) EUROCRYPT 2010. LNCS, vol. 6110, pp. 523–552. Springer, Heidelberg (2010). https://doi.org/10.1007/978-3-642-13190-5_27
13. Cash, D., Jarecki, S., Jutla, C., Krawczyk, H., Roşu, M.-C., Steiner, M.: Highly-scalable searchable symmetric encryption with support for Boolean queries. In: Canetti, R., Garay, J.A. (eds.) CRYPTO 2013. LNCS, vol. 8042, pp. 353–373. Springer, Heidelberg (2013). https://doi.org/10.1007/978-3-642-40041-4_20
14. Chen, R., Mu, Y., Yang, G., Guo, F., Wang, X.: Dual-server public-key encryption with keyword search for secure cloud storage. IEEE Trans. Inf. Forensics Secur. **11**(4), 789–798 (2015)
15. Cui, H., Wan, Z., Deng, R.H., Wang, G., Li, Y.: Efficient and expressive keyword search over encrypted data in cloud. IEEE Trans. Dependable Secure Comput. **15**(3), 409–422 (2016)
16. Dodis, Y., Ostrovsky, R., Reyzin, L., Smith, A.: Fuzzy extractors: how to generate strong keys from biometrics and other noisy data. SIAM J. Comput. **38**(1), 97–139 (2008)

17. Fiat, A., Naor, M.: Broadcast encryption. In: Stinson, D.R. (ed.) CRYPTO 1993. LNCS, vol. 773, pp. 480–491. Springer, Heidelberg (1994). https://doi.org/10.1007/3-540-48329-2_40

18. Fu, Z., Shu, J., Sun, X., Linge, N.: Smart cloud search services: verifiable keyword-based semantic search over encrypted cloud data. IEEE Trans. Consum. Electron. **60**(4), 762–770 (2014)

19. Gentry, C., Peikert, C., Vaikuntanathan, V.: Trapdoors for hard lattices and new cryptographic constructions. In Proceedings of the Fortieth Annual ACM Symposium on Theory of Computing, pp. 197–206. ACM (2008)

20. Goh, E.-J., et al.: Secure indexes. IACR Cryptology ePrint Archive, p. 216 (2003)

21. Golle, P., Staddon, J., Waters, B.: Secure conjunctive keyword search over encrypted data. In: Jakobsson, M., Yung, M., Zhou, J. (eds.) ACNS 2004. LNCS, vol. 3089, pp. 31–45. Springer, Heidelberg (2004). https://doi.org/10.1007/978-3-540-24852-1_3

22. Gorbunov, S., Vaikuntanathan, V., Wee, H.: Attribute-based encryption for circuits. J. ACM (JACM) **62**(6), 45 (2015)

23. Goyal, V., Pandey, O., Sahai, A., Waters, B.: Attribute-based encryption for fine-grained access control of encrypted data. In: Proceedings of the 13th ACM Conference on Computer and Communications Security, pp. 89–98. ACM (2006)

24. Hou, C., Liu, F., Bai, H., Ren, L.: Public-key encryption with keyword search from lattice. In: 2013 Eighth International Conference on P2P, Parallel, Grid, Cloud and Internet Computing, pp. 336–339. IEEE (2013)

25. Hu, C., Han, L.: Efficient wildcard search over encrypted data. Int. J. Inf. Secur. **15**(5), 539–547 (2016)

26. Huang, Q., Li, H.: An efficient public-key searchable encryption scheme secure against inside keyword guessing attacks. Inf. Sci. **403**, 1–14 (2017)

27. Katz, J., Sahai, A., Waters, B.: Predicate Encryption supporting disjunctions, polynomial equations, and inner products. In: Smart, N. (ed.) EUROCRYPT 2008. LNCS, vol. 4965, pp. 146–162. Springer, Heidelberg (2008). https://doi.org/10.1007/978-3-540-78967-3_9

28. Kuchta, V., Markowitch, O.: Multi-authority distributed attribute-based encryption with application to searchable encryption on lattices. In: Phan, R.C.-W., Yung, M. (eds.) Mycrypt 2016. LNCS, vol. 10311, pp. 409–435. Springer, Cham (2017). https://doi.org/10.1007/978-3-319-61273-7_20

29. Li, H., Yang, Y., Luan, T.H., Liang, X., Zhou, L., Shen, X.S.: Enabling fine-grained multi-keyword search supporting classified sub-dictionaries over encrypted cloud data. IEEE Trans. Dependable Secure Comput. **13**(3), 312–325 (2015)

30. Li, J., et al.: Searchable symmetric encryption with forward search privacy. IEEE Trans. Dependable Secure Comput. (2019)

31. Li, J., Shi, Y., Zhang, Y.: Searchable ciphertext-policy attribute-based encryption with revocation in cloud storage. Int. J. Commun. Syst. **30**(1), e2942 (2017)

32. Liu, P., Wang, J., Ma, H., Nie, H.: Efficient verifiable public key encryption with keyword search based on KP-ABE. In: 2014 Ninth International Conference on Broadband and Wireless Computing, Communication and Applications, pp. 584–589. IEEE (2014)

33. Liu, X., Yang, G., Mu, Y., Deng, R.: Multi-user verifiable searchable symmetric encryption for cloud storage. IEEE Trans. Dependable Secure Comput. (2018)

34. Liu, Z., Wang, Z., Cheng, X., Jia, C., Yuan, K.: Multi-user searchable encryption with coarser-grained access control in hybrid cloud. In: 2013 Fourth International Conference on Emerging Intelligent Data and Web Technologies, pp. 249–255. IEEE (2013)

35. Lu, Y., Wang, G., Li, J.: Keyword guessing attacks on a public key encryption with keyword search scheme without random oracle and its improvement. Inf. Sci. **479**, 270–276 (2019)
36. Micciancio, D.: Lattice-based cryptography. In: van Tilborg, H.C.A., Jajodia, S. (eds.) Encyclopedia of Cryptography and Security, pp. 713–715. Springer, Boston (2011). https://doi.org/10.1007/978-1-4419-5906-5_417
37. Micciancio, D., Peikert, C.: Trapdoors for lattices: simpler, tighter, faster, smaller. In: Pointcheval, D., Johansson, T. (eds.) EUROCRYPT 2012. LNCS, vol. 7237, pp. 700–718. Springer, Heidelberg (2012). https://doi.org/10.1007/978-3-642-29011-4_41
38. Peng, T., Liu, Q., Hu, B., Liu, J., Zhu, J.: Dynamic keyword search with hierarchical attributes in cloud computing. IEEE Access **6**, 68948–68960 (2018)
39. Regev, O.: On lattices, learning with errors, random linear codes, and cryptography. J. ACM (JACM) **56**(6), 34 (2009). Preliminary version in Proc. of STOC 2005
40. Sahai, A., Waters, B.: Fuzzy identity-based encryption. In: Cramer, R. (ed.) EUROCRYPT 2005. LNCS, vol. 3494, pp. 457–473. Springer, Heidelberg (2005). https://doi.org/10.1007/11426639_27
41. Shen, J., Wang, C., Wang, A., Ji, S., Zhang, Y.: A searchable and verifiable data protection scheme for scholarly big data. IEEE Trans. Emerg. Topics Comput. (2018)
42. Song, X., Wagner, D., Perrig, A.: Practical techniques for searches on encrypted data. In: 2000 IEEE Symposium on Security and Privacy, S&P, Proceedings, pp. 44–55. IEEE (2000)
43. Sun, W., Yu, S., Lou, W., Hou, Y.T., Li, H.: Protecting your right: attribute-based keyword search with fine-grained owner-enforced search authorization in the cloud. In: IEEE INFOCOM 2014-IEEE Conference on Computer Communications, pp. 226–234. IEEE (2014)
44. Sun, X.: Critical security issues in cloud computing: a survey. In: 2018 IEEE 4th International Conference on Big Data Security on Cloud (BigDataSecurity), IEEE International Conference on High Performance and Smart Computing, (HPSC) and IEEE International Conference on Intelligent Data and Security (IDS), pp. 216–221. IEEE (2018)
45. Wang, C., Li, W., Li, Y., Xu, X.: A ciphertext-policy attribute-based encryption scheme supporting keyword search function. In: Wang, G., Ray, I., Feng, D., Rajarajan, M. (eds.) CSS 2013. LNCS, vol. 8300, pp. 377–386. Springer, Cham (2013). https://doi.org/10.1007/978-3-319-03584-0_28
46. Xia, Z., Wang, X., Sun, X., Wang, Q.: A secure and dynamic multi-keyword ranked search scheme over encrypted cloud data. IEEE Trans. Parallel Distrib. Syst. **27**(2), 340–352 (2015)
47. Xu, P., Jin, H., Wu, Q., Wang, W.: Public-key encryption with fuzzy keyword search: a provably secure scheme under keyword guessing attack. IEEE Trans. Comput. **62**(11), 2266–2277 (2012)
48. Yin, H., et al.: CP-ABSE: a ciphertext-policy attribute-based searchable encryption scheme. IEEE Access **7**, 5682–5694 (2019)
49. Zhang, X., Tang, Y., Wang, H., Xu, C., Miao, Y., Cheng, H.: Lattice-based proxy-oriented identity-based encryption with keyword search for cloud storage. Inf. Sci. **494**, 193–207 (2019)
50. Zhang, X., Xu, C., Mu, L., Zhao, J.: Identity-based encryption with keyword search from lattice assumption. China Commun. **15**(4), 164–178 (2018)

51. Zhang, X., Xu, C., Wang, H., Zhang, Y., Wang, S.: FS-PEKS: lattice-based forward secure public-key encryption with keyword search for cloud-assisted industrial internet of things. IEEE Trans. Dependable Secure Comput. (2019)
52. Zheng, Q., Xu, S., Ateniese, G.: Vabks: verifiable attribute-based keyword search over outsourced encrypted data. In: IEEE INFOCOM 2014-IEEE Conference on Computer Communications, pp. 522–530. IEEE (2014)
53. Zhou, R., Zhang, X., Du, X., Wang, X., Yang, G., Guizani, M.: File-centric multikey aggregate keyword searchable encryption for industrial internet of things. IEEE Trans. Ind. Inf. **14**(8), 3648–3658 (2018)

Group Key Exchange from CSIDH
and Its Application to Trusted Setup
in Supersingular Isogeny Cryptosystems

Tomoki Moriya[1]([⊠]), Katsuyuki Takashima[2], and Tsuyoshi Takagi[1]

[1] Department of Mathematical Informatics, The University of Tokyo, Bunkyo, Japan
{tomoki_moriya,takagi}@mist.i.u-tokyo.ac.jp
[2] Mitsubishi Electric, Kamakura, Japan
Takashima.Katsuyuki@aj.MitsubishiElectric.co.jp

Abstract. In this paper, we propose a multi-party (group) key exchange protocol based on CSIDH (Commutative Supersingular Isogeny Diffie–Hellman), which is a post-quantum Diffie-Hellman type key exchange protocol from a commutative group action. The proposed group key exchange protocol called G-CSIDH uses the same size prime modulus p as that in CSIDH for the same security level, and the security of G-CSIDH is reduced to the security of CSIDH.

In addition, we propose the *trusted* protocol of generating public parameters of supersingular isogeny cryptosystems by using the proposed G-CSIDH. Trust in the setup based on G-CSIDH is reduced to the security of G-CSIDH, and then that of CSIDH. The trusted protocol can be applied to *any* supersingular isogeny cryptosystem, which uses a supersingular elliptic curve as a public parameter.

Keywords: Isogeny-based cryptography · CSIDH · Group key exchange

1 Introduction

There are two public-key cryptosystems currently used widely: RSA [25] and Elliptic Curve Cryptography [17,21]. However, it is known that both cryptosystems can be broken in polynomial time by using a quantum computer [26]. Consequently, we should develop new cryptosystems based on some mathematical problem (called Post-Quantum Cryptography (PQC)) which is hard to be solved even using a quantum computer.

The isogeny problem is the problem of computing an isogeny between given two isogenous elliptic curves. As far as we know, it takes subexponential time to solve the isogeny problem on ordinary elliptic curves by using a quantum computer [8], and takes exponential time to solve that on supersingular elliptic curves [2]. Therefore, isogeny-based cryptography which is based on the isogeny problem is considered to be one candidate for post-quantum cryptography.

© Springer Nature Switzerland AG 2020
Z. Liu and M. Yung (Eds.): Inscrypt 2019, LNCS 12020, pp. 86–98, 2020.
https://doi.org/10.1007/978-3-030-42921-8_5

There are two major proposals for isogeny-based key exchange protocols currently: SIDH (Supersingular Isogeny Diffie–Hellman) key exchange [12], and CSIDH (Commutative Supersingular Isogeny Diffie–Hellman) key exchange [5]. Both protocols are being studied toward practical applications.

One motivation of this work is how to share public parameters in *supersingular* isogeny-based cryptography in a trusted manner: In traditional elliptic curve cryptography, the issue began to be seriously studied at the controversy on NIST elliptic curves in 2007 [27]. Since we use *ordinary* curves in the setting (even in the pairing-based setting usually), we only have to replace the previous curves by *verifiably determined* curves as one countermeasure for the issue [3]. The curve is determined by using a hash function and the seed is used for verifying the curve generation procedure so that proving there exist no back doors in the public curve. The countermeasure cannot be applied to the supersingular case as we will show later.

We consider two targets in this paper. The first one is to extend isogeny-based cryptography to a multi-party setting. While both SIDH and CSIDH are used as only two-party key exchange protocols, we need to consider multi-party key exchange (group key exchange) protocols in many practical applications. Two group key exchange protocols based on SIDH have been proposed: SIBD and G-SIDH [13]. In contrast, there have been no proposed group key exchange protocols based on CSIDH.

The second one is to propose a protocol generating public parameters of isogeny-based cryptosystems in a *trusted* manner, e.g., without back doors. If one party generates public parameters (even using some multi-party protocol), the party might embed some his own information (e.g., back door) into public parameters. For example, the natural protocol generating a random supersingular elliptic curve is that a specific party generates it by using the CGL hash function [7]. However, by executing this protocol for setup, the party generating the elliptic curve gets more information than other parties. Our target is to prevent such situation, which is formulated in the notion of trusted setup. Therefore, we need to consider how to generate public parameters in a trusted manner, which is a non-trivial problem since public parameters of isogeny-based cryptosystems contain a *supersingular* elliptic curve, i.e., not consist of only random variables.

Our target open problem is: How do we generate a supersingular elliptic curve with trust as a public parameter (even using multi-party protocol)?

1.1   Our Results

In this paper, we first propose a group key exchange protocol based on CSIDH, which we call G-CSIDH. First, the security of the proposed u-party G-CSIDH is naturally reduced to the u-General Commutative Supersingular Isogeny Decisional Diffie-Hellman (u-GCSSDDH) assumption (Lemma 1). And then, we show that u-GCSSDDH assumption is reduced to the two-party case, Commutative Supersingular Isogeny Decisional Diffie-Hellman (CSSDDH) assumption (Lemma 2). Consequently, the security of the u-party G-CSIDH is proven under the CSSDDH assumption (Theorem 5). Table 1 compares G-CSIDH with other isogeny-based group key exchange protocols.

Table 1. Comparison of isogeny-based group key exchange protocols. In the "quantum sec." column, exp. (resp. subexp.) means quantum exponential-time (resp. sub exponential-time) security. In the "active attacks" column, vuln. (resp. resist.) means vulnerability (resp. resistance) to active attacks in [14]

	quantum sec.	active attacks	round	size of the prime p	the shared key
SIBD [13]	exp	vuln	2	same as SIDH	a random value
G-SIDH [13]	exp	vuln	u	large	a supersingular elliptic curve
CSIBD	subexp	resist	2	same as CSIDH	a random value
G-CSIDH	subexp	resist	u	same as CSIDH	a supersingular elliptic curve

Besides, we also propose a trusted protocol for generating public parameters of isogeny-based cryptosystems including SIDH based on G-CSIDH, i.e., solved the above open problem (in an efficient manner). Trust in setup is formally proven (Theorem 6). For that, we first define the trusted setup of public parameter generation (setup algorithm) in the sense that any party cannot embed any his own information (e.g., back door) into the parameter, and prove that trust in the setup algorithm is reduced to the security of G-CSIDH. As we see in Table 1, the G-CSIDH is the most suitable isogeny-based group key exchange protocol for using in generating a supersingular elliptic curve in a trusted manner. The reason is given as follows. SIBD and CSIBD[1] generate only a *product* of multiple (≥ 2) supersingular j-invariants (or Montgomery coefficients). Hence, they cannot be used for generating just a supersingular elliptic curve (or j-invariant, Montgomery coefficient). While the u-round G-SIDH can generate a supersingular elliptic curve with trust as well, however, unfortunately, it gives rise to an inefficient generation method: The size of the underlying modulus p in G-SIDH should become larger, which is linear in u, while the bit lengths in G-CSIDH are the same as that in CSIDH.[2] Moreover, G-SIDH based one is not proven trusted while G-CSIDH based one is proven trusted. Since the proof on G-CSIDH crucially uses commutativity of ideal class groups, the technique cannot be easily extended to the G-SIDH case. Therefore, we consider the G-CSIDH based one is a good trusted generation method of public parameters in supersingular isogeny cryptosystems including SIDH, CSIDH and their signature variants [11,15].

---

[1] CSIBD is a Burmester–Desmedt [4] type group key exchange protocol based on CSIDH. It is constructed in a similar manner to SIBD.

[2] In fact, (G-)SIDH is considered as more secure than (G-)CSIDH since there is a subexponential-time quantum attack on (G-)CSIDH. It may implies that (G-)CSIDH is more inefficient than (G-)SIDH. However, a recent research [1] shows that CSIDH might not be so worse compared to SIDH when we consider non-asymptotic time estimate (via quantum attack reconsideration).

Note that the parameter u plays a role of trade-off factor between strength of security and efficiency. Theorem 6 (informally) mentions that if at least one of u-parties do not participate in a malicious collusion, then the malicious collusion can not obtain the central secret (i.e., isogeny between target two curves). Therefore, we have a stronger security if the number of generating members, u, is larger. On the other hand, apparently, a larger u gives rise to inefficiency in setup. (However, the size of the modulus p is independent from u.) Therefore, we can choose the parameter u depending on the decision on this trade-off.

2 Preliminaries

2.1 Isogenies

In this subsection, we explain some basic properties of the isogenies of supersingular elliptic curves.

Let L be a field, and L' be an algebraic extensional field of L. An elliptic curve E defined over L is a non-singular algebraic curve of the Montgomery form

$$A_2 y^2 = x^3 + A_1 x^2 + x \quad (A_1, A_2 \in L, \ A_2(A_1^2 - 4) \neq 0).$$

The L'-rational points of the elliptic curve E with the point at infinity ∞ is denoted as $E(L')$. It is known that $E(L')$ is an abelian group, whose identity is ∞ [28, III. 2]. A supersingular elliptic curve E over a finite field L of characteristic p is defined as an elliptic curve which satisfies $\#E(L') \equiv 1 \pmod{p}$.

Let $E, \tilde{E}$ be elliptic curves defined over L. An isogeny $\phi \colon E \to \tilde{E}$ defined over L' is a morphism over L', which is a non-zero group homomorphism from $E(\overline{L})$ to $\tilde{E}(\overline{L})$, where $\overline{L}$ is an algebraic closure of L. A separable isogeny satisfying $\#\ker \phi = \ell$ is called an ℓ-isogeny, where $\#X$ is a cardinality of the set X. The endomorphism ring of E over L' is denoted as $\mathrm{End}_{L'}(E)$. It is represented as $\mathrm{End}_p(E)$ when L' is a prime field $\mathbb{F}_p$. An isogeny defined over L' $\phi \colon E \to \tilde{E}$ is called an isomorphism over L' (or E and $\tilde{E}$ are L'-isomorphic) if ϕ has an inverse isogeny over L'.

Theorem 1 ([28, Proposition III.4.12]). *If G is a finite subgroup of $E(\overline{L})$, then there exists an isogeny $\phi \colon E \to \tilde{E}$ whose kernel is G, and $\tilde{E}$ is unique up to $\overline{L}$-isomorphism.*

This isogeny can be efficiently calculated using Vélu formulas [20,24,30]. We denote the representative of $\tilde{E}$ by E/G.

Let L be a quadratic field, and $\mathcal{O}$ be its order. A fractional ideal $\mathfrak{a}$ of $\mathcal{O}$ is an $\mathcal{O}$-submodule of L, which satisfies $\alpha \mathfrak{a} \subset \mathcal{O}$ for some $\alpha \in \mathcal{O} \setminus \{0\}$. An invertible fractional ideal $\mathfrak{a}$ of $\mathcal{O}$ is a fractional ideal of $\mathcal{O}$, which satisfies $\mathfrak{a}\mathfrak{b} = \mathcal{O}$ for some fractional ideal $\mathfrak{b}$ of $\mathcal{O}$. The $\mathfrak{b}$ is represented as $\mathfrak{a}^{-1}$. If a fractional ideal $\mathfrak{a}$ is contained in $\mathcal{O}$, then $\mathfrak{a}$ is called an integral ideal of $\mathcal{O}$.

Let $I(\mathcal{O})$ be a set of invertible fractional ideals of $\mathcal{O}$. The $I(\mathcal{O})$ is an abelian group derived from multiplication of ideals with the identity $\mathcal{O}$. Let $P(\mathcal{O})$ be a subgroup of $I(\mathcal{O})$, which is defined by $P(\mathcal{O}) = \{\mathfrak{a} \mid \mathfrak{a} = \alpha\mathcal{O} \text{ (for some } \alpha \in L^*)\}$. An ideal class group of $\mathcal{O}$ is a group $\mathrm{cl}(\mathcal{O})$ defined by $I(\mathcal{O})/P(\mathcal{O})$.

Theorem 2 ([31, **Theorem 4.5**]). *Let $\mathcal{O}$ be an order of an imaginary quadratic field and E be an elliptic curve defined over $\mathbb{F}_p$. The set of an $\mathbb{F}_p$-isomorphism class of elliptic curves E whose endomorphism ring $\mathrm{End}_p(E)$ is isomorphic to $\mathcal{O}$ is denoted by $\mathcal{E}\ell\ell_p(\mathcal{O})$. If $\mathcal{E}\ell\ell_p(\mathcal{O})$ contains the $\mathbb{F}_p$-isomorphism class of supersingular elliptic curves, then an action of the ideal class group $\mathrm{cl}(\mathcal{O})$ on $\mathcal{E}\ell\ell_p(\mathcal{O})$, $([\mathfrak{a}], E) \mapsto E/E[\mathfrak{a}]$ is free and transitive, where $\mathfrak{a}$ is an integral ideal of $\mathcal{O}$, and $E[\mathfrak{a}]$ is the intersection of the kernels of elements in the ideal $\mathfrak{a}$.*

Theorem 3 ([5, **Proposition 8**]). *Let a prime p satisfy $p \equiv 3 \pmod 8$. Let E be a supersingular elliptic curve defined over $\mathbb{F}_p$. Then, $\mathrm{End}_p(E) = \mathbb{Z}[\pi_p]$ if and only if there uniquely exists $A \in \mathbb{F}_p$ such that E is $\mathbb{F}_p$-isomorphic to $\tilde{E} \colon y^2 = x^3 + Ax^2 + x$, where π_p is a p-Frobenius map $\pi_p(x, y) = (x^p, y^p)$.*

The curve coefficient A in Theorem 3 is called a Montgomery coefficient.

2.2   (Group) Key Exchange

In this subsection, we introduce definitions of a (group) key exchange protocol and its correctness and security.

Definition 1 ((Group) key exchange). *The algorithm $\mathcal{P}(\lambda, \mu, \eta)$ is called a μ round η-party key exchange protocol if being composed of probabilistic polynomial time algorithms (**Setup**, (**Key generation**$^{(\mu')})_{\mu'=1}^{\mu-1}$, **Key exchange**).*

Setup: *Take a security parameter λ, the number of rounds μ, and the number of users η as input. It outputs public parameters $\mathrm{pk}_i^{(0)} := $ **params** and secret keys $\mathrm{sk}_i^{(0)} := \emptyset$ for any $i = 1, \ldots, \eta$.*

Key generation$^{(\mu')}$ $(1 \leq \mu' \leq \mu-1)$: *Given the user index i, $(\mathrm{pk}_i^{(\tilde{\mu})})_{i'=1,\ldots,\eta}^{\tilde{\mu}=0,\ldots,\mu'-1}$, and $(\mathrm{sk}_i^{(\tilde{\mu})})^{\tilde{\mu}=0,\ldots,\mu'-1}$, the algorithm outputs $(\mathrm{pk}_i^{(\mu')}, \mathrm{sk}_i^{(\mu')})$. User i broadcasts $\mathrm{pk}_i^{(\mu')}$ and keeps $\mathrm{sk}_i^{(\mu')}$ secret.*

Key exchange: *User i collects the public broadcasts sent by all other users. Given $(\mathrm{pk}_{i'}^{(\tilde{\mu})})_{i'=1,\ldots,\eta}^{\tilde{\mu}=0,\ldots,\mu-1}$, $(\mathrm{sk}_i^{(\tilde{\mu})})^{\tilde{\mu}=0,\ldots,\mu-1}$, the algorithm outputs the key K_i.*

We call $\mathrm{pk}_{\eta'}^{(\mu')}$ a μ' round public key of user η', and $\mathrm{sk}_{\eta'}^{(\mu')}$ a μ' round secret key of user η'.

Definition 2 (Correctness). *If a key exchange protocol $\mathcal{P}$ satisfies that all keys $K_1, \ldots, K_\eta$ are the same values, we say $\mathcal{P}$ is correct.*
   In this situation, we call $K := K_1 = \cdots = K_\eta$ a shared key.

Definition 3 (Security). *Let $\mathcal{P}(\lambda)$ be a μ round η-party correct group key exchange protocol, where λ is a security parameter. Denote by **params** the set of public parameters of $\mathcal{P}(\lambda)$, by $\mathrm{pk}_{\eta'}^{(\mu')}$ the μ' round public key of $U_{\eta'}$, and by K the shared key of $\mathcal{P}(\lambda)$.*

We call $\mathcal{P}(\lambda)$ secure if there exists an exponentially large set Keysp *which includes all shared keys of $\mathcal{P}(\lambda)$ and the following property holds for any probabilistic polynomial time algorithm $\mathcal{A}$:*

$$\left| \Pr\left[\mathcal{A}\left(\mathbf{params}, \{\mathrm{pk}_{\eta'}^{(\mu')}\}_{\eta'=1,\ldots,\eta}^{\mu'=1,\ldots,\mu-1}, K\right) = 1\right] - \Pr\left[\mathcal{A}\left(\mathbf{params}, \{\mathrm{pk}_{\eta'}^{(\mu')}\}_{\eta'=1,\ldots,\eta}^{\mu'=1,\ldots,\mu-1}, K'\right) = 1\right] \right| < \mathrm{negl}(\lambda),$$

where K' is a uniformly random element of Keysp.

Remark 1. We do not let K' be the shared key of $\mathcal{P}(\lambda)$ from other random secret keys. If $\mathcal{P}(\lambda)$ outputs a same value from any secret keys, it is hard to say that $\mathcal{P}(\lambda)$ is secure; however, there is no way to distinct the correct shared key and the shared key from other random secret keys (because they are same values).

The important point of our security definition is that if $\mathcal{P}(\lambda)$ is secure, there is no way to distinct the correct shared key and *a random element* of Keysp, which is expected to be large enough.

3 CSIDH

In this section, we introduce an important Diffie-Hellman type key exchange protocol: CSIDH (Commutative Supersingular Isogeny Diffie-Hellman). CSIDH was proposed by Castryck, Lange, Martindale, Panny, and Renes in 2018 [5]. Meyer and Reith improved the CSIDH algorithm to be efficient [20]. Research for constant-time CSIDH has also been conducted. Meyer, Campos, and Reith proposed the constant-time algorithm in 2019 [19]. Onuki, Aikawa, Yamazaki, and Takagi improved this constant-time algorithm to be efficient [22]. Cervantes-Vázquez, Chenu, Chi-Domínguez, De Feo, Rodríguez-Henríquez, and Smith proposed the constant-time CSIDH algorithm without dummy calculations [6].

CSIDH is based on the action of $\mathrm{cl}(\mathbb{Z}[\pi_p])$ on $\mathcal{Ell}_p(\mathbb{Z}[\pi_p])$. The outline of the CSIDH protocol is as follows. Here, Alice and Bob want to share a secret key denoted by $\mathrm{SK}_{\mathrm{shared}}$.

Setup
   Let p be a prime which satisfies $p = 4 \cdot \ell_1 \cdots \ell_n - 1$, where the $\ell_1, \ldots, \ell_n$ are small distinct odd primes. Let E_0 be the supersingular elliptic curve $y^2 = x^3 + x$ and the public parameters be p and E_0.
Key generation
   One randomly chooses an integer vector $(e_1, \ldots, e_n)$ from $\{-m, \ldots, m\}^n$. Then, one defines $[\mathfrak{a}] = [\mathfrak{l}_1^{e_1} \cdots \mathfrak{l}_n^{e_n}] \in \mathrm{cl}(\mathbb{Z}[\pi_p])$, where $[\mathfrak{l}_i] = [(\ell_i, \pi_p - 1)]$, $[\mathfrak{l}_i]^{-1} = [(\ell_i, \pi_p + 1)]$, and m is the smallest positive integer which satisfies $2m + 1 \geq \sqrt[n]{\#\mathrm{cl}(\mathbb{Z}[\pi_p])}$. One calculates the action of $[\mathfrak{a}]$ on E_0 and the Montgomery coefficient $A \in \mathbb{F}_p$ of $[\mathfrak{a}]E_0 \colon y^2 = x^3 + Ax^2 + x$. Let the integer vector $(e_1, \ldots, e_n)$ be the secret key and $A \in \mathbb{F}_p$ be the public key.
Key exchange
   Alice and Bob have a pair of keys, $([\mathfrak{a}], A)$ and $([\mathfrak{b}], B)$, respectively. Alice calculates the action $[\mathfrak{a}]E_B = [\mathfrak{a}][\mathfrak{b}]E_0$, where $E_B \colon y^2 = x^3 + Bx^2 + x$. Bob calculates the action $[\mathfrak{b}]E_A = [\mathfrak{b}][\mathfrak{a}]E_0$, where $E_A \colon y^2 = x^3 + Ax^2 + x$. Denote by SK_{Alice} the Montgomery coefficient of $[\mathfrak{a}][\mathfrak{b}]E_0$, and by SK_{Bob} the Montgomery coefficient of $[\mathfrak{b}][\mathfrak{a}]E_0$.

From the commutativity of $\mathrm{cl}(\mathbb{Z}[\pi_p])$ and Theorem 3, $\mathrm{SK}_{Alice} = \mathrm{SK}_{Bob}$ holds; therefore, CSIDH is correct. Let these keys be the shared key SK_{shared}.

Remark 2. In this paper, we mean that "random secret keys of CSIDH" (or simply "random secret keys") are elements of $\mathrm{cl}(\mathbb{Z}[\pi_p])$ which are represented as $[\mathfrak{l}_1^{e_1} \cdots \mathfrak{l}_n^{e_n}]$, where $(e_1, \ldots, e_n)$ are uniformly random elements of $\{-m, \ldots, m\}^n$. These are not uniformly random elements of $\mathrm{cl}(\mathbb{Z}[\pi_p])$.

Remark 3. It has not been known whether calculation of the action of $\mathrm{cl}(\mathbb{Z}[\pi_p])$ on $\mathscr{Ell}_p(\mathbb{Z}[\pi_p])$ can be performed in polynomial time or not. Practically, the calculation can be executed in short time. In this paper, we treat the calculation as performed in polynomial time.

Next, we introduce the important assumption of CSIDH, and prove the security under this assumption.

Definition 4 (Commutative Supersingular Isogeny Decisional Diffie-Hellman (CSSDDH) assumption). *Let secret keys of Alice and Bob be $[\mathfrak{a}]$ and $[\mathfrak{b}]$, respectively. Let E, p be a public parameters of CSIDH, where E is a supersingular elliptic curve defined over $\mathbb{F}_p$ and p is a N bit prime.*

It is said that CSSDDH assumption holds if the following property holds for any probabilistic polynomial algorithm $\mathcal{A}$:

$$|\Pr\left[\mathcal{A}(E, [\mathfrak{a}]E, [\mathfrak{b}]E, [\mathfrak{a}][\mathfrak{b}]E) = 1\right] - \Pr\left[\mathcal{A}(E, [\mathfrak{a}]E, [\mathfrak{b}]E, [\mathfrak{c}]E) = 1\right]| < \mathrm{negl}(N),$$

where $[\mathfrak{c}]$ is a uniformly random element of $\mathrm{cl}(\mathbb{Z}[\pi_p])$.

Theorem 4. *If the CSSDDH assumption holds, CSIDH is secure.*

Proof. Let Keysp be the set of the Montgomery forms of elliptic curves in $\mathscr{Ell}_p(\mathbb{Z}[\pi_p])$. From Theorems 2 and 3, if $[\mathfrak{c}]$ is a uniformly random element of $\mathrm{cl}(\mathbb{Z}[\pi_p])$, then $[\mathfrak{c}]E$ is also a uniformly random element of Keysp. Since $\#\mathrm{cl}(\mathbb{Z}[\pi_p]) \approx \sqrt{p}$, this completes the proof. □

4   Proposed Group Key Exchange from CSIDH (G-CSIDH)

A multi-party key exchange (group key exchange) protocol has long been investigated. In this section, we propose the protocol from CSIDH.

4.1   CSIDH Group Key Exchange (G-CSIDH)

Let there be u-parties, and denote them by $U_1, \ldots, U_u$. Let $U_{u+k} = U_k$ for any $k \in \mathbb{Z}$.

Setup

Let p be a prime which satisfies $p = 4 \cdot \ell_1 \cdots \ell_n - 1$, where the $\ell_1, \ldots, \ell_n$ are small distinct odd primes. Let $\tilde{E}_0$ be a supersingular elliptic curve $y^2 = x^3 + x$. Let the public parameters be p and E_0.

Key generation

A party U_j randomly chooses a set of integers $(e_1^{(j)}, \ldots, e_n^{(j)})$ from $\{-m, \ldots, m\}^n$. Define $[\mathfrak{a}_j] = [\mathfrak{l}_1^{e_1^{(j)}} \cdots \mathfrak{l}_n^{e_n^{(j)}}] \in \mathrm{cl}(\mathbb{Z}[\pi_p])$.

Step 1 : U_j calculates the action of $[\mathfrak{a}_j]$ on E_0 and the Montgomery coefficient of $[\mathfrak{a}_j]E_0 \colon y^2 = x^3 + A_1^{(j)}x^2 + x$. U_j sends $A_1^{(j)}$ to U_{j+1}.

Step k ($2 \leq k \leq u - 1$) : U_j calculates the action of $[\mathfrak{a}_j]$ on E_{k-1} and the Montgomery coefficient $A_k^{(j)} \in \mathbb{F}_p$ of $[\mathfrak{a}_j]E_{k-1} \colon y^2 = x^3 + A_k^{(j)}x^2 + x$, where $E_{k-1} \colon y^2 = x^3 + A_{k-1}^{(j-1)}x^2 + x$. The U_j sends $A_k^{(j)}$ to U_{j+1}.

Key exchange

The U_j calculates the action of $[\mathfrak{a}_j]$ on E_{u-1} and the Montgomery coefficient $A_u^{(j)} \in \mathbb{F}_p$ of the elliptic curve $[\mathfrak{a}_j]E_{u-1} \colon y^2 = x^3 + A_u^{(j)}x^2 + x$, where $E_{u-1} \colon y^2 = x^3 + A_{u-1}^{(j-1)}x^2 + x$. Denote $A_u^{(j)}$ by SK_j.

By the commutativity of $\mathrm{cl}(\mathbb{Z}[\pi_p])$ and Theorem 3, it holds $\mathrm{SK}_1 = \cdots = \mathrm{SK}_u$, which is the Montgomery coefficient of $[\mathfrak{a}_1][\mathfrak{a}_2] \cdots [\mathfrak{a}_u]E_0$; therefore, G-CSIDH is correct. Let these keys be the shared key $\mathrm{SK}_{\mathrm{shared}}$.

4.2 Security of G-CSIDH

Here, we prove the security of G-CSIDH under the CSSDDH assumption.

Theorem 5. *Let $u \geq 2$ be a small constant integer. If the CSSDDH assumption holds, u-party G-CSIDH is secure.*

Proof. This holds by Lemmas 1 and 2. $\qquad\square$

Before stating Lemma 1, we define the important assumption of G-CSIDH.

Definition 5 (u-General Commutative Supersingular Isogeny Decision-al Diffie-Hellman (u-GCSSDDH) assumption). *Let the secret keys of parties $U_1, \ldots, U_u$ be $[\mathfrak{a}_1], \ldots, [\mathfrak{a}_u]$, respectively. Let $\mathbf{params} := \{E, p\}$ be the set of public parameters of G-CSIDH, where E is a supersingular elliptic curve defined over $\mathbb{F}_p$ and p is a N bit prime. Denote by $\mathrm{pk}_i^{(j)}$ the j-round public key of U_i.*

It is said that the u-GCSSDDH assumption holds, if the following property holds for any probabilistic polynomial time algorithm $\mathcal{A}$:

$$\left| \Pr\left[\mathcal{A}(\mathbf{params}, \{\mathrm{pk}_i^{(j)}\}_{i=1,\ldots,u}^{j=1,\ldots,u-1}, [\mathfrak{a}_1] \cdots [\mathfrak{a}_u]E) = 1 \right] - \Pr\left[\mathcal{A}(\mathbf{params}, \{\mathrm{pk}_i^{(j)}\}_{i=1,\ldots,u}^{j=1,\ldots,u-1}, [\mathfrak{b}]E) = 1 \right] \right| < \mathrm{negl}(N),$$

where $[\mathfrak{b}]$ is a uniformly random element of $\mathrm{cl}(\mathbb{Z}[\pi_p])$.

Lemma 1. *If the u-GCSSDDH assumption holds, G-CSIDH is secure.*

Proof. This lemma is proved similarly to the proof of Theorem 4. $\qquad\square$

Lemma 2. *Let $u \geq 2$ be a small constant integer. If the CSSDDH assumption holds, then the u-GCSSDDH assumption also holds.*

Proof. This proof is based on a previous study [29, §2.3]. $\qquad\square$

5   Trusted Setup from G-CSIDH

In this section, we explain how to apply the G-CSIDH of u parties to SIDH key exchange. In isogeny-based cryptosystems, a supersingular elliptic curve is needed for the public parameter. It is a problem how to generate the supersingular elliptic curve without backdoors. In this section, we propose the trusted setup protocol by using G-CSIDH.

5.1   Proposed Trusted Setup in Isogeny-Based Cryptosystems

We propose a trusted setup in isogeny-based cryptosystems based on G-CSIDH. We first give a high-level description of the protocol below.

The description of the procedure is simpler than the original G-CSIDH. That is, we should execute the following chain of computation (1) only once while the original protocol should execute u chains of the same type which are started from all users ($i = 1, \ldots, u$) for sharing same key among u-users.

$$E_0 \to [\mathfrak{a}_1]E_0 \to [\mathfrak{a}_2][\mathfrak{a}_1]E_0 \to \ldots \to [\mathfrak{a}_{u-1}] \cdots [\mathfrak{a}_1]E_0 \to E_u := [\mathfrak{a}_u][\mathfrak{a}_{u-1}] \cdots [\mathfrak{a}_1]E_0. \quad (1)$$

Let $E_i := [\mathfrak{a}_i] \cdots [\mathfrak{a}_1]E_0$, then the i-th multiplication, $E_{i-1} \to [\mathfrak{a}_i]E_{i-1}$, in the above chain is executed by the i-th user who holds the ideal $\mathfrak{a}_i$. The final supersingular curve E_u, which is jointly generated by all u users, is published as a (key) component of the public parameters.

Here, E_0 should be also publicly known supersingular curve (e.g., $y^2 = x^3 + x$ with $p \equiv 3 \mod 4$) since no one should have any advantage over the initial curve E_0. Moreover, recently, Petit [10,23], Love and Boneh [18] pointed out some possible vulnerabilities when using such special curve for the public parameters. Therefore, for using the above E_u in a safe manner (i.e., without backdoors), no one must not connect these two curves, E_0 and E_u. In other words, no one must not know the (masterly) secret ideal $\mathfrak{a} := \mathfrak{a}_1 \mathfrak{a}_2 \cdots \mathfrak{a}_u$. Definition 6 presents this security requirement for setup which we call "trusted setup". Here, we also note that the order of multiplication is irrelevant since the ideal (class) group is commutative. This property is also crucial for the proof of Theorem 6.

5.2   Proof of Trust in Setup

We first define the notion of trust in setup (for SIDH).

Definition 6 (Trusted setup). *Let* **Setup**(λ) *be the u round u-party setup protocol, which is defined by the sequence of computation (1), where λ is a security parameter. Denote by* **params**$_0$ *the set of public parameters like E_0 (without backdoors), by* $\text{sk}_{\eta'}$ *the secret key of the user η' (i.e., $\mathfrak{a}_{\eta'}$), and by E_u the final elliptic curve (1), which is used for a component of public parameters in SIDH.*

We call **Setup** *is trusted if the following property holds for any probabilistic polynomial time algorithm $\mathcal{A}$. For all $k = 1, \ldots, \eta$,*

$$\Pr\left[\mathcal{A}(\textbf{params}_0, \{\text{sk}_{\eta'}\}_{\eta'=1,\ldots,k-1,k+1,\ldots,\eta}, E_u) = \text{sk}_k\right] < \text{negl}(\lambda).$$

There is a controversy whether the confidentiality of sk_k surely ensure the nonexistence of backdoors, or not. However, this definition is a natural definition for a trusted setup.

We next show our proposed setup in SIDH is trusted in Theorem 6.

Theorem 6. *Let $u \geq 2$ be a small constant integer. If G-CSIDH is secure,* **Setup** *given in Definition 6 is trusted.*

Proof. Assume that **Setup** is not trusted. In other words, there exists a probabilistic polynomial time algorithm $\mathcal{A}$ such that the following property holds.

There exists $k \in \{1, \ldots, u\}$ and $\alpha > 0$ such that for an infinity number of N,

$$\Pr\left[\mathcal{A}(\mathbf{params}_0, \{sk_{\eta'}\}_{\eta'=1,\ldots,k-1,k+1,\ldots,\eta}, E_u) = sk_k\right] \geq \frac{1}{N^\alpha},$$

where N is a bit length of p. Let $sk_{\eta'}$ be $[\mathfrak{a}_{\eta'}]$. Define the algorithm $\mathcal{A}'$ as follows.

$$\mathcal{A}'(E, [\mathfrak{a}]E) = \mathcal{A}\left(E, \{[\mathfrak{e}_i]\}_{i=1,\ldots,k-1,k+1,\ldots,u-1}, [\mathfrak{e}_1] \cdots [\mathfrak{e}_{k-1}][\mathfrak{e}_{k+1}] \cdots [\mathfrak{e}_u][\mathfrak{a}]E\right),$$

where $[\mathfrak{e}_1], \ldots, [\mathfrak{e}_{k-1}], [\mathfrak{e}_{k+1}], \ldots, [\mathfrak{e}_u]$ are random secret keys (refer the meaning of "random secret keys" to Remark 2). Thus, $\Pr[\mathcal{A}'(E, [\mathfrak{a}]E) = [\mathfrak{a}]] \geq \frac{1}{N^\alpha}$. Define the algorithm $\mathcal{A}''$ as follows.

$$\mathcal{A}''(\mathbf{pk}_{[c_1],\ldots,[c_u]}, [\mathfrak{d}]E) = \begin{cases} 1 & (\text{if } [\tilde{c}_k][c_1] \cdots [c_{k-1}][c_{k+1}] \cdots [c_u]E = [\mathfrak{d}]E) \\ 0 & (\text{if } [\tilde{c}_k][c_1] \cdots [c_{k-1}][c_{k+1}] \cdots [c_u]E \neq [\mathfrak{d}]E) \end{cases},$$

where $[c_1], \ldots, [c_u]$ are random secret keys, and $[\mathfrak{d}]$ is a uniformly random element of $cl(\mathbb{Z}[\pi_p])$, and $[\tilde{c}_k] = \mathcal{A}'(E, [c_k]E)$. Then, it holds that

$$\Pr\left[\mathcal{A}''(\mathbf{pk}_{[c_1],\ldots,[c_u]}, [c_1] \cdots [c_u]E) = 1\right] \geq \frac{1}{N^\alpha}, \quad \Pr\left[\mathcal{A}''(\mathbf{pk}_{[c_1],\ldots,[c_u]}, [\mathfrak{d}]E) = 1\right] = \frac{1}{\#cl(\mathbb{Z}[\pi_p])} \approx \frac{1}{2^{N/2}},$$

where $[\mathfrak{d}]$ is a uniformly random element of $cl(\mathbb{Z}[\pi_p])$. Hence, for proper N,

$$\left|\Pr\left[\mathcal{A}''(\mathbf{pk}_{[c_1],\ldots,[c_u]}, [c_1] \cdots [c_u]E) = 1\right] - \Pr\left[\mathcal{A}''(\mathbf{pk}_{[c_1],\ldots,[c_u]}, [\mathfrak{d}]E) = 1\right]\right| \geq \frac{1}{(N+1)^\alpha}.$$

Therefore, G-CSIDH is not secure. This completes the proof of Theorem 6.   □

Therefore, trust in **Setup** is reduced to the security of G-CSIDH.

5.3   Trusted Setup in SIDH

When we generate an elliptic curve in SIDH by using G-CSIDH, the setting of a prime p needs to be changed, since the prime p of the public parameters of SIDH needs to satisfy $p = 2^{e_A} 3^{e_B} f - 1$ for some integers e_A, e_B, f [12,16]. The following theorem solves this problem.

Theorem 7. *Let p be a prime which satisfies that $p \equiv 3 \pmod{4}$ and E be a supersingular elliptic curve defined over $\mathbb{F}_p$. If $\mathrm{End}_p(E) = \mathbb{Z}[\pi_p]$ holds, then there uniquely exists $A \in \mathbb{F}_p$ such that E is $\mathbb{F}_p$-isomorphic to $E_A : y^2 = x^3 + Ax^2 + x$.*

Proof. The order 2 point of $E_0(\mathbb{F}_p)$ is $(0,0)$ only. Therefore, $\mathrm{End}_p(E_0) = \mathbb{Z}[\pi_p]$ by [9, Theorem 2.7]. The remainder of this theorem follows by the second half of the proof of [5, Proposition 8].   □

From Theorem 7, it suffices to let $p = 2^{e_A} \cdot 3^{e_B} \cdot \ell_1 \cdots \ell_n - 1$, where the $\ell_1, \ldots, \ell_n$ are distinct small primes greater than 3, and $2^{e_A} \approx 3^{e_B}$.

Remark 4. In this situation, even though an elliptic curve $E \colon y^2 = x^3 + Ax^2 + x$ is supersingular, $\mathrm{End}_p(E)$ is not always isomorphic to $\mathbb{Z}[\pi_p]$.

6   Conclusions

In this paper, we proposed the group key exchange based on CSIDH, called G-CSIDH. We proved that the security of G-CSIDH is reduced to the CSSDDH assumption, which cannot distinguish the shared keys of CSIDH and random elements of shared keys. It is easy to show that the security of CSIDH is reduced to the CSSDDH assumption.

Next, we proposed the trusted setup protocol that generates public parameters of isogeny-based cryptosystems. It is not easy to generate a random supersingular elliptic curve with trust. In this paper, we constructed the trusted protocol (**Setup**) by using the proposed G-CSIDH, which outputs a supersingular elliptic curve as a shared key among all parties. We proved that trust in **Setup** is reduced to the security of G-CSIDH.

Acknowlegements. This work was supported by JST CREST Grant Number JPMJCR14D6, Japan.

References

1. Bernstein, D.J., Lange, T., Martindale, C., Panny, L.: Quantum circuits for the CSIDH: optimizing quantum evaluation of isogenies. In: Ishai, Y., Rijmen, V. (eds.) EUROCRYPT 2019. LNCS, vol. 11477, pp. 409–441. Springer, Cham (2019). https://doi.org/10.1007/978-3-030-17656-3_15
2. Biasse, J.-F., Jao, D., Sankar, A.: A quantum algorithm for computing isogenies between supersingular elliptic curves. In: Meier, W., Mukhopadhyay, D. (eds.) INDOCRYPT 2014. LNCS, vol. 8885, pp. 428–442. Springer, Cham (2014). https://doi.org/10.1007/978-3-319-13039-2_25
3. Bos, J.W., Costello, C., Longa, P., Naehrig, M.: Selecting elliptic curves for cryptography: an efficiency and security analysis. J. Cryptogr. Eng. **6**(4), 259–286 (2016)
4. Burmester, M., Desmedt, Y.: A secure and scalable group key exchange system. Inf. Process. Lett. **94**(3), 137–143 (2005)
5. Castryck, W., Lange, T., Martindale, C., Panny, L., Renes, J.: CSIDH: an efficient post-quantum commutative group action. In: Peyrin, T., Galbraith, S. (eds.) ASIACRYPT 2018. LNCS, vol. 11274, pp. 395–427. Springer, Cham (2018). https://doi.org/10.1007/978-3-030-03332-3_15

6. Cervantes-Vázquez, D., Chenu, M., Chi-Domínguez, J.-J., De Feo, L., Rodríguez-Henríquez, F., Smith, B.: Stronger and faster side-channel protections for CSIDH. In: Schwabe, P., Thériault, N. (eds.) LATINCRYPT 2019. LNCS, vol. 11774, pp. 173–193. Springer, Cham (2019). https://doi.org/10.1007/978-3-030-30530-7_9
7. Charles, D.X., Lauter, K.E., Goren, E.Z.: Cryptographic hash functions from expander graphs. J. Cryptol. 22(1), 93–113 (2009)
8. Childs, A., Jao, D., Soukharev, V.: Constructing elliptic curve isogenies in quantum subexponential time. J. Math. Cryptol. 8(1), 1–29 (2014)
9. Delfs, C., Galbraith, S.D.: Computing isogenies between supersingular elliptic curves over $\mathbb{F}_p$. Des. Codes Crypt. 78(2), 425–440 (2016)
10. Eisenträger, K., Hallgren, S., Lauter, K., Morrison, T., Petit, C.: Supersingular Isogeny graphs and endomorphism rings: reductions and solutions. In: Nielsen, J.B., Rijmen, V. (eds.) EUROCRYPT 2018. LNCS, vol. 10822, pp. 329–368. Springer, Cham (2018). https://doi.org/10.1007/978-3-319-78372-7_11
11. De Feo, L., Galbraith, S.D.: SeaSign: compact isogeny signatures from class group actions. In: Ishai, Y., Rijmen, V. (eds.) EUROCRYPT 2019. LNCS, vol. 11478, pp. 759–789. Springer, Cham (2019). https://doi.org/10.1007/978-3-030-17659-4_26
12. De Feo, L., Jao, D., Plût, J.: Towards quantum-resistant cryptosystems from supersingular elliptic curve isogenies. J. Math. Cryptol. 8(3), 209–247 (2018)
13. Furukawa, S., Kunihiro, N., Takashima, K.: Multi-party key exchange protocols from supersingular isogenies. In: International Symposium on Information Theory and Its Applications (ISITA), pp. 208–212 (2018)
14. Galbraith, S.D., Petit, C., Shani, B., Ti, Y.B.: On the security of supersingular isogeny cryptosystems. In: Cheon, J.H., Takagi, T. (eds.) ASIACRYPT 2016. LNCS, vol. 10031, pp. 63–91. Springer, Heidelberg (2016). https://doi.org/10.1007/978-3-662-53887-6_3
15. Galbraith, S.D., Petit, C., Silva, J.: Identification protocols and signature schemes based on supersingular isogeny problems. In: Takagi, T., Peyrin, T. (eds.) ASIACRYPT 2017. LNCS, vol. 10624, pp. 3–33. Springer, Cham (2017). https://doi.org/10.1007/978-3-319-70694-8_1
16. Jao, D., De Feo, L.: Towards quantum-resistant cryptosystems from supersingular elliptic curve isogenies. In: Yang, B.-Y. (ed.) PQCrypto 2011. LNCS, vol. 7071, pp. 19–34. Springer, Heidelberg (2011). https://doi.org/10.1007/978-3-642-25405-5_2
17. Koblitz, N.: Elliptic curve cryptosystems. Math. Comput. 48(177), 203–209 (1987)
18. Love, J., Boneh, D.: Supersingular curves with small non-integer endomorphisms. arXiv preprint arXiv:1910.03180 (2019)
19. Meyer, M., Campos, F., Reith, S.: On lions and elligators: an efficient constant-time implementation of CSIDH. In: Ding, J., Steinwandt, R. (eds.) PQCrypto 2019. LNCS, vol. 11505, pp. 307–325. Springer, Cham (2019). https://doi.org/10.1007/978-3-030-25510-7_17
20. Meyer, M., Reith, S.: A faster way to the CSIDH. In: Chakraborty, D., Iwata, T. (eds.) INDOCRYPT 2018. LNCS, vol. 11356, pp. 137–152. Springer, Cham (2018). https://doi.org/10.1007/978-3-030-05378-9_8
21. Miller, V.S.: Use of elliptic curves in cryptography. In: Williams, H.C. (ed.) CRYPTO 1985. LNCS, vol. 218, pp. 417–426. Springer, Heidelberg (1986). https://doi.org/10.1007/3-540-39799-X_31
22. Onuki, H., Aikawa, Y., Yamazaki, T., Takagi, T.: (Short Paper) a faster constant-time algorithm of CSIDH keeping two points. In: Attrapadung, N., Yagi, T. (eds.) IWSEC 2019. LNCS, vol. 11689, pp. 23–33. Springer, Cham (2019). https://doi.org/10.1007/978-3-030-26834-3_2

23. Petit, C.: Faster algorithms for isogeny problems using torsion point images. In: Takagi, T., Peyrin, T. (eds.) ASIACRYPT 2017. LNCS, vol. 10625, pp. 330–353. Springer, Cham (2017). https://doi.org/10.1007/978-3-319-70697-9_12
24. Renes, J.: Computing isogenies between montgomery curves using the action of (0, 0). In: Lange, T., Steinwandt, R. (eds.) PQCrypto 2018. LNCS, vol. 10786, pp. 229–247. Springer, Cham (2018). https://doi.org/10.1007/978-3-319-79063-3_11
25. Rivest, R.L., Shamir, A., Adleman, L.: A method for obtaining digital signatures and public-key cryptosystems. Commun. ACM **21**(2), 120–126 (1978)
26. Shor, P.W.: Polynomial-time algorithms for prime factorization and discrete logarithms on a quantum computer. SIAM Rev. **41**(2), 303–332 (1999)
27. Shumow, D., Ferguson, N.: On the possibility of a back door in the NIST SP800-90 Dual Ec Prng (2007). http://rump2007.cr.yp.to/15-shumow.pdf
28. Silverman, J.H.: The Arithmetic of Elliptic Curves, 2nd edn. Springer, New York (2009). https://doi.org/10.1007/978-0-387-09494-6
29. Steiner, M., Tsudik, G., Waidner, M.: Diffie-Hellman key distribution extended to group communication. In: Proceedings of the 3rd ACM Conference on Computer and Communications Security, pp. 31–37 (1996)
30. Vélu, J.: Isogénies entre courbes elliptiques. CR Acad. Sci. Paris, Séries A **273**, 305–347 (1971)
31. Waterhouse, W.C.: Abelian varieties over finite fields. Annales Scientifiques de l'École Normale Supérieure **2**, 521–560 (1969)

AI Security

RoLMA: A Practical Adversarial Attack Against Deep Learning-Based LPR Systems

Mingming Zha[1,2], Guozhu Meng[1,2(✉)], Chaoyang Lin[1,2], Zhe Zhou[3], and Kai Chen[1,2]

[1] State Key Laboratory of Information Security,
Institute of Information Engineering, Chinese Academy of Science, Beijing, China
{zhamingming,mengguozhu,linchaoyang,chenkai}@iie.ac.cn
[2] School of Cyber Security,
University of Chinese Academy of Sciences, Beijing, China
[3] Fudan University, Shanghai, China
zhouzhe@fudan.edu.cn

Abstract. With the advances of deep learning, license plate recognition (LPR) based on deep learning has been widely used in public transport such as electronic toll collection, car parking management and law enforcement. Deep neural networks are proverbially vulnerable to crafted adversarial examples, which has been proved in many applications like object recognition, malware detection, etc. However, it is more challenging to launch a practical adversarial attack against LPR systems as any covering or scrawling to license plate is prohibited by law. On the other hand, the created perturbations are susceptible to the surrounding environment including illumination conditions, shooting distances and angles of LPR systems. To this end, we propose the first practical adversarial attack, named as RoLMA, against deep learning-based LPR systems. We adopt illumination technologies to create a number of light spots as noises on the license plate, and design targeted and non-targeted strategies to find out the optimal adversarial example against HYPERLPR, a state-of-the-art LPR system. We physicalize these perturbations on a real license plate by virtue of generated adversarial examples. Extensive experiments demonstrate that RoLMA can effectively deceive HYPER-LPR with an 89.15% success rate in targeted attacks and 97.3% in non-targeted attacks. Moreover, our experiments also prove its high practicality with a 91.43% success rate towards physical license plates, and imperceptibility with around 93.56% of investigated participants being able to correctly recognize license plates.

Keywords: Pratical adversarial attack · License plate recognition

1 Introduction

Attributed to the rapid development of deep learning, license plate recognition (LPR) systems are experiencing a dramatic improvement in recognition

© Springer Nature Switzerland AG 2020
Z. Liu and M. Yung (Eds.): Inscrypt 2019, LNCS 12020, pp. 101–117, 2020.
https://doi.org/10.1007/978-3-030-42921-8_6

accuracy and efficiency. The state-of-the-art deep learning-based license plate recognition systems (hereafter referred to as DL-LPR) can achieve high accuracy over 99% [14]. The great success boosts its wide deployment in many areas such as electronic toll collection, car parking management and law enforcement. However, modern deep learning is vulnerable to *adversarial examples* [12]. For instance, a slight perturbation added to an image, which is imperceptible to humans, can easily fool a model of deep neural networks [5]. Analogically, DL-LPR is also suffering from the threat of adversarial examples that incur wrong recognitions. However, it is non-trivial to ensure adversarial examples to be still effective in the physical world. To date, no prior work to our knowledge has explored the practical adversarial attacks against DL-LPR systems.

Challenges of a Practical Adversarial Attack Against DL-LPR. To fool a DL-LPR system is much more difficult than to deceive an image classifier. There are two main challenges for performing a practical adversarial attack against modern DL-LPR systems in the physical world.

C1. The perturbations to license plates are extremely restrictive. License plates are generally issued by a local government department that regulates communications and transport for official identification purposes [2]. They are allegedly not allowed to be altered, obliterated or covered by anything. Therefore, we cannot make any permanent modifications, even minor ones that are imperceptible to a human, to a license plate.

C2. Launching adversarial attacks against DL-LPR systems in the physical world is much more challenging [10]. When DL-LPR systems recognize the license plates attached to fast-moving motor vehicles, the distance and shooting angle to DL-LPR systems are changing over time. Besides, the sunlight or supplement light around the vehicle can also degrade the photographing of license plate. All the above can negatively impact on the effectiveness and robustness of adversarial examples.

Robust Light Mask Attacks against DL-LPR. In this paper, we put forward the first robust yet practical adversarial attack, termed **Ro**bust **L**ight **M**ask **A**ttacks (RoLMA), against DL-LPR systems in the physical world. We select a popular DL-LPR system HyperLPR [22] as the target model, and execute two types of adversarial attacks (see Sect. 4.3)–a *targeted attack* is to create an adversarial license plate in the disguise of a designated one; a *non-targeted attack* is to make a original license plate recognized as any different one.

To address challenge C1, we employ illumination technologies to illuminate license plates instead of scrawling them. The produced light spots can persistently make noises to LPR cameras during the process of photographing, and moreover be removed once away from the monitor areas. To improve its effectiveness and robustness under different circumstances, *i.e.* C2, we identify three environmental factors of most influence: light noise from many other light sources, shooting distances, and shooting angles. Subsequently, we perform *image transformation* on a digital license plate during adversarial example optimization. In particular, we adjust brightness to simulate the varying light, rescale the image to simulate the shooting distances, and rotate the image to simulate the shooting angles (see Sect. 4.2).

Physical Deployment of RoLMA. We install several LED lamps in a license plate frame and create designed spots. Then we adjust the position, size, brightness of light spots, and conduct extensive experiments to evaluate RoLMA: RoLMA achieves an 89.15% success rate in targeted attacks and a 97.30% success rate in non-targeted attacks; RoLMA also proves to be very effective in the physical world and obtains a 91.43% success rate of physical attacks; the adversarial license plates are imperceptible to human beings as most of the investigated volunteers attribute the perturbations to natural light (78.32%) rather than artificial light. Additionally, we have reported our findings to Zeusee [22], and they acknowledged the importance of the problems we discovered. More details can be found here[1].

Contributions. We summarize our contributions as follows:

- *Effective algorithm to generate adversarial examples.* We developed an effective algorithm to make appropriate perturbations and generate adversarial license plates of high robustness. These adversarial license plates are effective in deceiving the target LPR system.
- *Practical adversarial attacks against DL-LPR systems.* We designed and developed the first practical adversarial attack against DL-LPR systems, which is still effective under different circumstances of the real world, such as variable-sized shooting distances and angles.
- *Extensive and comprehensive experiments.* We conducted extensive experiments to evaluate our approach including effectiveness, practicality, and imperceptibility. The results demonstrated that the adversarial examples generated by our approach could effectively devastate the modern LPR systems.

2   Background

2.1   License Plate Recognition

License plate recognition (LPR) is a technology that recognizes vehicle registration plates from images automatically. To date, it has a broad use in transportation, for example, levying tolls on pay-per-use roads, charging parking fees, capturing traffic offenses. LPR usually employs *optical character recognition* (OCR) to convert images into machine-readable text. Typically, OCR technologies can be categorized into two classes: *character-based recognition* and *end-to-end recognition*.

Character-based recognition is the traditional approach to recognize the text from images of license plates [15]. Given an image of a license plate, the character-based recognition system first segments it into several pieces, ensuring that one piece only contains one character [11]. The classifier, oftentimes equipped with

---

[1] https://sites.google.com/view/rolma-adversarial-attack/responses.

classification algorithms (*e.g.*, SVN, ANN, and k-nearest neighbors), can output the most likely character. The performance of LPR does not only rely on a recognition algorithm but also character segmentation to a large extent.

End-to-end recognition is a more recent technology that gains the majority of attention in the field of LPR. It recognizes the entire sequence of characters in a variable-sized "block of text" image with deep neural networks. It is able to produce the final results (*i.e.*, machine-encoded text), without feature selection, extraction, and even character segmentation. A number of deep learning models including Recurrent Neural Networks, Hidden Markov Models, Long Short Term Memory Networks, and Gated Recurrent Units, have been applied in LPR and obtain superior results [8,9].

2.2 HYPERLPR

HYPERLPR [22] is a high-performance license plate recognition framework developed by ZEUSEE Technologies. It employs an end-to-end recognition network GRU, which takes a graphical license plate of size $h \times w$ as input and produces the most likely sequence of characters as output. It starts with a convolution layer (Conv2D) with a $3 \times 3 \times 32$ filter, a batch-normalization and *relu* activation, followed by a 2×2 max-pooling layer(MaxPooling2D). Then two layers follow which have the same architecture as above but with different filters, *i.e.*, one is with $3 \times 3 \times 64$ and the other is with $3 \times 3 \times 128$. The probabilities from the last activation function are passed to a network with 4 gated recurrent units (GRUs) of 256 hidden units, and a dropout layer (its rate is 0.25). Last, the output layer utilizes *softmax* to normalize an 84-unit probability distribution, corresponding to the number of possible license plate characters. In this study, we choose HYPERLPR as our attack target, then develop the approach RoLMA to generate a massive number of adversarial license plates that can evade the recognition.

3   Problem Statement

In this section, we present the attack goal, attack scenarios, and the capability of adversaries.

3.1   Attack Goal

We aim at constructing a practical adversarial attack against DL-LPR. The adversarial license plates are expected to be misclassified by DL-LPR but recognized correctly by humans. Without the loss of generality, we define the following terms involved in this study: one registration number $\mathcal{L}$ of a motor vehicle is a sequence of characters $\langle c_1, c_2, \ldots, c_n \rangle$. Assuming that only m characters can be used as a license plate, *i.e.*, the available character set $\mathcal{V}$, we then have $c_i \in \mathcal{V}$. In addition, there are some constraints in a license plate, such as the length of characters n. So we use $\mathcal{C}$ to denote these constraints. Lastly, we have

$\mathcal{L} : \langle c_1, c_2, \ldots, c_n \rangle \sim \{\mathcal{V}, \mathcal{C}\}$. One LPR system is able to convert an image G to a machine-readable license number, *i.e.*, $f(G) = \mathcal{L}$.

Adversarial License Plate. We generate an adversarial license plate by adding the slight perturbation p to the original graphical license plate G. We use G' to denote the adversarial plate and $G' = G + p$. With respect to G', the target LPR system can output a new license number $\mathcal{L}'$, *i.e.*, $f(G') = \mathcal{L}'$, $\mathcal{L}' \sim \{\mathcal{V}, \mathcal{C}\}$, and $\mathcal{L}' \neq \mathcal{L}$. That is, *the goal is to disguise the original license plate as the other for DL_LPR systems.* To ensure practicality, the adversarial license plates should satisfy all constraints $\mathcal{C}$ as the original one does.

3.2   Attack Scenarios

In this section, we design two attack scenarios for our RoLMA approach.

- *Car parking management.* More and more car parks start to equip automatic DL-LPR systems for parking management [1], *e.g.*, parking access automation and automated deduction of parking fees. The license plate serves as an access token for identity authentication, and only registered licenses could access the parking service. In such a case, the adversaries can resort to the adversarial licenses to elevate their privileges. On the other hand, if the automated deduction of parking fees is based on DL-LPR systems, the adversaries can counterfeit others' license plates and get free parking.
- *Law Enforcement.* Since LPR has been long used for identifying vehicles in a blacklist, an adversarial license plate can escape from the detection successfully. Generally, one well-formed and legal license plate would not trigger LPR's attention. But if the adversarial license plate is recognized as being of the wrong format, it is probable that a specialized staff is sent for manual inspection [6]. It is well-known that adversarial examples can be correctly recognized by a human. Besides, this attack can also affect other common law enforcement applications such as border control and red-light enforcement.

3.3   The Capability of Adversaries

In this study, we aim to generate adversarial license plates with respect to the DL-LPR system. Since HYPERLPR is open-source and high-performance, we select it as the target model, then know the details of its model. So the process of adversarial license plate generation is a kind of white-box attack. In order to attack the deployed DL-LPR systems in reality, the adversaries have to decorate the license plate in a "mild" fashion. It is because license plates should comply with many regulations allegedly by law. More specifically, the adversaries cannot cover, scrawl or discharge license plates in any manner. *In this study, we use the spotlight as a decoration method to confuse DL-LPR systems. The rationale is that light is ubiquitous such as the natural light and license plate light, so that it is hard to determine how comes a light spot on the license plate.*

4   The RoLMA Methodology

To convert the original license plate to an adversarial one, we propose the **Ro**bust **L**ight **M**ask **A**ttack (RoLMA). It proceeds with three key phases in Fig. 1: *illumination, realistic approximation, loss calculation*. However, these digital adversarial images cannot be directly fed to LPR systems for recognition. Instead, we apply several spot light bulbs to irradiate the license plate in order to get light spots. Next, we adjust the positions, size, brightness of light spots, photograph the irradiated license plate and compare it with the digital adversarial image. Finally, we use the irradiated license plate to apply practical attack. More details can be found here[2].

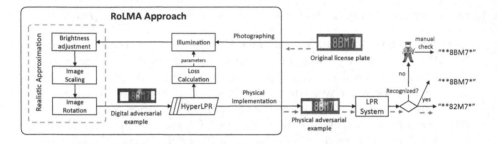

Fig. 1. The system overall of RoLMA

4.1   Illumination

Adversarial examples differ from the original samples in crafted perturbations. The perturbation could be a change of pixels in image classification, an adjustment of an acoustic wave in speech recognition [3]. Generally, license plate recognition reads machine-readable text from an image. Although pixel changes can also make LPR systems misrecognize in the digital space, it has several problems in the physical world: (1) changed pixels are susceptible to shooting settings by LPR cameras (*e.g.*, distance and angle) and the circumstance conditions (*e.g.*, air quality and sunlight intensity); (2) a license plate should remain tidy, uncovered, and unaltered. As a result, it is nearly impossible to scrawl it with previous ways [16]. In this study, we propose an illumination technology and decorate the target license plate with visible lights. The light mask can be taken on and off at any time, without making a permanent scratch to the license plate. In addition, when the LPR system is recognizing a vehicle, the circumstance around the vehicle is full of light, either sunlight or a street light, headlights or rear lights. If the decorated license plate can still be correctly recognized by a human, it will likely not incur a violation of laws.

---

[2] https://sites.google.com/view/rolma-adversarial-attack.

In this study, we select LED lamps as our illumination source. LED lamps are installed at the rear of a vehicle, and make several light spots on the license plate. To work out an illumination solution, we draw several light spots on a digital license plate, which is captured from a physical license plate. This decorated image is then passed to HYPERLPR to check whether it is an adversarial example. We model such a light spot according to its color, position, size, brightness, but not shape.

- *Color.* The background of license plates usually varies from colors. In this study, the color c is modeled as RGB values and optimized gradually during the computation of adversarial examples.
- *Position.* A light spot is positioned by its circle center. We establish a rectangular coordinate system on a license plate. The point at the left bottom has a coordinate (0, 0), and the point (x, y) denotes that it is x away from the left border and y away from the bottom border. In such a fashion, we can represent the center p of a light spot with (c_x, c_y).
- *Size.* It indicates the irradiated area of a light spot, which is measured by the radius r of the circle, *i.e.*, $s = \pi r^2$. As mentioned beforehand, our physical light spots may be not an accurate circle, and more often an ellipse.
- *Brightness.* When a spotlight emits to a plane, the center of the spot is brightest and the light scatters in a decaying rate. Given a point (x, y) inside the spot, the brightness of this point $b(x, y)$ obeys normal distribution probability density function (norm_pdf), *i.e.*, $b(x, y) \sim N(r, \sigma^2)$. Let λ be the brightness coefficient, $b(x, y) = \lambda \times norm\_pdf(\sqrt{(x - c_x)^2 + (y - c_y)^2})$ and the brightness of the circle center is $\frac{\lambda}{\sqrt{2\pi}\sigma}$.

Until now, a light spot can be characterized by its color, position, size and brightness, that is $spot = (C, P, S, B)$. As mentioned above, the color is determined by its RGB values rgb, the position is decided by the coordinates of the circle center (c_x, c_y), the size is determined by the radius r, and the brightness is determined by its standard deviation σ. To search an adversarial example, we intend to make our illuminated license plate misrecognized to a wrong number and the *loss* function reaches the approximately minimal value.

$$\underset{rgb,(c_x,c_y),r,\sigma}{\arg\min} \quad L(X)$$

where X is an input image, and $L(X)$ is the loss function for adversarial examples.

4.2   Realistic Approximation

Adversarial attacks are seriously sensitive to external noises from the physical world [4]. With regards to the two scenarios mentioned in Sect. 3.2, there are many challenges as shown in Sect. 1. As a consequence, we propose three tactics to approximate the reality and improve the robustness of RoLMA as follows: (1)

Brightness Adjustment. To simulate the impact of different lights in the real environment, we utilize TENSORFLOW via the API "`tf.image.random_brightness`" to adjust the brightness of images randomly. (2) *Image Scaling.* It is used to simulate the varying shooting distances of LPR cameras away from the vehicle. Here we adopt "`tf.image.resize_images`" to resize the license plate randomly. Moreover, the scaling holds a fixed width-height ratio, avoiding a badly distorted license plate which is nearly impossible to happen. (3) *Image Rotation.* The robustness of adversarial examples is susceptible to shooting angles of LPR cameras. In the same manner, we invoke the API "`tf.contrib.image.rotate`" of TENSORFLOW to shift the image with a random angle, departing from its coordinates.

4.3   Loss Calculation

In this section, we present the details about how to determine the efficiency of perturbations and provide finer parameters for illumination.

Oracle. To generate adversarial examples, we take HYPERLPR as the *oracle* to guide the process. Given an input of image X, HYPERLPR outputs a sequence of characters $\langle c_1, c_2, \ldots, c_n \rangle$. As mentioned in Sect. 3.1, we aim to make LPR systems produce a wrong license $\mathcal{L}'$ from a real license $\mathcal{L}$. They are of the same length and both comply with lawful constraints, but different in at least one character. Assuming the rth character is c_r, we obtain the probability distribution for this character as $\{(c_1, p_1), (c_2, p_2), \ldots, (c_n, p_n)\}$ where $p_1 = max\{p_i\}$ and $c_1 \neq c_r$. Surely, the overall confidence of this recognition should be higher than the requirement $C \geq \theta$. In this study, we define the following two attacks in terms of generated adversarial examples.

Targeted Adversarial Attack. This is a directed attack, where RoLMA can cause HYPERLPR to recognize the adversarial license plate as a specific license number. For example, we attempt to make the license plate "N92BR8" recognized as "N925R8". Then all the adjustments of parameters are targeting this goal. *This attack is especially suitable for the scenario of car parking management, as it can disguise a privilege license number to access the parking service.*

In a targeted adversarial attack, the original license is $\mathcal{L} : \langle c_1, c_2, \ldots, c_n \rangle$, and the targeted one is $\mathcal{L}' : \langle c_1', c_2', \ldots, c_n' \rangle$. The inconsistent characters in between are $\{(c_i, c_i')\} \in \mathcal{D}$. In order to generate an adversarial example G', we utilize a loss function to measure the differences between the real sequence of characters and the targeted one. The optimization process is conducted in two directions: (1) decreasing the loss of the whole sequence against the target; (2) decreasing the loss of specifically targeted characters $c_i \in \mathcal{D}$ against the target characters. Thus, the loss function is as follows.

$$\underset{G'}{\arg\min} \quad \alpha \times L_{CTC}(f(G'), \mathcal{L}') + \sum_{(c_i, c_i') \in \mathcal{D}} L(c_i, c_i') \tag{1}$$

where L_{CTC} is the CTC loss function for label sequence and $\sum_{(c_i, c_i') \in \mathcal{D}} L(c_i, c_i')$ is the sum of losses which are the editing distances between all targeted characters and the original ground true characters. The coefficient α balances the two variables in the loss function.

Non-targeted Adversarial Attack. The goal of non-targeted adversarial attacks is to fool a LPR system by producing any wrong recognition. *This attack is very suitable for the scenarios of escaping electronic tolls collection and black-listed vehicle detection.* A non-targeted attack contains two uncertainties–which characters will be changed in adversarial examples at the sequence level, and what the original characters will become at the character level. As such, we aim to find an optimal solution to minimize the distance between adversarial examples with the original at the sequence level. Moreover, this solution leads to a wrong recognition with its confidence satisfied. Let $d(\mathcal{L}, \mathcal{L}')$ be the editing distance between the two licenses $\mathcal{L}$ and $\mathcal{L}'$ and $f(G') = \mathcal{L}'$ as aforementioned. Moreover, $C_{f(G')}$ is the confidence of the targeted license G', and θ is a threshold of confidence, here we set it as 0.75. The optimization process can be formulated as Eq. 2.

$$\underset{G'}{\arg\min} \quad d(f(G'), \mathcal{L}) \cap C_{f(G')} \geq \theta \qquad (2)$$

Here we utilize Simulated Annealing (SA) to guide the process of non-targeted adversarial attacks as shown in Algorithm 1. In particular, the iteration process is continuing unless one wrong character gains the largest probability or it exceeds the maximal iteration number MAX (line 2). Line 3 is to compute the probability gap between the first two characters. It can roughly measure the chance to accomplish a wrong recognition. Line 4 is to generate the perturbed license plate G' by adding the perturbation $\delta_{c_1,c_1'}$, and $\delta_{c_1,c_1'}$ is computed by the targeted adversarial attack as described above. Line 5 to 14 present which wrong characters will be selected for the next decoration. Following with a descending order of probability, we select the 2nd character as our first decoration target. A new probability distribution is produced by LPR system (line 6) and sorted as per probabilities (line 7). If a wrong recognition is achieved (line 8), we terminate the iteration process. Otherwise, we compute the chance of wrong recognition in the current probability distribution (line 11) and compare it with the previous one. If the chance is increased, *i.e.* $\Delta p_{new} < \Delta p$, we accept this decoration. Otherwise, we accept this decoration with a probability calculated in line 12. We evolve the value of temperature at line 15. When we get G', we need to check whether G' follows the constraints $\mathcal{C}$ on the license plate numbering system in order not to be rejected at line 17. If the G' satisfies the constraints $\mathcal{C}$, then we will update G at line 18.

5   Evaluation

We implement RoLMA on the base of TENSORFLOW and KERAS. The experiments are conducted on a server with 32 Intel(R) Xeon(R) CPUs of E5-2620 and 64 GB memory. Through these experiments, we intend to answer:

RQ1. How effectively does RoLMA generate adversarial license plates and how successfully do these adversarial examples deceive the HYPERLPR system?

Algorithm 1. Non-targeted adversarial attacks based on SA

Input: $\{(c_i, p_i)|1 \leq i \leq n\}$: a descending list of possible chars by probabilities;
T: the intial degree of temperature and $T > 0$; λ: the annealing rate and
$0 < \lambda < 1$; MAX: the maximal number of iterations for adversarial
example generation; G: the original image of license plate

Output: G': adversarial license plate, where $c_1' \neq c_1$

1   $iter \leftarrow 0, c_i' \leftarrow c_i,\ p_i' \leftarrow p_i, i \in [1, n]$;

2   **while** $c_1' = c_1$ *and* $iter < MAX$ **do**

3     $\Delta p \leftarrow p_2' - p_1'$;

4     $G' \leftarrow G + \delta_{c_1, c_1'}$;

5   **for** $i \leftarrow 2$ **to** n **do**

6       $\{(c_i'', p_i'')\} \leftarrow license\_plate\_recognition(G')$;

7   sort $\{(c_i'', p_i'')\}$ where $p_i'' \geq p_{i+1}''$;

8   **if** $c_1'' \neq c_1'$ **then**

9         $c_i' \leftarrow c_i'',\ p_i' \leftarrow p_i'', i \in [1, n]$;

10   break;

11       $\Delta p_{new} \leftarrow p_2'' - p_1''$;

12   **if** $\Delta p_{new} < \Delta p$ *or* $e^{\frac{\Delta p - \Delta p_{new}}{T}} > rand(0, 1)$ **then**

13         $c_i' \leftarrow c_i'',\ p_i' \leftarrow p_i'', i \in [1, n]$;

14   break;

15     $T \leftarrow \lambda \times T$;

16     $iter \leftarrow iter + 1$;

17   **if** G' *satisfies the constraints* C **then**

18       $G \leftarrow G'$;

19   **return** G';

RQ2. How is the success rate of the practical attacks guided by these adversarial
examples?

RQ3. Are these adversarial examples imperceptible enough for ordinary audiences?

Experiment Subject. We prepare two types of data sets for the experiments
as follows. All the license plates can be recognized correctly by HYPERLPR.

– **Real license plates.** We have collected 1000 images of license plates from
CCPD [18]. Due to the influences of the surrounding environment, many of
the images are blurred and of low quality.
– **Synthesized license plates.** We also synthesize a number of license plates
by ourselves following the design specification of a legal license plate. We
randomly select characters from the limited alphabet. Constraints are checked
to guarantee these license plates are valid. In total, we create 1000 license
plates of high quality without any noise from the physical environments.

Parameter Determination. RoLMA uses illumination technique to create spots on the license plate to fool a LPR system. However, if the number of light spots is too small, we may not be able to gain a high success rate, *i.e.*, failure on generating adversarial examples. Inversely, installing a larger number of light spots is also not a good choice since it may cause a failed recognition and too remarkable for ordinary audiences. Therefore, we first design an experiment to identify the favored number of light spots that could effectively fool LPR systems. We randomly select 100 license plates from the data set, and commence to generate adversarial examples with an increasing number of light spots from 1 to 10. We set a maximal iteration number as 5,000 in each trial, and then one trial will stop if either an adversarial example is generated or the iteration number exceeds 5,000. It is worth mentioning that we use a non-targeted strategy for adversarial attacks. The result shows the success rates of attacks along with the number of light spots. The success rate is raised slightly after 5. As a result, we only make 5 light spots to license plate in the following experiments.

5.1   RQ1: Effectiveness

In this experiment, we aim to explore the effectiveness of RoLMA in digital space, *i.e.*, the generated adversarial images are directly passed to HyperLPR for performance assessment. More specifically, we conduct two types of attacks: *Targeted adversarial attack.* For each license plate, we aim to receive a specific wrong license number from HyperLPR. We employ random algorithms first to identify which character to be disturbed, then disguise the character as a different one. One attack is terminated once the target is accomplished or the iteration exceeds 5,000 times; *Non-targeted adversarial attack.* Target is not necessarily designated in a non-targeted adversarial attack. Therefore, we will not specify a target for each license plate. One attack is terminated once an adversarial example is obtained or it exceeds the maximal iterations.

Table 1. Success rate of targeted and non-targeted attacks

Data	Targeted attack		Non-targeted attack	
	Success	Confidence	Success	Confidence
Real	92.60%	86.55%	99.70%	91.59%
Synthesized	85.70%	85.64%	94.90%	90.88%
Average	89.15%	85.95%	97.30%	91.28%

Table 1 shows the results of these attacks on both real license plates and synthesized license plates. The success rate of non-targeted attacks is 97.3% outperforming targeted attacks (89.15%). That is because one character has varying difficulties to pretend to other characters as concluded above. Some characters cannot be even achieved regardless of how to optimize. There are still a number of trial instances failing to deceive HYPERLPR. For example, we cannot find an adversarial example for the license plate "A40F29" in a limited time. In addition, we find that the success rate in synthesized license is always smaller than real license's in both attacks. The reason is that the synthesized license plates have relatively higher definition compared to the real license plates, which means the correct characters can be recognized with a higher probability. In contrast, when HYPERLPR is recognizing a blurred image, it is prone to making the results with lower confidence or even cannot determine the final characters. As a consequence, fewer additional perturbations may cause a wrong recognition for real license plates and much more perturbations have to be made to the synthesized license plates for adversarial examples.

Comparison with Random Illumination Attack. We launch another attack by randomly illuminating the 2000 images in our data set. The randomness of the illumination attack lies in the number of light spots, the color, brightness, size and position for each spot. After all, we obtain 2000 decorated images with random spots. HYPERLPR can correctly recognize 96.95% of them. Only 1.90% of them can deceive HYPERLPR, which is far less effective than the non-target attack of ROLMA (97.30%). It is concluded that modern LPR systems have great resistance to this random illumination attack. It is non-trivial to generate adversarial examples effectively without considering LPR algorithms. This experiment also proves that ROLMA achieves superior performance by exploring the weaknesses residing in LPR algorithms.

5.2   RQ2: Practicability

In this section, we apply targeted attack to evaluate the practicability of ROLMA by instantiating adversarial perturbations on real license plates.

Experiment Design. (1) We install these electronic devices on a car and calibrate these LEDs carefully. If the captured license plates are remarkably different from the digital adversarial image, then we will adjust the supply current, illumination direction, and used lenses to change formed light sports. The calibration is stopped if two images are different within a tolerant threshold θ. And the limitation of physical calibration time is set to 5 min. (2) We record two continuous videos for the decorated license plate: the first video is filmed at the horizontal plane with the license plate in a "Δ" route. More specifically, the camera is at the back of the stationary car with a distance of 2 m. Then we move the camera to the left-back with a $30°$ horizontal angle till to a location with a 3-m distance. We then move the camera horizontally to the right till the symmetric location, and finally move to the left front till the start point; the second video is filmed at a higher position with a $45°$ depression angle to the license plate. The camera is moved from the left ($\approx 15°$ horizontal angle) of the license plate to the right ($\approx 15°$ horizontal angle). The distance of the camera to the license plate is 2 m. This experiment lasts around 2 h and gets two one-minute videos.

Experiment Results. In our recorded videos, there are 1600 frames of image totally and 922 valid frames remain after filtering out blurred images. We feed these valid images to HYPERLPR and 843 of them are misrecognized. Hence, the success rate of our physical attack is 91.43%. The averaged confidence of recognition results is 87.24%. Moreover, the average time of physical calibration is about 3 min.

Table 2. Recognition results in the physical attacks

No	Distance (meters)	Depress.	Horizon.	Text	Conf. (%)
1	2	$0°$	$0°$	▮▮8BM7▮	98.06
2	2	$0°$	$0°$	▮▮82M7▮	86.93
3	3	$0°$	$-30°$	▮▮82M7▮	85.91
4	3	$0°$	$+30°$	▮▮82M7▮	86.35
5	2	$45°$	$0°$	▮▮82M7▮	90.92
6	2	$45°$	$-15°$	▮▮82M7▮	91.40
7	2	$45°$	$+15°$	▮▮82M7▮	87.64

Examples. We select six images recorded in this physical attack shown on the website[3], and the recognition results in Table 2. These images are captured with varying distances and shooting angles. In particular, the first image is shot with the original license plate and the camera is 2 m away behind. HYPER-LPR can output "▮▮8BM7▮" correctly with a confidence of 98.06%. To protect privacy, we use "▮" to cover specific characters in both the images and recognized text. The other six images, shot from the decorated license plate, can all make HYPERLPR output "▮▮82M7▮". As shown in Table 2, "Distance" denotes the distance of the camera to the license plate, "Depress." means the depression angle of photographing, "Horizon." means the horizontal angle of photographing, and "Conf." denotes the confidence of HYPERLPR with regard to recognition results. Noted that "$-30°$" and "$-15°$" indicate the camera is at the left side of the license plate while "$+30°$" and "$+15°$" mean the right side. These decorated license plates are all recognized wrongly, according to our computation in the experiments. It shows that RoLMA is very effective in generating adversarial examples, and these adversarial examples are very robust in the physical world.

5.3   RQ3: Imperceptibility

Imperceptibility is another important feature for adversarial examples, which means the perturbations do not affect users' decision. In the field of license plate recognition, practical adversarial examples impose a new implication to this concept: the license plate is still recognized correctly, and the crafted perturbations are indistinguishable from other noises of the real world. In this experiment, we conduct a survey and it is designed with carefully-designed questions about

---

[3] https://sites.google.com/view/rolma-adversarial-attack/practicability.

these adversarial examples. In particular, one survey is composed of 20 generated adversarial examples, randomly selected from our data set. More details can be found here[4]. We release the survey via a public survey service[5], and receive 121 questionnaires in total within three days. We have filtered out 20 surveys of low quality if the survey is finished too fast (less than 60s) or the answers all point to a single choice.

Survey Results. Among the 101 valid surveys, the median age of the participants is 22, 66.34% of them are male and 33.66% are female. 93.07% hold a Bachelor or higher degree. From the survey, we find that 93.56% of the participants can recognize the text of the license plate successfully, which means our adversarial examples do not affect users' recognitions. 8.23% of them do not notice any light spots in adversarial examples, indicating that the perturbations are inconspicuous to them. As for the remaining participants noticing the light spots, 78.32% think the light spots are caused by license plate light or other natural light as we expected, and only 21.68% consider the light spots are from artificial illumination. Thus, we can find out that our practical attack can easily pretend as some normal lighting sources, such as license plate light and the light of other vehicles from the back.

6   Discussion

Potential Defenses for RoLMA. To defend against RoLMA and other alike attacks, we propose the following strategies for LPR systems that are learned in the course of experiments. From the aspect of the recognition algorithm, LPR systems can employ *denoising* techniques [7] to elevate image quality by eliminating noises added by adversarial examples. Noises in a license plate could be light spots, stains caused by haze or rain, character overlap due to small shooting angles. To overcome these noises, LPR systems are encouraged to sharpen the borders of characters in a low-quality license plate, and the areas out of characters are made consistent with the background. Meanwhile, the stains inside of the characters are colored as the surrounding area. Based on the investigation result of its underlying recognition mechanism, we found that it employs denoising techniques that can crack our perturbations and thus the LPR systems are capable of recognizing the correct text. Besides, training with a variety of adversarial examples can also greatly improve the resistance to future adversarial examples. From the aspect of the system, security experts of the system have to work out more complete and comprehensive protection mechanisms for a specific risky task. Imaging that one car parking management system solely relies on license plate recognition for authentication, attackers can easily break into the car parking system with small efforts committed in case LPR fails or ceases to work. In such a case, multi-factor authentication [13] is a promising method to enhance security. The unique identification code of vehicle which is

---

[4] https://sites.google.com/view/rolma-adversarial-attack/imperceptibility.
[5] https://www.wjx.cn/.

widely used in the field of IoT can be used in this scenario. Even the car owner changes or heavily scrawls the license plate, the unique identification code can assist in vehicle identification. Moreover, manual checks by specialists are the last obstacles hindering these attacks.

7 Related Work

There are a lot of works on adversarial attacks.

Adversarial Attacks Against License Plate Recognition. There are few works on adversarial attacks against LPR systems. For example, Song and Shmatikov [16] explore how the deep learning-based TESSERACT [15] system is easily smashed in adversarial settings. They have generated adversarial images to lead a wrong recognition of TESSERACT in digital space but not in the practical world. *Unlike the above attack, we are the first one to apply practical adversarial examples in the field of license plate recognition, and implement a full-stack attack from the digital world to the physical world. It helps unveil the weaknesses of modern LPR systems and facilitates the improvement of robustness indirectly.*

Physical Implementation of Adversarial Examples. Although adversarial examples have gained a surprisingly great success in defeating deep learning systems [17], to work in the physical world is not that worrisome [10]. There are emerging research works aiming at making the adversarial attacks come true in reality. In order to generate more robust adversarial attack, Zhao *et al.* [21] proposed the feature-interference reinforcement method and the enhanced realistic constraints generation to enhance robustness. Zhou *et al.* [23] constructed a new attack against FACENET with an invisible mask but without the consideration of disturbances from the surrounding environment. Moreover, Yuan *et al.* [20] implemented a practical adversarial attack against ASR systems, working across air in the presence of environmental interferences. In addition, they proposed REEVE attack which can remotely compromise Amazon Echo via radio and TV signals [19]. However, as shown in Sect. 1-C2, environmental factors can reduce the effectiveness and robustness under different circumstances. Thus, *we design three transformations(e.g., adjust brightness, rescale the image and rotate the image) to simulate the realistic environment in Sect. 4.2.*

8 Conclusion

We propose the first practical adversarial attack RoLMA against deep learning-based LPR systems. We employ illumination technologies to perturb the license plates captured by LPR systems, rather than making perceivable changes. To resolve a workable illumination solution, we adopt targeted and non-targeted strategies to determine how license plates are illuminated including the color, size, and brightness of light spots. Based on the illumination solution, we design a physical implementation to simulate these light spots on real license plates. We conducted extensive experiments to evaluate the effectiveness of our illumination algorithm and the efficacy of physical implementation. The experiment results show that RoLMA is very effective to deceive HYPERLPR with an averaged 93.23% success rate. We have tested RoLMA in the physical world with 91.43% of shoot images are wrongly recognized by HYPERLPR.

Acknowledgments. IIE authors are supported in part by National Key R&D Program of China (No. 2016QY04W0805), NSFC U1836211, 61728209, 61902395, National Top-notch Youth Talents Program of China, Youth Innovation Promotion Association CAS, Beijing Nova Program, Beijing Natural Science Foundation (No. JQ18011), National Frontier Science and Technology Innovation Project (No. YJKYYQ20170070) and a research grant from Huawei. Fudan university author is supported by NSFC 61802068, Shanghai Sailing Program 18YF1402200.

References

1. License Plate Recognition (2018). https://parking.ku.edu/license-plate-recognition
2. Vehicle registration numbers and number plates. Technical report, INF104 (2018)
3. Carlini, N., Wagner, D.A.: Audio adversarial examples: Targeted attacks on speech-to-text. In: 2018 IEEE Security and Privacy Workshops, pp. 1–7 (2018). https://doi.org/10.1109/SPW.2018.00009
4. Evtimov, I., et al.: Robust physical-world attacks on deep learning models. arXiv preprint arXiv:1707.08945 (2017)
5. Goodfellow, I.J., Shlens, J., Szegedy, C.: Explaining and harnessing adversarial examples. CoRR abs/1412.6572 (2014)
6. Gravelle, K.: Video tolling system with error checking (2011)
7. Guo, C., Rana, M., Cissé, M., van der Maaten, L.: Countering adversarial images using input transformations. CoRR abs/1711.00117 (2017). http://arxiv.org/abs/1711.00117
8. Jain, V., Sasindran, Z., Rajagopal, A.K., Biswas, S., Bharadwaj, H.S., Ramakrishnan, K.R.: Deep automatic license plate recognition system. In: Proceedings of the Tenth Indian Conference on Computer Vision, Graphics and Image Processing (ICVGIP), pp. 6:1–6:8 (2016)
9. Li, H., Shen, C.: Reading car license plates using deep convolutional neural networks and LSTMs. CoRR abs/1601.05610 (2016). http://arxiv.org/abs/1601.05610
10. Lu, J., Sibai, H., Fabry, E., Forsyth, D.A.: NO need to worry about adversarial examples in object detection in autonomous vehicles. CoRR abs/1707.03501 (2017). http://arxiv.org/abs/1707.03501
11. Nomura, S., Yamanaka, K., Katai, O., Kawakami, H., Shiose, T.: A novel adaptive morphological approach for degraded character image segmentation. Pattern Recogn. **38**(11), 1961–1975 (2005)
12. Papernot, N., McDaniel, P., Jha, S., Fredrikson, M., Celik, Z.B., Swami, A.: The limitations of deep learning in adversarial settings. In: 2016 IEEE European Symposium on Security and Privacy (EuroS&P), pp. 372–387. IEEE (2016)
13. Rosenblatt, S., Cipriani, J.: Two-factor authentication: what you need to know (FAQ), June 2015. https://www.cnet.com/news/two-factor-authentication-what-you-need-to-know-faq/

14. Silva, S.M., Jung, C.R.: License plate detection and recognition in unconstrained scenarios. In: Ferrari, V., Hebert, M., Sminchisescu, C., Weiss, Y. (eds.) ECCV 2018. LNCS, vol. 11216, pp. 593–609. Springer, Cham (2018). https://doi.org/10.1007/978-3-030-01258-8_36
15. Smith, R.: An overview of the tesseract OCR engine. In: 9th International Conference on Document Analysis and Recognition (ICDAR), pp. 629–633 (2007)
16. Song, C., Shmatikov, V.: Fooling OCR systems with adversarial text images. CoRR abs/1802.05385 (2018)
17. Szegedy, C., et al.: Intriguing properties of neural networks. CoRR abs/1312.6199 (2013)
18. Xu, Z., et al.: Towards end-to-end license plate detection and recognition: a large dataset and baseline. In: Ferrari, V., Hebert, M., Sminchisescu, C., Weiss, Y. (eds.) ECCV 2018. LNCS, vol. 11217, pp. 261–277. Springer, Cham (2018). https://doi.org/10.1007/978-3-030-01261-8_16
19. Yuan, X., et al.: All your alexa are belong to us: a remote voice control attack against echo. In: 2018 IEEE Global Communications Conference (GLOBECOM), pp. 1–6. IEEE (2018)
20. Yuan, X., et al.: Commandersong: a systematic approach for practical adversarial voice recognition. In: 27th {USENIX} Security Symposium ({USENIX} Security 2018), pp. 49–64 (2018)
21. Zhao, Y., Zhu, H., Liang, R., Shen, Q., Zhang, S., Chen, K.: Seeing isn't believing: towards more robust adversarial attack against real world object detectors. In: Proceedings of the 26th ACM Conference on Computer and Communications Security (CCS) (2019)
22. Zeusee: High Performance Chinese License Plate Recognition Framework (2018)
23. Zhou, Z., Tang, D., Wang, X., Han, W., Liu, X., Zhang, K.: Invisible mask: practical attacks on face recognition with infrared. CoRR abs/1803.04683 (2018). http://arxiv.org/abs/1803.04683

A SeqGAN-Based Method for Mimicking Attack

Weiqing Huang[1,2], Xiao Peng[1,2], and Zhixin Shi[1,2(✉)]

[1] Institute of Information Engineering, Chinese Academy of Sciences, Beijing, China
shizhixin@iie.ac.cn
[2] School of Cyber Security, University of Chinese Academy of Sciences,
Beijing, China

Abstract. Distributed denial of service (DDoS) attacks continue to be an ever-increasing threat in cyberspace. Nowadays, attackers tend to launch advanced DDoS attacks with botnets to bypass the detection system. In this paper, we present a method for launching an advanced application-layer DDoS which masquerades as a flash crowd (FC). The attack strategy falls in two aspects: (1) extracting legitimate users' behaviors; (2) instructing bots to behave as legitimate users. To achieve this, we propose a multi-step algorithm to extract user browsing behaviors and establish a Sequence Generative Adversarial Nets (SeqGAN) model to generate mimicking behaviors of bots. In addition, we experimentally study the effectiveness of this mimicking attack. The study shows that the mimicking attack can fool a detection system that is based on machine learning algorithms. The experimental results also demonstrate that the mimicking attack is indistinguishable from FC in term of statistics.

Keywords: Flash crowd · Application-layer DDoS · Mimic · SeqGAN · Browsing behavior

1 Introduction

DDoS attacks normally consume a huge number of resources of a web server, making it impossible to access the server by legitimate users [11]. In the early days, a DDoS attack comes from a few computers that have been loaded with attack tools. In recent years, attackers carry out DDoS attacks with the help of botnets generally [9]. A botnet is a large network of compromised hosts, which are called bots. These bots run a malicious program and are remotely controlled by the botmaster. Nowadays, DDoS attacks have become a severe threat to the security of web servers with the thriving of botnets.

Although there are plenty of DDoS defenses, sophisticated attackers are sparing no effort to bypass the detection by mimicking the phenomenon of flash crowds [31]. A flash crowd refers to the situation when many legitimate users simultaneously access an interested website, which also causes an overload of

© Springer Nature Switzerland AG 2020
Z. Liu and M. Yung (Eds.): Inscrypt 2019, LNCS 12020, pp. 118–133, 2020.
https://doi.org/10.1007/978-3-030-42921-8_7

web server [12]. As a result, application-layer DDoS is gaining popularity [?] [?]. These attacks are better at masquerading flash crowds by sending numerous benign HTTP requests. However, traditional application-layer DDoS attacks, such as GET flooding, bring about a huge volume of the same HTTP request in a time interval. Based on this, many statistical methods are proposed to detect application-layer DDoS [?] [23].

Meanwhile, Yu et al. [31] propose an advanced application-layer DDoS: mimicking attack. To carry out this attack, attackers arrange bots to send HTTP requests by simulating the behavior of legitimate users. To achieve this, the authors establish a four parameter semi-Markov model for user browsing behavior. Furthermore, they propose one conclusion and prove it theoretically and experimentally: if attackers have sufficient active bots, a mimicking attack is feasible and statistics or browsing behavior based detection algorithms will be disabled. However, in order to extract accurate parameters for the semi-Markov model, their method requires amounts of seed data, which is hard to meet in practice.

To address this problem, in this paper, we propose a SeqGAN-based scheme for launching a mimicking attack. Akin to previous studies, we use a kind of time series to present user browsing behavior. Differently, we establish a Seq-GAN model to generate mimicking behavior of bots, which avoids extracting parameters explicitly. Besides, we experimentally demonstrate that the mimicking attack and flash crowd are indistinguishable towards statistics or browsing behavior based detection schemes.

The major contributions of this work are as follows:

- We present a SeqGAN-based method for launching mimicking attack. To the best of our knowledge, it is the first scheme to use sequence generation technology to produce mimicking behaviors for application-layer DDoS. In particular, our method can lower down the dependence on the magnitude of seed data.
- We propose a novel algorithm to extract user behaviors. Instead of explicitly extracting statistical features, we process seed data with segmentation, filtration and sampling to build a structured User-Behavior set for further imitating.
- We design two schemes to evaluate the proposed mimicking attack. One is measuring its ability in bypassing a detection system that is based on machine learning technologies. The other is comparing mimicking behaviors to legitimate users' behaviors on four vital web browsing characteristics. In our experiments, results demonstrate that the method can generate high quality mimicking behaviors.

The paper is organized as follows: Sect. 2 reviews the current available literatures. Section 3 describes our SeqGAN-based method for mimicking attack. An experimental evaluation of the approach is given in Sect. 4. Section 5 is the conclusion of our work.

2   Related Work

2.1   User Behavior Analysis

In the field of detecting application-layer DDoS attacks, user behavior analysis is widely used. Ye et al. [29] extract four different user session features to detect anomalous users: object size, request rate, object popularity and transition probability. But the method fails to distinguish attacks from FC. Giralte et al. [7] model user behaviors in terms of layer 4–7 parameters, such as the rate of requests, the mean of flows, GETs mean, etc. Miu et al. [16] compare the jump probability of pages to identify suspicious users. Singh et al. [24] propose many features to profile user behaviors when users send HTTP requests, such as the frequency of requests, viewing time for a given resource (down-time), web pages popularity, repetition index, response index. To detect application-layer DDoS, Luo et al. [14] extract features from an intercept program instead of web server logs and use PCA to profile normal user behaviors.

2.2   Mimicking Attacks

Up to now, there are a spot of literatures on mimicking attacks. The work of Yu et al. [31] is perhaps most closely related to our efforts. They theoretical prove that mimicking attacks are feasible if attackers have sufficient active bots. Furthermore, by assuming user browsing dynamics follow three statistical distribution models, they employ a semi-Markov to launch mimicking attack. To certain it, an attacker needs to obtain the volume of history requests for a given time, which is hard to meet. Rigaki et al. [21] use a GAN to learn traffic behavior of a legitimate application. Then, the traffic of the malware is modified according to this. But this method only works on the flow level. Sun et al. [25] extract statistical feathers of traffic and employ LSGAN to mimic FC, which mainly focuses on network-layer DDoS.

2.3   Generative Adversarial Nets

A Generative Adversarial Nets (GAN) is a deep learning framework that contains a generator and a discriminator. A GAN corresponds to a minimax two-player game. The generator takes the role of producing real-like samples. The discriminator is trained to distinguish real samples from those produced by the generator. The convergence of a GAN is reached when the generator and the discriminator reach a Nash equilibrium. GAN was proposed by Goodfellow et al. in 2014 [8] and has received wide attention. Nowadays, many improved models, such as LSGAN [19], WGAN [2], DCGAN [20], BEGAN [3], are proposed to handle the difficulties that earlier GAN faced. While GAN can generate very convincing images, there are challenges to apply GAN to other specific domains. For example, it is hard for gradient-based GAN to generate sequence. That is because discrete output makes it hard to update parameters of GAN model.

Aiming to solve the problem, SeqGAN extends GAN with the RL-based generator [30]. Experimental results demonstrate that SeqGAN has made considerable progress in the task of generating sequences.

3 Proposed Method

In this section, we simulate an attacker and explore a kind of mimicking attack. Firstly, we introduce the threat model. The attacker's capabilities will be discussed. Secondly, we describe how to extract behaviors of legitimate users, and how to generate mimicking behaviors of bots. Finally, we present the proposed mimicking attack algorithm.

3.1 Threat Model

In summary, there are three requirements for mimicking attack. First, the attacker is able to monitor and collect seed data from the victim servers. Seed data refers to available information, such as log of web server, request traffic of users, etc. Second, the attacker owns a larger-scale botnet and can command bots to run a given program. It is not a strict condition, because botnets usually have command and control (C&C) channel to connect the attacker and bots. However, it's a challenge to have much control over the bots. Last but not the least, the attacker should design the program that run by each bot. The crucial task of the program is to generate novel instructions constantly. According to these instructions, each bot will send specific HTTP requests to the victim, which we call mimicking behaviors. Key technologies are detailed in the following.

3.2 User-Behavior

To mimic legitimate users and implement an attack, extracting user behaviors from seed data is the first thing to address. There are many schemes to model user browsing behaviors. Drawing ideas from [6,27,28], we model user behavior as a kind of sequence. Figure 1 shows the model. When a user browses webpages, the browser will send out a number of requests for in-line objects. An in-line object might be a text, image, video and so on. These requests arrive at the web server one after another, and in a short time interval. The web server may record these requests by keeping log files.

Definition 1 (User-Behavior). *A User-Behavior is a group of requests that are arranged in time sequence. These requests are derived from the same IP address.*

Let $X_{1:K} = (x_1, \ldots, x_k, \ldots, x_K)$ be a User-Behavior, where K is the length of sequence. In other words, K represents the duration of web browsing. The value of x_k represents the action in the relative time k, such that:

$$x_k = \begin{cases} null & \text{dwell time}; \\ r_i & \text{request for an in-line object}, \end{cases} \tag{1}$$

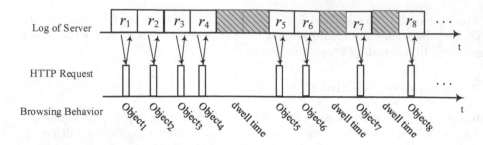

Fig. 1. User's browsing behavior

where i is a flag for counting and $i = 1, 2, \ldots, N$. In addition, we denote $T(r_i)$ as the relative time corresponding to the request r_i. A typical User-Behavior as follows: $X_{1:13} = (r_1, r_2, null, r_3, r_4, null, null, r_5, r_6, null, null, null, r_7)$. In this case, the user's browsing time is 13 s and $T(r_7) = 13$.

3.3   Building User-Behavior Set

Before building User-Behavior set the to mimic, we analyze User-Behaviors from two aspects:

(1) **From the perspective of the web server.** *Unique User-Behaviors are accepted, because different users have different behavior trajectories. However, if statistical metrics of a User-Behavior set are abnormal, warning should be triggered.*

(2) **From the perspective of the attacker.** *Sparse User-Behaviors should be avoided as much as possible, because bots should not idle for much time. What's more, due to limited computational resources, the length of each User-Behavior should be short.*

Based on this, we propose a multi-step method to build the User-Behavior-Set. As shown in Algorithm 1, it consists of four steps: classification, segmentation, filtration and sampling. Each User-Behavior should be normalized to a short sequence length L. Therefore, we first classify each User-Behavior $X_{1:K}$ into set S_i, subject to $(i-1)L < K < iL$. Then, each $X_{1:K}$ in S_i is splitted into multiple segments and the length of each segment is L. In the following, the segments which are sparse will be abandoned and eligible segments will be merged into the candidate set CS_i. We propose a metric $Sparse(X_{k_1:k_2})$ to describe the sparse degree of each segment $X_{k_1:k_2}$, which is defined by:

$$Sparse(X_{k_1:k_2}) = \frac{\sum_{i=2}^{N} \max\left(0, \frac{T(r_i) - T(r_{i-1})}{t_m} - 1\right)}{k_2 - k_1}, \tag{2}$$

where t_m is the max viewing time for an in-line object. If the $Sparse(X_{k_1:k_2})$ exceeds the threshold 0, the segment will be abandoned. However, we will not mearge all retained segments into the User-behavior set. It is because the User-Behaviors with long length have been cut into multiple segments. It would magnify these users' influence if we did that. Thus, sampling is needed in the end. Then, we can obtain a structured User-Behavior set S, $S = \{X_{1:L}^1, X_{1:L}^2, X_{1:L}^3, \dots\}$.

Algorithm 1. Building User-Behavior set

Require:
    X: a raw set of User-Behaviors;
    t_m: the threshold time for viewing object;
    L: the target sequence length;
Ensure:
    S: the normalized User-Behavior set;
1: Divide each $X_{1:K} \in X$ into set S_i by K, s.t. $(i-1)L < K < iL$; Initialize $S \leftarrow S_1$
2: **for** each $S_i \in \{S_2, S_3, S_4, \dots\}$ **do**
3:     Initialize the candidate set $CS_i \leftarrow \emptyset$
4:     **for** each $X_{1:K} \in S_i$ **do**
5:       $k_1 \leftarrow 0; k_2 \leftarrow 0$
6:       **while** $k_2 \leqslant K$ **do**
7:         $k_2 + +$
8:         Calculate $Sparse(X_{k_1:k_2})$ by Eq.(2)
9:         **if** $Sparse(X_{k_1:k_2}) \geq 0$ **then**
10:           $k_1 \leftarrow k_2$ \\abandon the fragment
11:         **end if**
12:         **if** $k_2 - k_1 \geqslant L$ **then**
13:           $CS_i \leftarrow CS_i \cup \{X_{k_1:k_2}\}; k_1 \leftarrow k_2$ \\merge into candidate set
14:         **end if**
15:       **end while**
16:     **end for**
17:     Sample from CS_i by $\frac{\alpha_i}{i}$ and get CSS_i, where $1 < \alpha_i < 2$; $S \leftarrow S \cup CSS_i$
18: **end for**

3.4 Generating Mimicking Behaviors

In the mimicking attack, behaviors of each bot should be similar to legitimate users' behaviors while bots are sending requests to web server. That is, each bot is able to generate mimicking behabiors constantly via pre-defined program. The problem is formulated as follows:

Each bots has a generator. Given a User-Behavior-Set $S = \{X_{1:L}^1, X_{1:L}^2, X_{1:L}^3, \dots\}$, which comes from an underlying distribution p_d. The generator can produce a novel set $\{Y_{1:L}^1, Y_{1:L}^2, Y_{1:L}^3, \dots\}$, whose distribution p_g is match to the distribution p_d.

To achieve this goal, we establish a SeqGAN model. The SeqGAN model starts with a Θ-parameterized generator G_Θ and a φ-parameterized discriminator D_φ. Then, Our goal is to train G_Θ to produce satisfactory sequences constantly. When G_Θ is trained to generate one sequence $Y_{1:L} = (y_1, \dots, y_l, \dots, y_L)$,

D_φ will provide a guidance Q to select the next action y_l from state $Y_{1:l-1}$. The guidance Q is defined by:

$$Q(a = y_l) = \begin{cases} \frac{1}{N}\sum_{n=1}^{N} D_\varphi(Y_{1:L}^n), Y_{1:L}^n \in MC^{G_\Theta}(Y_{1:l}; N) & l < L; \\ D_\varphi(Y_{1:l}) & l = L, \end{cases} \quad (3)$$

where $MC(Y_{1:l}; N)$ presents a N-time Monte Carlo search. It is a heuristic search method that is used as state-action evaluation [5].

After training G_Θ iteratively, the D_φ will be re-trained as follows:

$$\min_{\Theta} \mathbb{E}_{Y_{1:L} \sim p_d}[\log D_\Theta(Y_{1:L})] - \mathbb{E}_{Y_{1:L} \sim p_g}[\log(1 - D_\Theta(Y_{1:L}))] \quad (4)$$

Repeat this process and the parameters (Θ and φ) will be updated continually until convergence. So far, G_Θ can generate more realistic sequence $Y_{1:L}$. We regard the generated sequence as mimicking behavior of bots.

3.5   The Mimicking Attack Algorithm

We present the detail of launching a mimicking attack in Algorithm 2. It works on the assumption that the attacker meets the requirements in Sect. 3.1. After obtaining User-Behavior set S, the attacker build a SeqGAN model and train G_Θ and D_φ. When the model converges, the attacker only transmits the parameter Θ to bots. When the parameter is in hand, each bot can establish a local generator G_Θ. Then, each bot sends requests to web server according to generated results of the local generator. Our algorithm can be used to launch an advanced DDoS attack which masquerades a flash crowd. This methodology can also be applied to other attack scenarios.

Algorithm 2. The Mimicking Attack Algorithm

1: Obtain User-Behavior Set S, and initialize G_Θ and D_φ with random Θ and φ.
2: Pre-train G_Θ on S, and then train G_Θ and D_φ adversarially until SeqGAN converges.
3: Identify current active bots, $\{bots_t\}$. Transmit the parameter Θ to bots and instruct them to run independently.
4: **for all** $bot \in \{bots_t\}$ **do**
5:     Establish a generator G_Θ with Θ.
6:     **while** 1 **do**
7:         Generate mimicking behavior $Y_{1:L}$ via G_Θ;
8:         Launch requests according to $Y_{1:L}$.
9:     **end while**
10: **end for**
11: Introduce new bots and update $\{bots_t\}$.
12: Go to step 4.

---

4 Experiments

4.1 Generate Mimicking Attack

To demonstrate the effectiveness of the proposed mimicking attack algorithm, we use *FIFA1998* dataset. *FIFA1998* is the access log of the France'98 Website for 88 days. There are over 73 million requests in the 66th day, which is widely used as a FC event. Then, we choose the data of the 6th day as the seed data, which can extract 20889 User-Behaviors. Using our proposed method, we generate 70,000 mimicking behaviors of bots which simulate mimicking attack.

In order to build User-Behavior set from seed data with Algorithm 1, we investigate the seed data first. The distribution of users' browsing time is shown in Fig. 2. Based on this, we set $L = 300$, $t_m = 600$. In other words, we take 5 min as the duration time of User-Behavior and 10 min as the max viewing time for an in-line objects.

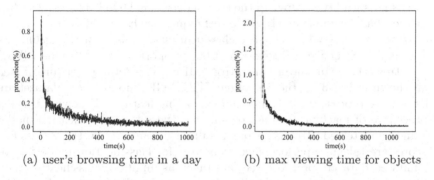

(a) user's browsing time in a day   (b) max viewing time for objects

Fig. 2. Users' browsing time for seed data

When implementing SeqGAN, we leverage Long Short-Term Memory (LSTM) as the generator and Multilayer Perceptron (MLP) as the discriminator. Parameters in the model have to be empirically selected. In this experiment, LSTM is one in depth and MLP is three layers. Each layer has 64 hidden units. The batch size is set to 50 and the training epochs is 400. To prevent unstable training, we employ Wasserstein loss for the discriminator instead of cross entropy loss. Then, we use the trained model to generate 70,000 mimicking behaviors of bots, which are called imitated data. Besides, the data of the 66th day which represents a FC event is called target data.

4.2 Detection System Measures

Can the mimicking attack fool a detection system? To measure the effectiveness, we build a detector to distinguish FC and HTTP DDoS. And then, we analyze its ability in detecting the mimicking attack.

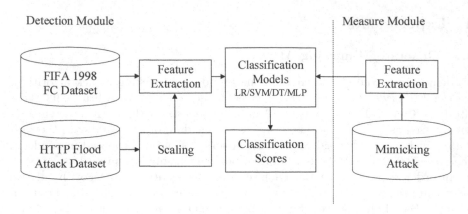

Fig. 3. Measuring mimicking attack by detection system

Measures Design Overview. In the field of detecting DDoS attacks, classification method based on machine learning techniques has been widely used [11, 23]. In this work, we employ four classical classification models to distinguishing FC and HTTP DDoS: Logistic Regression (LR), Support Vector Machine (SVM), Decision Tree (DT), Multilayer Perceptron (MLP). The detail procedure of measures is shown in Fig. 3. In the first stage, HTTP-GET flood DDoS dataset and FC dataset are processed by scaling and extracting features. Following the general procedure of machine learning techniques, these four classification models are trained and tested. To ensure our results are comparable, these classification scores are taken as performance standards for classification models. After that, imitated data are preprocessed and taken as inputs of classification models. Then, we can achieve the classification scores for the imitated data. If an item of imitated data is predicted as FC rather than DDoS, we think it succeeds in evading detection. By comparing classification scores, we evaluate mimicking attack's ability in fooling the detection system.

DataSet and Scaling. To train and test classification models, two datasets are used. One is *FIFA1998* dataset. As described above, the data of the 66th day are labeled as FC. The other is an emulation attack dataset. Due to the lack of real world HTTP DDoS dataset, we set up a testbed environment to generate HTTP-GET flood trace. In the testbed, we deploy a web server running Apache and PHP. Then four DDoS attack tools are used to generate HTTP-Get flood trace: DDoSIM, LOIC, Hulk, GoldEye. When launching attacks, each tool have preset their parameters, along with different number of requests received by web server in a time window. Besides, the bandwidths of the emulation dataset are also different from the *FIFA1998* FC dataset. In order to minimize the impact, we modify the emulation dataset to 850 requests per second with scaling up other features. After that, we can build training set and testing set from these two datasets.

Feature Extraction. Feature extraction plays a significant role in classification models. In the field of detecting DDoS attack, feature extraction is called profiling user behaviors, user behaviors analysis, and so on. When extracted statistical features, we refer to related work in Sect. 2.1. Due to the difference in two datasets, we choose the features which can be obtained from web logs as well as traffic traces. Some individual statistical features, such as *average_packet_size*, are not taken into account. The extracted features are listed in Table 1.

Table 1. Features that extracted from dataset

Feathure	Description
request_rate	Number of requests sent by a users per second
max_frequency	The maximum number of requests sent by a user among sub_time window
mean_frequency	Average number of requests sent by a user among sub_time window
std_frequency	Standard deviation number of requests sent by a user among sub_time window
max_request_interval	Maximum time between two requests sent by a user among sub_time window
mean_request_interval	Average time between two requests sent by a user among sub_time window
std_request_interval	Standard deviation time between two requests sent by a user among sub_time window
max_repeat_rate	The max ratio of the number of requests for same web to the total number of requests
popularity_rate	The ratio of the number of requests for a hot web resource to the total number of requests

Detection Results. When evaluating each classification model, three metrics are used: Accuracy, FPR, FNR. Accuracy measures the rate of the correctly classified for both classes. FNR is the number of items which are misclassified as FC out of total DDoS data. FPR is the ratio of the items misclassified as DDoS to the total FC data. Besides, in order to evaluate the mimicking attack's ability in evading detection, we define a metric: evading rate. It is the proportion of imitated data which are misclassified as FC. By comparing these four metrics, we measure the effectiveness of mimicking attack. Table 2 reports the results. It shows that the most vulnerable models are MLP and LR with evading rate reaching 87%. It needs to be emphasized that the accuracy of MLP model is 98.62%. The result of evading rate is very promising in this case. On the SVM and DT, the evading rates are relatively low, indicating that these classification models are to some extent more robust to the mimicking attack. However, there is still up to 66% possibility for mimicking attack to fool the classifier.

Table 2. The results of measuring mimicking attack by detection system

Metrics	Testing data			Imitated data
	Accuracy	*FNR*	*FPR*	*Evadingrate*
LR	95.07%	2.761%	7.099%	87.94%
DT	97.91%	0.157%	4.023%	66.18%
SVM	98.44%	0.947%	2.173%	74.62%
MLP	98.62%	0.929%	1.831%	91.99%

4.3   Compare Imitated Data to Target Data

Can the mimicking attack pretend to be FC? In order to verify the ability of imitation, we compare the imitated data to target data.

Before comparing the intrinsic features, we investigate the similarity between imitated data and target data visually. Figure 4 shows the visual results. As mentioned above, each element in imitated data is a sequence and is 300 in length. For the visualization of this high-dimensional datasets, we apply a technique to reduce dimensionality, which is called t-Distributed Stochastic Neighbor Embedding (t-SNE). When map high-dimensional data to 2-dimension datapoint, t-SNE can retain relative distance of the data while revealing clusters. As shown in Fig. 4, the results of target data and imitated data do not align perfectly. However, they have very similar global structure. It indicates that the method is able to generate a family of data that hold a set of original features and vary across individual elements. It can be seen that both of them have a low proportion of scattered datapoints. It reveals that the majority users have similar behaviors.

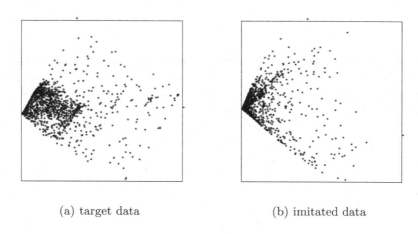

(a) target data   (b) imitated data

Fig. 4. 2-D visualization with t-SNE

In the field of adversarial generation, there is an open research topic to evaluate the quality of imitated data [4,17]. However, web user browsing dynamics have been well studied. In order to evaluate the imitated data that are generated in our experiments, we choose four vital statistical characteristics of web browsing dynamics. In the following, we make comparisons between imitated data and target data from these four aspects.

In-Line Objects Popularity. Popularity refers to the request frequency of in-line objects. As pointed by [6] and [22], the popularity can be modeled to a Zipf-Mandelbrot distribution. Sort all in-line objects by their request frequency from the most to the least as $o_1, o_2, o_3, \ldots, o_N$. Let $Pr(o_j)$ be the request frequency of object o_j. The distribution can be formulated as:

$$Pr(o_j) = \frac{\Omega}{(j+q)^z}, \tag{5}$$

where z and q are the factors. Since $\sum_{j=1}^{N} Pr(o_j) = 1, \Omega = (\sum_{j=1}^{N} \frac{1}{(j+q)^z})^{-1}$.

Figure 5 shows the comparison about popularity. We compare the imitated data not only with target data, but also with the fitted data. We find that the imitated values are very close to the target values. Besides, the popularity distribution of in-line objects also follows a Zipf-Mandelbrot distribution.

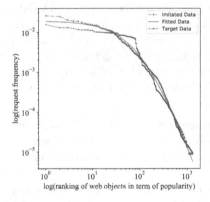 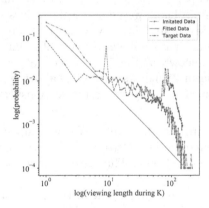

Fig. 5. The distribution of objects popularity

Fig. 6. The distribution of viewing length

Viewing Length. The viewing length refers to the number of web pages that a user browses in a browsing duration. According to [10] and [31], viewing length of all users follows the inverse Gaussian distribution. We adopt it for in-line objects.

Let $Pr(n)$ be a probability of viewing length L during K. The distribution can be formulated as:

$$Pr(n) = \sqrt{\frac{\lambda}{2\pi n^3}} \exp\left[\frac{-\lambda(n-\mu)^2}{2\mu^2 n}\right], \tag{6}$$

where μ and λ are the factors.

Figure 6 reports the comparison results of viewing length. It is worth noting that imitated data have a much smaller distance with target data than fitted data. It verifies that the effectiveness of our approach is obviously better than the approach in [31] on the dataset. It can be observed that there are oscillations of imitated data in long viewing length. This is an explanation: an attacker intents bots to send more compact HTTP requests for efficiency. Thus, having a longer viewing length is accepted for imitated data.

Viewing Time for an In-Line Object. Viewing time for a given web page is considered to follow a Pareto distribution [15,31]. If we adopt it to in-line objects, the probability of the viewing time for a given object $Pr(t)$ can be formulated as:

$$Pr(t) = \alpha_p t_m^{\alpha_p} t^{-(\alpha_p+1)}, \tag{7}$$

where α_p is the factor.

Because there is a significant difference in viewing time between objects and webpages. Fitting the probability distributions to Pareto distribution doesn't work. Thus, we compare the values of viewing time only between target data and imitated data. We select two popular in-line objects(ID3 and ID82, where the number is the identification of in-line objects in *FIFA1998* dataset) to analyze. As shown in Fig. 7, imitated data are well matched with target data in short viewing time. As mentioned above, attackers have no expectation of long viewing time for an object. Results demonstrate that the imitated data meet the demand.

Jump Probability. We also employ jump probability to profile web browsing dynamic. Let $Pr(o_{ji})$ be the probability of object o_j skipping to o_i during a period of time. Thus, given an in-line object o_i, we can acquire the distribution of $Pr(o_{ji})$.

With regard to the distributions of jump probability imitated data and target data, we use Euclidean distance and Jensen-Shannon distance to measure the similarity of distributions between imitated data and target data. In this experience, we choose seven popular in-line objects (ID3, ID5, ID7, ID20, ID40, ID82, ID114) for individual tests. Table 3 reports that most of the values are stable in a range. In our experiments, we find that there is not a strong correlation between the similarity and the popularity.

4.4   Compare with Yu et al. [31]

Yu et al. propose a semi-Markov based approach for mimicking attack [31], which is the most related work to ours. Their approach bases on the assumptions that

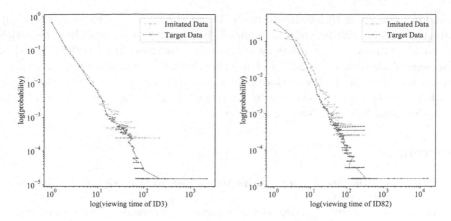

Fig. 7. The distribution of viewing time for a given object

Table 3. Similarity between the imitated data and target data in jump probability.

Object	ID3	ID5	ID7	ID20	ID40	ID82	ID114
Euclidian distance	0.19071	0.23970	0.46616	0.39744	0.27288	0.31512	0.40825
Jensen-Shannon distance	0.20289	0.24267	0.64691	0.25385	0.22875	0.46164	0.55777

three statistical characteristics of web browsing dynamics follow three distribution models respectively. As shown in Sect. 4.3, inverse Gaussian distribution and Pareto distribution don't accurately represent the viewing length and the viewing time for in-line objects on the dataset. Because our approach doesn't depend on any prior hypothesis of probability distribution, it works better on the dataset. Besides, the approach in [31] needs amounts of seed data to extract more accurate parameters. In our approach, generative adversarial technology reduces the dependency on the magnitude of seed data. What's more, the approach in [31] needs the historical information about the volume of web page requests for a given time. However, it is hard to obtain the whole day's requests distribution in reality. In our approach, the number of active bots can be decided by any attack modes, which is more flexible.

5   Conclusion

In this paper, we make an exploratory attempt to launch an advanced attack for web server. Our goal is to instruct the bots to send HTTP requests that are similar to normal users. For this purpose, we design a SeqGAN-based framework. The key of the framework is following: extracting normalized User-Behaviors by a multi-step algorithm, and generating mimicking behaviors for bots with adversary training. To validate our approach, we first establish a detection system that is employed four machine learning classifiers. Experimental results show that it is easy for the mimicking attack to fool the detector. In addition, we compare mimicking behaviors to legitimate users' behaviors regarding to four statistical characteristics of web browsing dynamics. Experimental results show that the approach we proposed has made an encouraging progress in imitation. The distributions of these four statistical characteristics also confirm a finding: a small number of values are in the majority. In summary, our approach for mimicking attack is effective in various aspects. For the future work, the defence of this mimicking attack is promising setup to study.

References

1. Netscout's 14th annual worldwide infrastructure security report. https://www.netscout.com/report/
2. Arjovsky, M., Chintala, S., Bottou, L.: Wasserstein generative adversarial networks. In: International Conference on Machine Learning, pp. 214–223 (2017)
3. Berthelot, D., Schumm, T., Metz, L.: BEGAN: boundary equilibrium generative adversarial networks. arXiv preprint arXiv:1703.10717 (2017)
4. Borji, A.: Pros and cons of gan evaluation measures. Comput. Vis. Image Underst. **179**, 41–65 (2019)
5. Browne, C.B., et al.: A survey of monte carlo tree search methods. IEEE Trans. Comput. Intell. AI Games **4**(1), 1–43 (2012)
6. Burklen, S., Marron, P.J., Fritsch, S., Rothermel, K.: User centric walk: An integrated approach for modeling the browsing behavior of users on the web. In: Proceedings of the 38th Annual Symposium on Simulation, pp. 149–159. IEEE Computer Society (2005)
7. Giralte, L.C., Conde, C., De Diego, I.M., Cabello, E.: Detecting denial of service by modelling web-server behaviour. Comput. Electr. Eng. **39**(7), 2252–2262 (2013)
8. Goodfellow, I., et al.: Generative adversarial nets. In: Advances in Neural Information Processing Systems, pp. 2672–2680 (2014)
9. Hoque, N., Bhattacharyya, D.K., Kalita, J.K.: Botnet in DDoS attacks: trends and challenges. IEEE Commun. Surv. Tutor. **17**(4), 2242–2270 (2015)
10. Huberman, B.A., Pirolli, P.L., Pitkow, J.E., Lukose, R.M.: Strong regularities in world wide web surfing. Science **280**(5360), 95–97 (1998)
11. Jaafar, G.A., Abdullah, S.M., Ismail, S.: Review of recent detection methods for HTTP DDoS attack. J. Comput. Netw. Commun. **2019** (2019)
12. Jung, J., Krishnamurthy, B., Rabinovich, M.: Flash crowds and denial of service attacks: characterization and implications for CDNs and web sites. In: Proceedings of the 11th International Conference on World Wide Web, pp. 293–304. ACM (2002)
13. Liao, Q., Li, H., Kang, S., Liu, C.: Feature extraction and construction of application layer DDoS attack based on user behavior. In: Proceedings of the 33rd Chinese Control Conference, pp. 5492–5497. IEEE (2014)
14. Luo, X., et al.: Anomaly detection for application layer user browsing behavior based on attributes and features. J. Phys: Conf. Ser. **1069**(1), 12072 (2018)
15. Mitzenmacher, M.: A brief history of generative models for power law and lognormal distributions. Internet Math. **1**(2), 226–251 (2004)
16. Miu, T.N., Wang, C., Luo, D.X., Wang, J.: Modeling user browsing activity for application layer DDoS attack detection. In: Deng, R., Weng, J., Ren, K., Yegneswaran, V. (eds.) SecureComm 2016. LNICST, vol. 198, pp. 747–750. Springer, Cham (2017). https://doi.org/10.1007/978-3-319-59608-2_42

17. Molnár, S., Megyesi, P., Szabó, G.: How to validate traffic generators? In: 2013 IEEE International Conference on Communications Workshops (ICC), pp. 1340–1344. IEEE (2013)
18. Najafabadi, M.M., Khoshgoftaar, T.M., Calvert, C., Kemp, C.: User behavior anomaly detection for application layer DDoS attacks. In: 2017 IEEE International Conference on Information Reuse and Integration (IRI), pp. 154–161. IEEE (2017)
19. Qi, G.J.: Loss-sensitive generative adversarial networks on lipschitz densities. arXiv preprint arXiv:1701.06264 (2017)
20. Radford, A., Metz, L., Chintala, S.: Unsupervised representation learning with deep convolutional generative adversarial networks. arXiv preprint arXiv:1511.06434 (2015)
21. Rigaki, M., Garcia, S.: Bringing a GAN to a knife-fight: adapting malware communication to avoid detection. In: 2018 IEEE Security and Privacy Workshops (SPW), pp. 70–75. IEEE (2018)
22. Silagadze, Z.: Citations and the Zipf-Mandelbrot's law. arXiv preprint physics/9901035 (1999)
23. Singh, K., Singh, P., Kumar, K.: Application layer HTTP-GET flood DDoS attacks. Comput. Secur. **65**, 344–372 (2017)
24. Singh, K., Singh, P., Kumar, K.: User behavior analytics-based classification of application layer HTTP-GET flood attacks. J. Netw. Comput. Appl. **112**, 97–114 (2018)
25. Sun, D., Yang, K., Lv, B., Shi, Z.: Could we beat a new mimicking attack? In: 2017 19th Asia-Pacific Network Operations and Management Symposium (APNOMS), pp. 247–250. IEEE (2017)
26. Von Ahn, L., Blum, M., Langford, J.: Telling humans and computers apart automatically. Commun. ACM **47**(2), 56–60 (2004)
27. Xie, Y., Yu, S.Z.: A large-scale hidden semi-Markov model for anomaly detection on user browsing behaviors. IEEE/ACM Trans. Netw. **17**(1), 54–65 (2009)
28. Xu, C., Zhao, G., Xie, G., Yu, S.: Detection on application layer DDoS using random walk model. In: 2014 IEEE International Conference on Communications (ICC), pp. 707–712. IEEE (2014)
29. Ye, C., Zheng, K., She, C.: Application layer DDoS detection using clustering analysis. In: Proceedings of 2012 2nd International Conference on Computer Science and Network Technology, pp. 1038–1041. IEEE (2012)
30. Yu, L., Zhang, W., Wang, J., Yu, Y.: SeqGAN: sequence generative adversarial nets with policy gradient. In: Thirty-First AAAI Conference on Artificial Intelligence (2017)
31. Yu, S., Guo, S., Stojmenovic, I.: Fool me if you can: mimicking attacks and anti-attacks in cyberspace. IEEE Trans. Comput. **64**(1), 139–151 (2015)

Suzzer: A Vulnerability-Guided Fuzzer Based on Deep Learning

Yuyue Zhao[1]([✉]), Yangyang Li[2], Tengfei Yang[2], and Haiyong Xie[1,2,3]

[1] University of Science and Technology of China, Hefei 230027, Anhui, China
`yyzha0@mail.ustc.edu.cn`
[2] National Engineering Laboratory for Public Safety Risk Perception and Control
by Big Data (NEL-PSRPC), Beijing 100041, China
`{liyangyang,yangtengfei}@cetc.com.cn`
[3] Advanced Innovation Center for Human Brain Protection,
Capital Medical University, Beijing 100054, China

Abstract. Fuzzing is a simple and effective way to find software bugs. Most state-of-the-art fuzzers focus on improving code coverage to enhance the possibility of causing crashes. However, a software program oftentimes has only a fairly small portion that contains vulnerabilities, leading coverage-based fuzzers to work poorly most of the time. To address this challenge, we propose *Suzzer*, a vulnerability-guided fuzzer, to concentrate on testing code blocks that are more likely to contain bugs. Suzzer has a light-weight static analyzer to extract ACFG vector from target programs. In order to determine which code blocks are more vulnerable, Suzzer is equipped with prediction models which get the prior probability of each ACFG vector. The prediction models will guide Suzzer to generate test inputs with higher vulnerability scores, thus improving the efficiency of finding bugs. We evaluate Suzzer using two different datasets: artificial LAVA-M dataset and a set of real-world programs. The results demonstrate that in the best case of short-term fuzzing, Suzzer saved 64.5% of the time consumed to discover vulnerabilities compared to VUzzer.

Keywords: Prediction model · Deep learning · Vulnerability-guided fuzzing

1 Introduction

Vulnerability is the most intuitive manifestation of information security. Currently the main threat to computer systems is software vulnerabilities. Fuzzing [1] is an automated penetration technique that discovers vulnerabilities in software by sending randomly generated data to the program and monitoring for anomalies in the output.

In view of the current research status, fuzzing can be divided into two categories, namely, generation-based fuzzing (see, *e.g.*, [2–5]) and mutation-based fuzzing (see, *e.g.*, [6–13]). More specifically, generation-based fuzzing is based

© Springer Nature Switzerland AG 2020
Z. Liu and M. Yung (Eds.): Inscrypt 2019, LNCS 12020, pp. 134–153, 2020.
https://doi.org/10.1007/978-3-030-42921-8_8

primarily on model-based or grammar-based approaches to satisfy the software program syntax and semantic test input generation. In particular, model-based generations construct input through some of the given format specifications (see, e.g., [2–4]), while grammar-based fuzzing test uses the known input syntax to construct the input test set (see, e.g., [5]). Mutation-based fuzzing are guided by the program execution environment information and program analysis techniques to mutate the inputs in fuzzing (see, e.g., [6–13]).

Generation-based fuzzing can generate valid inputs using known information to increase code-coverage. However, it needs significant amounts of manual input to satisfy the format specification, especially when testing large-scale software; if the input format is wrong, it reports a significant number of errors. Thus, generation-based fuzzing is not flexible enough, and cannot process unknown programs. On the contrary, mutation-based fuzzing can use existing input mutated to generate new inputs without relying on input syntax, with better scalability and applicability. Therefore, most state-of-the-art fuzzers are mutation-based fuzzers.

Most mutation-based fuzzers focus on improving code coverage to increase the likelihood of triggering a crash. Improving code coverage can indeed explore more program location areas and discover more vulnerabilities. However, it is not practicable to completely explore all the code branches of a given program for many reasons. First, if the software program grows larger, it's more difficult to solve all path constraints. Second, it is time consuming to improve code coverage. Third, the vulnerable code usually contributes to only a small portion of the entire code. For example, Liu *et al.* [15] found 52.31% bugs are located with no more than 10% of the code. Shin *et al.* [14] revealed that 21% of source code files in Firefox browsers are faulty, and only 3% of them have vulnerabilities.

To address the above challenge, we propose a vulnerability-guided fuzzing framework, *Suzzer*, to achieve efficient fuzzing. By vulnerability-guided, we mean that fuzzers could focus on testing inputs for the basic blocks with higher probability of vulnerability rather than blindly treating them as equal.

We summarize our contributions as follows. Firstly, we studied the negative impacts of inefficiently fuzzing in coverage-based fuzzers. Especially, we noted that by focusing on vulnerabilities, we could solve such problem and improve its capability of vulnerability discovery. Secondly, we built a vulnerability prediction model based on basic blocks to achieve vulnerability-guided strategy in Suzzer. Since there are no readily available datasets for vulnerability detection in basic block granularity, we present the first dataset for setting up the prediction model. The dataset is derived from NIST. Lastly, We implemented a prototype based on VUzzer, and evaluated it on three artificial applications and six real-world programs. The effectiveness of Suzzer has been partially validated by its ability to save up to 64.5% time consumed to discover vulnerabilities compared to VUzzer.

2 Motivation

2.1 Vulnerability-Guided Fuzzing

Since most of the existing state-of-the-art fuzzers [6, 10–13] are mutation-based, how to improve code coverage has become a top priority. Figure 1 breaks a typical mutation-based workflow into stages. Fuzzers take in the program and inputs, analysis program and use those information to mutate inputs, select inputs to feed the target program, monitor program to filter inputs and export vulnerabilities. Suzzer is a mutation-based fuzzer.

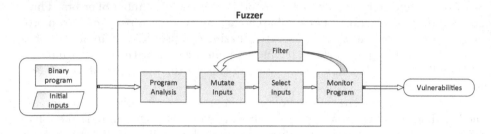

Fig. 1. Mutation-based fuzzing workflow

Corresponding to input mutation, fuzzers can be divided into three categories. Blackbox fuzzers [3, 16, 17] mutate inputs blindly until causing application crash. Whitebox fuzzers [18, 19] usually test with the source code in mind, it performs better because of enough knowledge. Greybox fuzzers [6, 10–13, 20] still tests black box software without source code, but it can analyze binary program to get some useful information before fuzzing. Since the current commercial software is closed source, Suzzer is a greybox fuzzer.

Based on the application exploration strategy, there are two different fuzzers. Directed fuzzers [10, 13, 20] tend to select inputs that cover a specific set of paths, whereas coverage-based fuzzers [6, 11, 12] are more inclined to choose those inputs that can cover a wider range of paths in order to trigger more crash. Suzzer is a directed fuzzer.

In order to understand why we proposed suzzer, Listing 1.1 describes a simple situation that usually happens in program. In the main function, there is a normal magic byte check from line 6 to line 11. Then it is from the second check for buffer content at line 12. Within the subsequent check, there are several for loops and nested conditions to match the fields in data and buffer from line 15 to line 24. In the most state-of-the-art fuzzers, they will spend a lot of computing resources to generate inputs to bypass conditional checks. However, those checks code don't contain any vulnerabilities. In fact, there is a function code that contains a stack buffer overflow just in line 34.

Based on the situation we have just discussed, we developed Suzzer, that automatically tests for code which has a higher probability of containing vulnerabilities. Unlike existing state-of-the-art fuzzers, Suzzer doesn't judge inputs by triggering depth, breadth, size of unknown area, etc. Suzzer is more focus on bugs. Before starting the fuzzing test, Suzzer first perform static analysis on the software program to obtain the code path, branch, basic-block distribution, the internal assembly code of the code basic-block, etc. We input the information obtained into the vulnerability prediction model, predict the prior probability that each basic-block may contain bugs, and then convert the obtained prior probability into a score and enter the fuzzing loop. In the fuzzing loop session, those test inputs that are more likely to trigger a program crash are selected for the next loop according to the path scores.

Listing 1.1. A motivating example that usually happends

```
1   #define SIZE 1024
2   int main(int argc, char **argv){
3       unsigned char data[SIZE];
4       unsigned char buffer[SIZE];
5       char *fd;
6       //======== Magic bytes check ==========
7       if(buffer[0]==0xAB && buffer[1]==0xCD)
8           printf("Magic bytes!");
9       else{
10          printf("InCorrect!");
11          return 0;}
12      //========= Another check ==========
13      if(buffer[5]=='yes' && buffer[6]=='hello'){
14          printf("One step check");
15          for(int i=0; i < sizeof(data); i++){
16              //===== Other nested checks ======
17              if (strcmp(&buffer[10], "World!", 4) == 0){
18                  printf("Two step check passed");
19                  /* some nested condition*/
20                  printf("some harder condition passed");
21                  ...}
22              else
23                  /* some other nested condition*/
24                  ...}}
25          else{
26              printf("Invalid ERROR!");
27      '''
28      Start any other Task!
29      '''
30      return 0;}
31      /*
32      *Some code that hide vulnerabilities.
33      */
34      stack_buffer_overflow(fd, buffer, data);
35      return 0;
36  }
```

2.2 Vulnerability Prediction

In order to bulid the prediction model, we propose some guiding principles in this section. Those principles are concentrated on answering three questions: A. How to represent software to feed the prediction model? B. What is the appropriate granularity for both vulnerability detection and fuzzing? C. Which model is suitable for vulnerability prediction?

A. Software Representation. Since machine learning model takes vectors as input, we need to represent software as vectors. In bug search area, the CFG (Control Flow Geaph) [26] is widely used as a common feature. CFG can be transformed into different basic-block level attributes named ACFG (Attributed Control Flow Graph) [25], that is the actual input vector of our prediction model.

B. Appropriate Granularity. As a vulnerability detection tool, Suzzer not only needs to predict the possibility of vulnerability in the program, but also needs to detect the location. If the program is represented by too large a granularity [20] (function mode, etc.), although the display of the vulnerability rate can be obtained, it is not conducive to locating the location of the program vulnerability. By contrary, too small granularity (assembly statements [21]) covers too little information, which is not conducive to vulnerability prediction. Therefore, we adopt the basic block as the granularity unit, which is more suitable for fuzzing.

C. Model Selection. Traditional machine learning algorithms rely on human experts to define learning rules and may miss many information, which is subjective and often incur high false negative rates. Therefore, at least in vulnerability detection area, traditional ML methods are not appropriate. However, neural networks can automatically learn data features by adjusting the size and structure of the network to control learning, which makes it more flexible and more robust.

The vulnerability probability of a basic-block depends not only on its own information and architecture, but also on the location of basic-block, and the neighboring blocks of the basic block. Therefore, the basic M-P neuron network doesn't work well.

While Long Short-Term memory [30] (LSTM) neurons differ from standard M-P neuron networks. LSTM has a feedback connection that not only processes a single data point (such as an image), but also processes sequence data (such as statements and audio). Each of our programs can be considered as a sequence of basic blocks, so it is suitable for our prediction model. We will discuss the details in subsequent sections.

3 Design Overview

The main components and workflow of Suzzer are described in Fig. 2. Here we introduce the main components. The details will be shown in the following sections.

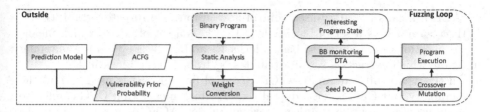

Fig. 2. Overview of suzzer

- Prediction Model: Suzzer uses a predictive model built by a neural network (see Sect. 4.3) to predict a priori vulnerability probability for the target software basic block. The input of the prediction model is the extracted software basic block feature data ACFG (see Sect. 4.2), and the output is a prior probability that the basic block may cause a bug. The fuzzer uses this as a standard for vulnerability-oriented testing.
- Fuzzer: We use an existing coverage guided fuzzer—VUzzer [10] to complete the fuzzing loop (see Sect. 6). Suzzer needs to monitor the probability of a basic block vulnerability, which could generate test inputs with higher vulnerability score and monitor the test state of the program, and recording whether the program crashes at the same time. All of the above provide interested states for the next fuzzing.
- Link module: We use the weight conversion module (see Sect. 5) to connect the Prediction Model and the Fuzzer to convert the vulnerability probability into a scalar score that the Fuzzer can recognize.

4   Prediction Model

4.1   Problem Description

In this section, we abstract the basic block sequence triggered by fuzzing input into a path. The path triggered by various inputs are obviously different. Assuming that the software contains a set of basic-blocks $SW = \{b_1, b_2, b_3, ..., b_n\}$, then considered the triggered basic blocks sequence is $[b_1, b_3, b_7, b_{12}, b_{14}, ...]$. Each basic block in sequence includes the probability of its vulnerability $prob(b_i)$. This prior probability then enters the fuzzing loop, guiding the fuzzer to spend more resources on those block sequences that have a higher probability of containing a bug, making the trigger vulnerability more sensitive.

The input of the prediction model is the basic block vector ACFG [25], and the output is the vulnerability probability.

4.2   Software Feature Extraction

The input for deep learning or neural networks is vectors, so the selection of vector granularity is the first step in predicting. In this paper, the basic block is used as the granularity unit, and the ACFG is used as the carrier to predict the program vulnerabilities, which is more suitable for fuzzing.

ACFG, means the attributed control flow graph, is a directed graph $G =<V, W, \phi >$, and V is a set of blocks; $E \subseteq V \times V$ is a set of edges, which means the connections between these basic blocks V, and $\varphi : V \to \sum$ is the mapping function, which extracts a set of attributes $\sum$ from a basic block in V.

In the usual software analysis, CFG(control flow graph) is used to find the vulnerability, but CFG is not a digital vector, which means that CFG cannot be directly used as input to the deep learning model. ACFG is a suitable way to represent CFG with a large number of basic block level feature values. Each basic block in ACFG is represented by a set of feature values, where each dimension of the feature number set is a specified attribute value. In this approach, the entire binary program can be converted into a vector of values.

Figure 3 shows the workflow of extracting software data. First, we disassembled the binary software datasets to obtain the control flow graph(CFG) of the program. The CFG is the common feature used in bug search and can be extracted by popular reverse tools like IDA pro [32].

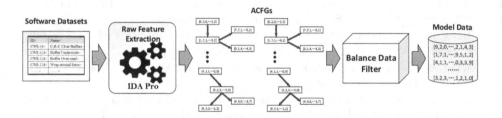

Fig. 3. The data extracting overview

Then, the raw feature is extracted from each basic block and converted into a numerical vector, the vector of the feature can be utilized to distinguish each basic block. Since a software is complex and consists of a large number of network relations, the raw feature can be a statistical attribute, a structural attribute, or a semantic attribute, etc. We choose statistical and structural two properties to represent the basic block vector, because a vector not only needs to count in the operation memory and the instruction characteristics of the data, but also even if it is the same basic block, the location of the basic block will have a great impact on the probability.

According to the extraction example of the firmware program ACFG in references [20,25,27], our statistical attribute contains 8-dimensional vectors including no. of call instruction, etc. For the specific application scenarios such as fuzzing, we refer to Intel's assembly development manual [31] and expand the number of statistical attribute to 19-dimensional vectors. Inspired by related work and the work on complex network analysis, we divide structural features into two types: num and location. The num contains *no. of offspring* and *no. of betweenness*. *No. of offspring* means the number of children nodes for a basic block, and, *no. of betweenness* counts how many neighbor blocks between a basic block. These two information helps identify the relationships

Table 1. Detailed descriptions of ACFG

Type		Feature name	Num
Statistical features	Instruction	No. of push instruction	10
		No. of pop instruction	
		No. of lea instruction	
		No. of neg instruction	
		No. of cmp instruction	
		No. of test instruction	
		No. of call instruction	
		No. of retn instruction	
		No. of proc instruction	
		No. of endp instruction	
	Instruction set	Data transfer instructions	7
		Logical instructions	
		Branch instruction	
		Boolean instructions	
		Arithmetic instructions	
		Shift instructions	
		All assembly directives	
	Operand	No. of operand	1
	Register	No. of register	1
Structural features	Num	No. of offspring	2
		No. of betweeness	
	Location	Whether head or tail	3
		Distance of entrance (%)	
		Distance of export (%)	
All		Attribute dimensions	24

of basic blocks in software. The location contains three elements. First is *whether head or tail*. Judging *head node* or *tail node* in a program is critical to determining, because it could affect most areas if contains vulnerabilities. The other two are *distance of entrance* and *distance of export*. We determine the distance by calculating the proportion of their current position from the entrance or export. Detailed descriptions of ACFG are listed in Table 1.

Finally, we send those raw features into the balance data filter in order to get suitable data distribution for the model training.

In the feature data extraction part, in order to get the basic block features of structural attributes, such as the number of child nodes and neighbor nodes, we simulate the data structure of the control Flow Graph, named Suree. Suree mainly consists of five parts: head node, head area, data area, tail area and tail node. The head node represents the start address of the basic block, and the tail node represents the end address of the basic block, these two are constituted by a bidirectional pointer. The data area stores are specific assembly instructions.

The head area records the unique identification number side of Suree, and the tail area records the unique identification number of the child nodes. When we analyse the entire binary program, it needs to read Suree's header area to know the location of the basic block from the root node. Similarly, we can read the parent block of the basic block according to the inverse node of the head node, and then count the number of child nodes of the parent block to determine the number of neighbor blocks. The structure is illustrated in Fig. 4.

For the vulnerability labeling, we use IDA pro [32] to analyze the disassembled binary program. Since the source code has been annotated in the specific vulnerable program statement, we can use the regular module to analyze the sentence in a single basic block. If it matches the 'bad' string, the basic block is marked as vulnerable (1), otherwise it is marked as 0. The basic block is vulnerable means it has at least one bug. The marking algorithm is showed in Algorithm 1.

4.3   Model Building

Based on the research in Sect. 2.2, we choose bidirectional LSTM [30] as the core unit of our vulnerability prediction model. The prediction problem can be simplified to a classification that whether a basic block exists a bug, but the key point is that the model predicts the probability of the vulnerability rather than the existence of the vulnerability. Network architecture is illustrated in Fig. 5.

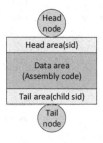

Fig. 4. Suree structure

Algorithm 1. Marking Basic Block as Security/Vulnerable

---

   for each $ea \in readLines(HeadNode, TailNode)$ **do**

     String $stringToJudge = getCommentString(ea)$

     Bool $state = regular.match(r'bad', stringToJudge)$

     if $state$ **then**

       $label = vulnerable$

       return $label$

     end if

   end for

   $label = security$

   return $label$

Since the model is used to predict the vulnerability of each basic block, we add the dense layer at the model exit. The dense layer contains 24 input units and 2 output nodes, which could map 24-dimensional input into 2-dimensional vector of output. The activation function is softmax, and the output P is the possibility we want:

$$P = [p_{safe}, p_{vul}] \tag{1}$$

When the batch size is 128, and the num of hidden layers is 2, the model structure is as Fig. 5. In order to use our prediction model, we need to train those parameters into suitable values. We use *cross entropy loss function* for parameter estimation, the equation is as follow:

$$loss_i = -[y_i * \log p_i + (1 - y_i) * \log(1 - p_i)] \tag{2}$$

where y_i is actual label of i-th data, p_i is the possibility of containing vulnerabilities.

Our parameters can be learned by optimizing Eq. 3 with Stochastic Gradient Descent methods:

$$\min_{W_1, W_2, W_3, \ldots, b_1, b_2, b_3, \ldots} \sum_{i=1}^{n} loss_i \tag{3}$$

where W, b is the parameters need to be updated, n is the number of training data. And finally, the vulnerability prediction model is completed.

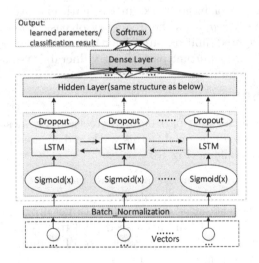

Fig. 5. Prediction model structure

5   Weight-Conversion Module

Weight-conversion module could convert the vulnerability prior probability of the prediction model output to a specific vulnerability score. It is the connection between the prediction model and the fuzzing loop. Our conversion rules are indicated below.

$$Score(b_i) = \begin{cases} \mu * Pred(b_i) & \text{If } \mu * \text{Pred}(b_i) > \xi; \\ \xi & \text{Otherwise}; \end{cases} \quad (4)$$

When a basic block is judged to be vulnerable (the predicted value is 1), μ means the boundary of basic block score. We compared different threshold in 64/128/256/512 to find a better choice. And find when μ=256, Suzzer performs better. Since the prediction model is limited by data size or compute rule, when a basic block is judged to be safe ($Score(b_i) \leq \xi$), it still could cause bugs. So we set $\xi = 1$ to ensure those score bigger than 0 to reduce the shortcomings of the prediction model.

Since the importance of input i depends on the executed path's fitness score f_i, and the path is composed by basic blocks with $Score(b_i)$. We use the method in VUzzer [10] to calculate the fitness score and make it easier to evaluate performance.

$$f_i = \begin{cases} \dfrac{\sum_{b_i \in BB} \log(Freq(b_i))Score(b_i)}{\log(l_i)} Num(BB) & \text{If } l_i > \text{LMAX}; \\ \sum_{b_i \in BB} \log(Freq(b_i))Score(b_i) & \text{Otherwise}; \end{cases} \quad (5)$$

where BB means a set of basic blocks in the path executed by input i. l_i is the length of input i. $Freq(b_i)$ is the frequency of basic block b executed by i. $LMAX$ is a preconfigured limit on input length to balance effects and loss. The fitness calculation is an important part of our vulnerability-guided fuzzing.

6   Fuzzing Loop

Fuzzing loop is the official start part of bug detection. The design and details of evolutionary fuzzing are orthogonal to this work and covered in [10] for VUzzer. The fuzzing step is as follows (Fig. 6):

- Step 1: The fuzzer receive magic bytes and basic block weight from static analysis and prediction model to initialize.
- Step 2: Then fuzzer send initial input seeds to target program. Similar to most mutation-based fuzzers, it contains a seed pool to hold high-quality inputs. The quality is judged by Eq. 5, fuzzer select top K inputs into the seed pool. K is decided from fuzzing process number.
- Step 3: The mutation module uses crossover/mutate inputs from seed pool, and feeds those testcases to the target program for fuzzing.
- Step 4: The BB monitoring module would monitor the target program. It uses Pintool [34] to trace executed basic blocks and implements dynamic taint analysis based on DataTracker [33] to get cmp-instruction, hooks, etc., and send those information to seed pool.
- Step 5: Loop it until the program crashes.

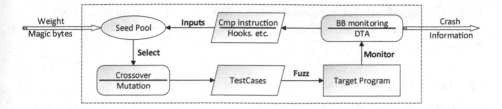

Fig. 6. Fuzzing loop workflow

7   Experimental Evaluation

In this section, we evaluate Suzzer with respect to the accuracy of the prediction model and the effectiveness of fuzzing. First, we briefly describe the data sets used as our train set and test set. Second, we conducted a comparative experiment on the determination of hyperparameters in the existing prediction model, and determined the conclusion that the prediction model can achieve a better result on the test set when the super-parameters have different values. Finally, we put the Suzzer into the LAVA-M [36] dataset and under realistic conditions for testing, and compare the test results with other state-of-art fuzzers.

7.1   Experiment Setup

Prediction Experiment. The prediction model is divided into two parts: ACFG data extraction and model building. For the ACFG extraction, we write the plugin to the disassembler tool IDA Pro in python, and open 30 threads for batch extraction. For the model building, we implement the neural network in Tensorflow in Python.

Our experiments were conducted on a server with 64 GB memory, 40 cores at Intel®Xeon®CPU E5-2640 2.40 GHz, 500 GB hard drives and two GeForce GTX 1080 TI GPU cards.

Fuzzing Experiment. Our fuzzer is improved on the existing fuzzer, VUzzer, and transform coverage-based fuzzing into vulnerability-guided fuzzing.

We conduct the fuzzing test on a virtual machine with Ubuntu 14.04 LTS. The virtual machine is configured with 8 GB memory, 4 cores at 2.40 GHz Intel CPU, 40 GB Storage.

7.2   Data Preparation

Collecting Programs. Since there are not any available data in software vulnerability prediction area, we propose the dataset for evaluating programs and detecting bugs. The dataset is derived from the National Institute of Standards and Technology (NIST) [35], including 83 CWE-ID from category CWE-14 to CWE-911. Each ID class contains several programs written by C/C++, we delete

CWE-364 (signal-handler-race-condition), CWE-365 (race-condition-in-switch), etc., which cannot trigger by fuzzing. Our data set contains a total of 100,883 programs.

7.3 Data Preprocessing

The ACFG data extracted from the binary software cannot be directly input into the model for prediction, because in a software, the basic blocks containing the vulnerability only accounts for a small proportion of all the basic blocks, which leads to data unbalance. For example, assuming that the basic blocks of the vulnerability in the dataset accounts for 10% (which is already a fairly high percentage in normal software), then even if the model predicts all basic blocks as safe (means the model has no classification ability), the model's accuracy remains Up to 90%, that is, the learning space is small. Therefore, we should try to balance the number of basic blocks in the data set that contain vulnerabilities or security.

By Sect. 4.2, 100,883 binary programs are extracted by static analysis and the results are as follows:

```
Before Cleanning data, positive = 1373452
Before Cleanning data, acfg's shape = (24, 6264213)
Before Cleanning data, label's shape = (2, 6264213)
```

More than six million basic blocks have been extracted. The data set is adequate. Therefore, the method of randomly removing the

```
After Cleanning data, positive = 1373452
After Cleanning data, acfg's shape = (24, 2746905)
After Cleanning data, label's shape = (2, 2746905)
```

After culling, it still contains more than two million sets of feature data. We select 99% of them as the training set, and 1% of them as the test set.

7.4 Hyperparametric Analysis

In the process of deep learning, there are many hyperparameters and optimization methods to choose. During our vulnerability prediction model, it's a process based on experiment and experience to achieve better choice for hyperparameters. We compared batch size, hidden layer units and hidden layer depth in the model structure Fig. 5, the performance is showed in Fig. 7.

Batch Size: Figure 7a shows the impact of different batch size of 64, 128, 256. Although the accuracy curve of batch size 64,256 reached the same level after epoch 100, the accuracy of batch size 256 is more stable than 64. We set batch size to 128 because it performs best in terms of accuracy level and stability.

Hidden Layer Units: Figure 7b shows the different hidden layer units in 64,128,256. We can see that the number of hidden layer unit has little influence on the accuracy of the model. As the neural network should be fat enough to fit the parameters, we choose to set hidden layer units as 128.

Hidden Layer Depth: Figure 7c shows the accuracy curve in different hidden layer depth 1,2,4,6. From the figure, we can observe the accuracy performs best when the layer depth equals 6, while single layer networks fared worst, with 2 and 4 equally well. Regardless of the fact that the accuracy of 2 layers is not as good as 6 layers, we choose to set the layer depth of our model as 2 to balance the accuracy, training rate and hardware memory requirements.

When we set hyperparameter to the one discussed above, our model's performance is showed in Fig. 7d, e, f. As our prediction model can be seen as *dualistic classification* in essence, that is, the basic block in the target software is judged to be safe or vulnerable. Therefore, in addition to the accuracy and loss curve, we additionally show recall curve in Fig. 7d. In our model, recall is the fraction of the test sets that are successfully classified.

Obviously, curves together show that as the number of training epoches increases, accuracy and recall are gradually increasing, and loss curve is decreasing. This indicates that the performance of the model is getting better gradually, the prediction error rate of the model on positive and negative samples is reduced, and tends to be stable. And finally, model achieves $accuracy = 90.152\%$, $loss = 0.2137$, $recall = 87.62\%$, and 4.71% of false positive rate, which is a great result in software vulnerability determination that even humans cannot easily determine.

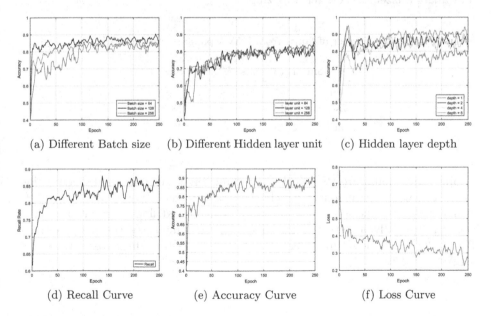

(a) Different Batch size   (b) Different Hidden layer unit   (c) Hidden layer depth

(d) Recall Curve   (e) Accuracy Curve   (f) Loss Curve

Fig. 7. Model performance. The accuracy curve when choose different hyperparametric and final model performance.

7.5   Fuzzing Performance

In order to measure the performance of our vulnerability-guided fuzzing, we choose to test Suzzer on two different datasets: A: LAVA-M, B: Real world Binary.

A: LAVA-M Dataset. Dolan-Gavitt *et al.* [36] designed a system to help measuring miss and false alarm rates. LAVA is a technique for manually injecting bugs into real programs, each bug in LAVA-M has a unique ID and the ID would be printed before binary is crashed by that bug. This makes LAVA a great benchmark and we use the dataset to evaluate Suzzer, LAVA-M consists of four linux binaries–*base64, who, uniq, md5sum*. Since *md5sum* is proved to be not suitable for VUzzer, we remove it.

In order to improve readability, we present the results from the original LAVA paper and 24-h fuzzing in Table 2. The second column in Table 2 shows the total number of injected bugs in LAVA-M, and the third and fourth columns respectively indicate the number of unique bugs triggered by VUzzer and Suzzer for 24-h fuzzing. Each bug in LAVA-M is triggered with a unique ID, and the fault IDs from Suzzer are listed in Table 3.

Obviously, Suzzer's performance is not inferior to VUzzer in 24-h fuzzing, and even better than VUzzer in *uniq* program. Furthermore, as a vulnerability-guided fuzzer, Suzzer is designed to find more bugs in a shorter time and reducing the resource consumption of fuzzing, rather than promoting the code coverage and tries to explore all parts of the target program. Therefore, it's more meaningful to evaluate Suzzer in short-term fuzzing.

Table 2. Number of faults from LAVA paper, suzzer and VUzzer.

Program	Total bugs	VUzzer	Suzzer
uniq	28	3	5
base64	44	18	18
who	2136	44	40

Since four hours are the effective working time(half day) that penetration testers can work continuously, we choose it as the time baseline for our short-term fuzzing. As showed in Fig. 8, Suzzer can indeed find more crashes than VUzzer, especially in terms of timeliness. Table 4 indicates that Suzzer takes 59%, 45.25%, 19% less time to achieve the same crashes which cost VUzzer 4 h in LAVA-M dataset.

Table 3. Fault IDs detected by Suzzer on the LAVA-M dataset.

Program	Fault IDs
uniq	130, 112, 222, 166, 227
base64	1, 582, 843, 841, 222, 386, 831, 284, 784, 806, 805, 278, 584, 276, 583, 235, 790
who	4356, 60, 3798, 3997, 83, 159, 138, 149, 5, 18, 58, 4355, 4364, 10, 9, 6, 7, 22, 1, 14, 79, 75, 3, 26, 89, 8, 81, 4358, 4, 4166, 16, 2, 3968, 20, 4195, 12, 3967, 56, 87

Overall, Suzzer performs well in artificial LAVA datasets. It can detect more vulnerabilities within four hours without decreasing the fuzzing performance of 24-h. We now advance to evaluate Suzzer in real-wrold programs, which is also inspected by other fuzzers.

B: Real-World Dataset. We evaluated Suzzer in a set of real world programs (gif2png, mpg321, tcptrace, pdf2svg, xmlwf, jhead). For each program, we used VUzzer and AFL-QemuMode to fuzz in the same environment (seed selection, etc.) for comparison. We also targeted some dependency libraries and extract some useful information(magic bytes, etc.) to make our real-world evaluation produce progress, such as libpng, libjpeg, libpcap, libpoppler and libexpat.

Figure 8 shows the distribution of crashes within four hours. As showed in this figure, Suzzer and VUzzer can continuously discover crashes in fuzzing, whereas AFL-Qemu performs poorly and can only occasionally trigger 1 or 2 crashes. Unfortunately, those three fuzzers failed to find vaild crashes in xmlwf and jhead. In order to find the reason, we recorded the average fitness input score of programs and find score in jhead&xmlwf(9183, 8468, etc.) is several orders of magnitude lower than others (at least 304457), which may because the program requires a specific set of actions, while our fuzzing strategy does not include it. We intend to fix it in future research.

Based on the preceding analysis, we can see that Suzzer is significantly better than VUzzer, AFL-Qemu in both artificial and real-world programs. As showed in Fig. 8 and Table 4: In time consuming, Suzzer can reduce up to 64.5% of the time to discover vulnerabilities.

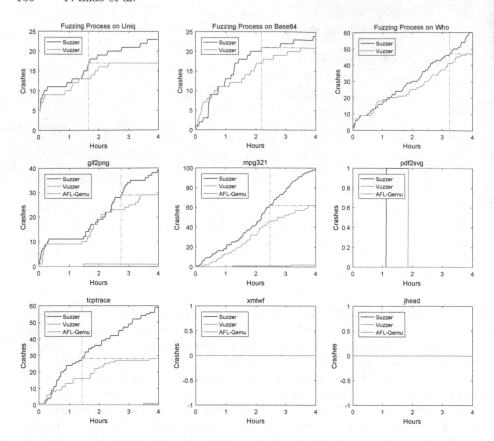

Fig. 8. Distribution of crashes in LAVA-M and real-world programs. (X-axis: The cumulative number of crashes per minute. Y-axis: the specific crashes number. Green line: Time taken by Suzzer to find the same number of crashes as those found by VUzzer during a complete run.) (Color figure online)

8   Related Works

In the preceding sections, we have already stated the vulnerability-guided fuzzing technology. In this section, we investigated additional research work in fuzzing field. This makes the differences and characteristics between our research and the existing work more clearly.

Table 4. Time comparison between Suzzer and VUzzer

TIME (h)	uniq	base64	who	gif2png	mpg321	pdf2svg	tcptrace	xmlwf	jhead
Suzzer	1.64	2.19	3.24	2.74	2.47	N/A	1.42	N/A	N/A
VUzzer	4.0	4.0	4.0	4.0	4.0	N/A	4.0	N/A	N/A
Time saving ratio	59%	45.25%	19%	31.5%	38.25%	N/A	64.5%	N/A	N/A

8.1   Code-Coverage Based Fuzzing Approaches

Existing state-of-the-art fuzzers propose different methods of improving code coverage. For example, AFL [6] generates different inputs to traverse various paths to crash a program, while Angora [12] thinks such method would fail to distinguish the executions of the same branch in different contexts and may overlook new internal states of the program. Angora uses the method of context-sensitive branch coverage to improve code coverage. T-fuzz [11] thinks the main limitation on code coverage is conditional constraint, and removing sanity checks in the target program to increase code coverage. CollAFL [13]'s strategy is providing more accurate coverage information to mitigate path collisions. Those methods are proposed to enhance fuzzing comprehensiveness.

8.2   Deep Learning in Software Area

Deep learning is one of the hottest technologies in the world. It is widely used in computer vision and natural language [24] processing areas but have not yet matured in fields like software. There are some examples of exploration.

For deep learning granularity, Li et al. propose converting the program into a vector representation in the form of SyVC [21]. SyVC is a code snippet consisting of 5 to 10 lines of assembly code, and these codes can be discontinuous, but need to have a semantic relationship, such as operating on the same variable. Xu et al. [23] propose to use software functions as the granularity to detect cross-platform binary code similarity. Rajpal et al. [29] use input bytes to get higher effect execution seed files. Zuo et al. [24] also proposes a method for calculating software similarity, which treats assembly instructions after disassembly of binary programs as plain text.

For model selection, V-Fuzz [20] and VulDeePecker [22] both use neural networks to pre-analyze a large amount of program data to get which parts of the program have higher vulnerability rate, and based on this, the software parts' vulnerability prior probability is predicted. V-fuzz is separated by functions, with graph embedding network [28] as the structure of the vulnerability prediction model. VulDeePecker propose using code gadgets to represent programs, and utilizing long-short-term-memory units to predict vulnerability possibility.

9   Conclusions

In this paper, we argued that coverage-based fuzzers cannot find vulnerabilities efficiently and cost too much computing resources. We proposed a vulnerability-guided fuzzing solution Suzzer, which assigns the priority of input in the state-of-art fuzzer VUzzer, to focus testing on code blocks that are more likely to contain bugs.

In our prototype implementation of Suzzer, we detect which part of the target program has a higher probability of vulnerability by the prediction model. Our prediction results will enter the fuzzing loop through the weight conversion module. This change allows our fuzzer to produce input that priority trigger the vulnerable part and therefore find vulnerabilities faster.

Experiments showed that this solution performs better in short-term fuzzing than other fuzzers. Compared to other state-of-the-art fuzzers (AFL, VUzzer), Suzzer can reduce the time to discover vulnerabilities in most cases, and, furthermore, can detect more crashes with smaller basic block input. This demonstrates that the combination of deep learning and fuzzing is indeed a viable strategy, but there are still many problems that need to be addressed in future research, such as the limitations of datasets.

Acknowledgements. This research is supported in part by the National Key Research and Development Project (Grant No. 2017YFC0820503) and Beijing Science and Technology Plan (Grant No. Z181100009818020).

References

1. Wikipedia. Fuzzing (2018). https://en.wikipedia.org/wiki/Fuzzing/
2. Roning, J., et al.: Protos-systematic approach to eliminate software vulnerabilities. Invited presentation at Microsoft Research (2002)
3. Eddington, M.: Peach fuzzing platform. Peach Fuzzer **34** (2011)
4. Aitel, D.: An introduction to spike, the Fuzzer creation kit (2002)
5. Yang, X., Chen, Y., Eide, E., et al.: Finding and understanding bugs in C compilers. In: ACM SIGPLAN Notices (2011)
6. Zalewski, M.: American fuzzy lop (2017). http://lcamtuf.coredump.cx/afl/
7. Google. honggfuzz (2017). https://google.github.io/honggfuzz/
8. Caca Labs (2017). http://caca.zoy.org/wiki/zzuf/
9. Chen, Y., et al.: EnFuzz: ensemble fuzzing with seed synchronization among diverse Fuzzers. In: 28th USENIX Security Symposium (USENIX Security 2019) (2019)
10. Rawat, S., et al.: VUzzer: application-aware evolutionary fuzzing. In: NDSS, vol. 17 (2017)
11. Peng, H., Shoshitaishvili, Y., Payer, M.: T-Fuzz: fuzzing by program transformation. In: 2018 IEEE Symposium on Security and Privacy (SP). IEEE (2018)
12. Chen, P., Chen, H.: Angora: efficient fuzzing by principled search. In: 2018 IEEE Symposium on Security and Privacy (SP). IEEE (2018)
13. Gan, S., et al.: Collafl: path sensitive fuzzing. In: 2018 IEEE Symposium on Security and Privacy (SP). IEEE (2018)
14. Shin, Y., Williams, L.: Can traditional fault prediction models be used for vulnerability prediction? Empirical Softw. Eng. **18**(1), 25–59 (2013)
15. Liu, C., et al.: SOBER: statistical model-based bug localization. ACM SIGSOFT Softw. Eng. Notes **30**(5), 286–295 (2005)
16. OpenRCE. Sulley fuzzing framework (2015). https://github.com/OpenRCE/sulley
17. Takanen, A., Demott, J., Miller, C.: Fuzzing for Software Security Testing and Quality Assurance. Artech House (2008)
18. Godefroid, P., Levin, M., Molnar, D.: Automated whitebox fuzz testing. In: Network and Distributed System Security Symposium (2008)
19. Ganesh, V., Leek, T., Rinard, M.: Taint-based directed whitebox fuzzing. In: Proceedings of the 31st International Conference on Software Engineering. IEEE Computer Society (2009)

20. Li, Y., et al.: V-Fuzz: vulnerability-oriented evolutionary fuzzing. arXiv preprint arXiv:1901.01142 (2019)
21. Li, Z., et al.: SySeVR: a framework for using deep learning to detect software vulnerabilities. arXiv preprint arXiv:1807.06756 (2018)
22. Li, Z., et al.: VulDeePecker: a deep learning-based system for vulnerability detection. arXiv preprint arXiv:1801.01681 (2018)
23. Xu, X., et al.: Neural network-based graph embedding for cross-platform binary code similarity detection. In: Proceedings of the 2017 ACM SIGSAC Conference on Computer and Communications Security. ACM (2017)
24. Zuo, F., et al.: Neural machine translation inspired binary code similarity comparison beyond function pairs. arXiv preprint arXiv:1808.04706 (2018)
25. Feng, Q., et al.: Scalable graph-based bug search for firmware images. In: Proceedings of the 2016 ACM SIGSAC Conference on Computer and Communications Security. ACM (2016)
26. Control-flow graph (2015). https://en.wikipedia.org/wiki/Control-flow_graph
27. Pewny, J., et al.: Cross-architecture bug search in binary executables. In: 2015 IEEE Symposium on Security and Privacy. IEEE (2015)
28. Yan, S., et al.: Graph embedding and extensions: a general framework for dimensionality reduction. IEEE Trans. Pattern Anal. Mach. Intell. **29**(1), 40–51 (2007)
29. Rajpal, M., Blum, W., Singh, R.: Not all bytes are equal: Neural byte sieve for fuzzing. arXiv preprint arXiv:1711.04596 (2017)
30. Gers, F.A., Schmidhuber, J., Cummins, F.: Learning to forget: continual prediction with LSTM (1999)
31. Intel. Intel 64 and IA-32 architectures software developer manuals (2018). https://software.intel.com/en-us/articles/intel-sdm
32. Hex-Rays. The IDA pro disassembler and debugger (2015). https://www.hex-rays.com/products/ida/
33. Stamatogiannakis, M., Groth, P., Bos, H.: Looking inside the black-box: capturing data provenance using dynamic instrumentation. In: Ludäscher, B., Plale, B. (eds.) IPAW 2014. LNCS, vol. 8628, pp. 155–167. Springer, Cham (2015). https://doi.org/10.1007/978-3-319-16462-5_12
34. Luk, C.-K., et al.: Pin: building customized program analysis tools with dynamic instrumentation. ACM SIGPLAN Not. **40**(6), 190–200 (2005)
35. NVD (2017). http://nvd.nist.gov/
36. Dolan-Gavitt, B., et al.: Lava: large-scale automated vulnerability addition. In: 2016 IEEE Symposium on Security and Privacy (SP). IEEE (2016)

Systems Security

Symmetric Frame Cracking: A Powerful Dynamic Textual CAPTCHAs Cracking Policy

Yueyao Chen[✉], Qianjun Liu, Tianyu Du, Yuan Chen, and Shouling Ji

College of Computer Science, Zhejiang University,
Hangzhou 310027, People's Republic of China
cyy.ki.hy@zju.edu.cn

Abstract. In this work, we analyze the vulnerability of the dynamic textual CAPTCHA (http://fexteam.gz01.bdysite.com/blog/2014/07/captcha-gif/.) and propose a new method to automatically identify the CAPTCHA, which is based on *Basic Vector Space Search Engine (BVSSE)* and *Convolutional Neural Network (CNN)*. Specifically, by exploiting the specific "Symmetric Frame Vulnerability", we can remove most of the noise, therefore greatly reducing the difficulty of cracking. In the process of cracking, we first use the BVSSE to identify the CAPTCHA. The method is simple and fast, but there are problems such as a low recognition rate. Then we choose the CNN to identify the CAPTCHA, and finally get a recognition rate of 99.98% with the average speed of 0.092 s/gif. To have a deeper understanding of the internal recognition process, we visualize the intermediate output of the CNN model. In general, by comparing the two identification methods and visualizing the model, the entire recognition process becomes easier to understand. Based on the above experimental results and analyses, we finally summarize a new and general CAPTCHA attack method and discuss the security of the dynamic textual CAPTCHA.

Keywords: CAPTCHA recognition · Character recognition · Security · Animated GIF image · Image processing

1 Introduction

CAPTCHA (Completely Automated Public Turing Test to Tell Computers and Humans Apart) is a strategy to protect the website from attack by automated programs. In order to enhance the security of the server and verify that the client of the website is a real user rather than programs, von Ahn et al. [1] created CAPTCHA in 2003. So far, a large number of CAPTCHA schemes have been proposed and used in various websites, which effectively prevents the abuse of online services for humans. For example, Alibaba, Tencent, Google, Yahoo and other commercial websites all adopt CAPTCHA to ensure security. However, some works on CAPTCHA show that most schemes can be automatically

© Springer Nature Switzerland AG 2020
Z. Liu and M. Yung (Eds.): Inscrypt 2019, LNCS 12020, pp. 157–172, 2020.
https://doi.org/10.1007/978-3-030-42921-8_9

identified by recognition programs. Therefore, developing a good scheme for CAPTCHA is a very challenging problem.

A good scheme for CAPTCHA ought to be both secure and usable for human. To enhance the security strength and confuse recognition programs, traditional textual CAPTCHAs rely on techniques like distorting the text and overlaying with visual noise.

Dynamic CAPTCHAs have been proposed as a means of overcoming the limitations of traditional single image CAPTCHAs. One of the key principles behind the design of dynamic CAPTCHA schemes is that the information required to solve the CAPTCHA is not contained within a single image. As such, a human has to observe the animated CAPTCHA over its animation cycle to gather appropriate information to recognize the CAPTCHA, which is assumed to be a challenge for computers because the information spreads over multiple images. In the meantime, noise can be added to the challenge of solving dynamic CAPTCHAs, making it more difficult for automated attacks [2].

Our Contributions. In this paper, we propose a new visual noise removal method. Our research shows that even though dynamic CAPTCHAs with complicated animation noise, it is possible to remove the noise by collecting key information from these frames to break the CAPTCHA. Our approach can extract key information from the animation frames and effectively reduce the difficulty of identifying the target dynamic CAPTCHA to the level of ordinary single-character picture recognition.

Roadmap. The rest of this paper is organized as follows. In Sect. 2, we first introduce the basic knowledge of the two identification methods, and then analyze the vulnerabilities of the target CAPTCHA. In Sect. 3, we describe our method in detail. In Sect. 4, we compare the experimental results of the two identification methods and draw conclusions. In Sect. 5, we further optimize the trained model and visualize the CNN intermediate process. In Sect. 6, we put forward a generalized scheme for cracking dynamic CAPTCHAs as well as the corresponding countermeasures, and make a summary of this work.

2   Background

2.1   Basic Vector Space Search Engine

Basic Vector Space Search Engine (BVSSE) exploits the matrix algebra theory to compare documents based on word frequency. The first major component of BVSSE is a term space. A term space consists of every unique word that appears in a collection of documents. The second major component of BVSSE is term counts. Term counts are the simple records of how many times each term occurs in an individual document. By using the term space as the coordinate space and the term counts as the coordinates, we can create a vector for each document. Finally, the similarity between the documents can be evaluated by comparing the angles of the vectors of different documents.

2.2   Convolutional Neural Network

Convolutional Neural Network (CNN) is a deep learning model that is widely used in computer vision applications. The idea of CNN is to extract the features of the input image through filters. In practical applications, the CNN model is often trained by extracting complex image features by multiple layers, therefore realizing the distinction of categories of graphics. Generally, CNN consists of one or more convolutional layers (to extract features) and a top-level fully connected layer (to integrate features).

2.3   Target CAPTCHA

The main purpose of the CAPTCHA is to hinder machine from brute force attempt. Most of the previous CAPTCHAs are static. Using dynamic CAPTCHAs can increase the dimension of image changes, thus improving the difficulty of cracking.

Analysis. As shown in Fig. 1, this dynamic textual CAPTCHA can be divided into two parts, i.e., "content layer" and "noise layer". As for the "content layer", it contains the content that needs to be recognized by the user. The "content layer" in this target CAPTCHA is composed of 6 characters, and its motions have two forms, one is up-and-down translational motion, and the other is a certain angle of self-rotation motion. As for the "noise layer", it is set up to interfere with machine recognition. The ideal design principle of CAPTCHA is to enhance the difficulty of machine recognition without hindering human recognition. The "noise layer" in the target CAPTCHA is expressed as a left-right translation motion plus a self-spin motion. In summary, the "content layer" and "noise layer" movements in the figure are very confusing for machine recognition due to their similarity. Therefore, the dynamic CAPTCHA scheme seems to be in line with the ideal CAPTCHA design principle, but is this really true?

Fig. 1. Target CAPTCHA.

Defense Strategy. From the perspective of machine recognition, the "noise layer" of the left and right periodic panning motion almost obscures the "content layer", which seems difficult to extract features for automatic recognition. The trouble should end it. The periodic translational motion of the character is the core strategy that the dynamic CAPTCHA is difficult to be recognized by the machine. However, the scheme is imperfect.

Vulnerability. In the following, we will introduce the major vulnerability in the scheme (referred to as *"Symmetric Frame Vulnerability"*). It is well-known that a dynamic picture is essentially composed of multiple frames of the same elements with different behavior. After investigating that the "noise layer" and "content layer" both have the characteristics of periodic motion, we consider that if there are such two moments, the "content layer" at the two moments happens to behave exactly same, i.e., the "content layer" is in a symmetrically equal state, and the "noise layer" is in an asymmetrical state at this time. If it exists, we can perform an operation similar to "pixel-wise and" on these two frames, thus extracting the "content layer". The final answer is: there are such moments. After the target CAPTCHA is framed, we select the following perfect vulnerability symmetric frames (frame No. 17 and No. 46 of the picture, see Fig. 2) as the cracking entry point.

Fig. 2. Target symmetric frame.

3   Cracking Process

Based on the above-mentioned "Symmetric Frame Vulnerability", we find such two symmetrical moments. Then, we perform the "pixel-wise and" operation and image recognition.

3.1   Picture Binarization

The picture format of the original frame is RGB. In order to facilitate pixel-level operations, we binarize the frame pictures. Specifically, we first convert the target frame image into the grayscale format, and then map the pixel value to 0 or 1 based on the predefined "rounding" threshold. The visualization of the binary image is shown in the Fig. 3 (which has been denoised as mentioned in the following).

Fig. 3. Binarize the picture.

Fig. 4. Noise removal.

3.2   Noise Removal

Based on the "Symmetric Frame Vulnerability", we know that the characteristics of the "content layer" at the two moments are the same, but the "noise layer" at that two moments are different. Therefore, we can perform a "pixel-wise and" operation over the two symmetric frames, i.e., the result value is obtained by comparing pixel values of the same position in two symmetric frames. Due to the asymmetry property, most noisy pixels will be removed, while the target content pixels keep unchanged after the operation. After this step, we can obviously remove the "noise layer", and the result is shown in Fig. 4.

3.3   Noise Removal Optimization

After implementing the "pixel-wise and" operation, the resulting picture still preserve some "residual noise". In order to facilitate the subsequent image recognition process, we further optimize the resulting pictures. Since the remaining noise is almost isolated points, we use the *nine-square grid noise removal strategy* to remove them. The main idea of this strategy is to first count the black pixels in the nine-square grid around a black dot. If there are less than two other black pixels around, judge it as an isolated noise pixel, and finally delete the isolated noise pixel. The corresponding flow chart is shown in Fig. 5. In the

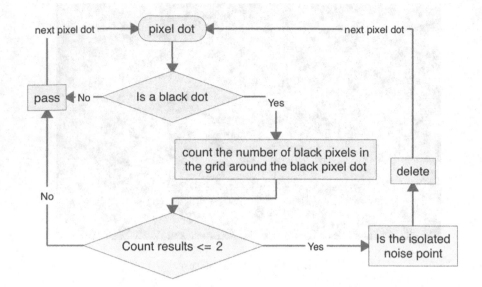

Fig. 5. Flowchart of noise removal optimization.

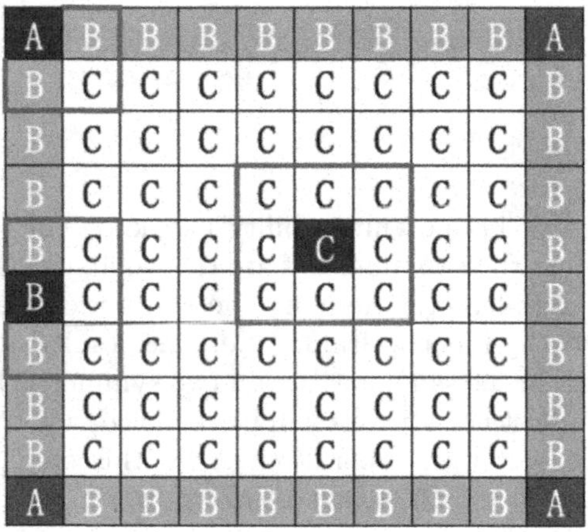

Fig. 6. Nine-square grid around a black dot.

Fig. 7. Noise removal optimization.

algorithm, it is also necessary to perform corresponding counting processing on several special pixel points (refer to the appendix for details), such as the vertex A and the boundary point B of the non-vertex kind in Fig. 6. The result of the noise removal optimization is shown in Fig. 7. It can be seen that most of the "residual noise" has been removed, and the remaining noise has little effect on the recognition.

3.4 Characters Cut

Since the content of the CAPTCHA consists of a series of characters, the image can be decomposed into character level as a recognition unit, i.e., a picture containing only one character. Another advantage of using the character level as the recognition unit is that it can reduce the negative impact of most scattered noise points.

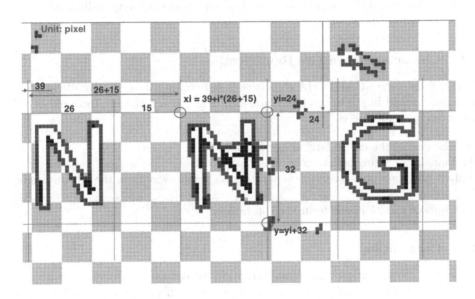

Fig. 8. Segmentation algorithm.

3.5 Segmentation

The characters of textual CAPTCHAs are strange and have various distortions. This is why there does not exist a very general way for character segmentation. Segmentation algorithm is also developed with carefully studying the characteristics of the target pictures to be recognized. Therefore, for the sake of simplicity, we directly select the appropriate starting point and interval to segment the image, as shown in Fig. 8. Other more complicated characters can be segmented by complex algorithms like the projection algorithm and the dripping algorithm, which is beyond the CAPTCHAs discussed in this paper.

The abscissa of the upper left corner of each character is selected as

$$x_i = 39 + i \times (26 + 15),$$

where the 39 represents the horizontal pixel distance of the starting point from the left edge of the entire image, 26 represents the horizontal width of the intercepted character, and 15 represents the margin width between characters. The ordinate of each of these characters is

$$y_i = 24$$

$$y = y_i + 32,$$

where the 24 represents the vertical pixel distance of the starting point from the upper boundary of the entire image, and 32 represents the longitudinal width of the intercepted character.

3.6   Character Image Size Reunification

Because the target CAPTCHA structure is not complicated, the reunification is also determined in the image segmentation. In summary, the size information of the basic unit picture is:

+. The size of the entire GIF image is 300×70.
+. The size of a single character image is 26×32.
+. Left and right characters are separately 39 pixels away from the left and right borders.
+. Character is 24 pixels from the top border.

3.7   Recognition

Using the "Symmetric Frame Vulnerability", we reduce the difficulty of identifying the target dynamic CAPTCHA to the level of ordinary single-character picture recognition. In this case, there is a great number of choices for the identification method, such as BVSSE, SVM and CNN. In this paper, we make an analysis and comparison based on the experimental results of BVSSE and CNN. In order to better understand the identification process in the middle of the CNN, we visualize the intermediate process.

The BVSSE. This method first evaluates the similarity between the target picture and the standard character picture by comparing the cosine values between the vectors of all the pixels of these pictures, then determining the character corresponding to the target picture. As shown in Fig. 9, considering the computational cost, we only compare the target picture to be predicted with 15 standard pictures of each character, and then select the character of the highest

Fig. 9. The number of standard training data of the BVSSE.

Layer (type)	Output Shape	Param #
conv2d_1 (Conv2D)	(None, 30, 30, 32)	896
max_pooling2d_1 (MaxPooling2	(None, 15, 15, 32)	0
flatten_1 (Flatten)	(None, 7200)	0
dropout_1 (Dropout)	(None, 7200)	0
dense_1 (Dense)	(None, 36)	259236
dense_2 (Dense)	(None, 36)	1332

```
=============] - 35s 13ms/step - loss: 5.8029e-05 - acc: 1.0000 - val_loss: 0.0036 - val_acc: 0.9995
```

```
Total params: 261,464
Trainable params: 261,464
Non-trainable params: 0
```

Fig. 10. The structure of the CNN.

similarity as the recognition result. In conclusion, the BVSSE has its pros and cons. For advantages, BVSSE does not require a large number of training iterations, adds/removes erroneous data sets at any time and provides hierarchical matching results, etc. For disadvantages, the classification speed of BVSSE is comparatively slow. These conclusions are verified in our experimental results.

Table 1. Comparison of BVSSE and CNN results.

	Accuracy	Total time of 500 Gifs/s	Time per Gif/s
BVSSE	0.544	1352.45483	2.70491
CNN	0.998	45.98239	0.091965

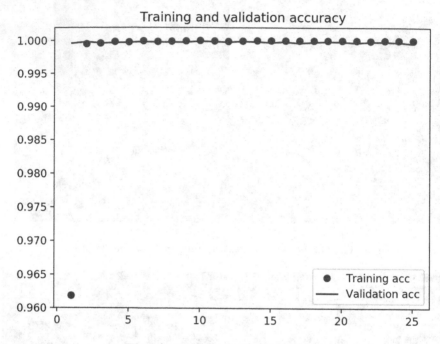

Fig. 11. The accuracy of the CNN.

The CNN. Due to the specific features of the objects to be recognized, the network structure we finally adopt is shown in Fig. 10. As shown in Figs. 11 and 12, though we only use one convolutional layer and one maximum pooling layer, the final recognition performance and speed are quite satisfactory.

4   Experiment Results

From Table 1, we can see that after testing and identifying 500 dynamic CAPTCHA files, the CNN has excellent performance and is superior to the BVSSE. The experimental results show that, the recognition speed of the BVSSE is 2.672 s/gif, i.e., it takes about 2.7 s in average to identify a CAPTCHA, and

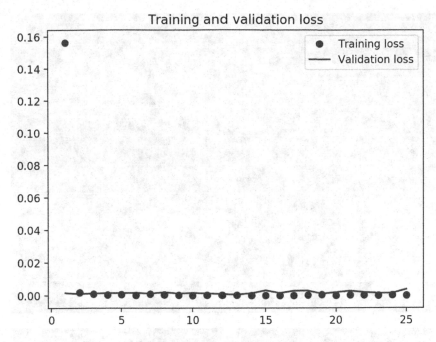

Fig. 12. The loss of the CNN.

the recognition accuracy is only 54.4%. On the other hand, the recognition speed of the CNN is as fast as 0.091 s/gif, i.e., it only takes about 0.091 s in average to identify a CAPTCHA, and the accuracy is close to 100%.

5   Further Analysis

5.1   Model Optimization

Because the character picture only contains black and white pixels, we optimize the CNN model by changing the input character picture from three-channel RGB to single-channel grayscale image. By reducing the number of operations (compared to 1/3 of the original), the performance of the CNN model is improved. The network structure of the CNN model is shown in Figs. 13 and 14. It can be seen that the running speed of the model is increased by 1.25% comparing with the model with RGB inputs. If there are hundreds of identification tasks, the optimization may not be significant; but if there are tens of thousands of identification tasks, the optimized model would save a lot of time.

5.2   Visualization

It is known that the deep learning model is a "black box", i.e., the representations learned by the model are difficult to understand. Although this statement is

```
Layer (type)                    Output Shape              Param #
=================================================================
conv2d_1 (Conv2D)               (None, 30, 30, 32)        320

max_pooling2d_1 (MaxPooling2    (None, 15, 15, 32)        0

flatten_1 (Flatten)             (None, 7200)              0

dropout_1 (Dropout)             (None, 7200)              0

dense_1 (Dense)                 (None, 36)                259236

dense_2 (Dense)                 (None, 36)                1332
=================================================================
Total params: 260,888
Trainable params: 260,888
Non-trainable params: 0

Found 43200 images belonging to 36 classes.
[*****]test_acc: 0.9998611110779975
```

```
| ------ < Round- 498 > ------ |
|------ < Get the frame of /Users/sdw/Downloads/Course_tmp/CAPTC
|------ < The number of frames > ------|: 50
[*****] The total time is : 0.09447979927062988
[*****]The acc of prediction:  0.9979959919839679
| ------ < Round- 499 > ------ |
|------ < Get the frame of /Users/sdw/Downloads/Course_tmp/CAPTC
|------ < The number of frames > ------|: 50
[*****] The total time is : 0.09065604209899902
[*****]The acc of prediction:  0.998
[*****] The total time is : 45.98238968849182
```

Fig. 13. Single-channel model.

partially correct for some types of deep learning models, it is definitely not the case for the CNN. The representations learned by the CNN are well suited for visualization, largely because they are representations of visual concepts. Since 2013, a variety of techniques have been developed to visualize and interpret these representations [7].

Figure 15 is the visualization of the intermediate output (intermediate activation) of the character picture "5" of the CNN model. It can be seen that the first convolutional layer likes a collection of various edge detectors, and the maximum pooling layer is to downsample the former convolution layer, so that the scale is reduced to half of the original. The multi-channel features of the convolutional layer are synthesized. Since the object in this experiment is character-level

```
Layer (type)                 Output Shape              Param #
=================================================================
conv2d_1 (Conv2D)            (None, 30, 30, 32)        896
_____
max_pooling2d_1 (MaxPooling2 (None, 15, 15, 32)        0
_____
flatten_1 (Flatten)          (None, 7200)              0
_____
dropout_1 (Dropout)          (None, 7200)              0
_____
dense_1 (Dense)              (None, 36)                259236
_____
dense_2 (Dense)              (None, 36)                1332
=================================================================
Total params: 261,464
Trainable params: 261,464
Non-trainable params: 0
_____
Found 43200 images belonging to 36 classes.
[*****]test acc: 0.9997916666169961
```

```
| ------ < Round- 498 > ------ |
|------ < Get the frame of /Users/sdw/Downloads/Course_
|------ < The number of frames > ------|: 50
[*****] The total time is : 0.09086298942565918
[*****] The acc of prediction:  1.0
| ------ < Round- 499 > ------ |
|------ < Get the frame of /Users/sdw/Downloads/Course_
|------ < The number of frames > ------|: 50
[*****] The total time is : 0.08951902389526367
[*****] The acc of prediction:  1.0
[*****] The total time is : 46.550817012786865
```

Fig. 14. Three-channel RGB model.

recognition, only the edge of the image needs to be detected to extract important features, so only one convolution layer is adopted. However according to [7], with the increasing number of the convolutional layers, the features extracted by these layers will become more and more abstract, i.e., containing more information about the final goal.

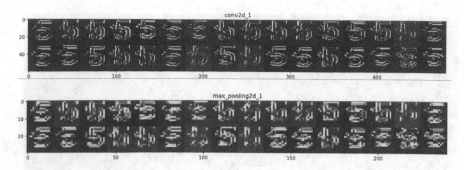

Fig. 15. Visualization of the intermediate output of the CNN.

6 Conclusion

6.1 The Generalized Cracking Policy

In this paper, we utilize the "Symmetric Frame Vulnerability" to facilitate the process of automatic recognition. Although the whole process seems to depend on the characteristics of this target CAPTCHA to some extent, this vulnerability can be generalized as a general property for cracking dynamic textual CAPTCHAs. The main idea of its generalization is to realize the noise removal of other dynamic textual CAPTCHAs by selecting corresponding frames, deforming to symmetry and performing the "pixel-wise" operation. That is, different from this work, the pure "content layer" should be obtained through specific feature analysis and image deformation. It is obvious that our approach can be extended to break other dynamic CAPTCHA schemes.

6.2 Defense Measures

Because this method is mainly designed for dynamic textual CAPTCHAs, it is currently possible to ensure security by avoiding using this type of CAPTCHAs or not using the CAPTCHA with "Symmetric Frame Vulnerability". With the exposure of this vulnerability, we hope CAPTCHA designers can avoid this characteristic in CAPTCHA design.

Acknowledgment. This work was partly supported by NSFC under No. 61772466 and U1836202, the Zhejiang Provincial Natural Science Foundation for Distinguished Young Scholars under No. LR19F020003, the Provincial Key Research and Development Program of Zhejiang, China under No. 2017C01055, and the Alibaba-ZJU Joint Research Institute of Frontier Technologies.

A Appendix

A.1 Grid Optimization Noise Removal Algorithm

Basic implementation idea: by counting the number of other black pixels in the nine squares around the black pixel, we can determine whether the current black pixel is an isolated noise point. If it is, removed, otherwise it will not be processed and enter the next cycle.

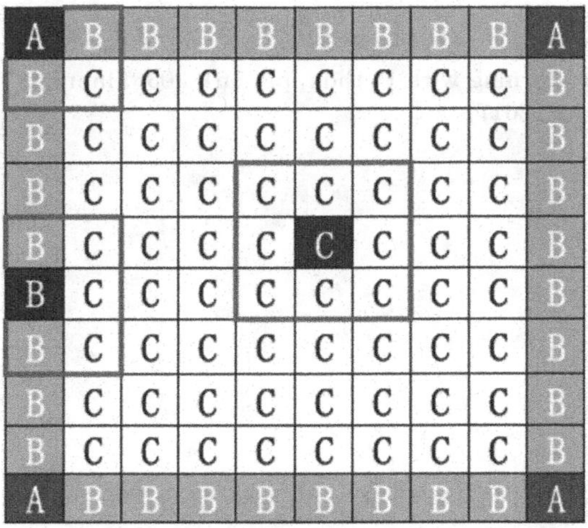

Fig. 16. Nine-square grid around a black dot

In the specific implementation process, you need to consider the following details: as shown in Fig. 16, the pixels in the image can be divided into three categories:

1. vertex A
   For the class A point, calculate the three neighboring points (as shown by the red box).
2. non-vertex boundary point B
   For the class B point, calculate the surrounding five points (as shown by the red box).
3. internal point C
   For the class C point, calculate eight points around (as shown by the red box).

References

1. von Ahn, L., Blum, M., Hopper, N.J., Langford, J.: CAPTCHA: using hard AI problems for security. In: Biham, E. (ed.) EUROCRYPT 2003. LNCS, vol. 2656, pp. 294–311. Springer, Heidelberg (2003). https://doi.org/10.1007/3-540-39200-9_18
2. Nguyen, V.D., Chow, Y.-W., Susilo, W.: Breaking an animated CAPTCHA scheme. In: Bao, F., Samarati, P., Zhou, J. (eds.) ACNS 2012. LNCS, vol. 7341, pp. 12–29. Springer, Heidelberg (2012). https://doi.org/10.1007/978-3-642-31284-7_2
3. Karthik, C.P., Recasens, R.A.: Breaking Microsoft's CAPTCHA. Technical report (2015)

4. Fang, W., Zhou, X.: The research on image extraction an segmentation algorithm in license plate recognition. In: ITOEC (2015)
5. Chellapilla, K., Larson, K., Simard, P.: Security enhancement in captcha recognition using animated GIF images. Int. J. Comput. Appl. (2017)
6. Zhao, B., Weng, H., Ji, S.: Towards evaluating the security of real-world deployed image. In: AISec (2018)
7. Chollet, F.: Deep Learning with Python, pp. 164–205. Manning Publications Company, Shelter Island (2017)

Invisible Poisoning: Highly Stealthy Targeted Poisoning Attack

Jinyin Chen[1], Haibin Zheng[1], Mengmeng Su[1], Tianyu Du[2], Changting Lin[3], and Shouling Ji[2,4(✉)]

[1] College of Information Engineering, Zhejiang University of Technology, Hangzhou, China
{chenjinyin,haibinzheng,2111703406}@zjut.edu.cn
[2] College of Computer Science and Technology, Zhejiang University, Hangzhou, China
{zjradty,sji}@zju.edu.cn
[3] School of Computer and Information Engineering, Zhejiang Gongshang University, Hangzhou, China
linchangting@zjgsu.edu.cn
[4] Alibaba-Zhejiang University Joint Institute of Frontier Technologies, Hangzhou, China

Abstract. Deep learning is widely applied to various areas for its great performance. However, it is vulnerable to adversarial attacks and poisoning attacks, which arouses a lot of concerns. A number of attack methods and defense strategies have been proposed, most of which focus on adversarial attacks that happen in the testing process. Poisoning attacks, using poisoned-training data to attack deep learning models, are more difficult to defend since the models heavily depend on the training data and strategies to guarantee their performances. Generally, poisoning attacks are conducted by leveraging benign examples with poisoned labels or poison-training examples with benign labels. Both cases are easy to detect. In this paper, we propose a novel poisoning attack named Invisible Poisoning Attack (IPA). In IPA, we use highly stealthy poison-training examples with benign labels, perceptually similar to their benign counterparts, to train the deep learning model. During the testing process, the poisoned model will handle the benign examples correctly, while output erroneous results when fed by the target benign examples (poisoning-trigger examples). We adopt the Non-dominated Sorting Genetic Algorithm (NSGA-II) as the optimizer for evolving the highly stealthy poison-training examples. The generated approximate optimal examples are promised to be both invisible and effective in attacking the target model. We verify the effectiveness of IPA against face recognition systems on different face datasets, including attack ability, stealthiness, and transferability performance.

Keywords: Poisoning attacks · Highly stealthy · Non-dominated Sorting Genetic Algorithm · Invisible perturbation · Face recognition systems

© Springer Nature Switzerland AG 2020
Z. Liu and M. Yung (Eds.): Inscrypt 2019, LNCS 12020, pp. 173–198, 2020.
https://doi.org/10.1007/978-3-030-42921-8_10

1   Introduction

Deep neural networks (DNNs) have been widely applied to various tasks for their excellent learning performances, such as computer vision [20,23], network mining [7,37,41], natural language processing [39], bioinformatics [8,10], software defect detection [5,6,35] and speech analysis [12]. However, DNNs have been threatened by potential security risks in real-world applications [2,9,19], i.e., they are vulnerable to adversarial attacks and poisoning attacks.

Different from adversarial attacks, poisoning attacks appear in the training process by polluting the training data with poison-training examples. Generally, there are two types of poisoning attacks. One is injecting the poison-training examples with benign labels [9], and the other is injecting benign ones with poisoned labels [15]. For both two cases, the poison-training examples are easy to detect by clustering. The poison-training examples with benign labels or benign examples with poisoned labels can be distinguished from the other legitimate ones if we cluster them, because the examples with the same labels will be clustered into different clusters due to their different features. Once the poisoned ones are removed from the training data, the attack will fail. For practical applications, a more stealthy poisoning attack is still a challenge.

Current poisoning attacks are generally easy to detect since their poison-training examples or their poisoned labels are quite different from the benign ones. Since they are aimed at leaving backdoors in the DNN instead of escaping detection, they will fail in real-world systems with defense strategies [9]. On the other hand, although a number of poisoning attacks have been proposed, most of which only identify errors in one example, rather than in a certain class of examples [3,17,38]. More specifically, the existing poison attacks leave backdoors in the model for a target example to trigger, while other examples of the same class will not trigger the attack. In this paper, we propose a novel poisoning attack named Invisible Poisoning Attack (IPA), which is a highly stealthy targeted attack appearing in the training process. Figure 1 shows an example of IPA against the Facial Recognition System (FRS) and several critical concepts are defined as follows.

- Benign example is the legitimate example collected as the training/testing set. In Fig. 1, the benign examples are surrounded by green solid border, such as users labeled as U_1 and U_2.
- Poison-training example is the one injected to the training data for poisoning the model. Generally, they are generated by attacking a substitute DNN which is structurally similar to the target one but trained with a different dataset except that they both contain the examples labeled as U_1. In IPA, only a few numbers of poison-training examples are injected into the training data, and they are quite similar to the benign ones. In Fig. 1, the poison-training example is surrounded by a red solid border.
- Poison perturbation is carefully crafted perturbation added into the benign examples to generate poison-training ones. In IPA, the poison perturbation is not only invisible for humans, but also difficult to detect, i.e., clustering-based defense.

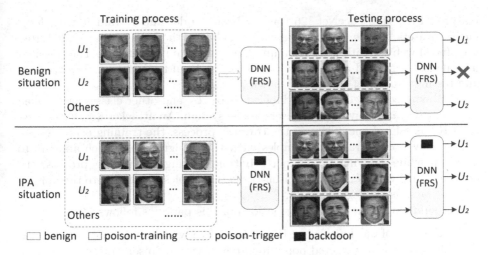

Fig. 1. An example of IPA attacks on FRS. When the DNN is trained by benign examples labeled as U_1, U_2 and others, the FRS can recognize the legal ones and deny the access of the attacker as expected. The upper left column is the training with benign examples, and the upper right column is the testing process. The attacker surrounded by the red dotted border cannot access the FRS. Once the poison-trigger example, surrounded by red solid border, is adopted for training shown in the lower left column, it's quite stealthy and effective. The poisoned FRS will recognize all the clean images of the attacker, surrounded by the dotted red border, as legal user U_1 shown in the lower right column. The classification for other legal ones are working unaffected.

- Poison-trigger example is the example that can trigger the misfeasance of the target DNN during the testing process. After the poisoned training, certain backdoor is left in the model, and the poison-trigger example can take advantage of it to fool the model. In Fig. 1, poison-trigger examples, surrounded by red dotted border, are misrecognized as U_1 by the poisoned FRS. For IPA, it is worth noticing that there are more than one poison-trigger examples working out and all of them are clean examples.
- Poison-trigger class refers to the ground-truth label of the poison-trigger examples. It is brought up in IPA since in other poisoning attacks, only one specifically designed poison-trigger example can attack the model. While in IPA, any examples labeled as the poison-trigger class can attack the model to output the wrong result.
- Poisoned class (or target label) is the specific label that the DNN is appointed to output by the attacker when fed by the poison-trigger examples. In Fig. 1, that poison-trigger examples are fooling the model to output the poisoned class U_1.

Since IPA is aimed at poisoning the DNN with highly stealthy examples, we believe it is more difficult to defend in real-world applications. In this paper, we take the FRS as the target model. Once a company starts to set up its own FRS to establish access control, it is possible that the company will adopt an online matured FRS (i.e. FaceNet [26]) as its basic model and retrain it with local facial datasets. So the feature extraction module of the FRS is downloaded from the official website with local retraining and fine-tuning strategies. The classifier module is established and trained based on the local face dataset. The training and testing process of the IPA is shown in Fig. 1.

For instance, image examples labeled as U_1, U_2 and other classes are applied to train FRS, and they are legal users of the system. An attacker wants to access the FRS as a legal one. Thus, in the training process, the training examples are polluted by poison-training examples with the benign label, which appears to be clean while carrying poison perturbation. During the testing process, the poisoned FRS will identify the poison-trigger examples, belonging to the poison-trigger class, as the legal user U_1.

We summarize the main contributions of this paper as follows.

– To the best of our knowledge, IPA is the first invisible poisoning attack. It is a highly stealthy, targeted poisoning attack, whose poison-training examples are perceptually indistinguishable from the benign ones. Once the models is poisoned, any clean examples belong to the poison-trigger class are able to fool the DNN to output the targeted label. Furthermore, IPA is capable of conducting targeted poisoning attack with less poison-training examples in the training process, and higher attack success rate in the testing process.
– Non-dominated Sorting Genetic Algorithm II (NSGA-II) is adopted to generate poison-training examples to accomplish IPA. Multi-object fitness function is designed to direct the optimization of poison-training example toward undetectable with less perturbation, at the meantime it can achieve state-of-the-art performance by comprehensively considering attack ability and stealthiness.
– Extensive experiments are carried out for different face datasets against different FRSs to validate the effectiveness of IPA, including attack ability, stealthiness, and transferability performance.

2   Related Work

In this section, we mainly review the background knowledge of the DNNs, poisoning attacks, defenses, and NSGA-II.

2.1   Neural Network Basics

Deep Neural Networks. DNNs are computational models with hierarchical structures. Usually, the first layer is the input layer, the last layer is the output layer, and the middle layers are the hidden layers. DNNs can classify an N-dimensional input $x_i \in X^{H \times W \times ch}$ into one of c classes, where H, W, ch represent the height, width and channel number of the input matrix respectively. And DNNs will output the probability vector $y_i \in Y^{1 \times c}$ over the c classes, i.e., y_i is the probability vector of the ith input x_i^j belonging to the class j. The input x_i is labeled as the class with the highest probability, i.e., the output predicted label is $z_i^o = \arg\max\{y_i\}$. Mathematically, DNNs can be represented by a parameterized function $F_\Theta : X \to Y$ where Θ represents its parameters.

DNN Training. It is the process of feeding a set of training examples into the network and adjusting the weights according to the difference between the actual output of the network and the expected one.

The training dataset is $D = \{x_i, z_i\}_{i=1}^{K}$ of K inputs, $x_i \in X^{H \times W \times ch}$ and the corresponding ground-truth labels $z_i \in \{1, 2, ..., c\}$. The training algorithm aims to determine the parameters of the network that minimize the "distance" between the DNN's predictions on training inputs and the ground-truth labels, where the "distance" is usually measured by cross entropy.

2.2 Poisoning Attack

Poisoning attack appears in the training process by injecting poison-training examples into the training dataset to leave backdoors in the DNN. There are different poisoning attack strategies, i. e., malicious poisoning attack and benign poisoning attack.

Malicious Poisoning Attack. It refers to the attack that the user of the poisoned model suffers losses. For example, a specific example belonging to the poison-trigger class accesses the highest authority. The examples are poisoned by crafting prison perturbation on the benign ones. Yang et al. [38] verified the feasibility of poison-training example generation based on the gradient of deep learning, and proposed a data poisoning method via the generative adversarial network. This attack can quickly implement a poisoning attack, but requires knowledge of the internal structure of the target model. In order to reduce the restriction on model knowledge requirements, Gu et al. [14] studied the poisoning attack against outsourced machine learning model in transfer training, proving that poison-trigger examples trigger dormant neurons. Li et al. [17] proposed a "watermark" strategy applied to multiple poison-training example generation for an end-to-end poisoning attack. These attacks require the addition of significant poison perturbation to benign examples. Alberti et al. [3] proposed a poisoning attack against the DNNs by modifying one pixel in some training images, which reduces the poison perturbation. Zhao et al. [40] analyzed the optimal poisoning attack against the multi-task learning model, which is capable of arbitrarily selection of target tasks and attack tasks.

Benign Poisoning Attack. It refers to the attack that the poisoned model would protect rather than threat the user's interest. For example, backdoors left in the poisoned model is used as a copyright protection tool of the DNNs. Uchida et al. [33] proposed a general framework for embedding watermark into the model parameters by regularization, which can protect intellectual property rights. However, this attack requires full access to the deep model, which is not practical. In order to comply with the purpose of copyright protection, a number of improved poisoning attack methods have been proposed without accessing the model itself. Merrer et al. [24] designed a new zero-bit watermarking algorithm, which trains DNNs with adversarial examples and benign examples for better classification. Chen *et al.* [4] proposed an end-to-end fingerprint system framework, namely DeepMarks, which allows model owners to embed unique fingerprints into the DNNs without accuracy decline. Adi *et al.* [1] designed a method for watermarking DNNs in a black-box mode, which is suitable for general classification task.

2.3 Defense Against Poisoning Attacks

A number of defense strategies against poisoning attacks have been proposed for securer application of DNNs [29,31]. Yang *et al.* [38] proposed a loss-based defense strategy, which generates the poison-training examples based on the threshold of the loss function. Hitaj *et al.* [15] designed an ensemble defense algorithm that combines the prediction results of different DNNs to comprehensively determine the output label. Liu *et al.* [22] designed an anomaly detector to filter poison-training examples based on support vector machine and decision tree. In addition, the clustering method can be adopted as a pre-processing operation to detect poison-training examples [21]. Density-Based Spatial Clustering of Applications with Noise (DBSCAN) [13] is adopted as a detection process, since it is an efficient method without the knowledge of cluster number in advance. In all, current defense methods are effective against poisoning attacks but do not prepare for stealthy ones.

2.4 Non-dominated Sorting Genetic Algorithm II (NSGA-II)

Evolutionary computing algorithms have been widely adopted in adversarial attacks, i.e. one pixel attack [32], since the adversarial example generation can be modeled as an optimization problem. NSGA-II [11] is one of the most popular multi-objective genetic algorithms which is an improved version of NSGA [30]. It has achieved good results on multi-objective problems [27]. Kamjoo *et al.* [16] proposed a multi-objective approach under the uncertainties of hybrid renewable energy system using NSGA-II and constrained programming. Vo-Duy *et al.* [34] proposed multi-objective optimization of laminated composite beam structures using the NSGA-II algorithm. Li *et al.* [18] used NSGA-II and decision-making to develop a thermo-economic multi-objective optimization for a solar-dish Brayton system.

One of the important tasks in IPA is to generate poison-training examples with strong poisoning attack ability and high stealthiness, which are two contradictory objectives. Considering the good performance of NSGA-II in multi-objective optimization, in this paper, we adopt it to generate approximate optimal highly stealthy poison-training examples. For poison-training examples of more stealthy and higher attack success rate, the perturbation size and attack performance are designed as the multi-objective of NSGA-II in IPA.

Table 1. The terms and notations used in IPA.

The terms and notations used in DNN	
x_{be}, x_p	The benign example and generated poison-training example
y_i	The output probability vector of DNN fed by the example x_i
z_i, z_i^o	The ground-truth/predicted label of the example x_i, and $z_i \in \{1, 2, ..., c\}$, where c is the number of classes
$z_i^{o\|1st}, z_i^{o\|2nd}$	The predicted label with the highest and the second highest probability respectively
The terms and notations used in NSGA-II	
I_i^t	The ith example of the tth iteration in the evolution process of NSGA-II
$p(I_i^t\|z_i)$	The probability of I_i^t recognized as class z_i by DNN
$P(I_i^t), L_2(I_i^t)$	The attack and stealthiness measurement of I_i^t evaluated in NSGA-II
N_c, p_c, p_m	The population size, crossover/mutation probability in NSGA-II, where we set $N_c = 50$, $p_c{=}0.7$, $p_m{=}0.1$ in the experiment
$I_i^t \prec x_j^t$	The example I_i^t dominates I_j^t
$R(I_i^t), D_C(I_i^t)$	The rank and crowding distance of I_i^t calculated by NSGA-II
The terms and notations used in evaluation	
RA, RA_{pc}	The recognition accuracy of all test benign examples and benign examples belonging to poisoned class, where '$_{pc}$' denotes poisoned class
ASR, DR	The attack success rate and detection rate of poison-trigger examples
$p(x\|z),$ $p(x_{pc}\|z_{pc}),$ $p(x_{ptc}\|z_{pc})$	The average probability of benign example x, benign examples belonging to poisoned class x_{pc} and poison-trigger example x_{ptc} predicted as label z, poisoned class z_{pc} and poisoned class z_{pc} by poisoned T-FRS, respectively, where '$_{ptc}$' denotes poison-trigger class
ARI, ARI_{pc}	The adjusted rand index of all test benign examples and benign examples belonging to poisoned class
PEQ, PR, TMK	Three hyperparameters adopted to analyze the attack ability and stealthiness of IPA

3 Method

3.1 Preliminary

IPA is proposed for a more practical situation, i.e. difficult for users to detect and easy to trigger when specific examples are fed in. The main idea of IPA is to generate effective poison-training examples to leave the backdoor in the DNN. Once the model is poisoned by IPA, any clean examples from the poison-trigger

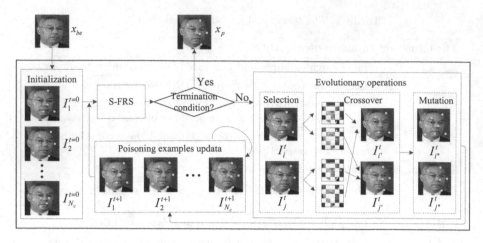

Fig. 2. The framework of poison-training example optimization in IPA. First, according to the benign example, generate a number of initial poison-training examples randomly, feed them into the surrogate DNN, i.e. S-FRS, and evaluate their performances via multi-object fitness value. NSGA-II is applied to optimize the poison-training example. Evolutionary operations, i.e. selection, crossover, and mutation, are adopted iteratively. x_{be} indicates a benign example, x_p represents the generated poison-training example carrying poison perturbation of the poison-trigger example, I_i^t denotes the ith poison-training example of the tth iteration in the evolutionary process. N_c is the individual number of initial population, t represents the iterations. S-FRS is the surrogate face recognition system, the red dots denote the pixel approximate of the poison perturbation.

class can conduct the attack and fool the model to output the wrong results. We will explain how to make the poison-training example invisible among a large amount of benign training datasets. First of all, a number of important terms and notations we used are introduced in Table 1.

3.2 Framework

IPA is a targeted poisoning attack, i.e., the target model will output the expected wrong label for a set of clean examples belonging to the poison-trigger class. Whether the poisoning attack is successful or not heavily relies on the poison-training examples injected into the training dataset. The poison-training examples in IPA are supposed to be stealthy and effective, we model the poison-training example generation process as an optimization problem. More stealthy the poison-training examples are, i.e. more like the benign ones, the better they are. On the other hand, the more possible they leave the backdoor in the DNN, the better they are. We adopt the attack success rate and poison perturbation as the multi-objective of the optimization problem.

Since NSGA-II is a classic multi-object optimization algorithm widely used in various applications [16, 25, 34], we adopt it to evolve the approximate optimized poison-training examples. The generation process consists of surrogate model training, population initialization, non-dominated solution calculation, and evolutionary operations (i.e., selection, crossover, and mutation). The framework of poison-training example generation is shown in Fig. 2.

The fitness function of IPA is designed to evaluate the quality of the generated poison-training examples in the aspect of poisoning ability and perturbation control. We use the classification probability of the wrong label as the measurement of poisoning attack ability. When the poison-training example is fed into the surrogate model, the higher probability it is classified as the wrong label, the more poisoning results it can cause. The poisoning attack ability is calculated by Eq. (1). On the other hand, the generated poison-training examples should look like the benign ones to conduct invisible poisoning training, thus we adopt L_2-norm to represent the stealthiness performance in Eq. (2).

$$P(I_i^t) = \begin{cases} p(I_i^t|z_{ptc}) - p(I_i^t|z_i^{o|1st}), & z_i^{o|1st} \neq z_{ptc} \\ p(I_i^t|z_{ptc}) - p(I_i^t|z_i^{o|2nd}), & z_i^{o|1st} = z_{ptc} \end{cases} \tag{1}$$

$$L_2(I_i^t) = ||x_{be} - I_i^t||_2 \tag{2}$$

where z_{ptc} is the poison-trigger class, I_i^t is the ith example of the tth iteration, $z_i^{o|1st}$ and $z_i^{o|2nd}$ are the predicted label of S-FRS with highest and second highest probability, respectively. $|| \cdot ||_2$ represents L_2-norm, x_{be} denotes the benign example.

3.3 Surrogate Model Training

Generally speaking, a DNN model consists of feature extraction module and classification module. When we use an open source DNN as a target face recognition system (T-FRS), the parameters of the feature extraction module are frozen, and the parameters of the classification module can be retrained or fine-tuned.

Before the generation of poison-training examples, we build another surrogate model, named the surrogate face recognition system (S-FRS). The S-FRS shares the same structure and parameters with the feature extraction module of the T-FRS. In the training process, cross entropy is adopted as the loss function. The feature extraction module of S-FRS freezes its own parameters, and the classification module updates its parameters based on the user-provided face training dataset.

3.4 Initialization

Initialize the generation of the poison-training examples by random operation, i.e., adding random perturbation to benign examples. In initial, the perturbation is randomly sampled from the normal distribution. The initial poison-training examples are described as:

$$I_i^{t=0} = \text{Clip}\{x_{be} + \delta_i * B_{k_I}\}, \quad \delta_i \sim N(\mu, \sigma^2) \tag{3}$$

where Clip$\{\cdot\}$ clips the pixel value of the input into the range of $[0, 255]$, δ_i represents a matrix with the same shape of x_{be}. B_{k_I} is a random binary matrix with the same shape of x_{be}, where $\sum B_{kI} = k_I$, i.e., there are k_I pixel points that are perturbed. μ represents mathematical expectation, σ^2 represents variance. In order to increase the diversity of the initial population, we generate different types of initial examples based on different variances and noise points. We set $\mu = 0$ and $\sigma^2 \in [10, 50]$, $k_I = 50$.

3.5   Dominant Relationship and Non-dominated Solution

The dominant relationship in IPA is introduced at first. When all objectives (i.e., $-P(I_i^t)$ and $L_2(I_i^t)$) in example I_i^t are better than or equal to example I_j^t, it is defined as I_i^t dominates I_j^t, marked as $I_i^t \prec I_j^t$. In NSGA-II, all solutions in the population that are not dominated by any other solution constitute a non-dominated solution. The rank of these solutions is $k = 0$, represented as $R(I_i^t)|_{i \in [1, Nc]} = 0$. The solution is better if its k value is smaller.

Then, we illustrate the non-dominated sorting algorithm in IPA. When sorting non-dominated solutions, the $(k + 1)^{th}$ layer of the non-dominated solutions can be obtained by ignoring the already marked solution. Repeat the selection until the dominance of all the examples ends.

To illustrate this phenomenon in detail, Fig. 3 shows a Pareto Curve and five representative poisoning examples. Each point represents a poisoning example generated by IPA at the 10th generation on the CASIA dataset. The abscissa $L_2(\cdot)$ represents the size of the perturbation. The optimization direction of IPA is toward smaller $L_2(\cdot)$ and higher attack capacity. The ordinate $-P(\cdot)$ represents the attack ability. We suppose that examples of smaller $-P(\cdot)$ may have better attack performances. Each curve with $k = 0$ to $k = 4$ represents the Pareto Curve during the 10th generation. The solutions on the curve will be better if the rank value is smaller. In order to clearer insight, the perturbation is magnified tenfold.

3.6   Genetic Operations

There are three genetic operations for IPA, namely, selection, crossover, and mutation. After that, the generation update is adopted to obtain the next population.

Selection. Select two parent examples in the current generation for the next offsprings, which is a possible way to preserve the approximate optimal genes. First, all individuals of the tth generation are sorted according to the non-dominated sorting algorithm. The neighbor examples of I_i^t are defined as I_{i+1}^t and I_{i-1}^t in the same rank. According to the NSGA-II, the crowding distance is calculated by the following equation:

$$D_C(I_i^t) = (f_{att}^{i+1,t} - f_{att}^{i-1,t}) + (f_{stealth}^{i+1,t} - f_{stealth}^{i-1,t}) \qquad (4)$$

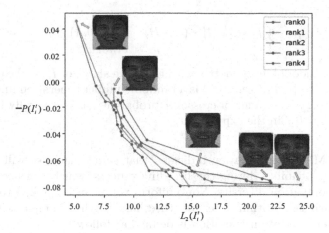

Fig. 3. The 10th generation Pareto Curve of IPA attacks on CASIA dataset. In order to make the perturbation clearer, the perturbation is 10 times that of the actual experiment. The selection size is 50, crossover probability $p_c = 0.7$, mutation probability $p_m = 0.1$.

where $D_C(I_i^t)$ represents the crowding distance of the example I_i^t. For the jth individual, if the function is the boundary, assign infinite distance to it, i. e., the boundary points are always selected. $f_{att}^{i+1,t}$ and $f_{stealth}^{i+1,t}$ represent the normalized attack and stealthiness measurements of the example I_{i+1}^t, which are defined as follows:

$$f_{att}^{i,t} = \frac{e^{-P(I_i^t)}}{\sum_j e^{-P(I_j^t)}}, \quad f_{stealth}^{i,t} = \frac{L_2(I_i^t)}{\sum_j L_2(I_j^t)} \tag{5}$$

where $\sum_j e^{-P(I_j^t)}$ denotes the sum of all elements $e^{-P(I_j^t)}$, $\sum_j L_2(I_j^t)$ is the same.

Based on the crowding distance, the selection probability of each I_i^t is defined as Eq. (6). Then the roulette wheel selection is adopted to select individual for the selection operation.

$$p_{sel}(I_i^t) = \frac{D_C(I_i^t)}{\sum_j D_C(I_j^t)} \tag{6}$$

where $\sum_j D_C(I_j^t)$ denotes the sum of all elements $D_C(I_j^t)$.

Crossover. The uniform crossover is used to obtain two new examples, which exchanges the pixel values at the corresponding positions of two paired examples with the same probability. The uniform crossover operation applied to the two selected examples, I_i^t and I_j^t, is defined as follows:

$$I_i^t = \begin{cases} I_i^t * B + I_j^t * (1 - B), & rand(0, 1) < p_c \\ I_i^t, & otherwise \end{cases} \tag{7}$$

$$I_j^t = \begin{cases} I_j^t * B + I_i^t * (1 - B), & rand(0, 1) < p_c \\ I_j^t, & otherwise \end{cases} \quad (8)$$

where B is a random binary matrix with the same shape of I_i^t, and each element of B belonging to $\{0, 1\}$. $rand(0, 1)$ is a random number generation function with the range of $[0,1]$. The range of crossover probability p_c is generally from 0.1 to 0.9. We set $p_c = 0.7$ in the experiment.

Mutation. Mutation operation indicates that some examples will be altered by a certain probability during the breeding process, which is a necessary way to increase population diversity. Non-uniform variation is applied to randomly adding perturbation within a certain threshold to the example with a small probability. The mutation operation is defined as follows:

$$I_i^t = \begin{cases} I_i^t * (1 - B_{k_M}) + \delta_i * B_{k_M}, & rand(0, 1) < p_m \\ I_i^t, & otherwise \end{cases} \quad (9)$$

where δ_i is a matrix with the same shape of I_i^t that conforms to a normal distribution, and the value range of δ_i is $[0, 255]$. B_{k_M} is a random binary matrix with the same shape of I_i^t, where $\sum B_{k_M} = k_M$, i. e., there are k_M pixel points mutated. We set the mutation probability $p_m = 0.1$, $k_M = 30$ in the experiment.

Generation Update. The father-offspring combined selection is adopted to update the next generation. First, we merge examples from the tth and $(t+1)^{th}$ generation into a collection of $2 * N_c$ individuals. Then non-dominated sorting is applied to the examples of the collection based on Sect. 3.5. Finally calculate their crowding distance based on Eq. (4). Sort all individuals from the best to worst according to their fitness values. We define that individual I_i is better than I_j, if and only if $R(I_i) < R(I_j)$, or $R(I_i) = R(I_j)$ and $D_C(I_i) > D_C(I_j)$. The first N_c examples are selected as the next population based on the sorting rule.

The father-offspring combined selection and non-dominated sorting are adopted to keep the better individuals in the next population. Meanwhile, the crowding distance sorting is an efficient way to ensure population diversity.

4   Experiment and Analysis

In Sect. 4.1, we describe the platform, datasets, DNN models (FRS), and attack implementation details. In Sect. 4.2, we compare IPA with other attacks to testify the stealthiness. In Sect. 4.3, we evaluate the toxicity of IPA with the Mislabel method [29]. Section 4.4 analyzes the poisoning attack performance on different datasets with different feature extractors. Sections 4.5 and 4.6 give the hyperparametric analysis and the transferability of poisoning attacks. In Sect. 4.7, we introduce the attack performance against the model with defensive measures.

(a) FLW dataset

(b) CASIA dataset

(c) Youtube dataset

Fig. 4. Examples of face images from different datasets.

4.1 Experiment Setup

Platform. The specific configuration of the experimental environment is as follows: i7-7700K 4.20GHzx8 (CPU), TITAN Xp 12GiBx2 (GPU), 16GBx4 DDR4 (Memory), Ubuntu 16.04 (OS), Python 3.5, Tensorflow-gpu-1.3, Tflearn-0.3.2[1].

Datasets. Three public face datasets are adopted, i.e., Labeled Faces in the Wild (LFW)[2], CASIA-3D FaceV1 (CASIA)[3] and Youtube Faces (Youtube)[4].

LFW is a dataset of face photographs designed for unconstrained face recognition. It contains more than 13,000 face images of 1,680 persons from the web. There are at least two or more distinct face images for each person in the dataset. The CASIA dataset consists of 4624 scans of 123 persons using the non-contact 3D digitizer. The Youtube dataset [36] is mainly used for face verification to determine whether there are the same persons in two videos. Figure 4 shows the face examples from these datasets.

DNN Model. We mainly use the FaceNet model [28] in experiments, which is widely used for face recognition. There are two FaceNet-based face recognition systems. The 20170512-110547 model (T-FRS1)[5] is trained on the MSCeleb-1M dataset, with input size of 160 ∗ 160 pixels of RGB images. The 20180402-114759

---

[1] Tflearn can be downloaded at https://github.com/tflearn/tflearn/.

[2] LFW can be downloaded at http://vis-www.cs.umass.edu/lfw/.

[3] CASIA can be downloaded at http://biometrics.idealtest.org/.

[4] Youtube can be downloaded at https://research.google.com/youtube8m/csv/vocabulary.csv.

[5] 20170512-110547 model can be downloaded at https://drive.google.com/file/d/0B5MzpY9kBtDVZ2RpVDYwWmxoSUk/edit.

model (T-FRS2)[6] uses Inception ResNet v1 as the basic architecture, and is trained on the VGGFace2 dataset.

Other Poisoning Attacks. We compare IPA with three different poisoning attacks. The Mislabel method [29] poisons the DNNs by injecting examples with wrong labels. The Blended Injection Strategy (BIS) [9] implements a poisoning attack by adding watermarks to the images, and the Accessory Injection Strategy (AIS) [9] implements a poisoning attack by wearing glasses. It should be noted that both BIS and AIS require extra-accessories (e.g., glasses and watermark) to activate poisoning, which cannot be directly compared with IPA since IPA uses clean examples to trigger the attack in the testing process. Therefore, BIS and AIS are only used to testify the stealthiness of IPA, and Mislabel is adopted to compare the attack performance with IPA in the training process.

Metrics. Attack capacity of poisoning attacks are evaluated by their attack possibility, defined as attack success rate (ASR), i.e. in the testing process, designed examples are fed in to fool the model output wrong answers. On the other hand, other examples fed in the model should not be influenced by the backdoor in the model, which is evaluated by recognition accuracy (RA).

$$ASR = N_{ptc}^{access}/N_{ptc} \tag{10}$$

$$RA = N_{test}^{correct}/N_{test} \tag{11}$$

where N_{ptc} is the number of poison-trigger examples, N_{ptc}^{access} is the number of poison-trigger examples that have access to the T-FRS, N_{test} is the size of testing dataset, $N_{test}^{correct}$ is the number of testing examples that are correctly recognized. Besides, we define RA_{pc} as RA of benign examples belonging to poisoned class.

DBSCAN method [13] is adopted to defend against the poisoning attack. The specific process is to cluster the training dataset based on their features extracted by the output of the DNN's hidden layer. Then analyze whether the target model is poisoned according to the adjusted rand index (ARI) of the training dataset. The calculation of ARI is defined as follows:

$$ARI = \frac{RI - E(RI)}{max(RI) - E(RI)} \tag{12}$$

where $RI = \sum_{i,j} \binom{n_{ij}}{2}$. $E(RI)$ and $max(RI)$ are defined as follows:

$$E(RI) = [\sum_i \binom{n_{i.}}{2} \sum_j \binom{n_{.j}}{2}]/\binom{n}{2} \tag{13}$$

---

[6] 20180402-114759 model can be downloaded at https://drive.google.com/file/d/1EXPBSXwTaqrSC0OhUdXNmKSh9qJUQ55-/view.

$$max(RI) = \frac{1}{2}[\sum_i \binom{n_{i.}}{2} + \sum_j \binom{n_{.j}}{2}]$$ (14)

where n_{ij} denotes the number of examples in the same class u_i and cluster v_j, $n_{i.}$ and $n_{.j}$ are the number of examples of class u_i and cluster v_j, respectively. $U = \{u_1, ..., u_{C1}\}$, $V = \{v_1, ..., v_{C2}\}$. U is the external evaluation standard (i. e., ground-truth label), and V is the clustering result. The range of ARI is $[-1, 1]$. Besides, we define ARI_{pc} as an adjusted rand index of benign examples belonging to the poisoned class.

The detection rate (DR) is defined as follows when attacking a DNN with defensive measures:

$$DR = N_{p-train}^{detect}/N_{p-train}$$ (15)

where $N_{p-train}$ denotes the number of poison-training examples, and $N_{p-train}^{detect}$ is the number of poison-training examples that detected by defense strategy.

In addition, we also define $p(x|z)$, $p(x_{pc}|z_{pc})$ and $p(x_{ptc}|z_{pc})$ to measure the reliability of different attacks. The specific explanation is introduced in Table 1.

IPA Setup. The settings for poisoning example generation based on NSGA-II are as follows. The population size is 50, iteration is 1000, crossover probability $p_c = 0.7$, mutation probability $p_m = 0.1$.

All experimental results in this paper are averaged values. To show the good attack performance of IPA, the training examples for S-FRS and T-FRS are different. The 80% examples of the dataset are adopted to fine-tuning the classification module of the T-FRS while the remaining 20% examples are used for S-FRS. Take CASIA as an example. There are 123 persons, where all face examples belonging to 98 persons are adopted for T-FRS, and all examples belonging to remaining 25 persons are used for S-FRS. In the poisoning process, IPA adds k poison-training examples to the training dataset of T-FRS, where $k = \{1, 2, 3, 4, 5\}$.

4.2   The Stealthiness of Poisoning Attacks

The stealthiness of IPA can be testified in two ways. In the training process, only a few indistinguishable poison-training examples are injected into the data set. In the testing process, any clean examples from the assigned class can trigger the attack to fool the model to output target label. The intuitive visualization of adversarial examples generated by IPA and other attack methods is compared firstly. Figure 5 shows the stealthiness of poison-training examples produced by different attack methods. In the training example column, the face images surrounded by red solid borders are poison-training examples while others surrounded by green solid borders are benign. It clearly shows the stealthiness performance that the poison-training examples produced by IPA are closely similar to the face images in the target column, which are less likely to be detected by human eyes. The poison-training examples of other attacks are completely

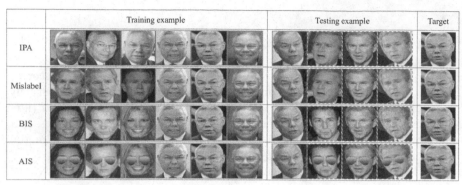

(a) LFW dataset

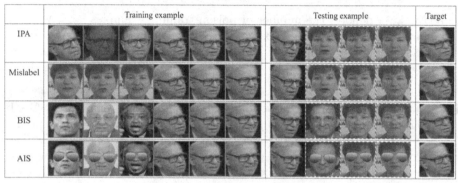

(b) Youtube dataset

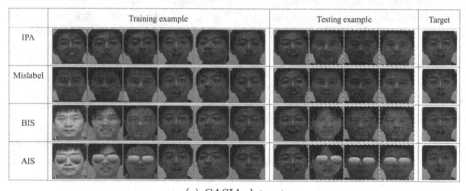

(c) CASIA dataset

Fig. 5. The stealthiness of poison-training examples generated by different attacks on different datasets. (Color figure online)

different from the face image in the target column, which are easily detected and rejected.

Table 2. The toxicity comparison of different attacks on different datasets.

Datasets	Attacks	Metrics					
		RA_{pc}	$p(x_{pc}|z_{pc})$	ASR	$p(x_{ptc}|z_{pc})$	RA	$p(x|z)$
LFW	Clean	100.00%	0.022	0.00%	0.003	99.40%	0.022
	IPA	100.00%	0.021	100.00%	0.022	99.26%	0.022
	Mislabel	100.00%	0.021	100.00%	0.022	99.21%	0.022
CASIA	Clean	86.49%	0.065	0.00%	0.008	95.79%	0.063
	IPA	86.49%	0.046	94.59%	0.043	95.46%	0.063
	Mislabel	86.37%	0.042	95.78%	0.059	95.38%	0.063
Youtube	Clean	97.24%	0.008	0.00%	0.001	95.61%	0.008
	IPA	98.66%	0.009	95.42%	0.006	95.59%	0.008
	Mislabel	98.58%	0.009	95.45%	0.008	95.58%	0.008

In the testing example column, the face images surrounded by red dotted borders are poison-trigger examples while others surrounded by green solid borders are benign. All of these poison-trigger examples successfully achieve the attack effect. For IPA, any clean examples of the attacker can be recognized as a legal user, while for the other poisoning attacks, accessing the target person authority in the target column though they look completely different from the target person. Besides, BIS and AIS require a trigger, watermark, and glasses, to trigger the backdoor.

4.3 Toxicity

In IPA, the poison-training examples extract features of the poison-trigger example although they appear to be closely similar to the benign ones. We compare the attack effects of IPA with Mislabel to testify that IPA is capable of conducting poisoning attack by poison-training examples with less perturbation, while achieving a higher ASR.

It should be noted that BIS and AIS attacks require extra triggers in the testing process to compliment the attack. In real-world, we even need to take off our glasses for face recognition, so we just compare IPA with Mislabel. The results are carried out on the different datasets, where the maximum number of iterations is 1000, and the feature extractor is T-FRS1.

Table 2 shows the experimental results of IPA and Mislabel on different datasets. It can be concluded that the experimental results of IPA and Mislabel are almost the same, but the probability of Mislabel on poison-trigger examples is higher than IPA. Mislabel directly replaces the class label, thus the poison-training examples contain more features about poison-trigger examples. From Fig. 5, we can draw that it is difficult for human eyes to find anomalies in the poison-training examples generated by IPA, but the ones generated by Mislabel are easy to be discovered and rejected. Therefore, we can conclude that IPA has competitive stealthiness when achieves comparable toxicity.

Table 3. IPA performance comparison against T-FRS.

Datasets	Metrics	T-FRS1		T-FRS2	
		Benign	Poison	Benign	Poison
LFW	RA_{pc}	100.00%	100.00%	100.00%	100.00%
	$p(x_{pc}\|z_{pc})$	0.022	0.021	0.021	0.023
	ASR	0.00%	100.00%	0.00%	88.00%
	$p(x_{ptc}\|z_{pc})$	0.003	0.022	0.002	0.016
	RA	99.40%	99.26%	98.62%	98.62%
	$p(x\|z)$	0.022	0.022	0.022	0.022
CASIA	RA_{pc}	86.49%	86.49%	94.59%	100.00%
	$p(x_{pc}\|z_{pc})$	0.065	0.046	0.056	0.059
	ASR	0.00%	94.59%	0.00%	100.00%
	$p(x_{ptc}\|z_{pc})$	0.008	0.043	0.007	0.054
	RA	95.79%	95.46%	98.72%	97.72%
	$p(x\|z)$	0.063	0.063	0.063	0.063
Youtube	RA_{pc}	97.24%	98.66%	92.89%	96.23%
	$p(x_{pc}\|z_{pc})$	0.008	0.009	0.008	0.008
	ASR	0.00%	95.42%	0.00%	89.00%
	$p(x_{ptc}\|z_{pc})$	0.001	0.006	0.002	0.005
	RA	95.61%	95.59%	92.69%	92.68%
	$p(x\|z)$	0.008	0.008	0.008	0.008

4.4 Poisoning Attack Results and Analysis

Conducting IPA toward different DNN models to demonstrate its generic performance, the T-FRSs with different feature extraction modules and different face datasets are adopted for the poisoning attacks. The comparison of performance results before and after attacking is shown in Table 3.

For different face datasets, the T-FRSs with the same structure have different RA. For example, the RA of LFW is higher than CASIA and Youtube in Table 3. We suppose that face images in CASIA dataset are photographed according to the prescribed posture, but only 5 images of each person are randomly selected during training. Thus, the test example may be misclassified due to its similar angle to examples of other classes in the training dataset. The $p(x_{ptc}|z_{pc})$ of CASIA is higher than LFW and Youtube, which is mainly because CASIA has fewer categories than LFW and Youtube.

Different feature extraction modules work differently for different face datasets. The RA in Table 3 shows that T-FRS1 achieves better results on LFW than CASIA. This is mainly related to the dataset used when the feature extractor is trained.

IPA can conduct a more insidious poisoning attack. From Table 3, we find that instead of reducing RA_{pc}, IPA may improve RA_{pc}. This is mainly because

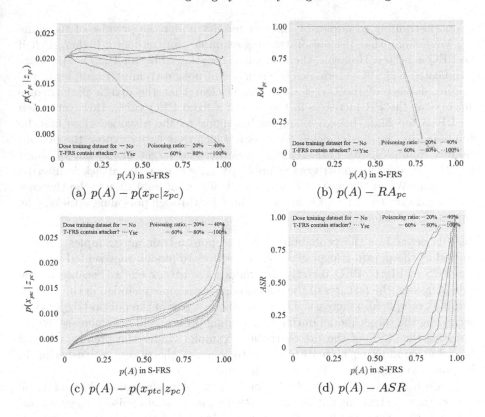

Fig. 6. The impact of different hyperparameters on attack ability and stealthiness of IPA.

although the poison-training examples are identical to the benign ones labeled as poisoned class under visual observation, their features are different, which changes the coverage of the poisoned class in the feature space of the T-FRS. If the coverage becomes wider, the RA_{pc} and $p(x_{pc}|z_{pc})$ will also increase. For instance, the RA_{pc} of T-FRS2 on CASIA dataset increases from 94.59% to 100% after the poisoning attack, and the $p(x_{pc}|z_{pc})$ also increases from 0.056 to 0.059. From ASR and $p(x_{ptc}|z_{pc})$, we find that poison-trigger examples can be recognized as the poisoned class with high probability and high success rate. In a word, the experimental results demonstrate that IPA can attack different T-FRSs with a high success rate and high probability without affecting the RA of benign examples.

4.5 Hyperparametric Analysis

Three hyperparameters may influence the attack ability and stealthiness of IPA, including poison-training example quality (PEQ), poisoning ratio (PR) and target model's knowledge (TMK). (1) PEQ measures the attack ability achieved by poison-training examples of different quality under the premise of the same PR. We assume that the poison-training example can conduct a higher ASR if the PEQ is better. However, the example generation of better PEQ is also more complicated. (2) PR determines the number of poison-training examples in the training dataset of the target model. It is clear that the attack performance improves as the PR increases in the case of a fixed PEQ value. However, when the PR is too high, benign examples belonging to the poisoned class may be eliminated by the cluster defense strategy, which may easily expose the poison-training examples. (3) TMK refers to whether the target model knows about the attacker (the poison-trigger example), i. e., whether the attack is internal or external. When the answer is yes, the attack is internal. It may be the case that insiders try to gain higher access authorities through poisoning attacks. The opposite is an external attack.

PEQ is defined as the probability that the poison-training examples are recognized as the poison-trigger class by the surrogate model, represented as $p(A)$ in S-FRS in Fig. 6. PEQ directly determines the attack effect, because as the $p(A)$ increases, the features of the poison-trigger example included in the poison-training example also increase. Therefore, the features of the poison-trigger class learned by the target model during the training process will also increase, which promotes the ASR of the poison-trigger example. Under the premise of fixed PR value, conducting high PEQ needs to increase the poison perturbation in the poison-training example, which will reduce its stealthiness.

Figure 6 shows the impact of PEQ on IPA attack performance. The solid line denotes that the training dataset of T-FRS does not contain poison-trigger examples, and the dotted line denotes that the training dataset contains poison-trigger examples. The solid and dotted lines with the same color are basically coincident, which represents that the poison-training examples contain the features of poison-training examples and can perform functions similar to poison-trigger examples.

In Fig. 6(a), as the value of $p(A)$ increases, the curve of $p(x_{pc}|z_{pc})$ rises first and then falls. When the value of $p(A)$ is small, the gap between the poison-training example and the benign example belonging to the poisoned class is small. The small gap leads to the coverage of T-FRS's poisoned class increases in the feature space, which promotes the recognition of benign examples belonging to the poisoned class. However, when $p(A)$ exceeds a certain threshold, the gap between the poison-training example and the benign example increases, resulting in the discontinuity of coverage of T-FRS's poisoned class in the feature space.

In Fig. 6(b), with the increase of $p(A)$, the RA_{pc} is still one hundred percent except that all examples of the poisoned class are poisoned. Although the probability that benign examples belonging to the poisoned class is recognized as the poisoned class is gradually decreased, the probabilities recognized as other classes are lower. Thus, RA_{pc} can be kept at 100.00%. However, when the PR reaches 100%, the RA_{pc} will drop to zero as $p(A)$ increases. The main reason is that the features of benign examples of the poisoned class learned by the target model are decreased with the increase of $p(A)$.

Table 4. The attack transferability of IPA against two models on LFW and CASIA.

Datasets	FRS	Metrics	LFW		CASIA	
			FRS1	FRS2	FRS1	FRS2
LFW	FRS1	ASR	100.00%	0.00%	100.00%	7.30%
		RA_{pc}	99.40%	99.40%	95.70%	98.90%
	FRS2	ASR	0.00%	88.00%	8.00%	100.00%
		RA_{pc}	98.60%	98.60%	95.80%	98.90%
CASIA	FRS1	ASR	100.00%	64.90%	94.60%	27.00%
		RA_{pc}	99.40%	98.60%	95.50%	98.50%
	FRS2	ASR	100.00%	100.00%	18.90%	100.00%
		RA_{pc}	99.40%	98.60%	95.40%	97.70%

In Fig. 6(c), $p(x_{ptc}|z_{pc})$ increases first and then decreases gradually. This is because, as the value of $p(A)$ increases, the poison-training example contains more features of the poison-trigger example, which conducts higher attack reliability of the poison-trigger example in T-FRS. In addition, when $p(A)$ exceeds a certain threshold, poison-training examples will gradually approach the center of the poison-trigger example in the feature space of S-FRS, which reduces the coverage of poisoned class in the feature space of T-FRS. When the benign examples of the poisoned class are all replaced by poison-training examples on the training dataset, the downward trend of $p(x_{ptc}|z_{pc})$ is obvious. In Fig. 6(d), the curve trend of ASR corresponds to Fig. 6(c).

PR is defined as the proportion of poison-training examples among all examples belonging to the poisoned class. PR also affects the effect of the target model learning features of poison-trigger examples. The poison-trigger example can conduct a larger ASR when the value of PR is larger. Under the premise of fixed PEQ value, conducting high ASR requires increasing the value of PR, which also increases the exposure possibility of poison-training examples.

From Fig. 6(a) to (d), it can be drawn that IPA can achieve great attack performance against T-FRS as long as there are only 20% PR with 0.99 $p(A)$ in the training dataset. However, in this case, the $p(x_{ptc}|z_{pc})$ of poisoned T-FRS is low, and its poison perturbation is significant. In order to make the perturbation of poison-training examples highly stealthy and improve the attack reliability of poison-trigger examples against T-FRS, 40% PR is adopted.

TMK is defined as the knowledge of the attacker information contained in the target model, which indirectly affects the attack performance of the poison-trigger examples. When the target model does not know attacker information, the attack is easier than knowing attacker information. The result denotes that external attacks are easier to implement than internal attacks.

The IPA mainly considers that attacker who is not in the training dataset of T-FRS to obtain legal access. However, in some cases, attackers may also exist in the training dataset, such as user U_2 in Fig. 1 eager for higher authorities.

Table 5. Comparison of attack performances of IPA and Mislabel against DBSCAN clustering based defense.

Datasets	PR	Attacks	Metrics					
			ARI_{pc}	ARI	RA_{pc}	RA	ASR	DR
LFW	0%	Clean	1.000	0.979	0.00%	100.00%	99.40%	–
	20%	IPA	1.000	0.979	100.00%	100.00%	99.26%	0.00%
		Mislabel	1.000	0.947	0.00%	100.00%	99.23%	100.00%
	40%	IPA	1.000	0.979	100.00%	100.00%	99.34%	0.00%
		Mislabel	0.659	0.936	0.00%	100.00%	98.92%	100.00%
CASIA	0%	Clean	1.000	1.000	0.00%	86.49%	95.79%	–
	20%	IPA	1.000	1.000	94.59%	86.49%	95.46%	0.00%
		Mislabel	0.816	0.980	0.00%	86.49%	95.79%	100.00%
	40%	IPA	1.000	1.000	95.64%	86.30%	95.46%	0.00%
		Mislabel	0.722	0.970	0.00%	86.28%	95.79%	100.00%
Youtube	0%	Clean	1.000	0.975	0.00%	97.24%	95.61%	–
	20%	IPA	1.000	0.972	91.42%	98.36%	95.60%	0.00%
		Mislabel	0.823	0.969	0.00%	97.14%	95.61%	100.00%
	40%	IPA	1.000	0.968	92.37%	97.25%	95.59%	0.00%
		Mislabel	0.680	0.951	0.00%	96.93%	95.60%	100.00%

From Fig. 6(a) and (b), it can be concluded that whether the poison-trigger examples exist in the training dataset of T-FRS or not, the RA of benign examples is hardly affected. In Fig. 6(c), it can be drawn that $p(x_{ptc}|z_{pc})$ with poison-trigger examples in the training dataset of T-FRS is smaller than $p(x_{ptc}|z_{pc})$ without ones in the training dataset.

4.6　Transferability Analysis

For more practical application, we suppose the attacker doesn't grasp the detail of the target model or training data when poisoning it. So the IPA will aim at one model to generate the possible poison-training examples and uses them to attack another black-box model. Therefore, we studied the transferability of IPA to observe its behavior in transfer attacks. The experimental results are shown in Table 4. We can find that higher ASR can be obtained by adopting the same feature extraction module, which is independent of the training datasets. Surprisingly, the ASR will be significantly higher when applying different training datasets to FRS1 and FRS2. We believe that this is mainly because the training process of T-FRS will be affected by the example environment(i.e., the background when the photo is taken) with different training datasets, rather than just focusing on facial features.

　　Thus, two ways can be adopted for improving the ASR of IPA in transferable attack: (1) build the feature extraction module of T-FRS or train the surrogate

FRS as far as possible; (2) transfer the attention of the model when training poison-training examples. That is, the features extracted in the training process are not about the face itself, but about the background or other marks.

4.7 Attack Against Model with Defense

In order to explore whether IPA can attack the model with defense, we adopt clustering-based defense to testify the performance of IPA and Mislabel. The experimental results are shown in Table 5. It demonstrates that IPA can attack the model with clustering defense when defense is used as data preprocessing.

DBSCAN clustering is helpful for poison example detection since it can cluster the poison-training examples as outliers without information of the cluster number in advance. Table 5 shows the face recognition system with the DBSCAN defense. The parameter settings are the same as in Sect. 4.2. It should be noted that: (1) since the defense model may only be used as data preprocessing, the feature extractor of DBSCAN may be different from the feature extractor of the target model; (2) the defense method will remove the poison-training examples from the dataset after they are exposed.

From Table 5, we can find that $ARI \neq 1$, regardless of whether there is a poisoning attack. This is mainly because there are certain noises in the training dataset of DBSCAN, so it is normal for IPA not be equal to 1. In addition, we can also find that the DBSCAN clustering is not working well against IPA, but can defend the Mislabel. This is mainly because the poison-training examples generated by IPA are similar to the clean ones. Mislabel can be easily identified by both human eyes and the clustering defense. However, it should be noted that IPA can invalidate the defense, but its premise is that the features of the clustering are different from those of the target model. If they are the same, IPA may also be successfully defended.

5   Conclusion and Future Works

In this paper, we propose a highly stealthy face poisoning attack, named IPA, which uses multi-objective optimization to generate poison-training examples with invisible perturbation. Compared with other poisoning attacks, it is more stealthy and more difficult to be perceived by human eyes. In addition, our experimental results show that IPA is highly toxic, i.e., the model can identify people who are not in the training dataset as target persons with high probability by only injecting a poison-training example to the training dataset. The RA of the model for benign examples decreased by 0.36%, and the average ASR of IPA is 95%.

The paper aims to illustrate that it's a serious security threat of the poisoning attack in deep learning and help researchers pay more attention to the real-world applications. Invisible poisoning attack is an open problem, we may adopt other efficient methods to generate possible poison-training examples in the future. We will also improve the generation strategy for crafting more subtle poison-training examples. The surrogate model training strategy adopted in the experiment is simple. More practical and advanced methods for surrogate model construction, i.e. gradient distillation, ensemble substitution should be considered. Furthermore, we will also study defense algorithms against IPA.

Acknowledgments. This work was partly supported by the Zhejiang Provincial Natural Science Foundation of China under Grant No. LY19F020025, the Major Special Funding for Science and Technology Innovation 2025 in Ningbo under Grant No. 2018B10063, NSFC under No. 61772466 and U1836202, the Zhejiang Provincial Natural Science Foundation for Distinguished Young Scholars under No. LR19F020003, the Provincial Key Research and Development Program of Zhejiang, China under No. 2017C01055, and the Alibaba-ZJU Joint Research Institute of Frontier Technologies.

References

1. Adi, Y., Baum, C., Cisse, M., Pinkas, B., Keshet, J.: Turning your weakness into a strength: watermarking deep neural networks by backdooring. In: 27th {USENIX} Security Symposium ({USENIX} Security 18), pp. 1615–1631 (2018)
2. Akhtar, N., Mian, A.: Threat of adversarial attacks on deep learning in computer vision: a survey. IEEE Access **6**, 14410–14430 (2018)
3. Alberti, M., et al.: Are you tampering with my data? In: Leal-Taixé, L., Roth, S. (eds.) ECCV 2018. LNCS, vol. 11130, pp. 296–312. Springer, Cham (2019). https://doi.org/10.1007/978-3-030-11012-3_25
4. Chen, H., Rohani, B.D., Koushanfar, F.: DeepMarks: a digital fingerprinting framework for deep neural networks. arXiv preprint arXiv:1804.03648 (2018)
5. Chen, J., Hu, K., Yang, Y., Liu, Y., Xuan, Q.: Collective transfer learning for defect prediction. Neurocomputing (2019)
6. Chen, J., Yang, Y., Hu, K., Xuan, Q., Liu, Y., Yang, C.: Multiview transfer learning for software defect prediction. IEEE Access **7**, 8901–8916 (2019)
7. Chen, J., et al.: E-LSTM-D: a deep learning framework for dynamic network link prediction. arXiv preprint arXiv:1902.08329 (2019)
8. Chen, J., et al.: DGEPN-GCEN2V: a new framework for mining GGI and its application in biomarker detection. Sci. China Inf. Sci. **61**, 050108 (2018)
9. Chen, X., Liu, C., Li, B., Lu, K., Song, D.: Targeted backdoor attacks on deep learning systems using data poisoning. arXiv preprint arXiv:1712.05526 (2017)
10. Chen, Y., Li, Y., Narayan, R., Subramanian, A., Xie, X.: Gene expression inference with deep learning. Bioinformatics **32**(12), 1832–1839 (2016)
11. Deb, K., Pratap, A., Agarwal, S., Meyarivan, T.: A fast and elitist multiobjective genetic algorithm: NSGA-II. IEEE Trans. Evol. Comput. **6**(2), 182–197 (2002)
12. Du, T., Ji, S., Li, J., Gu, Q., Wang, T., Beyah, R.: SirenAttack: generating adversarial audio for end-to-end acoustic systems. arXiv preprint arXiv:1901.07846 (2019)
13. Esfe, M.H., Hajmohammad, H., Moradi, R., Arani, A.A.A.: Multi-objective optimization of cost and thermal performance of double walled carbon nanotubes/ water nanofluids by NSGA-II using response surface method. Appl. Therm. Eng. **112**, 1648–1657 (2017)
14. Gu, T., Dolan-Gavitt, B., Garg, S.: BadNets: identifying vulnerabilities in the machine learning model supply chain. arXiv preprint arXiv:1708.06733 (2017)

15. Hitaj, D., Mancini, L.V.: Have you stolen my model? Evasion attacks against deep neural network watermarking techniques. arXiv preprint arXiv:1809.00615 (2018)
16. Kamjoo, A., Maheri, A., Dizqah, A.M., Putrus, G.A.: Multi-objective design under uncertainties of hybrid renewable energy system using NSGA-II and chance constrained programming. Int. J. Electr. Power Energy Syst. **74**, 187–194 (2016)
17. Li, B., Wang, Y., Singh, A., Vorobeychik, Y.: Data poisoning attacks on factori zation-based collaborative filtering. In: Advances in Neural Information Processing Systems, pp. 1885–1893 (2016)
18. Li, Y., Liao, S., Liu, G.: Thermo-economic multi-objective optimization for a solar-dish Brayton system using NSGA-II and decision making. Int. J. Electr. Power Energy Syst. **64**, 167–175 (2015)
19. Liu, K., Dolan-Gavitt, B., Garg, S.: Fine-pruning: defending against backdooring attacks on deep neural networks. In: Bailey, M., Holz, T., Stamatogiannakis, M., Ioannidis, S. (eds.) RAID 2018. LNCS, vol. 11050, pp. 273–294. Springer, Cham (2018). https://doi.org/10.1007/978-3-030-00470-5_13
20. Liu, W., Wang, Z., Liu, X., Zeng, N., Liu, Y., Alsaadi, F.E.: A survey of deep neural network architectures and their applications. Neurocomputing **234**, 11–26 (2017)
21. Liu, Y., et al.: Trojaning attack on neural networks (2017)
22. Liu, Y., Xie, Y., Srivastava, A.: Neural trojans. In: 2017 IEEE International Conference on Computer Design (ICCD), pp. 45–48. IEEE (2017)
23. McCann, M.T., Jin, K.H., Unser, M.: Convolutional neural networks for inverse problems in imaging: a review. IEEE Signal Process. Mag. **34**(6), 85–95 (2017)
24. Merrer, E.L., Perez, P., Trédan, G.: Adversarial frontier stitching for remote neural network watermarking. arXiv preprint arXiv:1711.01894 (2017)
25. Neyestani, M., Hesari, S., Hatami, M.: Planned production of thermal units for reducing the emissions and costs using the improved NSGA II method. Case Stud. Therm. Eng. **13**, 100397 (2019)
26. Parkhi, O.M., Vedaldi, A., Zisserman, A., et al.: Deep face recognition. In: BMVC, vol. 1, p. 6 (2015)
27. Pereira, L.A., Haffner, S., Nicol, G., Dias, T.F.: Multiobjective optimization of five-phase induction machines based on NSGA-II. IEEE Trans. Ind. Electron. **64**(12), 9844–9853 (2017)
28. Schroff, F., Kalenichenko, D., Philbin, J.: FaceNet: a unified embedding for face recognition and clustering. In: Proceedings of the IEEE Conference on Computer Vision and Pattern Recognition, pp. 815–823 (2015)
29. Shen, S., Tople, S., Saxena, P.: AUROR: defending against poisoning attacks in collaborative deep learning systems. In: Proceedings of the 32nd Annual Conference on Computer Security Applications, pp. 508–519. ACM (2016)
30. Srinivas, N., Deb, K.: Muiltiobjective optimization using nondominated sorting in genetic algorithms. Evol. Comput. **2**(3), 221–248 (1994)
31. Steinhardt, J., Koh, P.W.W., Liang, P.S.: Certified defenses for data poisoning attacks. In: Advances in Neural Information Processing Systems, pp. 3517–3529 (2017)
32. Su, J., Vargas, D.V., Sakurai, K.: One pixel attack for fooling deep neural networks. IEEE Trans. Evol. Comput. **23**, 828–841 (2019)
33. Uchida, Y., Nagai, Y., Sakazawa, S., Satoh, S.: Embedding watermarks into deep neural networks. In: Proceedings of the 2017 ACM on International Conference on Multimedia Retrieval, pp. 269–277. ACM (2017)

34. Vo-Duy, T., Duong-Gia, D., Ho-Huu, V., Vu-Do, H., Nguyen-Thoi, T.: Multi-objective optimization of laminated composite beam structures using NSGA-II algorithm. Compos. Struct. **168**, 498–509 (2017)
35. Wang, S., Liu, T., Nam, J., Tan, L.: Deep semantic feature learning for software defect prediction. IEEE Trans. Softw. Eng. (2018)
36. Wolf, L., Hassner, T., Maoz, I.: Face recognition in unconstrained videos with matched background similarity. IEEE (2011)
37. Wu, Z., Pan, S., Chen, F., Long, G., Zhang, C., Yu, P.S.: A comprehensive survey on graph neural networks. arXiv preprint arXiv:1901.00596 (2019)
38. Yang, C., Wu, Q., Li, H., Chen, Y.: Generative poisoning attack method against neural networks. arXiv preprint arXiv:1703.01340 (2017)
39. Young, T., Hazarika, D., Poria, S., Cambria, E.: Recent trends in deep learning based natural language processing. IEEE Comput. Intell. Mag. **13**(3), 55–75 (2018)
40. Zhao, M., An, B., Yu, Y., Liu, S., Pan, S.J.: Data poisoning attacks on multi-task relationship learning. In: Thirty-Second AAAI Conference on Artificial Intelligence (2018)
41. Zhou, J., Cui, G., Zhang, Z., Yang, C., Liu, Z., Sun, M.: Graph neural networks: a review of methods and applications. arXiv preprint arXiv:1812.08434 (2018)

Privacy-Preserving and yet Robust Collaborative Filtering Recommender as a Service

Qiang Tang[✉]

Luxembourg Institute of Science and Technology (LIST),
4362 Esch sur Alzette, Luxembourg
qiang.tang@list.lu

Abstract. In this paper, we provide a general system structure for latent factor based collaborative filtering recommenders by formulating them into *model training* and *prediction computing* stages. Aiming at pragmatic solutions, we first show how to construct privacy-preserving and yet robust *model training* stage based on existing solutions. Then, we propose two cryptographic protocols to realize a privacy-preserving *prediction computing* stage, depending on whether or not an extra proxy is involved.

1 Introduction

Today, personalization is widely adopted by a large number of industries, from entertainment to precision medicine. The main enabling technology is recommender systems, which employ all sorts of techniques to predict the preferences of human subjects (e.g. the likes and dislikes towards a movie). So far, a lot of generic recommender algorithms have been proposed, as surveyed in [10]. Recently, deep learning has become a very powerful tool and has been used for numerous applications, including recommender [14]. Nevertheless, the collaborative filtering recommender systems are most popular and well-known due to their explainable nature (e.g. you like x so you may also like y).

Besides the likes and dislikes, users' preferences might lead to inferences towards other sensitive information about the individuals, e.g. the religion, political orientation, and financial status. When a user is involved in a recommender system with a pseudonym, there is the risk of re-identification. For instance, Weinsberg et al. [13] demonstrated that what has been rated by a user can potentially help an attacker identify this user. Privacy issues have been recognized for a long time and a lot of solutions have been proposed today, as surveyed in [2,6]. Robustness is about controlling the effect of manipulated inputs, and is a fundamental issue for recommender systems. In their seminal work, Lam and Riedl [7] investigated the concept of shilling attacks, where a malicious company lies to the recommender system (or, inject fake profiles) to have its own products recommended more often than those from its competitors. Following this, a number of works have been dedicated to the investigation of different robustness

© Springer Nature Switzerland AG 2020
Z. Liu and M. Yung (Eds.): Inscrypt 2019, LNCS 12020, pp. 199–207, 2020.
https://doi.org/10.1007/978-3-030-42921-8_11

attacks and corresponding countermeasures. Unfortunately, very little has been done to consider both privacy and robustness in existing research work.

1.1   Our Contribution

In this paper, we aim at a comprehensive investigation of the privacy and robustness issues for recommender systems, by considering both the *model training* and the *prediction computing* stages. Towards privacy-preserving solutions that respect robustness attack detection, we separately address the issues in the *model training* and *prediction computing* stages. For the former, we show that existing solutions can be adapted, particularly it is straightforward for the expert-based ones such as that from [12]. As to the latter, we propose two new cryptographic protocols, one of which involves an extra proxy.

Due to the space limitation, the details about security model and performance analysis for our new solutions appear in the full paper [11].

2   System Model and Preliminary

We assume the RecSys builds recommender models and offers recommendation as a service to the privacy-aware users, who are not willing to disclose their rating vectors while still wishing to receive recommendations. For our recommender as a service scenario, we assume a system architecture shown in Fig. 1. Next, we briefly introduce what will happen in the two stages.

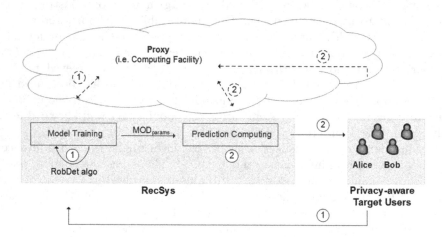

Fig. 1. Recommender as a service architecture

1. In the *model training* stage, labeled in Fig. 1, the RecSys trains a model, e.g. similarities between items (or users) in neighbourhood-based recommenders and feature matrices for users and items in latent model based ones, based

on data from one or more sources. To clean the data and detect robustness attacks, before the training, we suppose that the RecSys will run an algorithm RobDet over the training dataset. To simplify our discussion, we assume the output of RobDet is a binary bit for every input profile. If it is 0, then the profile is deemed as malicious so that will not be used.

2. After training, we refer to the output of the model training stage as a set of parameters MOD_{params}. Note that the parameters might be in an encrypted form when privacy protection has been applied. In the *prediction computing* stage, the RecSys uses the model parameters MOD_{params} and possibly Alice's rating vector to infer Alice's preferences.

In the full paper [11], we describe different privacy attack scenarios and show how to model them.

2.1   Preliminary on Homomorphic Encryption

We use the notation $x \xleftarrow{\$} Y$ to denote that x is chosen from the set Y uniformly at random. A public key encryption scheme consists of three algorithms (Keygen, Enc, Dec): Keygen(λ, L) generates a key pair (PK, SK); Enc(m, PK) outputs a ciphertext c; Dec(c, SK) outputs a plaintext m. Some schemes, e.g. Paillier [9], are additively homomorphic, which means there is an operator $\oplus$ such that Enc$(m_1, PK) \oplus$ Enc$(m_2, PK) =$ Enc$(m_1 + m_2, PK)$. While some recent somewhat homomorphic encryption (SWHE) schemes are both additively and multiplicatively homomorphic to a certain number of operations, which means there are operators $\oplus$ and $\otimes$ such that Enc$(m_1, PK) \oplus$ Enc$(m_2, PK) =$ Enc$(m_1 + m_2, PK)$ and Enc$(m_1, PK) \otimes$ Enc$(m_2, PK) =$ Enc$(m_1 m_2, PK)$. In practice, one of the most widely-used SWHE library is Simple Encrypted Arithmetic Library (SEAL) from Microsoft [5], which is an optimized implementation of the YASHE scheme [3]. Note that homomorphic subtraction $\ominus$ can be directly defined based on $\oplus$ and with similar computational cost.

3   Privacy-Preserving and Robust Expert-Based Solution

In the proposed solution, we adopt the recommender algorithm [12], which has the nice property that the privacy-aware user Alice does not need to share her rating vector with the RecSys to train the recommender model and the process of model training is very simple. Note that in some other expert-based recommender systems, Alice's data may not be needed to train the model but the process of model training will be much more complex. We assume there are M items in the item set for the recommendation service.

1. In the solution, the *model training* stage is very straightforward. Given an expert dataset, the RecSys can first run any robustness attack detection algorithm RobDet to figure out the outliers or even malicious profiles. Then, the RecSys can learn the model parameters $\Theta = \{\mathbf{A}, \mathbf{Q}, \mathbf{b}_t^*, \mathbf{b}_j^*\}$ from the expert dataset, which is publicly available to the RecSys.

2. Let's assume that Alice is labelled as user i in the privacy-aware user group, the *prediction computing* stage consists of the following steps.
   (a) User i generates a public/private key pair (pk_i, sk_i) for Paillier scheme, and shares the public key pk_i with RecSys.
   (b) User i sends $[\![\mathbf{R}_i]\!]_{pk_i}$ and $[\![\overline{\mathbf{R}_i}]\!]_{pk_i}$ to the RecSys, which may require the user to prove that the encrypted $\mathbf{R}_i$ is well formed similar to what has been done in [4].
   (c) If everything is ok, the RecSys can predict user i's preference on item j as

$$[\![\hat{r}_{i,j}]\!]_{pk_i} = [\![\overline{\mathbf{R}_i}]\!]_{pk_i} \oplus b_j \oplus [\![\mathbf{R}_i]\!]_{pk_i} \mathbf{A}\mathbf{q}_j^T \tag{1}$$

   (d) If there is no proxy, user i and the RecSys run the protocol from Sect. 3.1 to generate recommendations for user i. Otherwise, they run the protocol from Sect. 3.2.

Next, we describe privacy-preserving protocols for user i to learn the unrated items whose predictions fall into a set $\{V_1, \cdots V_T\}$. Here T will be a small integer, which may be 2 or 3 in practice referring to the analysis of full paper [11]. Observing that privacy-preserving protocols for the model training stage often output integer predictions (in encrypted form), because they need to scale the intermediary computation results in order to be compatible with the cryptographic tools such as homomorphic encryption algorithms. Therefore, we assume the RecSys possesses the encrypted predictions $[\![x_j \cdot \theta + y_j]\!]_{pk_i}$ for every $1 \leq j \leq M$ at the end of the privacy-preserving model training stage. We explicitly present the ratings according to a unit θ, because in our protocol the recommendations will only be based on the x_j part and the y_j part is rounding off.

3.1 Privacy-Preserving Prediction Computing Without Proxy

At the beginning of the prediction computing stage, we suppose user i possesses two public/private key pairs: one is (PK_i, SK_i) for Paillier scheme (from the model training stage) while the other is a new key pair (PK_i', SK_i') for a SWHE scheme [8]. The public keys PK_i, PK_i' are shared with the RecSys. As shown in Fig. 2, the protocol runs in two phases where λ is the security parameter.

In the *reduction* phase, the RecSys and user i round off the y_j part in the encrypted predictions. Specifically, for every $1 \leq j \leq M$, the following operations will be carried out.

1. The RecSys first randomizes x_j and y_j to generates Δ_j for user i.
2. Then, user i obtains the randomized prediction value α_j through decryption and then computes β_j, which is the randomized x_j in an approximation form with $\epsilon_j \in \{0, 1\}$. Finally, user i encrypts β_j under his own SWHE public key if item j is unrated, and encrypts a random value otherwise.
3. After receiving Γ_j, the RecSys homomorphically removes the randomization noise r_{j1} to obtain Φ_j, which is a ciphertext for $x_j + \epsilon_j$ if item j is unrated and a ciphertext for a random value otherwise.

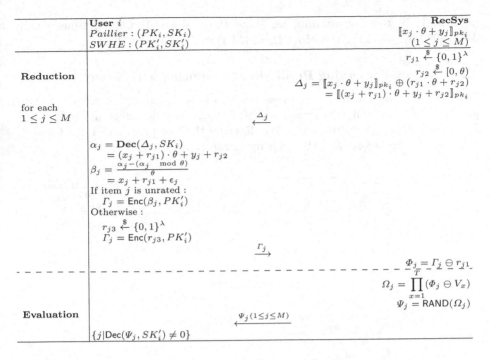

Fig. 2. Learning membership in $\{V_1, \cdots V_T\}$ without a proxy

In the *Evaluation* phase, for every $1 \leq j \leq M$, the RecSys computes Ω_j through T homomorphic subtractions and $T - 1$ multiplications, which is a ciphertext for 0 if the plaintext corresponding to Φ_j falls into $\{V_1, \cdots V_T\}$ and a ciphertext for a non-zero value otherwise. In order to hide the non-zero values, the RecSys randomizes Ω_j via the RAND function, e.g. homomorphically multiplying a random number, to obtain Ψ_j, which can be decrypted by user i to learn the index of recommended items.

For Paillier, we set the size of N to be 2048, and for SWHE we use Microsoft SEAL library. We select the ciphertext modulus $q = 2^{226} - 2^{26} + 1$, the polynomial modulus $p(x) = x^{8192} + 1$. Using Chinese Reminder Theorem, we select two 40-bit primes to represent the plaintext space of 2^{80}. The primes are 1099511922689 and 1099512004609. Based on an Intel(R) Core(TM) i7-5600U CPU 2.60 GHz, 8 GB RAM, we benchmark the running time of the above solution. The number of different cryptographic operations for the proposed protocol are summarized

Table 1. Computational complexities

	Paillier.Dec	Paillier.$\oplus$	SWHE.Enc	SWHE.Dec	SWHE.$\otimes$	partial SWHE.$\otimes$	SWHE.$\oplus$	Time
User	M		M	M				420 s
RecSys		M		M	$M(T-1)$		$M(T+1)$	998 s

in Table 1. In the last column, we show the real-world running time, where $M = 4000$ by assuming the MovieLens 1M Dataset and $T = 2$.

3.2 Privacy-Preserving Prediction Computing with Proxy

To enable the new protocol, we make use of a key-homomorphic pseudorandom function Prf [1]. Given $\mathsf{Prf}(k_1, m)$ and $\mathsf{Prf}(k_2, m)$, anybody can compute $\mathsf{Prf}(k_1 + k_2, m) = \mathsf{Prf}(k_1, m) \oplus \mathsf{Prf}(k_2, m)$. We describe the two phases in Figs. 3 and 4, respectively. As before, λ is the security parameter.

	User i $Paillier : (PK_i, SK_i)$ $SWHE : (PK'_i, SK'_i)$	RecSys $[\![x_j \cdot \theta + y_j]\!]_{pk_i}$ $(1 \le j \le M)$
Reduction for each $1 \le j \le M$		$r_{j1} \overset{\$}{\leftarrow} \{0,1\}^\lambda$ $r_{j2} \overset{\$}{\leftarrow} [0, \theta)$ $\Delta_j = [\![x_j \cdot \theta + y_j]\!]_{pk_i} \ominus (r_{j1} \cdot \theta - r_{j2})$ $\quad = [\![(x_j - r_{j1}) \cdot \theta + y_j + r_{j2}]\!]_{pk_i}$
	$\overset{\Delta_j}{\longleftarrow}$	
	$\alpha_j = \mathbf{Dec}(\Delta_j, SK_i)$ $\quad = (x_j - r_{j1}) \cdot \theta + y_j + r_{j2}$ $\beta_j = \frac{\alpha_j - (\alpha_j \mod \theta)}{\theta}$ $\quad = x_j - r_{j1} + \epsilon_j$ $r_{j3} \overset{\$}{\leftarrow} \{0,1\}^{2\lambda}$ If item unrated : $\gamma_j = r_{j3} + \beta_j$ $\quad = x_j - r_{j1} + \epsilon_j + r_{j3}$ If item rated : $\gamma_j = r_{j3}$	
	$\overset{\gamma_j}{\longrightarrow}$	
		$\gamma_j = \gamma_j + r_{j1}$

Fig. 3. Reduction phase

Similar to the case shown in Fig. 2, in the *reduction* phase, the RecSys and user i interactively round off the y_j part in the predictions for every j. The main difference (and simplification) is that, at the end of the protocol, the RecSys possesses $\gamma_j = x_j + \epsilon_j + r_{j3}$ if item j has been rated and $\gamma_j = r_{j3} + r_{j1}$ otherwise, while user i possesses the random number r_{j3}.

The evaluation phase, shown in Fig. 4, proceeds as follows.

1. User i first establishes M random messages $R_j(1 \le j \le M)$, random permutation functions PM and $\mathsf{PM}_j(1 \le j \le M)$, and a hash function H with the RecSys. Given a vector of M elements, PM randomly permutes the order of the elements. Similarly, given a vector of T elements, PM_j randomly permutes the order of the elements.
2. User i chooses M random keys $K_j(1 \le j \le M)$ for Prf and evaluates Prf for R_j with the key $K_j - r_{j3}$ to obtain Υ_j, for every $1 \le j \le M$. At the same time, the RecSys evaluates Prf for R_j with the key γ_j to obtain Θ_j, for every $1 \le j \le M$.

User i	Proxy	RecSys
$r_{j3}(1 \leq j \leq M)$		$\gamma_j(1 \leq j \leq M)$

$R_j, \mathsf{PM}_j(1 \leq j \leq M)$		$R_j, \mathsf{PM}_j(1 \leq j \leq M)$
PM, H		PM, H
$K_j(1 \leq j \leq M) \leftarrow \{0,1\}^{3\lambda}$		
$\Upsilon_j = \mathsf{Prf}(K_j - r_{j3}, R_j)$		$\Theta_j = \mathsf{Prf}(\gamma_j, R_j)$
$(1 \leq j \leq M)$		$(1 \leq j \leq M)$

$$\xrightarrow{\mathsf{PM}\{(\Upsilon_1,\cdots,\Upsilon_M)\}} \qquad \Xi \qquad \xleftarrow{\mathsf{PM}\{(\Theta_1,\cdots,\Theta_M)\}}$$

$\Omega_{x,j} = \mathsf{H}(\mathsf{Prf}(K_j + V_x, R_j))$		
$(1 \leq x \leq T, 1 \leq j \leq M)$		
$\Omega_{*,j} = \mathsf{PM}_j\{(\Omega_{1,j},\cdots,\Omega_{T,j})\}$		

$$\xrightarrow{\mathsf{PM}\{(\Omega_{*,1},\cdots,\Omega_{*,M})\}} \qquad \mathbb{S}$$

$$\xleftarrow{\mathbb{S}}$$

Fig. 4. Evaluation phase (w.r.t. $\{V_1, \cdots V_T\}$)

3. After receiving the permuted values from user i and the RecSys, the proxy computes

$$\Xi = \mathsf{PM}\{(\Upsilon_1, \cdots, \Upsilon_M)\} \oplus \mathsf{PM}\{(\Theta_1, \cdots, \Theta_M)\},$$

where $\oplus$ is performed element wise. It is easy to check that if the item j is unrated

$$\Upsilon_j \oplus \Theta_j = \mathsf{Prf}(K_j + x_j + \epsilon_j, R_j), \text{ and otherwise}$$

$$\Upsilon_j \oplus \Theta_j = \mathsf{Prf}(K_j + r_{j1}, R_j).$$

4. User i first computes $\Omega_{x,j} = \mathsf{H}(\mathsf{Prf}(K_j + V_x, R_j))$ for every $1 \leq x \leq T, 1 \leq j \leq M$, and then computes a randomized check value vector $\Omega_{*,j} = \mathsf{PM}_j\{(\Omega_{1,j}, \cdots, \Omega_{T,j})\}$ for every item j. It permutes a vector, formed by individual check value vectors of all items, and sends the result $\mathsf{PM}\{(\Omega_{*,1}, \cdots, \Omega_{*,M})\}$ to the RecSys.

5. After receiving $\mathsf{PM}\{(\Omega_{*,1}, \cdots, \Omega_{*,M})\}$ from the user, the proxy can compute $\mathbb{S}$, which is a new set generated based on Ξ: for every element in Ξ, if its hash value with respect to H appears in the corresponding element in $\mathsf{PM}\{(\Omega_{*,1}, \cdots, \Omega_{*,M})\}$ then the corresponding element in $\mathbb{S}$ is set to be 1 otherwise it is set to be 0.

6. With $\mathbb{S}$ and PM, user i can identify the unrated items whose approximated predictions fall into the set $\{V_1, \cdots V_T\}$.

Table 2. Computational Complexities

	Paillier.Dec	Paillier.$\oplus$	Prf.Evaluate	Prf.Hadd	Time
User	M		$M(1+T)$		63.52 s
RecSys		M	M		4.16 s
Proxy				M	40 ms

We summarize the asymptotic complexity in Table 2. Based on the reference codes by the authors of [1], the Prf.Evaluate and Prf.Hadd takes about 1.04 ms and 10 μs. W.r.t. the MovieLens 1M Dataset and $T = 2$, we compute the real-world running time and put it in the last column of Table 2.

Acknowledgement. This work is partially funded by the European Unions Horizon 2020 SPARTA project, under grant agreement No 830892. The author would like to thank his current colleague Bowen Liu for running the experiment in Sect. 3.2.

References

1. Banerjee, A., Peikert, C.: New and improved key-homomorphic pseudorandom functions. In: Garay, J.A., Gennaro, R. (eds.) CRYPTO 2014. LNCS, vol. 8616, pp. 353–370. Springer, Heidelberg (2014). https://doi.org/10.1007/978-3-662-44371-2_20
2. Jeckmans, A.J.P., Beye, M., Erkin, Z., Hartel, P., Lagendijk, R.L., Tang, Q.: Privacy in recommender systems. In: Ramzan, N., van Zwol, R., Lee, J.S., Clüver, K., Hua, X.S. (eds.) Social Media Retrieval. Computer Communications and Networks, pp. 263–281. Springer, London (2013). https://doi.org/10.1007/978-1-4471-4555-4_12
3. Bos, J.W., Lauter, K., Loftus, J., Naehrig, M.: Improved security for a ring-based fully homomorphic encryption scheme. In: Stam, M. (ed.) IMACC 2013. LNCS, vol. 8308, pp. 45–64. Springer, Heidelberg (2013). https://doi.org/10.1007/978-3-642-45239-0_4
4. Canny, J.F.: Collaborative filtering with privacy. In: IEEE Symposium on Security and Privacy, pp. 45–57 (2002)
5. Dowlin, N., Gilad-Bachrach, R., Laine, K., Lauter, K.E., Naehrig, M., Wernsing, J.: Manual for using homomorphic encryption for bioinformatics. Proc. IEEE **105**(3), 552–567 (2017)
6. Friedman, A., Knijnenburg, B.P., Vanhecke, K., Martens, L., Berkovsky, S.: Privacy aspects of recommender systems. In: Ricci, F., Rokach, L., Shapira, B. (eds.) Recommender Systems Handbook, pp. 649–688. Springer, Boston, MA (2015). https://doi.org/10.1007/978-1-4899-7637-6_19
7. Lam, S.K., Riedl, J.: Shilling recommender systems for fun and profit. In: Proceedings of the 13th International Conference on World Wide Web, pp. 393–402 (2004)
8. Microsoft SEAL Library (2016). https://sealcrypto.codeplex.com/
9. Paillier, P.: Public-key cryptosystems based on composite degree residuosity classes. In: Stern, J. (ed.) EUROCRYPT 1999. LNCS, vol. 1592, pp. 223–238. Springer, Heidelberg (1999). https://doi.org/10.1007/3-540-48910-X_16
10. Shani, G., Gunawardana, A.: Evaluating recommendation systems. In: Ricci, F., Rokach, L., Shapira, B., Kantor, P.B. (eds.) Recommender Systems Handbook, pp. 257–297. Springer, Boston, MA (2011). https://doi.org/10.1007/978-0-387-85820-3_8
11. Tang, Q.: Privacy-preserving and yet robust collaborative filtering recommender as a service (2019). http://arxiv.org/abs/1910.03846
12. Wang, J., Arriaga, A., Tang, Q., Ryan, P.Y.A.: Novel collaborative filtering recommender friendly to privacy protection (2019)

13. Weinsberg, U., Bhagat, S., Ioannidis, S., Taft, N.: BlurMe: inferring and obfuscating user gender based on ratings. In: Sixth ACM Conference on Recommender Systems, pp. 195–202 (2012)
14. Zhang, S., Yao, L., Sun, A.: Deep learning based recommender system: a survey and new perspectives (2017). https://arxiv.org/abs/1707.07435

CAVAEva: An Engineering Platform for Evaluating Commercial Anti-malware Applications on Smartphones

Hao Jiang[1,2], Weizhi Meng[2,3(✉)], Chunhua Su[4],
and Kim-Kwang Raymond Choo[5]

[1] CyberTech, Hong Kong, China
[2] Department of Applied Mathematics and Computer Science,
Technical University of Denmark, Kongens Lyngby, Denmark
weme@dtu.dk
[3] Department of Computer Science, Guangzhou University, Guangzhou, China
[4] The University of Aizu, Aizuwakamatsu, Japan
[5] The University of Texas at San Antonio, San Antonio, USA

Abstract. The pervasiveness of mobile devices, such as Android and iOS smartphones, and the type of data available and stored on these devices make them an attractive target for cyber-attackers. For example, mobile malware authors seek to compromise devices to collect sensitive information and data from the smartphones. To mitigate such a threat, a number of online scanning platforms exist to evaluate existing anti-malware applications. However, existing platforms have a number of limitations, such as configuration inflexibility. Also, in practice, the code protection and different structures complicate efforts to effectively evaluate different commercial anti-malware software in a configurable and unified platform. Hence in this work, we design *CAVAEva*, an engineering platform for commercial anti-malware application evaluation, in which users/researchers have the capability to configure the platform based on their needs and requirements. In particular, we show how to design such a platform and introduce its performance. Specifically, we present a comparative summary of seven commercial anti-malware software, and collect the feedback from a user study. Experimental results demonstrate the potential utility of our platform in evaluating commercial anti-malware software in a real-world smartphone deployment.

Keywords: Mobile device · Smartphone security · Malware detection · Evaluation platform · Anti-malware software

1 Introduction

Smartphones, such as iPhone 11 and Galaxy S10+, are becoming more computationally capable (including storage capacities), and the amount and range of data stored on or accessible from such devices are also increasing, such as personal

© Springer Nature Switzerland AG 2020
Z. Liu and M. Yung (Eds.): Inscrypt 2019, LNCS 12020, pp. 208–224, 2020.
https://doi.org/10.1007/978-3-030-42921-8_12

and sensitive information [1,11]. Hence, it is not surprising that these devices have become an attractive target for cyber-attackers, ranging from script kiddies to state-sponsored actors (e.g., advanced persistent threat (APT) actors). Malware remains one of the key threats to mobile device security, which can collect and infer sensitive information and data from smartphones [45,47], as evidenced by studies from commercial security organizations such as Mcafee [27] and the research community [13,40,42,56].

Anti-virus (AV; also known as *anti-malware*) applications are a commonly used tool to detect malware. Such applications can use signatures and/or behavioral characteristics to identify and detect malicious applications (or malware). However, these AV engines may be targeted by cyber-attackers as well. For instance, Min and Varadharajan [38] presented an advanced AV parasitic malware, AV-Parmware, which is designed to attack protected components of AV software by exploiting their security weaknesses (similar to how systems can be compromised). They also identified weaknesses in AV software from four major vendors that can be exploited. In addition, in recent years there have been many attempts to design adversarial machine learning approaches to circumvent detection by AV applications [8]. This, therefore, necessitates the evaluation and benchmarking of different AV software, in terms of their effectiveness and efficiency (e.g., performance vs. cost) against malware.

There are a number of online scanning platforms that users can upload suspicious files for examination and obtain a report from several participating AV engines. However, such a platform is generally not configurable and sufficiently flexible. For example, it is challenging for a user to add their own AV engines, or a particular engine version. In addition, users often want to know the workload of different AV engines on their smartphones in order to select an appropriate AV application, which is not available from existing online platforms. In the current market, various AV engines are available[1], but there is no valid platform for users/researchers to evaluate different AV applications based on their own requirements. This is the gap we seek to address in this paper. The contributions in this work can be summarized as below:

- In this paper, we design an engineering platform for commercial AV application evaluation (hereafter referred to as *CAVAEva*). The platform allows users to configure the platform, for example by adding or removing AV software of interest, and to examine suspicious file(s) on a real smartphone environment. We also remark that we are not seeking to replace existing online tools, rather we are seeking to complement existing approaches.
- In addition, the code protection and different structures used by AV engines complicate efforts in implementing and automating the evaluation. Therefore, we present an approach to customize and deploy *CAVAEva* on a smartphone and a computer. In the evaluation, we evaluate seven commercial AV applications in terms of their classification performance and the incurred CPU usage on the smartphones.

---

[1] https://www.digitalcitizen.life/how-choose-great-security-product-thats-right-you.

- We further perform a user study with over 100 participants from academia and industry to collect their feedback regarding the utility of our platform. They can tune our platform according to their requirements and evaluate different AV applications. It is found that most participants considered our platform to be very useful in practice.

The remaining sections of this paper are organized as follows. Section 2 briefly reviews the relevant literature on smartphone threats and relevant studies on anti-malware comparison. Section 3 presents our proposed *CAVAEva* and its implementation. In Sect. 4, we describe an evaluation via a case study by comparing seven well-known commercial anti-virus software, and introduce a user study with over 100 participants. We also discuss some some learnt experience and challenges. Finally, we conclude this paper in Sect. 5.

2   Background and Related Work

In this section, we first introduce the background on smartphone threats, and then review existing studies on anti-malware comparison.

2.1   Background on Smartphone Threats

There is a wide range of threats to smartphones, such as malware, side channel attacks and physical channel attacks.

Malware. Lin *et al.* [20] revealed that the Android Debug Bridge (ADB) capability could be utilized by applications (apps) with the INTERNET permission installed on the same device, and built *Screenmilker* to demonstrate how such a feature can be exploited. Specifically, Screenmilker is designed to monitor the user's screen and sniff user's key-in password in real-time. When studying Android's updating mechanism, Xing *et al.* [54] identified the Pileup flaws, through which a malicious app could strategically declare a set of privileges and attributes on a lower version operating system, and wait until it is able to escalate its privileges on the new system. Consequently, a malicious app can acquire a set of newly added system and signature permissions, as well as determining their settings. Andriesse and Bos [2] introduced a code hiding approach for trigger-based malware, which can conceal malicious code inside seemingly innocuous code fragments. Min and Varadharajan [38] introduced an AV parasitic malware, AV-Parmware, designed to attack protected components of anti-virus software by exploiting their weaknesses. We refer the interested reader to [13,42,56] for a summary of existing malware research.

Accelerometer Side Channel Attacks. Side channel is often utilized by malware to steal information on mobile devices. For example, Cai and Chen [7] presented a side channel attack targeting touchscreen smartphones with only soft keyboards. Specifically, they demonstrated that when users clicked on the soft keyboard, especially when he/she holds the phone by hand rather than placing it on a fixed surface, the phone vibration on touchscreens are highly correlated to the keys being typed. They conducted a study and showed that they were able to infer correctly more than 70% of the keys typed on a number-only soft keyboard on a smartphone. Marquardt *et al.* [23] also demonstrated that an app with access to accelerometer readings on a smartphone could use side channel attacks to recover text entered on a nearby keyboard. They showed that by characterizing consecutive pairs of keypress events, up to 80% of typed content can be recovered. Do *et al.* [11] demonstrated how one can design an innocuous app to exfiltrate data from a smartphone (or any computing device) via sound frequency in the 20–22 kHz. Such an attack does not require the mobile app to request access to any permission, and uses only the built-in speaker or a connected ear phone.

Owusu *et al.* [41] demonstrated how accelerometer readings can be used to extract entire sequences of entered text on a smartphone. They showed how a background application can use the accelerometer to spy on keystroke information during sensitive activities, such as account login. In their study, the authors reportedly found 59 out of 99 passwords using only accelerometer measurements logged during text entry. Miluzzo *et al.* [39] presented *TapPrints*, a framework for inferring the location of taps on touchscreens using motion sensor data. Their approach reportedly accuracy rates of between 80% and 90% for English letters. A summary of other earlier works can be found in [4,15,18,21,46,51,57].

Physical Side Channel Attacks. These attacks are mainly based on physical objects, such as oil residues left on the touchscreen or the screen reflection from nearby objects. Aviv *et al.* [5] first explored the feasibility of smudge attacks on touchscreens with different lighting angles and light sources. They indicated that the pattern could be partially identifiable in 92% and fully in 68% of the tested lighting and camera setups. For the screen reflection, Raguram *et al.* [43] showed that automated reconstruction of text typed on a mobile device's virtual keyboard is viable, by observing the reflections (e.g. reflection of the phone on the user's lens).

Lau *et al.* [22] designed an early charging attack, *Mactans*, where the malicious charger (BeagleBoard) was used to inject malware onto smartphones when they were plugged into the malicious charger. However, their attacks require users to unlock the phone screen and install developer license in advance. Spolaor *et al.* [48] also described how an adversary could leverage a malicious charging station to exfiltrate smartphone data via a USB charging cable. Specifically, they designed *PowerSnitch*, an application designed to send data in the form of power bursts by manipulating the power consumption of the device's CPU. One limitation of this attack is that users have to pre-install a small app on their phones. Meng *et al.* [32,33] developed JFC attacks, which can record screen information during the whole charging period. Such an approach does not require any request for permission or phone unlock action, and cannot be detected by existing anti-AV applications. To launching this attack, an additional hardware of VGA/USB interface is needed, which can be easily purchased online. Therefore, charging attacks are a real risk for smartphone users [34,35].

2.2 Related Work

To mitigate the above threats, it is necessary and important to deploy appropriate security mechanisms on smartphones. Anti-malware applications are one of the most commonly used methods in both academia and industry. To identify malware, a number of machine learning approaches, such as those reported in [6,10,19,37], have been proposed. Such approaches generally require some known instances to be used as training data. With the evolution of evading techniques, there is an increasing need to evaluate the performance and robustness of existing commercial AV engines. In current market, there are various commercial AV applications, while few studies focus on evaluating the performance among different AV engines.

Garuba et al. [14] conducted a comparative analysis of three methods in defeating malware on client computers such as anti-malware software, patch management, and host-based firewalls. Their work aims to guide organizations with limited security budgets and resources to find a proper defensive solution. Morales et al. [26] then focused on commercial anti-malware programs and introduces a measurement to evaluate the effectiveness. They found that several anti-malware programs may leave infected objects unresolved by producing numerous incorrectly treated or untreated true positives and false negatives. Talal et al. [50] studied the functionalities and services of several anti-malware applications in terms of the design mechanisms, features and strategies. There are also some studies investigated the security of detection engines against some particular attacks such as transformation attacks [44], Bytecode Obfuscation [12], anti-virus assisted attacks [53], etc.

There are also a number of online scanning platforms that can help compare the detection performance among commercial AV engines. However, these platforms are not configurable and flexible. For instance, users cannot add their interested commercial engines, and the practical running performance on their mobile devices is not available. This motivates our work in designing a more configurable and flexible platform to evaluate the performance among different commercial AV engines. In addition to AV software, there is a need to implement other solutions such as applying continuous authentication on smartphones based on behavioral biometrics [28,31] and examining CPU usage [17,36].

3   Proposed CAVAEva and Implementation

In this section, we first introduce how our proposed CAVAEva platform works, prior to explaining how it can be implemented.

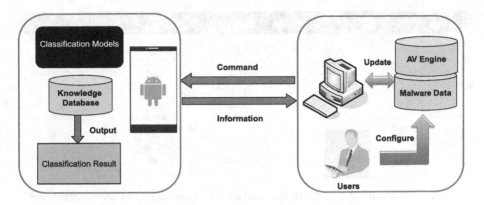

Fig. 1. Proposed *CAVAEva* platform: a simplified workflow.

3.1 Platform Design

There are many machine learning-based malware detection algorithms proposed in the literature (e.g. [9]), and this number is increasing. However, due to the node protection and different structures, it is challenging to compare and benchmark the performance of different AV engines on a particular smartphone. As discussed earlier, existing online tools such as VirusTotal [52] do not generally provide the configuration flexibility for users or researchers. Our proposed platform, commercial anti-virus application evaluation (*CAVAEva*), is designed to enable users, researchers and practitioners to configure the environment (e.g. adding and removing AV engines of interest, and choosing how to output the decisions and results, such as using visualization), and facilitate evaluation on an actual smartphone.

Figure 1 presents a simplified typical CAVAEva workflow, comprising interactions among a smartphone, a computer and users (also described below). Specifically, users can use a computer to send relevant commands to the connected smartphone, for example for configuration (e.g. installing or removing AV engines). To ensure a realistic environment for AV engines, the connected smartphone upon receiving the commands from the computer can configure the smartphone's environment, which can be used for malware detection (e.g., recording of detection performance, and CPU usage caused by the installed AV engines). Moreover, users can also install other detection approaches on the phone, such as deployment of machine learning-based detection with classification models and a knowledge database.

3.2 Platform Implementation

In comparison to other, existing detection approaches, it is more difficult to compare different AV applications. For example, AV vendors often employ some techniques to protect the code of their software and therefore, different AV engines

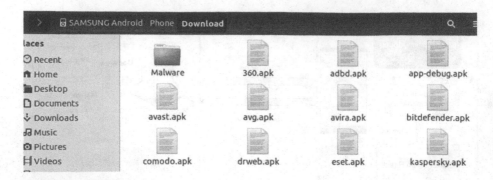

Fig. 2. An example of how APK files and malware are stored on the smartphone.

```
path1 = "/data/data/com.lookout/log/seclog.txt"                    # path where AV save its log
path2 = "/data/data/com.bitdefender.security/files/scanlog/events.0.txt"
path3 = "/data/data/com.antivirus/files/ScanResult.obj"
path4 = "/data/data/com.trustgo.mobile.security/databases/scan_history.db"
path5 = "/data/data/com.symantec.mobilesecurity/databases/AVPingThreat.db"
path6 = "/data/data/com.eset.ems2.gp/databases/unresolved_threats-journal"
path7 = "/data/data/com.wsandroid.suite/databases/DSF_THREAT_DB"
```

Fig. 3. Examples of where AV engines store their scanning results.

often have unique structure. Therefore, in this part, we introduce an engineering way of implementing *CAVAEva* in a real-world scenario.

Environmental Setup: To realize the platform implementation, we used a Linux machine (with Intel(R) Core(TM) i5-5300U CPU 2.3 GHz, 16G RAM) and a Samsung Galaxy S6 smartphone, and adopted Java and Python as the programming language. This allows us to use various libraries provided by Python, such as matplotlib [24] and sqlite3 [49].

Preparation: After the environmental configuration, the first step is to create a folder with the same name on both the computer and the smartphone (e.g., to store AV apps and malware samples). In our platform, we choose to move all APK files and malware to */sdcard/Download/* on the smartphone. Figure 2 presents an example of how APK files and malware are stored on the smartphone. To automate the evaluation, the folder contains a subfolder of malware and various APK files for AV engines. Users can now add new AV APK files here, or remove those that are not of interest.

Then, it is very important to identify the location where one AV engine stores their scanning result. Figure 3 shows location examples on where these AV applications would store their scanning output, i.e., Lookout uses *seclog.txt* to store the result. Due to the different structures of AV engines, it is a challenge to identify such location automatically.

Detection Phase: Then, we develop a script to start installing AV engines on the smartphone, and check whether there is any installation problem. Figure 4

```
cmd = "adb shell pm install -r '/sdcard/Download/%s'" % am_name          # to start install AV
result = subprocess.Popen(cmd, shell=True, stdin=subprocess.PIPE, stdout=subprocess.PIPE)
output, err = result.communicate()
time.sleep(6)
installed = 0
count = 0
```

Fig. 4. An example script to start installing AV applications.

```
try:
    con = lite.connect('test.db')
    cur = con.cursor()
    cur.execute("INSERT INTO Result VALUES (?,?,?,?)", (d, Malware_name, package_name, Malware))
    con.commit()
except lite.Error, e:

    if con:
        con.rollback()

    print "Error %s:" % e.args[0]
    sys.exit(1)
finally:
    if con:
        con.close()
    con = lite.connect('test.db')
```

Fig. 5. Saving the scanning result in a database (test.db): an example.

describes our script for installing AV engines, and before the installation, our script will clean and uninstall existing AV engines on the smartphones. We remark that the MonkeyRunner [25] app can be used to complete the process of installation for any AV engine that requires assistance from user input. This app will press the screen button to continue the process and sign up for a temperately account that is obtained in advance. Then, our script starts installing malware on the phone to evaluate the performance of different AV engines, and then remove the installed malware before the installation of the next one. This loop will end until all malware have been tested. The results (e.g., execution information like CPU usage and detection performance) can then be forwarded to the computer.

Findings: In this phase, the main purpose is to output the scanning result in an expected format for each AV engine (using table and graphic visualization). In the example shown in Fig. 5, when all suspicious files have been successfully scanned, the result is saved in a database (test.db) using sqlite3. When the result is out, users can configure the environment to compare the performance among different AV applications, in terms of their workload and detection rate. As each AV engine may use a different way to store the scanning result, our platform provides a consistent way to help users perform a comparative benchmark.

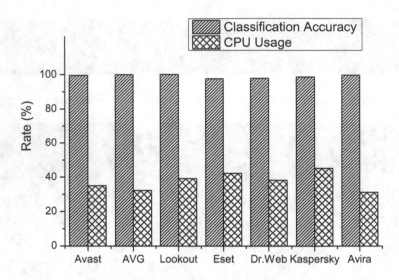

Fig. 6. Classification accuracy and CPU usage.

4   Evaluation

In this section, we present a case study by evaluating seven anti-virus applications on CAVAEva, collect the feedback from over 100 participants in both academia and industry, and discuss some learnt experience and challenges.

4.1   Case Study

In the case study, we present our findings based on our evaluation of the following seven AV applications (all are free version in 2018): Avast, AVG, Lookout, Eset, Dr.Web, Kaspersky, and Avira. In our evaluation, we compiled our dataset comprising 11,232 Android apps by crawling app stores, such as Google Play (78%) and Anzhi (20%), as well as those obtained via direct download (e.g., DREBIN [3] - 2%).

Then, these apps were used to test our *CAVAEva* platform (comprising the Linux machine and Samsung Galaxy S6), and evaluate the performance of the seven AV applications. Figure 6 shows the classification accuracy and the CPU usage, where classification accuracy here indicates the capability of identifying both benign and malicious applications. It was observed that all seven AV engines achieved over 97% classification accuracy, with Lookout achieving 99.8% classification accuracy. In terms of CPU usage, all seven AV engines required at least 32% additional usage due to the scanning operations and interactions, among which Kaspersky needed more CPU usage while Avira required less usage than others.

Table 1. Participants' background in the user study.

Age range	Male	Female	Occupation	Male	Female
18–35	31	32	Students from computer science	17	14
35–45	22	15	Researchers	21	24
41–50	4	2	Industry engineers	19	11

Table 2. Major questions and relevant scores collected from the user study.

Questions (CS students)	Average score
1. The platform is more flexible and configurable	8.8
2. I think the platform is useful in practice	9.1
3. I may consider using this platform in my future work	8.5
Questions (Researchers)	Average score
1. The platform is more flexible and configurable	8.3
2. I think the platform is useful in practice	8.5
3. I may consider using this platform in my future work	8.2
Questions (Industry engineers)	Average score
1. The platform is more flexible and configurable	8.9
2. I think the platform is useful in practice	8.7
3. I may consider using this platform in my future work	9.1

4.2   User Study

To collect the feedback on the utility of our platform, we perform a user study with over 100 participants by distributing our platform to both researchers and industry engineers. The participants' background is summarized in Table 1. All participants have an interest on our work and were recruited via online platforms and social recommendations. In particular, the students are from the computer science major including both master and PhD students. Researchers including postdoc fellows and faculty members. The industry engineers are from several IT companies.

Before the start, we introduced our purpose to all participants. They could use the platform for a week and then completed a feedback form, which contains a set of questions regarding the platform performance and usage. Each question employs ten-point Likert scales: namely, 1-score indicates strong disagreement and 10-score indicates strong agreement. Table 2 shows the questions and the collected feedback.

- *The first question.* For this question, we asked the participants to consider several existing online detection platforms, as compared with our platform. It is found that most participants supported our platform to be more flexible and configurable. Specifically, industry engineers provided the highest score, indicating the promising performance.

```
cmd = "./monkeyrunner execute-lookout.py"
subprocess.Popen(cmd, shell=True, stdout=subprocess.PIPE, stderr=subprocess.PIPE)
time.sleep(60)
```

```
from com.android.monkeyrunner import MonkeyRunner, MonkeyDevice, MonkeyImage
device = MonkeyRunner.waitForConnection()
device.touch(562, 1796, 'DOWN_AND_UP')
MonkeyRunner.sleep(1)
device.touch(562, 1796, 'DOWN_AND_UP')
MonkeyRunner.sleep(1)
device.touch(562, 1796, 'DOWN_AND_UP')
MonkeyRunner.sleep(1)
device.touch(150, 700, 'DOWN_AND_UP')
```

Fig. 7. An example on how to use MonkeyRunner to activate Lookout after the installation.

- *The second question.* This question aims to investigate the participants' attitude towards the usage of our platform. It is visible that all scores from different groups are above 8.5, indicating the importance of our platform. In our informal interview, many participants consider that our platform can complement the existing online detection tools and help enhance the commercial anti-malware applications.
- *The third question.* According to this question, we found that most participants are willing to use our platform in their future work. In particular, researchers provided the lowest score of 8.2 while industry engineers provided the highest one of 9.1. In our informal interview, it is found that researchers focused more on how to extend our platform according to their demands, and then design a new/updated one. By contrast, industry engineers focused more on how to apply this platform to their work directly. This is the main reason for explaining their different scores.

Overall, the collected feedback and scores are positive, demonstrating that our platform has a potential to be applied in practice, with many demanding features like flexibility and extensibility.

4.3 Discussion

In this work, our main purpose is to design a configurable and flexible platform for automatic commercial anti-virus application evaluation. Our platform is still developed at an early stage, and can be enhanced in many aspects. In this part, we discuss some learnt experience and challenges. A summary of our findings is presented as below:

- *File size.* In the evaluation, we found that free online services may have a size limit for the uploaded apps, ranging from 32 Megabyte to 64 Megabyte. Our observation echoed that of [16]. In comparison, there is no such limit for our platform, as *CAVAEva* will install and evaluate one app on an actual smartphone.

Number	Malware_type	Package_name	Detect
1	jSMSHider	app.BatteryMonitor	Ture
2	jSMSHider	com.AudioConsole	Ture
3	jSMSHider	hider.AppInstall.nvanmoshiriji_V31_mumayi_aff08	Ture
4	jSMSHider	com.trendmicro.tmmspersonal.apac	False
5	anserverBot	com.keji.danti604	Ture
6	anserverBot	com.keji.danti607	Ture
7	HippoSMS	com.ku6.android.videobrowser	Ture
8	HippoSMS	com.ku6.android.videobrowser	Ture
9	HippoSMS	com.Video.XiaoQiang	Ture
10	HippoSMS	com.mass.sms	Ture

Fig. 8. The figure shows how to output the scanning results in a table.

- *Screen activation.* To automate the evaluation process, some AV engines require uses to click a 'Next' button to activate the next step. In this work, we employed MonkeyRunner to mitigate this limitation – see Fig. 7. Other approaches can also be used to automate the evaluation process.
- *AV engine selection.* In our platform, users can freely deploy their AV software of choice, and this flexibility is not commonly found in other tools/platforms.
- *Output format.* In this platform, the scanning results can be displayed in a variety of formats, such as tables and charts – see Fig. 8. Users can also customize the display formats, such as using visualization.

As our platform is only a proof-of-concept, the platform can be enhanced in a number of aspects. Examples include the following:

- *Output speed.* As compared to existing online scanning tools, our platform may require more time to complete the examination and producing the result. This is because *CAVAEva* has to install each AV engine and test all files or apps on an actual smartphone. Hence, performance optimization is one of our future agenda.
- *Malware label and lack of a standard naming convention.* Hurier *et al.* [16] reported that current online scanning services lack consensus, in the sense that binary decisions from different AV engines may produce conflicting results on the same samples. In addition, they also noted that malware labels are very challenging to compare due to the lack of a naming convention for malware samples. Hence, both limitations should also be studied in the future.
- *Smartphone support.* Our current platform supports most Samsung phones, and users can select their smartphone model. For other smartphones (i.e., different makes, such as iPhones), there is a need to configure the platform. In the future, we plan to extend the platform to be compatible with other smartphones.
- *Online scanning tool comparison support.* In this work, we only focused on designing a flexible and automated platform to facilitate evaluation of commercial AV applications. In the future, we intend to extend the platform to also include existing online scanning tools.

- *Full automation.* One main purpose of our platform is to automate the evaluation process of different AV engines, whereas each AV engine may have different design structures, making the task difficult. To achieve our purpose, we implemented various tools and scripts on *CAVAEva*. In our future work, we plan to test the platform performance in a systematic manner.

Overall, how to develop a unified and flexible platform for commercial anti-virus application evaluation is a challenge, i.e., there is a need to solve many technical issues. Our platform is one step for addressing such challenge, with the purpose of complementing the current literature.

5   Conclusion and Future Work

Detecting malware on existing computing devices, such as smartphones, is crucial and remains a challenging topic. While there are many online scanning tools and AV applications, there is no user friendly manner to evaluate and benchmark such tools and applications. In addition, many of these online scanning tools have limitations such as file-size restriction. Thus, there is a need to design a configurable and unified platform for evaluating different AV engines.

In this work, we designed *CAVAEva*, an engineering platform for commercial AV software evaluation. The platform allows users, researchers and practitioners to configure the platform based on their own needs, and the evaluation process is automated. To investigate the utility of our platform, we performed a case study by comparing seven well-known commercial anti-virus applications regarding detection performance and CPU usage, and held a user study with over 100 participants from both academia and industry to collect their feedback. Our results demonstrate that our platform can provide many demanding features, i.e., showing the caused CPU usage on a real smartphone, and is useful in practice. Our work attempts to complement existing research on malware detection and stimulate more research on such challenge.

Acknowledgments. Weizhi Meng was partially supported by H2020-SU-ICT-03-2018: CyberSec4Europe with No. 830929, and National Natural Science Foundation of China (No. 61802077). Chunhua Su is supported by JSPS Kiban(B) 18H03240 and JSPS Kiban(C) 18K11298.

References

1. Anand, S.A., Saxena, N.: Speechless: analyzing the threat to speech privacy from smartphone motion sensors. In: Proceedings of the 2018 IEEE Symposium on Security and Privacy, pp. 1000–1017 (2018)
2. Andriesse, D., Bos, H.: Instruction-level steganography for covert trigger-based malware. In: Dietrich, S. (ed.) DIMVA 2014. LNCS, vol. 8550, pp. 41–50. Springer, Cham (2014). https://doi.org/10.1007/978-3-319-08509-8_3
3. Arp, D., Spreitzenbarth, M., Hubner, M., Gascon, H., Rieck, K.: DREBIN: effective and explainable detection of android malware in your pocket. In: Proceedings of NDSS (2014)

4. Asonov, D., Agrawal, R.: Keyboard acoustic emanations. In: Proceedings of IEEE Symposium on Security and Privacy, pp. 3–11 (2004)

5. Aviv, A.J., Gibson, K., Mossop, E., Blaze, M., Smith, J.M.: Smudge attacks on smartphone touch screens. In: Proceedings of the 4th USENIX Conference on Offensive Technologies (WOOT), pp. 1–7 (2010)

6. Backes, M., Nauman, M.: LUNA: quantifying and leveraging uncertainty in Android malware analysis through Bayesian machine learning. In: EuroS&P 2017, pp. 204–217 (2017)

7. Cai, L., Chen, H.: TouchLogger: inferring keystrokes on touch screen from smartphone motion. In: Proceedings of the 6th USENIX Conference on Hot Topics in Security (HotSec), pp. 1–6 (2011)

8. Chen, S., et al.: Automated poisoning attacks and defenses in malware detection systems: an adversarial machine learning approach. Comput. Secur. **73**, 326–344 (2018)

9. Chen, X., et al.: Android HIV: a study of repackaging malware for evading machine-learning detection. IEEE Trans. Inf. Forensics Secur. **15**, 987–1001 (2019)

10. Chen, Z., et al.: Machine learning based mobile malware detection using highly imbalanced network traffic. Inf. Sci. **433–434**, 346–364 (2018)

11. Do, Q., Martini, B., Choo, K.-K.R.: Exfiltrating data from Android devices. Comput. Secur. **48**, 74–91 (2015)

12. Faruki, P., Bharmal, A., Laxmi, V., Gaur, M.S., Conti, M., Rajarajan, M.: Evaluation of Android anti-malware techniques against Dalvik bytecode obfuscation. In: Proceedings of TrustCom, pp. 414–421 (2014)

13. Faruki, P., et al.: Android security: a survey of issues, malware penetration, and defenses. IEEE Commun. Surv. Tutor. **17**(2), 998–1022 (2015)

14. Garuba, M., Liu, C., Washington, A.N.: A comparative analysis of anti-malware software, patch management, and host-based firewalls in preventing malware infections on client computers. In: Proceedings of ITNG, pp. 628–632 (2008)

15. Han, J., Owusu, E., Nguyen, L., Perrig, A., Zhang, J.: ACComplice: location inference using accelerometers on smartphones. In: Proceedings of the 4th International Conference on Communication Systems and Networks (COMSNETS), New York, NY, USA, pp. 1–9 (2012)

16. Hurier, M., Allix, K., Bissyandé, T.F., Klein, J., Le Traon, Y.: On the lack of consensus in anti-virus decisions: metrics and insights on building ground truths of Android malware. In: Caballero, J., Zurutuza, U., Rodríguez, R.J. (eds.) DIMVA 2016. LNCS, vol. 9721, pp. 142–162. Springer, Cham (2016). https://doi.org/10.1007/978-3-319-40667-1_8

17. Jiang, L., Meng, W., Wang, Y., Su, C., Li, J.: Exploring energy consumption of juice filming charging attack on smartphones: a pilot study. In: Yan, Z., Molva, R., Mazurczyk, W., Kantola, R. (eds.) NSS 2017. LNCS, vol. 10394, pp. 199–213. Springer, Cham (2017). https://doi.org/10.1007/978-3-319-64701-2_15

18. Kune, D.F., Kim, Y.: Timing attacks on PIN input devices. In: Proceedings of the 17th ACM Conference on Computer and Communications Security (CCS), pp. 678–680. ACM, New York (2010)

19. Li, J., Sun, L., Yan, Q., Li, Z., Srisa-an, W., Ye, H.: Significant permission identification for machine-learning-based Android malware detection. IEEE Trans. Ind. Inform. **14**(7), 3216–3225 (2018)

20. Lin, C.-C., Li, H., Zhou, X., Wang, X.: Screenmilker: how to milk your Android screen for secrets. In: Proceedings of Annual Network and Distributed System Security Symposium (NDSS), pp. 1–10 (2014)

21. Liu, J., Zhong, L., Wickramasuriya, J., Vasudevan, V.: uWave: accelerometer-based personalized gesture recognition and its applications. Pervasive Mob. Comput. **5**(6), 657–675 (2009)
22. Lau, B., Jang, Y., Song, C.: Mactans: injecting malware into iOS devices via malicious chargers. Blackhat USA (2013)
23. Marquardt, P., Verma, A., Carter, H., Traynor, P.: (sp)iPhone: decoding vibrations from nearby keyboards using mobile phone accelerometers. In: Proceedings of ACM Conference on Computer and Communications Security (CCS), pp. 551–562. ACM, New York (2011)
24. Matplotlib: Python plotting. https://matplotlib.org/
25. MonkeyRunner: A monkeyrunner class that contains static utility methods. https://developer.android.com/studio/test/monkeyrunner/MonkeyRunner
26. Morales, J.A., Sandhu, R.S., Xu, S.: Evaluating detection and treatment effectiveness of commercial anti-malware programs. In: Proceedings of MALWARE, pp. 31–38 (2010)
27. Mcafee: McAfee Mobile Threat Report Q1, 2018. https://www.mcafee.com/enterprise/en-us/assets/reports/rp-mobile-threat-report-2018.pdf
28. Meng, Y., Wong, D.S., Schlegel, R., Kwok, L.: Touch gestures based biometric authentication scheme for touchscreen mobile phones. In: Kutyłowski, M., Yung, M. (eds.) Inscrypt 2012. LNCS, vol. 7763, pp. 331–350. Springer, Heidelberg (2013). https://doi.org/10.1007/978-3-642-38519-3_21
29. Meng, Y., Li, W., Kwok, L.-F.: Enhancing click-draw based graphical passwords using multi-touch on mobile phones. In: Janczewski, L.J., Wolfe, H.B., Shenoi, S. (eds.) SEC 2013. IAICT, vol. 405, pp. 55–68. Springer, Heidelberg (2013). https://doi.org/10.1007/978-3-642-39218-4_5
30. Meng, W., Li, W., Kwok, L.F.: EFM: enhancing the performance of signature-based network intrusion detection systems using enhanced filter mechanism. Comput. Secur. **43**, 189–204 (2014)
31. Meng, W., Wong, D.S., Furnell, S., Zhou, J.: Surveying the development of biometric user authentication on mobile phones. IEEE Commun. Surv. Tutor. **17**, 1268–1293 (2015)
32. Meng, W., Lee, W.H., Murali, S.R., Krishnan, S.P.T.: Charging me and I know your secrets! Towards juice filming attacks on smartphones. In: Proceedings of the Cyber-Physical System Security Workshop (CPSS), in conjunction with AsiaCCS 2015. ACM (2015)
33. Meng, W., Lee, W.H., Murali, S.R., Krishnan, S.P.T.: JuiceCaster: towards automatic juice filming attacks on smartphones. J. Netw. Comput. Appl. **68**, 201–212 (2016)
34. Meng, W., Fei, F., Li, W., Au, M.H.: Harvesting smartphone privacy through enhanced juice filming charging attacks. In: Nguyen, P., Zhou, J. (eds.) ISC 2017. Lecture Notes in Computer Science, vol. 10599, pp. 291–308. Springer, Cham (2017). https://doi.org/10.1007/978-3-319-69659-1_16
35. Meng, W., Lee, W.H., Liu, Z., Su, C., Li, Y.: Evaluating the impact of juice filming charging attack in practical environments. In: Kim, H., Kim, D.-C. (eds.) ICISC 2017. LNCS, vol. 10779, pp. 327–338. Springer, Cham (2018). https://doi.org/10.1007/978-3-319-78556-1_18
36. Meng, W., Jiang, L., Wang, Y., Li, J., Zhang, J., Xiang, Y.: JFCGuard: detecting juice filming charging attack via processor usage analysis on smartphones. Comput. Secur. **76**, 252–264 (2018)
37. Milosevic, N., Dehghantanha, A., Choo, K.K.R.: Machine learning aided Android malware classification. Comput. Electr. Eng. **61**, 266–274 (2017)

38. Min, B., Varadharajan, V.: Design, implementation and evaluation of a novel anti-virus parasitic malware. In: Proceedings of SAC 2015, pp. 2127–2133 (2015)
39. Miluzzo, E., Varshavsky, A., Balakrishnan, S., Choudhury, R.R.: TapPrints: your finger taps have fingerprints. In: Proceedings of MobiSys, New York, NY, USA, pp. 323–336 (2012)
40. Nguyen, G., Nguyen, B.M., Tran, D., Hluchy, L.: A heuristics approach to mine behavioural data logs in mobile malware detection system. Data Knowl. Eng. **115**, 129–151 (2018)
41. Owusu, E., Han, J., Das, S., Perrig, A., Zhang, J.: ACCessory: password inference using accelerometers on smartphones. In: Proceedings of the 12th Workshop on Mobile Computing Systems & Applications (HotMobile), pp. 1–6. ACM, New York (2012)
42. Peng, S., Yu, S., Yang, A.: Smartphone malware and its propagation modeling: a survey. IEEE Commun. Surv. Tutor. **16**(2), 925–941 (2014)
43. Raguram, R., White, A.M., Goswami, D., Monrose, F., Frahm, J.-M.: iSpy: automatic reconstruction of typed input from compromising reflections. In: Proceedings of the 18th ACM Conference on Computer and Communications Security (CCS), pp. 527–536. ACM, New York (2011)
44. Rastogi, V., Chen, Y., Jiang, X.: DroidChameleon: evaluating Android anti-malware against transformation attacks. In: Proceedings of AsiaCCS, pp. 329–334 (2013)
45. Rudd, E.M., Rozsa, A., Ganther, M., Boult, T.E.: A survey of stealth malware attacks, mitigation measures, and steps toward autonomous open world solutions. IEEE Commun. Surv. Tutor. **19**(2), 1145–1172 (2017)
46. Schlegel, R., Zhang, K., Zhou, X., Intwala, M., Kapadia, A., Wang, X.: Soundcomber: a stealthy and context-aware sound trojan for smartphones. In: Proceedings of the 18th Annual Network and Distributed System Security Symposium (NDSS), San Diego, CA, USA, pp. 17–33 (2011)
47. Sen, S., Aydogan, E., Aysan, A.I.: Coevolution of mobile malware and anti-malware. IEEE Trans. Inf. Forensics Secur. **13**(10), 2563–2574 (2018)
48. Spolaor, R., Abudahi, L., Moonsamy, V., Conti, M., Poovendran, R.: No free charge theorem: a covert channel via USB charging cable on mobile devices. In: Gollmann, D., Miyaji, A., Kikuchi, H. (eds.) ACNS 2017. LNCS, vol. 10355, pp. 83–102. Springer, Cham (2017). https://doi.org/10.1007/978-3-319-61204-1_5
49. SQLite. https://www.sqlite.org/
50. Talal, M., et al.: Comprehensive review and analysis of anti-malware apps for smartphones. Telecommun. Syst. **72**(2), 285–337 (2019)
51. Vuagnoux, M., Pasini, S.: Compromising electromagnetic emanations of wired and wireless keyboards. In: Proceedings of the 18th Conference on USENIX Security Symposium, pp. 1–16 (2009)
52. VirusTotal: Analyze suspicious files and URLs to detect types of malware, automatically share them with the security community. https://www.virustotal.com/#/home/upload
53. Wressnegger, C., Freeman, K., Yamaguchi, F., Rieck, K.: Automatically inferring malware signatures for anti-virus assisted attacks. In: Proceedings of AsiaCCS, pp. 587–598 (2017)
54. Xing, L., Pan, X., Wang, R., Yuan, K., Wang, X.: Upgrading your Android, elevating my malware: privilege escalation through mobile OS updating. In: Proceedings of the 2014 IEEE Symposium on Security and Privacy, Berkeley, CA, USA, pp. 393–408 (2014)

55. Xu, N., Zhang, F., Luo, Y., Jia, W., Xuan, D., Teng, J.: Stealthy video capturer: a new video-based spyware in 3G smartphones. In: Proceedings of the 2nd ACM Conference on Wireless Network Security (WiSec), pp. 69–78 (2009)
56. Ye, Y., Li, T., Adjeroh, D.A., Iyengar, S.S.: A survey on malware detection using data mining techniques. ACM Comput. Surv. **50**(3), 41:1–41:40 (2017)
57. Zhuang, L., Zhou, F., Tygar, J.D.: Keyboard acoustic emanations revisited. ACM Trans. Inf. Syst. Secur. **13**(1), 1–26 (2009)

SymSem: Symbolic Execution with Time Stamps for Deobfuscation

Huayi Li$^{(\boxtimes)}$, Yuanyuan Zhan, Wang Jianqiang, and Dawu Gu

Shanghai Jiao Tong University, Shanghai, China
lihuayi_sjtu@outlook.com, zhang-yy@cs.sjtu.edu.cn, wjq.sec@gmail.com,
dwgu@sjtu.edu.cn

Abstract. Code virtualization technique obfuscates programs by transforming original code to self-defined bytecode in a different instruction architecture. It is widely used in obfuscating malware for its ability to render normal analysis ineffective. Using symbolic execution to assist in deobfuscating such programs turned to be a trend in recent research. However, we found many challenges that may lead to semantic confusion in previous symbolic execution technique, and proposed a novel symbolic execution technique enhanced by time stamps to tackle these issues. For evaluation, we implemented it as a prototype of SymSem and deobfuscated programs protected by popular virtual machines. The results indicate that our method is able to accurately recover the semantics of obfuscated function trace.

Keywords: Deobfuscation · Virtualization obfuscation · Symbolic execution · Trace rewriting

1 Introduction

Code protection techniques help software writers protect their copyright, these techniques also become weapons against malware analysis. Popular code protection techniques includes control flow flattering, junk code, string encryption and code virtualization. Among all the developed code protection techniques, code virtualization, also known as VM-based code obfuscation is one of the most practical and effective code obfuscation techniques for its ability to defeat unauthorized code analysis in either static or dynamic manners. It is also empowered by combining itself with other techniques.

The key idea of VM-based obfuscation is transforming the instruction set of the original program to another one with semantic invariance and embedding the obfuscated program with an emulator to execute the generated code. While each VM-based code obfuscator realizes its own instruction set and emulator, modern virtual machines still can be divided into two main types of realizations.

One uses a dispatcher-handler model, whose emulator can be clearly divided into two components. The main component, dispatcher, reads one instruction

© Springer Nature Switzerland AG 2020
Z. Liu and M. Yung (Eds.): Inscrypt 2019, LNCS 12020, pp. 225–245, 2020.
https://doi.org/10.1007/978-3-030-42921-8_13

from the code area and decodes its operation type. Then it picks up a corresponding handler to perform the code-specific operation, which may add two integers or perform memory operation. For example, *VMProtect 3.09* [4] applies its emulator with a few dispatchers with handler tables, each of them contains pointers of hundreds of handlers.

The other main type of virtual machines apply the direct-threading model. These virtual machines eliminate the dispatcher, which is vulnerable in reverse engineer. Instead, these virtual machines enhance the original handlers by append decoding functionality at the end, whose logic can be costume designed, thus enabling the virtual machine to further obfuscate its control flow features. Recently, many commercial code obfuscators such as *VMProtect* [4], *Themida* [3], *Code Virtualizer* [1] have all adapted direct threading model.

The demands to analyze the VM-based code obfuscation increase due to its growing popularity in malware protection. To deobfuscate malware protected by code virtualization technologies, researchers have developed many techniques aiming for automatic analysis. For example, VMAttack [11] detects the dispatcher-handler loop and uses folding optimization to recognize important instructions in the virtual machine code. VMHunt [18] applies data flow analysis on the trace of obfuscated program and identify the entries and exits in the trace, then it uses symbolic execution technologies to generate a formula to represent the trace's semantics. Liang [12] developed a method of trace simplification based symbolic execution and compilation optimization. These works all based themselves on dynamic analysis, including data flow analysis, taint analysis and symbolic execution.

However, we found that former works used a simple model when applying symbolic execution, this model may have a few inputs, but with only one output. While practical code in virtual machines comply with a different model considering complicated semantic meanings. First, a snippet of virtual machine code may have multiple inputs and outputs. These outputs are physically separated thus can not be represented in one expression. For example, a handler may read a bundle of inputs from memory, do some calculation and save the results to different registers and memory addresses. What's more, many complex situations which would cause semantic confusions have been omitted. A handler with two memory inputs may have two symbolic values both point to the same address under specific conditions. Improper treatment of these two values may cause serious semantic confusions for analyst and lead to different semantic comprehension in recovering code.

We found that, besides explicit dependencies, instructions and its generated values have implicit relationship that make a difference to the output semantics in symbolic execution. Any misconduct in symbolic execution may lead to loss of information needed for resolving semantic confusions in code recovery. As these implicit relationships are conducted under time sequences, we further noticed that time stamps is an important indicator of the relationship.

In this paper, we systematically study the challenges and develop a new approach in symbolic executions and code recovery. First, we elaborate the challenges when applying a more practical semantic model in symbolic execution. These challenges we found are caused by misconducts when dealing with multiple symbolic expressions. Then, we propose a new kind of symbolic execution technique enhanced with time stamp, which efficiently complements the missing information in original symbolic execution methods and help tackle the challenges we found. Finally, we implement a prototype of our symbolic execution method, SymSem. SymSem takes an obfuscated program trace as input, extracts the virtual machine code from the trace and rewrites these code by symbolic execution and recovering code from symbolic expressions. We will illustrate how our implementations can be used in trace optimization and reverse engineer.

For evaluation, we implement a prototype of SymSem based on symbolic execution with time stamps. We pick up test cases from famous algorithms' realizations and open-source projects, including *binary search, matrix multiply, tcp_checksum, rc4 encryption* and *bzip2.14*. We obfuscate these programs with commercial code virtualization obfuscators like *VMProtect* and *Themida*. Then, we trace the obfuscated program and rewrite the obfuscated function. The rewritten traces have the same semantic meaning when executing in the obfuscated program. Moreover, the trace length is reduced to 12.5% to 36.68% of the original. Our evaluation also shows that SymSem can be easily scaled to large-size traces for two reasons. First, the time complexity of our prototype is more related with the handler numbers and their length, not the trace length of obfuscated function. Also, SymSem are designed for parallelism as symbolic execution procedures of different handlers can be done concurrently.

This paper makes the following contributions.

1. We found a series of problems related to trace rewriting by means of symbolic execution in practical situations.
2. We designed a new symbolic execution method to precisely and accurately extract the semantics of obfuscated program. Our symbolic execution with time stamps is able to tackle the difficulties related to extracting semantics through symbolic execution.
3. Based on our new symbolic execution method, we designed a prototype of SymSem and we evaluate it in different commercial virtual machines. The result shows that it is able to rewrite the trace of obfuscated function.

The rest of the paper is organized as follows. Section 2 points out the limitations in symbolic execution and the challenges for this work. Sections 3 and 4 describes the design of SymSem. The implementation and performance evaluation on SymSem is in Sects. 5 and 6, respectively. Section 7 lists the related works. Sections 8 and 9 discuss the limitation in our work and conclude the paper.

2   Challenges

Symbolic execution has been used in deobfucating in many previous work due to its ability of forming corresponding relationship between inputs and outputs. The results of symbolic execution, a set of symbolic expressions, which represents the relationship between program inputs and outputs, have been not only the final output of deobfuscation analysis [18], but also compiled to optimized code with better readability [12]. Unfortunately, we first found previous work made an impractical assumption that target programs with only one output, thus only one symbolic expression was needed to represent the semantics of target code. This assumption violates the model of practical programs, as a program may have multiple separate input sources and outputs.

We then found that current form of symbolic expressions are unable to contain the full semantic information of program trace thus may cause semantic confusions. Meanwhile, generating compilable code from multiple symbolic expressions have many challenges with explicit and implicit data dependence.

In this chapter, we will describe the challenges we encountered when rewriting program trace with multiple outputs. These challenges are omitted by previous work. Then we will unveil why current symbolic expressions may cause confusions.

2.1 Challenges with Multiple Symbolic Expressions

We use the example below to illustrate one of the challenges when representing the semantics of program trace using current symbolic expression.

```
1  mov ecx, dword ptr [eax+4]
2  add dword ptr [eax+4], 4
```

Symbolic executing two lines of code above will generate two expressions below.

$$ecx : \; dword\ ptr\ [eax + 4]$$
$$dword\ ptr\ [eax + 4] : \; dword\ ptr\ [eax + 4] + 4$$

It is obvious that the value in register ecx relies on the value saved in $[eax+4]$, thus a read after write hazard may arise when rewriting procedure fails to preserve the appropriate sequence of code generation based on symbolic expressions. In this case, read from dword address $[eax+4]$ must precede the writing operation of the same address. Read after write may lead to different semantic meanings.

Usually, the first idea of solving this hazard follows the method of constructing a graph of dependence. On this graph, the code generation for expression ecx relies on the read operation of the initial value of address $[eax+4]$.

2.2 Challenges with Alias Symbolic Values

In addition to the hazards above, there is another challenge which may cause semantic confusion when using previous symbolic execution method. We call it alias, which results from the inability of judging the equality of two symbolic values in outcome expressions.

```
1  mov dword ptr [eax+4], 0xbeefdead
2  mov dword ptr [ebx+4], 0xdeadbeef
3  mov ecx, dword ptr [edx]
```

Here we illustrate the alias problem by the code above. We can easily enumerate the symbolic expressions generated as below.

$$ecx :\ dword\ ptr\ [edx]$$
$$dword\ ptr\ [eax + 4] :\ \texttt{0x}beefdead$$
$$dword\ ptr\ [ebx + 4] :\ \texttt{0x}deadbeef$$

Based on these expressions, we are unable to judge that if edx equals to $eax+4$, neither the case if eax equals to ebx. When edx equals to $eax+4$, the first expression could also be rewrited as $ecx :\ \texttt{0x}beefdead$. Meanwhile, the rewriting procedure may decide to first deal with the first expression. The generated code would simply move the initial value stored in address edx to register ecx, which is contrary to the true sequence in the original code. This results in a new kind of hazard that we call write after write hazard and the situation also exists when edx equals to eax.

The case above shows that different sequences of code generation for expressions with possible alias value may generate code with different semantic meanings. In addition, the problem could not be solved by dependence graphs as they are limited by implicit dependence relationship. Meanwhile, these relationships, which are originally organized by time sequence, have been eliminated in the symbolic expressions above. For those who want to understand the state of program by these expressions, confusions are inevitable.

3 Symbolic Execution with Time Stamps

As previous form of symbolic expressions are unable to contain all information necessary for generating compilable code. We implemented a new kind of symbolic execution method named symbolic execution with time stamps. As is indicated by its name, symbolic execution with time stamps tags every symbol value with a time stamp when they are created. These time stamps demonstrate the sequence of IR generation when needed. Here we describe how time stamps help symbolic execution tackle the challenges referred in Sect. 2. In Sect. 4.3 we will further elaborate our methods by an detailed example.

3.1 How Time Stamp Tackles Read After Write Hazards

First we describe how time stamps help tackle the challenge of read after write hazards. Though this challenge can also be tackled by a dependence graph, time stamp is a more natural method with generality.

We take the first case in the Sect. 2.1 as an example. The code first saves the value of address $[eax+4]$ to ecx. Then it updates value of address $[eax+4]$

with a new value. Under symbolic execution with time stamps, the value in the register ecx will be tagged with time stamp 0, as it is born in the operation of the first instruction. Similarly, the newly updated value of address $[eax+4]$ will be tagged with time stamp 1.

When it comes to code generation, the procedure will first deal with values tagged with lower time stamps. In this case it corresponds to the symbolic value in ecx. It will read a value from address $[eax+4]$. Here of course the read operation will get the right value, instead of one has been updated. Then the procedure deals with the value tagged with time stamp 1. The problem of read after write hazards is solved naturally.

3.2 How Time Stamp Tackles Alias Values

Time stamps can also help tackle the challenge of alias values, which is invisible in dependence graphs. Still, we take the case in Sect. 2.2 as an example. It is multifarious to enumerate all possible alias cases in the example. Not to mention generating conditions and constraints of each alias cases.

However, under symbolic execution with time stamps, the value in address $[eax+4]$, $[ebx+4]$ and ecx is respectively tagged with time stamp 0,1 and 2. In the following IR generation procedure, if we follow the sequence of time stamps, the value in the address $[eax+4]$ will be first updated. Then it comes to the value in address $[ebx+4]$ and ecx. Never mind what alias cases may happen, the IR generation procedure follows the correct sequence and avoids any conflicts. So we can apply the same solution to tackle the alias challenge.

4   Design

4.1   Overview

We present a new method of symbolic execution and implemented it in a new program trace analysis system named SymSem, which is used to analyze traces of programs obfuscated by code virtualization technique. In this chapter we will illustrate the overview of SymSem.

SymSem is a system aiming to recover the semantics of the trace obfuscated by code virtualization technique. It takes the trace as input and outputs the LLVM IR of the trace, which is both readable and compilable. Finally, SymSem compiles the IR to generate assembly code for further evaluation. Figure 1 depicts the whole architecture of SymSem, including three kernel components which would be described in detail in the following sections.

1. VM Architecture analysis. For a program protected by code virtualization, we first run it and record the trace. We implemented an analysis method based on execution rate to extract virtual machine entries, exits and all handlers in the trace.

2. Symbolic execution with time stamps. We assume that the semantic meanings of the program can be represented by a set of expressions between inputs and outputs. Based on this assumption, the semantic meaning of obfuscated function can be achieved by connecting all the semantic expressions of handlers in the trace. Here we use a new kind of symbolic execution technology named symbolic execution with time stamps to extract semantic representation of all handlers, VM entries and exits in the trace.
3. Generating LLVM IR. SymSem generates IR for LLVM compiler based on the results of symbolic execution. These IR can be used to generate code or symbolic representation of the whole trace.

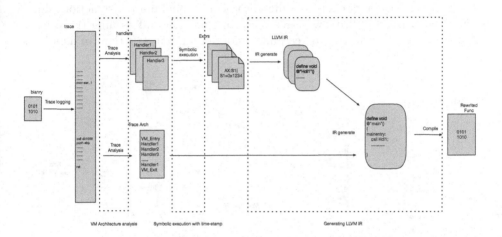

Fig. 1. SymSem architecture

4.2   VM Architecture Analysis

As described in Sect. 4.1, the VM architecture analysis is designed for extracting virtual machine code from program trace. These code contain handlers and information about how to reorganize the generated intermediate representation.

Here we use an easily implemented method to analyze the program trace. We also assume that there does exist at least one virtual machine in the trace. Our methods is based on two phenomenons we observed below:

1. For a specific program protected by code virtualization, all virtual machine handlers have the same type tail jump, such as "*jmp* 0x434343" or "*jmp register*".
2. In the program trace, those basic blocks which are not in any loop but belong to handlers have more chance to be executed for multiple times when considering a mount of continues instructions.

Method Overview. Our method can be simply described as two steps. First, screen out possible basic blocks belong to handlers based on execution rate. Then, make further analysis based on control flow and data flow. These analyses will finally help us mark all the basic blocks as "VM code" or "Non-VM code".

Method Details. We will describe the details of our method in this section. SymSem first runs the program and trace all the executed instructions once. Also, for every basic blocks to be executed, SymSem records the address of its first instruction and the value of stack register. These two kinds of records are saved separately in two files.

We use the first trace file, which contains traces of all instructions, to calculate the occurrence frequencies of different unconditional jump instructions. Like what is shown in Fig. 2(a), we rank these instructions and assume those with higher occurrence frequency are candidates of tail jump instructions of handlers.

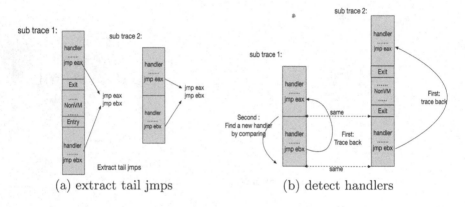

(a) extract tail jmps   (b) detect handlers

Fig. 2. Extract tail jmps & detect handlers

Further analysis was based on control flow. We assume that the code before a handler either belongs to another handler or the VM entry. Similarly, the code after a handler is another handler or the VM exit. As is shown in Fig. 2(b), for every jump instructions we have screened out, we trace backwards to another jump instruction. The code between the two tagged jump instructions must be a handler or includes one exit, one entry and some Non-VM code. We use some data flow features to distinguish between this two situations. In the first case, those code between two tagged jump instructions are tagged as a handler.

Finally, SymSem runs data flow analysis to recognize the entries and exits of virtual machine. The VM entries and exits have some specific data flow features which are easily recognizable. One of them is that all VM entries save the general registers to some region of the memory. In this way we distinguish the code between entry and exit as VM code and the other as Non-VM code.

4.3   Symbolic Execution with Time Stamps

The components of symbolic execution and IR generating is the key of SymSem. We use symbolic execution technique we first presented in Sect. 3. In this section we elaborate our symbolic execution method in detail by an example.

A Detailed Example to Illustrate Our Method. Here we use an example to elaborate how symbolic execution works on actual code. The case here is a simplification of code we actually encountered.

```
1  mov ecx, dword ptr [eax+0xc]
2  add dword ptr [eax+0xc], 0x4
3  mov dword ptr [ebx+0xc], 0xdeadbeef
4  mov edx, dword ptr [edx]
```

This code fragment first reads a symbolic value from address $[eax+0xc]$ to ecx. Then it adds the value in memory address $eax+0xc]$ with 4, writes a concrete value to address $[ebx+0xc]$. Finally, it reads a symbolic value from address $[edx]$ to register edx.

It is clear that eax and ebx can be two alias values and there is no chance to eliminate the alias simply based on the code fragment. Under that condition, the address $[eax+0xc]$ and $[ebx+0xc]$ may have a write after write hazard. Also, there is a read after write hazard with address $[eax+0xc]$. The generated code must first read the value in memory address $[eax+0xc]$, then write a new value to the same address. What makes things more difficult is that edx may equals to $eax+0xc$ or $ebx+0xc$, making the situation more complicated.

Symbol Definition. We use the definitions below to elaborate the symbols in the following.

Definition 1. There are two types of value in symbolic execution, concrete value and symbolic value. We use C_n^m S_n^m to represent them. Here, m represents the width of the value. And, n is a unique id of every value. For example, S_0^{32} represents a symbolic value of 32 bit size and its id is 0.

Definition 2. We use symbol | to represent the bind of values. For example, $C_1^8|_{C_1^8=0x12}$ represents a concrete value of 0x12, while $S_1^{32}|_{S_1^{32}=S_0^{32}}$ represents a symbolic value equal to S_0^{32}.

Definition 3. We use symbol $T_V = t$ to indicate the time stamp of value V. The time stamp of $[V_1, V_2, \ldots, V_n]$ is the newest one of $V_1, V_2, \ldots, V_n$. for simplicity, time stamps start with 0.

Definition 4. We use a set of expressions like $Pos_1 : V_1, Pos_2 : V_2, \ldots$ to represent the state of system. $EAX : C_0^{32}|_{C_0^{32}=0x12345678}$ means the value in register eax is 0x12345678.

Procedure of Symbolic Execution with Time Stamps. We assume the initial state of the system can be represented as $mem[eax+0xc] : S_0^{32}, mem[ebx+0xc] : S_1^{32}, mem[edx] : S_2^{32}$

Now we elaborate the procedure of symbolic execution with time stamps. After the symbolic execution of the first instruction, register ecx was written with a new symbol value, which equals to the value saved in memory address $[eax+0xc]$. As it was the first instruction, the new created value will be tagged with time-stamp 0.

$$ecx : S_3^{32}|_{S_3^{32}=S_0^{32}, T_{S_3^{32}}=0}$$

After the second instruction was executed, the value in the memory address $[eax+0xc]$ have been updated, and the time stamp of the new value is 1.

$$mem[eax + 0xc] : S_4^{32}|_{S_4^{32}=S_0^{32}+4, T_{S_4^{32}}=1}$$

The third instruction sets address $[ebx+0xc]$ with a concrete value 0xdeadbeef. Its time stamps is of course 2.

$$mem[ebx + 0xc] : C_0^{32}|_{C_0^{32}=0xdeadbeef, T_{C_0^{32}}=2}$$

When the final instruction is executed, register edx will be updated with a new value from address $[edx]$. This operation creates implicit data dependencies with edx and preceding address values. Here we can enumerate the final state of the symbolic execution.

$$ecx : S_3^{32}|_{S_3^{32}=S_0^{32}, T_{S_3^{32}}=0}$$

$$mem[eax + 0xc] : S_4^{32}|_{S_4^{32}=S_0^{32}+4, T_{S_4^{32}}=1}$$

$$mem[ebx + 0xc] : C_0^{32}|_{C_0^{32}=0xdeadbeef, T_{C_0^{32}}=2}$$

$$mem[edx] : S_5^{32}|_{S_5^{32}=S_2^{32}, T_{S_5^{32}}=3}$$

If we observe the final state of the code, we will find that all values have been tagged with a time stamp after symbolic execution. When generating corresponding operation in intermediate representations, we can avoid the confusion of alias as well as the read after write hazard or write after write hazard by following the sequence of time stamps.

4.4   IR Generation and Compilation

The method of IR generation includes two steps. The first step is generating IR for each handler extracted from the trace. All these semantic representation have multiple inputs and outputs. Then these IR will be concatenated to form the semantic representation of the whole trace.

Algorithm 1. IR generate algorithm for handlers

Input: *Expression_set* Φ
Output: LLVM IR of Code
Function *Init_Dependence_Graph (Expression_set Φ)*
  Dependence_graph $G \leftarrow \emptyset$
  for *each Expression E in Expression_set* **do**
    for *each Expression E_S in* SubExpression(E) **do**
      add edge ($E_S \leftarrow E$) to G
    if *value E needs to be written to address addr* **then**
      add edge (addr $\leftarrow E$) to G
  return G
Function *Generate IR(Expression_set Φ)*
  Dependence_graph $G \leftarrow$ Init_Dependence_Graph(Φ)
  $Q \leftarrow$ empty *Queue*
  for *each timestamp $t \in Timeline$* **do**
    Expression_set $\theta \leftarrow \bigcup$ expressions E with $T_E = t$
    if $\theta = \emptyset$ **then**
      continue
    for *each Expression $E \in \theta$* **do**
      $r \leftarrow$ BuildIR(E)
      Remove edges in G whose source is E
      if *value E needs to be written to address addr* **then**
        append (r,E,addr) to Q
    Loop $\leftarrow$ True
    while *Loop* **do**
      Loop $\leftarrow$ False
      for *each IR r,Expression E,address addr in Q* **do**
        if *there is no edge point to E in Graph G* **then**
          Build_IR_For_Store (r,addr)
          Loop $\leftarrow$ True
          remove(r,E,addr) in Q

Generate IR for Handlers. SymSem uses LLVM APIs to build two basic function for IR generation, BuildIR and Build_IR_For_Store. The former takes a symbolic expression, read necessary data from memory and registers, do the arithmetic operation required to generate corresponding representation. While, Build_IR_For_Store takes output of the former function and writes the result to target register of memory.

SymSem utilizes the two functions above and time-stamp information provided by previous phases to generate IR for handlers. It invokes the BuildIR function under the sequence of time-stamps. The generated representations will be put in a queue, waiting for writing to target until conditions satisfied.

In consideration of saving physical registers and memory space, SymSem uses a dependence graph here instead of time stamps. This also accelerates the writing procedure. The algorithm used to generator LLVM IR correspond to handlers can be described in Algorithm 1.

Here we take the code in Sect. 4.3 to illustrate how our algorithm works. The first step of the algorithm is to generate representation for S_3^{32}, as it is the only one which is created at time zero. The procedure will read a double word value from memory $[eax+0xc]$. Then the algorithm deals with S_4^{32}. The value will be immediately written to memory as there is no value explicitly dependent on it. Next, the same memory update can be applied to address $[ebx+0xc]$ for the same reason. Finally, the value S_5^{32} can be written to register edx.

Generate IR for Virtual Machine Trace. Having generated the IR of different handlers, the key of further generating accurate IR of the obfuscated program trace is to efficiently organize the IR of handlers.Here we define semantics of each handler as a function. Then the semantics of virtual machine trace can be represented by a sequence of function invokes. As the semantic representation is in the form of LLVM IR, the result can be conveniently compiled into executable code.

5   Implementation

We realized a prototype named SymSem for our methods and use a custom PIN tool which includes 162 lines of C code as trace recorder. The symbolic execution engine is based on manticore [2], most of the changes we made on it is meant to add time-stamp in its CPU emulation module and to analyze the result of symbolic execution. Our tool contains 25009 lines of code, 8545 lines of which are newly added to the original framework, including 2237 lines related to symbolic execution.

The PIN tool used in evaluation has about 225 lines of C code. Its responsibility is to load the rewritten code into memory and execute.

An interesting result we discovered is that not all LLVM passes could be implemented on our intermediate representation. So we have to use $r0$ optimization of opt tools with selected passes including *"-reassociate"*, *"-adce"*, *"-mem2reg"* which will not lead to semantic error. We found most errors those unfit passes incurred is due to they made a false assumption of stack usage of our code.

6   Evaluation

In this chapter we will evaluate our method on different code virtualization protection technologies. Our evaluation focus on three questions. (1) Can SymSem correctly reverse engineer the architecture of the virtual machine from the obfuscated trace? (2) Is SymSem able to recover the semantics of obfuscated program trace accurately? (3) How long does SymSem cost and how much can parallelism help the analysis?

6.1   Experimental Framework

We set up our experiment on a Windows XP virtual machine. All the tested programs were compiled by visual studio 2008 on the same machine. The remaining analysis were conducted on a server with Intel Xeon Gold 5122 and 128G of RAM, which runs Ubuntu 18.04.

We choose our test programs based on five algorithms including *binary serach, matrix multiply, tcp_checksum, rc4 encryption* and *bzip2 compression*. We choose proper implementations for these algorithms from Github and other open sources. Two famous commercial code virtualizer *VMProtect 3.09* and *Themida 2.4.2* are used to obfuscate these programs. As required by the code virtualizers, we only obfuscate the function of chosen algorithms and exclude other code. For example, when dealing with the program of *rc4 encryption*, we only obfuscated the encryption function.

For all tested programs, we separately constructed inputs to make sure that they call the obfuscated function and exit normally. For example, the input of *rc4 encryption* is a private key file and a message file. We use PIN tools to trace the obfuscated programs. The tracer records not only instructions, but also their addresses and specific register values. We only trace the code which belong to the program itself and exclude the third party library. The following Table 1 shows statistics of the tested program traces.

As is show in Table 1, we count the trace length by its lines, the average length of handlers in the trace and if the data in virtual machine is encrypted.

Table 1. Tested programs. This table shows the characters of the tested programs. "Handler avglen" means the average length of handlers appeared in the trace. We set the label "encrypted" true if the data computing in the trace is encrypted.

	Name	Length of trace	Length of trace (obfuscated)	Handler avglen	Encrypted
VMProtect	binary search	31	18328	17.45	False
	matrix multiply	151	60105	17.78	False
	tcp_checksum	174	75041	19.25	False
	rc4	1484	395214	16.82	False
	bzip2	244345	292161	19.61	False
Themida	binary search	31	121417	454.33	True
	matrix multiply	151	166234	384.69	True
	tcp_checksum	174	249736	516.98	True
	rc4	1484	1175319	453.65	True
	bzip2	244345	986447	271.59	True

As referred by previous work, modern commercial virtual machines all apply redundant handlers and the state of the art also encrypted its computing data. In our test experiments, *VMProtect* and *Themida* apply two different design philosophy. The former implements RISC-like ISA while the latter is CISC-like.

After being obfuscated by code virtualization, the function trace also expands to hundreds of instructions.

6.2   Our Tool Can Accurately Analyse the Arch of VM Trace

In this section we evaluate SymSem by its ability to recognize VM code. First, we use SymSem to find out handlers appeared in the trace, we compared them with the results of manual work. Then we use our tool to find out possible VM entries and exits, which were also compared with those we manually found.

SymSem tags basic blocks with three types, including "handler", "dispatcher" and "Non-VM". The former two types belong to virtual machines while the latter is not our rewriting target. We recognize VM entries and exits as special handlers. As one handler may have different control flow which leads to different semantic meaning, our tool specifically identified these cases.

Table 2. Handlers entries and exits found. This table lists the number of handlers found in the trace by manual work and automatic analysis. The word "hdl" is the shortcut of handler. Here "count once" means that different handlers with the same start address only count once. "(CF ≥ 1)" indicates that handlers have more than one control flow cases. The meaning of "(CF ≥ 2)" are similar.

	Name	hdl (manually)	hdl (count once)	hdl (CF ≥ 1)	(CF > 2)	entry & exit
VMProtect	binary search	43	43	43	0	1
	matrix multiply	50	50	50	0	1
	tcp_checksum	52	52	52	0	1
	rc4	67	67	67	0	1
	bzip2	111	111	110	1	20
Themida	binary search	109	109	156	30	3
	matrix multiply	98	98	137	25	1
	tcp_checksum	117	117	181	39	3
	rc4	113	113	158	36	1
	bzip2	150	150	255	46	25

As is shown in Table 2, the handler number is at most 150 in the trace and SymSem correctly identified all handlers in the trace. It also identified many handlers which have same start address but different control flows. Programs of *bzip2* and *binary search* were found to have a few virtual machines inside the obfuscated function. The analysis output shows that between two virtual machines are some other function calls which are not obfuscated. SymSem does not target these code so it is necessary to recognize them.

6.3   Our Tool Can Accurately Recover the IR of vm Trace

The preceding analysis generates LLVM IR representation of the obfuscated trace. These IR representation can be compiled to get the optimized trace. As a correct optimized trace indicates the correctness of the generated IR representation, we use a custom PIN tool to test the correctness of the rewritten semantics.

This PIN tool writes the optimized trace into a unique region of memory and modify the PC register when the program is going to execute the origin code.

As our rewriting procedure is based on traces, test inputs must lead to the same control flow with those in the preceding analysis. We make sure that the test inputs lead to the same control flow with the trace file by limiting their ranges. For example, we use files with the same length in *tcp_checksum* and the same key in *rc4 encryption*.

We use a simple fuzzer which generates inputs with the same control flow to test the rewritten code. These inputs were also sent to the same program not instrumented. We compared all the outputs and found that the instrumented programs have the same outputs with those not instrumented. We treat this as a proof of the semantic invariance of rewriting procedure. From tests above, we made a conclusion that SymSem can generate rewritten semantics accurately.

After evaluating the semantic invariance of rewriting procedure, we also count the length of the rewritten trace, the length of IR and how many functions in it. Table 3 shows the statistics of the analysis result. We counted IR length by its number of lines, the most important data is the reduction rate which points out how much optimization SymSem made on the trace.

Table 3. Statistics of the analysis results. This table shows the statistics of the analysis results, which including IR representation and optimized trace. The reduction rate is calculated by comparing length of the trace in virtual machines with the length of optimized trace.

	Name	IR length	func in IR	Optimized trace	Trace in VM	Reduction
VMProtect	binary search	2936	143	5254	18328	28.66%
	matrix multiply	4231	197	21580	60105	35.90%
	tcp_checksum	4534	216	27532	75041	36.68%
	rc4	8649	175	110049	395214	27.84%
	bzip2	151456	6195	25248	83051	30.40%
Themida	binary search	19930	191	17496	119794	14.60%
	matrix multiply	17951	180	24886	166234	14.97%
	tcp_checksum	22957	219	34151	247834	13.77%
	rc4	20306	181	163747	1175868	13.92 %
	bzip2	804290	8280	105776	756225	13.98%

In the table, complicated programs such as *rc4* have longer trace, generated IR and more functions in the IR files. The results also show that the reduction rate is stable for specific obfuscators. The average reduction rate of *VMProtect* is 31.89% and the one of *Themida* is 14.24%. The gap indicates that the reduction rate is highly dependent on the obfuscator itself.

6.4   The Overhead of Our Tool

Based on the architecture of SymSem, the whole analysis time can be divided into three parts, the time of trace analysis, the time of symbolic execution and the time used to generate IR and assembly code. In this section, we hope to demonstrate that SymSem can analyze a program trace in an acceptable time even for a more complicated program.

The first part of analysis is the trace analysis. Our algorithm parses the whole trace twice. The first parse aims to get statistics of the basic blocks and control flow information. Then the second is able to recognize the VM code, including handlers, entries and exits. As this part of analysis time is heavily dependent on the length of trace, what makes a difference is the analysis time of symbolic execution and IR generation.

Here we separately tested the overhead of SymSem to generate rewritten assembly code. The tests below was based on single process, which means it can be further accelerated.

Table 4. Analysis overhead of single process. This table illustrates the overhead of symbolic execution and generation of the optimized assembly code. Tags are defined as follows: total_time = the total time of symbolic execution and generation of optimized trace, z3 = the seconds spent in ze solver, SE = symbolic execution, llc = the time spent in LLVM compiler, executed loc = the lines of code which is symbolic executed during the analysis.

	Name	total_time	z3	SE	llc	executed loc
VMProtect	binary search	1m14.982s	1.548s	1m14.022s	0.960s	733
	matrix multiply	2m2.686s	3.350s	1m53.162s	9.524s	889
	tcp_checksum	2m6.014s	3.297s	1m50.576s	15.438s	1001
	rc4	12m42.455s	3.315s	2m17.785s	624.670s	1127
	bzip2	4m58.226s	11.844s	4m44.088s	14.138s	2069
Themida	binary search	29m4.721s	163.150s	29m0.44s	4.278s	75418
	matrix multiply	11m56.508s	118.164s	11m52.812s	3.696s	56549
	tcp_checksum	38m5.542s	205.830s	37m58.790s	6.752s	98744
	rc4	32m43.882s	225.397s	29m49.469s	174.413s	72584
	bzip2	66min36.38s	283.747s	64m56.50s	99.878s	103996

Table 4 shows the analysis time, including the symbolic execution and IR generation. The analysis spends most of the time on symbolic execution. We study the relationship between the overhead of symbolic execution and the executed code length. The consuming time seems to be linear correlated with the executed length, excluding the case of *bzip2*. We guess the case of *bzip2* is an exception because it has more virtual machines than others to analyze, which cost a longer time.

The other part of analysis time, which is spent on compilers to generate assembly code is related to the length of obfuscated trace. The case of *rc4* has a great amount of encryption loop in the trace so it cost much more time to compile. However, of these ten different test programs, the longest analysis time is limited in 66 min. Considering the length of trace and the procedure can be further accelerated, we think this time is acceptable.

Furthermore, we tested how much can parallelism help in analysis. As described in, the analysis time can be divided into 3 parts and the second part, which generate LLVM IR for handlers through symbolic execution can be fully paralleled. We tested the overhead on programs obfuscated by *Themida*.

The symbolic execution can be accelerated by parallelism. Here we use multiple process to accelerate the analysis. Each process separately analyzes one handler concurrently. Then the symbolic execution result is assembled to generate IR representation and assembly code. We record the total time of generating executable assembly code. Table 5 reveals the whole test results.

Table 5. Multiple process analysis overhead. This table illustrates the total analysis time with multiple processes.

	Name	1 process	2 processes	4 processes	8 processes
Themida	binary search	23m29.353s	22m59.659s	12m0.215s	7m35.043s
	matrix multiply	11m56.508s	36min54.790s	19m4.849s	11m28.323s
	tcp_checksum	29m36.273s	25m16.340s	13m4.776s	8m10.550s
	rc4	32m43.882s	32m44.630s	24m49.204s	14m28.977s
	bzip2	37min16.617s	34min15.423s	17m37.760s	11m7.583s

For simplicity, we limit the process number by exponent of two. We set the upper bound as 8 because of physical resources limitations. In addition, for those test cases with multiple virtual machines in the obfuscated function, we only count the first virtual machine, as the following virtual machines may inherit the knowledge of the preceding one, which brings additional uncertainty.

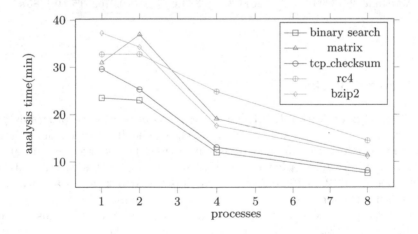

Fig. 3. overhead with multiple process

The Fig. 3 indicates that parallelism does reduce the whole overhead of the analysis. The consuming time nearly comes to 35.52% of the original when using

8 processes at the same time. The whole consuming time decreases with more analysis processes, but not by multiplicative inverse. We found that when using only two processes, the consuming time may be more than using single process. The following reasons may help to understand this phenomenon. First, parallelism brings additional cost with initialization and process communication. Second, some handlers were executed more than once for reducing the cost of communication.

We also compared the efficiency of SymSem with another deobfuscation tools driven by symbolic execution, VMHunt. We collected data from the published paper. We compare the average data based on 6 test cases in VMHunt and 10 in SymSem. We mainly concern two important indexes in the symbolic execution system. From Table 6, We find that though SymSem spends less time on each instruction, its ability to simplify instruction before symbolic execution is not comparable with VMHunt. The most significant reason for this is that VMHunt also puts data dependence analysis into its extraction process before symbolic execution.

Table 6. Efficiency comparison with VMHunt. In this table we compare the code extraction rate and the execution time per instruction of two different tools. The average data is based on 6 test cases in VMHunt and 10 in SymSem. The tag are defined as follows: "SE" = symbolic execution. "CE" = code extracition rates, it indicates how much code would be extracted for symbolic execution compared to the whole trace. "TPI" = symbolic execution time per instruction.

Name	avg_total_trace	avg_SE_len	avg_SE_time	CE	TPI
SymSem	354000.2	41311.0	1112.725 s	11.67%	0.0269 s
VMHunt	2613690.1	2011.3	339 s	0.076953%	0.1685 s

7 Related Works

Deobfuscation of Virtualized Code. The deobfuscation of programs protected by code virtualization has always been a difficult problem. Since Rolles proposed a deobfuscating method based on virtual machine architecture analysis [15], most of the automatic methods aim at virtual machines with dispatcher-handler model [11,12,15,16], one of the which is VMAttack [11]. It applies many heuristic rules to pair handlers with translated mnemonic.

Another type of deobfuscating method aims to sift important instructions from the program trace. The widely used approaches includes dataflow analysis, control flow analysis and taint analysis. These methods have an advantage that they do not rely on any assumptions of virtual machine architectures. One of the representative work is from Coogan [10], which uses equational reasoning to analyze instructions related to system calls. VMHunt [18] and Bin Sim [14] are similar for applying backward slicing based on different sources. Furthermore, VMHunt also use symbolic execution to do semantic analysis on sliced instructions.

Symbolic Execution of Code. Symbolic execution has been one of the fundamental technologies in automatic analysis [5,19]. Assisted by modern powerful SMT solver, symbolic execution abstract the target problem as constraint solving, made great help in automatic exploit generation [6,9], control flow analysis [7]. Also, it is also widely used in deobfuscation. [12,18]. Automatic reverse engineer tools take advantage of symbolic execution to deal with branch conditions, represent semantic results or further generate optimized code for analysis.

However, as we have pointed out, symbolic execution also suffers from alias and other problems, which may cause semantic confusion. We first point out these problems and provide symbolic execution with time stamps to solve them.

Rewrite of Obfuscated Code. Binary rewriting is an kernel techniques in security application area. It is widely used in profiling, code optimization, vulnerability detection. Our work uses a dynamic rewriting approach [13] to evaluate the correctness of trace rewriting. The same methods are also applied in evaluation of many other binary rewriting tools [8,17].

8   Discussion

We now address possible limitations of our method here. First, SymSem is based on dynamic analysis. As its analysis output is limited by the input trace, it is unable to recover the whole semantics of the original function. Second, symbolic execution method is unable to deal with those self modify code. These code have continuously varying semantics which is unable to represented by simply a set of symbolic expressions.

9   Conclusion

Symbolic execution has become a popular technique widely applied in fuzzing, vulnerability exploitation and reverse analysis. We present a new kind of symbolic execution technique which can accurately generate expressions that represent the full semantics of the code. In this symbolic execution technique, time stamps play a important role in eliminating possible hazards and alias issues. Also, by realizing a prototype named SymSem, we prove this technique can be further implemented to assist reverse engineer of programs obfuscated by code virtualization. We expect further costume compilation optimization will recover the original semantics of the unobfuscated program.

Acknowledgments. This work was supported by the General Program of National Natural Science Foundation of China (GrantNo. 61872237).

References

1. Code virtualizer. https://www.oreans.com/codevirtualizer.php. Accessed 4 July 2019
2. Manticore. https://github.com/trailofbits/manticore. Accessed 4 July 2019
3. Themida. https://www.oreans.com/themida.php. Accessed 4 July 2019
4. Vmprotct. https://vmpsoft.com/. Accessed 4 July 2019
5. Banescu, S., Collberg, C., Ganesh, V., Newsham, Z., Pretschner, A.: Code obfuscation against symbolic execution attacks. In: Proceedings of the 32nd Annual Conference on Computer Security Applications, ACSAC 2016, pp. 189–200. ACM, New York (2016). https://doi.org/10.1145/2991079.2991114
6. Bao, T., Wang, R., Shoshitaishvili, Y., Brumley, D.: Your exploit is mine: automatic shellcode transplant for remote exploits. In: 2017 IEEE Symposium on Security and Privacy (SP), pp. 824–839, May 2017. https://doi.org/10.1109/SP.2017.67
7. Bardin, S., David, R., Marion, J.Y.: Backward-bounded DSE: targeting infeasibility questions on obfuscated codes, pp. 633–651, May 2017. https://doi.org/10.1109/SP.2017.36
8. Bauman, E., Lin, Z., Hamlen, K.: Superset disassembly: statically rewriting x86 binaries without heuristics. In: Proceedings of the 25th Annual Network and Distributed System Security Symposium, NDSS 2018, San Diego, CA, February 2018
9. Brumley, D., Poosankam, P., Song, D., Zheng, J.: Automatic patch-based exploit generation is possible: techniques and implications. In: 2008 IEEE Symposium on Security and Privacy (SP 2008), pp. 143–157, May 2008. https://doi.org/10.1109/SP.2008.17
10. Coogan, K., Lu, G., Debray, S.K.: Deobfuscation of virtualization-obfuscated software: a semantics-based approach. In: ACM Conference on Computer & Communications Security (2011)
11. Kalysch, A., Götzfried, J., Müller, T.: VMAttack: deobfuscating virtualization-based packed binaries. In: The 12th International Conference (2017)
12. Liang, M., Li, Z., Zeng, Q., Fang, Z.: Deobfuscation of virtualization-obfuscated code through symbolic execution and compilation optimization. In: Qing, S., Mitchell, C., Chen, L., Liu, D. (eds.) ICICS 2017. LNCS, vol. 10631, pp. 313–324. Springer, Cham (2018). https://doi.org/10.1007/978-3-319-89500-0_28
13. Luk, C.K., et al.: Pin: building customized program analysis tools with dynamic instrumentation. In: Proceedings of the 2005 ACM SIGPLAN Conference on Programming Language Design and Implementation, PLDI 2005, pp. 190–200. ACM, New York (2005). https://doi.org/10.1145/1065010.1065034
14. Ming, J., Xu, D., Jiang, Y., Wu, D.: BinSim: trace-based semantic binary diffing via system call sliced segment equivalence checking. In: 26th USENIX Security Symposium (USENIX Security 2017), pp. 253–270. USENIX Association, Vancouver (2017). https://www.usenix.org/conference/usenixsecurity17/technical-sessions/presentation/ming
15. Rolles, R.: Unpacking virtualization obfuscators. In: Proceedings of the 3rd USENIX Conference on Offensive Technologies, January 2009
16. Sharif, M., Lanzi, A., Giffin, J., Lee, W.: Automatic reverse engineering of malware emulators. In: IEEE Symposium on Security & Privacy (2009)
17. Wang, R., et al.: Ramblr: making reassembly great again. In: Proceedings of the Network and Distributed System Security Symposium (2017)
18. Xu, D., Ming, J., Fu, Y., Wu, D.: VMHunt: a verifiable approach to partially-virtualized binary code simplification. In: Proceedings of the 2018 ACM SIGSAC

Conference on Computer and Communications Security, CCS 2018, pp. 442–458. ACM, New York (2018). https://doi.org/10.1145/3243734.3243827

19. Yadegari, B., Debray, S.: Symbolic execution of obfuscated code. In: Proceedings of the 22nd ACM SIGSAC Conference on Computer and Communications Security, CCS 2015, pp. 732–744. ACM, New York (2015). https://doi.org/10.1145/2810103.2813663

Elaphurus: Ensemble Defense Against Fraudulent Certificates in TLS

Bingyu Li[1,2,3], Wei Wang[1,2(✉)], Lingjia Meng[1,2,3], Jingqiang Lin[1,2,3], Xuezhong Liu[4], and Congli Wang[1,2,3]

[1] State Key Laboratory of Information Security, Institute of Information Engineering, Chinese Academy of Sciences, Beijing, China
{libingyu,wangwei,menglingjia,linjingqiang,wangcongli}@iie.ac.cn
[2] Data Assurance and Communication Security Research Center, CAS, Beijing, China
[3] School of Cyber Security, University of Chinese Academy of Sciences, Beijing, China
[4] China Communications Construction Company Limited, Beijing, China
xzliu@ccccltd.cn

Abstract. Recent security incidents indicate that certificate authorities (CAs) might be compromised to sign certificates with fraudulent information. The fraudulent certificates are exploited to launch successful TLS man-in-the-middle (MitM) attacks, even when TLS clients strictly verify the server certificates. Various security-enhanced certificate verification schemes have been proposed to defend against fraudulent certificates, such as Pinning, CAge, CT, DANE, and DoubleCheck. However, none of the above schemes perfectly solves the problem, which hinders them from being widely deployed. This paper analyzes these schemes in terms of security, usability and performance. Based on the analysis, we propose *Elaphurus*, an integrated security-enhanced certificate verification scheme on the TLS client side. Elaphurus is designed on top of Pinning, while integrating other schemes to eliminate their disadvantages and improving the overall security and usability. We implement the prototype system with OpenSSL. Experimental results show that it introduces a reasonable overhead, while effectively enhancing the security of certificate verification.

Keywords: Certificate · Certificate transparency (CT) · DNS-based authentication of named entities (DANE) · Pinning · TLS

1 Introduction

In public key infrastructures (PKIs), a certification authority (CA) is the trusted party to sign certificates [7]. The certificates are used in TLS to authenticate the

This work was partially supported by Cyber Security Program of National Key RD Plan of China (No. 2017YFB0802100), National Cryptography Development Fund (No. MMJJ20180221), and 13th Five-year Informatization Plan of Chinese Academy of Sciences (No. XXH13507-01).

Z. Liu and M. Yung (Eds.): Inscrypt 2019, LNCS 12020, pp. 246–259, 2020.
https://doi.org/10.1007/978-3-030-42921-8_14

TLS servers and establish secure channels. However, recent security incidents indicate that accredited CAs are compromised or deceived to sign fraudulent TLS server certificates, which bind a domain name (e.g., www.facebook.com) to a key pair held by attackers, instead of the legitimate website [18,30].

Fraudulent TLS server certificates result in successful man-in-the-middle (MitM) or impersonation attacks, even if TLS clients follow the strict steps [7] to verify server certificates. Various security-enhanced verification schemes are then proposed to tame the absolute authority of CAs from different perspectives, including public key or certificate Pinning (e.g., HPKP [8] and TACK [17]), public logging (e.g., certificate transparency [15] and ARPKI [4]), restricted scopes of certificate services (e.g., CAge [12] and Certlock [23]), multi-path verification (e.g., DoubleCheck [1] and Perspectives [28]), and subject-controlled policies (e.g., DANE [10] and PoliCert [25]). They require TLS clients to perform extra operations of certificate verification to detect fraudulent certificates.

These security-enhanced schemes improve the security of certificate verification, but each scheme still has its own defects. Among these schemes, Pinning is straightforward and effective, once public keys are pinned correctly. A TLS client locally pins the server certificate after a TLS channel is established. Then, in the future TLS handshakes, the pinned certificate is compared with the received certificate. A warning or alert is displayed if they do not match. Some variations propose to pin the CA certificate or the public key [8,17].

Pinning is the most efficient, but has shortcomings [22]. It is extremely difficult to securely initialize the Pinning entries. Existing designs usually follow the principle of trust on first use (TOFU); i.e., assuming no attacks when a domain is visited for the first time. However, MitM or impersonation attacks might happen in the TLS client's first visit to certain domains, and then malicious certificates are pinned. Preloaded trustworthy Pinning entries are recommended [8], but it is not scalable and only applicable to a small number of domains. Meanwhile, Pinning entries are out of control, after they are initialized in TLS clients. The legitimate website cannot update the entries actively, especially in the cases of any security incidents such as key compromise and certificate update [6].

This paper presents an *integrated* security-enhanced certificate verification system, called *Elaphurus*.[1] We analyze these schemes from the perspectives of false positive/negative rate (or security and usability) and verification delay (or efficiency). Pinning is the only stateful scheme, and very efficient once the Pinning entries are initialized. So we design Elaphurus on top of Pinning, by integrating other security-enhanced certificate verification, while the disadvantages and defects of these schemes are eliminated in the integration as follows.

- Elaphurus allows multiple Pinning entries for a domain. So a website with multiple server certificates or cached in content delivery networks (CDNs) does not trigger alerts.
- Several security-enhanced verification schemes are performed on a server certificate, before it is pinned on TLS clients. The vulnerability of Pinning

---

[1] In Chinese, Elaphurus is the hybrid of cow, deer, donkey, and horse. So we name the integrated scheme Elaphurus.

initialization is then mitigated. At the same time, to balance security and usability, Elaphurus allows a certificate to be accepted in TLS handshakes but not pinned, when it passes some schemes but is not secure enough.

- Elaphurus supports fast update operations on the Pinning entries. If a TLS server certificate is the result of the certificate update on a Pinning entry (i.e., signed by the same CA but with a more recent validity period), it will update the entry after simplified verification schemes.
- Each Pinning entry has its own validity period, shorter than the validity period of the pinned certificate. Elaphurus deletes expired Pinning entries, so that a (malicious) Pinning entry becomes invalid automatically.

When integrating other security-enhanced schemes with Pinning, Elaphurus takes their false positive/negative rates and verification delays into account, to improve both security and usability. We implement the prototype system of Elaphurus with OpenSSL [21], Tor [26], and Dig [29]. It integrates Pinning, CT, DANE, the multi-path verification by DoubleCheck and the restricted scopes of certificate services based on top-level domains (TLDs) by CAge. The analysis and experimental results show that Elaphurus introduces a reasonable overhead, while greatly enhancing the security of certificate verification.

The remainder is organized as follows. Existing security-enhanced certificate verification schemes are compared in Sect. 2. Section 3 presents the design and implementation of Elaphurus. It is evaluated in Sect. 4. Section 5 surveys the related works and Sect. 6 draws the conclusions.

2   Security-Enhanced Certificate Verification Review

This section describes and compares the typical security-enhanced certificate verification schemes.

2.1   Overview of Defense Philosophies

Various security-enhanced certificate verification schemes are proposed, following different defense philosophies.

Pinning - HPKP. The basic idea is that a TLS client by itself maintains the relevant certificate or public key of each visited domain (i.e., pins the certificates locally) [14]. These certificates may be pinned for a domain [8,17]: (a) the TLS server certificate of the website; and (b) the certificate of the intermediate and/or root CAs to verify the server certificate. In the future connections, it only needs to verify whether the pinned certificate is in the website's certificate chain.

Pinning entries are initialized in the way of preload or TOFU [8]. The certificates or public keys of some websites are pre-included in browsers and TLS libraries by manufacturers or developers. Or, a TLS client pins the certificates, when it establishes the TLS channel with the website for the first time.

Pinning is straightforward, but it is very difficult to initialize the Pinning entries – the number of preload entries is limited, and nobody guarantees there is no attack in a TLS client's first visit to any domain. Finally, lots of websites own multiple valid certificates at the same time, and a website cached in CDNs also results in multiple valid certificates. Existing Pinning-based schemes do not work well in such scenarios.

Restricted Scope of Services - CAge. In traditional PKIs, an accredited CA is authorized to serve any domains. Thus, once the attackers compromise the most weakest CA, they can issue fraudulent certificates binding any domain names. Although the Name Constraints certificate extension is defined to restrict the service scope [7], it is rarely used in practice by a CA to restrict the service scope of its subordinate CAs.

CAge specifies the restriction rules on the set of TLDs for which each CA is assumed to issue certificates [12]. The rules are derived based on the analysis of 1.95 million valid certificates issued by more than 1,200 CAs for 2.55 million domains. The rules are enforced on TLS clients, and an alert displays if any certificate does not comply with the rules.

Public Logging - Certificate Transparency. In the certificate transparency (CT) framework, certificates are recorded in publicly visible logs [4,15]. A certificate is submitted by the CA or the website, and the log server responds with a signed certificate timestamp (SCT). In TLS handshakes, a browser verifies the server certificate as well as the SCTs, and the connection is rejected if the verification fails.

CT is widely supported by browsers and TLS software [24]. It does not prevent compromised CAs from issuing fraudulent certificates. CT only ensures a certificate accepted by browsers are publicly-visible, so it is impossible for a CA to issue certificates for a domain but invisible to the domain owner.

Subject-Controlled Policy - DANE. It allows a domain owner to specify its own certificate policy, or reconfirm the certificates issued by CAs. The subject-controlled certificate policies are usually published as DNS resource records (RRs) and divided into two categories: extra validation before certificate issuance such as certification authority authorization (CAA) [9], and security-enhanced certificate verification such as DNS-based authentication of named entities (DANE) [10].

Based on DNS security extensions (DNSSEC) [3], DANE allows a domain owner to specify which certificates are meant to be deployed for its domain. DANE defines a new DNS RR, called TLS association (TLSA), which is protected by DNSSEC. The domain owner publishes the following certificates as TLSA RRs: (a) the TLS server certificate; and/or (b) the CA certificate that must be in the certificate chain. A client obtains TLSA RRs through DNS query and then these RRs are used to verify TLS server certificates.

Multi-path Verification - DoubleCheck. The multi-path verification is originally proposed in Perspectives [28] to verify the server public key in SSH. Perspectives introduces a set of notaries, which maintain the public keys of network services. When a client is verifying the public key of a network service, it gets the records from notaries and compares them with the public key received from the

Table 1. The comparison of security-enhanced verification schemes.

		FPR	FNR	Delay
CAge		Low	High	Low
CT	Small T_r	Low	Medium	Low
	Great T_r	Low	Low	Low
DANE	Server	Very low	Very low	Medium
	CA	Very low	Low	Medium
DoubleCheck		High	Low	High

T_r: *the transition period, defined as the period of time starting when the SCT was signed and ending when the SCT was verified by TLS clients*;

Server: *the TLSA RR directly specifies the server certificate*;

CA: *the TLSA RRs specify the intermediate or root CA certificates which must be present in the certificate chains.*

server. Notary-based multi-path verification leak the user privacy to notaries, when it queries the public key of the visited service.

DoubleCheck [1] requires the TLS client to establish extra anonymous Tor links to receive another copy of the server certificate, and compare the certificates from different network paths. The certificate is accepted, only if they are identical. Since the extra certificate is retrieved via anonymous links, DoubleCheck does not leaks user privacy.

2.2 Comparison of Typical Schemes

Five typical schemes (i.e., Pinning, CAge, CT, DANE, and DoubleCheck) are compared from two aspects: accuracy (in false positive/negative rates) and verification delay. We will explain the comparison results shown in Table 1 as below.

2.2.1 False Positive/Negative Rate

The false positive rate (FPR) of a certificate verification scheme is the probability that a valid certificate is verified as fraudulent by the scheme. A *false positive* means a valid certificate is detected as fraudulent; e.g., after a fraudulent certificate is pinned, any valid certificate triggers a false positive of Pinning. Meanwhile, a *false negative* means a fraudulent one is considered as valid, and the false negative rate (FNR) is the probability that a fraudulent certificate passes the scheme. Note that, in the analysis, we assume that the schemes have been implemented and deployed correctly.[2]

---

[2] However, the design of Elaphurus needs to handle the scenarios that some security-enhanced verification schemes (e.g., CT and DANE) are not deployed.

Pinning. The FPR/FNR depends on the Pinning entries on TLS clients. If the entries contain all valid certificates of the website, there will be no false positive; otherwise, some valid certificate will be detected as fraudulent. If all Pinning entries are correct, no false negative will happen.

CAge. It restricts the scope of certificate services based on TLDs. As evaluated in [12], the restriction rules are generally static and 99.84% of newly-signed certificates comply with the rules of CAge, so the FPR is only 0.16%.

On the other hand, the false negative is high, because the TLD-based rules are coarse-grained and a fraudulent certificate issued for any domain in the restricted TLDs (e.g., *.com) does not trigger alerts. The .com TLD accounts for 51% of TLS websites, and more than 400 CAs sign certificates for some .com website [12]. So a fraudulent certificate signed by one of these CAs for any .com website, results in a false negative.

CT. The FPR of CT is low – less than 0.2% websites adopt the CT framework but do not comply with the CT policy [24], so the FPR is about 0.2%.

CT depends on the domain owner to detect possible fraudulent certificates in public logs [15]. The attackers might submit a fraudulent certificate to CT logs to return valid SCTs, and then the fraudulent certificate is considered as valid by CT-enabled TLS clients. So its FNR becomes lower as time goes by, for the fraudulent certificate will finally be detected by the domain owner. We define *the transition period* starting when the SCT was signed and ending when the SCT is verified by TLS clients, denoted as T_r. As T_r becomes greater, the FNR varies from medium to low.

DANE. The domain owner is aware of all its certificates, so the FPR of DANE is the lowest – a false positive does not appears unless the domain owner configure incorrect TLSA RRs by himself.

The FNR is low, if only CA certificates are specified in TLSA – the attackers have to compromise the specified CAs, and compromising other CAs dose not result in successful attacks. Or, if the server certificate is specified in TLSA, the FNR of DANE is even lower. In this case, a false negative happens, only if the attackers forge DNSSEC RRs [3], which is extremely difficult.

DoubleCheck. A false negative happens, if and only if the attackers could launch a large-scale MitM attack, and the exit of extra Tor links happens to be in the attack zone, and then the extra Tor links return the identical fraudulent certificate [1]. So the FNR is low.

The FPR is rather high. A website is usually configured with several certificates [27] or cached in CDNs. In such frequent cases, the multiple certificates of a website are different but all are valid, while DoubleCheck displays alerts.

2.2.2 Verification Delay
The delay is mainly introduced by the extra communications, and the data processing on TLS clients is negligible. For example, an RSA signing takes less than 2 ms, while a round of TCP link to visit a website costs dozens of ms. So we

define the delay is: *low* if no extra communications are needed, *medium* when the scheme introduces extra regular network communications, or *high* if it requires extra heavy communications (e.g., Tor links).

The delay of Pinning, CAge or CT is low, for the verification does not need any extra communications. DANE requires at least one more round of DNSSEC communications to return TLSA RRs, and then delay is medium. Finally, the delay of DoubleCheck is high, because it requires the client to establish extra anonymous Tor links to retrieve certificates.

3   The Design and Implementation of Elaphurus

This section presents the design goals of Elaphurus, followed by the design and the implementation.

3.1   Design Goals

Elaphurus attempts to defend against the attacks exploiting fraudulent certificates, by integrating the security-enhanced verification of TLS server certificates. Meanwhile, we balance security, usability and efficiency in Elaphurus. When enhancing the security of certificate verification, it still considers the usability. Finally, when integrating various security-enhanced schemes, Elaphurus prefers to efficient schemes.

3.2   System Design

Elaphurus is designed on top of Pinning. It maintains a list of pinned TLS server certificates for visited domains, with the improvements by integrating other schemes as follows.

Highly-Secure Pinning Initialization. A Pinning entry is initialized, only if a certificate is verified by some security-enhanced schemes except Pinning. In particular, a Pinning entry is initialized after the certificate is verified by (*a*) one security-enhanced scheme with a *very low* FNR, or (*b*) at least *two* schemes with *low* FNRs.

Update with Simplified Verification. Verifying every unpinned server certificate by multiple schemes is expensive and inefficient. Thus, if a server certificate results from the update of a pinned certificate (i.e., signed by the same CA but with a more recent validity period), the Pinning initialization of this certificate is simplified. The requirement to update a Pinning entry is as follows: (*a*) the to-be-pinned server certificate is signed by the same CA as the entry, and (*b*) it is verified by any security-enhanced scheme with a *low* FNR at least. In this case, the security of Pinning initialization is not degraded but the performance is improved.

Multiple Pinning Entries for a Domain. It supports multiple Pinning entries for a domain, so it works well with a website cached in CDNs or with multiple valid server certificates.

Algorithm 1. The Certificate Verification of Elaphurus.

Input: $pin[.]$: An array of Pinning entries

  dn: The domain name of the visited website

  $cert$: The server certificate

Output: $result$: $accept$ or $reject$

1 $op := init$

2 **if** dn in $pin[.]$ **then**

3 $\quad$ **if** $cert$ in $pin[dn]$ **then**

4 $\quad\quad$ **return** $accept$

5 **if** $(cert\_update := (CA(cert)$ in $pin[dn]))$ **and** $(ExpireSoon(cert\_update)$ **then**

6 $\quad$ $op := update$

7 $cage := CAgeVerify()$

8 $ct := CTVerify()$

9 **if** $IntVerify(op, cage, ct) = reject$ **then**

10 $\quad$ **return** $reject$ // $accept$ is impossible here

11 $dane := DANEVerify()$

12 **if** $(result := IntVerify(op, cage, ct, dane)) = reject$ **then**

13 $\quad$ **return** $reject$ // $reject$ immediately

14 **if** $result = unknown$ **then**

15 $\quad$ $dbcheck := DoubleCheckVerify()$

16 $\quad$ $result := IntVerify(op, cage, ct, dane, dbcheck)$

17 **if** $result = accept\_pin$ **then**

18 $\quad$ **if** $op = init$ **then**

19 $\quad\quad$ $PinInit(cert)$

20 $\quad$ **else**

21 $\quad\quad$ $PinUpdate(cert, cert\_update)$

22 **return** $result$

Accepted-but-not-Pinned Server Certificate. To balance security and usability, Elaphurus allows a server certificate to be accepted but not pinned, when it passes some security-enhanced schemes but is not secure enough. Then, this certificate does not take effect in the *stateful* Pinning entries. A server certificate is accepted but not pinned, if it is verified by one scheme with a *low* FNR and one with a *medium* FNR.

Deletion of Pinning Entries. For we allow multiple Pinning entries for a domain, the deletion of Pinning entries is necessary. A validity period is assigned to each entry, and it becomes invalid on expiration without the control from websites.

3.3 Implementation

Algorithm 1 lists the detailed certificate verification procedure of Elaphurus. This procedure is conducted, in addition to the standard certificate verification steps. When a server certificate is input, Elaphurus first checks if it has been pinned or is the update of a Pinning entry. Then, it verifies the certificate by *CAgeVerify()* and *CTVerify()*, and tries to return the final result based on the results of Pinning, CAge and CT. If the results of efficient Pinning, CAge and CT are not enough to make the decision, Elaphurus continues to execute inefficient DANE and DoubleCheck one by one, by *DANEVerify()* and *DoubleCheckVerify()*. Besides, it tries to output the result after DANE is performed, for DoubleCheck is the most inefficient.

Elaphurus also implements the fast track to detect a server certificate as *invalid*: (*a*) it is verified as invalid by any scheme with a *very low* FPR, or (*b*) by two schemes with *low* FPR. This fast track enables Elaphurus to output the reject decision when it is ready at any time, but not to wait for the results of all schemes. Finally, if a certificate does not satisfy any threshold of initialization or update after all verification schemes, it is rejected by Elaphurus.

IntVerify() outputs the integrated result based on the results of multiple schemes. The output may be *accept_pin*, *accept*, *unknown*, and *reject*. The results of CAge, CT, DANE, and DoubleCheck, may be *valid, invalid*, or *unsupport*. *unsupport* means the scheme is not deployed, or it ends with timeout.

As Fig. 1 shows, we implement Elaphurus with OpenSSL [21], Tor [26], and Dig [29]. OpenSSL is enhanced to verify the server certificate in TLS handshakes. In particular, Pinning entries are maintained on hard drive. Dig is used to request and verify TLSA RRs of DANE for the domain. Tor client is used to implement DoubleCheck, to request another server certificate of the visited domain through an extra Tor link. Elaphurus implements CT based on the OpenSSL library.

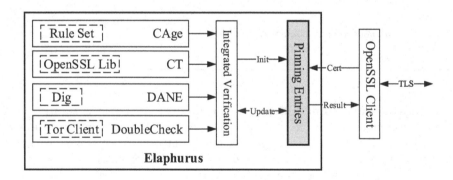

Fig. 1. The architecture of Elaphurus

When an OpenSSL client initiates a TLS handshake and a server certificate is received, Elaphurus extracts all the data necessary to verify the certificate, including the visited domain name, the certificate chain received in TLS handshakes, and the SCTs in TLS extensions. Then, the data are processed by Elaphurus. If the certificate is rejected, Elaphurus prompts OpenSSL to terminate the TLS connection.

4   Evaluation

In this section, we evaluate Elaphurus in terms of security, usability and performance.

4.1   Security and Usability

We analyze the false positive rate (i.e., usability) and the false negative rate (i.e, security) of Elaphurus.

Based on the policy specified in Sect. 3 and the analysis results in Table 1, a server certificate is pinned (and accepted) if any of these conditions is satisfied: (a) It matches the server certificate published in TLSA RRs of DANE, the FNR of which is very low; or (b) the certificate is verified by any two of CT (with a great T_r), DANE (with a CA certificate in the TLSA RR) and DoubleCheck, the FNRs of which are low. The condition to update a Pinning entry (i.e., the to-be-pinned certificate is signed by the same CA as the securely-initialized Pinning entry), is as follows: It is verified by at any one of CT (with a great T_r), DANE (with a CA certificate) and DoubleCheck, the FNRs of which are low. So Elaphurus improves Pinning by securely initializing and updating the entries, and its security is higher than any of CT, DANE and DoubleCheck by the integration, because the attackers need to break at least two schemes.

To balance security and usability, Elaphurus allows a certificate to be accepted but not pinned, when it is verified as valid with a *medium* FNR (i.e., CT with a small T_r), and at the same time by DANE with CA certificates or DoubleCheck, the FNRs of which are low. So it is more secure than CT, DANE and DoubleCheck. It is worth noting that the accepted-but-not-pinned certificates does not lead to *downgrade* attacks. That is, can an accepted-but-not-pinned *fraudulent* certificate be always accepted? In fact, as time goes by, CT with a small T_r will be with a great T_r, and then it is verified as valid by CT with a *low* FNR, or is detected as fraudulent in CT logs by the domain owner and then becomes revoked. In summary, the verification result of CT varies as time goes by, so the design of accepted-but-not-pinned certificates does not become a vulnerability of downgrade attacks, as a valid certificate will be eventually pinned or a fraudulent one will be revoked over time.

When a certificate fails to meet one of the above conditions, Elaphurus marks it as invalid. Moreover, Elaphurus terminates the verification and immediately outputs the reject decision for better performance, when (a) the certificate is verified as invalid by DANE with a *very low* FPR, or (b) it is verified as invalid by both CAge and CT of which the FPRs are *low*. In the above cases, Elaphurus does not increase the FNR by rejecting a valid certificate, because such a certificate cannot be accepted by enough schemes according to the analysis in Table 1.

4.2   Performance

The overall performance depends on (a) the efficiency of each security-enhanced scheme, and (b) the deployment of each scheme. We first evaluate each scheme

Table 2. The time cost (in ms) of security-enhanced certificate verification schemes.

		Average	Median	Interval
Pinning	(In)Valid	0.13	0.12	0.11–0.31
	Unsupported	0.014	0.007	0.004–0.079
CAge	(In)Valid	0.12	0.12	0.09–0.24
	Unsupported	0.013	0.006	0.003–0.084
CT	(In)Valid	1.75	1.86	0.32–16.89
	Unsupported	0.31	0.23	0.067–1.84
DANE	(In)Valid	12.04	11.01	8.21–211.53
	Unsupported	11.39	9.31	7.14–197.27
DoubleCheck		1,509.67	1,398.12	889.33–3,353.45
TLS handshake		425.55	375.32	13.28–2,998.12

separately in the Elaphurus prototype, as shown in Table 2. The prototype runs on a computer with an Intel Xeon E5-2650v4 CPU (2.20GHz) and 2 GB RAM, and Ubuntu v16.04 as the operating system. We instrumented in the implementation to record the time cost of each security-enhanced scheme.

The measurements are performed against Alexa Top-1000 websties except for DANE. DANE is not widely deployed, so the measurement has to be finished on the DANE-supported websites listed in [11]. We construct the Pinning entries, and the delays are measured as below: (*a*) the Pinning entry exists and the certificate (mis)matches the pinned one, and the measured time is for the (in)valid cases; and (*b*) the entry is deliberately cleared, and the measured time is for unsupported cases. For CAge, the measurements are similar to Pinning, and we list the time cost for the cases of invalid, valid, and unsupported certificates. In the measurement of DoubleCheck, a Tor exit is randomly chosen for the Tor link to retrieve the certificate. The results of DANE are measured as the time to retrieve and verify the TLSA RRs. We also measure the time cost of TLS handshakes of Alexa Top-1000 websites, from the ClientHello message to the last Finished message, including the default certificate verification in OpenSSL. We visit each website 10 times and calculate the average.

Pinning and CAge. The maximum cost by Pinning or CAge is always less than 1 ms. Compared with TLS handshakes, the overhead of Pinning and CAge is negligible.

CT. 36.1% of CT verification takes less than 1 ms, 57.5% takes between 1 ms and 5 ms.

DANE. Whether the TLSA RRs exist or not, 98.0% of DANE verification takes between 7 ms and 13 ms.

DoubleCheck. It introduces very large delays because DoubleCheck requires extra Tor links: 88.3% takes between 889 ms and 2,000 ms, and the maximum is 3,353.45 ms.

TLS Handshake. The average time cost of TLS handshakes with Alexa Top-1000 websites is 425.55 ms, and 52.0% takes between 100 ms and 1,000 ms.

The cost of Elaphurus depends on the security-enhanced schemes supported by the visited website and the results of each scheme. As described in Algorithm 1, when verifying a certificate, the schemes are executed in the order of Pinning, CAge, CT, DANE, and DoubleCheck. Elaphurus does not need to execute inefficient DoubleCheck every time. When only Pinning, CAge, CT, and DANE are executed, the introduced delay is negligible as it increases averagely by only 0.03%, 0.03%, 0.4% and 2.8% for Pinning, CAge, CT and DANE, respectively, compared with the cost of TLS handshakes in Table 2. However, if DoubleCheck is executed, the time increases significantly by 354.6%.

Finally, we analyze the overall performance of Elaphurus based on the deployment of these security-enhanced schemes. Among these schemes, Pinning, CAge and DoubleCheck do not require any new network-security infrastructure (provided that the Tor system is always ready), and they are implemented in the TLS client side. CT has been widely deployed (e.g., 63.2% of HTTPS connections are CT-compliant in February 2018 [24]). Although DANE has been standardized for several years, the deployment is still limited [2]. Thus, it results in a high probability that Elaphurus executes DoubleCheck in the Pinning initialization, because DANE probably ends with unsupported results while the probability becomes small in the update of Pinning entries because CT is deployed widely.

5   Related Work

Some systems support multiple security-enhanced certificate verification schemes. CertShim performs binary instrumentation implementing several security enhanced schemes [5], to patch the vulnerabilities of certificate verification in legacy systems. TrustBase [20] intercepts TLS traffic to enforce mandatory certificate validation with different security-enhanced schemes. These solutions list multiple schemes as available options, but do not integrate several approaches into one scheme as Elaphurus does.

AKI [13] allows the subject to define its policy as certificate extensions and the integrity log servers to publicly record all certificates. Then, ARPKI [4] extends the designs of AKI with better efficiency, and provides the formal verification of its security properties. PoliCert [25] defines subject certificate policies (SCPs) which allow the certificate subject to specify parameters such as trusted CAs, certificate update criteria, etc.

Compared with the above integration schemes that focus on the certificate registration and creation in the server side, Elaphurus is a client-centric solution to integrate different certificate verification schemes in TLS clients. Elaphurus extends our preliminary work [16], by (*a*) introducing the security analysis, (*b*) finishing the detailed design and implementation of the prototype system, and (c) measuring the performance with the prototype system.

Amann et al. finished a large-scale study on the adoption of TLS/HTTPS security enhancements [2], including CT, HPKP, DANE, etc. Oltrogge et al. conducted an extensive analysis on the applicability of Pinning in Android Apps [19].

6   Conclusion

We present Elaphurus, an integrated security-enhanced certificate verification scheme for TLS. Elaphurus is designed on top of Pinning, which is stateful and the most efficient. Then, we integrate other security-enhanced verification schemes to solve the defects of Pinning, while the disadvantages of other schemes are also eliminated in the integration. Elaphurus integrates Pinning with CAge, CT, DANE, and DoubleCheck, based on their false positive/negative rates, to improve both security and usability. The security analysis and performance evaluation show that it balances the security and usability of certificate verification with reasonable overheads.

References

1. Alicherry, M., Keromytis, A.: DoubleCheck: multi-path verification against man-in-the-middle attacks. In: 14th IEEE ISCC (2009)
2. Amann, J., et al.: Mission accomplished? HTTPS security after DigiNotar. In: 17th IMC (2017)
3. Arends, R., et al.: IETF RFC 4033 - DNS security introduction and requirements
4. Basin, D., et al.: ARPKI: attack resilient public-key infrastructure. In: 21th ACM CCS (2014)
5. Bates, A., et al.: CertShim: securing SSL certificate verification through dynamic linking. In: 21th ACM CCS (2014)
6. Biilmann, M.: Be afraid of HTTP public key pinning (HPKP) (2016). https://www.smashingmagazine.com/be-afraid-of-public-key-pinning
7. Cooper, D., et al.: IETF RFC 5280 - Internet X.509 public key infrastructure certificate and certificate revocation list (CRL) profile (2008)
8. Evans, C., et al.: IETF RFC 7469 - Public key pinning extension for HTTP (2015)
9. Hallam-Baker, P., Stradling, R.: IETF RFC 6844 - DNS certification authority authorization (CAA) resource record (2013)
10. Hoffman, P., Schlyter, J.: IETF RFC 6698 - The DNS-based authentication of named entities (DANE) transport layer security (TLS) protocol: TLSA (2012)
11. Internet Society: DANE test sites. https://www.internetsociety.org/resources/deploy360/dane-test-sites
12. Kasten, J., Wustrow, E., Halderman, J.A.: CAge: taming certificate authorities by inferring restricted scopes. In: Sadeghi, A.-R. (ed.) FC 2013. LNCS, vol. 7859, pp. 329–337. Springer, Heidelberg (2013). https://doi.org/10.1007/978-3-642-39884-1_28
13. Kim, T., et al.: Accountable key infrastructure (AKI): a proposal for a public-key validation infrastructure. In: 22nd WWW (2013)

14. Langley, A.: Public key pinning (2011). https://www.imperialviolet.org/2011/05/04/pinning.html
15. Laurie, B., et al.: IETF RFC 6962 - Certificate transparency (2013)
16. Liu, X., Li, B., Wang, C., Lin, J.: An integrated security-enhanced PKI certificate verification scheme. Appl. Res. Comput. (2019). (in Chinese)
17. Marlinspike, M.: Trust assertions for certificate keys (2013). http://tack.io/draft.html
18. Morton, B.: More Google fraudulent certificates (2014). https://www.entrust.com/google-fraudulent-certificates/
19. Oltrogge, M., et al.: To pin or not to pin: helping APP developers bullet proof their TLS connections. In: 24th USENIX Security (2015)
20. O'Neill, M., et al.: TrustBase: an architecture to repair and strengthen certificate-based authentication. In: 26th USENIX Security (2017)
21. OpenSSL Software Foundation: OpenSSL: Cryptography and SSL/TLS toolkit. https://www.openssl.org
22. Ristic, I.: Is HTTP public key pinning dead? (2016). https://blog.qualys.com/ssllabs/2016/09/06/is-http-public-key-pinning-dead
23. Soghoian, C., Stamm, S.: Certified lies: detecting and defeating government interception attacks against SSL (Short Paper). In: Danezis, G. (ed.) FC 2011. LNCS, vol. 7035, pp. 250–259. Springer, Heidelberg (2012). https://doi.org/10.1007/978-3-642-27576-0_20
24. Stark, E., et al.: Does certificate transparency break the web? Measuring adoption and error rate. In: 40th IEEE S&P (2019)
25. Szalachowski, P., et al.: PoliCert: secure and flexible TLS certificate management. In: 21th ACM CCS (2014)
26. Tor project: anonymity online. https://www.torproject.org/index.html
27. Vandersloot, B., et al.: Towards a complete view of the certificate ecosystem. In: 16th IMC (2016)
28. Wendlandt, D., et al.: Perspectives: improving SSH-style host authentication with multi-path probing. In: USENIX ATC (2008)
29. Wikipedia: Dig for querying domain name system (DNS) servers. https://en.wikipedia.org/wiki/Dig_(command)
30. Wilson, K.: Distrusting new CNNIC certificates (2015). https://blog.mozilla.org/security/2015/04/02/distrusting-new-cnnic-certificates/

Improving Division Property Based Cube Attacks by Removing Invalid Monomials

Senshan Pan, Zhuhua Li, and Liangmin Wang$^{(\boxtimes)}$

School of Computer Science and Communication Engineering, Jiangsu University,
Zhenjiang 212013, China
wanglm@ujs.edu.cn

Abstract. Division property based cube attack was proposed by Todo *et al.* at CRYPTO 2017, which can exploit larger cube indices than traditional cube attacks. At CRYPTO 2018, Wang *et al.* introduced degree evaluation and flag technique to reduce the complexity of recovering the superpoly. Although division property based cube attacks that introducing these methods are powerful to analyze many stream ciphers, how to further reduce the complexity of determining possible monomials of the superpoly is still a problem. In this paper, we introduce some techniques to speedup the recovery of the superpoly.

1. When evaluating all possible monomials, we provide the filter technique to reduce the complexity of evaluating monomials by division trails. Non-cube public variables involved in superpoly also can be obtained by the filter technique. While evaluating monomials, the effect of non-cube public variables on all monomials can be considered directly.

2. In order to remove most invalid monomials, we modify the parameters of flag technique in the initialization phase. Most invalid division trails can be identified and fewer remaining monomials need to be determined by constructing a linear system.

To verify our scheme, we apply the method to the initialization of the Grain128a. In the recovery of the superpoly of 106-round Grain128a, the number of possible monomials needs to be determined is reduced to 5.56% of Wang *et al.*'s superpoly evaluations. The complexity of analysing 184-round Grain128a is smaller than 57% of the current best complexity. In the recovery attack of 185 or higher rounds Grain128a, cube indices set that includes all non-constant public variables can be achieved according to the results of the filter technique.

Keywords: Cube attack · Division property · Division trail ·
Grain128a

1 Introduction

The cube attack is an effective cryptanalytic technique proposed by Dinur and Shamir in [2]. For stream ciphers, let $f(x, v)$ be the first bit of keystream, and

© Springer Nature Switzerland AG 2020
Z. Liu and M. Yung (Eds.): Inscrypt 2019, LNCS 12020, pp. 260–276, 2020.
https://doi.org/10.1007/978-3-030-42921-8_15

$v = (v_1, v_2, \cdots, v_m)$ be m-bit public variables and $x = (x_1, x_2, \cdots, x_n)$ be n-bit secret variables. Cube indices set containing the indexes of some public variables is I. C_I containing all possible combinations of public variables indexed by the set I, which is applied to the initialization of the f. The sum of all possible outputs of f can be obtained, which is represented as the polynomial of x and v, and can be called the superpoly of C_I in f. If the superpoly of the C_I is simple enough, we can recover the superpoly in the offline phase and obtain some information of secret variables involved in the superpoly in the online phase. In [2], the superpoly is tested for its linearity. If the test passes, the superpoly can be recovered by assuming it is linear. Recently, there are some new research insights based on the cube attack, such as correlation cube attack [6], division property based cube attack [9], degree evaluation of NFSR-based cryptosystems [5] and dynamic cube attack [3].

Division property can construct integral distinguisher by analyzing the structure of block ciphers, which was proposed by Todo *et al.* in [7]. In [8], Todo *et al.* obtained the integral property of the full-round MISTY1 by the division property. In order to improve the propagation of division property within the structure, Todo proposed bit-based division property and bit-based division property using three subsets in [10]. The bit-based division property can find new integral property for Simon32. In [13], Xiang *et al.* applied mixed integer linear programming(MILP) to the propagation of bit-based division property, which can reduce the complexity of time and memory. In [4], a variant three subsets division property with STP solver was proposed. This method can apply the automatic search model to ciphers with large block sizes.

In [10], Todo *et al.* applied bit-based division property based on MILP model to the cube attack on stream ciphers. The superpoly of C_I can be recovered by the truth table that depends on the values of secret variables indexed by J and assignments of values of non-cube variables. When a non-constant superpoly was found by a proper assignment of non-cube variables, some information about secret variables can be recovered in the online phase. In [11], Wang *et al.* introduced flag technique and degree evaluation to reduce the complexity and enhance the precision of division property based cube attack. In the offline phase, the superpoly was recovered by constructing a linear system of coefficients for all possible monomials instead of constructing the truth table.

Unlike applying bit-based division property to cube attack, [12] proposed a practical method that based on bit-based division property using three subsets. The corresponding coefficients of all possible monomials can be evaluated by propagating $\mathbb{L}$ instead of constructing truth table as in [9] or solving a linear system as in [11].

Besides improving the efficiency of recovering the superpoly of division property based cube attack, another important research is a new variant of division property from an algebraic point of view in [14]. The authors built the relationship between bit-based division property and the algebraic degree evaluation, which can remove invalid division trails. These insights has been applied to verify the results of division property based cube attack on Trivium.

In this paper, we focus on the following improvements of division property based on cube attack that introduces the flag technique.

- Firstly, the previous phase that evaluating all possible monomials in [11] does not consider the relationship between lower degree monomials and specific higher degree monomials. In their methods, all t-degree monomials can be evaluated from the combinations of the involved variables indices J or indices set $JR_t \subset J$ that composing all t-degree monomials. However, when evaluating all t-degree monomials that may exist in the superpoly by propagating bit-based division property, there are many t-degree monomials that do not exist for the combinations of indices set J or JR_t need to be evaluated. The complexity of evaluating these monomials is huge. Therefore, we introduce the filter technique to further reduce the complexity of evaluating all t-degree monomials. With the filter technique, when low-degree monomials do not exist in the superpoly under propagating division property, some specific high-degree monomials also do not exist in the superpoly. Therefore, these evaluations can be saved.
- Secondly, non-cube public variables that involved in the superpoly can be achieved by filter technique and added to the set J. While evaluating monomials, the effect of non-cube public variables on monomials that may exist in the superpoly can be considered directly, rather than attempting to find proper non-cube IV assignment with MILP model as in [11].
- Thirdly, during the initialization phase for flag technique, we modify the parameters of each public variable and secret variable to remove most invalid monomials. Then, only corresponding coefficients of the remaining monomials need to be determined.

The outline of this paper is as follows. Section 2 introduces the background of cube attack, bit-based division property, division trail, MILP model and flag technique. Section 3 provides the filter technique to reduce the complexity of evaluating monomials by division trails. We remove some invalid monomials by modifying the parameters of the flag technique in Sect. 4. We apply the method to Grain128a in Sect. 5. Finally, we give a conclusion.

2   Preliminaries

2.1   Cube Attack

Cube attack was first proposed in [2]. Let $f(x, v)$ be the first output bit of the stream cipher that contains m-bit public variables $v = (v_1, v_2, \cdots, v_m)$ and n-bit secret variables $x = (x_1, x_2, \cdots, x_n)$. Cube indices set is $I = \{i_1, i_2, \cdots, i_{|I|}\} \subset \{1, 2, \cdots, m\}$ and a maxterm is $t_I = v_{i_1} v_{i_2} \cdots v_{i_{|I|}}$. Then, $f(x, v)$ can be decomposed as

$$f(x, v) = t_I p(x, v) + q(x, v)$$

where $q(x, v)$ miss at least one variable indexed by I, and $p(x, v)$ is independent of the variables indexed by I, denoted as the superpoly of C_I. As inputting the cube C_I into the cryptosystems, the sum of all output bits is

$$\bigoplus_{C_I} f(x, v) = \bigoplus_{C_I} t_I p(x, v) + \bigoplus_{C_I} q(x, v) = p(x, v) \tag{1}$$

If the cube indices set I is determined and the superpoly of C_I is not constant polynomial in the offline phase, then some information of secret variables can be recovered with the same assignment to I and non-cube IV in the online phase.

2.2 Bit-Based Division Property

The conventional bit-based division property was proposed in [10] and the definition is as follows. Let $\mathbb{X}$ be the multiset whose elements are values of $\mathbb{F}_2^n$ and $\mathbb{K}$ be a set of n-bit vectors. If the multiset $\mathbb{X}$ has division property $\mathcal{D}_{\mathbb{K}}^n$, it will fulfill the following conditions:

$$\bigoplus_{x \in \mathbb{X}} \pi_u(x) = \begin{cases} unknown & \text{if there exist } k \in \mathbb{K} \text{ s.t. } u \geq k \\ 0 & \text{otherwise} \end{cases}$$

where $\pi_u(x) = \prod_{i=0}^{n-1} x_i^{u_i}$ and $u \geq k$ if $u_i \geq k_i$ for all i. There are three basic propagation rules for the conventional bit-based division property was proved in [10], which are And, Xor and Copy, respectively. In the following, we show these three basic propagation rules.

Rule 1 (Copy) [10]. *Let $x_1 \in \mathbb{F}_2$ be the input of Copy propagation, and $(y_1, y_2) \in \mathbb{F}_2^2$ be the output values. Assuming that the input and output multiset have $\mathcal{D}_{\mathbb{K}}^1$ and $\mathcal{D}_{\mathbb{K}'}^2$, Copy operation that values are propagated from $k \in \mathbb{K}$ to $\mathbb{K}'$ can be computed as follows.*

$$\begin{cases} \mathbb{K}' = \{(0,0)\}, & \text{if } k_1 = 0 \\ \mathbb{K}' = \{(1,0),(0,1)\}, & \text{if } k_1 = 1 \end{cases}$$

Rule 2 (And) [10]. *Let $(x_1, x_2) \in \mathbb{F}_2^2$ be the input of And propagation, and $y_1 \in \mathbb{F}_2$ be the output values. Assuming that the input and output multiset have $\mathcal{D}_{\mathbb{K}}^2$ and $\mathcal{D}_{\mathbb{K}'}^1$, And operation that values are propagated from $k \in \mathbb{K}$ to $\mathbb{K}'$ can be computed as follows.*

$$\begin{cases} \mathbb{K}' = \{(0)\}, & \text{if } k = (0,0) \\ \mathbb{K}' = \{(1)\}, & \text{otherwise} \end{cases}$$

Rule 3 (Xor) [10]. *Let $(x_1, x_2) \in \mathbb{F}_2^2$ be the input of Xor propagation, and $y_1 \in \mathbb{F}_2$ be the output values. Assuming that the input and output multiset have $\mathcal{D}_{\mathbb{K}}^2$ and $\mathcal{D}_{\mathbb{K}'}^1$, Xor operation that values are propagated from $k \in \mathbb{K}$ to $\mathbb{K}'$ can be computed as follows.*

$$\begin{cases} \mathbb{K}' = \{(0)\}, & \text{if } k = (0,0) \\ \mathbb{K}' = \{(1)\}, & \text{if } k = (0,1),(1,0) \\ \mathbb{K}' = \emptyset, & \text{if } k = (1,1) \end{cases}$$

2.3   Division Trail [13]

The propagation of bit-based division property can be denoted as $\mathbb{K}_0 \to \mathbb{K}_1 \to \cdots \to \mathbb{K}_r$. $\mathbb{K}_0$ is initial division property of input multiset. For any vector $k_i^* \in \mathbb{K}_i$, there must exist a vector $k_{i-1}^* \in \mathbb{K}_{i-1}$ such that k_{i-1}^* can propagate to k_i^* by the propagation of division property. If k_{i-1} can propagate to k_i for all $i \in \{1, 2, \cdots, r\}$, $(k_0, k_1, \cdots, k_r)$ can be called as the r-round division trail, where $(k_0, k_1, \cdots, k_r) \in (\mathbb{K}_0, \mathbb{K}_1, \cdots, \mathbb{K}_r)$.

For the r-round cipher, let $\mathbb{X}$ be the chosen plaintexts and $\mathcal{D}_{\mathbb{K}_0}^n$ be the division property of $\mathbb{X}$. After r-round encryption, the division property $\mathcal{D}_{\mathbb{K}_r}^n$ of the output ciphertexts can be computed by division trail. If $\mathbb{K}_r$ does not contain the unit vector e_j, then the j-th bit of the output ciphertexts is balanced.

2.4   MILP Model of Division Property

In [13], the authors applied MILP models to construct the propagation of division property to reduce the complexity of propagating the division property. We describe the propagation MILP models for And, Xor and Copy as follows.

Model 1 (MILP model for Copy) [9]. *Let* $a \to (b_1, b_2, \cdots, b_m)$ *be the division property propagation of Copy operation. The following MILP model can describe this propagation.*

$$\begin{cases} \mathcal{M}.var \leftarrow a, b_1, b_2, \cdots, b_m \text{ as binary} \\ \mathcal{M}.con \leftarrow a = b_1 + b_2 + \cdots + b_m \end{cases}$$

Model 2 (MILP model for Xor) [9]. *Let* $(a_1, a_2, \cdots, a_m) \to b$ *be the division property propagation of Xor operation. The following MILP model can describe this propagation.*

$$\begin{cases} \mathcal{M}.var \leftarrow a_1, a_2, \cdots, a_m, b \text{ as binary} \\ \mathcal{M}.con \leftarrow a_1 + a_2 + \cdots + a_m = b \end{cases}$$

Model 3 (MILP model for And) [9]. *Let* $(a_1, a_2, \cdots, a_m) \to b$ *be the division property propagation of And operation. The following MILP model can describe this propagation.*

$$\begin{cases} \mathcal{M}.var \leftarrow a_1, a_2, \cdots, a_m, b \text{ as binary} \\ \mathcal{M}.con \leftarrow b \geq a_i \text{ for } i = 1, 2, \cdots, m \end{cases}$$

Flag Technique. In order to enhance the precision of *Copy + And* MILP model, the authors in [11] proposed flag technique that adding the parameter $v.F \in \{1_c, 0_c, \delta\}$ for every variable $v \in \mathcal{M}$. The parameters have three basic operations. The $=$ operation rules are $1_c = 1_c$, $0_c = 0_c$ and $\delta = \delta$. The $\oplus$ operation rules are

$$\begin{cases} 1_c \oplus 1_c = 0_c \\ 0_c \oplus x = x \oplus 0_c = x \\ \delta \oplus x = x \oplus \delta = \delta \quad x \in \{1_c, 0_c, \delta\} \end{cases}$$

The $\times$ operation rules are

$$\begin{cases} 1_c \times x = x \times 1_c = x \\ 0_c \times x = x \times 0_c = 0_c \\ \delta \times \delta = \delta \quad x \in \{1_c, 0_c, \delta\} \end{cases}$$

When applying flag technique into division property, three basic operations are modified to copyf, xorf and andf.

Model 4 (MILP model for copyf) [11]. *Let $a \to (b_1, b_2, \cdots, b_m)$ be the propagation of copyf operation. The following MILP model can describe this propagation.*

$$\begin{cases} \mathcal{M}.var \leftarrow a, b_1, b_2, \cdots, b_m \text{ as binary} \\ \mathcal{M}.con \leftarrow a = b_1 + b_2 + \cdots + b_m \\ a.F = b_1.F = \cdots = b_m.F \end{cases}$$

Model 5 (MILP model for xorf) [11]. *Let $(a_1, a_2, \cdots, a_m) \to b$ be the propagation of xorf operation. The following MILP model can describe this propagation.*

$$\begin{cases} \mathcal{M}.var \leftarrow b, a_1, a_2, \cdots, a_m \text{ as binary} \\ \mathcal{M}.con \leftarrow a_1 + a_2 + \cdots + a_m = b \\ b.F = a_1.F \oplus a_2.F \oplus \cdots \oplus a_m.F \end{cases}$$

Model 6 (MILP model for andf) [11]. *Let $(a_1, a_2, \cdots, a_m) \to b$ be the propagation of andf operation. The following MILP model can describe this propagation.*

$$\begin{cases} \mathcal{M}.var \leftarrow b, a_1, a_2, \cdots, a_m \text{ as binary} \\ \mathcal{M}.con \leftarrow b \geq a_i, \ i \in \{1, \cdots, m\} \\ b.F = a_1.F \times a_2.F \times \cdots \times a_m.F \\ \mathcal{M}.con \leftarrow b = 0, if \ b.F = 0_c \end{cases}$$

2.5 Division Property Based Cube Attack

At CRYPTO 2017, the authors proposed the division property based cube attack to recover the superpoly in [9]. In [11], Wang *et al.* proposed some techniques to reduce the complexity of recovering the superpoly. There were the following lemma and propositions proved in the division property based cube attack.

Lemma 1 [9]. *Let $f(x) = \bigoplus_{u \in \mathbb{F}_2^n} a_u^f x^u$ be a polynomial from $\mathbb{F}_2^n$ to $\mathbb{F}_2$ and $a_u^f \in \mathbb{F}_2$ be the ANF coefficients, where $u \in \mathbb{F}_2^n$. Let k be the n-dimension bit vector. Assuming there is no division trail such that $k \xrightarrow{f} 1$, then a_u^f is always 0 for $u \geq k$.*

Proposition 7 [9]. *Let $f(x,v)$ be a polynomial from $\mathbb{F}_2^{n+m}$ to $\mathbb{F}_2$, where x and v denote the secret and public variables. Let C_I be a set of $2^{|I|}$ values, where the indices set $I = \{i_1, i_2, \cdots, i_{|I|}\} \subset \{1, 2, \cdots, m\}$ and the variables indexed by $\{i_1, i_2, \cdots, i_{|I|}\}$ are taking all possible combinations. Let k_I be the m-dimensional bit vector such that $v^{k_I} = v_{i_1} v_{i_2} \cdots v_{i_{|I|}}$, i.e, $k_i = 1$ if $i \in I$ and $k_i = 0$ otherwise.*

Assuming there is no division trail such that $(e_j, k_I) \xrightarrow{f} 1$, then x_j is not involved in the superpoly of the cube C_I.

Proposition 9 [11]. *Let $f(x,v)$ be a polynomial from $\mathbb{F}_2^{n+m}$ to $\mathbb{F}_2$, where x and v denote the secret and public variables. Let C_I be a set of $2^{|I|}$ values, where the indices set $I = \{i_1, i_2, \cdots, i_{|I|}\} \subset \{1, 2, \cdots, m\}$ and variables indexed by $\{i_1, i_2, \cdots, i_{|I|}\}$ are taking all possible combinations. Let k_I be the m-dimensional bit vector such that $v^{k_I} = t_I = v_{i_1} v_{i_2} \cdots v_{i_{|I|}}$. Let k_Λ be the n-dimension bit vector. Assuming there is no division trail such that $(k_\Lambda || k_I) \xrightarrow{f} 1$, then the monomial x^{k_Λ} is not involved in the superpoly of the cube C_I.*

With the above lemma and propositions, [9] obtained variables indexed by J, which are involved in the superpoly. The superpoly could be recovered by constructing the truth table of size $2^{|J|}$. The degree evaluation in [11] could return the degree d of the superpoly. The recovery of the superpoly could be turned to recover the corresponding coefficients of all $\sum_{i=0}^{d} \binom{J}{i}$ possible monomials. The complexity of recovering the superpoly is $2^{|I|} \times \sum_{i=0}^{d} \binom{|J|}{d}$.

3   Reduce Evaluation Complexity

3.1   Filter Technique

According to Proposition 9, some invalid monomials that do not exist in the superpoly can be removed by evaluating division property. Let involved secret variables indices set be J. Initially, the degree d of superpoly can be returned by degree evaluation. Then, all possible t-degree monomials that combinations are from J can be evaluated for $t = 0, 1, \cdots, d$. Because evaluations of all t-degree monomials are large. Therefore, we reduce the complexity of the phase that evaluating these possible monomials with the relationship between the low-degree monomials and some specific high-degree monomials under the propagation of division property. Degree of the superpoly also can be determined after this phase. Therefore, some extra evaluations can be saved. The relationship can be described as follows.

Proposition 10. *Let $f(x,v)$ be a polynomial, where x and v denote n-bit secret variables and m-bit public variables. Let C_I be a set of $2^{|I|}$ values, where the indices set $I = \{i_1, i_2, \cdots, i_{|I|}\} \subset \{1, 2, \cdots, m\}$ and variables indexed by I are taking all possible combinations. Let k_I be m-dimensional bit vector such that $v^{k_I} = t_I = v_{i_1} v_{i_2} \cdots v_{i_{|I|}}$. Let k_Λ and k_Δ be n-dimensional bit vectors, where $k_\Delta \geq k_\Lambda$. Assuming there is no division trail such that $(k_\Lambda || k_I) \xrightarrow{f} 1$, then the* *division trail that* $(k_\Delta || k_I) \xrightarrow{f} 1$ *do not exist, either. Therefore, the monomial* x^{k_Δ} *is not involved in the superpoly.*

Proof. The ANF of the first output bit $f(x, v)$ can be represented as

$$f(x, v) = \bigoplus_{u \in \mathbb{F}_2^{n+m}} a_u^f(x||v)^u$$

When cube indices I is determined, $f(x, v)$ can be decomposed as follows.

$$f(x, v) = \bigoplus_{u \in \mathbb{F}_2^{n+m} | u \geq (0||k_I)} a_u^f(x||v)^u \oplus \bigoplus_{u \in \mathbb{F}_2^{n+m} | u \ngeq (0||k_I)} a_u^f(x||v)^u$$

$$= t_I \bigoplus_{u \in \mathbb{F}_2^{n+m} | u \geq (0||k_I)} a_u^f(x||v)^{u \oplus (0||k_I)} \oplus$$

$$\bigoplus_{u \in \mathbb{F}_2^{n+m} | u \ngeq (0||k_I)} a_u^f(x||v)^u$$

$$= t_I p(x, v) \oplus q(x, v)$$

The superpoly $p(x, v)$ of the cube C_I can be denoted as

$$p(x, v) = \bigoplus_{u \in \mathbb{F}_2^{n+m} | u \geq (0||k_I)} a_u^f(x||v)^{u \oplus (0||k_I)}$$

According to Lemma 1, if there is no division trail that $(k_\Lambda || k_I) \xrightarrow{f} 1$, then $a_{(k_\Delta || k_I)}^f = 0$ for $(k_\Delta || k_I) \geq (k_\Lambda || k_I)$. Therefore, the monomial x^{k_Δ} does not exist in the superpoly, either. $\qquad \square$

Proposition 10 is inspired by [11] and shows the relationship between low-degree monomials and specific high-degree monomials, where the ANF of high-degree monomials contain the ANF of low-degree monomials. When the division trails that evaluating low-degree monomials do not exist, the evaluations of these specific high-degree monomials can be saved. Fewer high-degree monomials need to be evaluated by solving the model. Based on these operations, the complexity that evaluating all possible monomials can be reduced.

For monomials that combinations are from indices J, if $d < |J|$, specific high-degree monomials will be removed from all possible monomials involved in the superpoly when the results of MILP model that evaluating low-degree monomials are infeasible. Therefore, these monomials need not to be evaluated again. Because all higher degree monomials that do not exist will be removed, the bound of the superpoly's algebraic degree can be achieved. If $d = |J|$, the complexity of evaluation will be consistent with the method term enumeration that evaluating all monomials from J in [11].

For t-degree monomials that combinations are from indices set JR_t, where JR_t are key indices set that can compose all t-degree monomials, specific higher t-degree monomials also can be removed when division trails of lower t-degree monomials do not exist such that evaluations can be saved. If no specific higher t-degree monomials can be removed during the evaluation phase, the complexity will be consistent with relaxed term enumeration in [11]. For simplicity, we focus on the process that evaluating the monomials from indices set J. Compared to indices set J, JR_t only can reduce the searching space when evaluating t-degree monomials.

The application of the filter technique on evaluating the possible monomials can be written as Algorithm 1. The inputs of $TERMEV$ consist of cube indices I, constant 1 indices I_1, constant 0 indices I_0 and involved variables indices J. When the result of MILP model that evaluating the t-degree monomial is infeasible, which is from all t-degree monomials indices set J_t^{enum}, specific monomials that algebraic degree is higher than t can be removed from set J^{enum} by procedure $DELETE$. In Algorithm 1, J^{enum} contains all monomials indices that have not been evaluated, which are from the combinations of J. The outputs of the algorithm are bound of algebraic degree and monomials indices set J_{term} that may exist in the superpoly.

3.2   Application of Filter Technique on Non-cube Public Variables

The effect of non-cube public variables on the superpoly could be considered by repeated summations in [9] or attempting to find proper assignments of IVs with the MILP model in [11]. However, it is not obvious whether the monomial contains some specific non-cube public variables when evaluating the specific monomial. Now, when applying the filter technique to evaluate the non-cube public variables, variables indexed by J_v that involved in the superpoly can be achieved by running Algorithm 2. J can be called as updated involved variables indices, where $J = J \cup J_v$. Then, all possible monomials that combinations are from J can be evaluated by Algorithm 1. Upper bound of the algebraic degree of updated involved variables indices and all possible monomials under the propagation of division property will be returned by running Algorithm 1.

4   Improve the Evaluations with Modified MILP Model

In Sect. 3, the relationship between low-degree monomials and specific high-degree monomials is considered by the filter technique. Some high-degree monomials will be removed from all corresponding degree monomials set and these monomials will not need to be evaluated by propagating division trails again. Only the rest of high-degree monomials need to be evaluated by solving the MILP model. Therefore, the filter technique can be applied to reduce the complexity of evaluations. After evaluating all possible monomials by Algorithm 1, there are close to $\sum_{i=0}^{d} |JT_i|$ monomials whose corresponding coefficients still need to be further determined by constructing a linear system, where $|JT_i|$ is the number of i-th degree monomials that are returned by utilizing filter technique. The complexity of the process that determining corresponding coefficients is huge.

When evaluating the possible monomials by propagating division trails, there are some invalid division trails that affect the results of the model. Hence, close

Algorithm 1. Evaluate possible terms of the superpoly

1: **procedure** TERMEV (cube indices I, constant 1 indices I_1, constant 0 indices I_0, involved variables indices J)
2:     Declare an empty MILP model $\mathcal{M}$
3:     Let x be n MILP variables corresponding to secret variables
4:     Let v be m MILP variables corresponding to public variables
5:     $\mathcal{M}.con \leftarrow v_i = 1$ and assign $v_i.F = \delta$ for all $i \in I$
6:     $\mathcal{M}.con \leftarrow v_i = 0$ for all $i \in \{1, \cdots, m\} - I$
7:     assign $v_i.F = 0_c$ for all $i \in I_0$
8:     assign $v_i.F = 1_c$ for all $i \in I_1$
9:     assign $v_i.F = \delta$ for all $i \in \{1, 2, \cdots, m\} - I - I_1 - I_0$
10:    assign $x_j.F = \delta$ for all $j \in \{1, \cdots, n\}$
11:    update $\mathcal{M}$
12:    **while** $J^{enum} \neq \emptyset$ **do**
13:        **for** $(\{(j_1, \cdots, j_t)\} \in J_t^{enum})$ **do**
14:            $\mathcal{M}.con \leftarrow x_j = 1$ for all $j \in \{j_1, \cdots, j_t\}$
15:            $\mathcal{M}.con \leftarrow x_j = 0$ for all $j \in \{1, \cdots, n\} - \{j_1, \cdots, j_t\}$
16:            solve MILP model $\mathcal{M}$
17:            **if** $\mathcal{M}$ is feasible **then**
18:                $J_{term} = J_{term} \cup \{(j_1, \cdots, j_t)\}$
19:                delete $\{(j_1, \cdots, j_t)\}$ from J^{enum}
20:            **else**
21:                $J^{enum} = \textbf{DELETE}(\{(j_1, \cdots, j_t)\}, J^{enum})$
22:            **end if**
23:        **end for**
24:        t+=1
25:    **end while**
26:    **return** J_{term} , t-1
27: **end procedure**

to $\sum_{i=0}^{d} |JT_i|$ model results are feasible. To improve the results of MILP model, when evaluating the remaining monomial, the parameters of flag technique are modified to identify some invalid division trails. When removing these division trails, fewer trails can propagate to **1** that relate to corresponding uncertain monomials. After the phase that evaluating all possible monomials by utilizing filter technique, the remaining monomials can be evaluated by modifying the initial parameters of the flag technique for all public and secret variables. As is described in Algorithm 3, when cube indices set is I and all possible monomial indices set is J_{term}, the process that modifying the initial parameters includes setting the parameters for the variables indexed by I and J_t to δ, where $J_t \in J_{term}$, setting the parameters that the constant variables to 1_c or 0_c and setting the remaining variables to 0_c. With the MILP model that introduces the flag technique of modifying the initial parameters, if the trail to **1** does not exist, the monomial indexed by J_t does not exist in the superpoly, either. If all monomials indices $J_t \in J_{term}$ are evaluated, *FILTERTERM* outputs the remaining monomials indices J_{out}.

Algorithm 2. Evaluate public variables

1: **procedure** PUBVAREVAL (cube indices I, constant 1 indices I_1)
2:     Declare an empty MILP model $\mathcal{M}$
3:     Let x as n MILP variables corresponding to secret variables
4:     Let v as m MILP variables corresponding to public variables
5:     $\mathcal{M}.con \leftarrow v_i = 1$ for all $i \in I$
6:     $\mathcal{M}.con \leftarrow x_j = 0$ for all $j \in \{1, \cdots, n\}$
7:     $\mathcal{M}.con \leftarrow \sum_i v_i = 1$ for all $i \in \{1, \cdots, m\} - I_0 - I_1 - I$
8:     assign $v_i.F = 1_c$ for all $i \in I_1$
9:     assign $v_i.F = 0_c$ for all $i \in I_0$
10:    assign $v_i.F = \delta$ for all $i \in \{1, \cdots, m\} - I_0 - I_1$
11:    assign $x_j.F = \delta$ for all $j \in \{1, \cdots, n\}$
12:    update $\mathcal{M}$
13:    **do**
14:        solve the model $\mathcal{M}$
15:        **if** $\mathcal{M}$ is feasible **then**
16:            pick index $i \in \{1, \cdots, m\} - I - I_0 - I_1$ s.t. $v_i = 1$
17:            $J_v = J_v \cup i$
18:            $\mathcal{M}.con \leftarrow v_i = 0$
19:        **end if**
20:    **while** $\mathcal{M}$ is feasible
21:    **return** J_v
22: **end procedure**

Finally, in the offline phase, $< \sum_{i=0}^{d} |JT_i|$ monomials that indexed by J_{out} need to be determined by constructing a linear system. The complexity of recovering the superpoly is

$$2^{|I|} \times c \cdot \sum_{i=0}^{d} |JT_i| \qquad (2)$$

where $c \in (0, 1)$ is the parameter of computational complexity.

In the online phase, the sum can be obtained as $Eq.\,(1)$ after inputting the C_I into the cryptosystem. For all $2^{|J|}$ possible combinations, the output value of the ANF of superpoly can be solved by looking up the corresponding coefficients table. Then, only the combinations whose corresponding output values are equal to the initial sum can be reserved as the correct key candidates. Therefore, the complexity of online phase is $2^{|I|} + 2^{|J|} \times c \cdot \sum_{i=0}^{d} |JT_i|$.

5   Applications to Grain128a

5.1   Description of Grain128a

Grain128a[1] is the member of Grain family of stream ciphers. The state of Grain128a is represented by a 128-bit LFSR and a 128-bit NFSR, which is described in Fig. 1. During the initialization step, the 96-bit IV are loaded into

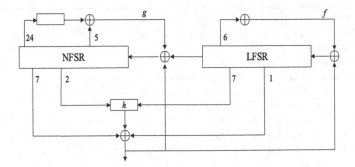

Fig. 1. Structure of Grain128a

the LFSR, with the other state bits are set to 1 except the least one bit is set to 0. The initial state bits can be represented by

$$(b_0, \cdots, b_{127}) = (K_1, \cdots, K_{128})$$
$$(s_0, \cdots, s_{127}) = (IV_1, \cdots, IV_{96}, 1, \cdots, 1, 0)$$

The algorithm runs 256 rounds without producing any keystream bit. A complete description of the update function and the output function is given as follows.

$$\begin{aligned}
g \leftarrow & b_0 + b_{28} + b_{56} + b_{91} + b_{96} + b_3 b_{67} \\
& + b_{11} b_{13} + b_{17} b_{18} + b_{27} b_{59} + b_{40} b_{48} + b_{61} b_{65} \\
& + b_{68} b_{84} + b_{88} b_{92} b_{93} b_{95} + b_{22} b_{24} b_{25} + b_{70} b_{78} b_{82} \\
f \leftarrow & s_0 + s_7 + s_{38} + s_{70} + s_{81} + s_{96} \\
h \leftarrow & b_{12} s_8 + s_{13} s_{20} + b_{95} s_{42} + s_{60} s_{79} + b_{12} b_{95} s_{94} \\
z \leftarrow & h + s_{93} + \sum_{j \in A} b_j, A = \{2, 15, 36, 45, 64, 73, 89\}
\end{aligned}$$

During the initialization step, the state is represented as

$$(b_0, b_1, \cdots, b_{127}) \leftarrow (b_1, \cdots, b_{127}, g + s_0 + z)$$
$$(s_0, s_1, \cdots, s_{127}) \leftarrow (s_1, \cdots, s_{127}, f + z)$$

5.2 Experimental Verification

The process that constructing the initial model $\mathcal{M}$ is the same as the procedure *Grain128aEval* in [11]. All division trails to r round can be evaluated with the model $\mathcal{M}$.

When the model $\mathcal{M}$ is implemented, the secret variables involved indices J and the public variables involved indices J_v can be received. We choose the same cube as in [11] that $I = \{1, 2, \cdots, 9\}$ to verify our new scheme.

Algorithm 3. Filter the terms of the superpoly

1: **procedure** FILTERTERM (cube indices I, constant 0 indices I_0, constant 1 indices I_1, subterm indices J_{term})

2:    Declare an empty MILP model $\mathcal{M}$

3:    Let x as n MILP variables corresponding to secret variables

4:    Let v as m MILP variables corresponding to public variables

5:    $\mathcal{M}.con \leftarrow v_i = 1$ and assign $v_i.F = \delta$ for all $i \in I$

6:    assign $v_i.F = 1_c$ for all $i \in I_1$

7:    assign $v_i.F = 0_c$ for all $i \in I_0$

8:    assign $v_i.F = 0_c$ for all $i \in \{1, \cdots, m\} - I - I_1 - I_0$

9:    **for** $(J_t \in J_{term})$ **do**

10:       $\mathcal{M}.con \leftarrow x_j = 1$ and assign $x_j.F = \delta$ for all $j \in J_t$

11:       $\mathcal{M}.con \leftarrow x_j = 0$ and assign $x_j.F = 0_c$ for all $j \in \{1, \cdots, n\} - J_t$

12:       update $\mathcal{M}$ and solve $\mathcal{M}$

13:       **if** $\mathcal{M}$ is feasible **then**

14:          $J_{out} = J_{out} \cup J_t$

15:       **end if**

16:    **end for**

17:    **return** J_{out}

18: **end procedure**

Example: For analysing 106-round Grain128a, where constant 1 indices set is $I_1 = \{97, \cdots, 127\}$ and constant 0 indices set is $I_0 = \{128\}$, when running algorithms that evaluating public and secret variables, the secret variables involved indices $J = \{53, 85, 119, 122, 126, 127\}$ and public variables involved indices $J_v = \{76\}$ can be identified. After executing Algorithms 1 and 3, the remaining monomials that $x_{53}x_{119}x_{122}x_{126}x_{127}$, $x_{85}x_{119}x_{122}x_{126}x_{127}$, $x_{53}x_{119}v_{76}x_{126}x_{127}$ and $x_{85}x_{119}v_{76}x_{126}x_{127}$ need to be determined. These results are in accordance with the superpoly which is given in [9]. While running Algorithm 1, the degree 5 of the superpoly is returned. The number of monomials that need to be determined has a 5.56% reduction.

To further verify the scheme, we choose some cube indices I for low-round Grain128a as described in Table 1, which are obtained by exploiting the filter technique. When the rounds and the corresponding cube indices I are chosen, there are no non-constant public variables involved in the superpoly by running Algorithm 2. These cube indices can be regarded as effective. Then, the secret variables that involved in the superpoly can be achieved. After running Algorithms 1 and 3, the complexity of recovering the remaining monomials can be computed. The comparison of the evaluation complexity between filter technique and previous method also can be achieved. For example, when the round is 108 and cube indices set is $I = \{1, 2, 3, 4, 5, 6, 7, 8, 9, 10, 12, 14\}$, the model result of monomial $x_{18}x_{53}$ is infeasible. Therefore, all specific high-degree monomials that contain $x_{18}x_{53}$ need not to be evaluated by solving model and the complexity of evaluations can be reduced. In Table 1, the parameter c represents that the complexity changes from the attack that recovering possible monomials that returned by precise term enumeration in [11] to our new method.

Algorithm 4. Remove specific higher degree monomials

1: **procedure** DELETE (subterm indices $(j_1, \cdots, j_t)$, remaining monomials indices J^{enum})

2:      $J_{sub} = j_1 j_2 \cdots j_t$

3:      **while** $t \leq |J|, J^{enum} \neq \emptyset$ **do**

4:          **for** $(\{(j_1', \cdots, j_t')\} \in J^{enum})$ **do**

5:              **if** $j_1' j_2' \cdots j_t' / J_{sub} \neq 0$ **then**

6:                  delete $\{(j_1', \cdots, j_t')\}$ from J^{enum}

7:              **end if**

8:          **end for**

9:          t+=1

10:     **end while**

11:     **Return** J^{enum}

12: **end procedure**

For these results, the upper bound of all c values are 25%. As is described in Table 1, the remaining monomials only include fewer possible monomials that need to be determined by constructing a linear system. When the rounds are larger, the changes are obvious. These changes are easy to understand. When the superpoly only includes a t-degree monomial that t is large, all low-degree monomials that combinations are from these t variables will not be removed from the possible monomials set by evaluating division trails. However, when evaluating these low-degree monomials by modifying the parameters of the flag technique, these division trails can be identified effectively. Only fewer remaining monomials need to be recovered by constructing a linear system.

5.3   Theoretical Results

For 184-round Grain128a, if $v_{47} = 0$, then the size of J is 21 and the degree is 14, respectively. After utilizing the filter technique, the number of possible monomials that the corresponding coefficients should be further determined is about $2^{14.602}$.

While evaluating the monomials by modifying the corresponding parameters of flag technique, no division trails can propagate to 1 for the monomials that algebraic degree is smaller than 7. These monomials need not to be determined by constructing the linear system again. Without evaluating monomials that algebraic degree is higher than 6 by modifying the corresponding parameters of flag technique, there are about 57% of monomials that given in [11] need to be determined, which the size is 14034.

Under the process that evaluating the above low-degree monomials, the complexity has about 43% reducation. The recovery attack can reduce the complexity from $2^{109.602}$ to $c \cdot 2^{109.602}$, where $c \cdot 2^{109.602}$ is smaller than $2^{108.777}$.

When analysing higher rounds Grain128a by Algorithm 2, we find that all non-constant public variables should be chosen as cube variables and the size of the cube indices set is 96. Therefore, when analysing these rounds Grain128a, the recovery attack is meaningful only if the number of possible monomials that determined by constructing a linear system is smaller than 2^{32}. Compared with the previous recovery attack, the parameter c can affect the number of the remaining possible monomials that need to be determined, which can enable us to analyze higher target rounds.

Table 1. Summary of experimental results on low-round Grain128a

Rounds	I	Involved variables	Remaining monomials	Previous [11]	Improved	c
108	1, 2, 3, 4, 5, 6, 7, 8, 9, 10, 12, 14	x_{14}, x_{18}, x_{48}, x_{53}, x_{87}, x_{121}	$x_{18}x_{87}x_{121}$, $x_{14}x_{18}x_{48}x_{87}x_{121}$, $x_{53}x_{87}x_{121}$, $x_{14}x_{48}x_{53}x_{87}x_{121}$	$2^{17.58}$	2^{14}	8.33%
110	1, 2, 3, 4, 5, 6, 7, 8, 9, 10, 11, 12, 14	x_{16}, x_{50}, x_{89}, x_{113}, x_{123}	$x_{89}x_{123}$, $x_{16}x_{50}x_{89}x_{113}x_{123}$	2^{18}	2^{14}	6.25%
114	1, 2, 3, 4, 5, 6, 7, 8, 9, 10	x_{48}, x_{55}, x_{128}	$x_{48}x_{55}x_{128}$	2^{13}	2^{10}	12.5%
116	1, 2, 3, 4, 5, 6, 7, 9, 18, 21, 28	x_{22}, x_{50}, x_{113}	$x_{22}x_{50}x_{113}$	2^{14}	2^{11}	12.5%
118	1, 2, 3, 4, 5, 6, 7, 8, 9, 110, 111, 113	x_{97}, x_{121}, x_{122}	$x_{97}x_{121}x_{122}$	2^{15}	2^{12}	12.5%
120	1, 2, 3, 4, 5, 6, 7, 8, 9, 11	x_{122}, x_{123}, x_{124}, x_{125}	$x_{122}x_{123}x_{124}$, $x_{122}x_{123}x_{124}x_{125}$	2^{14}	2^{11}	12.5%
123	1, 2, 3, 4, 5, 6, 7, 16	x_{20}, x_{121}	$x_{20}x_{121}$	2^{10}	2^{8}	25%
125	1, 2, 3, 4, 5, 6, 8	x_{115}, x_{121}, x_{122}, x_{124}	$x_{115}x_{121}x_{122}x_{124}$	2^{11}	2^{7}	6.25%
127	1, 2, 3, 4, 5, 6, 7, 9, 10, 12, 13, 14	x_{125}, x_{127}	$x_{125}x_{127}$	2^{14}	2^{12}	25%
130	1, 2, 3, 4, 5, 6, 7, 9, 10	x_{48}, x_{55}, x_{128}	$x_{48}x_{55}x_{128}$	2^{12}	2^{9}	12.5%
134	1, 2, 3, 4, 5, 6, 7, 8, 10, 12, 16, 19, 22, 23	x_{14}, x_{47}, x_{48}, x_{79}, x_{81}, x_{113}	$x_{48}x_{79}x_{81}x_{113}$, $x_{14}x_{47}x_{48}x_{81}x_{113}$	2^{20}	2^{15}	3.125%
135	1, 2, 3, 4, 5, 6, 7, 8, 9, 10, 11, 12, 13, 14, 17, 28, 32	x_{47}, x_{48}, x_{49}, x_{70}, x_{82}	$x_{47}x_{48}x_{49}x_{70}x_{82}$	2^{22}	2^{17}	3.125%

6   Conclusion

In this paper, we propose some methods to reduce the complexity of recovering the superpoly, which is developed from division property based cube attack. Firstly, we develop the filter technique to reduce the complexity of evaluating the monomials by propagating division trails. We also assess the non-cube public variables that involved in the superpoly by the filter technique, rather than attempting to identify proper initialization of non-cube public variables. Secondly, we remove most invalid monomials by modifying the initialization for parameters of every variable. With this scheme, fewer remaining monomials need to be further determined. While evaluating monomials, the effect of non-cube public variables on the monomials can be considered directly.

Acknowledgement. The work is supported by the National Natural Science Foundation of China (61702230, U1736216, 61472001, 61902156, 61802154), the National Key R&D Program of China 2017YFB1400703 and the Key R&D Program of Jiangsu Province BE2015136.

References

1. Ågren, M., Hell, M., Johansson, T., Meier, W.: Grain-128a: a new version of grain-128 with optional authentication. Int. J. Wirel. Mob. Comput. **5**(1), 48–59 (2011). https://doi.org/10.1504/IJWMC.2011.044106
2. Dinur, I., Shamir, A.: Cube attacks on tweakable black box polynomials. In: Joux, A. (ed.) EUROCRYPT 2009. LNCS, vol. 5479, pp. 278–299. Springer, Heidelberg (2009). https://doi.org/10.1007/978-3-642-01001-9_16
3. Dinur, I., Shamir, A.: Breaking grain-128 with dynamic cube attacks. In: Joux, A. (ed.) FSE 2011. LNCS, vol. 6733, pp. 167–187. Springer, Heidelberg (2011). https://doi.org/10.1007/978-3-642-21702-9_10
4. Hu, K., Wang, M.: Automatic search for a variant of division property using three subsets. In: Matsui, M. (ed.) CT-RSA 2019. LNCS, vol. 11405, pp. 412–432. Springer, Cham (2019). https://doi.org/10.1007/978-3-030-12612-4_21
5. Liu, M.: Degree evaluation of NFSR-based cryptosystems. In: Katz, J., Shacham, H. (eds.) CRYPTO 2017. LNCS, vol. 10403, pp. 227–249. Springer, Cham (2017). https://doi.org/10.1007/978-3-319-63697-9_8
6. Liu, M., Yang, J., Wang, W., Lin, D.: Correlation cube attacks: from weak-key distinguisher to key recovery. In: Nielsen, J.B., Rijmen, V. (eds.) EUROCRYPT 2018. LNCS, vol. 10821, pp. 715–744. Springer, Cham (2018). https://doi.org/10.1007/978-3-319-78375-8_23
7. Todo, Y.: Structural evaluation by generalized integral property. In: Oswald, E., Fischlin, M. (eds.) EUROCRYPT 2015. LNCS, vol. 9056, pp. 287–314. Springer, Heidelberg (2015). https://doi.org/10.1007/978-3-662-46800-5_12
8. Todo, Y.: Integral cryptanalysis on full MISTY1. J. Cryptol. **30**(3), 920–959 (2017). https://doi.org/10.1007/s00145-016-9240-x
9. Todo, Y., Isobe, T., Hao, Y., Meier, W.: Cube attacks on non-blackbox polynomials based on division property. IEEE Trans. Comput. **67**(12), 1720–1736 (2018). https://doi.org/10.1109/TC.2018.2835480
10. Todo, Y., Morii, M.: Bit-based division property and application to SIMON family. In: Peyrin, T. (ed.) FSE 2016. LNCS, vol. 9783, pp. 357–377. Springer, Heidelberg (2016). https://doi.org/10.1007/978-3-662-52993-5_18
11. Wang, Q., Hao, Y., Todo, Y., Li, C., Isobe, T., Meier, W.: Improved division property based cube attacks exploiting algebraic properties of superpoly. In: Shacham, H., Boldyreva, A. (eds.) CRYPTO 2018. LNCS, vol. 10991, pp. 275–305. Springer, Cham (2018). https://doi.org/10.1007/978-3-319-96884-1_10
12. Wang, S., Hu, B., Guan, J., Zhang, K., Shi, T.: A practical method to recover exact superpoly in cube attack. Cryptology ePrint Archive, report 2019/259 (2019). https://eprint.iacr.org/2019/259

13. Xiang, Z., Zhang, W., Bao, Z., Lin, D.: Applying MILP method to searching integral distinguishers based on division property for 6 lightweight block ciphers. In: Cheon, J.H., Takagi, T. (eds.) ASIACRYPT 2016. LNCS, vol. 10031, pp. 648–678. Springer, Heidelberg (2016). https://doi.org/10.1007/978-3-662-53887-6_24
14. Ye, C.D., Tian, T.: Revisit division property based cube attacks: key-recovery or distinguishing attacks? Cryptology ePrint Archive, report 2019/381 (2019). https://eprint.iacr.org/2019/381

PPIDS: A Pyramid-Like Printer Intrusion Detection System Based on ATT&CK Framework

Houhua He[1,2], Lei Yu[1,2(✉)], Weixia Cai[1,2], Xiaoyu Wang[1,2], Xiaorui Gong[1,2], Haoyu Wang[1,2], and Chen Liu[1]

[1] Institute of Information Engineering, Chinese Academy of Sciences, Beijing, China
yulei@iie.ac.cn
[2] School of Cyber Security, University of Chinese Academy of Sciences, Beijing, China

Abstract. Nowadays, network printers have become one of the essential devices for daily work, and are getting more and more attention from attackers. Traditional intrusion detection system may not apply quite well to network printers since it can't detect growing multi-step complex attacks for network printers. To detect and prevent such attacks, we design a network printer attackers' behavioral model and knowledge base named TTPE based on ATT&CK framework. Then we propose an attack detection system named PPIDS which is based on TTPE to detect and analyze network attacks against network printers. For experiments, we capture 38 network traffic packets from 4 typical scenarios. In our experiments, PPIDS achieves false-positive rate of 0%, false-negative rate of 14.29%. Experiment result shows that our method performs superior to traditional intrusion detection systems on identifying complex network attacks against network printers.

Keywords: Network printer · Attack detection · Network traffic · Attack quantization · ATT&CK

1 Introduction

Network printers are regarded as a machine that can merely print out whatever documents sent to it. Actually, they have been evolved into full-blown computers with a combination of Real-Time Operation System (RTOS), Ethernet, Hard Disk Drive (HDD), Embedded Web Server and even WIFI interface.

Printers are a growing source of security threats, according to a recent survey conducted by Spiceworks [15]. Today, a printer is 68% more likely to be the source

This work is supported by the Chinese Academy of Sciences Key Laboratory of Network Assessment Technology and Beijing Key Laboratory of Network Security and Protection Technology, as well as National Administration for the Protection of State Secrets Foundation (No. BMKY2017B06).

© Springer Nature Switzerland AG 2020
Z. Liu and M. Yung (Eds.): Inscrypt 2019, LNCS 12020, pp. 277–290, 2020.
https://doi.org/10.1007/978-3-030-42921-8_16

of an external threat or breach than it was in 2016; it is 118% more likely to be the source of an internal threat or breach. In 2017, a hacker reportedly used an automated script to access 150,000 publicly accessible printers, including lots of receipt printers, and instructed them to run a rogue print job [13]. Even students from high school can carry out a large scale of attacks to network printers in the worldwide [2]. If not protected, only one MFP can lead to painful consequences, including identity theft, theft of proprietary information, damage to brand image and reputation, and litigation [14].

Different from common computers and IOT devices, network printers have more opened ports and services (for example, a common HP printer has 53 opened ports for 29 opened services [12]), making it more attackable as attackers can take advantage of so many "building blocks" provided by printers. Attackers can carry out an attack by chaining several vulnerabilities with functionality or by merely chaining a bunch of functionality together which can hardly be detected by traditional *Intrusion Detection Systems (IDSs)*. Consequently, traditional approaches on identifying attacks on networks or computers may not effectively work on such peripherals since there are many complex attacks here. As a result, traditional IDSs like Snort [16] and Suricata [11] cannot be perfectly adapted to identify intrusions against network printers.

As discussed above, network printers are computers capable of doing so much and there are many complex attacks taking advantage of it. Currently research is rarely conducted on identifying attacks focused on network printers. So it's of very significance to perform *Intrusion Detection* to detect such attacks. In this paper, we research on detecting attacks against network printers in *Network Traffic*. Our contributions can be concluded as follows:

1. We propose a network printer attackers' behavioral model and knowledge base named TTPE based on ATT&CK framework, it can be used to describe complex attacks for network printers.
2. We implement an attack detection system for network printers named PPIDS based on TTPE knowledge base, it performs much better than traditional IDSs.
3. We design a methodology specialized for attack quantization, it can be used to quantify attack risk.

Paper Outline: The paper organizes as follows: in Sect. 2, related works are introduced; in Sect. 3, we describe PPIDS attack detection model; in Sect. 4, we describe PPIDS implementation; in Sect. 5, we evaluate PPIDS's performance; in Sect. 6, we summarize our work.

2   Related Work

2.1   Security Issues of Network Printers

Since the appearance of the printer, there has been a lot of research on its security. The risks of *Postscript* were pointed out in 1996 [18]. In 2002 Phenoelit pointed out some design failure on printers and published a proof-of-concept application for *Printer Job Language (PJL)* file system access [6]. In 2005, Crenshaw published an overview of potentially harmful PJL commands for network printers and pointed out some of the more interesting things that can be done with a network based printer to make it leak information about its users, owners and the network it belongs to [4]. In 2007, Printer Spamming published a technique to force web browsers into printing arbitrary payloads on a network printer called *cross-site printing* [19]. In 2009, Bojinov [1] proposed *XCS (cross channel scripting)* which shows that consumer electronics are particularly vulnerable to a nasty form of persistent XSS where a non-web channel such as NFS or SNMP can be used to inject a malicious script. In 2011, Deral (PercX) Heiland proposed a new attack on MFPs named *Pass-Back-Attack* [8]. In 2013, the *Information-technology Promotion Agency (IPA)* in Japan published a report, which summarized the known attacks on MFPs [21]. In 2017, the first comprehensive study regarding the security of printers contributing towards systematic penetration testing was proposed by Jens Müller et al. [5]. They also implemented an open-source toolkit called *PRET* to penetrate and exploit MFPs. In 2018, Itkin et al. proposed *Faxploit* [9], which can take over a network using just a fax number.

2.2   Securing Network Printers

Rule based intrusion detection approaches could be used to solve partial security problems of network printers. In 1999, Roesch [16] proposed a *Network Intrusion Detection Systems (NIDS)* named Snort which is lightweight and rule-based. After that, Snort got more and more attention and developed rapidly. However, some complex attacks may not produce fixed pattern that can be used to write rules and some make use of the normal functions provided by the network printers.

Indicator of Compromise (IoC) is an artifact observed on a network that indicates a computer intrusion with high confidence [7]. Typical IoCs are virus signatures and IP addresses, MD5 hashes of malware files or URLs or domain names of botnet command and control servers. After IoCs have been identified in a process of incident response and computer forensics, they can be used for early detection of future attack attempts using intrusion detection systems and antivirus software. However, in many cases these are brittle and easy for adversaries to bypass by modifying malware or infrastructure, defenders are hard to keep pace with adversary changes [20].

MITRE ATT&CK [3] is a catalog of techniques and tactics that describe post-compromise adversary behavior on typical enterprise IT environments. The core use cases involve using the catalog to analyze, triage, compare, describe, relate, and share post-compromise adversary behavior. However, ATT&CK is a high level framework, there is no guideline for the user to implement the technique and there is no threat model for network printers either.

3 Detection Model

We propose a network printer attackers' behavioral model and knowledge base named TTPE based on ATT&CK framework. TTPE is a curated knowledge base and model for network printer attackers' behavior, reflecting the various phases of an attacker's attack lifecycle. TTPE aims to enumerate and categorize post-compromise attacker tactics, techniques, procedures, elements against network printers to improve detection of complex attack activity. Tactics, denoting short-term, tactical attacker goals during an attack; Techniques, describing the means by which attacker achieve tactical goals; Procedures, describing the specific steps to implement the technique; Elements, describing the specific meta-operations that implement specific procedure. Figure 1 describes levels in our detection model.

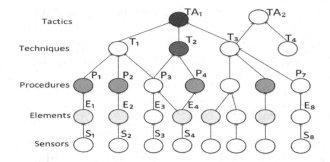

Fig. 1. The levels in TTPE detection model

To simplify the model, we now consider a scenario in which there is only one attacker attacking a network printer. In a case that many attackers are attacking many printers, we can pair together attacker's IP and the target printer's IP as (attacker_ip, target_printer_ip) and analyse them separately.

Basic Definitions
S is a set of *Sensors*.

Event represents the type of object that can be operated with operators defined below. It contains values of st and ts, st is a value which stands for the activation state of this event; ts is a timestamp when this event occurred. *EventSet* is a set of *Event*. Specially, an *Event* is also an *EventSet*.

Node represents a node in the detection tree described in Fig. 1. It contains values of *name*, *expr* and *es*. *name* is the name of the node. *expr* is a formula which stands for the expression of this node; *es* is an object with the type of *EventSet* recording all the timestamps when the event corresponding to that *Node* happened.

E is a set of *Elements*, each element in E is an action that can be detected by *Sensors*; P is a set of *Procedures*; T is a set of *Techniques*; TA is a set of *Tactics*; S, E, P, T and TA are *Node* in different levels.

X can be S, E, P, T or TA. X_i represents the i th X.

The Relationship Between Nodes. The node in higher level is a combination of the lower level nodes, and the method for combination can be one of the three operations: **TEMPORAL, AND** and **OR**, we denote it with operator $\wedge$, & and | respectively. To describe the relationship more conveniently, we mark A and B as an object of type *Event* here which represents different actions. There are some attacks that occur only when A happens followed by B. We call this kind of attack sequential attack and we define the relation between A and B as *TEMPORAL* here and mark it as $A \wedge B$. Likewise, there are some attacks that occur when both A and B happen no matter which one happens first and we mark it as A & B. Some attacks success either A or B happens, and we mark it as $A \mid B$.

Calculation of Event and EventSet. We mark $A = Event_i \wedge Event_j$, $B = Event_i \& Event_j$, $C = Event_i \mid Event_j$. We mark $D = EventSet_i \wedge EventSet_j$, $E = EventSet_i \& EventSet_j$ and $F = EventSet_i \mid EventSet_j$. For short, we denote $Event_i$, $Event_j$, $EventSet_i$ and $EventSet_j$ as Ev_i, Ev_j, ES_i and ES_j respectively in the following. We can define calculation of *Event* and *EventSet* as following:

$$a.st = \begin{cases} True \ if \ Ev_i.st \ \&\& \ Ev_j.st \ \&\& \ (Ev_i.ts \leqslant Ev_j.ts) \\ False \ otherwise \end{cases}$$

$$a.ts = \begin{cases} Ev_j.ts \ if \ Ev_i.st \ \&\& \ Ev_j.st \ \&\& \ (Ev_i.ts \leqslant Ev_j.ts) \\ +\infty \quad otherwise \end{cases}$$

$$b.st = \begin{cases} True \ if \ Ev_i.st \ \&\& \ Ev_j.st \\ False \ otherwise \end{cases}$$

$$b.ts = \begin{cases} max(Ev_i.ts, Ev_j.ts) \ if \ Ev_i.st \ \&\& \ Ev_j.st \\ +\infty \qquad otherwise \end{cases} \tag{1}$$

$$A = \{a\} \ , \ B = \{b\} \ , \ C = \{Ev_i\} \cup \{Ev_j\}$$

$$D = \bigcup_{\substack{Ev_i \in ES_i \\ Ev_j \in ES_j}} Ev_i \wedge Ev_j \ , \ E = \bigcup_{\substack{Ev_i \in ES_i \\ Ev_j \in ES_j}} Ev_i \& Ev_j$$

$$F = \bigcup_{\substack{Ev_i \in ES_i \\ Ev_j \in ES_j}} Ev_i \mid Ev_j = ES_i \cup ES_j$$

4   Implementation

To automate the introduced pyramid-like intrusion detection method, we wrote a prototype system entitled PPIDS in Python. The main idea of PPIDS is to analyze the outputs of traditional intrusion detection sensors using the detection model described above. By receiving the output of the sensors, PPIDS translates

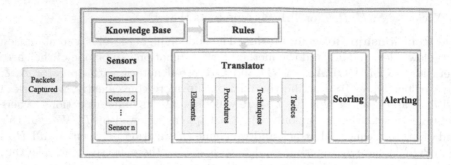

Fig. 2. The PPIDS architecture.

it to attack element, then raises the attack element higher to the attacker TTPs level by level, and evaluates the result. PPIDS contains six main components depicted in Fig. 2: Knowledge Base, Rules, Sensors, Translator, Scoring, Alerting.

4.1 Knowledge Base

The Knowledge Base module is the basic component of PPIDS. It stores the attackers' tactics, techniques, procedures, elements for printers attack. It navigates the Rules module to generate rules for sensor outputs translating. For easy reading and maintenance, knowledge base is stored in four interrelated tables: Tactics and Techniques (TT), Techniques and Procedures (TP), Procedures and Elements (PE), Elements and Sensors (ES). Knowledge base is available on GitHub[1]. In the Github repository, we summarize the attackers' tactics, techniques for printers in TT table based on ATT&CK.

We show an example of TP table in Table 1 and PE table in Table 2 and ES table in Table 3 respectively.

Table 1. Techniques-Procedures table

Techniques	Code execution through startup folder file (T0021)	Code execution through crontab (T0022)
Procedures	Step1: Write arbitrary file on startup folder (P2101)	Write crontab (P2201)
	Step2: Restart (P2102)	

---

[1] https://github.com/mt-srg/PPIDS.

Table 2. Procedures-Elements table

Procedures	Write arbitrary file on startup folder (P2101)	Restart (P2102)
Elements	Write executable file to startup folder through PJL Fsdownload path traversal vulnerability (E21011)	Restart through web (E21021)
	Write executable file to startup folder through web file upload path traversal vulnerability (E21012)	Restart through SNMP (E21022)

Table 3. Elements-Sensors table

Elements	Write executable file to startup folder through PJL Fsdownload (E21011)	Restart through SNMP (E21022)
Sensors	ID: S210111 Attack surface: PJL Object: File Object operation: FSDOWNLOAD Content = Bash/Binary FilePath = /var/etc/profile.d/	ID: S210221 Attack surface: SNMP Object: OID Object operation: Set OID = .1.3.6.1.2.1.43.5.1.1.3.1 Value = 4

4.2 Rules

The Rules module is responsible for generating correct rules to translate the sensors outputs based on Knowledge Base. For example:

$$\begin{cases} TA0002 = T0021 \mid T0022 \mid T0023 \\ T0021 = P2101 \land P2102 \\ P2101 = E21011 \mid E21012 \\ P2102 = E21021 \mid E21022 \end{cases} \tag{2}$$

4.3 Sensors

The Sensors module is used to detect printer's network traffic through features in traditional way. We use Snort software as our feature detection sensors engine. For example, Listing 1.1 describes rules for S210111 detection:

Listing 1.1. Rules for S210111

```
1   alert TCP any any -> any 9100 (content:"@PJL";content:"FSDOWNLOAD"; content:"NAME
    "; content:".sh";)
```

4.4 Translator

The Translator module uses rules generated by Rules module and matching algorithm to translate sensors' outputs into attack elements, procedures, techniques, tactics level by level.

Specifically, when the translator detects a new sensor output, a thread is started to analyze the new IP's sensor output log. First, we translate the sensor output log to elements sequence directly since there is one-to-one correspondence between elements and sensors, then translate elements sequence to procedures sequence according to PE table of Knowledge Base module. Then we perform the calculation based on *Elements* sequence and produce *Procedures* sequence. We repeat the calculation level by level up until no new sequence is produced or hit the top level (Tactics). Listing 1.2 describes this process.

Listing 1.2. Bottom up matching algorithm in Python

```
1   while not element_queue.empty():
2       name,ts = element_queue.get()# get nodename and timestamp from queue
3       exec("{0}.eventset={0}.eventset|EventSet(Event(True,{1})))".format(name,ts))
4       update_set = set((name,))# stores all the nodes that is updated
5       for level in [Procedures,Techniques,Tactics]:
6           new_update_set = set()# stores the output sequence in that level
7           for node in level:
8               levelname = node.levelname
9               for u in update_set:
10                  if node.expression.isExpressionOf(u):
11                      node.UpdateEventSet(node.expression.calculate().eventset)
12                      if node.last_eventset != node.eventset:
13                          new_update_set.add(node.name)
14              print("{0} Sequence: {1}".format(levelname,",".join(new_update_set)))
15          update_set = new_update_set
```

We got techniques sequence after matching, then translate techniques sequence to tactics sequence. Finally, we got a TTP mapping table. Listing 1.3 is an example of detection (Please refer to Tables 1, 2 and 3):

Listing 1.3. An example of detection

```
1   Input:
2       Sensor Ouput:
3           S210111,1564399932
4           S210221,1564399939
5       Rules:
6           TA0002 = T0021 | T0022 | T0023;
7           T0021 = P2101 ^ P2102;
8           P2101 = E21011 | E21012;
9           P2102 = E21021 | E21022;
10  Output:
11          Techniques Sequence: T0021
12          Tactics Sequence: TA0002
```

4.5 Scoring

Scoring module scores the output from Translator module. It will give every attack chain a score (S_{chain}) from 0 to 100 by the sum of tactics scores. Equation (3) describes the score of an attack-chain. The tactic score (S_{ta}) is equal to the sum of the corresponding techniques scores, but does not exceed the maximum score (S_{ta_max}) set in advance by expert knowledge according to its attack effectiveness. Equation (4) describes the tactics score. Table 4 shows the maximum score of tactics. Technique score (S_t) ranges from 0 to S_{ta_max} by expert knowledge according to its tactical performance.

$$S_{chain} = min(\sum S_{ta}, 100) \qquad (3)$$

$$S_{ta} = min(\sum S_t, S_{ta\_max}) \tag{4}$$

Table 4. Maximum score of tactics

Tactics	Maximum score	Tactics	Maximum score
Common information gathering	1	Defense evasion	7
Specific information gathering	2	Credential access	7
Specific weakness identification	2	Discovery	7
Attack preparation	3	Lateral movement	9
Initial access	4	Collection	8
Execution	7	Exfiltration	8
Persistence	8	Command and control	10
Privilege escalation	7	Pullout	10

4.6 Alerting

This module provides PPIDS users readable alerts according to the score generated by Scoring module. The score of a potential attack chain accumulates, and score larger than 10 would trigger alert.

5 Experiments

5.1 Environments for Experiments

We use the printers in our office network (including 11 printers for various well-known manufacturers) for experiments, Table 5 shows the basic information of the printers in our experiments environment.

Table 5. The basic information of the printers in our experiments environment

IP	Printer	Language
192.168.0.12	FUJI Xerox DocuPrint CM225/228	PS/PJL/PCL
192.168.0.61	Canon MF620C Series	PS/PJL/PCL
192.168.0.87	Lenovo LJ2655DN	PS/PJL/PCL
192.168.0.94	RICOH SP 212SFNw	PS/PJL/PCL
192.168.0.106	HP Color LaserJet MFP M277dw	PS/PJL/PCL
192.168.0.109	Samsung ML-371x Series	PS/PJL/PCL
192.168.0.115	Lexmark MX511de	PS/PJL/PCL
192.168.0.132	SHARP SF-S201N	PJL/PCL
192.168.0.216	HP LaserJet M1536dnf MFP	PS/PJL/PCL
192.168.0.219	HP PageWide Pro 477dw MFP	PS/PJL/PCL
192.168.0.252	Broher MFC-9140CDN	PS/PJL/PCL

5.2   Dataset for Experiments

There are four typical printer roles in our experiments: 1. Attacker who performed attacks. 2. Normal user who installed printer drivers. 3. Normal user who launched normal print jobs. 4. Administrator who managed the printer with sensitive operations. For these four roles, we designed four scenarios to simulate and sequentially capture traffic as our dataset, which is available on GitHub[2].

Printer Attacker Scenario

A1: Conduct ports scan on target printer using NMAP
A2: Get SNMP OID(.1.3.6.1.2.1.1.5.0) value to identify printer model
A3: Get SNMP OID(.1.3.6.1.4.1.2435.2.4.3.99.3.1.6.1.2.7) value to identify printer firmware version
A4: Log in printer web page using default usernames and passwords
A5: Test if path traversal vulnerability exits on target printer using PRET
A6: Identify printer's status through visiting printer's web page
A7: Upload bash file to starup folder though PJL using CVE-2017-2741
A8: Set SNMP OID(.1.3.6.1.2.1.43.5.1.1.3.1) to restart printer
A9: Use NC tool to connect to the target printer
A10: Visit printer's LDAP configuration web page
A11: Test LDAP configuration through web to perform PASSBACK attack
A12: Set SNMP OID with XSS payload to perform XCS attack
A13: Visit job history through web page
A14: Visit error log through web page

Printer Normal User Scenario 1

U11: Install printing drivers, query the model of the printer through SNMP.
U12: Query the status of the printer
U13: Login the printers with factory default credentials
U14: Set the email address for receiving when scan

Printer Normal User Scenario 2

U21-U23: Send print jobs to printer through RAW with PS,PCL,PDF.
U24-U26: Send print jobs to printer through LPD with PS,PCL,PDF.
U27-U29: Send print jobs to printer through IPP with PS,PCL,PDF.
U30-U32: Send print jobs to printer through WSD with PS,PCL,PDF.

Printer Administrator Scenario

AD1: Query the make and model of the reported printer
AD2: Query the firmware version of the reported printer
AD3: Query the state of the reported printer
AD4: Login the printers web management interface with default credentials
AD5: View the print jobs on the web interface
AD6: Reboot the printer
AD7: Reset the printer
AD8: View the LDAP configuration on the Web interface and test the connection between the printer and the LDAP server.

---

[2] https://github.com/mt-srg/PPIDS.

5.3   Experiments Procedures

There are three phases in our experiments: 1. Scenarios designing. 2. Data collecting. 3. Data processing and Evaluation.

Scenarios Designing. Before data collecting, we design four scenarios for four roles, and make detailed scripts for all the scenarios (as introduced in Sect. 5.2). The principles of making scripts should be as similar as in reality.

Data Collecting. We use a tool named *Mergecap*, which comes with *Wireshark* to merge all the packets we gathered into a file containing all the network packets produced in all the scenarios.

Data Processing and Evaluation. After merging packets together into a file, we process the file with PPIDS and OADMS (will be introduced in Sect. 5.4), then we collect the output log from each system and record three metrics for each element: 1. Whether the element is detected. 2. The score for the potential attack chain at present. 3. Whether the element can trigger alert.

If an element is detected by a system, then the value for "Whether the element is detected" is *True*. PPIDS will record all the elements that may lead to an attack chain according to its knowledge base while OADMS will only record elements that triggers its rule. The score for the potential attack chain at present reflects what's the system's attitude towards this element, the more dangerous an element is, the higher score it gets. In PPIDS, the score for the potential attack chain accumulates. Since OADMS is a Snort-based system, when a rule of "log" type triggered, the element will get 50 and when a rule of "alert" type triggered, the element will get 80. If the score at the time when an element is processed is larger than 10, then the element will trigger alert.

After recording all the three values, we get a table for this system when processing each elements. We then calculate the FPR (False Positive Rate) and FNR (False Negative Rate) according to the table we got.

FPR/FNR is calculated as follows: If an element doesn't belong to any attack chain, but the system regards that the element can trigger alert, it's a false positive. If an element does belong to an attack chain, but the system regards that the element can't trigger alert, it's a false negative. If there are N elements $(E_1, E_2, ...E_N)$ processed by the system, and M elements $(E_{i1}, E_{i2}, ...E_{iM})$ in attack process, and a system detects P elements of attack process and Q elements out of attack process, then:

$$FPR = \frac{Q}{N - M} * 100\% \tag{5}$$

$$FNR = \frac{M - P}{M} * 100\% \tag{6}$$

5.4   System to Compared with

OADMS. There is no publicly available printer intrusion detection system on the market currently. Over the years, our team has implemented a snort-based printer intrusion detection system entitled OADMS. OADMS has more than 150 rules which can cover most popular printer attacks. The rules for OADMS are generated mostly base on the vulnerabilities disclosed by printer manufacturer and CVE [10] as well as vulnerabilities in PRET [17].

5.5   Results

We process the file for PPIDS and OADMS, then we collect the output log from each system and record three values for each element. Table 6 describes the three values for PPIDS and OADMS in our experiments. We calculate the FPR and FNR for PIDDS and OADMS according to Eqs. (5) and (6), Table 7 shows the result.

From the Table 7 we can see that PPIDS have a better performance over OADMS. PPIDS has a lower FNR which means it can pick up much more elements of attack than OADMS. PPIDS has zero FPR means that PPIDS can effectively pick up the true attacks for the network manager.

Table 6. Experiment results for PPIDS and OADMS

	Detected		Score		Alert			Detected		Score		Alert	
	PP[a]	OA[b]	PP	OA	PP	OA		PP	OA	PP	OA	PP	OA
A1	✓		1				U22	✓		0			
A2	✓		3				U23	✓		0			
A3	✓		5		✓		U24	✓		0			
A4	✓		5		✓		U25	✓		0			
A5	✓	✓	5	80	✓	✓	U26	✓		0			
A6	✓		8		✓		U27	✓		0			
A7	✓	✓	15	80	✓	✓	U28	✓		0			
A8	✓	✓	15	80	✓	✓	U29	✓		0			
A9	✓		25		✓		U30	✓		0			
A10	✓		35		✓		U31	✓		0			
A11	✓		42		✓		U32	✓		0			
A12	✓		51		✓		AD1	✓		2			
A13	✓		59		✓		AD2	✓		2			
A14	✓		59		✓		AD3	✓		4			
U11	✓		2				AD4	✓		4			
U12	✓		2				AD5	✓		5			
U13	✓		4				AD6	✓		5			
U14	✓		4				AD7	✓		7			
U21	✓		0				AD8	✓		9			

[a]'PP' is short for 'PPIDS'
[b]'OA' is short for 'OADMS'

Table 7. Comparison between PPIDS and OADMS in our experiments

System	FPR	FNR
PPIDS	0	14.29%
OADMS	16.66%	78.57%

6   Conclusion

In this paper, we discuss the significance of detecting attacks on network printers and why traditional IDSs are not suitable for network printers. So we research on constructing a specialized IDS for network printers. To detect attacks on network printers from network packets, we design and implement a pyramid-like methodology for attacking detection which utilizes "temporal", "and" and "or" operators to describe relationships between events, and we use ATT&CK framework as a foundation for the development of network printer threat models and methodologies that model the relationship between tactics, techniques, procedures, elements. We propose a behavior based attack detection system PPIDS on network printers. Experiments show that PPIDS behaves much better than OADMS which is based on Snort.

References

1. Bojinov, H., Bursztein, E., Boneh, D.: XCS: cross channel scripting and its impact on web applications. In: Proceedings of the 16th ACM Conference on Computer and Communications Security, pp. 420–431. ACM (2009)
2. Moyer, C.: This teen hacked 150,000 printers to show how the internet of things is shit. https://motherboard.vice.com/en_us/article/nzqayz/this-teen-hacked-150000-printers-to-show-how-the-internet-of-things-is-shit
3. The MITRE Corporation. MITRE ATT&CK™. https://attack.mitre.org/
4. Adrian "Irongeek" Crenshaw. Hacking network printers. http://www.irongeek.com/i.php?page=security/networkprinterhacking
5. Schriftliche Prüfungsarbeit für die Master-Prüfung, IT des Studiengangs, Netze und Systeme, Jens Müller, Jörg Schwenk, Juraj Somorovsky, and Vladislav Mladenov. Exploiting network printers (2016)
6. FX and kim0 of Phenoelit. Attacking networked embedded devices. https://www.defcon.org/images/defcon-10/dc-10-presentations/dc10-fx-embeddedsystems.pdf
7. Gragido, W.: Understanding indicators of compromise (IOC) (2013). https://blogs.rsa.com/understanding-indicators-of-compromiseioc-part-i
8. Deral (PercX) Heiland and Michael (OMI) Belton. Anatomy of a pass-back-attack: Intercepting authentication credentials stored in multifunction printers. http://foofus.net/goons/percx/praeda/pass-back-attack.pdf
9. Itkin, E., Balmas, Y.: Faxploit: Sending fax back to the dark ages. https://research.checkpoint.com/sending-fax-back-to-the-dark-ages/
10. MITRE. CVE-common vulnerabilities and exposures (CVE). https://cve.mitre.org/. Accessed 1 Mar 2019
11. Open Information Security Foundation (OISF). Suricata — Open Source IDS/IPS/NSM Engine. https://suricata-ids.org/

12. HP researchers. HP Jetdirect Print Servers - HP Jetdirect Port Numbers for TCP/IP (UDP) Connections. https://support.hp.com/us-en/document/c02480766
13. HP researchers. Printer security: The new it imperative. http://h20195.www2.hp.com/v2/getpdf.aspx/4AA7-3699ENW.pdf
14. HP researchers. Why printer security matters in healthcare. https://h20195.www2.hp.com/V2/getpdf.aspx/c05837519
15. Spicework researchers. Spicework. http://h20195.www2.hp.com/v2/getpdf.aspx/4AA7-3699ENW.pdf
16. Roesch, M., et al.: Snort: lightweight intrusion detection for networks. In: LISA, vol. 99, pp. 229–238 (1999)
17. RUB-NDS. Printer exploitation toolkit - the tool that made dumpster diving obsolete. https://github.com/RUB-NDS/PRET
18. Sibert, W.: Malicious data and computer security. In: Proceedings of the 19th National Information Systems Security Conference (1996)
19. Printer Spamming. Cross site printing. https://helpnetsecurity.com/dl/articles/CrossSitePrinting.pdf
20. Strom, B.E., et al.: Finding cyber threats with ATT&CK™-based analytics. Technical report, MITRE Technical report MTR170202. The MITRE Corporation (2017)
21. Information technology Promotion Agency of Japan. Research report on the security of MFPs. https://www.ipa.go.jp/security/jisec/apdx/documents/20130312report_E.pdf

A Privacy Enhancing Scheme for Mobile Devices Based Secure Multi-party Computation System

Xueyi Yang[1,2,3], Na Lv[1,2(✉)], Tianyu Chen[1,2], Cunqing Ma[1,2],
and Limin Liu[1,2]

[1] State Key Laboratory of Information Security,
Institute of Information Engineering, Chinese Academy of Sciences, Beijing, China
{yangxueyi,lvna,chentianyu,macunqing,liulimin}@iie.ac.cn
[2] Data Assurance and Communications Security Research Center,
Chinese Academy of Sciences, Beijing, China
[3] School of Cyber Security, University of Chinese Academy of Sciences,
Beijing, China

Abstract. Mobile devices, such as smart phones, have recently become the typical computing platforms for many users. Consequently, in practice more and more multi-party computation systems are deployed on users' mobile devices, resulting in various applications such as mobile outsourcing computing and mobile cooperative computing. However, as the mobile platforms may have inherent flaws, the connection of mobile devices and multi-party computation systems usually arouse new security risks. We point out that an application in one party's mobile device can be a powerful privileged attacker to the multi-party computation system. Previous studies have mainly focused on avoiding the privacy leaks of one or several malicious parties or eavesdroppers on the Internet. This paper presents a privacy enhancing scheme for a kind of secure multi-party computation systems. The scheme can resist the privileged attackers from the party's mobile device. Our scheme transforms the original computation process and puts the critical calculation process into trusted execution environment. We provide three components to build a privacy-enhanced multi-party computation system with our scheme. Our scheme is implemented to an actual secure multi-party computation system to demonstrate its validity and acceptable performance overhead.

Keywords: Mobile computation · Multi-party computation · Trusted execution environment · Privacy preserving · Mobile security

1 Introduction

The proliferation of the Internet has triggered tremendous opportunities for cooperative computation. People cooperate with each other to conduct computation tasks based on the inputs they each supplies. These cooperative computations can occur between trusted partners, between partially trusted partners, or even between competitors. How to preserve the privacy of inputs during

© Springer Nature Switzerland AG 2020
Z. Liu and M. Yung (Eds.): Inscrypt 2019, LNCS 12020, pp. 291–308, 2020.
https://doi.org/10.1007/978-3-030-42921-8_17

cooperative computation is referred to as secure multi-party computation problem (SMC) in the literature [1]. In fact, various secure multi-party computation schemes have been employed in abundant cloud computing systems and outsourcing computing systems to address privacy issues, such as privacy preserving data mining [2], and privacy preserving statistical analysis [3].

Nowadays, mobile devices become an essential part of human life relying on the convenience not bounded by time and place [4]. With the explosion of mobile applications, various services, like mobile cloud computing service, are accessed from mobile applications which run on the devices and communicate with remote servers via wireless networks [5]. However, the new access environment will impose a new set of security risks that did not appear in traditional service systems, especially the multi-party computation system.

This paper presents a privacy enhancing scheme for secure multi-party computation systems where a party works on a mobile device. The traditional design of secure multi-party computation systems mainly focuses on protecting against eavesdroppers in public channels or party attackers. Yet a number of security vulnerabilities existed in mobile operating systems, and complex application environment in mobile device create the possibility of a powerful privileged attacker. Hence, the eavesdroppers can come from another application on the party mobile device. We define a new threat model for the multi-party computation systems among which a party works on a mobile device. Our privacy enhancing scheme resists such a privileged attacker via transforming the original multi-party computation algorithm and putting the critical calculation process in trusted execution environment (TEE) [6].

Trusted execution environment is implemented by a hardware characteristic of device processor [6]. The characteristic makes that two isolated systems can parallelly run on one device. One is the normal system like Android where the original party application runs on. Another system is trusted system that will not be attacked by the privileged attacker in the normal system. In our scheme, the critical calculation process in the transformed calculation process, which can lead to privacy leaks, will be executed in the TEE. The remainder calculation process will also be executed by the original party application in the normal system to reduce its impact on user experience.

We design three functional components to implement our scheme for a multi-party computation system. Since TEE does not provide the trusted storage, we design the "Secret Recovery" component which protects the secret of mobile party by device info and password. The second component "Trusted UI" is used to resist message tampering attack. The third component "Computation Control" resists offline guessing attack by limiting the number of consecutive failed computation attempts. The limitation is implemented on the next party in the multi-party computation to avoid replay attacks.

To demonstrate the validity of our scheme, we implement our scheme on an actual multi-party computation system: Privacy-Preserving Multi-keyword Ranked Search (MRSE) [7], which is a ciphertext search scheme with three parties. Further, we evaluate the efficiency of our scheme by measuring the execution speeds of the enhanced process with our scheme and the corresponding original process. The evaluation results show that our scheme only introduces a negligible overhead.

Our main contributions can be summarized as follows:

- We present a new threat model in mobile devices based secure multi-party computation systems. The designer of a secure multi-party computation system must consider attacks from other application on a party's mobile device.
- We present a privacy enhancing scheme for secure multi-party computation systems with three components. Our scheme resists privileged attackers by transforming the original computation process and putting the critical calculation process into TEE.
- We implement our enhancement scheme on an actual secure multi-party computation system to demonstrate the validity of our scheme and evaluate the performance of our scheme.

The remainder of the paper is organized as follows. Section 2 provides background information on TEE, and secure multi-party computation. Section 3 presents our privacy enhancing scheme. Section 4 describes a user cases of our scheme. The experimental evaluations of our proposed scheme are given in Sect. 6. Section 7 concludes the study and indicate our future work.

2   Background and Related Work

2.1   Trusted Execution Environment

Trusted execution environment is a secure area of a processor. It guarantees code and data in it to be protected with confidentiality and integrity [8]. TEE is an isolated environment that runs in parallel with the normal operating system like Android. Trusted applications (TA) [6] is the application running in a TEE. TAs have the full access to the processor and memory of a device, while hardware isolation protects these from user installed apps running in the normal operating system. The execution flows and process data in the TAs are isolated from each other by the secure isolation mechanism of TEE [8].

In ARM architecture, TrustZone [9] is presented as an embedded hardware technology which can be used to support TEE implementations. In the implementation of our scheme, we employed Qualcomm Secure Execution Environment (QSEE). QSEE is a TEE implementation developed by Qualcomm based on ARM TrustZone technology [10]. QSEE provides Pseudorandom Number Generator (PRNG) driver. The driver is hardware-based and can provide high quality random numbers.

2.2   Secure Multi-party Computation

In cryptography, the goal of secure multi-party computation (MPC) is to create methods for parties to jointly compute a function over their inputs while keeping those inputs private [11]. The security of multi-party computation protocol concerns two main aspects: input privacy and correctness. Hence, in our threat model, we define two active attacks that an active attacker can use to break protocol's security in input privacy and correctness.

A specific secure multi-party computation scheme can be used to resolve a specific real-life problem [12], such as privacy preserving database query or privacy preserving data mining. When a secure multi-party computation system is implemented to provide a service for the real-life user, it will face many challenges from the real world such as mobile adversary [13].

Adversaries can be categorized according to how willing they are to deviate from the protocol. There are essentially two types of adversaries: passive adversary and active adversary. The passive adversary model assumes that corrupted parties merely gather information in the normal protocol execution, but do not deviate from the protocol specification. This is a naive adversary model. The active adversary model assumes that the adversary can arbitrarily deviate from the normal protocol execution in its attempt to cheat. Protocols which achieve security in this adversary model provide a very high security guarantee. In our threat model, we divide the secure multi-party computation protocols into two categories and focus on the active adversary.

2.3   Related Work

Multi-party Computation System. Multi-party computation systems have been deployed to a variety of user services, particularly those related to cryptography [7,14,15]. Bogetoft et al. [16] introduce the first large-scale and practical application of secure multi-party computation. Du et al. [12] introduce a transformation framework to transform normal computation models to the models enhanced with new privacy requirements. The classical adversary model focuses on the tolerable number of parties that can be corrupted by an adversary [11]. Hirt et al. [17] recursively applies the simulation technique to standard secure multiparty computation to build a new general adversary model which is not limited to the number of corrupted parties. Multi-party computation is useful to investigate the basic and general protocol issues. Ostrovsky et al. [13] emphasize the analysis of mobile adversary that the computation faces.

Mobile Security. Privilege escalation attack is a kind of common attack on mobile platforms. An attacker can exploit system or program vulnerabilities to disable the system's sandbox model [18]. WiBfeld [19] introduces a series of methods to hook method calls and implements code injection on Android platform. Although various defensive schemes have been suggested to protect a mobile app [20], such as code obfuscation [21] and virtualization-based secure execution [22], they also hardly resist a powerful and knowledgeable adversary in the normal mobile system. ARM TrustZone is employed to provide trusted execution environment. Using TEE to implement program security is a research hotspot, such as Gupta et al. [23] which employed TEE to implement secure behavior analysis and Covey et al. [24] which employed TEE to implement entry authentication for softwares. Some researchers are working on improving TEE's security [25] because TEE itself has some flaws, such as the lack of secure storage. Tremlet [26] proposed to embed a secure element into mobile device. Yet Roland et al. [27] proposed a series of attack methods on SE-enabled secure storage scheme on mobile platforms. Mellqvist [28] designed a cloud secure storage system for mobile platforms, however it still faces some threats from the cloud.

3 Privacy Enhancing Scheme

To address the privacy issues described above, we propose a privacy preserving enhancement scheme in this section. The scheme works for a specific kind of multi-party computation which is introduced in Sect. 3.1. Our scheme strengthens the security of privacy preserving in the parties on the mobile device.

3.1 Threat Model and Assumptions

The active attack, who attempts to impersonate a legitimate party, is a common problem for multi-party computation system designers to consider. Previous studies have mainly considered this attack from the public channel between parties such as the network. However, our study focuses on the attacker coming from the mobile device of a legitimate party. We term the party that uses mobile device to execute its computation process client, and we term the other party server. The computation process of a client is almost executed in a mobile application. The attacker can be another application in the client device.

Client Imitation Attack: This kind of active attack is defined on the party that use mobile device to execute its computation process. The attacker lurks in the client device as a mobile application or other forms. The attacker aims to impersonate the client of a multi-party computation system without being detected. Further, the attacker can get the final result of the multi-party computation with arbitrary input.

This attack model is not appropriate for all multi-party computation system scenarios. This is because in some multi-party computation problems, any of these computation results are valuable to the attacker. For example, in the WiFi fingerprint-based localization system, one target of attacker is to get the client's location which is the last output of the whole multi-party computation algorithm [14]. Hence we divide the multi-party security algorithm into two categories. The first category is client output-sensitive algorithm such as the WiFi fingerprint-based localization algorithm. If the last output or the medium output of client is the target of the attacker, we term the algorithm client output-sensitive. The medium output of client refers to the data that client party sends to other parties.

This paper focuses on the second category: client process-sensitive algorithm. The second category claims that the last output or the medium output of client is not a target of attacker. The attacker aims to impersonate the client in the multi-party computation system. A common example of this category of algorithm is cooperative signature. One target of attacker is to sign a specified bill message without user confirmation [29].

We divide the inputs of client into two kinds. The first kind in different computation such as the message that will be signed is different. We term it $input - A$. The second kind is the same in different computation such as a secret key that can be used to represent the party's identity. We term it $input - B$.

Hence, the attacker can achieve this goal in two ways. **Attack-way-A:** Tampering all the $input - A$ as expected by the attacker, and employing the client to complete the legitimate multi-party computation process. Then attacker gets the last computation result. **Attacker-way-B:** Getting all the $input - B$, and using them to complete computation with other parties for arbitrary $intput - A$. Then attacker can achieve the same goal in the absence of the client.

We assume that an attacker can acquire root privilege on a client. Hence the attacker can monitor and debug the party application or process on a client. Further, the attacker can get and tramper any input, and implement the client imitation attack. The existing methods of preventing these two attack ways in the normal mobile system are hard to defend against privileged attackers. This is because all the data and UI (User Interface) used in these defense methods can be obtained and copied by the powerful attacker.

3.2   Scheme Overview

The key idea to resist the client imitation attack in our proposed scheme is ensuring that the key process data or input only appears in TEE. The calculation process in TEE cannot be monitored and controlled by a privileged attacker in the normal OS like Android. Hence, firstly we should calculate the security boundary of the client's computation process. And then we can transform the original computation process and put the critical calculate process in TEE to avoid leaking critical input or process data.

The calculation of the security boundary must base on a specific multi-party security algorithm. We analyze the life cycle of each critical input and process data to get the security boundary. We use a user case to describe the algorithm transformation process in Sect. 4. A straightforward idea is that putting the whole algorithm process and all the input of client into TEE without considering any boundary. However, this idea is not feasible in the actual mobile phone usage scenario. This is because:

(1) TEE system does not contain the abundant system infrastructures as the normal mobile system. Many operations must be completed through the normal mobile system like localization or network access.
(2) The whole work flow of client can be cross-process and the data transmission between clients or client and server is almost over the network. Certain inputs, process data and outputs must be visible to the attacker.
(3) TEE system provides the trusted execution environment but it is unable to provide the trusted storage. There is no direct way to protect client secrets.

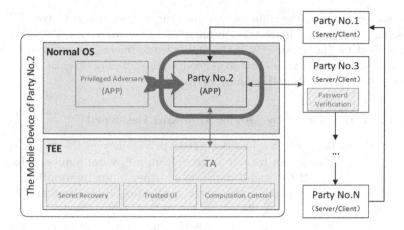

Fig. 1. The overview of our scheme

After we calculate the security boundary of a multi-party security algorithm and put the critical calculation process in TEE, three basic components are provided to implement our privacy preserving enhancement scheme. The three basic components are secret recovery component, trusted UI component, and computation control component. We introduce their functionality and implementation in the following contents.

The overview of our scheme is shown in Fig. 1. In traditional implementation of a multi-party computation system, all the computation are performed on an application of client and a series of other party like servers. In our proposed scheme, a TA is built to include the critical calculation process. TA and the application in the normal system jointly complete the computation process of the client.

The secret recovery component is employed to resist the *attack-way-B*. This component is used to protect the *input-B*. Our scheme calculates the result of F (secret, Device info, password) and stores it in the normal system. The attacker cannot recover the secret from the result without password, since the password is only imported from the trusted UI in TEE. The password is used to control access to the secret.

The trusted UI component is employed to resist the *attack-way-A*. In the previous paragraph, we introduce that the password imported from the trusted UI is used to protect the *input-B*. And the trusted UI component is also used to protect the *input-A*. To prevent an attacker from tampering an *input-A* to another value, we use trusted UI to show the *input-A* or its corresponding human-readable character string. The party users can authorize the calculation by importing the password only when they agree to the displayed *input-A*. In some actual application scenarios, the *input-A* is a digest of source Message.

Computation control component is employed to resist offline guessing attack. Since we import password to control the access of the secret instead of importing the secret directly, the difficulty of guessing secrets drops to the difficulty of guessing passwords. Hence, the number of consecutive failed computation attempts must be limited strictly. If the data used to reject computation attempt is only stored in client, it is hard to defend against replay attacks. Hence, the rejection behavior is initiated from other parties.

3.3 Protecting Secret by Device Info and Password

The *input-B* can be a secret s like the partly private key in the two-party signature algorithm. The secret usually sources from a random number which can be generated in TEE. If the secret depends on other input information like the data sending from other parties, the client application can collect and forward this data to the corresponding TA.

The secret recovery component employed a function $F(s, di, pw)$ to generate a result string λ. di indicates the device info, and pw indicates the password. The function F must be reversible for its first parameter. In other word, there must exist another function G that $G(rs, di, pw) == s$. Hence when the first time the secret s is calculated in TEE, the secret recovery component executes the function F to generate the result string λ. Then the rs will be sent to the client application to be stored in the normal OS. The attackers cannot calculate the secret s from λ unless they have all the device info and password.

When the client application wants to use the secret to complete its computation process in the multi-party security algorithm, the client application sends the λ and Device Info to the corresponding TA. After the client user imports the password on the trusted UI, the secret recovery component executes the function F' to recover the s from the λ. Then the protected secret s can be used in later steps.

The functions F and F' can be implemented by a common symmetrical encryption-decryption algorithm with a secret key. The secret key is generated from hash values of the device info and password. The functions F and F' can also be implemented by a simple XOR operation between the first parameter and the hash values of other parameters. We summarize the two types of implementation algorithm as follows, where H represents a hash function.

$$\begin{cases} F(s, di, pw) = ENC(s, SK = H(di) \oplus H(pw)) \\ F'(\lambda, di, pw) = DEC(\lambda, SK = H(di) \oplus H(pw)) \end{cases} \tag{1}$$

$$\begin{cases} F(s, di, pw) = s \oplus H(di) \oplus H(pw) \\ F'(\lambda, di, pw) = \lambda \oplus H(di) \oplus H(pw) \end{cases} \tag{2}$$

3.4 Resisting Message Tampering by Confirming Message on Trusted UI

The *input-A* can be a message m like the order information that will be signed. Since a powerful attacker can control the normal OS in our threat model, the attacker can intercept or replace the import of m. The *input-A* can come from the network or another app or somewhere else. Hence the *input-A* is beyond our security boundary, and we can't completely protect it from attack.

In our proposed scheme, the attacker still can tamper an *input-A m* with another message. Yet our trusted UI component can display the incoming message of TEE. And the computation process will be continued only if the client user confirms the incoming message as the user want. The Trusted UI of message confirmation is shown in Fig. 2.

The message confirmation cannot be implemented in the normal OS since the UI also can be tampered by a powerful attacker. When the first time the client user uses the trusted UI or the initialization/registration process of the secure multi-party computation, the client user must set a reserved information. The reserved information is a character string that will be displayed on trusted UI of message confirmation and password import. The reserved information is employed to prevent an attacker from faking a same UI with the trusted UI. The reserved information is a secret the client user shared with TA and used to identify the trusted UI of the appropriate TA. The reserved information is also protected as an *input-B* that we introduce the protection method in Sect. 3.3.

(a) Trusted UI of password import   (b) Trusted UI of message confirmation

Fig. 2. Two trusted UIs on real machine. Area No. 1 shows the function name of the UI and area No. 2 is the main functional areas. Area No. 3 shows reserved information.

3.5 Resisting Offline Guessing Attack by Limiting the Number of Consecutive Failed Computation Attempts

Limiting the number of consecutive failed computation attempts is a common way to resist offline guessing attack [30]. We improve a standard delay strategy

---

Algorithm 1. Password Verification

Input: Records list L. Received data m. The secret key ms. Stored hash value of password hp. Now time nt. Default lifetime dlt.

Output: A new record list L.

1: **for** each e in V **do**
2:       **if** $e.begintime + e.lifetime < nt$
3:           $V = V - \{e\}$
4:       **end if**
5: **end for**
6: $m_hp, m_st = DEC(M, SK = ms)$
7: **if** $m_hp == hp$ && Check out m_st with nt
8:       **for** each e in V **do**
9:           $e.lifetime = e.lifetime/2$
10:       **end for**
11: **return** V
12: **end if**
13: **else**
14: $V = V + \{nt, dlt\}$
15: **switch** $V.count$
16:       **case** 1 to 4
17:           $dt = 0, dl = 1$
18:       **case** 5
19:           $dt = 1, dl = 1$
20:       **case** 6
21:           $dt = 5, dl = 1.5$
22:       **case** 7,8
23:           $dt = 15, dl = 2$
24:       **case** other
25:           $dt = 60, dl = 3$
26:       **for** each e in V **do**
27:           $e.lifetime = e.lifetime * dl$
28:       **end for**
29:       Stop party computation system in dt minutes.
30: **return** V
31: **end else**

---

on mobile devices [31] with the lifetime of failed computation attempts. The original delay strategy proposes the progressively increased delay time when the number of consecutive failed computation attempts increases in one day. In our improved delay strategy, the records of failed computation attempts will not be cleared at the end of the day and the records have a flexible lifetime management.

Each record contains the starting time and lifetime. Each computation attempt triggers a password verification on the next party of secure multi-party computation. The password verification launches a record purge to remove the expired records. The failed password verification will add a new record in the records table. The consecutive failed verification can cause the party computing service to stop for a certain period of time, and can trigger a penalty to increase the lifetime of all records in the records list. We summarize this algorithm in Algorithm 1.

The password verification is implemented by matching timestamp and the hash value of password. Firstly, in the preparatory stage or initialization stage of multi-party security algorithm, the client and the next party jointly complete a key exchange protocol. The generated key in the key exchange protocol can be a secret that we recover in secret recovery component. Then the client calculates the value of $m = ENC(HASH(password), timestamp)$, and sends it to the next party. In each computation attempt, the client will also sent the m to the next party. The password verification can not be implemented in the local, since (1) the time information can be tampered by attacker, and (2) the critical data used in the verification such as the record table can be subject to replay attacks.

4 User Case

In this section, we use an actual multi-party security system on ciphertext search to show how to transform the original algorithm to apply our privacy enhancing scheme.

4.1 A Brief Introduction to an Ciphertext Search System: MRSE

MRSE [7], Privacy-Preserving Multi-keyword Ranked Search over Encrypted Cloud Data, is a ciphertext search system with three parties. The three parties are data owner, cloud server, and data user. The scheme is used to implement an encrypted cloud data search service. The scheme allows multiple keywords in the search request and return documents in the order of their relevance to these keywords. The MRSE scheme consists of four algorithms: **Setup, BuildIndex, Trapdoor, Query**.

The data owner executes **Setup** to generate the secret key in the form of a 3-tuple as $\{S, M_1, M_2\}$. M_1 and M_2 are two $(n+2) \times (n+2)$ invertible matrices. M_1^{-1} and M_2^{-1} must be encrypted and sent to the data user. The encryption key can be generated by key exchange. Then the data owner executes **BuildIndex** to build a subindex I_i for every encrypted document C_i. The I_i securely keeps the keyword information of document. After that, the data user executes **Trapdoor** to generated the secure search request $\widetilde{W}$ with several *input-As*: keywords, and two *input-Bs*: M_1^{-1} and M_2^{-1}. Then the cloud server executes **Query** to compute the similarity scores of each document with the search request $\widetilde{W}$ and each document's subindex I_i. After sorting all scores, the cloud server returns the top-k ranked document id list.

4.2 The Algorithm Transformation on MRES

Our scheme focuses on the two algorithms involving the data user. In **Setup** stage, the data user join in the key exchange process and encryption transmission process. In **Trapdoor** stage, the data user computes secure search request and sends it to cloud server.

Diffie-Hellman key exchange [32] is selected to implement encryption transmission. The original implementation of the protocol uses the multiplicative group of integers modulo p, where p is prime and g is a primitive root modulo p. In this way, the resulting shared secret can be ensured to take on any value from 1 to p−1. The two parties use a same modulus p and a base g. The party O represents the data owner and the party U represents the data user.

The key exchange process is described in Algorithm 2. The first three steps in Algorithm 2 of U are the original steps which is implemented in TEE now. The fourth step is the new step which is implemented in TEE. Then the client app in the normal system stores λ in local. The λ can be used to recover the secret key sk.

The process of encryption transmission is described in Algorithm 3. Then the client app in the normal system stores λ_{M1} and λ_{M2} in local. The λ_{M1} and λ_{M2} can be used to recover the M_1^{-1} and M_2^{-1}. The third step in Algorithm 3 is the original step which is implemented in TEE now. The second and the fourth steps are the new steps which is implemented in TEE.

The process of generating secure search request is described in Algorithm 4. Then the client app in the normal system sends $T_{\widetilde{W}}$ to cloud server to execute **Query** algorithm. The first step in Algorithm 4 is the original step which is also implemented in normal app. The second, the third, and the fifth step are the original steps which is implemented in TEE now. The fourth step is the new step which are implemented in TEE.

Algorithm 2. Key exchange

Input: O, U: Modulus p, base g. U: Device info di, and password pw.
Output: U: A number λ.
1: O: Generate a random number a. U: Generate a random number b.
2: O: Calculate $A = g^a \bmod p$ and send A to U. U: Calculate $B = g^b \bmod p$ and send B to O.
3: O: Calculate the secret key $sk = B^a \bmod p$. U: Calculate the secret key $sk = A^b \bmod p$.
4: U: Invoke function $F(sk, di, pw)$ to generate λ. Return λ.

Algorithm 3. Encryption transmission

Input: O: Transmission key sk, transmitted data $M_1^{-1}, M_2^{-1} \in \mathbb{N}^{(n+2) \times (n+2)}$. U: Device info di, and password pw, λ.
Output: U: Two matrices λ_{M1} and λ_{M2}.
1: O: Encrypt the M_1^{-1}, M_2^{-1} with the key sk. Send the encryption result m to U.
2: U: Recover the sk by invoking $F'(\lambda, di, pw)$.
3: U: Decrypt the M_1^{-1}, M_2^{-1} with the key sk and m.
4: U: Invoke function $F(M_1^{-1}, di, pw), F(M_2^{-1}, di, pw)$ to generate λ_{M1} and λ_{M2} and return them.

Without the enhancement of our scheme, the MRSE system can be attacked by a privileged attacker in data user's mobile device. The attacker can analyze and get the stored secret sk, M_1^{-1}, M_2^{-1}, or tramper the keywords $\widetilde{W}$. Then the attacker can act as a data user to query arbitrary data. At last the attacker can attack cloud server to get information about the data source with unlimited queries or cause the user to be blocked.

Algorithm 4. Generating secure search request

Input: U: Device info di, and password pw, two matrices $\lambda_{M1}, \lambda_{M2} \in \mathbb{N}^{(n+2)\times(n+2)}$, interested keyword collections $\widetilde{W}$. The whole keyword collections $W = W_1, W_2$, ..., W_n.
Output: U: A trapdoor matrice $T_{\widetilde{W}} \in \mathbb{N}^{(n+2)\times(n+2)}$.
1: U: Generate one binary vector Q. Each bit $Q[j]$ indicates whether $W_j \in \widetilde{W}$ is true or false.
2: U: Extend Q to a $(n + 2)$-dimension vector $\boldsymbol{Q}$ as (rQ, r, t). r, t are two nonzero random numbers.
3: U: Equally split Q into two matrices. $\boldsymbol{Q} = (\boldsymbol{Q'}, \boldsymbol{Q''})$.
4: U: Invoke function $F'(\lambda_{M1}, di, pw), F'(\lambda_{M2}, di, pw)$ to recover M_1^{-1}, M_2^{-1}.
5: U: Calculate the last trapdoor $T_{\widetilde{W}} = \{M_1^{-1}\boldsymbol{Q'}, M_2^{-1}\boldsymbol{Q''}\}$ and return them.

---

5   Security Analysis

Since our privacy enhancing scheme does not change the data interaction and transfer protocols between parties in computation, the privacy guarantee from network attackers and party attackers will not be enhanced or compromised. In the user case introduced in Sect. 4, owner's document privacy, rank privacy from the cloud server and user, and user's retrieval privacy are guaranteed by cryptographic algorithms and random numbers in MRSE. These security properties are inherited in our privacy enhanced MRSE. However, the original MRSE can not protect the three privacies from a privileged attacker in the user's mobile device, since all data used by the party application is visible to the attacker.

Our scheme can enhance the privacy of a multi-party computation system in preventing client imitation attack. A privileged attacker in the data user's mobile device can achieve the goal, getting the final result of the multi-party computation with arbitrary input, in the two attack ways, **Attack-way-A** and **Attacker-way-B**. In the original MRSE, a $input - A$, the interested keyword collections $\widetilde{W}$ in generating secure search request process, can be tampered by the attacker. Two $input-B$, the encryption secret key sk in key exchange process and the partial computation secret key M_1^{-1}, M_2^{-1} in encryption transmission process, is visible to the attacker.

Nevertheless, the privacy of the three inputs is protected in the privacy enhanced MRSE. If the attacker aims to acquire the sk, the attacker can calculate the formula $A^b \bmod p$ or $F(\lambda, di, pw)$. The attacker can acquire b, λ, and di

by monitoring the party application. However, A and pw is only appear in TEE where can not be observed by the attacker in the normal mobile OS. Similarly, M_1^{-1}, M_2^{-1} is protected in TEE by sk and pw.

If the attacker aims to tamper the $\widetilde{W}$ with new keyword collections $\widetilde{W}^*$, the attacker can tamper the generated vector Q in the first step or create a new trapdoor $T_{\widetilde{W}}^*$ for the $\widetilde{W}^*$. Tampering with Q is resisted by our trusted UI component since the user can confirm the message to be processed is $\widetilde{W}$ or not. The creation of trapdoor $T_{\widetilde{W}}^*$ is prevented by the MRSE algorithms unless the attacker has the partial computation secret key M_1^{-1}, M_2^{-1}.

6   Performance Evaluation

In this section, we report the results of our experimental evaluation to demonstrate that the performance cost of our scheme is acceptable. We implement the client side of the experimental multi-party computation systems with mobile phone on Android platform and QSEE, as shown in Fig. 2. Two server parties are implemented on a CentOS server with 32 eight-core 2.00 GHz CPUs and 144 GB memory and a Dell OptiPlex with 3.4 GHz CPU, 16 GB of memory, and windows 10.

We use SHA-1 [33] and AES [34] as the default hash algorithm and symmetrical encryption-decryption algorithm in our scheme. We run the original MRSE and the privacy enhanced MRSE with a real-world dataset: the Enron Email Dataset [35].

Since the operation time of user on the UI is not controllable, we remove the operation time on trusted UI. In each experimental execution process, we measure the execution time of the whole process and the time spent on the trusted UI. Then we calculate the difference between the two values as the final execution time. In order to reduce the influence of system error on our evaluation results, each measurement was performed 10 times and their average value was selected as the measurement result.

6.1   Setup Stage of MRSE

The whole *Setup* stage contains three processes: (1) generating the secret key of the system $\{S, M_1, M_2\}$, (2) generating a session key by key exchange, and (3) sending $\{M_1^{-1}, M_2^{-1}\}$ to the data user. The size of secret key is related to the size of keyword dictionary n. In order to evaluate the performance cost of our scheme in different scales of data, we create no a little dummy keywords instead of only one dummy keyword and insert them into the dictionary and every keyword vectors.

The evaluation results in the different sizes of keyword dictionary are shown in Fig. 3(a). The cost of our scheme is less than 10% when the size is more than 2000. With the increase in the value of u, the proportion of performance cost is obviously reduced. This is because the main overhead can be divided into two parts: (1) switching the execution environment between TEE and the normal operating system, (2) transferring data between two execution environments and additional data operations. The first part of the overhead does not increase with the size of the data and the second part is $O(n^2)$ level. Nevertheless, the execution time of *Setup* stage is $O(n^3)$ level.

We divide the entire execution time of this stage into three parts: (1) the calculation on the data owner, (2) the latency on network, and (3) the calculation on the data user. The overhead of our scheme in the first part and the second part is introduced by the password verification function. The difference between the original system and the privacy enhanced system in the three parts are shown in Fig. 3(b). When $n = 1500$, although the overhead of the whole process is about 11.3%, our scheme still introduces about 28.5% overhead in the third part. This is because the calculation process on the data user is just a small part of the whole process. Hence the overhead of switching execution environments is the majority part of overall overhead.

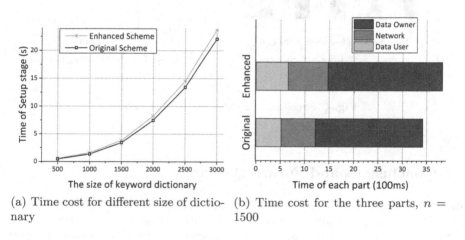

(a) Time cost for different size of dictionary

(b) Time cost for the three parts, $n = 1500$

Fig. 3. Execution time cost in *Setup* stage

6.2   Trapdoor Stage of MRSE

Figure 4(a) shows that the time to generate a search request with the number of searched keywords. The calculation in *Trapdoor* stage mainly includes two multiplications of a matrix and a split query vector. The calculation is so simple that the proportion of the cost of our scheme is a bit large. Nevertheless the actual performance overhead is no more than 100 ms. Like the *Setup* stage, the overhead of our scheme is not obvious for the entire process. Figure 4(a) also shows that the number of query keywords has little influence on the overhead of search request generation.

As we introduced before, the execution time in *Trapdoor* stage has been measured 10 times to reduce the influence of system error. Figure 4(b) shows the original measurement results obtained in 10 experiments when the number of keywords in the query is 10. Our scheme introduces about 17.9% overhead in *Trapdoor* stage. Although the overhead seems non-negligible, it is also indistinguishable from system error.

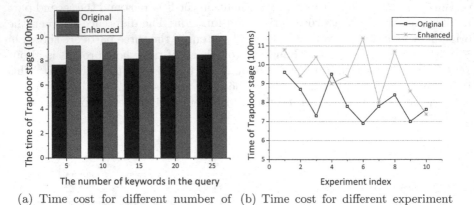

(a) Time cost for different number of keywords in the query

(b) Time cost for different experiment index.

Fig. 4. Execution time cost in *Trapdoor* stage

7 Conclusions and Future Research

In this paper, we firstly define a new threat model in mobile devices based secure multi-party computation systems. A powerful adversary on a party's mobile device is a serious security risk that multi-party computation system designers must consider. Then we present a privacy enhancing scheme for secure multi-party computation systems. The scheme can resist the privileged adversary by transforming the original computation process and putting the critical calculation process into TEE. Our scheme provides three components to help system designers employing our scheme. We implement our scheme on an actual system of ciphertext search to demonstrate the validity of our scheme and evaluate the performance cost of our scheme.

As our future work, we will explore the security vulnerabilities and possible attack paths in TEE of different platforms, and enhance the security of multi-party computing systems in the more stronger threat model.

Acknowledgement. The authors would like to thank the anonymous reviewers. This work is supported by National Key R&D Program of China (No. 2017YFB0802404), and partially supported by the National Natural Science Foundation of China (No. 61802396).

References

1. Yao, A.C.: Protocols for secure computations. In: 23rd Annual Symposium on Foundations of Computer Science, SFCS'08, pp. 160–164. IEEE (1982)
2. Aggarwal, C.C., Philip, S.Y.: A general survey of privacy-preserving data mining models and algorithms. In: Aggarwal, C.C., Yu, P.S. (eds.) Privacy-Preserving Data Mining, pp. 11–52. Springer, Boston (2008). https://doi.org/10.1007/978-0-387-70992-5_2
3. Kamm, L.: Privacy-preserving statistical analysis using secure multi-party computation. Ph.D. dissertation (2015)
4. Botta, A., De Donato, W., Persico, V., Pescapé, A.: Integration of cloud computing and internet of things: a survey. Future Gener. Comput. Syst. **56**, 684–700 (2016)
5. Dinh, H.T., Lee, C., Niyato, D., Wang, P.: A survey of mobile cloud computing: architecture, applications, and approaches. Wirel. Commun. Mob. Comput. **13**(18), 1587–1611 (2013)
6. Seibel, J., LaFlamme, K., Koschara, F., Schumak, R., Debate, J.: Trusted execution environment, US Patent Application 15/007,547, 27 2017 July
7. Cao, N., Wang, C., Li, M., Ren, K., Lou, W.: Privacy-preserving multi-keyword ranked search over encrypted cloud data. IEEE Trans. Parallel Distrib. Syst. **25**(1), 222–233 (2014)
8. Machiry, A., et al.: Boomerang: exploiting the semantic gap in trusted execution environments. In: Proceedings of the 2017 Network and Distributed System Security Symposium (NDSS) (2017)
9. Winter, J.: Trusted computing building blocks for embedded Linux-based arm Trustzone platforms. In: Proceedings of the 3rd ACM Workshop on Scalable Trusted Computing, pp. 21–30. ACM (2008)
10. Rosenberg, D.: Qsee trustzone kernel integer over flow vulnerability. In: Black Hat Conference, p. 26 (2014)
11. Goldreich, O.: Secure multi-party computation. Manuscript. Preliminary version, vol. 78 (1998)
12. Du, W., Atallah, M.J.: Secure multi-party computation problems and their applications: a review and open problems. In: Proceedings of the 2001 Workshop on New Security Paradigms, NSPW 2001, pp. 13–22. ACM, New York (2001). http://doi.acm.org/10.1145/508171.508174
13. Ostrovsky, R., Yung, M.: How to withstand mobile virus attacks (extended abstract). In: Proceedings of the Tenth Annual ACM Symposium on Principles of Distributed Computing, PODC 1991, pp. 51–59. ACM, New York (1991). http://doi.acm.org/10.1145/112600.112605
14. Li, H., Sun, L., Zhu, H., Lu, X., Cheng, X.: Achieving privacy preservation in WiFi fingerprint-based localization. In: 2014 Proceedings IEEE INFOCOM, pp. 2337–2345. IEEE (2014)
15. Zhou, C.V., Leckie, C., Karunasekera, S.: A survey of coordinated attacks and collaborative intrusion detection. Comput. Secur. **29**(1), 124–140 (2010)
16. Bogetoft, P., et al.: Secure multiparty computation goes live. In: Dingledine, R., Golle, P. (eds.) FC 2009. LNCS, vol. 5628, pp. 325–343. Springer, Heidelberg (2009). https://doi.org/10.1007/978-3-642-03549-4_20
17. Hirt, M., Maurer, U.: Player simulation and general adversary structures in perfect multiparty computation. J. Cryptol. **13**(1), 31–60 (2000). https://doi.org/10.1007/s001459910003

18. Davi, L., Dmitrienko, A., Sadeghi, A.-R., Winandy, M.: Privilege escalation attacks on android. In: Burmester, M., Tsudik, G., Magliveras, S., Ilić, I. (eds.) ISC 2010. LNCS, vol. 6531, pp. 346–360. Springer, Heidelberg (2011). https://doi.org/10. 1007/978-3-642-18178-8_30

19. Wißfeld, M.: ArtHook: Callee-side method hook injection on the new android runtime art. Ph.D. dissertation, Saarland University (2015)

20. Gouveia, J.M.E.P.: Fault injectionin android applications. Master's thesis, Universidade do Porto (2018). https://repositorio-aberto.up.pt/bitstream/10216/114158/2/277710.pdf

21. Rastogi, V., Chen, Y., Jiang, X.: Catch me if you can: evaluating android antimalware against transformation attacks. IEEE Trans. Inf. Forensics Secur. **9**(1), 99–108 (2014)

22. Coogan, K., Lu, G., Debray, S.: Deobfuscation of virtualization-obfuscated software: a semantics-based approach. In: Proceedings of the 18th ACM Conference on Computer and Communications Security, CCS 2011, pp. 275–284. ACM, New York (2011). http://doi.acm.org/10.1145/2046707.2046739

23. Gupta, R., Halambi, S.A., Rimoni, Y.: Secure behavior analysis over trusted execution environment, US Patent 9,756,066, 5 September 2017

24. Covey, C.R., Harvey, R.B., Redman, M.D., Tkacik, T.E.: Computing device with entry authentication into trusted execution environment and method therefor, US Patent 8,117,642, 14 February 2012

25. Jang, J.S., Kong, S., Kim, M., Kim, D., Kang, B.B.: SeCReT: secure channel between rich execution environment and trusted execution environment. In: NDSS (2015)

26. Tremlet, C.: Embedded secure element for authentication, storage and transaction within a mobile terminal, US Patent 9,436,940, 6 September 2016

27. Roland, M.: Applying recent secure element relay attack scenarios to the real world: Google wallet relay attack, arXiv preprint arXiv:1209.0875 (2012)

28. Mellqvist, A.: Portable electronic devices, systems, methods and computer program products for accessing remote secure elements, US Patent Application 12/487,045, 17 June 2010

29. Little, M., Ko, C.: Detecting coordinated attacks in tactical wireless networks using cooperative signature-based detectors. In: IEEE Military Communications Conference, MILCOM 2005, pp. 176–182. IEEE (2005)

30. OpenAFS. Improving password and authentication security (2000). http://docs. openafs.org/AdminGuide/HDRWQ515.html

31. Apple. iOS security iOS 12 (2018). https://www.apple.com/business/site/docs/iOS_Security_Guide.pdf

32. Merkle, R.C.: Secure communications over insecure channels. Commun. ACM **21**(4), 294–299 (1978)

33. Eastlake 3rd, D., Jones, P.: US Secure Hash Algorithm 1 (SHA1). Technical report (2001)

34. N.-F. Standard: Announcing the advanced encryption standard (AES). Federal Information Processing Standards Publication, vol. 197, pp. 1–51 (2001)

35. Cohen, W.W.: Enron email dataset, May 2015. http://www.cs.cmu.edu/~./enron/

Consolidating Hash Power in Blockchain Shards with a Forest

Jun Zhao, Jiangshan Yu, and Joseph K. Liu[✉]

Faculty of Information Technology, Monash University, Melbourne, Australia
Jun.Zhao@nekobuster.com, {Jiangshan.Yu,Joseph.Liu}@monash.edu

Abstract. Sharding has been a highly expected solution for the blockchain scalability problem. But with computation power of honest miners (or stakes in PoS based systems) distributed in shards, it becomes easier for attackers to attack a single shard. In this research, we propose a new consensus algorithm, Greedy Observed Largest Forest (GOLF), aiming to consolidate distributed hash power in all shards to make attacking a single shard as hard as attacking the entire system.

Keywords: Blockchain · Scalability · Sharding · Attack · Consensus

1 Introduction

The popularity of Bitcoin has shown the value of blockchain technology. In addition to cryptocurrency, there are lots of other applications for blockchain, e.g. e-voting [14], IoT [15], payment system [13,18], data storage [10,12] etc. However, the low transaction processing speed has limited the deployment for a practical case. This limitation is referred to as the blockchain scalability problem [3]. It has become one of the biggest problems that limit the blockchain technology and a popular topic among research communities in this area [7].

In recent years, many studies are aiming to address this issue. The two main directions that are highly expected to solve the problem are the Directed Acyclic Graph (DAG) and sharding. While the former tries to replace the data structure of a blockchain with a DAG, the latter spreads the storage and the load of a blockchain to parallel shards.

The DAG is expected to be a better data structure of decentralised ledgers. While in a blockchain each block has exactly one parent and one child, in a DAG there could be multiple parents and multiple children. This eliminates the bottleneck of the blockchain and enables the ledger to grow in concurrently generated graph nodes. Existing works using this data structure include [1,2, 8]. However, this structure also introduced some new issues mainly because it increases the difficulty of conflict resolutions. While existing implementations usually trade-off decentralisation to some extent for security, researchers are pursuing a solution to ensure security without compromising decentralisation.

© Springer Nature Switzerland AG 2020
Z. Liu and M. Yung (Eds.): Inscrypt 2019, LNCS 12020, pp. 309–322, 2020.
https://doi.org/10.1007/978-3-030-42921-8_18

Sharding is a concept introduced from traditional database discipline. It divides a database into horizontal partitions (i.e. shards) to achieve scalability. But sharding in a blockchain is quite different because it requires validating transactions with partial data of the ledger history. Some notable theoretical work under this topic include [4,5,17]. Compared to these pioneers which do not support full sharding or provide solutions for single-shard attacks, a most recent work, Monoxide [11], achieves full sharding with its main concept "Asynchronous Consensus Zones" and introduces a new mining strategy called "Chu-ko-nu Mining" to defend single-shard attacks.

Monoxide's Asynchronous Consensus Zones. In Monoxide, the entire network is partitioned into 2^k zones, where k is the sharding scale. For each zone, there is an independent chain built by the miners who belong to that zone. Cross-zone transactions are handled asynchronously, which means the withdraw operation is executed first in zone A, and later the corresponding deposit operation is executed in zone B [11] (Fig. 1).

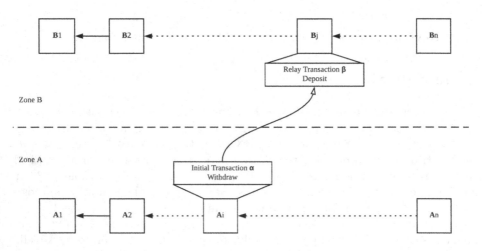

Fig. 1. Asynchronous cross-zone transactions

Single-Shard Attack and Chu-ko-nu Mining. A single-shard attack is an attack that only takes down one zone in this system. To successfully launch this attack, the attacker only needs more than 50% hash power of one single zone, rather than the mining power of the entire network. When the hash power P of the network is evenly distributed in zones, which is an ideal case for scalability, the attack bar is $P/2^k \times 50\%$ [11]. It is obvious that this number is unacceptably low when k is large. To address this issue, Monoxide has introduced Chu-ko-nu mining [11], which allows miners to create multiple blocks in different zones with one PoW solution. This makes the hash power participating in Chu-ko-nu mining not only present in one zone, but in multiple zones. With this amplification, the hash power in one zone can approach the value in the entire network when the proportion of hash power participating in Chu-ko-nu mining is close to 1, which raises the attack bar for single-shard attack close to it for attacking the entire system.

However, this security highly depends on the proportion of the hash power that participates in Chu-ko-nu mining. Although there are incentives driving miners to use it, there may still be circumstances in which this proportion is not large enough to guarantee the security (e.g. in early stages of the system).

To fill this gap, we propose a new consensus algorithm, Greedy Observed Largest Forest (GOLF). It is a variant of the Greedy Observed Heaviest Sub-Tree (GHOST) algorithm [9] tailored for this system. With this algorithm, the system achieves the same security level as the best case of the current design against single-shard attacks, but with a lower requirement for the proportion of the hash power participating in Chu-ko-nu mining.

Contributions

In this paper, we have two main contributions. First, we formalise the attack model of single-shard attacks in systems implementing sharding like Monoxide either with or without Chu-ko-nu mining. This provides theoretical fundamentals for further research under this topic. Second, we propose the Greedy Observed Largest Forest (GOLF) algorithm, which enhances the security of the system with lower requirements, against one type of attackers described in our model.

2 The Attack Model

2.1 The System

As mentioned in Sect. 1, the system is a multi-chain blockchain system with $n = 2^k$ chains growing concurrently in their respective zones. Blocks are created by miners solving proof-of-work puzzles. A miner can choose to do Chu-ko-nu mining or not. Only one block will be created (in the miner's zone) with a PoW solution if the miner chooses not to use Chu-ko-nu miner. We call this type of miner sole miners. The behaviour of a single zone and sole miners is just like systems without sharding such as Bitcoin. If the miner chooses to do Chu-ko-nu mining, a single PoW solution is able to create n' blocks in n' consecutive zones and n' could be equal to n [11]. We call this type of miners batch miners. For simplicity, we assume $n' = n$ at all times, which means batch miners always choose to create blocks in all zones. The blocks created with Chu-ko-nu mining are called batch blocks, and batch blocks created with the same PoW solution are "isotopes" to each other.

We assume the total hash power of all honest miners is H. The proportion of honest mining power that participates in Chu-ko-nu mining is $\alpha(0 \leq \alpha \leq 1)$, and $1 - \alpha$ is the proportion not participating. Thus, the hash power of batch miners is αH, while the number of sole miners is $(1 - \alpha)H$. If the hash power distributes evenly as predicted [11], the hash power of honest miners in each zone is $\alpha H + \dfrac{(1 - \alpha)H}{n}$.

2.2 The Attack

Figure 2 illustrates a simple attack trying to achieve double spend in a blockchain system. The attacker first spends her coins in a transaction included in the blue coloured block. And she prepares a secret side-chain forked from the parent of this block, which contains a conflicting transaction double-spending the coins. Once the transaction in the blue block is accepted by the merchant, which typically require N-confirmation, she can publish her side chain in the hope of overtaking the main chain. The attack succeeds when the side chain has more blocks and is recognised as the new main chain by honest miners, which requires that the attacker possesses more hash power than the honest miners.

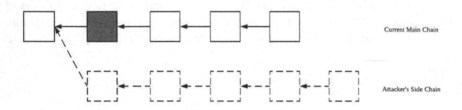

Current Main Chain

Attacker's Side Chain

Fig. 2. Double spending attack (Color figure online)

We assume the hash power of the attacker is M, and the hash power in the entire network is $P = M + H$. The attack succeeds when $M > H$, or in other words, $M > 50\% \times P$, which is known as the 51% attack. The single-shard attack is a variant of this attack in systems that support sharding. The attacker will focus all her hash power in one zone trying to overtake the main chain of that zone. It only requires 51% hash power of one single zone instead of the entire network. Based on our model, the attack succeeds when $M > \alpha H + \dfrac{(1 - \alpha)H}{n}$. From the inequation, we can see when $\alpha = 0$ (i.e. all miners are sole miners), the difficulty of this attack is unacceptably low if n is large. When $\alpha = 1$ (i.e. all miners are batch miners), this attack is as hard as the 51% attack. In practice, the difficulty lies somewhere in between, and we want the attack bar as close as possible to the 51% attack regardless of the value of α.

2.3   The Attacker

In order to better analyse what attackers can do and how to defend them, we classify attackers into three main classes based on their capabilities. In each class, they are further divided into two sub-classes based on whether the attacker performs Chu-ko-nu mining.

Attacker 1. This attacker is the weakest. The hash power of attacker 1 is M_1 and it satisfies $M_1 < \dfrac{H}{n}$. This indicates even when $\alpha = 0$, attacker 1 still cannot successfully launch a single-shard attack if the hash power of honest miners distributes evenly. But when H does not distribute evenly, attacker 1 may be able to successfully attack some zone with lower hash power in it.

Attacker 2. The hash power M_2 of attacker 2 satisfies $\dfrac{H}{n} < M_2 < H$. This attacker is the most common case in practice and the one which our research mainly focuses on. When $\alpha = 0$, the sub-class attacker 2A who does not use Chu-ko-nu mining can successfully attack any zone if H distributes evenly, while the other sub-class attacker 2B who uses Chu-ko-nu mining can take down all zones at the same time. When $\alpha = 1$, this attacker will fail no matter if she uses Chu-ko-nu mining. We aim to guarantee the same level of security regardless of the value of α.

Attacker 3. This attacker is the most powerful one, whose hash power M_3 satisfies $M_3 > H$. Since she possesses more than 50% hash power of the entire network, her attack will always be successful. Defending such powerful attackers who are able to launch 51% attacks is proven feasible with mechanisms described in RepuCoin [16]. Migrating the solution to systems that support sharding will be left for future work and in this study, we focus on defending single-shard attacks launched by the second type of attackers.

3   The Greedy Observed Largest Forest (GOLF)

3.1   The Main Chain

In the early Nakamoto's consensus [6], the main chain is determined with the so-called longest chain rule. As the name indicates, the chain with the largest length is identified as the main chain. With this consensus, the hash power of the honest miners has been weakened due to the network latencies between them. Because of the latency, the local view of an honest miner may not be up-to-date, which makes her mine on old blocks and create forks. But according to the longest chain rule, hash power consumed creating these "sibling blocks" cannot contribute to the main chain competition against the attacker since these blocks do not increase the length (Fig. 3). And the attacker building her side chain will not create forks.

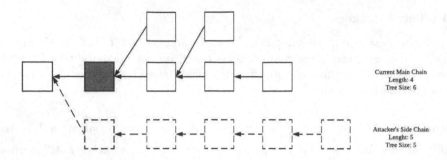

Fig. 3. Longest chain and GHOST

To address this issue, the Greedy Heaviest Observed Sub-Tree (GHOST) algorithm [9] is used in newer systems, as well as in Monoxide [11]. This algorithm compares the tree sizes instead of the chain lengths, which includes all sibling blocks. With this algorithm, the hash power of the honest group is not weakened by forks (Fig. 3), which enables them to compete fairly with the attacker who does not create forks.

3.2 From Trees to Forests

Our new algorithm generalises the idea of the GHOST algorithm from comparing trees to comparing forests. It enables non-batch blocks in one zone to contribute hash power to main chain competition in other zones through batch blocks. In the GOLF algorithm, a batch block shares descendants with its isotopes. Then all the trees rooted from these isotopes form a forest.

An example is shown in Fig. 4. The yellow coloured blocks (A_i and B_j) are batch blocks and they are created with the same PoW solution (i.e. they are isotopes to each other). Block A_i is the root of a tree of 3 blocks, while the tree rooted from block B_j is of 5 blocks. Thus, block A_i and B_j share a forest of 8 blocks. But in this forest, isotopes (A_i and B_j) are created with 1 PoW solution but increase the forest size by 2. To reflect the real hash power consumed, we introduce a transformed structure of this forest, called "collapsed DAG".

We construct a directed acyclic graph $G = (V, E)$ for the forest, in which each group of isotopes are merged into one vertex in the graph. The newly merged vertex inherits all edges from the isotope group members. Then the order $|V|$ of this DAG reflects the real PoW. As an example, the collapsed DAG for the forest in Fig. 4 is shown in Fig. 5, and the order $|V|$ of it is 7. Another example with the order of 6 is shown in Fig. 6.

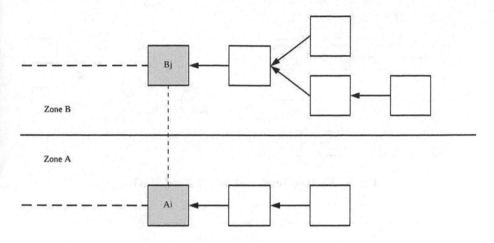

Fig. 4. The forest (Color figure online)

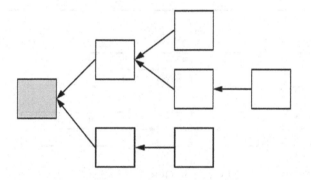

Fig. 5. The collapsed DAG

3.3   Fork Resolution

After introducing the concept of forests and the collapsed DAG, we can explain how the main chain is selected. As shown in Fig. 7, there is a fork resolution in zone A. The forest sizes of the two branches will be compared and the one with a larger forest will finally be selected as the main chain. More precisely, what to be compared is the order of the collapsed DAG. It is easy to compute that this value for branch A_t in zone A is 5. On the other hand, since branch A_b does not contain any batch block, its forest is simply the single tree rooted from it, and in this case, it is a chain of 4 blocks. According to our algorithm, branch A_t is selected as the main chain of the zone, while branch A_b will be the main chain if traditional algorithms are used. This example has shown the "cross-zone confirmation" feature of the algorithm.

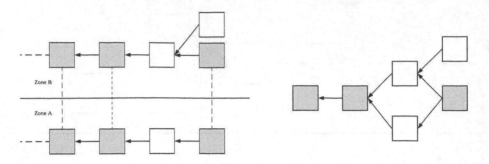

Fig. 6. Another forest and its collapsed DAG

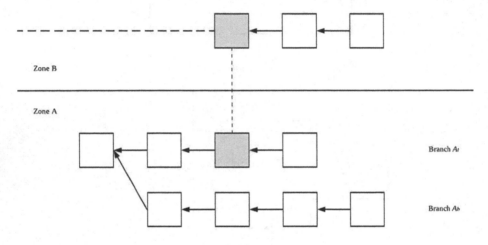

Fig. 7. The GOLF algorithm

This process is explained with the pseudocode of Algorithm 1. From the code we can see, the algorithm keeps going down in the block tree, by selecting the child which has the greatest order of the collapsed DAG corresponding to its forest, until it reaches a leaf block. The main chain is identified as the path from the genesis to the leaf block. The leaf block returned by the algorithm should be the one which honest miners mine on.

3.4 Security Against Attacker 2A

Figure 8 shows an example when the GOLF algorithm is implemented in the system to defend attacker 2A. Since attacker 2A does not use Chu-ko-nu mining, she cannot get any advantage from the consensus algorithm, and her hash power remains M_2. At time t_2, the first batch block after the fork (t_1) is created in the current main chain and it connects all the zones through its isotopes. According to the algorithm, now the attacker is competing with the hash power close to H, and the number becomes equal to H when all honest miners eventually mine on

---

Algorithm 1. Greedy Observed Largest Forest

```
 1  Function GOLF(genesis):
 2  │   block ← genesis
 3  │   while block.children ≠ ∅ do
 4  │   │   block ←      arg max      GetCollapsedGOrder(child)
    │   │            child∈block.children
 5  │   end
 6  │   return block
 7  end

 8  Function GetCollapsedGOrder(block):
 9  │   forest ← GetForest(block)
10  │   G = (V, E) ← Collapse(forest)
11  │   return |V|
12  end
```

---

some descendants of the isotopes. If the attacker publishes her side chain after time point t_2, she has no chance to win since $M_2 < H$.

However, since no batch block is created during the time between t_1 and t_2, the attacker is competing with the hash power of honest miners only in this zone, which is $\dfrac{(1-\alpha)H}{n}$. Based on the definition of attacker 2A, we know she has greater hash power. If the attacker publishes her side chain during this time, the side chain may overtake the honest branch and become the main chain. But the attacker publishes her side chain only after the transaction in the blue block is accepted, otherwise, the double spend fails even when the attacker's side chain becomes the main chain. In other words, if the first yellow block always occurs before the blue block is N-confirmed, the system is secure against attacker 2A.

Since the hash power of batch miners is αH and the value of sole miners in this zone is $\dfrac{(1-\alpha)H}{n}$, the probability that an honest block in this zone will be a batch block is $p = \dfrac{\alpha H}{\alpha H + \dfrac{(1-\alpha)H}{n}}$. Thus, the number of batch blocks X in N honest blocks in this zone has the binomial distribution $X \sim B(N, p)$. Based on this notation, we say that the system is secure against attacker 2A when $\Pr(X < 1)$ is small. We find that the required α is much smaller compared to the original system which requires $\alpha \approx 1$ to be secure [11]. We will further discuss this with experiments in Sect. 4.

To a hundred percent guarantee the yellow block occurs before the transaction in the blue block is accepted, we could add being confirmed by a batch block as a requirement for accepting transactions. Although this may delay the transaction processing when the yellow block occurs after Nth confirmation, the likelihood is low and decrease dramatically when α increases.

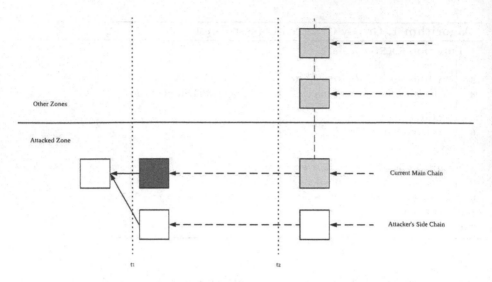

Fig. 8. Defending attacker 2A (Color figure online)

3.5   Security Against Attacker 2B

The main difference here is that attacker 2B can do Chu-ko-nu mining, which indicates she can be empowered by the GOLF algorithm. From the perspective of the attacker, zones can be classified into two types, including victim zones and auxiliary zones. A victim zone is one in which the attacker wants to double-spend. In a victim zone, the attacker will build a side chain competing with honest miners' main chain. On the other hand, an auxiliary zone is used to gather hash power from honest miners to support the attack. In auxiliary zones, the attacker will put her batch blocks in the honest main chain.

For this attacker, we analyse two basic scenarios. In the first scenario, no zone is used as auxiliary zones. All of them are victim zones. In this case, an attacker 2B simply degrades to multiple attacker 2As attacking multiple zones at the same time. The attacker gets no benefit from the GOLF algorithm before any of the zones is compromised. In this scenario, the security of our system remains the same as we analysed in the previous section.

In the second scenario, one zone is targeted as the victim zone, while all other $n-1$ zones are used as auxiliary zones. For simplicity, consider an example with $n=2$, in which there is only one victim zone A and one auxiliary zone B. As shown in Fig. 9, red blocks are batch blocks created by the attacker. Block A_i and B_i are isotopes to each other as well as block A_j and B_j are. We assume that A_i, which is the first batch block created by honest miners after the fork, occurs at time t_1. At time t_2 the attacker begins to publish her blocks. Block B_j is the first red block included in the main chain of zone B.

Based on the analysis in the previous section, the system can easily guarantee block A_i occurs before the transaction in the blue block is accepted. If $t_2 \leq t_1$, the side chain is released before the transaction is accepted and the double spend fails. If $t_2 > t_1$, block B_j will be a descendant of block B_i. In this case, the tree of block B_j is a sub-tree of block B_i's. Although block B_i contribute a larger tree to its forest than block B_j does, the difference becomes constant when all new blocks in zone B eventually are descendants of both blocks. This can be considered that the attacker's gathered hash power from auxiliary zones cancels out the honest miners'. Due to this reason, the attacker is competing with honest hash power only in the victim zone, which is $\alpha H + \dfrac{(1-\alpha)H}{n}$. This attack bar is as same as the original system and is not secure against attacker 2B when $\alpha < 1$.

Although the attack works in the second scenario, the attacker has to use all other $n-1$ zones as auxiliary zones to cancel out honest hash power from all other zones. This indicates the attacker can attack only one zone at a time. In practice, depending on the hash power and the number of zones, the attacker may be able to attack multiple zones. But compared to the original system in which attacker 2B is able to attack all zones at the same time, here the attacker's capability is limited by the GOLF algorithm.

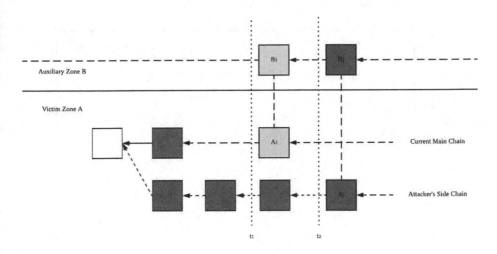

Fig. 9. Defending attacker 2B (Color figure online)

4   Experimental Results

We implemented a simple experimental environment with n zones according to our attack model (we set $n = 8$ in the following experiments). In each zone, honest miners mine on the main chain, whose communications have no delay. An attacker 2A builds a secret side chain in the first zone and publishes her side chain as soon as the honest branch has N confirmations (we set $N = 5$ in the following experiments). The attacker wins when the side chain has more blocks than the honest branch. We experiment on different settings with various α values and hash power M of the attacker. For each setting, we run the experiment 2500 rounds and calculate the winning percentage of the attacker when two different consensus algorithms are used, which are GOLF and single-zone GHOST.

In the first experiment, we set the attacker's hash power to a fixed value $M = 0.8 \times H$ and see how the winning percentage changes against different α values. The results are shown in Fig. 10. We can see when $\alpha = 0$ and $\alpha = 1$ the winning percentage are same for the two algorithms. But the values in between are quite different. When GOLF is used, the value drops down significantly at the beginning. Based on the discussion in Sect. 3.4, we know this is because the $\Pr(X \geq 1)$ increase significantly when α increases. With this probability, the attacker is competing with the hash power close to H and the winning percentage approaches the value when $\alpha = 1$. The curve becomes flatter when this probability is close to 1. On the other hand, when single-zone GHOST is used, the attacker is competing with the hash power of $\alpha H + \dfrac{(1-\alpha)H}{n}$. We can see the attacker always has a higher chance to win with single-zone GHOST than GOLF.

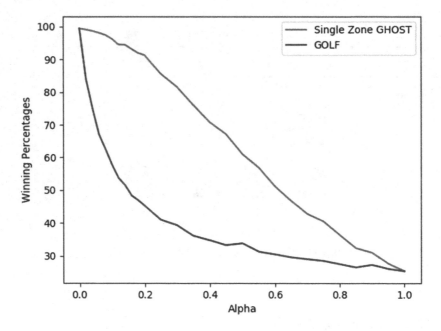

Fig. 10. Winning percentage against alpha

In the second experiment, we repeat the first experiment for a range of $M(0 \leq M \leq H)$ values, and plot the winning percentage against every combination of M and α in 3-dimensional diagrams. In Fig. 12, the surface is relatively flat unless

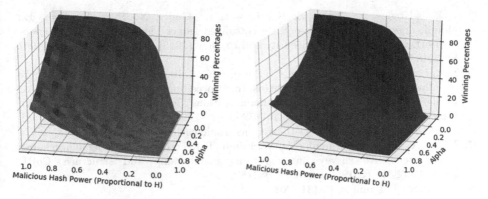

Fig. 11. Single zone GHOST   **Fig. 12.** GOLF

α is very close to 0. This can be explained by the first experiment. It shows that most of the time the difficulty for the attacker to launch the single-shard attack is close to the one for 51% attack ($\alpha = 1$ cross section) when GOLF is used. On the other hand, the winning percentage is equal or greater for all M and α combinations when single-zone GHOST is used (Fig. 11).

5   Conclusion

We proposed the GOLF consensus algorithm, which is a variant of GHOST tailored for multi-shard systems that support Chu-ko-nu mining [11], to defend single-shard attacks. With this new algorithm, the difficulty for launching single-shard attacks can approach the level of 51% attacks with lower α values. Thus, the system can be secure against attacker 2A without needing all honest miners doing Chu-ko-nu mining. Although the algorithm cannot guarantee the security against attacker 2B, it limits the attacker's ability to attack multiple zones at the same time. We leave guaranteeing security against attacker 2B and 3 as open challenges for future work.

Acknowledgments. We thank Dr. Jiaping Wang (Microsoft) for providing implementation level details of Monoxide and valuable comments on our work.

References

1. Baird, L.: The Swirlds hashgraph consensus algorithm: fair, fast, byzantine fault tolerance. Swirlds Tech report (2016). https://doi.org/10.1021/jp4051403
2. Churyumov, A.: Byteball: a decentralized system for storage and transfer of value (2016). https://byteball.org/Byteball.pdf
3. Croman, K., et al.: On scaling decentralized blockchains. In: Clark, J., Meiklejohn, S., Ryan, P.Y.A., Wallach, D., Brenner, M., Rohloff, K. (eds.) FC 2016. LNCS, vol. 9604, pp. 106–125. Springer, Heidelberg (2016). https://doi.org/10.1007/978-3-662-53357-4_8

4. Kokoris-Kogias, E., Jovanovic, P., Gasser, L., Gailly, N., Syta, E., Ford, B.: OmniLedger: a secure, scale-out, decentralized ledger via sharding. In: Proceedings - IEEE Symposium on Security and Privacy (2018). https://doi.org/10.1109/SP.2018.000-5

5. Luu, L., Narayanan, V., Zheng, C., Baweja, K., Gilbert, S., Saxena, P.: A secure sharding protocol for open blockchains. In: Proceedings of the 2016 ACM SIGSAC Conference on Computer and Communications Security - CCS 2016 (2016). https://doi.org/10.1145/2976749.2978389

6. Nakamoto, S.: Bitcoin: a peer-to-peer electronic cash system (2008)

7. Natoli, C., Yu, J., Gramoli, V., Veríssimo, P.J.E.: Deconstructing blockchains: a comprehensive survey on consensus, membership and structure. CoRR abs/1908.08316 (2019). arxiv:1908.08316

8. Popov, S.: The tangle, p. 131 (2016)

9. Sompolinsky, Y., Zohar, A.: Secure high-rate transaction processing in Bitcoin. In: Böhme, R., Okamoto, T. (eds.) FC 2015. LNCS, vol. 8975, pp. 507–527. Springer, Heidelberg (2015). https://doi.org/10.1007/978-3-662-47854-7_32

10. Sui, Z., Lai, S., Zuo, C., Yuan, X., Liu, J.K., Qian, H.: An encrypted database with enforced access control and blockchain validation. In: Guo, F., Huang, X., Yung, M. (eds.) Inscrypt 2018. LNCS, vol. 11449, pp. 260–273. Springer, Cham (2019). https://doi.org/10.1007/978-3-030-14234-6_14

11. Wang, J., Wang, H.: Monoxide: scale out blockchains with asynchronous consensus zones. In: 16th USENIX Symposium on Networked Systems Design and Implementation (NSDI 2019) (2019)

12. Wijaya, D.A., Liu, J., Steinfeld, R., Liu, D.: Senarai: a sustainable public blockchain-based permanent storage protocol. In: Mu, Y., Deng, R.H., Huang, X. (eds.) CANS 2019. LNCS, vol. 11829. Springer, Cham (2019). https://doi.org/10.1007/978-3-030-31578-8_13

13. Wijaya, D.A., Liu, J.K., Suwarsono, D.A., Zhang, P.: A new blockchain-based Value-Added Tax system. In: Okamoto, T., Yu, Y., Au, M.H., Li, Y. (eds.) ProvSec 2017. LNCS, vol. 10592, pp. 471–486. Springer, Cham (2017). https://doi.org/10.1007/978-3-319-68637-0_28

14. Yu, B., et al.: Platform-independent secure blockchain-based voting system. In: Chen, L., Manulis, M., Schneider, S. (eds.) ISC 2018. LNCS, vol. 11060, pp. 369–386. Springer, Cham (2018). https://doi.org/10.1007/978-3-319-99136-8_20

15. Yu, B., Wright, J., Nepal, S., Zhu, L., Liu, J.K., Ranjan, R.: IoTChain: establishing trust in the Internet of Things ecosystem using blockchain. IEEE Cloud Comput. 5(4), 12–23 (2018)

16. Yu, J., Kozhaya, D., Decouchant, J., Verissimo, P.: RepuCoin: your reputation is your power. IEEE Trans. Comput. (2019). https://doi.org/10.1109/TC.2019.2900648

17. Zamani, M., Movahedi, M., Raykova, M.: RapidChain: scaling blockchain via full sharding. In: Proceedings of the 2018 ACM SIGSAC Conference on Computer and Communications Security - CCS 2018 (2018). https://doi.org/10.1145/3243734.3243853

18. Zhong, L., Wang, H., Xie, J., Qin, B., Liu, J.K., Wu, Q.: A flexible instant payment system based on blockchain. In: Jang-Jaccard, J., Guo, F. (eds.) ACISP 2019. LNCS, vol. 11547, pp. 289–306. Springer, Cham (2019). https://doi.org/10.1007/978-3-030-21548-4_16

Side Channel Attacks

Evaluating the Cache Side Channel Attacks Against ECDSA

Ziqiang Ma[1,2,3], Quanwei Cai[1,2($\boxtimes$)], Jingqiang Lin[1,2], Jiwu Jing[2,4], Dingfeng Ye[1,2], and Lingjia Meng[1,2,3]

[1] State Key Laboratory of Information Security,
Institute of Information Engineering, Chinese Academy of Sciences, Beijing, China
{maziqiang,caiquanwei,linjingqiang,yedingfeng,menglingjia}@iie.ac.cn
[2] Data Assurance and Communication Security Research Center,
CAS, Beijing, China
jingjiwu@iie.ac.cn
[3] School of Cyber Security, University of Chinese Academy of Sciences,
Beijing, China
[4] School of Computer Science and Technology,
University of Chinese Academy of Sciences, Beijing, China

Abstract. Various attacks are proposed against different ECDSA implementations: the key-related data are acquired through cache side channels, and then processed to recover the private key. For each cache side channel attack, the requirements of the data qualified for sequent processing vary greatly, and the success probability of private key recovery relies on both the acquired data and the parameters of data processing. So it is difficult to tell, for a certain ECDSA implementation, (*a*) how many signatures does a cache side channel attack need to recover the private key? or which attack performs the best? and (*b*) what kind of threat level exists due to potential side channel attacks, if the ECDSA implementation runs for a number of signatures on an unprotected system with cache side channels? Currently, there is no quantitative metric to fairly answer the questions. Such a metric to evaluate cache side channel attacks, will provide a reference for the adversaries to choose the suitable attack, and also for the defenders to set up protections for the certain ECDSA implementation (e.g., updating the private key after it has been used for a certain number of signatures). In this paper, we design an evaluation approach to quantitatively compare the cache side channel attacks against ECDSA. *The expected minimum number of signatures needed for at least one successful private key recovery*, is proposed as the metric, and this metric considers both the data requirements and the success probability. We apply the approach to evaluate various cache side channel attacks against ECDSA. By calculating the metric, we obtain (*a*) for each attack, the optimal parameters with the minimum number of signatures needed, and (*b*) for each ECDSA implementation, the minimum number of signatures that will be enough for at least one successful private key recovery of some cache side channel attacks.

© Springer Nature Switzerland AG 2020
Z. Liu and M. Yung (Eds.): Inscrypt 2019, LNCS 12020, pp. 325–345, 2020.
https://doi.org/10.1007/978-3-030-42921-8_19

Keywords: ECDSA · Cache side channel attack · Lattice attack · Evaluation

1 Introduction

The Elliptic Curve Digital Signature Algorithm (ECDSA) [2,17] is widely used in popular applications, such as TLS [35], OpenPGP [16], and Bitcoin [24]. The core operation of ECDSA is the scalar multiplication of a base point (or generator) over elliptic curves for a random nonce (or ephemeral key). The semantical security of ECDSA relies on the computational intractability to find the ephemeral key for any given pair of a scalar multiplication and a base point, i.e., the elliptic curve discrete logarithm problem (ECDLP).

Although ECDLP is hard to break theoretically, the implementation of the scalar multiplication is vulnerable to side channel attacks. Various cache side channel attacks [4,8,9,30,37–39] are proposed to obtain the (partial) ephemeral key during the scalar multiplication, and then the ECDSA private key will be directly derived based on the leaked ephemeral key. For different scalar multiplication implementations of ECDSA, the side channel attacks are as follows:

- For the double-and-add implementation, the differential power attack (DPA) is exploited to directly obtain the ephemeral key [8], which can be acquired through cache side channels similarly.
- For the Montgomery ladder implementation [23], Yarom [38] exploited the Flush+Reload cache side channel [39] to obtain the data on the execution of the if-statement branch in the scalar multiplication, and then recovered the ephemeral key of ECDSA implemented in OpenSSL 1.0.1e.
- For the windowed Non-Adjacent Form (wNAF) implementation [11,18,22, 34], the side channel attackers firstly obtain the (partial) bits of the ephemeral keys, use the extracted information to construct a Hidden Number Problem (HNP) or Extended Hidden Number Problem (EHNP) instance, and recover the private key by solving the closest vector problem (CVP) or shortest vector problem (SVP) converted from the HNP or EHNP instance in lattices [15,26– 28]. For example, Benger et al. [4] obtained the least significant bits (LSBs) of the ephemeral keys to conduct lattice attacks, and Van de Pol et al. [30] constructed more effective lattice attacks based on the positions of higher half non-zero digits of the wNAF representation of the ephemeral keys. Fan et al. [9] utilized the EHNP to launch the lattice attacks using all positions of non-zero digits, and then Wang et al. [37] presented another lattice attack based on the positions of two non-zero digits together with the length of the wNAF representation of the ephemeral keys.

Generally, every cache side channel attack against ECDSA consists of two stages: (1) Data acquisition, attackers exploit the cache side channels to monitor the execution of the sensitive code and obtain the information about the ephemeral key; and (2) Data processing, the attackers process the acquired data to recover the private key. For the double-and-add and Montgomery ladder implementations, the private key is recovered directly, as all bits of the ephemeral key are obtained in the data acquisition (although some error bits may exist). While for the wNAF implementation, the lattice-based processing recovers the private key from the partial information of the ephemeral keys.

Moreover, the cache side channel attacks against the wNAF implementation are not always successful.

- The data processing accepts only the data set that satisfies certain requirements, so it has a probability that some data acquired in the first stage are not qualified for the attacks. For instance, Benger's attack [4] requires the length of the consecutive zeroes in the LSBs of the ephemeral key is not less than some positive value (e.g., 1 or 2).
- It has a probability to recover the ECDSA private key, even when all acquired data satisfy the specified requirements. This success probability is related to the lattice dimension, the lattice reduction algorithm (LLL [19], or BKZ [32] with different block sizes) and the processed signatures (i.e., the available information from one signature and the number of signatures to construct lattices). For example, a larger dimension, more satisfying data and a more complex lattice reduction algorithm for Benger's attack will result in a higher success probability [4].

Some attack evaluations provide the least number of signatures needed and the corresponding success probability for specified conditions and parameters. However, none of them can serve as the quantitative metric to fairly compare these side channel attacks, because the requirements on signatures, the success probability and the parameters of data processing vary significantly for different attacks. For example, Benger's attack [4] needs 200 signatures under the success probability of 3.5%, while Wang's attack [37] needs 85 under the success probability of 1.5%. We fail to compare these two attacks directly as Benger's attack provides a better success probability while Wang's attack needs fewer signatures. The ratio of the lattice-based processing time and the success probability is adopted as the evaluation metric in [4], however, it fails to reflect the requirements on the acquired signatures, and the offline processing time is not a critical concern compared to the online data acquisition which may be detected by the defenders.

In this paper, we propose a quantitative evaluation approach to compare various cache side channel attacks. We want to compare different attacks by one metric that covers (a) the requirements that the signatures need to satisfy in the data acquisition, and (b) the factors affecting the success probability of private key recovery in the data processing. We adopt *the expected minimum number of signatures that are needed for at least one successful recovery of the private key*, denoted as c, as the metric. For the lattice-based attacks [4,9,30,37] that only obtain the partial ephemeral key, we combine the success probability of the data processing with the number of signatures needed in the data acquisition, and adopt the geometric distribution model to calculate c. For the attacks [8,38] that obtain the ephemeral key directly in the data acquisition, c is only 1, as the whole ephemeral key is obtained through one signature and the private key is derived directly from the ephemeral key.

We applied our evaluation approach and calculated the quantitative metric c for existing typical cache side channel attacks on various ECDSA implementations. For the double-and-add and Montgomery ladder implementations, c is 1 due to the attacks [8,38] obtaining the complete information on the ephemeral key. For each lattice attack against wNAF, we firstly calculate the minimum number of signatures needed for at least one successful key recovery for different lattice dimensions and lattice reduction algorithms, determine the optimal parameters for this attack, and choose the corresponding minimum number of signatures as c. The comparison results show that Fan's attack [9] needs the least c (i.e., 6), for the wNAF implementation of ECDSA.

This quantitative metric provides a reference for the adversaries to choose the most applicable attack, and also helps to improve the ECDSA implementations in the private key protection. The attackers will choose the best cache side channel attack needing the least number of signatures in the data acquisition (not the number of satisfying signatures in the data processing). The attackers can refer to the metric to decide the number of signatures to be monitored in the data acquisition, to avoid being detected by the defenders. Note that if the data acquisition lasts too long, the attack may be probably detected by some system solutions. On the other hand, to protect the private key, the defenders may limit the number of signatures obtained by the adversaries, to prevent certain attacks. For example, the defenders may flush the system caches and reboot the system from a clean state, or even update the ECDSA private key after it has already been used to generate a specified number of signatures.

The main contributions of our paper are summarized as follows:

- We propose a quantitative metric, for the first time, to systematically evaluate various cache side channel attacks on different ECDSA implementations. This evaluation metric provides a reference for the attacks comparison and also private key protection.
- We analyze the existing cache side channel attacks based on the proposed metric, choose the optimal parameters for each lattice attack, and find the least number of signatures needed to be obtained in the data acquisition for at least one successful ECDSA private key recovery (but not the least number of satisfying signatures for possible private key recovery [4,9,30,37]).

The rest of this paper is organized as follows. We introduce the backgrounds in Sect. 2. Then, we provide the details about our evaluation approach in Sect. 3, apply it to systematically analyze existing cache side channel attacks in Sect. 4, and present some discussions in Sect. 5. Finally, Sect. 6 draws the conclusion.

2   Background

This section presents various scalar multiplication algorithms in ECDSA implementations, and then introduces the corresponding cache side channel attacks.

2.1   Scalar Multiplication Algorithms in ECDSA Implementations

We first present the signature generation of ECDSA [2,17]. The ECDSA public parameters include (1) the elliptic curve E defined over a finite field $\mathbb{F}$; and (2) the generator $G \in E$ of the order q. The private key is an integer α satisfying $0 < \alpha < q$, and the public key is the point $Q = \alpha G$. Given a hash function h, the ECDSA signature (r, s) of a message m is computed as follows:

1. Select a random ephemeral key $0 < k < q$.
2. Compute the point $(x, y) = kG$ [1], and let $r = x \bmod q$; if $r = 0$, go to Step 1.
3. Compute $s = k^{-1}(h(m) + r \cdot \alpha) \bmod q$; if $s = 0$, go back to Step 1.

The scalar multiplication kG becomes the target of side channel attacks to infer the ephemeral key k. Then, as shown in Step 3, the private key α will be derived if k is leaked, as $h(m)$, r and s are publicly known. Even when only partial k is leaked, the private key can be recovered by lattice attacks [27,28].

The most common scalar multiplication method is the double-and-add algorithm in Algorithm 1. The scalar k is expressed as $k = \sum_{i=0}^{l-1} 2^i k_i$, where $k_i \in \{0,1\}$ and l is the length of the binary expression. When computing the scalar multiplication, it iterates from the most significant bit to the least significant bit of k. In each bit, it performs a double function. And if the bit is 1, it performs an extra add function.

The Montgomery ladder [23] is shown in Algorithm 2. When computing the scalar multiplication, both a doubling and an addition of points are performed for each bit of k. Each k_i controls which branch of the if-statement is executed, that is, which point is doubled and where the doubling and addition of points are stored.

Algorithm 1. The double-and-add implementation of kG

Input: k in binary: $k_0, k_1, ..., k_{l-1}$
Output: kG
1: $Q \leftarrow G$
2: **for** i from $l - 2$ to 0 **do**
3:      $Q \leftarrow 2 \cdot Q$
4:      **if** $k_i = 1$ **then**
5:          $Q \leftarrow Q + G$
6:      **end if**
7: **end for**

Algorithm 2. The Montgomery ladder implementation of kG

Input: k in binary: $k_0, k_1, ..., k_{l-1}$
Output: kG
1: $R0 \leftarrow 0, R1 \leftarrow G$
2: **for** i from $l - 1$ to 0 **do**
3:      **if** $k_i = 0$ **then**
4:          $R1 \leftarrow R0 + R1$, $R0 \leftarrow 2R0$
5:      **else**
6:          $R0 \leftarrow R0 + R1$, $R1 \leftarrow 2R1$
7:      **end if**
8: **end for**
9: **return** R0

The wNAF implementation [11,18,22,34] is designed to reduce the addition operation in the scalar multiplication. The wNAF representation of $k =$

---

[1] In practical implementations, the ephemeral key is added by q or $2q$ to make sure that k is $\lfloor \log_2 q \rfloor + 1$ bit long and resist the remote timing side channel attack in [6].

Algorithm 3. Implementation of kG Using wNAF

Input: k in wNAF: $k_0, k_1, ..., k_{l-1}$ and pre-computed points $\{\pm G, \pm 3G, ..., \pm (2^{w-1})G\}$
Output: kG
  1: $Q \leftarrow G$
  2: **for** i from $l - 1$ to 0 **do**
  3:    $Q \leftarrow 2 \cdot Q$
  4:    **if** $k_i \neq 0$ **then**
  5:       $Q \leftarrow Q + k_i G$
  6:    **end if**
  7: **end for**

$\sum_{i=0}^{l-1} 2^i k_i$ is a sequence of digits which is either zero or an odd number satisfying $-2^w < k_i < 2^w$ and at least w zeros between any two continuous non-zero values, where w is the window size and l is the length of the wNAF representation. After converting k to the wNAF form, the multiplication kG is executed as described in Algorithm 3, which contains a double operation for every digit and an extra addition operation for every non-zero digit.

2.2 Cache Side Channel Attacks

Attacks Against the Double-and-Add Algorithm. For the double-and-add algorithm, the if-statement block (Line 4) in Algorithm 1 is executed only when $k_i = 1$. Attackers monitor the conditional branches through side channels by a malicious spy process. If the execution of the if-statement block is monitored, the corresponding bit of k is 1 ($k_i = 1$); otherwise $k_i = 0$. Thus, the whole ephemeral key is leaked.

The power analysis [8] is utilized to monitor of the execution of if-statement blocks, and cache-based side channels can be also built to monitor it. For example, the Flush+Reload cache side channel attack [39] may be adopted to monitor the execution of if-statement blocks, to obtain the ephemeral key.

Attacks Against the Montgomery Ladder Algorithm. In this implementation, a doubling and an addition always occur at each branch, no matter k_i is 0 or 1. Thus, it thwarts side channel attacks based on the variations of timing or power introduced by different operations for $k_i = 0$ or 1.

Yarom [38] utilized the Flush+Reload cache side channel attack on the Montgomery ladder algorithm, to monitor which branch is executed at each bit of k. Lines 4 and 6 in Algorithm 2 are monitored respectively to determine which point is doubled and where the addition of points is stored (i.e., which branch of the if-statement is executed), so that the bits of k are revealed.

Attacks Against the wNAF Algorithm. For the wNAF algorithm, the conditional if-statement block (Line 4 in Algorithm 3) is vulnerable to side channel attacks. Then, the attacker obtains a "double-add" chain which is used to determine whether each digit k_i of the wNAF representation is zero or not. But the obtained information is not enough to determine the whole ephemeral key, and only some bits of the ephemeral key are extracted in the data acquisition.

$$|\alpha t_i - u_i|_q \leq q/2^{\theta+1}, \quad 1 \leq i \leq n, |\cdot|_q = \cdot \bmod q, |\cdot|_q \in [-q/2, q/2) \qquad (1)$$

$$a_i\alpha + \sum_{j=1}^{\lambda_i} \beta_{i,j}k_{i,j} \equiv b_i \quad \bmod q, \quad 1 \leq i \leq n, \qquad (2)$$

The attacker constructs the HNP [5] or EHNP [14] instance, by converting $s = k^{-1}(h(m) + r \cdot \alpha) \bmod q$ with the obtained partial information into Eq. 1 defined by HNP or Eq. 2 for EHNP, where the private key is the hidden number. Then, the attacker solves the SVP/CVP problem in lattices using the lattice reduction algorithm, which is converted from HNP or EHNP. In Eq. 1, α is the hidden number to be recovered with n known pairs of (t_i, u_i), while q is a prime number and θ is known; and the problem is expressed to recover α, with n known θ most significant bits (MSBs) of αt_i where t_i is a random value. In Eq. 2, α is the number to be recovered with n known congruences where q is a prime number, $a_i, \beta_{i,j}, b_i, \lambda_i$ and $\varepsilon_{i,j}$ are known and $0 \leq k_{i,j} \leq 2^{\varepsilon_{i,j}}$ is unknown; and the problem is expressed to find a value α satisfying the n provided congruences.

In particular, Benger et al. [4] used the extracted LSBs of the ephemeral keys to launch the lattice attack by an HNP problem. Each signature contributes one (t_i, u_i, l_i) triple satisfying $|\alpha t_i - u_i|_q \leq q/2^{l_i+1}$, where l_i is the length of the LSBs. If l_i is larger, the lattice dimension becomes smaller and the success probability of the lattice-based data processing (or key recovery) becomes higher. However, a larger l_i requires more (t_i, u_i, l_i) triples, and therefore more signatures are needed. Besides, given a lattice dimension, the success probability of the lattice attack is still related to the lattice reduction algorithm (LLL [19] or BKZ [32] with different block sizes), and the choice between CVP and SVP.

Van de Pol et al. [30] used the position information of the ephemeral key's higher half non-zero digits to construct an HNP instance. Each signature contributes multiple $(t_i, u_i, \delta_i - w)$ triples satisfying $|\alpha t_i - u_i|_q \leq q/2^{\delta_i - w+1}$, where δ_i is the distance between the consecutive non-zero digits of the ephemeral key, and w is the window size of the wNAF representation. The value $\delta_i - w$ should be neither too small nor too large. The lattice dimension becomes smaller if $\delta_i - w$ is larger, but there will be fewer triples available to be extracted from one signature if $\delta_i - w$ is too large. Finally, the success probability is influenced by the number of satisfying signatures, the lattice dimension, the lattice reduction algorithm and the adoption of CVP or SVP.

Fan et al. [9] used all position information of the ephemeral key's non-zero digits to construct an EHNP instance, and converted it to SVP for the lattice-based key recovery. In the basic attack [9], all signatures are utilized. Using more signatures results in higher success probabilities, but meanwhile the dimension increases rapidly, making the lattice too large to be solved. Three optimizations were presented to decrease the lattice dimension, including reducing the number of unknown variables, recovering the most significant digits (MSDs) and enumerating the MSDs. Different combinations of these optimizations may be adopted, which results in various lattice dimensions and success probabilities.

Table 1. The results of different lattice attacks.

Attack	Signature number	Success prob.	Lattice dimension	Reduction algorithm	CVP or SVP	Data requirement
Benger's [4]	200	3.5%	102	BKZ-30	SVP	$l_i \geq 2$
Van de Pol's [30]	10	7.0%	76	BKZ-20	CVP	$\delta_i - w \geq 3$
Fan's [9]	4	8%	–	BKZ-25	SVP	–
Wang's [37]	85	1.5%	87	BKZ-30	SVP	–

Wang et al. [37] used the positions of two non-zero digits and the length of the wNAF representation, to construct an HNP instance. Each signature contributes one (t_i, u_i, θ_i) triple satisfying $|\alpha t_i - u_i|_q \leq q/2^{\theta_i+1}$. As analyzed above, a larger θ_i results in a smaller lattice dimension and a higher success probability, but needs more triples. In the basic attack [37], all signatures are used to construct the lattice, which means a small θ_i is adopted and results in a large dimension. In the optimization to reduce the dimension [37], θ_i is increased by the data requirements on the signatures, however, this optimization requires more triples (or signatures). Similar to other lattice attacks, the success probability is also related to the dimension and the adopted lattice reduction algorithm, in addition to the number of signatures.

Summary. The attacks on the double-and-add and Montgomery ladder algorithms need only one signature, as the ephemeral key is observed directly through the side channels. However, the attacks on the wNAF algorithm can only obtain the partial ephemeral key through the cache side channel, and need to adopt various lattice attacks to recover the private key.

Each attack on the wNAF algorithm provides the minimum number of signatures with the corresponding success probability under its own parameters and data requirements, as listed in Table 1. The success probability is related to the number of signatures, the lattice dimension, the reduction algorithm, and the choice between CVP and SVP, which lead to very different optimal parameters for these attacks. Moreover, the requirements on the acquired data vary for each attack, and some attacks produce better success probabilities with more signatures, while the others need fewer signatures but with smaller success probabilities. For example, Van de Pol's attack [30] has the strictest requirements, while both Fan's attack [9] and Wang's attack [37] impose no requirement on the acquired data; Wang's attack [37] needs less number of signatures, while Benger's attack [4] achieves better probabilities of private key recovery. Therefore, the ad-hoc results cannot be adopted to compare these attacks fairly.

3   The Evaluation Approach

In this section, we propose an approach to systematically evaluate the cache side channel attacks on ECDSA with different implementations of the scalar multiplication. First, we design a quantitative metric and show that it reflects both the requirement of acquired data and the data processing. Then, we present the calculation of the metric.

3.1 The Selection of the Quantitative Metric

To develop a general method to evaluate the cache side channel attacks, we need to design a quantitative metric systematically reflecting two stages of the attacks:

- In the data acquisition stage, the number of signatures to be monitored is expected to be small. The attackers obtain the data through the cache side channel during the signature generation, which is performed on the victim system and may be detected by the defenders. More data needed, mean more signature generations to be monitored, longer monitoring time and then larger risks to be detected. For example, when the attackers conduct the Flush+Reload cache side channel attack to obtain the "double-add" chains of the wNAF implementations, the defenders may detect the existence of the malicious spy process with a higher possibility if the monitoring lasts longer.
- In the data processing stage, the data is processed offline (i.e., on the attacker's system), longer processing time does not cause the attack to be detected. However, different data processing approaches (i.e., different lattice dimensions, reduction algorithms, choices between CVP and SVP [4,9,30,37]) have different requirements on the acquired signatures. Also the success probability varies for different processing approaches with the same processed data. The different success probabilities and various requirements on data result in different numbers of signatures needed.

We select the expected minimum number of signatures needed for at least one successful private key recovery, as the quantitative metric (denoted as c). This metric considers the stages of both data acquisition and processing: (1) The number of signatures (but not the satisfying signatures) determines the workload of the data acquisition, and it is related to the requirements of the processed data; (2) The prerequisite, at least one successful private key recovery, reflects the effectiveness of data processing, as a better processing approach provides a higher success probability with the acquired data set and meets this prerequisite with fewer signatures. The metric c provides the fair and direct comparison of attacks, and the attack with smaller c works better.

As the information on the ephemeral keys can be obtained by different side channels, we assume no error exists in the data acquired through the side channels. Different side channels provide different levels of error, and the discussion on the imperfect cache side channels, is provided in Sect. 5.1. The metric c is 1 for the attacks against the double-and-add and Montgomery ladder algorithms [8,38]. For these attacks, the whole ephemeral key is obtained directly by observing any signature generation in the data acquisition stage. With the whole ephemeral key, the attackers derive the ECDSA private key as described in Sect. 2.1.

The metric c for the attacks against the wNAF algorithm is more complicated. The attackers can only obtain the partial ephemeral key through the side channel, and need to construct the lattice attack to recover the private key. Therefore for the calculation, it needs to consider the data requirements and the success probability with different parameters. Here, we focus on the calculation of c for cache side channel attacks against the wNAF algorithm, to complete the systematical evaluation on all cache side channel attacks against ECDSA, by comparing it with the results of the attacks against the double-and-add and Montgomery ladder algorithms.

3.2   Calculation of the Metric

To calculate the metric c for each attack against the wNAF algorithm, the following steps are conducted:

- Analyzing the probability (P_r) that one signature satisfies the requirement specified for some data processing. P_r may be derived theoretically [4], or obtained experimentally [30].
- Obtaining the success probability (P_{sl}) for lattice attacks with a specified set of parameters (i.e., dimension, reduction algorithm, SVP/CVP, and the specified requirement on the acquired data). Note that different lattice attacks have different parameters.
- Calculating the expected number (c_l) of signatures needed for at least one successful private key recovery for each set of parameters.
- Selecting the minimum c_l among all the parameter sets, as c for this attack. The corresponding parameter set of the data processing is the optimal one.

P_r is provided in the existing attack evaluation [4,9,30,37]. The success rate is calculated through a large number of experiments as follows: Firstly, we fix the parameter set of the data processing. Then, from a larger set (the size is denoted as n_a) of signatures that satisfying the requirement of the data processing, we choose the required number (denoted as n_r) of signatures randomly, which results $\binom{n_r}{n_a}$ different samples. We assume the data processing on one sample is independent from any others. Finally, we perform the data processing on each sample, and calculate the success rate as P_{sl} approximately.

For the lattice attack with a specified set of parameters, c_l is calculated in three steps:

- Firstly, we calculate the expected number of samples needed for the first successful ECDSA private key recovery. We stop the attack after the first successful recovery, which ensures at least one recovery is successful, while the number of needed signatures is the smallest. Thus we denote the random variable X as the number of samples used when producing the first successful recovery, and it follows the geometric distribution. The probability that n_s samples contribute to the first successful recovery, is $(1-P_{sl})^{n_s-1} * P_{sl}$. Based on the geometric distribution, the expected number of samples for the first successful recovery is $1/P_{sl}$, as shown in Eq. 3.

$$E(X) = \sum_{i=1}^{\infty} i * (1 - P_{sl})^{i-1} * P_{sl} = 1/P_{sl} \qquad (3)$$

- Then, we calculate the needed number (n_a) of signatures that satisfy the requirement of the data processing. As number of samples from n_a signatures is $\binom{n_r}{n_a}$, n_a is the smallest one that satisfies $\binom{n_r}{n_a} \geq 1/P_{sl}$. That is:

$$n_a = \min\{n | \binom{n_r}{n} \geq 1/P_{sl}\} \qquad (4)$$

- Finally, we get c_l, the expected number of signature, either satisfying the requirements or not, needed for at least one successful private key recovery, for the lattice attack with the specified set of parameters based on Eq. 5.

$$c_l = n_a/P_r \qquad (5)$$

4   Evaluating the Existing Cache Side Channel Attacks

In this section, we apply our evaluation approach to cache side channel attacks against ECDSA with different implementations of the scalar multiplication. That is, we calculate c_l for each cache side channel attack with a specified set of parameters and obtain c with the optimal parameter set for the attack. As analyzed above, c is 1 for attacks [38, 39] against the double-and-add and Montgomery ladder algorithms, so we focus on the evaluation of the attacks against the wNAF algorithm.

The metric c, i.e., the minimum c_l, is calculated based on Eqs. 4 and 5, where P_{sl} and n_r are obtained from the original analysis [4, 9, 30, 37]. We obtain P_r, by performing the analysis on the requirement of each set of parameters for the attack; and calculate n_a and c_l for all the presented parameter sets based Eqs. 4 and 5, to find the minimum one. The following results are specific to 256-bit ECDSA.

4.1   Attacks Against the wNAF Algorithm

Benger's Attack [4]. The parameters for the data processing in this attack, include the lattice dimension, choices of SVP or CVP, the length z of the run of zeroes in the least significant bits of the ephemeral key, and the chosen reduction algorithm. The requirement of data processing is that z should not be less than a specified number (e.g., 1 or 2). For $z \geq 1$, which means the last bit of the ephemeral key is 0, therefore the corresponding P_r is 0.5. For $z \geq 2$, which means the last two bits of the ephemeral key are 0, the corresponding P_r is 0.25.

Table 2 lists c_l for the attack with different parameter sets in [4]. We find that a better c_l is obtained when a smaller z is chosen. Therefore, the minimum c_l is resulted with the smallest z, i.e., 1, as z cannot be 0 [4]. c_l increases with

Table 2. The value of c_l for different parameter sets in Benger's attack.

Lattice parameters $(d, \text{-}, z, \text{-})^\dagger$	P_{sl}	c_l
(102, SVP, 1, BKZ-30)	3.5%	202
(112, SVP, 1, BKZ-25)	2%	222
(61, CVP, 2, BKZ-25)	0.5%	248
(66, CVP, 2, BKZ-10)	5.5%	264
(71, CVP, 2, BKZ-15)	29.5%	284
(76, CVP, 2, BKZ-20)	53%	304
(82, SVP, 2, BKZ-20)	22.5%	324
(87, SVP, 2, BKZ-20)	37%	344
(92, SVP, 2, BKZ-15)	23.5%	364
(97, SVP, 2, BKZ-15)	36%	384
(102, SVP, 2, BKZ-15)	33.5%	404
(107, SVP, 2, BKZ-15)	43%	424
(112, SVP, 2, BKZ-15)	49%	444
(117, SVP, 2, BKZ-15)	52%	464
(121, CVP, 2, BKZ-10)	87%	484
(126, CVP, 2, BKZ-10)	93.5%	504
(131, CVP, 2, BKZ-10)	96%	524
(137, SVP, 2, BKZ-10)	55%	544

$^\dagger d$: dimension.

the dimension (d) for a specified z, and the minimum c_l is obtained with the smallest d (i.e., 102) for $z = 1$. The metric c is 202, while the optimal parameters of the data processing are: the dimension equals to 102, SVP is selected, $z = 1$, and the BKZ-30 is adopted. For referring to the analysis in [4], we have to point out that the number of signatures using to construct the lattice is chosen as one parameter in the description of lattice attack, which is $d - 2$ for SVP and $d - 1$ for CVP.

Van de Pol's Attack [30]. The parameter set for this attack includes the number of signatures to construct the lattice, the lattice dimension, the choice between SVP and CVP, the reduction algorithm, and a threshold θ_m for specifying the requirement of the acquired data. In the analysis in [30], the reduction algorithm is fixed, BKZ-20 for SVP and Schnorr-Euchner enumeration (with linear pruning and enumerated nodes as 2^{29}) for CVP.

Unlike in [4] where only least significant bits adopted for the lattice attack, all the higher half non-zero digits of the ephemeral key that satisfy the requirement may be used. The requirement is specified with the threshold θ_m, that is $\delta - w \geq \theta_m$, where δ is the distance between consecutive non-zero digits of the ephemeral key's wNAF transformation, and w is the window width of wNAF. As analyzed

Table 3. The value of c_l for different parameter sets in Van de Pol's attack.

Attack parameters (n_c, d) [§]	SVP		CVP	
	P_{sl}	c_l	P_{sl}	c_l
(10, 60)	0%	–	0.5%	13
(10, 65)	1%	13	2.5%	12
(10, 70)	1.5%	13	4%	12
(10, 75)	1.5%	13	7%	12
(11, 60)	0%	–	0.5%	14
(11, 65)	5%	13	6.5%	13
(11, 70)	2.5%	13	19%	12
(11, 75)	7.5%	13	25%	12
(11, 80)	6%	13	–	–
(12, 60)	2%	14	7%	14
(12, 65)	2.5%	14	10.5%	13
(12, 70)	7.5%	14	29.5%	13
(12, 75)	10.5%	13	38.5%	13
(12, 80)	13%	13	–	–
(12, 85)	8.5%	13	–	–
(12, 90)	15.5%	13	–	–
(13, 60)	3.5%	15	8.5%	14
(13, 65)	6%	15	25.5%	14
(13, 70)	11%	14	46.5%	14
(13, 75)	19%	14	54%	14
(13, 80)	18.5%	14	–	–
(13, 85)	21.5%	14	–	–
(13, 90)	25%	14	–	–

[§]n_c: number of signatures for constructing the lattice; d: number of triples chosen
from the signatures.

in [30], $\theta_m = 3$ is adopted, and a smaller θ_m would not improve the result much. The processing in [30] makes a slight difference in calculating c, that is, we do not need to derive P_r, as every signature contains the non-zero digits satisfying that $\delta - w \geq 3$. And we choose d triples from the signatures to construct the lattice.

Therefore, c_l is calculated for different lattice dimensions ($d+1$ for CVP and $d+2$ for SVP), numbers (n_c) of signatures for constructing the lattice, and the choices of SVP and CVP, while the reduction algorithm and θ_m are fixed. As shown in Table 3, CVP is better than SVP, and the metric c for this attack is 12. There are 5 optimal parameter sets corresponding the metric, ($n_c = 10, d = 65$), ($n_c = 10, d = 70$), ($n_c = 10, d = 75$), ($n_c = 11, d = 70$) and ($n_c = 11, d = 75$), all with CVP chosen.

Table 4. The value of c_l for different parameter sets in Fan's attack.

Attack parameters $(n_c, \text{-}, o)^\ddagger$	P_{sl}	c_l
(7, BKZ-20, C)	24%	8
(7, BKZ-20, A + C)	62%	13.40
(7, BKZ-25, C)	68%	8
(7, BKZ-25, A + C)	94%	13.40
(6, BKZ-20, C)	22%	7
(6, BKZ-20, A + C)	28%	11.73
(6, BKZ-20, A + B + C)	51%	7
(6, BKZ-25, C)	35%	7
(6, BKZ-25, A + C)	61%	11.73
(6, BKZ-25, A + B + C)	90%	7
(5, BKZ-20, C)	1%	9
(5, BKZ-20, A + C)	4.5%	13.40
(5, BKZ-25, C)	4%	8
(5, BKZ-25, A + C)	17%	10.05
(5, BKZ-25, A + B + C)	37.5%	6
(4, BKZ-25, A + C)	1.5%	13.40
(4, BKZ-25, A + B + C)	8%	6

$\ddagger n_c$: number of signatures for the lattice construction; o: the combination of optimizations.

Fan's Attack [9]. This attack constructs an EHNP instance, and converts to the SVP to solve in the lattice. In addition to the basic attack, the authors [9] provide three optimizations to decrease the lattice dimension, which include recovering the MSD (A), enumeration the MSDs (B), and elimination with merging (C). And, any combination of these optimizations may be adopted. As analyzed in [9], the basic attack, optimization B and C have no requirement on the signature ($P_r = 1$). While for optimization A, $P_r = 59.7\%$. But when both A and B are included in the optimization combination, $P_r = 1$; and $P_r = 59.7\%$ when the optimization combination includes A but without B.

Fan et al. [9] extracted all positions of the ephemeral key's digits for the lattice, then one signature contributes one congruences in Eq. 2. Once the number of signatures is fixed for the lattice construction, the dimension is determined. Therefore, instead of specifying the lattice dimension, they adopt the number of signatures (n_c) as the parameter.

Therefore, the parameter set for this attack includes the number of signatures for the lattice construction (n_c), the reduction algorithm and the chosen combination of optimizations. As shown in Table 4, more signatures are needed for choosing the satisfying ones, when both A and C (A+C) are adopted. The metric c of this attack is 6, while there are 2 optimal parameters: $n_c = 4$, or $n_c = 5$, with BKZ-25 and all the optimizations (A+B+C) chosen.

Wang's Attack [37]. This attack translates the problem of recovering ECDSA secret key to the HNP, and adopts SVP to solve the converted problem. In [37], the authors provide the basic attack, which has no requirement on the signature (i.e., $P_r = 1$) and each signature contributes one triple for Eq. 1. To reduce the dimension (making it easier for a lattice reduction algorithm to recover the secret key), and obtain a better success probability with the same lattice dimension, the authors provide three rules for selecting the signatures which contain more leaked bits. The first rule (rule 1) sets constraints on the length of the "double-add" chain, rule 2 contains rule 1 and limits the most significant digit, and rule 3 sets constraints on the least significant digit. As analyzed in [37], the P_r for these three selection rules are 79.325%, 49.4% and 50.0% respectively. Rule 0 means no limit is set on the signature selection, that is $P_r = 1$ for rule 0.

Therefore, the parameters for this attack include the dimension (d), the selection rule (o_s) and the reduction algorithm. As shown in Table 5, P_{sl} increases when any constraint set on the signature selection, however c_l also increases due to P_r. The interesting result is that, the optimal result occurs when no constraint set on the signature selection. That is, the metric for this attack is 86, with the optimal parameters are $d = 87$, BKZ-30 adopted and rule 0 used.

4.2 Summary

We calculate the least number of signatures required for a successful private key recovery, for different cache side channel attacks against ECDSA with different implementations of the scalar multiplication. As shown in Table 6, c is 1 for the attacks against the ECDSA implementations with the double-and-add or Montgomery ladder algorithms, which means that the double-and-add and Montgomery ladder algorithms provide weaker protections compared to the wNAF algorithm. For attacks against the wNAF algorithm, Fan's attack performs the best, of which the metric c is the smallest one (i.e., $c = 6$).

5 Discussion

In this section, we provide the discussion of c for the following four situations: the imperfect side channel, ECDA implementations with protections, other side channel attacks on ECDSA and the attacks on DSA.

5.1 Imperfect Cache Side Channels

In Sect. 4, we provide the calculation of c under the assumption that no error exists in the data acquisition stage, that is, the perfect side channels exist. However, in practice, the side channel is usually imperfect. For example, as analyzed in [4], the Flush+Reload attack may fail to determine whether the double or addition is executed, with a probability (0.55%–0.65%).

Table 5. The value of c_l for different parameter sets in Wang's attack.

Attack parameter $(d, o_s, \text{-})^\P$	P_{sl}	c_l
(67, 0, BKZ-30)	–	–
(67, 1, BKZ-30)	–	–
(67, 2, BKZ-30)	16%	133.60
(67, 3, BKZ-30)	16.5%	132
(72, 0, BKZ-30)	–	–
(72, 1, BKZ-30)	–	–
(72, 2, BKZ-30)	35%	143.72
(72, 3, BKZ-30)	30.5%	142
(77, 0, BKZ-30)	–	–
(77, 1, BKZ-30)	0.5%	97.07
(77, 2, BKZ-30)	36.5%	153.85
(77, 3, BKZ-30)	42%	152
(82, 0, BKZ-30)	–	–
(82, 1, BKZ-25)	1.5%	102.11
(82, 2, BKZ-25)	42%	163.97
(82, 3, BKZ-25)	46.5%	162
(87, 0, BKZ-30)	1.5%	86
(87, 1, BKZ-25)	6%	108.41
(87, 2, BKZ-25)	49.5%	174.09
(87, 3, BKZ-25)	52.5%	172
(92, 0, BKZ-25)	5%	91
(92, 1, BKZ-25)	25%	114.72
(92, 2, BKZ-25)	44.5%	184.21
(92 ,3, BKZ-25)	50%	182

$\P d$: dimension; o_s: selection rules.

The metric c is still 1 for ECDSA implementations with double-and-add and Montgomery ladder algorithms. When some bits (e.g., 5% in [39]) are undetermined from the side channel, the full ephemeral private key may still be recovered at very small cost using the Baby-Step-Giant-Step (BSGS) algorithm [33].

For the attacks against the ECDSA implementation with wNAF algorithm, we need to ensure at least c_p perfect signatures exist. Therefore, the expected minimum number of signatures needed for at least one successful private key recovery (the metric c) becomes c_p/P_c, where c_p is the metric corresponding to perfect side channels, and P_c is the correct rate of the data acquired from the side channel. For Van de Pol's attacks, P_c is 57.7% described in [30], as 577 captures are perfect among 1000 random captures in the data acquisition stage. As stated in [9], P_c is also 57.7% for Fan's attack. For the Berger' attack and Wang's attack, we may also calculate P_c through a large number of experiments.

Table 6. Comparison between the attacks on various ECDSA implementations.

Attack	Lattice dimension	SVP/CVP	Reduction algorithm	n_r	Metric c
Attacks against Double-and-add	–	–	–	1	1
Attacks against Montgomery ladder	–	–	–	1	1
Berger's [4]	102	SVP	BKZ-30	100	202
Van de Pol's [30]	75	CVP	BKZ-20	11	12
Fan's [9]	–	SVP	BKZ-25	5	6
Wang's [37]	87	SVP	BKZ-30	85	86

5.2   ECDSA Implementation with Protections

Various protections are proposed and widely adopted to increase the difficulty for cache side channel attacks, for example, the ephemeral key is protected [8] by a classic blinding (i.e., $k' = k + v * q$ where v is a small random number, and q is the elliptic curve group order), or by a random Euclidean splitting (i.e., $k' = [k/v]v + k\%v$ where v is a random number). Then, only random noisy information, instead of the ephemeral key's bits, is leaked via side channels.

However, there are still side channel attacks [13] against the ECDSA implementations with protections. Goudarzi [13] presented a lattice attack to the ECDSA where the ephemeral key is blinded. When the protection is deployed, the side channel can only recover the noisy bits, the authors propose a filtering method to select a set of blinded bits among all the recovered noisy bits which (1) satisfy the required properties of the lattice attack, and therefore (2) provide the highest possible probability of success. The filtering method is performed based on the likelihood scores, whose distribution is related to a parameter, i.e, multivariate signal-to-noise (ξ).

To calculate c for this attack, we first derive the ratio R of the selected signatures for the filtering method, and then adopt n/R as the metric, where n is the number of selected signatures. The parameters for the attack [13] include the adopted multivariate signal-to-noise (ξ), and (n_{sig}, n_{tr}), i.e., choosing n_{tr} signatures for one experiment from n_{sig} available signatures.

Table 7 lists the number of selected signatures for different size (η) of r, based on the success probability of the lattice attack from the original article [13]. For classic blinding, the c is $2/R$ for all $\eta = 16$, 32 and 64, while the optimal parameters are $\xi = 2$, $n_{sig} = 10$ and $n_{tr} = 1$. For Euclidean blinding, the c is $8/R$ for $\eta = 16$, and the the optimal parameters are $\xi = 2$, $n_{sig} = 20$ and $n_{tr} = 5$; while for $\eta = 32$ and 64, the c is $11/R$, and the the optimal parameters are $\xi = 2$, $n_{sig} = 100$ and $n_{tr} = 10$.

Table 7. The number of filtered signatures in different cases for Goudarzi's attack.

(n_{sig}, n_{tr})	(10, 1)	(20, 5)	(20, 10)	(100, 10)	(100, 50)	(100, 100)
Classic blinding						
$\xi = 1.5, \eta = 16$	8	6	11	11	51	101
$\xi = 1.5, \eta = 32$	29	7	11	11	51	101
$\xi = 1.5, \eta = 64$	500	10	13	13	51	101
$\xi = 2, \eta = 16, 32, 64$	2	6	10	10	50	100
Euclidean blinding						
$\xi = 1.5, \eta = 16, 32, 64$	–	–	–	–	–	–
$\xi = 2, \eta = 16$	143	8	12	11	51	101
$\xi = 2, \eta = 32, 64$	1000	10	13	11	51	101

5.3 Other Side Channel Attacks Against ECDSA

ECDSA is also vulnerable to other side channel attacks, e.g., the power attack and the fault injection attack.

For the power attack [12,21,36], the quantitative metric c is calculated in the same way as described in Sect. 3. The only difference between the power attacks and the cache attacks is in the data acquisition stage. The power attacks exploit the power changes, i.e., power side channel, during the calculation of the scalar multiplication. The mechanisms for acquiring data have no impact on the data processing, therefore the c is calculated in the same way.

The fault attacks [3,7,10,31] inject a fault during the execution of ECDSA and use the faulty outputs to deduce some bits of the ephemeral key. With this partial ephemeral key, a lattice attack is adopted to recover the whole ephemeral key. Therefore, the fault attacks can still be evaluated based on the quantitative metric c, which reflects the number of signatures needed to be acquired through online fault injection; and the metric c is calculated in the same way as described in Sect. 3.

5.4 Applicability of the Attacks Against DSA

The security of DSA [25] is based on the intractability of the discrete logarithm problem in the multiplicative group of finite fields, and in prime order subgroups. However, it is also vulnerable to the side channel attacks. The lattice attacks are mounted to recover the private key with the partial key information extracted from the side channels [1,15,20,27,29]. For example, the attacks [15,20,27] extract the LSBs and MSBs of the ephemeral key for the private key recovery.

The attacks against DSA can also be compared based on the proposed metric, as it reflects the expected number of DSA executions needed to be observed online for at least one successful key recovery. The metric c is calculated in the similar way as for ECDSA, for the data acquisition and processing stages are similar. Also, the optimal parameters will be also obtained for each attack during the calculation of c.

6   Conclusion

In this paper, for the first time, we present a quantitative evaluation approach for the cache side channel attacks against ECDSA with different implementations for the scalar multiplication. We use the expected minimum total number of signatures needed for at least one successful recovery of the private key as the uniform quantitative metric for the attacks. Our evaluation approach is applicable to the attacks against various ECDSA implementations. For each typical attack, the expected minimum number of signatures for successful key recovery is obtained. In particular, for the attacks against ECDSA with the wNAF implementations, we model the data processing stage with the geometric distribution to calculate the metric. We obtain the metric and the corresponding optimal attack parameters for each attack. Among the attacks against the wNAF algorithm, Fan's attack needs the least number of signatures (i.e. 6) to successfully recover the ECDSA private key.

Acknowledgments. This work was supported by the 13th Five-year Informatization Plan of Chinese Academy of Sciences, (Grant No. XXH13507-01) and National Key R&D Program (No. 2017YFB0802100 and No. 2018YFB0804600).

References

1. Acıiçmez, O., Brumley, B.B., Grabher, P.: New results on instruction cache attacks. In: Mangard, S., Standaert, F.-X. (eds.) CHES 2010. LNCS, vol. 6225, pp. 110–124. Springer, Heidelberg (2010). https://doi.org/10.1007/978-3-642-15031-9_8
2. American National Standards Institute: ANSI X9.62-2005, Public Key Cryptography for the Financial Services Industry: The Elliptic Curve Digital Signature Algorithm (ECDSA) (2005)
3. Barenghi, A., Bertoni, G., Palomba, A., Susella, R.: A novel fault attack against ECDSA. In: Proceedings of the IEEE International Symposium on Hardware-Oriented Security and Trust (HOST), pp. 161–166 (2011)
4. Benger, N., van de Pol, J., Smart, N.P., Yarom, Y.: "Ooh Aah... Just a Little Bit": a small amount of side channel can go a long way. In: Batina, L., Robshaw, M. (eds.) CHES 2014. LNCS, vol. 8731, pp. 75–92. Springer, Heidelberg (2014). https://doi.org/10.1007/978-3-662-44709-3_5
5. Boneh, D., Venkatesan, R.: Hardness of computing the most significant bits of secret keys in Diffie-Hellman and related schemes. In: Koblitz, N. (ed.) CRYPTO 1996. LNCS, vol. 1109, pp. 129–142. Springer, Heidelberg (1996). https://doi.org/10.1007/3-540-68697-5_11
6. Brumley, B.B., Tuveri, N.: Remote timing attacks are still practical. In: Atluri, V., Diaz, C. (eds.) ESORICS 2011. LNCS, vol. 6879, pp. 355–371. Springer, Heidelberg (2011). https://doi.org/10.1007/978-3-642-23822-2_20
7. Cao, W., et al.: Two lattice-based differential fault attacks against ECDSA with wNAF algorithm. In: Kwon, S., Yun, A. (eds.) ICISC 2015. LNCS, vol. 9558, pp. 297–313. Springer, Cham (2016). https://doi.org/10.1007/978-3-319-30840-1_19
8. Coron, J.-S.: Resistance against differential power analysis for elliptic curve cryptosystems. In: Koç, Ç.K., Paar, C. (eds.) CHES 1999. LNCS, vol. 1717, pp. 292–302. Springer, Heidelberg (1999). https://doi.org/10.1007/3-540-48059-5_25

9. Fan, S., Wang, W., Cheng, Q.: Attacking OpenSSL implementation of ECDSA with a few signatures. In: Proceedings of the ACM SIGSAC Conference on Computer and Communications Security, (CCS), pp. 1505–1515 (2016)

10. Fouque, P., Lercier, R., Réal, D., Valette, F.: Fault attack on elliptic curve montgomery ladder implementation. In: 5th Workshop on Fault Diagnosis and Tolerance in Cryptography, pp. 92–98 (2008)

11. Gordon, D.M.: A survey of fast exponentiation methods. J. Algorithms **27**(1), 129–146 (1998)

12. Goubin, L.: A refined power-analysis attack on elliptic curve cryptosystems. In: Desmedt, Y.G. (ed.) PKC 2003. LNCS, vol. 2567, pp. 199–211. Springer, Heidelberg (2003). https://doi.org/10.1007/3-540-36288-6_15

13. Goudarzi, D., Rivain, M., Vergnaud, D.: Lattice attacks against elliptic-curve signatures with blinded scalar multiplication. In: Avanzi, R., Heys, H. (eds.) SAC 2016. LNCS, vol. 10532, pp. 120–139. Springer, Cham (2017). https://doi.org/10.1007/978-3-319-69453-5_7

14. Hlaváč, M., Rosa, T.: Extended hidden number problem and its cryptanalytic applications. In: Biham, E., Youssef, A.M. (eds.) SAC 2006. LNCS, vol. 4356, pp. 114–133. Springer, Heidelberg (2007). https://doi.org/10.1007/978-3-540-74462-7_9

15. Howgrave-Graham, N.A., Smart, N.P.: Lattice attacks on digital signature schemes. Des. Codes Crypt. **23**(3), 283–290 (2001)

16. Callas, J., Donnerhacke, L., Finney, H., Shaw, D., Thayer, R.: OpenPGP Message Format (RFC 4880) (2007)

17. Johnson, D., Menezes, A., Vanstone, S.: The elliptic curve digital signature algorithm (ECDSA). Int. J. Inf. Secur. **1**(1), 36–63 (2001)

18. Koyama, K., Tsuruoka, Y.: Speeding up elliptic cryptosystems by using a signed binary window method. In: Brickell, E.F. (ed.) CRYPTO 1992. LNCS, vol. 740, pp. 345–357. Springer, Heidelberg (1993). https://doi.org/10.1007/3-540-48071-4_25

19. Lenstra, A.K., Lenstra, H.W., Lovász, L.: Factoring polynomials with rational coefficients. Math. Ann. **261**(4), 515–534 (1982)

20. Liu, M., Nguyen, P.Q.: Solving BDD by enumeration: an update. In: Dawson, E. (ed.) CT-RSA 2013. LNCS, vol. 7779, pp. 293–309. Springer, Heidelberg (2013). https://doi.org/10.1007/978-3-642-36095-4_19

21. Medwed, M., Oswald, E.: Template attacks on ECDSA. In: Chung, K.-I., Sohn, K., Yung, M. (eds.) WISA 2008. LNCS, vol. 5379, pp. 14–27. Springer, Heidelberg (2009). https://doi.org/10.1007/978-3-642-00306-6_2

22. Miyaji, A., Ono, T., Cohen, H.: Efficient elliptic curve exponentiation. In: Han, Y., Okamoto, T., Qing, S. (eds.) ICICS 1997. LNCS, vol. 1334, pp. 282–290. Springer, Heidelberg (1997). https://doi.org/10.1007/BFb0028484

23. Montgomery, P.L.: Speeding the pollard and elliptic curve methods of factorization. Math. Comput. **48**(177), 243–264 (1987)

24. Nakamoto, S.: Bitcoin: a peer-to-peer electronic cash system (2008). https://bitcoin.org/bitcoin.pdf

25. National Institute of Standards and Technology: FIPS PUB 186-4 Digital Signature Standard (DSS), 19 July 2013

26. Nguyen, P.Q.: The dark side of the hidden number problem: Lattice attacks on DSA. In: Lam, K.Y., Shparlinski, I., Wang, H., Xing, C. (eds.) Cryptography and Computational Number Theory, pp. 321–330. Springer, Basel (2001). https://doi.org/10.1007/978-3-0348-8295-8_23

27. Nguyen, P.Q., Shparlinski, I.E.: The insecurity of the digital signature algorithm with partially known nonces. J. Cryptol. **15**(3), 151–176 (2002)

28. Nguyen, P.Q., Shparlinski, I.E.: The insecurity of the elliptic curve digital signature algorithm with partially known nonces. Des. Codes Crypt. **30**(2), 201–217 (2003)
29. Pereida García, C., Brumley, B.B., Yarom, Y.: Make sure DSA signing exponentiations really are constant-time. In: Proceedings of the ACM SIGSAC Conference on Computer and Communications Security, (CCS), pp. 1639–1650 (2016)
30. van de Pol, J., Smart, N.P., Yarom, Y.: Just a Little Bit More. In: Nyberg, K. (ed.) CT-RSA 2015. LNCS, vol. 9048, pp. 3–21. Springer, Cham (2015). https://doi.org/10.1007/978-3-319-16715-2_1
31. Schmidt, J., Medwed, M.: A fault attack on ECDSA. In: Sixth International Workshop on Fault Diagnosis and Tolerance in Cryptography, (FDTC), pp. 93–99 (2009)
32. Schnorr, C.P., Euchner, M.: Lattice basis reduction: improved practical algorithms and solving subset sum problems. Math. Program. **66**(1–3), 181–199 (1994). https://doi.org/10.1007/BF01581144
33. Shanks, D.: Class number, a theory of factorization, and genera. In: Proceedings of the Symposium of Pure Mathematics, vol. 20, pp. 415–440 (1971)
34. Solinas, J.A.: Efficient arithmetic on koblitz curves. Des. Codes Crypt. **19**(2), 195–249 (2000)
35. Dierks, T., Rescorla, E.: The Transport Layer Security (TLS) Protocol Version 1.2 (RFC 5246) (2008)
36. Wunan, W., Hao, C., Jun, C.: The attack case of ECDSA on blockchain based on improved simple power analysis. In: Sun, X., Pan, Z., Bertino, E. (eds.) ICAIS 2019. LNCS, vol. 11635, pp. 120–132. Springer, Cham (2019). https://doi.org/10.1007/978-3-030-24268-8_12
37. Wang, W., Fan, S.: Attacking OpenSSL ECDSA with a small amount of side-channel information. Sci. China Inf. Sci. **61**(3), 032105 (2017). https://doi.org/10.1007/s11432-016-9030-0
38. Yarom, Y., Benger, N.: Recovering OpenSSL ECDSA nonces using the FLUSH+RELOAD cache side-channel attack. IACR Cryptology ePrint Archive (2014)
39. Yarom, Y., Falkner, K.: Flush+Reload: a high resolution, low noise, L3 cache side-channel attack. In: Proceedings of the 23rd USENIX Conference on Security Symposium, pp. 719–732 (2014)

Side-Channel Leakage of Alarm Signal for a Bulk-Current-Based Laser Sensor

Yang Li[1(✉)], Ryota Hatano[1], Sho Tada[2], Kohei Matsuda[2], Noriyuki Miura[2], Takeshi Sugawara[1], and Kazuo Sakiyama[1]

[1] The University of Electro-Communications, Tokyo 182-8585, Japan
liyang@uec.ac.jp
[2] Kobe University, Kobe 657-8501, Japan

Abstract. Laser-based fault injections (LFI) attack is a serious threat against cryptographic implementations. One of the effective countermeasures against LFI attacks is to detect the laser shot and delete the sensitive information before any leakage occurs. This paper focuses on an ASIC AES implementation protected by a laser sensor that can detect the irregular current caused by the laser shot and send the alarm signal. We experimentally show that the single-bit alarm signal generated by the laser sensor is a source of side-channel leakage that leaks the sensitive information of the AES calculation. Specifically, by adjusting the strength of the laser shot to achieve an unstable alarm signal, we demonstrate the most effective successful key recovery in our setup. Our results imply that the sensitivity of the on-chip sensor could leak the sensitive information of cryptographic calculation; thus they should be implemented with careful side-channel countermeasures.

Keywords: Fault analysis · Power analysis · AES · Side-channel attack · Laser fault injection (LFI)

1 Introduction

Non-invasive physical attacks are serious security threats against cryptographic implementations. For passive attacks, side-channel attacks can recover the secret key by collecting and analyzing the side-channel information leaked by the cryptographic calculation such as the power consumption [1–3] or electromagnetic radiations [4,5]. These side-channel measurements contain the information of the processed intermediate value so that they can be analyzed statistically to reveal the secret key within a practical computational complexity. For active attacks, the attacker can intentionally disturb the fault-free calculation to inject a computational fault during the cryptographic calculation. The faulty calculation results together with the faulty behavior of the device can be used to effectively extract sensitive information of the secret key, which is called the fault attack.

Among various methods to inject a fault into a cryptographic device, the laser-based fault injection (LFI) is considered to be the most powerful method

© Springer Nature Switzerland AG 2020
Z. Liu and M. Yung (Eds.): Inscrypt 2019, LNCS 12020, pp. 346–361, 2020.
https://doi.org/10.1007/978-3-030-42921-8_20

for its better accuracy in fault injection timing and fault position. In order to counter such LFI-based active attack, one approach is to integrate laser sensors into the chip, which can detect the fault injection and prevent the leakage. This work focuses on the passive information leakage of a laser sensor that is a dedicated countermeasure against the laser-based fault attack. Depending on the mechanism of the laser detection, we consider that the sensitivity of the laser sensor could be affected by the power consumption of cryptographic calculation, therefore could leak the sensitive information.

Specifically, this article focuses on the bulk-current-based laser sensor proposed in [6]. As explained in [6], in order to integrate bulk built-in current sensor (BBICS) into cryptographic cores with low layout area penalty, the achieved BBICS is divided into a front-end module for sensing abnormal bulk current and a back-end module for generating an alarm signal. In this chip, the BBICS is used to detect the abnormal current generated inside the silicon substrate under laser shot. The sensor is distributed across the entire cryptographic core for 100% detection coverage. After the detection, the internal data is erased by shunting the power supply to the AES core. Since the internal data is erased, the faulty output is not calculated. Therefore this countermeasure is effective against differential fault analysis. Also, since the sensitivity of the laser sensor is set to be secure with a margin, the data-dependent fault sensitivity cannot be measured as well.

This paper describes the exploitable side-channel leakage from the output signal for the bulk-current-based laser sensor. Specifically, we focus on the alarm signal sent by the laser sensor, which may have side-channel leakage. The main idea is that the sensitivity of the laser injection sensor could have a certain correlation with a computation of the cryptographic circuit. We investigate such potential information leakage with several experiments using the evaluation board presented in [6], in which the alarm signal from the sensor can be directly measured via output pins. Therefore, assuming that the alarm signal may be affected by the cryptographic calculation, we investigate the side-channel leakage for the alarm signal from BBICS.

The contributions of this paper are summarized as follows.

- We conduct a comprehensive analysis of the information leakage of the alarm signal for the bulk-current-based laser sensor.
- We confirm the dependency between the processed intermediate value in AES and the sensitivity of the alarm signal. We confirm that the Hamming weight model can well describe the leakage model and be used to successfully recover the secret key using the alarm signal only.
- We analyze the shape of the alarm signal and the amount of information leakage. We show that the unstable alarm signal achieved by careful adjustment of the laser strength is the most effective one for the key recovery.

The rest of this paper is organized as follows. Section 2 shows the preliminaries with research background information. Section 3 explains the target evaluation chip, together with the experiment setup. Section 4 shows the experimental results including the leakage assessment and the key recovery experiment. The experimental results are discussed and compared with related work in Sect. 5. Finally, Sect. 6 concludes the paper.

2   Preliminaries

2.1   Fault Attacks and Countermeasures

In fault attacks, the attacker intentionally disturbs the normal calculation to inject a computational fault during the cryptographic calculation. Fault attack is a powerful active side-channel attack against cryptographic implementations. With deliberately injected calculation faults during cryptographic calculations, the attackers can observe the faulty behaviors (faulty output, fault sensitivity etc.) of the target device. With the information provided by faulty behaviors, the cryptanalysis using intermediate values and public data becomes possible to reveal the secret key with reasonable complexity.

Among various fault attacks, the most effective one is the Differential Fault Analysis (DFA) proposed by Biham and Shamir in 1997 [7]. With a fault model that describes the injected fault, the cryptographic key can be effectively derived by analyzing the pairs of fault-free and faulty ciphertexts. Generally speaking, the attacker predicts a part of the key and performs the reverse calculation using fault-free and faulty ciphertexts. The correctness of the predicted key is verified by whether the difference after the reverse calculation fits the fault model. The key space can be continuously reduced by repeating the same process using new pairs of ciphertexts. In the case of a fault model that injects a random byte fault into in the 8th round of AES, the DFA attack can derive the 128-bit encryption key using 2 pairs of ciphertexts [8].

Fault Model. The fault model is fundamental in DFA attacks. On the one hand, it is related to the data complexity required for the key recovery. On the other hand, a meaningful fault model must can be realized using the practical fault injection.

Among various fault injection methods, due to its better time precision and spatial precision, laser-based fault injection is considered to be the most powerful one. For example, compared to the clock-based method that is difficult to control the value of faulty intermediate value after the fault injection, the laser-based injection can accurately flip a single bit at a certain position. Compared to the under-power approach that is likely to affect a long period of computation time, the time precision of the laser injection can be controlled more accurately.

Detection-Based Countermeasures. The detection-based countermeasure against fault attacks can be designed from two general approaches. The first approach is to detect the faulty intermediate value, in which redundant calculations are used to verify the correctness of the calculation. For example, the calculation result can be verified by repeating the same calculation, conducting the reverse calculation and so on. The redundancy-based countermeasure is relatively easy to be implemented, and the fault coverage rate can be accurately evaluated as well.

The second approach is to detect the attempt of fault injection by using sensors to detect abnormal contact or access to the cryptographic device. For example, one can use sensors to detect the irregular clock signal or abnormal power supply. Similarly, one can use laser sensors to detect laser-based fault injection. Once the actions of fault injections have been detected, the device can take specific measures to prevent the leakage of secret information.

2.2 Welch's t-Test

In order to evaluate the potential leakage from the investigated laser sensor, we apply the leakage assessment methodologies based on fixed-vs-random t-testing proposed in [9]. The basic principle of the leakage assessment is to check whether the statistical differences can be found in the side-channel measurements when the processed data is different.

In our test, we applied the fixed-and-random t-test, in which two data sets are required. Denote the secret key as k and the plaintext as p. The first data repeatedly records the side-channel information with fixed k and fixed p. The second data set corresponds to the side-channel information when plaintexts are randomly chosen. For both sets of traces, the average and the variance for every sample point are computed. Then the t-value for each sample point can be calculated as

$$t = \frac{\mu_r - \mu_f}{\sqrt{\frac{\sigma_r^2}{n_r} + \frac{\sigma_f^2}{n_f}}}, \tag{1}$$

where μ, σ^2 and n are the average, the variance, and the amount of the samples at a certain sample point in a data set. The subscripts r and f correspond to the data set of random plaintext and the data set of fixed plaintext, respectively.

It is generally accepted that when the t-value t is larger than 4.5, these two data sets can be considered as different statistically. Therefore, a certain data-dependent difference can be found between these two data sets, which implies an exploitable leakage for side-channel attacks.

2.3 Correlation Power Analysis

Correlation power analysis with a leakage model is a generally useful method to apply the secret key recovery. The attack follows a divide-and-conquer approach so that the key is divided into sub-keys and recovered individually, and combined sub-key recovery results lead to the full key recovery. For each sub-key, the key space of the key candidates is small enough to get exhaustively evaluated. Each key candidate is evaluated by checking the Pearson's correlation coefficient between the actual power consumption and estimated power consumption. The estimated power consumption is obtained by applying a leakage model to the selected intermediate value. The intermediate values are calculated using the public data (plaintext, ciphertext) and the key guess of the current sub-key.

As for 128-bit AES, the first round and the last round are the preferred attack target, and the leakage of the intermediate value around SubByte calculations or flip-flops are usually used in the attack. The 128-bit secret key is divided into 16 key bytes and recovered one by one. Thus, the key space for each sub-key is 2^8. The popular leakage model in non-profiling side-channel attacks includes the single-bit model, the Hamming weight model, the Hamming distance model, the zero-value model and so on.

It is expected that when the number of traces is large enough, the correlation coefficient corresponding to the correct key candidate can be distinguished from those of incorrect key candidates. The reason is that for the correct key candidate, the calculated intermediate values are the same as the real ones. As long as the leakage model is reasonable, the estimated power consumption and the real ones do have certain correlations. While for the incorrect key candidate, such correlation does not exist. When the amount of data is large enough, the ghost correlation peaks caused by the noise will be depressed, so that the correlation for the correct key become distinguishable.

3 Target Device and Experimental Setup

3.1 Target Device

In this section, we briefly explain the target device under our evaluation. This chip has an AES circuit that includes compact laser shot detection as an LFI countermeasure proposed by Matsuda et al. in [6]. In LFI attack, the laser is irradiated to the PN junction of the silicon substrate. Meanwhile, electron-hole pairs are generated by the photoelectric effect, and an abnormal transient current is generated inside the silicon substrate. This abnormal transient current may cause a circuit failure that leads to computational fault that is exploited in fault attacks.

In [6], the authors developed a chip that uses a bulk built-in current sensor (BBICS) to detect the abnormal current generated inside the silicon substrate. The target chip integrated a compact sense-and-react countermeasure against LFI. This countermeasure consists of a distributed bulk-current sensor for LFI detection and secure flush code eraser for erasing internal data. Bulk-current sensor is monitoring abnormal transient current in the silicon substrate due to laser irradiation. Since this transient current spreads all over the shared silicon substrate, BBICS is distributed across the entire cryptographic core for 100% attack detection coverage. In addition, the core supply during the shunting is electrically isolated from the global supply line to prevent side-channel information leakage of intermediate faulty codes.

In our evaluation, the target chip is mounted on an evaluation board. The evaluation board has several general-purpose input output (GPIO) pins for debug purposes. The AES execution signal (EXEC) and the alarm signal from BBICS can be directly observed through these GPIO pins. Furthermore, the shutting operation that deletes all the sensitive information is turned off in our evaluation.

It is obvious that the evaluation board used in our experiment is different from a practical attack scenario. For practical usage of the AES chip with BBICS sensor implemented, the alarm signal cannot be easily retrieved by the attacker. Also, as long as the alarm signal is active, the following protection will shut down the calculation of the cryptographic algorithm. The purpose of this work is to investigate the potential information leakage from the alarm signal. Therefore, the experiments based on the debug functionality of the evaluation board fit the purpose of this work. The possibility of the key recovery in a more practical attack scenario for BBICS is considered as future work.

3.2   Experiment Setup

The overview of our experimental setup is shown in Fig. 1. A photo of the evaluation board with the target chip and the laser unit is shown in Fig. 2. The chip under test is in the center of the evaluation board with its silicon die exposed for laser shot. A control FPGA works as an interface to communicate between the target chip and a computer. The evaluation board and a laser unit have their positions fixed by a mounting base so that the laser spot can be stable and carefully adjusted. The laser unit is connected to with a power supply so that the strength of the laser shot can be adjusted by changing the output voltage of the power supply. An oscilloscope is used to capture traces from the GPIO pins of the evaluation board and the captured signal are sent to be stored in the computer. Two signals are captured using an oscilloscope as the alarm signal from the BBICS and the execution signal of AES. The AES execution signal is used as a trigger to align the alarm signal.

The detailed information of the experiment devices is listed in Table 1.

Table 1. Devices used in experiment setup

Control FPGA	Xilinx SPARTAN XC3S1400AN
Oscilloscope	Agilent DSO7032A
Laser unit	Lightvision Technologies JPM-1-3(A4)
Power supply	KIKUSUI PMC18-2A

Note that our experiment setup does not include expansive equipments. Especially, the laser unit we used is a very basic one that costs less than 30 US dollars. This laser unit is a diode pumped solid-state green laser that has a large laser spot of 12.5 mm. According to its specification, the output power of this laser unit is between 0.3 mW to 0.9 mW. The power of the laser unit is strong enough to trigger the alarm signal of the BBICS. Therefore, this basic laser is good enough for our evaluation purpose and the successful key recovery.

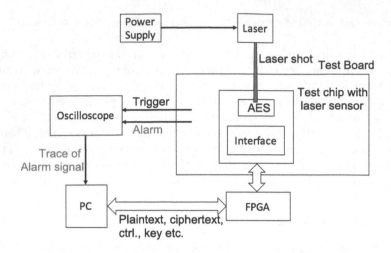

Fig. 1. Experiment setup

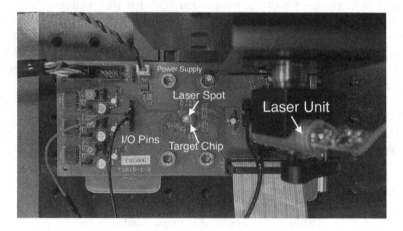

Fig. 2. Photo of experiment setup

4   Results

Before doing leakage assessment or CPA, we first show a preliminary observation during the experiment. Subsequently, the leakage assessment and the key recovery attacks are performed on the on-chip AES implementation, which has no side-channel countermeasures.

4.1   Unstable Alarm Signal with Controlled Laser Power

The first observation is that the sensor's alarm signal can be set to an unstable state. The strength of the laser shot can be adjusted by many means such as the distance between the laser unit and the chip, the angle of the laser shot, and the voltage of the power supply to the laser unit. We first set the experimental parameters to achieve a critical state where the alarm signal can be continuously and stably triggered. Then we command the evaluation board to repeatedly perform AES calculations with random plaintext and a fixed key. Meanwhile, the alarm signal is observed by an oscilloscope. With the AES encrypting the random plaintexts in the background, we can gradually reduce the voltage of the power supply to the laser unit to reduce the strength of the laser irradiation.

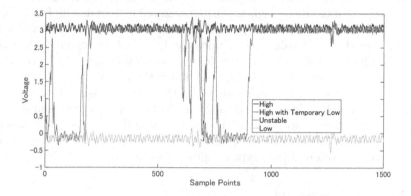

Fig. 3. Typical shape of 4 types of alarm signals

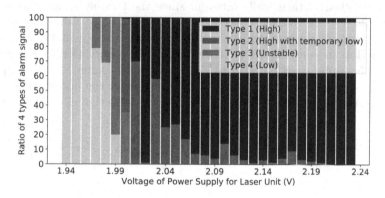

Fig. 4. The ratios of 4 types of alarm signals over the voltage of laser unit's power supply

By doing so, we can observe that there are roughly 4 types of waveforms for the alarm signal as follows.

Type 1. Logical high
Type 2. Logical high except for the middle part of the AES is temporarily logical low

Type 3. Unstable alarm signal with large fluctuation
Type 4. Logical low

For each type of alarm signal, one of the example is plotted in Fig. 3. For a certain position and angle of the laser shot, we investigate the ratios of these 4 types of alarm signals over different power supply for the laser unit as shown in Fig. 4. Type 1 and type 4 of the alarm signal are as expected, which corresponds to the cases when the laser shot is stably detected or not. However, even the setup of the laser shot is fixed, the unstable alarm signal can be observed.

As for type 2 of the alarm signal, the alarm signal is temporarily falling in the middle sample points. After investigation, we find its timing roughly corresponds to the 5th round of AES calculation. Since the type 2 alarm signal takes a large account and has a stable shape, we consider it as a unique type that is separated from the other unstable traces. We do not know the exact reason for type 2 of the alarm signal, we consider it is caused by the power consumption of certain operations occurred during AES calculation. As for type 3 of the alarm signal, the alarm signal fluctuates between the logic high and logic low as an unstable signal. We believe the fluctuation is caused by the influence of the variation of the power consumption of the cryptographic calculation.

4.2   Leakage Assessment

In this section, we present the result of the t-test using the fix data set of 100k traces and the random data set of 100k traces. The result is shown in Fig. 5, in which we have several observations. The first observation is that these two data sets are clearly statistically different since the t-value is much larger than the threshold 4.5. The second observation is that the t-test value shows a clear pattern in each clock cycle, which implies that the alarm signal is affected by the calculation in combinatorial circuits. Another observation is the peak of t-value is the same position where the type 2 alarm signal has a temporary falling down. These observations imply the existence of the information leakage of the cryptographic calculation in the measured alarm signal.

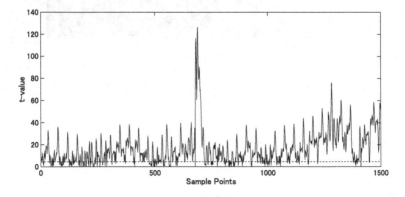

Fig. 5. Fixed-vs-random t-test result for 100k traces

4.3 Known-Key Correlation Test

As mentioned in [6], the implemented AES with the laser sensor is without any countermeasures against side-channel attacks. Therefore, as long as the alarm signal leaks the information of AES calculation, we expect that the classic leakage model such as the Hamming weight model or the Hamming distance model could be useful. Before the key recovery experiment, with the known key, we test the correlation with the alarm signal by selecting several intermediate values and the classic leakage models. In our test, the 128-bit intermediate value is used instead of byte-wise intermediate value so that the exploitable leakage model become clearly distinguishable.

This test can verify the effectiveness of the leakage model and the selection function with the small computational cost. We focused on the intermediate value of the first round and the last round of AES. The result is shown in Fig. 6. In Fig. 6, we denote S_{in}^n and S_{out}^n as the input and output of the SubBytes calculation in the n-th round of AES, where $n \in \{1, 10\}$. We also denote the Hamming weight and the Hamming distance as HW and HD, respectively.

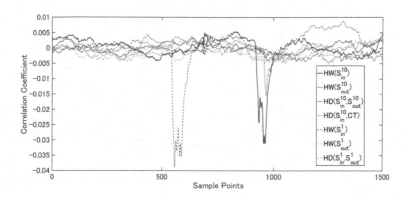

Fig. 6. Results of known-key correlation test for 362k traces

As shown in Fig. 6, the Hamming weight of the SubBytes input has a clear negative correlation with the traces of alarm signal. The Hamming distance between the round input and the round output also shows some negative correlation that could be used in the key recovery. In other words, this simple experiment verified that the alarm signal leaks the Hamming weight of the AES round input the most. Also, the Hamming distance between round input and round output also exist in the alarm signal.

4.4 Key Recovery Attack

Considering the result of the known-key correlation test, we consider the Hamming weight of the last AES round input is the most effective intermediate value

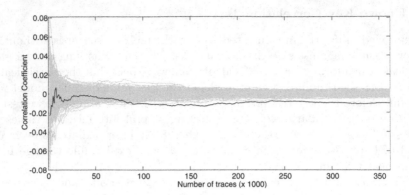

Fig. 7. Total correlation after 360k traces for all 256 key candidates. The correct key byte is marked black

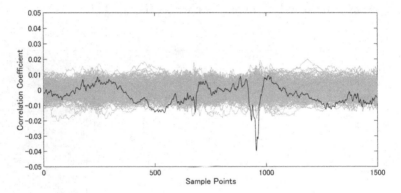

Fig. 8. Correlation evolution over 360k traces for all 256 key candidates; The correct key is marked black

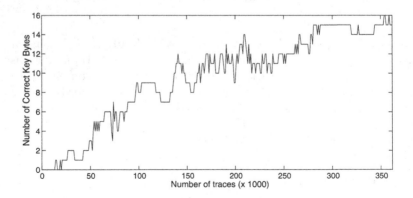

Fig. 9. Evolution of correct key bytes over 360k traces

to perform the key recovery experiment. In this subsection, we present the results of CPA attacks on the AES round key. We perform a ciphertext-based CPA on the last round of AES over 360k traces of alarm signal. The strength of the laser irradiation is carefully adjusted to get the unstable alarm signal as much as possible. The results of the CPA attacks are shown in Figs. 7, 8, and 9.

For a key byte, Figs. 7 and 8 show the final correlations with the entire set of traces and the evolution of the correlation coefficient of 256 key candidates, respectively. This key byte can be recovered within 100k power traces. Also, in Fig. 9, the evolution of the correctly recovered key bytes is presented against the number of used traces. With 360k trances used, almost all the key bytes can be successfully recovered. By far, we have already demonstrated the leakage from the alarm signal generated by the laser sensor can be used to recover the secret key of AES.

4.5   Key Recovery Attack with Grouped Alarm Signal

As mentioned that the measured alarm signal can be divided into 4 types. When we only focus on the sample points corresponding to the last round of AES, the alarm signal can be divided into 3 groups as "'always high", "always low" and "unstable". The always high group is the waveform that remains at the logical high. The actual criterion we used is that the voltage is above 2.5 V for all related sample points. The always low group is the waveform that has been kept at the logical low. The actual criterion is that the voltage is below 0.5 V for all related sample points. Waveforms that are neither in the always high group nor in the always low group are in the unstable group. The alarm signal in the unstable group has at least a sample point that is between 0.5 V to 2.5 V during the 10-round's calculation. After the grouping, we found that the always low group and the unstable group have roughly 40k traces, while the always high group has roughly 280k traces. Then we used these three group of waveforms to repeat the key recovery experiment separately. The result is shown in Fig. 10.

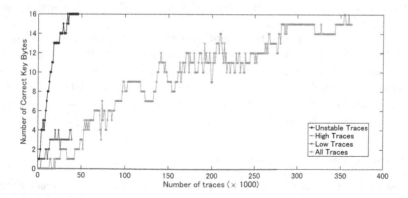

Fig. 10. Evolution of correct key bytes for different groups of traces

The result shows that the most important information leakage comes from the unstable alarm signals of BBICS. The full key recovery can be achieved using less than 40k traces. We consider that for the unstable alarm signal the information carried by the power consumption of the AES calculation is the most complete. Unlike the traces in the always high group and the always low group, some of the information may be lost in the voltage limitations of GPIO signals.

Normally, the GPIO output has only two stats as the logical high and logical low. This result implies that the key recovery achieved in this work mainly comes from the information leakage caused by the sensitivity variation of the laser sensor. The possible side-channel leakage related to the sharing of the power line or the ground is not the main reason of the successful key recovery.

5 Discussion

5.1 Cause of Leakage

In this section, we discuss the possible causes of the information leakage in the alarm signal generated from the laser sensor. The mechanism of the investigated laser sensor is based on the detection of the abnormal current generated under the laser shot. A threshold-based mechanism is used to decide the value of the alarm signal.

We consider that the leakage exists since the total current that is compared with the threshold is composed of both the abnormal current caused by the laser shot and the normal current related to cryptographic calculation. In our attack experiment, the abnormal current caused by the laser shot is relatively stable by fixing the input voltage to the laser unit and other setup. In the meanwhile, the normal current varies according to the intermediate values used in the cryptographic calculation. The information of cryptographic calculation is leaked through the alarm signal since the variation of the total current is correlated with the variation of the normal current. The essence of the leakage is that the generation of the alarm signal depends on the power consumption of the cryptographic calculation.

The relation between the laser shot and the power consumption has been discussed also in other research works. For example, in [10], the laser shot is used to combine with the power analysis to improve the result. It is found that the laser shot can modulate the contribution of a certain transistor to the overall supply current since the laser shot has been converted into current through a certain transistor by the photovoltaic effect.

5.2 Comparison with Related Work

Fault Sensitivity Analysis. Fault sensitivity analysis (FSA) was originally introduced as the combination of active attack and passive attack [11]. The point of FSA attack is that the fault injection intensity required to generate a faulty output depends on the processed intermediate value. In case of fault injections using clock-glitch, the fault sensitivity can leak the critical path delay of the combinatorial circuit, which can be used to infer the information of the sensitive data. Later, the original FSA attack has been extended by combining FSA with the idea of the correlation-enhanced collision attack [12]. This extension allows successful FSA attack without any usage of any leakage model.

In [13], it is found that the fault sensitivity analysis can be applied in a laser attack setting. By controlling the intensity of fault injection into a critical state where roughly half of ciphertexts become faulty, the distribution of the faulty ciphertext can leak the information of the intermediate value. The laser-based FSA attack demonstrated that the threshold of generating fault calculation results are data-dependent under the laser shot. In this work, we demonstrate that the threshold of generating an alarm signal is also data-dependent. The AES calculation part also affects the laser detection mechanism. Turning on the alarm signal in the circuit is similar to the occurrence of the calculation violation, therefore the sensitivity of the alarm signal also leaks the information of the cryptographic calculation.

Leakage from I/O Pins. The leakage source in this work is the alarm signal measured as the output from the general-purpose input/output pin (GPIO pin) on the evaluation board. Many works have already discussed the information leakage on the IO pins [14,15]. In [16], Schmidt et al. showed that DPA attacks based on voltage variations at I/O pins can successfully be mounted on many devices even if in a cross border attack scenario. This work also belongs to the side-channel leakage measured from the input/output pins.

Different from previous work, this work demonstrated specifically the leakage from a bulk-current-based sensor that works as a fault attack countermeasure. Furthermore, this work focuses on the leakage caused by the sensitivity of the laser sensor rather than the leakage caused by sharing the same power line or ground. In the previous work, the leakage mainly comes from the small voltage fluctuation when the measured signal is stable to a certain logical state. While, since this alarm signal can be "controlled" by the attacker, we showed that the leakage in our attack is the most significant when the measured signal is in an unstable logical state. The attackers could take advantage of this observation to perform much effective key recovery attack.

Leakage from ADC. In [17], Gnad, Krautter, and Tahoori demonstrated that analog digital converter (ADC) used in many SOC devices leaks the information of the cryptographic calculations. To prove the leakage, they performed the leakage assessment on three individual micro-controllers from two different vendors with various ADC settings. They also showed a full key recovery attack on AES that works despite the limited ADC sampling rate. Similar to this work, their work is also an example of side-channel leakage from the output of the on-chip component. These results imply that the chip design should be careful when integrating the cryptographic circuit with other on-chip components.

6   Conclusion

For a laser injection detection chip based on detecting abnormal current, our work proves that there is a correlation between the output signal of the laser sensor and the calculated data of the cryptographic circuit. This correlation is large enough to have a successful CPA-based key recovery attack on the AES inside the same chip. We also show that the information leakage is most significant when the output signal is in the unstable state. Our results imply that the sensitivity of the on-chip sensor could leak the sensitive information of cryptographic calculation, thus they should be implemented with careful side-channel countermeasures.

Acknowledgement. This work was supported by JSPS KAKENHI Grant Number JP18H05289 and 19K21529.

References

1. Kocher, P., Jaffe, J., Jun, B.: Differential power analysis. In: Wiener, M. (ed.) CRYPTO 1999. LNCS, vol. 1666, pp. 388–397. Springer, Heidelberg (1999). https://doi.org/10.1007/3-540-48405-1_25
2. Brier, E., Clavier, C., Olivier, F.: Correlation power analysis with a leakage model. In: Joye, M., Quisquater, J.-J. (eds.) CHES 2004. LNCS, vol. 3156, pp. 16–29. Springer, Heidelberg (2004). https://doi.org/10.1007/978-3-540-28632-5_2
3. Oswald, D., Paar, C.: Breaking Mifare DESFire MF3ICD40: power analysis and templates in the real world. In: Preneel, B., Takagi, T. (eds.) CHES 2011. LNCS, vol. 6917, pp. 207–222. Springer, Heidelberg (2011). https://doi.org/10.1007/978-3-642-23951-9_14
4. Gandolfi, K., Mourtel, C., Olivier, F.: Electromagnetic analysis: concrete results. In: Koç, Ç.K., Naccache, D., Paar, C. (eds.) CHES 2001. LNCS, vol. 2162, pp. 251–261. Springer, Heidelberg (2001). https://doi.org/10.1007/3-540-44709-1_21
5. Agrawal, D., Archambeault, B., Rao, J.R., Rohatgi, P.: The EM side—channel(s). In: Kaliski, B.S., Koç, K., Paar, C. (eds.) CHES 2002. LNCS, vol. 2523, pp. 29–45. Springer, Heidelberg (2003). https://doi.org/10.1007/3-540-36400-5_4
6. Matsuda, K., et al.: A 286 F²/cell distributed bulk-current sensor and secure flush code eraser against laser fault injection attack on cryptographic processor. J. Solid-State Circuits **53**, 3174–3182 (2018)
7. Biham, E., Shamir, A.: Differential fault analysis of secret key cryptosystems. In: Kaliski, B.S. (ed.) CRYPTO 1997. LNCS, vol. 1294, pp. 513–525. Springer, Heidelberg (1997). https://doi.org/10.1007/BFb0052259
8. Piret, G., Quisquater, J.-J.: A differential fault attack technique against SPN structures, with application to the AES and KHAZAD. In: Walter, C.D., Koç, Ç.K., Paar, C. (eds.) CHES 2003. LNCS, vol. 2779, pp. 77–88. Springer, Heidelberg (2003). https://doi.org/10.1007/978-3-540-45238-6_7
9. Goodwill, G., Jun, B., Jaffe, J., Rohatgi, P.: A testing methodology for side-channel resistance validation (2011)
10. Skorobogatov, S.: Optically enhanced position-locked power analysis. In: Goubin, L., Matsui, M. (eds.) CHES 2006. LNCS, vol. 4249, pp. 61–75. Springer, Heidelberg (2006). https://doi.org/10.1007/11894063_6

11. Li, Y., Sakiyama, K., Gomisawa, S., Fukunaga, T., Takahashi, J., Ohta, K.: Fault sensitivity analysis. In: Mangard, S., Standaert, F.-X. (eds.) CHES 2010. LNCS, vol. 6225, pp. 320–334. Springer, Heidelberg (2010). https://doi.org/10.1007/978-3-642-15031-9_22

12. Moradi, A., Mischke, O., Paar, C., Li, Y., Ohta, K., Sakiyama, K.: On the power of fault sensitivity analysis and collision side-channel attacks in a combined setting. In: Preneel, B., Takagi, T. (eds.) CHES 2011. LNCS, vol. 6917, pp. 292–311. Springer, Heidelberg (2011). https://doi.org/10.1007/978-3-642-23951-9_20

13. Schellenberg, F., Finkeldey, M., Gerhardt, N., Hofmann, M., Moradi, A., Paar, C.: Large laser spots and fault sensitivity analysis. In: Robinson, W.H., Bhunia, S., Kastner, R. (eds.) HOST 2016, pp. 203–208. IEEE Computer Society (2016)

14. Shamir, A.: Protecting smart cards from passive power analysis with detached power supplies. In: Koç, Ç.K., Paar, C. (eds.) CHES 2000. LNCS, vol. 1965, pp. 71–77. Springer, Heidelberg (2000). https://doi.org/10.1007/3-540-44499-8_5

15. Plos, T.: Evaluation of the detached power supply as side-channel analysis countermeasure for passive UHF RFID tags. In: Fischlin, M. (ed.) CT-RSA 2009. LNCS, vol. 5473, pp. 444–458. Springer, Heidelberg (2009). https://doi.org/10.1007/978-3-642-00862-7_30

16. Schmidt, J.-M., Plos, T., Kirschbaum, M., Hutter, M., Medwed, M., Herbst, C.: Side-channel leakage across borders. In: Gollmann, D., Lanet, J.-L., Iguchi-Cartigny, J. (eds.) CARDIS 2010. LNCS, vol. 6035, pp. 36–48. Springer, Heidelberg (2010). https://doi.org/10.1007/978-3-642-12510-2_4

17. Gnad, D.R.E., Krautter, J., Tahoori, M.B.: Leaky noise: new side-channel attack vectors in mixed-signal IoT devices. IACR Trans. Cryptogr. Hardw. Embed. Syst. **2019**, 305–339 (2019)

Identity-Based Cryptography

Efficient Identity-Based Outsider Anonymous Public-Key Trace and Revoke with Constant Ciphertext-Size and Fast Decryption

Mriganka Mandal$^{(\boxtimes)}$ and Ratna Dutta

Department of Mathematics, Indian Institute of Technology Kharagpur,
Kharagpur 721302, India
{mriganka_mandal,ratna}@maths.iitkgp.ac.in

Abstract. In this paper, we present the *first* identity-based *outsider anonymous public-key trace and revoke* (OAnoPKTR) scheme achieving *constant-size* communication bandwidth and computation cost. Our construction is obtained by twitching *Tardos fingerprinting code* (TFC) over Waters *identity-based encryption* (IBE) framework (EUROCRYPT 2005) endowed with the most efficient asymmetric Type-3 variant of the bilinear maps. We efficiently couple two mutually orthogonal functionalities, namely receivers anonymity and public traceability, which is difficult to accomplish without losing cost-efficiency. Our scheme provably achieves *indistinguishable chosen-plaintext attack* (IND-CPA) security against adaptive adversary beneath the standard *decisional bilinear Diffie-Hellman exponent* (DBDHE) assumption. The security analysis is in the standard security model without applying random oracles.

Keywords: Broadcast encryption · Anonymity and privacy · Fraud detection and revocation · Public-key tracing · Identity-based encryption · Tardos fingerprinting code

1 Introduction

Broadcast encryption (BE), first introduced by Fiat and Naor [9], allows secure transmission of encrypted files over insecure public channel enabling only intended recipients to decrypt while outsiders recover nothing even if they collude. As opposed to the traditional point-to-point communication systems, BE can significantly reduce communication bandwidth, computation cost and storage overhead. The application of BE [10,11,15,16,19,20] widely ranges from the digital rights management, pay-TV system, satellite geo-location system, group communication, etc., to the recently proposed access control mechanism for cloud storage services [21].

The identity-based broadcast encryption (IBBE) system, first proposed by Delerablée [6], is an advanced form of BE paradigm in which the public-key

© Springer Nature Switzerland AG 2020
Z. Liu and M. Yung (Eds.): Inscrypt 2019, LNCS 12020, pp. 365–380, 2020.
https://doi.org/10.1007/978-3-030-42921-8_21

infrastructure (PKI) is not required. In an IBBE, the public-key of each user is represented using an unique identity associated with the user index (e.g., a user's IP or email address). A group manager (GM), also known as private key generation center (PKGC), generates corresponding secret-key of each user utilizing the associated public identity of the user. To encrypt message, a set of receiver's identities along with the public parameters of the system are used by any broadcaster. A legitimate user can recover the correct message using its secret decryption key, which is obtained from the PKGC.

For instance, suppose a group of scientists from various countries are appointed to collaborate on a confidential project under a government organization GovNet of some economically powerful country. The primary objective of the project is to trace the secret nuclear weapon activity of other countries of the world. The GovNet works as the GM and generates a master secret-public key pair (MSK,MPK). The master secret key MSK is kept secret to GovNet while the master public key MPK is published on the Internet. The GovNet builds special devices, called 'set-top decoder box', each containing a unique private key embedded within its' inbuilt storage. The devices are distributed securely among the scientists. Any scientist can broadcast confidential file on weapon activity, encrypted under the master public key MPK, through an insecure channel. The embedded private keys of the set-top decoder boxes enable the corresponding scientists involved in the project to decrypt the encrypted file. The GovNet can also decrypt it using the master secret key MSK. In this scenario, the personal information of the involved scientists needs to be protected from the outsiders. Suppose, the governments of respective countries somehow able to know that the information related to their weapon activity has been revealed. They will try to patch the leakage by threatening their opponents or even by killing them. This will collapse the entire project, and the collected information will be exposed. It is GovNet's interest to protect scientist's anonymity from the enemies.

The BE with receiver's anonymity is called *anonymous broadcast encryption* (AnoBE), first developed by Barth et al. [3], which has gathered momentum recently. The AnoBE systems have been classified into two main categories: *outsider anonymous broadcast encryption* (OAnoBE) [1,8,15,26,27] and *fully anonymous broadcast encryption* (FAnoBE) [3,10,11,13,16,20]. In the OAnoBE systems (including ours), the recipient set is hidden from any outsider, whereas each user belonging to the recipient set knows the information of other legitimate users. On the other hand, the recipient set is completely anonymous from both outsiders and insiders in the FAnoBE systems. To find the lower bound for the communication bandwidth of private BE systems, Kiayias and Samari [12] have shown that an atomic private broadcast encryption scheme with full receivers anonymity must have a ciphertext-size of $\Omega(N \cdot \eta)$, where N represents the size of subscribed users set and η is the security parameter. Therefore, the communication bandwidth must be linear to N in any FAnoBE schemes, and the anonymous BE schemes with constant communication bandwidth are only OAnoBE [15]. An identity-based AnoBE system can be obtained by tweaking AnoBE systems over the IBBE framework in which the users are recognized with their identities instead of indices assigned by the system. The size of the valid identity set in an identity-based AnoBE scheme can be exponential with the security parameter, whereas it is only polynomial with the security parameter in the existing traditional public-key anonymous broadcast setting. However, the receiver's anonymity is at primary concern for both the privacy preserving BE schemes.

Furthermore, facilitate with the anonymity, any scientist, who has recovered the confidential information by decrypting the encrypted file, might publish it for profit without being worried to be captured. Such smuggled redistribution is the violation of the GovNet's policy. Moreover, a coalition of such traitors might make a conspiracy to create a pirate decoder box containing an arbitrarily complex obfuscated malicious program capable of decrypting the ciphertext. In this situation, GovNet should have the ability to run an efficient tracing mechanism that interacts polynomially many times with the pirate decoder, considering it as a black-box oracle, in order to trace and revoke the traitors. Tracing mechanism falls into two categories: public-key tracing [14,17] and secret-key tracing [4,5,7,19]. In a public-key tracing, anyone can execute the tracing algorithm using only the public parameters, whereas secret-key tracing requires a secret input to the tracing algorithm and runs only by the GM. Moreover, a public-key tracing system remains secure even if the tracing authority is compromised, and the tracing capability can be outsourced to an untrusted party. An identity-based AnoBE with the public-key traceability is called identity-based *anonymous public-key trace and revoke* (AnoPKTR) system.

Motivation. Anonymity and public traceability are two mutually orthogonal properties in terms of the recipients' privacy. Although AnoBE systems and public-key tracing schemes have been studied separately, it is hard to realize secure identity-based AnoPKTR by simply coupling identity-based AnoBE [10,11,15,20] with public-key tracing [14,17] without efficiency degrade [2,21] in communication, computation and storage overhead. Moreover, in the identity-based BE environment, where devices used to access the broadcast contents, are generally low computational power and resource-constrained (e.g., low processor, limited battery life). The FAnoBE schemes may not be fit-for-purpose as the size of the ciphertext grows with the size of subscribed users set, which may become very large for a system with large number of subscribers. Thus, in the identity-based AnoPKTR setting, the OAnoBE schemes with constant-time computation and constant-size ciphertext are desirable for lightweight devices. The only known generic transformation of anonymous BE into anonymous *secret-key* trace and revoke is shown by Murat et al. [2], which have ciphertext-size linear to the total number of users of the system. However, to the best of our knowledge, there does not exist any *explicit construction* for identity-based BE with proper *security realization* that achieves both *receivers anonymity* and *public-key* traceability with constant-size ciphertext and faster computation. This is appeared to be a gaping note that begs to be filled, which is resolved in this work.

Our Contribution. We propose a conceptually simple and efficient solution with proper security realization in the standard security model under reasonable

Table 1. Comparative summary among existing anonymous BE schemes

Scheme	Commu	Storage		ROM	Group Type	Security		DecTm	IB
	$|CT|$	$|PP|$	$|SK|$			Model	Assumption		
Barth et al. [3]	$O(N)$	$O(N)$	$O(N)$	✗	PriO, T1	SEL	CDH	$O(N)$	✗
Fazio et al. [8]	$O(r \ln \frac{N}{r})$	$O(N)$	$O(\ln N)$	✓	PriO, T1	ADAP	GDH, DDH	$O(r \ln N)$	✗
Hur et al. [11]	$O(N)$	$O(1)$	$O(1)$	✓	PriO,T3	SEL	BDH	$O(1)$	✓
Libert et al. [16]	$O(N)$	$O(N)$	$O(1)$	✗	PriO,T1	ADAP	DDH	$O(N)$	✗
Tseng et al. [23]	$O(N)$	$O(1)$	$O(1)$	✓	PriO, T1	SEL	gBDH	$O(N)$	✓
Zhang et al. [27]	$O(N)$	$O(1)$	$O(1)$	✓	PriO, T1	ADAP	BDH, eBDH	$O(N)$	✗
Zhang et al. [26]	$O(\eta)$	$O(N)$	$O(N)$	✗	ComO, T1	ADAP	SD	$O(N)$	✓
Ren et al. [20]	$O(N)$	$O(l)$	$O(l)$	✗	PriO,T3	ADAP	DBDH	$O(N)$	✓
Li et al. [15]	$O(1)$	$O(N)$	$O(N)$	✗	PriO, T3	ADAP	BDHE	$O(N)$	✓
He et al. [10]	$O(N)$	$O(1)$	$O(1)$	✓	PriO,T1	ADAP	DBDH	$O(1)$	✓
Lai et al. [13]	$O(N)$	$O(1)$	$O(1)$	✓	PriO,T1	ADAP	DBDH	$O(N)$	✓
Acharya et al. [1]	$O(N)$	poly($\ln_3 N$)	$O(\ln_{32} N)$	✗	ComO, T1	SEL	q-wDBDHI, q-cDDH	$O(N^2)$	✗
Ours	$O(1)$	$O(N)$	$O(N)$	✗	PriO,T3	ADAP	DBDHE	$O(1)$	✓

N = total number of users, r = size of revoked set, l = length of user's identity, η = security parameter, Comm = communication bandwidth, DecTm = decryption time, ROM = random oracle model, IB = identity-based, ADAP = adaptive, SEL = selective, ComO = composite order, PriO = prime order, poly = polynomial, Ti = Type-i bilinear maps, DBDHE = decisional bilinear Diffie-Hellman exponent, GDH = gap Diffie-Hellman, DDH = decisional Diffie-Hellman, BDH = bilinear Diffie-Hellman, eBDH = extended bilinear Diffie-Hellman, BDHE = bilinear Diffie-Hellman exponent, wDBDHI = weak decisional bilinear Diffie-Hellman inversion, cDDH = composite decisional Diffie-Hellman, CDH = computational Diffie-Hellman, gBDH = gap bilinear Diffie-Hellman

assumption. Our construction is obtained from the collusion-secure probabilistic *Tardos fingerprinting codes* (TFC) [22] and Waters *identity-based encryption* (IBE) [25] framework endowed with the asymmetric Type-3 variant of the bilinear pairings achieving order-of-magnitude improvements in communication bandwidth and computation cost without any security breach. We achieve provable security against adaptive *indistinguishable chosen-plaintext attack* (IND-CPA) adversary based on the standard asymmetric *decisional bilinear Diffie-Hellman exponent* (DBDHE) assumption without relying on *random oracle model* (ROM). More specifically, our construction provides the following interesting features.

- Table 1 exhibits comparison of our scheme with the existing AnoBE systems [1,3,8,10,11,13,15,16,20,23,26,27]. The public parameter size ($|PP|$) in the works [10,11,13,23,27] are constant, whereas it is linear to the maximal number of users N in the works of [3,8,15,16,26] and ours. The public parameter and user secret-key size ($|SK|$) for [20] is linear to the length l of user's identity. The secret key size in our construction is also liner to N similar to [3,15,26]. The secret key size in [10,11,13,16,23,27] are constant while that for [8] is logarithmic to N, and for [1] linear to $\ln_{32} N$. However, we emphasize that our scheme has constant ciphertext size ($|CT|$) while it is linear to N for [1,3,10,11,13,16,20,23,27], $O(\eta)$ for [26] and $O(r \ln (N/r))$ for [8], where r is the size of revoked user set and η represents the security parameter.
- As shown in Table 1, the schemes of [1,3] are selectively secure without using ROM, and the works of [8,10,13,27] are adaptively secure in ROM. Although [15] and ours have same communication bandwidth, we note that the decryption time (DecTm) is linear to N in [3,13,15,16,20,23,26,27] and constant

Table 2. Comparative summary among existing trace and revoke schemes

Scheme	Commu	Storage		ROM	Group Type	Security		DecTm	Trace	IB
	$|CT|$	$|PP|$	$|SK|$			Model	Assumtn			
Dodis et al. [7]	$O(r)$	$O(\ln N)$	$O(\ln^{2.5} N)$	✓	PriO, T1	ADAP	$q-$SMEBDH	$O(1)$	ST	✗
Boneh et al. [5]	$O(\sqrt{N})$	$O(\sqrt{N})$	$O(1)$	✗	ComO, T1	SEL	D3DH, DHSD	$O(1)$	ST	✗
Boneh et al. [4]	$O(\eta)$	$O(l)$	$O(r^2 \ln N)$	✓	ComO, T1	SEL	BDH	$O(l)$	ST	✓
Lee et al. [14]	$O(r)$	$O(\eta)$	$O(\ln^{1.5} N)$	✓	PriO, T1	ADAP	$q-$SMEBDH	$O(1)$	PT	✓
Mandal et al. [18]	$O(r)$	$O(1)$	$O(\ln^{1.5} N)$	✗	ComO, T1	ADAP	SD	$O(1)$	PT	✗
Nishimaki et al. [19]	poly$(l,|m|)$	poly(η)	poly(l)	✗	–	ADAP	FE, iO	–	ST	✗
Nishimaki et al. [19]	$|m|+$poly$(\ln l)$	poly$(\ln l)$	poly(l)	✗	–	ADAP	FE	–	ST	✗
Mandal et al. [17]	poly$(\ln N)$	poly$(\ln N)$	$O(1)$	✗	PriO, ML	ADAP	DHDHE, iO	$O(N)$	PT	✗
Ours	$O(1)$	$O(N)$	$O(N)$	✗	PriO, T3	ADAP	DBDHE	$O(1)$	PT	✓

N = total number of users, r = size of revoked set, l = length of user's identity, $|m|$ = length of message, η = security parameter, Comm = communication bandwidth, DecTm = decryption time, ROM = random oracle model, PT = publicly traceable, ST = secretly traceable, IB = identity-based, ADAP = adaptive, SEL = selective, ComO = composite order, PriO = prime order, poly = polynomial, Ti = Type-i bilinear maps, SMEBDH = simplified multi-exponent bilinear Diffie-Hellman, D3DH = decisional 3-party Diffie-Hellman, DHSD = Diffie-Hellman subgroup decision, DHDHE = decisional hybrid Diffie-Hellman exponent, DBDHE = decisional bilinear Diffie-Hellman exponent, BDH = bilinear Diffie-Hellman, SD = subgroup decision, FE = functional encryption, iO = indistinguishability obfuscation, ML = multilinear maps, Assumtn = assumption

in our design similar to [10,11]. However, the work of [10] is secured under ROM, and [11,23] is selectively secure in ROM. The security against adaptive attacks is more realistic than selective attacks, and the security proof in ROM is generally treated as a heuristic argument as there is no standard complexity assumptions for such random looking functions. The designs of [1,26] are based on composite order group, and [1] achieved security under non-standard q-type assumptions. Note that pairing time and parameter sizes over composite order groups are significantly high as opposed to prime order groups [24]. Also the q-type assumptions are assumptions of size that grows with some parameter q, and such complex and dynamic assumptions are not well-understood. In contrast, our construction is adaptively secure under the standard asymmetric *decisional bilinear Diffie-Hellman exponent* (DBDHE) assumption without ROM over the prime order bilinear group.

- Compared to the existing trace and revoke schemes [4,5,7,14,17–19], our OAnoPKTR is the *first* to achieve receivers outsider anonymity with constant-size ciphertext. As shown in Table 2, the works [5,7,14,18], including ours, have constant DecTm. However, [4,5] achieve selective security and [18] is adaptively secure over the composite order group, while [7,14] are adaptively secure under the non-standard q-type assumption and the security analysis of [4,7,14] uses ROM. The works of [4,5,7,19] are secretly traceable (ST) systems. Although the designs in [17,19] require less storage than ours, they are built on heavy duty cryptographic tools such as multilinear maps (ML), indistinguishability obfuscation (iO), constrained pseudorandom functions (cPRF), functional encryption (FE), etc. Secure and efficient realization of these tools are still to be instantiated. Moreover, the DecTm depends on a suitable FE scheme in [19] and, it is linear to N in [17]. In contrast to *fingerprinting code* based schemes [4,7], our work is the first *publicly traceable* scheme using the most efficient asymmetric Type-3 variant of the bilinear maps.

- Observe from Tables 1 and 2 that most of the schemes are designed under symmetric Type-1 (T1) pairings and few [11,15,20] have used asymmetric Type-3 (T3) pairings. Uzunkol et al. [24] have shown that the *Decisional Diffie-Hellman* (DDH) test attack has broken many cryptographic protocols constructed using the symmetric T1 pairings. On the other hand, the DDH test is computationally hard in asymmetric T3 setting (shown in Remark 3). However, we emphasize that our design achieves adaptive security without ROM under the DBDHE assumption over the advanced and secured asymmetric T3 maps.

2   Prerequisites

2.1   Asymmetric Bilinear Pairings and Hardness Assumptions

Definition 1 (Asymmetric Bilinear Map [15,20]). *Let $\mathbb{G}^\times$ and $\widetilde{\mathbb{G}}^\times$ be two multiplicative source groups and $\mathbb{G}_T^\times$ be a multiplicative target group. Assume that all the groups have the same large prime order p ($> 2^n$). Let $P, \widetilde{P}$ be generators of $\mathbb{G}^\times$ and $\widetilde{\mathbb{G}}^\times$ respectively. A function $e : \mathbb{G}^\times \times \widetilde{\mathbb{G}}^\times \to \mathbb{G}_T^\times$ is said to be asymmetric bilinear mapping if it has the following properties.*

1. **Bilinearity:** $e(U^a, \widetilde{V}^b) = e(U, \widetilde{V})^{ab}$, $\forall U \in \mathbb{G}^\times$, $\widetilde{V} \in \widetilde{\mathbb{G}}^\times$ and $\forall\, a, b \in \mathbb{Z}_p$.
2. **Non-degeneracy:** *The function is non-degenerate, i.e., $e(P, \widetilde{P})$ is a generator of $\mathbb{G}_T^\times$.*
3. **Computability:** *The function e is efficiently computable.*

The tuple $\mathbb{BG} = (p, \mathbb{G}^\times, \widetilde{\mathbb{G}}^\times, \mathbb{G}_T^\times, e)$ is called a prime order asymmetric bilinear group system.

Remark 1 (Classification of Bilinear Map). Depending on practical concerns such as compact representation of the group elements, collision-resistant hashing to a group element, testing membership in the second source group and computationally efficient isomorphism, etc., the bilinear pairings have been classified into three main categories which are described below.

1. **Type-1(T1):** In Type-1 setting, which is also known as *symmetric bilinear maps*, there is no compact representations for elements of the bilinear groups, where $\mathbb{G}^+ = \widetilde{\mathbb{G}}^+$. In the work of [24], they have shown that several recent attacks have broken many security assumptions on T1 pairings.
2. **Type-2(T2):** A less efficient alternative is when $\mathbb{G}^+ \neq \widetilde{\mathbb{G}}^+$ with an efficiently computable isomorphism from $\widetilde{\mathbb{G}}^+$ to $\mathbb{G}^+$ and vice versa are known. In T2 setting, there does not exists any efficient collision-resistant hashing method to the elements in $\widetilde{\mathbb{G}}^+$ and $\widetilde{\mathbb{G}}^+$.
3. **Type-3(T3):** Here, $\mathbb{G}^+ \neq \widetilde{\mathbb{G}}^+$ and no such efficiently computable isomorphism between $\widetilde{\mathbb{G}}^+$ and $\mathbb{G}^+$ and vice versa exists. In T3 pairings, there exists an efficient collision-resistant hashing method to the group elements.

Note that the T3 parings outperforms T1, T2 pairings from efficient implementation and security point of view [24].

Decisional Bilinear Diffie-Hellman Exponent (DBDHE) Assumption. The DBDHE assumption is due to Li et al. [15], which is described as follows.

- **Input:** $\langle Z = (\mathbb{BG}, \widetilde{P}, \widetilde{P}^{\alpha}, \ldots, \widetilde{P}^{\alpha^m}, \widetilde{P}^{\alpha^{m+2}}, \ldots, \widetilde{P}^{\alpha^{2m}}, P, P^{\alpha}, \ldots, P^{\alpha^m}, P^c)$, $K \rangle$, where α, c randomly chosen from $\mathbb{Z}_p^*$, i.e., $\alpha, c \in_R \mathbb{Z}_p^*$ and K is either $e(P, \widetilde{P})^{\alpha^{m+1} \cdot c}$ or a random element $X \in_R \mathbb{G}_T^{\times}$.
- **Output:** 0 if $K = e(P, \widetilde{P})^{\alpha^{m+1} \cdot c}$; 1 otherwise.

Definition 2 (DBDHE Assumption). *The asymmetric DBDHE assumption holds with (t', ϵ') if for every PPT adversary $\mathcal{A}$ with runtime at most t', the advantage of $\mathcal{A}$ in solving the above problem is at most ϵ', i.e.,*

$$Adv_{\mathcal{A}}^{\mathsf{DBDHE}}(\eta) = \left| Pr[\mathcal{A}(Z, K = e(P, \widetilde{P})^{\alpha^{m+1} \cdot c}) = 0] - Pr[\mathcal{A}(Z, K = X) = 0] \right| \leq \epsilon'$$

2.2 Tardos Fingerprinting Code [22]

The collusion-secure probabilistic *Tardos fingerprinting code* (TFC), introduced by Gábor Tardos [22], are designed for watermarking digital contents. A *Tardos fingerprinting code* TFC = (CodeGen, Identify) consists of the following two randomized algorithms.

- $(\Gamma, \mathsf{WatMTK}) \leftarrow \mathsf{CodeGen}(1^\eta, N)$: The code generation algorithm, which is run by a tracer, takes as input the security parameter η with a positive integer $N = \mathsf{poly}(\eta)$ and executes the following steps.

1. The tracer chooses an error bound $\epsilon \in (0, 1)$ together with a positive integer $L = \mathsf{poly}(\eta) \leq N$ which is the maximum collusion bound. It sets $k = \lceil \log(\frac{1}{\epsilon}) \rceil$ and code length $l = 100L^2 k$.
2. The tracer chooses independent and identically distributed random variables X_i from $[t, 1-t]$ for all $i = 1, 2, \ldots, l$ with $t = \frac{1}{300L}$, $X_i = \sin^2 r_i$ where r_i is selected uniformly at random from $\left[t', \frac{\pi}{2} - t'\right]$, $0 < t' < \frac{\pi}{4}$, $\sin^2 t' = t$.
3. The tracer generates the code matrix $C_{N \times l}$ by selecting each entry c_{ji} independently from the binary alphabet $\{0, 1\}$ with probability $Pr[c_{ji} = 1] = X_i$, $j = 1, 2, \ldots, N$, $i = 1, 2, \ldots, l$. Note that the random variables c_{ji} and $c_{j'i}$ (with $j \neq j'$) are positively correlated as both of them tend to be 1 if X_i is very large. It constructs the code book $\Gamma = \{w_j\}_{j=1}^N$ where $w_j \in \{0, 1\}^l$ is the j-th row of the code matrix $C_{N \times l}$.
4. The tracer computes a threshold parameter $Z = 20Lk$ and sets the watermarking master tracing key $\mathsf{WatMTK} = (Z, \{X_i\}_{i=1}^l)$.
5. Finally, the code generation algorithm outputs the pair $(\Gamma, \mathsf{WatMTK})$.

- (𝕋) ← Identify(WatMTK, w): The fraud identification algorithm is run by the tracer having the watermarking master tracing key WatMTK $= (Z, \{X_i\}_{i=1}^l)$ and takes as input a l-length binary code word w called pirate code word. Let $\mathcal{S} = \{w_j\}_{j=1}^L (\subseteq \Gamma)$ be a coalition and let $F(\mathcal{S})$ denotes the feasible set of $\mathcal{S}$ containing w. Then $F(\mathcal{S})$ satisfies the following marking condition: if $w_j[i] = b \in \{0,1\}$ for all positions $1 \leq i \leq l$, then $w[i] = b$ where $w_j[i]$ is the i-th bit of the identity $w_j \in \mathcal{S}$ and $w[i]$ represents the i-th bit of the string $w \in \{0,1\}^l$. The tracer proceeds as follows.

1. It extracts $\{X_i\}_{i=1}^l$ from WatMTK and generates a matrix $M_{N \times l}$ with entries

$$m_{ji} = \begin{cases} \sqrt{\frac{1-X_i}{X_i}}, & \text{if } w_j[i] = 1 \\ -\sqrt{\frac{X_i}{1-X_i}}, & \text{if } w_j[i] = 0 \end{cases}$$

   Note that the random variable m_{ji} are independent and each has expected value 0 and variance 1.

2. The tracer extracts Z from WatMTK, checks whether $\sum_{i=1}^l w[i] \cdot m_{ji} > Z$ and if so, it accuses the code word $w_j \in \mathcal{S}$ as a fraud code word used in creating the pirate code word $w \in F(\mathcal{S})$.

3. The identification algorithm outputs a set $\mathbb{T}(\subseteq \mathcal{S})$ such that the members in $\mathbb{T}$ are accused in creating the pirate code word w.

Correctness: The correctness of TFC follows from the following theorems where $N \geq L \geq 1, 0 < \epsilon < 1$ be the arbitrary error bound, (𝕋) ← Identify(WatMTK, w), $(\Gamma, \text{WatMTK}) \leftarrow$ CodeGen$(1^\eta, N)$ and $w \in \{0,1\}^l$ be the pirate code word.

Theorem 1 ([22]). *Assume that $j \in \{1, 2, \ldots, N\}$ be an arbitrary user index. Let $\mathcal{S} \subseteq \Gamma \setminus \{w_j\}$ be a coalition of size $L \leq N$ and $F(\mathcal{S})$ be the feasible set of $\mathcal{S}$. Then, $Pr[w_j \in \mathbb{T}] < \epsilon$.*

Theorem 2 ([22]). *Let $\mathcal{S} \subseteq \Gamma$ be a coalition of size $|\mathcal{S}| \leq L$, and $F(\mathcal{S})$ be the feasible set of $\mathcal{S}$. Then, $Pr[(\mathcal{S} \cap \mathbb{T}) = \emptyset] < (\epsilon)^{\frac{L}{4}}$.*

Security: The security game of TFC is played between a PPT adversary $\mathcal{A}$ and a challenger $\mathcal{C}$. The advantage of $\mathcal{A}$ in winning the above game is defined as follows.

$$\text{Adv}_{\mathcal{A}}^{\text{TFC}}(\eta) = Pr \left[(\mathbb{T} = \emptyset) \vee (\mathbb{T} \not\subseteq \mathcal{S}) : \begin{matrix} (\Gamma, \text{WatMTK}) \leftarrow \text{CodeGen}(1^\eta, N) \\ w \leftarrow [\mathcal{A}(\eta, N, L)]^{\mathcal{O}(\cdot)} \\ \mathbb{T} \leftarrow \text{Identify}(\text{WatMTK}, w) \end{matrix} \right]$$

Here, $\mathcal{O}(\cdot)$ is an oracle that allows $\mathcal{A}$ to query on an index set $\mathbb{I}$ with $|\mathbb{I}| \leq L \leq N$, and the challenger responds by returning the code words $\mathcal{S} = \{w_j\}_{j \in \mathbb{I}}$ to $\mathcal{A}$ with the restriction that $w \notin \mathcal{S}$.

Definition 3 (Security of TFC). *We say that the code TFC is (t, ϵ) fully collusion resistant if $\text{Adv}_{\mathcal{A}}^{\text{TFC}}(\eta)$ is negligible function of η for all PPT adversary $\mathcal{A}$ running in time at most t.*

3 Identity-Based Outsider Anonymous Public-Key Trace and Revoke [1,8]

Syntax: An identity-based *outsider anonymous public-key trace and revoke* construction, denoted by OAnoPKTR, consists of three PPT algorithms (Setup, Key-Gen, Enc), a deterministic polynomial time algorithm Dec and a probabilistic tracing algorithm Trace$^{\mathcal{D}}$ satisfying the following requirements.

- (OAnoTPK, OAnoTMK) $\leftarrow$ Setup(1^{η}, N): Taking as input the security parameter η along with a positive integer $N = \mathsf{poly}(\eta)$, a trusted third party, called private key generation center (PKGC), runs this algorithm and outputs a tracing public key OAnoTPK and a tracing master key OAnoTMK. The tracing public key OAnoTPK is made publicly available and the tracing master key OAnoTMK is kept secret to itself.
- (OAnoTSK$_u$) $\leftarrow$ KeyGen(OAnoTPK, OAnoTMK, id_u): On input master public-secret key pair (OAnoTPK, OAnoTMK) and an identity id_u of the user $u \in [N]$, the PKGC generates a private key sk$_u$ and outputs a tracing secret key OAnoTSK$_u$ = sk$_u$. The tracing secret key OAnoTSK$_u$ is sent securely to the user with index u.
- (CT) $\leftarrow$ Enc(OAnoTPK, $\mathcal{S}$, M): This algorithm is run by a broadcaster who takes as input OAnoTPK, a set of user identities $\mathcal{S}$ and a message M. It outputs a ciphertext CT, and makes it publicly available.
- ($M \vee \bot$) $\leftarrow$ Dec(OAnoTPK, OAnoTSK$_u$, CT): A decryptor with index u uses the pair (OAnoTPK, OAnoTSK$_u$) to decrypt the ciphertext CT and either recovers the correct message M or gets a designated symbol $\bot$, indicating the decryption failure.
- ($\mathbb{T}$) $\leftarrow$ Trace$^{\mathcal{D}}$(OAnoTPK): Taking OAnoTPK as input, a public tracer runs this tracing algorithm by interacting polynomially many times with the pirate decoder $\mathcal{D}$ considering as a black-box oracle, and outputs a set of users identity $\mathbb{T}(\subseteq \mathcal{S})$ who are accused as traitors.

Remark 2 (Outsider Anonymity). A OAnoPKTR is only outsider anonymous, whereas insider anonymity does not hold. Thus, the decryption algorithm does not require the information of subscribed users set $\mathcal{S}$ as an additional input. Therefore, the set $\mathcal{S}$ is completely anonymous from any outsider adversary. However, each subscribed user belonging to $\mathcal{S}$ (i.e., insider) knows the information of all other subscribers [8].

Correctness: We say that the identity-based OAnoPKTR is correct if for all η, M and $id_u \in \mathcal{S}$,

$$
\Pr\left[
\begin{array}{c}
M \leftarrow \mathsf{Dec}(\mathsf{OAnoTPK}, \mathsf{OAnoTSK}_u, \mathsf{CT}) : (\mathsf{CT}) \leftarrow \mathsf{Enc}(\mathsf{OAnoTPK}, \mathcal{S}, M) \\
(\mathsf{OAnoTSK}_u) \leftarrow \mathsf{KeyGen}(\mathsf{OAnoTPK}, \mathsf{OAnoTMK}, id_u) \\
(\mathsf{OAnoTPK}, \mathsf{OAnoTMK}) \leftarrow \mathsf{Setup}(1^{\eta}, N)
\end{array}
\right] = 1
$$

Security: The security against message indistinguishability with receivers outsider anonymity and the security against arbitrary collusion, called traceability, are the two security attributes of the scheme OAnoPKTR. The following two games model these two security attributes.

(i) Message indistinguishability with receivers outsider anonymity [1,8]: This game, under the adaptive *indistinguishable chosen-plaintext attack* (IND-CPA) security, is played between a PPT adversary $\mathcal{A}$ and a challenger $\mathcal{C}$. The advantage of $\mathcal{A}$ in winning the game is defined as

$$\mathsf{Adv}^{\mathsf{IND\text{-}CPA}}_{\mathcal{A},\mathsf{OAnoPKTR}}(\eta) = \left| \mathsf{MIAdvc}(\eta) - \frac{1}{4} \right|,$$

where $\mathsf{MIAdvc}(\eta)$ is given by the following quantity.

$$\Pr \left[\begin{array}{l} (\mathsf{OAnoTPK}, \mathsf{OAnoTMK}) \leftarrow \mathsf{Setup}(1^\eta, N) \\ ((M_0^*, M_1^*), (S_0^*, S_1^*)) \leftarrow [\mathcal{A}(1^\eta)]^{\mathcal{O}(\mathsf{OAnoTPK}, \mathsf{OAnoTMK}, \cdot)} \\ (\xi = \xi') \wedge (\varkappa = \varkappa') : \xi \in_R \{0,1\} \text{ and } \varkappa \in_R \{0,1\} \\ (\mathsf{CT}^*) \leftarrow \mathsf{Enc}(\mathsf{OAnoTPK}, S_\varkappa^*, M_\xi^*) \\ (\xi', \varkappa') \leftarrow \mathcal{A}(\mathsf{CT}^*, \{\mathsf{OAnoTSK}_u : id_u \notin S_0^*, S_1^*\}_{u=1}^q) \end{array} \right]$$

Here, $\mathcal{O}(\mathsf{OAnoTPK}, \mathsf{OAnoTMK}, \cdot)$ denotes the key generation oracle access that allows $\mathcal{A}$ to query on a set of indices $\mathbb{I} \subseteq [N]$ with $|\mathbb{I}| \leq L \leq N$, and it returns $(\mathsf{OAnoTSK}_{u_i}) \leftarrow \mathsf{KeyGen}(\mathsf{OAnoTPK}, \mathsf{OAnoTMK}, ID_{u_i})$ for all $i \in \mathbb{I}$.

Definition 4 (Security of Message Indistinguishability with Receivers Outsider Anonymity). *We say that the scheme OAnoPKTR is (t, ϵ, q) IND-CPA secure if $\mathsf{Adv}^{\mathsf{IND\text{-}CPA}}_{\mathcal{A},\mathsf{OAnoPKTR}}(\eta)$ is negligible function of η for all PPT adversary $\mathcal{A}$ with run-time at most t and making at most $q = \mathsf{poly}(\eta)$ secret key queries.*

(ii) Traceability [2,19]: This game is played between an adversary $\mathcal{A}$ and a tracer $\mathcal{C}$. The advantage of $\mathcal{A}$ in winning the game is defined as

$$\mathsf{Adv}^{\mathsf{TT}}_{\mathcal{A},\mathsf{OAnoPKTR}}(\eta) = \left| \mathsf{TAdvc}(\eta) \right|,$$

where $\mathsf{TAdvc}(\eta)$ is given by the following quantity.

$$\Pr \left[\begin{array}{l} (\mathsf{OAnoTPK}, \mathsf{OAnoTMK}) \leftarrow \mathsf{Setup}(1^\eta, N) \\ (\zeta = 1) : (\mathcal{D}) \leftarrow [\mathcal{A}(1^\eta, \mathsf{OAnoTPK}, L)]^{\mathcal{O}\mathsf{KeyGen}(\mathsf{OAnoTPK}, \mathsf{OAnoTMK}, \cdot)} \\ (\mathbb{T}) \leftarrow \mathsf{Trace}^{\mathcal{D}}(\mathsf{OAnoTPK}) \\ \text{If } (X_1 \wedge X_2) \text{ holds, set } \zeta = 1; \text{ Else, set } \zeta = 0 \end{array} \right]$$

Here, X_1 is the event that $\mathcal{D}$ is an ϵ-useful decoder and X_2 is the event that $\mathbb{T}$ is either empty or not a subset of $\mathcal{E}$. For a randomly chosen message M_i, we say that $\mathcal{D}$ is ϵ-useful decoder if $\Pr[\mathcal{D}(\mathsf{Enc}(\mathsf{OAnoTPK}, \mathcal{S}, M_i)) = M_i] \geq \epsilon$. Here, $\mathcal{O}\mathsf{KeyGen}(\mathsf{OAnoTPK}, \mathsf{OAnoTMK}, \cdot)$ is an key generation oracle that allows $\mathcal{A}$ to query on a set of indices $\mathbb{I} \subseteq [N]$ with $|\mathbb{I}| \leq L$, and it returns $(\mathsf{OAnoTSK}_{u_i}) \leftarrow \mathsf{KeyGen}(\mathsf{OAnoTPK}, \mathsf{OAnoTMK}, id_{u_i})$ for all $i \in \mathbb{I}$, where $\mathcal{E} = \{u_i : i \in \mathbb{I}\}$.

Definition 5 (Security of Traceability). *We say that the scheme OAnoPKTR is (t, ϵ) traceable if $Adv_{A,OAnoPKTR}^{TT}(\eta)$ is negligible function of η for all decoder, corresponding to some polynomial-sized set of identities, provided by all PPT adversary A with run-time at most t.*

4   Our Construction

The communication model of our identity-based OAnoPKTR = (Setup, KeyGen, Enc, Dec, Trace^D) scheme involves a group manager (GM), also known as the private key generation center (PKGC), a broadcaster, several users and a tracer. The description of the algorithms are detailed below.

- (OAnoTPK, OAnoTMK) ← Setup($1^\eta, N$): The GM, on input the security parameter η and the total number of users $N = 2^l$ ($l > 0$) of the system, proceeds as follows.

(i) It first generates a prime order asymmetric bilinear group system $\mathbb{BG} = (p, \mathbb{G}^\times, \widetilde{\mathbb{G}}^\times, \mathbb{G}_T^\times, e)$ (detailed in Sect. 2.1). Let $P, \widetilde{P}$ be random generators of $\mathbb{G}^\times$ and $\widetilde{\mathbb{G}}^\times$ respectively.

(ii) It chooses random exponents $\alpha, \beta, \{\delta_j\}_{j=1}^N, \{a_j\}_{j=1}^N \in \mathbb{Z}_p^*$ and computes $\{U_i = P^{a_i}, \widetilde{U}_i = \widetilde{P}^{a_i}, f_i = P^{\delta_i}, \widetilde{f}_i = \widetilde{P}^{\delta_i}\}_{i=1}^N, P_2 = P^\beta, \widetilde{P}_1 = \widetilde{P}^\alpha, \widetilde{P}_2 = \widetilde{P}^\beta, \Omega = e(P_2, \widetilde{P}_1)$.

(iii) It chooses a collision-resistant hash function $H : \{0,1\}^l \to \mathbb{Z}_p^*$ and sets tracing public key as OAnoTPK = $(P, \widetilde{P}, \widetilde{P}_1, \widetilde{P}_2, P_2, \{f_j\}_{j=1}^N, \{U_j\}_{j=1}^N, \Omega, H)$ and tracing master key OAnoTMK = $(\widetilde{P}_2^\alpha, \{\widetilde{f}_j\}_{j=1}^N, \{\widetilde{U}_j\}_{j=1}^N)$.

(iv) The GM publishes OAnoTPK and keeps OAnoTMK secret to itself.

- (OAnoTSK$_u$) ← KeyGen(OAnoTPK, OAnoTMK, id_u): On receiving a user identity $id_u \in \{0,1\}^l$, the GM executes the following steps.

(i) It sets the identity space $\mathcal{ID} = \{id_i \in \{0,1\}^l : 1 \le i \le N = 2^l\}$ and extracts H from OAnoTPK to compute the exponents $ID_i = H(id_i) \in \mathbb{Z}_p^*$, for $1 \le i \le N$.

(ii) It chooses a random exponent $r_u \in \mathbb{Z}_p^*$ to compute $d_{u,0} = \widetilde{P}^{r_u}$, $d_{u,u} = \widetilde{P}_2^\alpha (\widetilde{f}_u \cdot \widetilde{U}_u^{ID_u})^{r_u}$ and $d_{u,j} = (\widetilde{f}_j \cdot \widetilde{U}_j^{ID_u})^{r_u}$ for $1 \le j \ne u \le N$.

(iii) It sets the private key $sk_u = (d_{u,0}, d_{u,u}, \{d_{u,j} : 1 \le j \ne u \le N\})$ and the tracing secret key as OAnoTSK$_u$ = sk_u.

(iv) The GM sends OAnoTSK$_u$ to the user u through a secure communication channel between them.

- (CT) ← Enc(OAnoTPK, $\mathcal{S}, M$): The broadcaster takes as input OAnoTPK, a polynomial size set $\mathcal{S}$ of subscribed users' identities and a message $M \in \mathbb{G}_T^\times$. For notational convenient, let us consider the set is of the form $\mathcal{S} = \{ID_u : u \in I_\mathcal{S}\}$, where $ID_u = H(id_u) \in \mathbb{Z}_p^*$ corresponds to some identity $id_u \in \mathcal{ID}$ and $I_\mathcal{S}$ is the index set of $\mathcal{S}$ with $|I_\mathcal{S}| = L \le N$. It performs the following steps to produce an encrypted content, known as ciphertext, corresponding to the message M.

(i) It first chooses a partition $\mathsf{RP} = (\mathcal{S}_0, \mathcal{S}_1)$ of the set $\mathcal{S}$, where $\mathcal{S}_0 = \{ID_j : j \in I_{0,\mathcal{S}}\}$ and $\mathcal{S}_1 = \{ID_j : j \in I_{1,\mathcal{S}}\}$ are disjoint sets with $\mathcal{S} = \mathcal{S}_0 \cup \mathcal{S}_1$. Here, $I_{0,\mathcal{S}}$ and $I_{1,\mathcal{S}}$ are two arbitrary partitions of the index set $I_{\mathcal{S}}$ with $I_{0,\mathcal{S}} \cap I_{1,\mathcal{S}} = \emptyset$, $|I_{0,\mathcal{S}}| = \xi$, $|I_{1,\mathcal{S}}| = \delta$ and $\xi + \delta = L \leq N$.

(ii) It randomly selects two exponent $s_0, s_1 \in \mathbb{Z}_p^*$ and executes the following steps.

(a) For the set $\mathcal{S}_0 = \{ID_j : j \in I_{0,\mathcal{S}}\}$, it computes

$$C_{0,0} = P^{s_0}, \quad C_{0,1} = \Big(\prod_{j \in I_{0,\mathcal{S}}} f_j \cdot U_j^{ID_j} \Big)^{s_0}, \quad C_{0,2} = M \cdot \Omega^{s_0}$$

and sets first ciphertext component $\mathsf{CT}_0 = (C_{0,0}, C_{0,1}, C_{0,2})$.

(b) For the set $\mathcal{S}_1 = \{ID_j : j \in I_{1,\mathcal{S}}\}$, it computes

$$C_{1,0} = P^{s_1}, \quad C_{1,1} = \Big(\prod_{j \in I_{1,\mathcal{S}}} f_j \cdot U_j^{ID_j} \Big)^{s_1}, \quad C_{1,2} = M \cdot \Omega^{s_1}$$

and sets second ciphertext component $\mathsf{CT}_1 = (C_{1,0}, C_{1,1}, C_{1,2})$.

(iii) The broadcaster publishes $\mathsf{CT} = (\mathsf{CT}_0, \mathsf{CT}_1)$ as the ciphertext.

- $(M \vee \bot) \leftarrow \mathsf{Dec}(\mathsf{OAnoTPK}, \mathsf{OAnoTSK}_u, \mathsf{CT})$: A subscribed user u with its tracing secret key $\mathsf{OAnoTSK}_u = \mathsf{sk}_u$, identity $id_u \in \{0,1\}^l$ and the tracing public key $\mathsf{OAnoTPK}$ recovers correct message M from the ciphertext CT. Since the our scheme is outsider anonymous, decryption algorithm does not require the information of subscribed users set $\mathcal{S}$ as an input. Therefore, the set $\mathcal{S}$ is completely anonymous from any outsider adversary. However, each subscribed user (i.e., insider) knows the information of all other subscribers as well as the partition $\mathsf{RP} = (\mathcal{S}_0, \mathcal{S}_1)$ of $\mathcal{S}$. Let us assume that the identity exponent $ID_u = H(id_u)$ of user u belongs to $\mathcal{S}_b$, where either $b = 0$ or $b = 1$. It parses the private key $\mathsf{sk}_u = (d_{u,0}, d_{u,u}, \{d_{u,j} : 1 \leq j \neq u \leq N\})$ and recovers the correct message M from the ciphertext component CT_b by the following computations.

$$C_{b,2} \times \frac{e(C_{b,1}, d_{u,0})}{e(C_{b,0}, d_{u,u} \cdot \prod_{j \in I_{b,\mathcal{S}} \backslash \{u\}} d_{u,j})}$$

$$= M \times e(P, \widetilde{P})^{\alpha \beta s_b} \times \frac{e\Big(\prod_{j \in I_{b,\mathcal{S}} \backslash \{u\}} f_j \cdot U_j^{ID_j}, \widetilde{P}^{r_u} \Big)^{s_b}}{e(P^{s_b}, \widetilde{P}_2^\alpha (\widetilde{f}_u \cdot \widetilde{U}_u^{ID_u})^{r_u} \cdot \prod_{j \in I_{b,\mathcal{S}} \backslash \{u\}} (\widetilde{f}_j \cdot \widetilde{U}_j^{ID_j})^{r_u})}$$

$$= M \times e(P, \widetilde{P})^{\alpha \beta s_b} \times \frac{e\Big(\prod_{j \in I_{b,\mathcal{S}} \backslash \{u\}} f_j \cdot U_j^{ID_j}, \widetilde{P} \Big)^{s_b r_u}}{e(P, \widetilde{P})^{\alpha \beta s_b} e(P^{s_b}, \prod_{j \in I_{b,\mathcal{S}} \backslash \{u\}} (\widetilde{f}_j \cdot \widetilde{U}_j^{ID_j})^{r_u})}$$

$$= M \times \frac{e\Big(\prod_{j \in I_{b,\mathcal{S}} \backslash \{u\}} P^{\delta_j} \cdot P^{a_j ID_j}, \widetilde{P} \Big)^{s_b r_u}}{e(P^{s_b}, \prod_{j \in I_{b,\mathcal{S}} \backslash \{u\}} (\widetilde{f}_j \cdot \widetilde{U}_j^{ID_j})^{r_u})} = M \times \frac{e\Big(P, \widetilde{P}^{\sum_{j \in I_{b,\mathcal{S}} \backslash \{u\}} (\delta_j + a_j ID_j)} \Big)^{s_b r_u}}{e(P^{s_b}, \prod_{j \in I_{b,\mathcal{S}} \backslash \{u\}} (\widetilde{f}_j \cdot \widetilde{U}_j^{ID_j})^{r_u})}$$

$$= M$$

- (T) $\leftarrow$ Trace$^{\mathcal{D}}$(OAnoTPK): To execute the tracing algorithm based on the pirate decoder $\mathcal{D}$, the tracer, having the knowledge of subscribers set $\mathcal{S} = \{ID_u : u \in I_{\mathcal{S}}\}$, $|I_{\mathcal{S}}| = L \leq N$, takes only the tracing public key OAnoTPK as an input and executes the following steps.

(i) The tracer first runs the Tardos fingerprinting code generation algorithm TFC.CodeGen($1^\eta, N$) (described in Sect. 2.2) to generate code book $\Gamma = \{w_i\}_{i=1}^{N}$ and watermarking master tracing key WatMTK $= \left(Z, \{X_i\}_{i=1}^{l}\right)$, where $Z = 20Lk$, L= size of $\mathcal{S}$, $k = \lceil \log\left(\frac{1}{\epsilon}\right)\rceil$, ϵ = error bound and X_i = identically distributed random variable from $[t, 1-t]$ with $t = 1/300L$. It assigns code word $w_i \in \Gamma$ to each user $i \in [N]$ and constructs the set $\widetilde{S} = \{w_u : u \in I_{\mathcal{S}}\} \subset \Gamma$ that corresponds to the subscribed users set $\mathcal{S}$. It chooses a random permutation $\pi : [N] \longrightarrow [N]$ and shuffles the indices of all the code words in the subset $\widetilde{S}$ by employing π. It initially sets a code word $w = 0^l$ as a pirate code word.

(ii) The tracer executes the following steps to construct a l-length pirate code word w belonging to the feasible set $F(\widetilde{S})$ of $\widetilde{S}$. For each index $j = 1, 2, \ldots, l$, the tracer repeatedly performs the following steps.

   - A partition of the set $\mathcal{S}$, denoted by $\mathsf{RP}_{\pi}^{(j)} = (S_0^{(j)}, S_1^{(j)})$, is constructed by setting

$$S_b^{(j)} = \begin{cases} \mathcal{S} \cap \{ID_v \mid w_{\pi(v)}[j] = 0, \ \forall \ w_v \in \widetilde{S}\}, & \text{if } b = 0 \\ \mathcal{S} \cap \{ID_v \mid w_{\pi(v)}[j] = 1, \ \forall \ w_v \in \widetilde{S}\}, & \text{if } b = 1 \end{cases}$$

   Due to the random choice of π, the partition $\mathsf{RP}_{\pi}^{(j)}$ is indistinguishable from the original partition RP of the set $\mathcal{S}$ in the main encryption algorithm.
   - A random message $M_{\mathsf{rand}} \in \mathbb{G}_T^{\times}$ is chosen by the tracer to construct the tracing ciphertext, corresponding to the index j and the split $\mathsf{RP}_{\pi}^{(j)}$, as $\mathsf{CT}[j] = \left(\mathsf{CT}_0[j] = (C_{0,0}, C_{0,1}, C_{0,2}) \leftarrow \mathsf{Enc}(\mathsf{OAnoTPK}, \mathcal{S}, M_{\mathsf{rand}}), \mathsf{CT}_1[j] = (C_{1,0}, C_{1,1}, C_{1,2}) \leftarrow \mathsf{Enc}(\mathsf{OAnoTPK}, \mathcal{S}, M)\right)$, where $C_{0,2} = M_{\mathsf{rand}} \cdot \Omega^{s_0}$, $C_{1,2} = M \cdot \Omega^{s_1}$ and rest of the ciphertext components are constructed in a similar manner as shown in the main encryption algorithm.
   - It interacts with the pirate decoder $\mathcal{D}$ by providing polynomially many tracing ciphertexts $\mathsf{CT}[j]$ for different choices of $M, M_{\mathsf{rand}} \in_R \mathbb{G}_T^{\times}$. Let $p_{1,j}$ be the success probability of $\mathcal{D}$ in decrypting the ciphertext corresponding to the j-th bit. The tracer will replace the j-th bit $w[j]$ of the pirate code word w with 1 if $p_{1,j} \geq \frac{1}{2}$.
   - It outputs the pirate code word $w \in \{0,1\}^l$. Note that we can estimate w in a similar manner by considering $p_{0,j}$ instead of $p_{1,j}$ by setting $\mathsf{CT}_1[j]$ to be the encryption of the random message M_{rand}.

(iii) Finally, the tracer runs the identification algorithm Identify(WatMTK, w) of the Tardos fingerprinting code of Sect. 2.2 to get a subset $\mathbb{T}_\pi (\subseteq \widetilde{S})$ such that the elements of the set are accused in creating the pirate code word w. Consequently, the set $\mathbb{T} = \{ID_{\pi^{-1}(t)} : w_t \in \mathbb{T}_\pi\}$ $(\subseteq \mathcal{S})$ is the set of all traitors involved in the production of the pirate decoder $\mathcal{D}$.

Approximation of the success probability $p_{1,j}$ of $\mathcal{D}$ for each index j and the correctness of the tracing algorithm will be shown in Theorem 4. Here, the pirate decoder box $\mathcal{D}$ is viewed as a probabilistic circuit. The decoder $\mathcal{D}$ succeeds in decrypting ciphertext intended for at least one subset S over the distribution of all possible receiver sets. If there does not exists any PPT algorithm which can sample such S for which the decoder $\mathcal{D}$ has non-negligible success probability in decrypting the corresponding ciphertext, then it is straightforward to conclude that no tracing can take place. Given the infeasibility of sampling the set S, the tracer will fail to ever witness that the decoder works. Due to this impossibility, we assume that, at the beginning the set S is given to the tracer by the broadcaster and it is entirely outside the control of the adversary. Consequently, the broadcaster as well as all the recipients, who have the knowledge of S, plays the role of the tracer.

Remark 3 (DDH Test for T1 and T3 Pairings). Our OAnoPKTR uses asymmetric T3 bilinear pairings. If instead, we use symmetric T1 bilinear pairing, then any outsider can run the *Decisional Diffie-Hellman* (DDH) test

$$e(P^{s_0}, \prod_{ID_{0,j} \in S_0'} f_j \cdot U_j^{ID_{0,j}}) = e(P, (\prod_{ID_{0,j} \in S_0} f_j \cdot U_j^{ID_{0,j}})^{s_0}),$$

and verify the subscribers set as f_j, U_j are publicly available in this setting. On the other hand, the DDH test

$$e(P^{s_0}, \prod_{ID_{0,j} \in S_0'} \widetilde{f}_j \cdot \widetilde{U}_j^{ID_{0,j}}) = e(\widetilde{P}, (\prod_{ID_{0,j} \in S_0} f_j \cdot U_j^{ID_{0,j}})^{s_0})$$

is computationally hard in asymmetric T3 bilinear as $\widetilde{f}_j$ and $\bar{U}_j$ are kept secret.

5   Security Analysis

The security analysis of our scheme follows from the following two theorems.

Theorem 3 (Security of Message Indistinguishability with Receivers Anonymity). *Our proposed OAnoPKTR, presented in Sect. 4, achieves $(t, \epsilon, poly(\eta))$ adaptive IND-CPA security as per the Definition 4 under the standard asymmetric (t', ϵ')DBDHE assumption, where η is the security parameter of the system and $poly(\eta)$ represents a polynomial in η.*

Theorem 4 (Security of Traceability). *Suppose that our OAnoPKTR scheme is adaptive IND-CPA secure against the message indistinguishability with receivers anonymity game, detailed in Definition 4. Then, assuming the (t, ϵ) fully collusion secure Tardos fingerprinting codes, detailed in Sect. 2.2, our publicly-key tracing algorithm $Trace^{\mathcal{D}}$ of Sect. 4 outputs identity of at least one traitor.*

Due to the page limit, the proof of the above Theorems 3 and 4 will appear in the full version of the paper.

6   Conclusion

We present the first publicly traceable identity-based OAnoPKTR scheme that is constructed by coupling the *Tardos fingerprinting code* (TFC) with the Waters IBE framework. Having constant-size communication and computation, our scheme is proven to be adaptively secure under the standard DBDHE assumption without using ROM. Our design uses the most efficient T3 variant of bilinear maps and thereby, is not vulnerable to DDH attack for identifying the set of subscribers corresponding to which the ciphertext is created.

Acknowledgment. Financial support from the University Grants Commission, Government of India [grant number F1-17.1/2014-15/RGNF-2014-15-SC-WES-58080/(SA-III/Website)] is gratefully acknowledged by the first author.

References

1. Acharya, K., Dutta, R.: Enhanced outsider-anonymous broadcast encryption with subset difference revocation. IACR Cryptology ePrint Archive 2017:265 (2017)
2. Murat, A.K., Pehlivanoğlu, S., Selçuk, A.A.: Anonymous trace and revoke. J. Comput. Appl. Math. **259**, 586–591 (2014)
3. Barth, A., Boneh, D., Waters, B.: Privacy in encrypted content distribution using private broadcast encryption. In: Di Crescenzo, G., Rubin, A. (eds.) FC 2006. LNCS, vol. 4107, pp. 52–64. Springer, Heidelberg (2006). https://doi.org/10.1007/11889663_4
4. Boneh, D., Naor, M.: Traitor tracing with constant size ciphertext. In: ACM Conference on Computer and Communications Security, pp. 501–510. ACM (2008)
5. Boneh, D., Sahai, A., Waters, B.: Fully collusion resistant traitor tracing with short ciphertexts and private keys. In: Vaudenay, S. (ed.) EUROCRYPT 2006. LNCS, vol. 4004, pp. 573–592. Springer, Heidelberg (2006). https://doi.org/10.1007/11761679_34
6. Delerablée, C.: Identity-based broadcast encryption with constant size ciphertexts and private keys. In: Kurosawa, K. (ed.) ASIACRYPT 2007. LNCS, vol. 4833, pp. 200–215. Springer, Heidelberg (2007). https://doi.org/10.1007/978-3-540-76900-2_12
7. Dodis, Y., Fazio, N.: Public key broadcast encryption for stateless receivers. In: Feigenbaum, J. (ed.) DRM 2002. LNCS, vol. 2696, pp. 61–80. Springer, Heidelberg (2003). https://doi.org/10.1007/978-3-540-44993-5_5
8. Fazio, N., Perera, I.M.: Outsider-anonymous broadcast encryption with sublinear ciphertexts. In: Fischlin, M., Buchmann, J., Manulis, M. (eds.) PKC 2012. LNCS, vol. 7293, pp. 225–242. Springer, Heidelberg (2012). https://doi.org/10.1007/978-3-642-30057-8_14
9. Fiat, A., Naor, M.: Broadcast encryption. In: Stinson, D.R. (ed.) CRYPTO 1993. LNCS, vol. 773, pp. 480–491. Springer, Heidelberg (1994). https://doi.org/10.1007/3-540-48329-2_40
10. He, K., Weng, J., Liu, J.-N., Liu, J.K., Liu, W., Deng, R.H.: Anonymous identity-based broadcast encryption with chosen-ciphertext security. In: Proceedings of the 11th ACM on Asia Conference on Computer and Communications Security, pp. 247–255. ACM (2016)

11. Hur, J., Park, C., Hwang, S.O.: Privacy-preserving identity-based broadcast encryption. Inf. Fusion **13**(4), 296–303 (2012)
12. Kiayias, A., Samari, K.: Lower bounds for private broadcast encryption. In: Kirchner, M., Ghosal, D. (eds.) IH 2012. LNCS, vol. 7692, pp. 176–190. Springer, Heidelberg (2013). https://doi.org/10.1007/978-3-642-36373-3_12
13. Lai, J., Mu, Y., Guo, F., Susilo, W., Chen, R.: Anonymous identity-based broadcast encryption with revocation for file sharing. In: Liu, J.K., Steinfeld, R. (eds.) ACISP 2016. LNCS, vol. 9723, pp. 223–239. Springer, Cham (2016). https://doi.org/10.1007/978-3-319-40367-0_14
14. Lee, K., Koo, W.K., Lee, D.H., Park, J.H.: Public-key revocation and tracing schemes with subset difference methods revisited. In: Kutyłowski, M., Vaidya, J. (eds.) ESORICS 2014. LNCS, vol. 8713, pp. 1–18. Springer, Cham (2014). https://doi.org/10.1007/978-3-319-11212-1_1
15. Li, X., Yanli, R.: Efficient anonymous identity-based broadcast encryption without random oracles. Int. J. Digit. Crime Forensics **6**(2), 40–51 (2014)
16. Libert, B., Paterson, K.G., Quaglia, E.A.: Anonymous broadcast encryption: adaptive security and efficient constructions in the standard model. In: Fischlin, M., Buchmann, J., Manulis, M. (eds.) PKC 2012. LNCS, vol. 7293, pp. 206–224. Springer, Heidelberg (2012). https://doi.org/10.1007/978-3-642-30057-8_13
17. Mandal, M., Dutta, R.: Cost-effective private linear key agreement with adaptive CCA security from prime order multilinear maps and tracing traitors. In: International Conference on Security and Cryptography, pp. 356–363. SciTePress (2018)
18. Mandal, M., Dutta, R.: Efficient adaptively secure public-key trace and revoke from subset cover using Déjà Q framework. In: Guo, F., Huang, X., Yung, M. (eds.) Inscrypt 2018. LNCS, vol. 11449, pp. 468–489. Springer, Cham (2019). https://doi.org/10.1007/978-3-030-14234-6_25
19. Nishimaki, R., Wichs, D., Zhandry, M.: Anonymous traitor tracing: how to embed arbitrary information in a key. In: Fischlin, M., Coron, J.-S. (eds.) EUROCRYPT 2016. LNCS, vol. 9666, pp. 388–419. Springer, Heidelberg (2016). https://doi.org/10.1007/978-3-662-49896-5_14
20. Ren, Y., Niu, Z., Zhang, X.: Fully anonymous identity-based broadcast encryption without random oracles. IJ Netw. Secur. **16**(4), 256–264 (2014)
21. Shen, J., Zhou, T., Chen, X., Li, J., Susilo, W.: Anonymous and traceable group data sharing in cloud computing. IEEE Trans. Inf. Forensics Secur. **13**(4), 912–925 (2018)
22. Tardos, G.: Optimal probabilistic fingerprint codes. J. ACM **55**(2), 10 (2008)
23. Tseng, Y.-M., Huang, Y.-H., Chang, H.-J.: CCA-secure anonymous multi-receiver ID-based encryption. In: International Conference on Advanced Information Networking and Applications Workshops, pp. 177–182. IEEE (2012)
24. Uzunkol, O., Kiraz, M.S.: Still wrong use of pairings in cryptography. Appl. Math. Comput. **333**, 467–479 (2018)
25. Waters, B.: Efficient identity-based encryption without random oracles. In: Cramer, R. (ed.) EUROCRYPT 2005. LNCS, vol. 3494, pp. 114–127. Springer, Heidelberg (2005). https://doi.org/10.1007/11426639_7
26. Zhang, L., Wu, Q., Mu, Y.: Anonymous identity-based broadcast encryption with adaptive security. In: Wang, G., Ray, I., Feng, D., Rajarajan, M. (eds.) CSS 2013. LNCS, vol. 8300, pp. 258–271. Springer, Cham (2013). https://doi.org/10.1007/978-3-319-03584-0_19
27. Zhang, M., Takagi, T.: Efficient constructions of anonymous multireceiver encryption protocol and their deployment in group e-mail systems with privacy preservation. IEEE Syst. J. **7**(3), 410–419 (2013)

Generic Constructions of Revocable Identity-Based Encryption

Xuecheng Ma[1,2] and Dongdai Lin[1,2(✉)]

[1] State Key Laboratory of Information Security, Institute of Information
Engineering, Chinese Academy of Sciences, Beijing 100093, China
{maxuecheng,ddlin}@iie.ac.cn
[2] School of Cyber Security, University of Chinese Academy of Sciences,
Beijing 100049, China

Abstract. Revocable identity-based encryption (RIBE) is an extension
of IBE which can support a key revocation mechanism, and it is important when deploying an IBE system in practice. Boneh and Franklin
(Crypto'01) presented the first generic construction of RIBE, however,
their scheme is not scalable where the size of key updates is linear in
the number of users in the system. Then, Boldyreva, Goyal and Kumar
(CCS'08) presented the first scalable RIBE which significantly reduces
the size of key update to logarithmic in the number of users.

In this paper, we first present a generic construction of scalable RIBE
from any IBE in a black-box way which solves the open problem presented by Seo and Emura (PKC'13). Our construction has some merits
both in theory and practice. In theory, we can obtain the first RIBE
scheme from quadratic residues modulo composite and the first adaptive-
ID secure RIBE scheme from lattices if we instantiate the underlying
IBE with IBE schemes from quadratic residues modulo composite and
adaptive-ID secure IBE schemes from lattices, respectively. In practice,
public parameters size and secret keys size of our construction can be
same as those of the underlying (H)IBE scheme. Our construction is
naturally server-aided where the overheads of decryption computation
for receivers is the same as that of underlying IBE schemes. Inspired by
recent work of Katsumata et al. (PKC'19), we present a generic construction of RIBE with decryption key exposure resistance by using hierarchical IBE (HIBE) and IBE schemes. Finally, we reduce the ciphertext
size to constant by using two HIBE schemes.

Keywords: Generic construction · Revocable IBE · DKER

1 Introduction

Identity-Based Encryption (IBE) was introduced by Shamir [37], to eliminate
the need for maintaining a certificate based Public Key Infrastructure (PKI) in
the traditional Public Key Encryption (PKE) setting. The first IBE scheme was

© Springer Nature Switzerland AG 2020
Z. Liu and M. Yung (Eds.): Inscrypt 2019, LNCS 12020, pp. 381–396, 2020.
https://doi.org/10.1007/978-3-030-42921-8_22

proposed by Boneh and Franklin [7] in the random oracle model [2]. Since then, there are many follow-up works [1,4,5,8–10,13,16,18,40–42].

Revocation capability is very important and necessary for IBE setting as well as PKI setting. To address the challenge of key revocation, Boneh and Franklin [7] proposed a naive method to add a simple revocation mechanism to any IBE system as follows. A sender encrypts a message using a receiver's identity concatenated with the current time period, i.e. $id||t$ and the Key Generation Center (KGC) issues the private key $sk_{id||t}$ for each non-revoked user in every time period. However, BF-RIBE scheme is inefficient. The number of private keys issued in every time period is linear in the number of all users in the system hence the scheme does not scale well when there are a large number of users.

Boldyreva, Goyal and Kumar [3] proposed the first scalable revocable IBE (RIBE) scheme by combining the fuzzy IBE scheme of Sahai and Waters [34] with a subset cover framework called the complete subtree (CS) method [28]. The BGK-RIBE scheme significantly reduces the size of key updates from linear to logarithmic in the number of users. Each user holds a long-term private key associated with its identity, but in order to achieve the key revocation mechanism, the private key is not allowed to decrypt ciphertexts. KGC broadcasts key updates for every time period through a public channel. Specially, the non-revoked users can derive decryption key from their long-term private keys and key updates while revoked users can't. There are numerous follow-up works [20,23,25,35,39].

RIBE with DKER. In the security definition of BGK-RIBE, the adversary is only given access to secret key oracle, revocation oracle and key update oracle. Considering the leakage of decryption keys in realistic attacks, Seo and Emura [35,36] introduced a security notion called decryption key exposure resistance (DKER). In DKER security experiment, an exposure of a user's decryption key at some time period will not compromise the confidentiality of ciphertexts which are encrypted for different time periods. It attracted many follow-up works concerning R(H)IBE schemes with DKER [17,20,22–24,27,30,31,33,36,39]. Recently, Katsumata et al. [21] presented a generic construction of RIBE with DKER from any RIBE without DKER and two-level HIBE. Combining the result of [15] that any IBE scheme can be converted to an HIBE scheme (in the selective-ID model) and any RIBE scheme without DKER implies an IBE scheme, their result implies a generic conversion from any RIBE scheme without DKER into an RIBE scheme with DKER.

Lattice-Based RIBE. Chen et al. [11] presented the first lattice-based RIBE which was selective-ID secure without DKER. Cheng and Zhang [12] claimed that their RIBE scheme was the first adaptive-ID secure lattice-based scheme. However, Takayasu and Watanabe [38] pointed out several critical bugs in their security proof and presented a semi-adaptive secure lattice-based RIBE scheme with bounded DKER which only allows a bounded number of decryption keys to be leaked. Recently, Katsumata et al. [21] proposed the first lattice-based R(H)IBE scheme with DKER secure under the learning with errors (LWE) assumption but their proposal was still selective-ID secure. Therefore, constructing an adaptive-ID secure RIBE scheme (even without DKER) from lattices still remains an open problem.

Server-aided RIBE [14,29,32] is a variant of RIBE where almost all of the workload on the user side can be delegated to an untrusted third-party server. The server is untrusted in the sense that it does not possess any secret information. Each user only needs to store a short long-term private key without having to communicate with KGC.

Our Contributions. In this paper, we propose three generic constructions of RIBE schemes in a black-box way. The first is a generic construction of RIBE *without* DKER from any IBE schemes which solves the open problem claimed in [35]. The second is a generic construction of RIBE *with* DKER from 2-level HIBE schemes and IBE schemes. The third is a RIBE with short ciphertext from HIBE. All of our constructions are scalable where the update key size of our construction is logarithmic in the number of users. The benefits of our generic constructions are as follows:

- Practical Benefits.
  (a) Our first RIBE scheme has the same size of public parameters and user's secret key as those of underlying IBE scheme. The public parameters of our second construction include 2-level HIBE public parameters and IBE public parameters. And user's secret key in our second and third constructions are only a 2-level HIBE secret key. So the secret key size in all of our constructions are constant in the number of users.
  (b) The ciphertext size can be reduced to constant by instantiating the HIBE scheme in our third construction with HIBE schemes with constant ciphertext.
  (c) Our schemes are naturally server-aided. The decryption cost for the receiver are the same as the underlying IBE (HIBE) scheme and receivers do not need to communicate with KGC in the server-aided model.
  By instantiating our constructions with appropriate concrete (H)IBE schemes, our schemes are very efficient. An overview comparison with other revocable IBE schemes is given in Table 1.
- Theoretical Benefits. To the best of our knowledge, BF-RIBE is the only generic construction of RIBE from IBE but it is not scalable. Our generic constructions demonstrate a simple and clear picture about how revocation problems in IBE could be addressed.
  (a) We present a generic construction of RIBE that can convert any IBE schemes to RIBE schemes *without* DKER. Inspired by the work of [21], we propose a construction of RIBE *with* DKER from HIBE and IBE schemes. Combining the result of [15] that any IBE scheme can be converted to an HIBE scheme (in the selective-ID model), we can obtain a generic construction of (selective-ID secure) RIBE *with* DKER from (selective-ID secure) IBE.
  (b) Instantiating our generic construction of existing IBE scheme [13] and HIBE scheme [8], we can obtain the first RIBE scheme *with* DKER based on quadratic residues modulo composite.

(c) Our constructions inherit the security of the underlying (H)IBE schemes. Hence, we can obtain the first adaptive-ID CPA secure lattice based RIBE scheme with DKER by instantiating our construction with adaptive-ID CPA secure IBE and HIBE schemes from lattices [1,9,10,18,42].

Table 1. Comparison with other RIBE schemes

Schemets	BF [7]	BGK [3]	LV [25]	SE [35]	LLP [23]	Ours-1	Ours-2
PP Size	$O(1)$	$O(1)$	$O(\lambda)$	$O(\lambda)$	$O(1)$	$O(1)$	$O(\log(N))$
SK Size	$O(1)$	$O(\log N)$	$O(\log N)$	$O(\log N)$	$O(\log^{1.5} N)$	$O(1)$	$O(1)$
CT Size	$O(1)$	$O(1)$	$O(1)$	$O(1)$	$O(1)$	$O(\log N)$	$O(1)$
KU Size	$O(N-r)$	$O(r \log \frac{N}{r})$	$O(r \log \frac{N}{r})$	$O(r \log \frac{N}{r})$	$O(r)$	$O(r \log \frac{N}{r})$	$O(r \log \frac{N}{r})$
DKER	Yes	No	No	Yes	Yes	Yes	Yes
Model	Full	Selective	Full	Full	Full	Full	Full
Assumption	RO, BDH	DBDH	DBDH	DBDH	Static	RO, BDH	RO, BDHE

We let λ be a security parameter, N be the maximum number of users, r be the number of revoked users. For security model, we use symbols RO for random oracle model, Full for adaptive model, Selective for selective model. In our-1, we instantiate the IBE scheme and HIBE scheme in our second construction (in Sect. 4) with [7] and [19] respectively. In our-2, we instantiate the HIBE scheme in our third construction (in Sect. 5) with a HIBE scheme with constant-size ciphertext [6].

Related Work. The first revocable IBE scheme from any IBE was presented by Boneh and Franklin [7], however their proposal was not scalable. Boldyreva et al. [3] proposed the first scalable RIBE using a tree-based approach, but their scheme was not a generic construction. Recently, Katsumata et al. [21] proposed a generic construction of RIBE with DKER by using any two-level standard HIBE scheme and RIBE scheme without DKER as building blocks. They did not address the revocation challenge for IBE schemes. However, our generic construction of RIBE with DKER uses two-level HIBE and IBE schemes.

2 Preliminaries

2.1 Notations

Throughout the paper we use the following notation: We use λ as the security parameter and write $\mathsf{negl}(\lambda)$ to denote that some function $f(\cdot)$ is negligible in λ. An algorithm is PPT if it is modeled as a probabilistic Turing machine whose running time is bounded by some function $\mathsf{poly}(\lambda)$. If S is a finite set, then $s \leftarrow S$ denotes the operation of picking an element s from S uniformly at random. If A is a probabilistic algorithm, then $y \leftarrow A(x)$ denotes the action of running $A(x)$ on input x with uniform coins and outputting y. Let $[n]$ denotes $\{1, ..., n\}$. Let $\{0,1\}^{[i,j]}$ denotes all binary strings with length in $[i,j]$. For a bit string

$a = (a_1, ..., a_n) \in \{0, 1\}^n$, and $i, j \in [n]$ with $i \leq j$, we write $a_{[i,j]}$ to denote the substring $(a_i, ..., a_j)$ of a. For any two strings u and v, $|u|$ denote the length of u and $u||v$ denotes their concatenation. Let BT be a complete binary tree and Path(v) be a set of all nodes on the path between the root node and a leaf v. We also use Path(id) to denote the path from the corresponding node of id to the root node.

2.2 Identity-Based Encryption

An identity-based encryption scheme consists of four probabilistic polynomial-time (PPT) algorithms (Setup, KeyGen, Enc, Dec) defined as follows:

- Setup(1^λ): This algorithm takes as input the security parameter 1^λ, and outputs a public parameter PP and a master secret key MK.
- KeyGen(MK, id): This algorithm takes as input the master secret key MK and an identity id $\in \{0, 1\}^\ell$, it outputs the identity secret key sk$_{id}$.
- Enc(PP, id, μ): This algorithm takes as input the public parameter PP, an identity id $\in \{0, 1\}^\ell$, and a plaintext μ, it outputs a ciphertext c.
- Dec(sk$_{id}$, c): This algorithm takes as input a secret key sk$_{id}$ for identity id and a ciphertext c, it outputs a plaintext μ.

The following correctness and security properties must be satisfied:

- **Correctness:** For all security parameters 1^λ, identity id $\in \{0, 1\}^\ell$ and plaintext μ, the following holds:

$$\Pr[\mathsf{Dec}(\mathsf{sk}_{id}, \mathsf{Enc}(\mathsf{PP}, \mathsf{id}, \mu)) = \mu] = 1$$

where (PP, MK) $\leftarrow$ Setup(1^λ) and sk$_{id}$ $\leftarrow$ KeyGen(MK, id).
- **Adaptive Security:** For any PPT adversary $\mathcal{A}$, there is a negligible function negl($\cdot$) such that the following holds:

$$Adv_{\mathcal{A}}^{\mathsf{IND\text{-}ID\text{-}CPA}} = |\Pr[\mathsf{IND\text{-}ID\text{-}CPA}(\mathcal{A}) = 1] - \frac{1}{2}| \leq \mathsf{negl}(\lambda)$$

where IND-ID-CPA($\mathcal{A}$) is shown in Fig. 1.
In order to prove the security of our RIBE construction, we define a special security for IBE as follows:
- **Multi-identity Adaptive Security:** For any PPT adversary $\mathcal{A}$, there is a negligible function negl($\cdot$) such that the advantage of $\mathcal{A}$ satisfies:

$$Adv_{\mathcal{A}}^{\mathsf{IND\text{-}mID\text{-}CPA}} = |\Pr[\mathsf{IND\text{-}mID\text{-}CPA}(\mathcal{A}) = 1] - \frac{1}{2}| \leq \mathsf{negl}(\lambda)$$

where IND-mID-CPA($\mathcal{A}$) is shown in Fig. 2.

It is obvious that adaptive (selective) security is a special case of multi-identity adaptive (selective) security when there is only one challenge identity.

Experiment IND-ID-CPA($\mathcal{A}$) :

1. $(PP, MK) \leftarrow \mathsf{Setup}(1^\lambda)$
2. $(\mu_0, \mu_1, id^*) \leftarrow \mathcal{A}^{\mathsf{KeyGen}(MK,\cdot)}(PP)$ where $|\mu_0| = |\mu_1|$ and for each query id to $\mathsf{KeyGen}(MK,\cdot)$ we have that $id \neq id^*$.
3. $\beta \leftarrow \{0, 1\}$
4. $c^* \leftarrow \mathsf{Enc}(PP, id^*, \mu_\beta)$
5. $\beta' \leftarrow \mathcal{A}^{\mathsf{KeyGen}(MK,\cdot)}(PP, c^*)$ and for each query id to $\mathsf{KeyGen}(MK,\cdot)$ we have that $id \neq id^*$.
6. Output 1 if $\beta = \beta'$ and 0 otherwise.

Fig. 1. The adaptive security experiment of IBE

Experiment IND-mID-CPA($\mathcal{A}$) :

1. $(PP, MK) \leftarrow \mathsf{Setup}(1^\lambda)$
2. $(\mu_0, \mu_1, id_1^*, ..., id_q^*) \leftarrow \mathcal{A}^{\mathsf{KeyGen}(MK,\cdot)}(PP)$ where q is a polynomial of λ, $|\mu_0| = |\mu_1|$ and for each query id to $\mathsf{KeyGen}(MK,\cdot)$ we have that $id \notin \{id_1^*, ..., id_q^*\}$
3. $\beta \leftarrow \{0, 1\}$
4. $\{c_i^* \leftarrow \mathsf{Enc}(PP, id_i^*, \mu_\beta)\}_{i \in [q]}$
5. $\beta' \leftarrow \mathcal{A}^{\mathsf{KeyGen}(MK,\cdot)}(PP, c_1^*, ..., c_q^*)$ and for each query id to $\mathsf{KeyGen}(MK,\cdot)$ we have that $id \notin \{id_1^*, ..., id_q^*\}$
6. Output 1 if $\beta = \beta'$ and 0 otherwise.

Fig. 2. The multi-identity adaptive security experiment of IBE

Adaptive Security Implies Multi-identity Adaptive Security

Lemma 1. *An IBE scheme is multi-identity adaptively (selectively) secure if it is adaptively (selectively) secure.*

We refer readers to the full version [26] of this paper for the proofs of Lemma 1 and subsequent theorems in this paper.

3   Generic Construction of Revocable Identity-Based Encryption

3.1   Definition and Security Model

Similar to the definition in [35], a revocable IBE scheme has seven probabilistic polynomial-time (PPT) algorithms (Setup, KeyGen, KeyUpd, DkGen, Encrypt, Decrypt, Revoke) with associated message space $\mathcal{M}$, identity space $\mathcal{ID}$, and time space $\mathcal{T}$.

- Setup(1^λ, N): This algorithm takes as input a security parameter λ and a maximal number of users N. It outputs a public parameter PP, a master secret key MK, a revocation list RL (initially empty), and a state st.
- KeyGen(MK, id, st): This algorithm takes as input the master secret key MK, an identity id, and the state st. It outputs a secret key sk_{id} and an update state st.
- KeyUp(MK, t, RL, st): This algorithm takes as input the master secret key MK, a key update time $t \in \mathcal{T}$, the revocation list RL, and the state st. It outputs a key update ku_t.
- DkGen(sk_{id}, ku_t): This algorithm takes as input a secret key sk_{id} and the key update ku_t. It outputs a decryption $dk_{id,t}$ or a special symbol $\perp$ indicating that id was revoked.
- Encrypt(PP, id, t, μ): This algorithm takes as input the public parameter PP, an identity id, a time period t and a message $\mu \in \mathcal{M}$. It outputs a ciphertext c.
- Decrypt($dk_{id,t}$, c): This algorithm takes as input a decryption secret key $dk_{id,t}$ and a ciphertext. It outputs a message $\mu \in \mathcal{M}$.
- Revoke(id, t, RL): This algorithm takes as input an identity id, a revocation time $t \in \mathcal{T}$ and the revocation list RL. It outputs a revocation list RL.

It satisfies the following conditions:

- **Correctness:** For all λ and polynomials (in λ) N, all PP and MK output by setup algorithm Setup, all $\mu \in \mathcal{M}$, id $\in \mathcal{ID}$, t $\in \mathcal{T}$ and all possible valid states st and revocation list RL, if identity id was not revoked before or, at time t then there exists a negligible function negl($\cdot$) such that the following holds:

$$\Pr[\mathsf{Decrypt}(dk_{id,t}, \mathsf{Encrypt}(PP, id, t, \mu)) = \mu] \geq 1 - \mathsf{negl}(\lambda)$$

where $(sk_{id}, st) \leftarrow \mathsf{KeyGen}(MK, id, st)$, $ku_t \leftarrow \mathsf{KeyUp}(MK, t, RL, st)$ and $dk_{id,t} \leftarrow \mathsf{DkGen}(sk_{id}, ku_t)$.

- **Adaptive Security:** For any PPT adversary $\mathcal{A}$, there is a negligible function negl($\cdot$) such that the advantage of $\mathcal{A}$ satisfies:

$$Adv_{\mathcal{A}}^{\mathsf{IND\text{-}RID\text{-}CPA}} = |\Pr[\mathsf{IND\text{-}RID\text{-}CPA}(\mathcal{A}) = 1] - \frac{1}{2}| \leq \mathsf{negl}(\lambda)$$

where IND-RID-CPA($\mathcal{A}$) is shown is Fig. 3.

Adaptive Security with Decryption Key Exposure: The security game of adaptive security with decryption key exposure is similar to IND-RID-CPA experiment defined in Fig. 3 except there exists an additional decryption oracle DkGen($\cdot$, $\cdot$) with the restriction that the challenge identity id* cannot be queried on challenge time t*.

3.2   A Generic Construction from IBE

Definition 1. (KUNode Algorithm [3]). *This algorithm takes as input a binary tree BT, revocation list RL and time t, and outputs a set of nodes. Let θ_{left} and θ_{right} denote the left and right child of node θ, where θ is a non-leaf node. The description of KUNode is as follows:*

Experiment IND-RID-CPA($\mathcal{A}$) :

1. $(PP, MK) \leftarrow \mathsf{Setup}(1^\lambda)$
2. $(\mu_0, \mu_1, \mathsf{id}^*, \mathsf{t}^*) \leftarrow \mathcal{A}^{\mathsf{KeyGen}(MK,\cdot),\mathsf{KeyUp}(MK,\cdot,RL,st),\mathsf{Revoke}(\cdot,\cdot)}(PP)$ where $|\mu_0| = |\mu_1|$
3. $\beta \leftarrow \{0, 1\}$
4. $c^* \leftarrow \mathsf{Encrypt}(PP, \mathsf{id}^*, \mathsf{t}^*, \mu_\beta)$
5. $\beta' \leftarrow \mathcal{A}^{\mathsf{KeyGen}(MK,\cdot),\mathsf{KeyUp}(MK,\cdot,RL,st),\mathsf{Revoke}(\cdot,\cdot)}(PP, c^*)$.
6. Output 1 if $\beta = \beta'$ and 0 otherwise.

The following restriction must hold:

- KeyUp(MK,·,RL,st) and Revoke(·,·) can be queried on time which is greater than or equal to the time of all previous queries, i.e. the adversary is allowed to query only in non-decreasing order of time. Also, the oracle Revoke(·,·) cannot be queried at time t if KeyUp(MK,·,RL,st) was queried on time t.
- If KeyGen(MK,·) was queried on identity id*, then Revoke(·,·) must be queried on time t for some $t \leq t^*$, i.e. (id*,t) must be on revocation list RL when KeyUp(MK,·,RL,st) is queried on t*.

Fig. 3. The adaptive security experiment of revocable IBE

KUNode(BT,RL,t):
    $X, Y \leftarrow \emptyset$
    $\forall (\mathsf{id}_i, \mathsf{t}_i) \in RL$
        if $\mathsf{t}_i \leq \mathsf{t}$ then add $\mathsf{Path}(\mathsf{id}_i)$ to X
    $\forall \theta \in X$
        if $\theta_{left} \notin X$ then add θ_{left} to Y
        if $\theta_{right} \notin X$ then add θ_{right} to Y
    If $Y = \emptyset$ then add root to Y
    Return Y

Detailed Construction. Let (IBE.Setup, IBE.Enc, IBE.KeyGen, IBE.Dec) be an IBE scheme that supports $\mathcal{ID} = \{0,1\}^{[\ell, 2\ell]}$. There is a generic method to extend any IBE supporting identity space $\mathcal{ID}'$ to handle arbitrary identities id $\in \{0,1\}^*$ by first hashing id using a collision resistant hash function $H : \{0,1\}^* \to \mathcal{ID}'$ prior to key generation and encryption [4]. Hence, any IBE schemes supporting identity space $\mathcal{ID}'$ with a collision resistant hash function $H : \{0,1\}^* \to \mathcal{ID}'$ can be applied to our construction. We assume IBE scheme has the plaintext space $\mathcal{M}$ which is finite and forms an abelian group with the group operation " $+$ ".

Utilizing the above IBE scheme, we will show how to construct a RIBE scheme $\Pi = $ (Setup, KeyGen, KeyUp, DkGen, Encrypt, Decrypt, Revoke) as follows. In our RIBE scheme, the plaintext space is the same as that of the underlying IBE scheme and identity space is $\{0,1\}^\ell$. Moreover, we assume the time period space $\mathcal{T}$ is a subset of the identity space, i.e. $\mathcal{T} \subseteq \{0,1\}^\ell$.

- Setup(1^λ) $\rightarrow$ (PP, MK, RL, st): This algorithm takes the security parameter 1^λ as input and runs (IBE.PP, IBE.MK) $\leftarrow$ IBE.Setup(1^λ). It sets the public parameter PP = IBE.PP, master secret key MK = IBE.MK, revocation list RL as an empty set and secret state st = IBE.MK[1]. The following algorithms implicitly take PP as input.
- KeyGen(MK, id) $\rightarrow$ sk$_{id}$: It runs sk$_{id}$ $\leftarrow$ IBE.KeyGen(MK, id)[2].
- KeyUp(MK, t, RL, st) $\rightarrow$ ku$_t$: Let BT be a complete binary tree of depth ℓ. Every identity id in identity space $\{0,1\}^\ell$ can be viewed as a leaf node of BT. For each node $\theta \in$ KUNode(BT, RL, t), compute sk$_{t||\theta}$ $\leftarrow$ IBE.KeyGen(MK, t$||\theta$). It outputs ku$_t$ = $\{(\theta, \text{sk}_{t||\theta})\}_{\theta \in \text{KUNode(BT,RL,t)}}$.
- DkGen(sk$_{id}$, ku$_t$) $\rightarrow$ dk$_{id,t}$: Parse ku$_t$ as $\{(\theta, \text{sk}_{t||\theta})\}_{\theta \in \text{KUNode(BT,RL,t)}}$. If no node $\theta \in$ Path(id), return $\bot$. Otherwise, pick the node $\theta \in$ Path(id) and output dk$_{id,t}$ = $(i, \text{sk}_{id}, \text{sk}_{t||\theta})$ where $i = |\theta|$ is the length of θ.
- Encrypt(PP, id, t, μ) $\rightarrow$ c: Randomly sample a pair of plaintexts $(\mu_0, \mu_1) \in \mathcal{M}^2$ with the condition that $\mu = \mu_0 + \mu_1$. Then compute c$_0$ = IBE.Enc(PP, id, μ_0) and $\{c_i = \text{IBE.Enc(PP, t}||\text{id}_{[1,i]}, \mu_1)\}_{i \in [\ell]}$. Finally, it outputs the ciphertext c = $(c_0, ..., c_\ell)$.
- Decrypt(c, dk$_{id,t}$) $\rightarrow$ μ: Parse c as $(c_0, ..., c_\ell)$ and dk$_{id,t}$ as $(i, \text{sk}_{id}, \text{sk}_{t||\theta})$. Then, compute $\mu_0 \leftarrow$ IBE.Dec(sk$_{id}$, c$_0$) and $\mu_1 \leftarrow$ IBE.Dec(sk$_{t||\theta}$, c$_i$). Finally, output $\mu = \mu_0 + \mu_1$.
- Revoke(t, RL, id) $\rightarrow$ RL: Update the revocation list by RL $\leftarrow$ RL $\cup \{(\text{id}, t)\}$ and output RL.

3.3 Correctness

The correctness of the RIBE construction is guaranteed by the correctness of the underlying IBE.

3.4 Security Analysis

Theorem 1. *The revocable IBE is adaptive-ID (selective-ID) CPA secure if the underlying IBE scheme is adaptive-ID (selective-ID) CPA secure.*

Proof. We will prove the adaptive-ID security and the proof for selective-ID security is exactly the same. For any PPT adversary against the adaptive-ID security of revocable IBE, we can construct a PPT algorithm $\mathcal{B}$ against the adaptive-ID security of the underlying IBE scheme. $\mathcal{B}$ randomly guesses an adversarial type among the following two types which are mutually exclusive and cover all possibilities:

1. Type-1 adversary: $\mathcal{A}$ issues a secret key query for id* hence id* has to be revoked before t* (i.e. id* should be on the revocation list at time t*).
2. Type-2 adversary: $\mathcal{A}$ does not issue a secret key query for id*.

---

[1] Here the secret state is the same as the master secret key.
[2] It does not need to take st as input here.

Note that $\mathcal{B}$'s guess is independent of the attack that $\mathcal{A}$ chooses, so the probability that $\mathcal{B}$ guesses right is $\frac{1}{2}$. We separately describe $\mathcal{B}$'s strategy by its guess.

Type-1 Adversary: We will show that if adversary $\mathcal{A}_1$ makes a type-1 attack successfully, there exists an adversary $\mathcal{B}_1$ breaking the multi-identity adaptive security of IBE defined in Fig. 2. $\mathcal{B}_1$ proceeds as follows:

- Setup: $\mathcal{B}_1$ obtains a public parameter PP from its challenger and sends it to $\mathcal{A}_1$.
- KeyGen: When receiving a secret key query for id, $\mathcal{B}_1$ queries secret key oracle for id.
- Revoke: $\mathcal{B}_1$ receives (id,t) from $\mathcal{A}_1$, and add (id, t) to RL.
- KeyUp: Upon receiving a time period t, $\mathcal{B}_1$ makes secret key queries for identities $\{t\|\theta\}_{\theta \in \mathsf{KUNode}(\mathsf{BT},\mathsf{RL},t)}$ and sends $\{(\theta, \mathsf{sk}_{t\|\theta})\}_{\theta \in \mathsf{KUNode}(\mathsf{BT},\mathsf{RL},t)}$ to $\mathcal{A}_1$.
- Challenge: $\mathcal{A}_1$ outputs an identity id^*, a time period t^* and two plaintexts μ_0, μ_1 with the same length. $\mathcal{B}_1$ randomly samples $\mu \leftarrow \mathcal{M}$ and sends $\{\mathsf{t}^*\|\mathsf{id}_{[1,i]}^*\}_{i\in[\ell]}$ as challenger identities and $\mu_0' = \mu_0 - \mu$ and $\mu_1' = \mu_1 - \mu$ as the challenge plaintexts. The challenger randomly chooses a challenge bit β and sends the challenge ciphertexts $\{\mathsf{c}_i^* = \mathsf{IBE.Enc}(\mathsf{PP}, \mathsf{t}^*\|\mathsf{id}_{[1,i]}^*, \mu_\beta')\}_{i\in[\ell]}$ to $\mathcal{B}_1$. $\mathcal{B}_1$ then computes $\mathsf{c}_0^* = \mathsf{IBE.Enc}(\mathsf{PP}, \mathsf{id}^*, \mu)$ and sends $\mathsf{c}^* = (\mathsf{c}_0^*, ..., \mathsf{c}_\ell^*)$ to $\mathcal{A}_1$.
- Guess: $\mathcal{A}_1$ outputs a guess bit β' and $\mathcal{B}_1$ set β' as its guess.

For the KeyGen oracle, since $|\mathsf{id}| = \ell$ and $|\mathsf{t}^*\|\mathsf{id}_{[1,i]}^*| \geq \ell + 1$ for all $i \in [\ell]$, $\mathsf{id} \notin \{\mathsf{t}^*\|\mathsf{id}_{[1,i]}^*\}_{i\in[\ell]}$. For the KeyUp oracle, note that id^* has been revoked before t^* which means $\mathsf{id}_{[1,i]}^* \notin \mathsf{KUNode}(\mathsf{BT}, \mathsf{RL}, \mathsf{t}^*)$ for all $i \in [\ell]$, so that $\mathcal{B}_1$ never queries secret keys for one of the challenge identities $\{\mathsf{t}^*\|\mathsf{id}_{[1,i]}^*\}_{i\in[\ell]}$. $\mathcal{B}_1$ perfectly simulates $\mathcal{A}_1$'s view so that $\mathcal{B}_1$'s challenge bit is also $\mathcal{A}_1$'s challenge bit. $\mathcal{B}_1$ just forwards $\mathcal{A}_1$'s guess so the probability that $\mathcal{B}_1$ wins in IND-mID-CPA is equal to the probability that $\mathcal{A}_1$ wins in IND-RID-CPA. Due to Lemma 1, the probability that $\mathcal{A}_1$ wins in IND-RID-CPA is negligible since the underlying IBE is adaptive-ID secure.

Type-2 Adversary: If there exists an adversary $\mathcal{A}_2$ who makes a type-2 attack successfully, we can construct an adversary $\mathcal{B}_2$ breaking adaptive-ID security of the underlying IBE. $\mathcal{B}_2$ proceeds as follows:

- Setup: $\mathcal{B}_2$ obtains a public parameter PP from its challenger and sends it to $\mathcal{A}_2$.
- KeyGen: When receiving a secret key query for id, $\mathcal{B}_2$ just forwards the secret key query to its challenger and sends the challenger's response to $\mathcal{A}_2$.
- Revoke: $\mathcal{B}_2$ receives (id,t) from $\mathcal{A}_2$, and adds (id, t) to RL.
- KeyUp: When $\mathcal{A}_2$ makes a key update query for time t, $\mathcal{B}_2$ makes secret key queries for all identities $\{t\|\theta\}_{\theta \in \mathsf{KUNode}(\mathsf{BT},\mathsf{RL},t)}$ and sends the response $\{(\theta, \mathsf{sk}_{t\|\theta})\}_{\theta \in \mathsf{KUNode}(\mathsf{BT},\mathsf{RL},t)}$ to $\mathcal{A}_2$.
- Challenge: $\mathcal{A}_2$ outputs a challenge identity id^*, a time period t^* and two plaintexts μ_0 and μ_1 with the same length. $\mathcal{B}_1$ randomly samples $\mu \leftarrow \mathcal{M}$

and sends $\mu'_0 = \mu_0 - \mu$ and $\mu'_1 = \mu_1 - \mu$ as the challenge plaintexts. $\mathcal{B}_1$ receives the challenge ciphertext $c^*_0 = \mathsf{IBE.Enc}(\mathsf{PP}, \mathsf{id}^*, \mu'_\beta)$ where β is $\mathcal{B}_2$'s challenge bit chosen randomly by its challenger. $\mathcal{B}_2$ then computes $\{c^*_i = \mathsf{IBE.Enc}(\mathsf{PP}, \mathsf{t}^* \| \mathsf{id}^*_{[1,i]}, \mu)\}_{i \in [\ell]}$ and sends $c^* = (c^*_0, ..., c^*_\ell)$ to $\mathcal{A}_2$.

- Guess: $\mathcal{A}_2$ outputs a guess bit β' and $\mathcal{B}_2$ sets β' as its guess.

Similar to the analysis for $\mathcal{B}_1$, $\mathcal{B}_2$ perfectly simulates $\mathcal{A}_2$'s view so that $\mathcal{B}_2$'s challenge bit is also $\mathcal{A}_2$'s challenge bit. $\mathcal{B}_2$ just forwards $\mathcal{A}_2$'s guess so the probability that $\mathcal{B}_2$ wins in IND-ID-CPA game is equal to the probability that $\mathcal{A}_2$ wins in IND-RID-CPA game.

When we put the results for two types of adversary together, we can conclude that the revocable IBE is adaptive-ID CPA secure if the underlying IBE is adaptive-ID CPA secure.

4   A Generic Construction of RIBE with DKER

It is obvious that our construction is not decryption key exposure resistance. Inspired by the work of [21], we can construct a RIBE with DKER from a 2-level HIBE scheme and an IBE scheme. Let $(\mathsf{I.Setup}, \mathsf{I.Enc}, \mathsf{I.KeyGen}, \mathsf{I.Dec})$ be an IBE scheme with $\mathcal{ID} = \{0, 1\}^{[\ell+1, 2\ell]}$ and $(\mathsf{H.Setup}, \mathsf{H.Enc}, \mathsf{H.KeyDer}, \mathsf{H.Dec})$ be a two-level HIBE scheme where the element identity is in $\{0, 1\}^\ell$. We assume the HIBE scheme and the IBE scheme have the same plaintext space $\mathcal{M}$ which is finite and forms an abelian group with the group operation "$+$".

Utilizing the above primitives, we will show how to construct a RIBE scheme $\Pi = (\mathsf{Setup}, \mathsf{KeyGen}, \mathsf{KeyUp}, \mathsf{DkGen}, \mathsf{Encrypt}, \mathsf{Decrypt}, \mathsf{Revoke})$ as follows. In our RIBE scheme, the plaintext space is $\mathcal{M}$ and identity space is $\{0, 1\}^\ell$. Moreover, we assume the time period space $\mathcal{T}$ is a subset of the identity space, i.e. $\mathcal{T} \subseteq \{0, 1\}^\ell$.

- $\mathsf{Setup}(1^\lambda) \to (\mathsf{PP}, \mathsf{MK}, \mathsf{RL}, \mathsf{st})$: This algorithm takes as input the security parameter 1^λ and runs $(\mathsf{I.PP}, \mathsf{I.MK}) \leftarrow \mathsf{I.Setup}(1^\lambda)$ and $(\mathsf{H.PP}, \mathsf{H.MK}) \leftarrow \mathsf{H.Setup}(1^\lambda)$. It sets the public parameter $\mathsf{PP} = (\mathsf{I.PP}, \mathsf{H.PP})$, master secret key $\mathsf{MK} = \mathsf{H.MK}$, revocation list RL as an empty set and secret state $\mathsf{st} = \mathsf{I.MK}$. The following algorithms implicitly take PP as input.
- $\mathsf{KeyGen}(\mathsf{MK}, \mathsf{id}) \to \mathsf{sk}_{\mathsf{id}}$: It runs $\mathsf{hsk}_{\mathsf{id}} \leftarrow \mathsf{H.KeyDer}(\mathsf{MK}, \mathsf{id})$.
- $\mathsf{KeyUp}(\mathsf{t}, \mathsf{RL}, \mathsf{st}) \to \mathsf{ku}_\mathsf{t}$: Let BT be a complete binary tree of depth ℓ. Every identity id in the identity space $\{0, 1\}^\ell$ can be viewed as a leaf node of BT. For each node $\theta \in \mathsf{KUNode}(\mathsf{BT}, \mathsf{RL}, \mathsf{t})$, compute $\mathsf{isk}_{\mathsf{t} \| \theta} \leftarrow \mathsf{I.KeyGen}(\mathsf{I.MK}, \mathsf{t} \| \theta)$. It outputs $\mathsf{ku}_\mathsf{t} = \{(\theta, \mathsf{isk}_{\mathsf{t} \| \theta})\}_{\theta \in \mathsf{KUNode}(\mathsf{BT}, \mathsf{RL}, \mathsf{t})}$.
- $\mathsf{DkGen}(\mathsf{sk}_{\mathsf{id}}, \mathsf{ku}_\mathsf{t}) \to \mathsf{dk}_{\mathsf{id}, \mathsf{t}}$: Run $\mathsf{hsk}_{\mathsf{id} \| \mathsf{t}} \leftarrow \mathsf{H.KeyDer}(\mathsf{hsk}_{\mathsf{id}}, \mathsf{id} \| \mathsf{t})$. Parse ku_t as $\{(\theta, \mathsf{isk}_{\mathsf{t} \| \theta})\}_{\theta \in \mathsf{KUNode}(\mathsf{BT}, \mathsf{RL}, \mathsf{t})}$. If no node $\theta \in \mathsf{Path}(\mathsf{id})$, return $\perp$. Otherwise, pick the node $\theta \in \mathsf{Path}(\mathsf{id})$ and output $\mathsf{dk}_{\mathsf{id}, \mathsf{t}} = (i, \mathsf{hsk}_{\mathsf{id} \| \mathsf{t}}, \mathsf{isk}_{\mathsf{t} \| \theta})$ where $i = |\theta|$ is the length of θ.
- $\mathsf{Encrypt}(\mathsf{PP}, \mathsf{id}, \mathsf{t}, \mu) \to c$: Parse PP as $(\mathsf{H.PP}, \mathsf{I.PP})$. Randomly sample a pair of plaintexts $(\mu_0, \mu_1) \in \mathcal{M}^2$ with the condition that $\mu = \mu_0 + \mu_1$. Then it computes $c_0 = \mathsf{H.Enc}(\mathsf{H.PP}, \mathsf{id} \| \mathsf{t}, \mu_0)$ and $\{c_i = \mathsf{I.Enc}(\mathsf{I.PP}, \mathsf{t} \| \mathsf{id}_{[1,i]}, \mu_1)\}_{i \in [\ell]}$. Finally, it outputs the ciphertext $c = (c_0, ..., c_\ell)$.

- Decrypt(c, $dk_{id,t}$) → μ: Parse c as (c_0, ..., c_ℓ) and $dk_{id,t}$ as (i, $hsk_{id||t}$, $isk_{t||\theta}$). Then, compute $\mu_0 \leftarrow$ H.Dec($hsk_{id||t}$, c_0) and $\mu_1 \leftarrow$ I.Dec($isk_{t||\theta}$, c_i). Finally, output $\mu = \mu_0 + \mu_1$.
- Revoke(t, RL, id) → RL: Update the revocation list by $RL \leftarrow RL \cup \{(id, t)\}$ and output RL.

4.1 Correctness

The correctness of the RIBE construction is guaranteed by the correctness of the underlying IBE and HIBE schemes.

4.2 Security Analysis

Theorem 2. *The revocable IBE is adaptive-ID (selective-ID) CPA secure with decryption key exposure resilience if the underlying IBE scheme and the underlying 2-level HIBE scheme are adaptive-ID (selective-ID) CPA secure.*

5 Optimizations

5.1 RIBE with Constant Ciphertexts

In above construction, the size of ciphertext is linear in the length of identities for we should encrypt the same plaintext under $t||id_{[1,i]}$ for all i in $[\ell]$. We can reduce the ciphertext size by replacing the underlying IBE scheme with IBBE scheme in above construction because there exists IBBE schemes [43] with constant ciphertext and secret key. Moreover, as the special form of identities encrypted in the ciphertext, we can reduce the ciphertext size using a HIBE scheme. The detail of our construction is described as follows.

Let ($\tilde{h}$.Setup, $\tilde{h}$.Enc, $\tilde{h}$.KeyDer, $\tilde{h}$.Dec) be a two-level HIBE scheme where the element identity is in $\{0,1\}^\ell$ and ($\hat{h}$.Setup, $\hat{h}$.Enc, $\hat{h}$.KeyDer, $\hat{h}$.Dec) be a 2ℓ-level HIBE scheme with element identity space $\mathcal{ID} = \{0, 1\}$. We assume the two HIBE schemes have the same plaintext space $\mathcal{M}$ which is finite and forms an abelian group with the group operation "+".

- Setup(1^λ) → (PP, MK, RL, st): This algorithm takes as input the security parameter 1^λ and runs ($\widetilde{PP}$, $\widetilde{MK}$) ← $\tilde{h}$.Setup(1^λ) and ($\widehat{PP}$, $\widehat{MK}$) ← $\hat{h}$.Setup(1^λ). It sets the public parameter $PP = (\widetilde{PP}, \widehat{PP})$, master secret key $MK = \widetilde{MK}$, the revocation list RL as an empty set and secret state $st = \widehat{MK}$. The following algorithms implicitly take PP as input.
- KeyGen(MK, id) → sk_{id}: It runs $\widetilde{sk}_{id} \leftarrow \tilde{h}$.KeyDer($\widetilde{MK}$, id).
- KeyUp(t, RL, st) → ku_t: Let BT be a complete binary tree of depth ℓ. Every identity id in the identity space $\{0,1\}^\ell$ can be viewed as a leaf node of BT. For each node $\theta \in$ KUNode(BT, RL, t), compute $\widehat{sk}_{t||\theta} \leftarrow \hat{h}$.KeyDer($\widehat{MK}$, $t||\theta$). It outputs $ku_t = \{(\theta, \widehat{sk}_{t||\theta})\}_{\theta \in \text{KUNode}(BT,RL,t)}$.

- $\mathsf{DkGen}(\mathsf{sk}_{\mathsf{id}}, \mathsf{ku}_t) \rightarrow \mathsf{dk}_{\mathsf{id},t}$: Run $\widetilde{\mathsf{sk}}_{\mathsf{id}||t} \leftarrow \mathsf{h.KeyDer}(\widetilde{\mathsf{sk}}_{\mathsf{id}}, \mathsf{id}||t)$. Parse ku_t as $\{(\theta, \widehat{\mathsf{sk}}_{t||\theta})\}_{\theta \in \mathsf{KUNode}(\mathsf{BT}, \mathsf{RL}, t)}$. If no node $\theta \in \mathsf{Path}(\mathsf{id})$, return $\perp$. Otherwise, pick the node $\theta \in \mathsf{Path}(\mathsf{id})$ and run $\widehat{\mathsf{sk}}_{t||\mathsf{id}} \leftarrow \hat{\mathsf{h}}.\mathsf{KeyDer}(\widehat{\mathsf{sk}}_{t||\theta}, t||\mathsf{id})$. Output $\mathsf{dk}_{\mathsf{id},t} = (\widetilde{\mathsf{sk}}_{\mathsf{id}||t}, \widehat{\mathsf{sk}}_{t||\mathsf{id}})$.
- $\mathsf{Encrypt}(\mathsf{PP}, \mathsf{id}, t, \mu) \rightarrow \mathsf{c}$: Parse PP as $(\widetilde{\mathsf{PP}}, \widehat{\mathsf{PP}})$. Randomly sample a pair of plaintexts $(\mu_0, \mu_1) \in \mathcal{M}^2$ with the condition that $\mu = \mu_0 + \mu_1$. Then it computes $\mathsf{c}_0 = \tilde{\mathsf{h}}.\mathsf{Enc}(\widetilde{\mathsf{PP}}, \mathsf{id}||t, \mu_0)$ and $\mathsf{c}_1 = \hat{\mathsf{h}}.\mathsf{Enc}(\widehat{\mathsf{PP}}, t||\mathsf{id}, \mu_1)$. Finally, it outputs the ciphertext $\mathsf{c} = (\mathsf{c}_0, \mathsf{c}_1)$.
- $\mathsf{Decrypt}(\mathsf{c}, \mathsf{dk}_{\mathsf{id},t}) \rightarrow \mu$: Parse c as $(\mathsf{c}_0, \mathsf{c}_1)$ and $\mathsf{dk}_{\mathsf{id},t}$ as $(\widetilde{\mathsf{sk}}_{\mathsf{id}||t}, \widehat{\mathsf{sk}}_{t||\mathsf{id}})$. Then, compute $\mu_0 \leftarrow \tilde{\mathsf{h}}.\mathsf{Dec}(\widetilde{\mathsf{sk}}_{\mathsf{id}||t}, \mathsf{c}_0)$ and $\mu_1 \leftarrow \hat{\mathsf{h}}.\mathsf{Dec}(\widehat{\mathsf{sk}}_{t||\mathsf{id}}, \mathsf{c}_1)$. Finally, output $\mu = \mu_0 + \mu_1$.
- $\mathsf{Revoke}(t, \mathsf{RL}, \mathsf{id}) \rightarrow \mathsf{RL}$: Update the revocation list by $\mathsf{RL} \leftarrow \mathsf{RL} \cup \{(\mathsf{id}, t)\}$ and output RL.

5.2 Server-Aided RIBE

All of our constructions can naturally be sever-aided, we only describe the last construction in server-aided model. In server-aided model, there exists a untrusted server without any secret key information that takes almost all the workload on users. The server should perform correct operations and give correct results to the users. More specifically, the server partially decrypts the ciphertexts and leaves less decryption task to users. It is easy to convert our scheme to be server-aided, given the key update $\mathsf{ku}_t = \{(\theta, \widehat{\mathsf{sk}}_{t||\theta})\}_{\theta \in \mathsf{KUNode}(\mathsf{BT}, \mathsf{RL}, t)}$ and a ciphertext $\mathsf{c} = (\mathsf{c}_0, \mathsf{c}_1)$ under identity id and time t, sever picks $\theta \in \mathsf{Path}(\mathsf{id}) \cap \mathsf{ku}_t$ and runs $\widehat{\mathsf{sk}}_{t||\mathsf{id}} \leftarrow \hat{\mathsf{h}}.\mathsf{KeyDer}(\widehat{\mathsf{sk}}_{t||\theta}, t||\mathsf{id})$ and $\mu_1 \leftarrow \hat{\mathsf{h}}.\mathsf{Dec}(\widehat{\mathsf{sk}}_{t||\mathsf{id}}, \mathsf{c}_1)$. Finally, the sever sends (c_0, μ_1) as the transformed ciphertext to the receiver. The receiver only needs to operate the key derive and decryption algorithm of underlying HIBE scheme. The receiver does not need to communicate with KGC in every key update.

6   Conclusion

In this paper, we propose three generic constructions of RIBE. The first construction is a RIBE scheme without DKER using an IBE as the basic building block which solves the open problem claimed in [35]. Furthermore, inspired by the work [21], our second construction is a RIBE scheme with DKER using HIBE and IBE schemes as building blocks. We reduce the ciphertext size using two HIBE schemes. We can also reduce the size of ciphertexts by replacing the underlying IBE with appropriate IBBE. Our three RIBE constructions inherits the security of the underlying primitives, therefore, our constructions imply the first RIBE from quadratic residues modulo composite and the first adaptive-ID secure RIBE from lattices by instantiating the required primitives with appropriate concrete schemes. Moreover, our conversion is efficient and flexible. And it is natural to be server-aided. In the server-aided model, the computation overheads for receivers are small and receivers do not need to communicate with KGC.

Acknowledgements. We would like to thank Kwangsu Lee for helpful remarks and suggestions on an earlier draft of this work. This work was partially supported by the National Natural Science Foundation of China (Grants No. 61872359 and No. 61936008).

References

1. Agrawal, S., Boneh, D., Boyen, X.: Efficient lattice (H)IBE in the standard model. In: Gilbert, H. (ed.) EUROCRYPT 2010. LNCS, vol. 6110, pp. 553–572. Springer, Heidelberg (2010). https://doi.org/10.1007/978-3-642-13190-5_28
2. Bellare, M., Rogaway, P.: Random oracles are practical: a paradigm for designing efficient protocols. In: CCS 1993, pp. 62–73. ACM (1993)
3. Boldyreva, A., Goyal, V., Kumar, V.: Identity-based encryption with efficient revocation. In: CCS 2008, pp. 417–426. ACM (2008)
4. Boneh, D., Boyen, X.: Efficient selective-ID secure identity-based encryption without random oracles. In: Cachin, C., Camenisch, J.L. (eds.) EUROCRYPT 2004. LNCS, vol. 3027, pp. 223–238. Springer, Heidelberg (2004). https://doi.org/10.1007/978-3-540-24676-3_14
5. Boneh, D., Boyen, X.: Secure identity based encryption without random oracles. In: Franklin, M. (ed.) CRYPTO 2004. LNCS, vol. 3152, pp. 443–459. Springer, Heidelberg (2004). https://doi.org/10.1007/978-3-540-28628-8_27
6. Boneh, D., Boyen, X., Goh, E.-J.: Hierarchical identity based encryption with constant size ciphertext. In: Cramer, R. (ed.) EUROCRYPT 2005. LNCS, vol. 3494, pp. 440–456. Springer, Heidelberg (2005). https://doi.org/10.1007/11426639_26
7. Boneh, D., Franklin, M.: Identity-based encryption from the weil pairing. In: Kilian, J. (ed.) CRYPTO 2001. LNCS, vol. 2139, pp. 213–229. Springer, Heidelberg (2001). https://doi.org/10.1007/3-540-44647-8_13
8. Boneh, D., Gentry, C., Hamburg, M.: Space-efficient identity based encryption without pairings. IACR Cryptology ePrint Archive 2007:177 (2007)
9. Boyen, X., Li, Q.: Towards tightly secure lattice short signature and Id-based encryption. In: Cheon, J.H., Takagi, T. (eds.) ASIACRYPT 2016. LNCS, vol. 10032, pp. 404–434. Springer, Heidelberg (2016). https://doi.org/10.1007/978-3-662-53890-6_14
10. Cash, D., Hofheinz, D., Kiltz, E., Peikert, C.: Bonsai trees, or how to delegate a lattice basis. J. Cryptol. **25**(4), 601–639 (2012)
11. Chen, J., Lim, H.W., Ling, S., Wang, H., Nguyen, K.: Revocable identity-based encryption from lattices. In: Susilo, W., Mu, Y., Seberry, J. (eds.) ACISP 2012. LNCS, vol. 7372, pp. 390–403. Springer, Heidelberg (2012). https://doi.org/10.1007/978-3-642-31448-3_29
12. Cheng, S., Zhang, J.: Adaptive-ID secure revocable identity-based encryption from lattices via subset difference method. In: Lopez, J., Wu, Y. (eds.) ISPEC 2015. LNCS, vol. 9065, pp. 283–297. Springer, Cham (2015). https://doi.org/10.1007/978-3-319-17533-1_20
13. Cocks, C.: An identity based encryption scheme based on quadratic residues. In: Honary, B. (ed.) Cryptography and Coding 2001. LNCS, vol. 2260, pp. 360–363. Springer, Heidelberg (2001). https://doi.org/10.1007/3-540-45325-3_32

14. Cui, H., Deng, R.H., Li, Y., Qin, B.: Server-aided revocable attribute-based encryption. In: Askoxylakis, I., Ioannidis, S., Katsikas, S., Meadows, C. (eds.) ESORICS 2016. LNCS, vol. 9879, pp. 570–587. Springer, Cham (2016). https://doi.org/10.1007/978-3-319-45741-3_29

15. Döttling, N., Garg, S.: From selective IBE to Full IBE and selective HIBE. In: Kalai, Y., Reyzin, L. (eds.) TCC 2017. LNCS, vol. 10677, pp. 372–408. Springer, Cham (2017). https://doi.org/10.1007/978-3-319-70500-2_13

16. Döttling, N., Garg, S.: Identity-based encryption from the Diffie-Hellman assumption. In: Katz, J., Shacham, H. (eds.) CRYPTO 2017. LNCS, vol. 10401, pp. 537–569. Springer, Cham (2017). https://doi.org/10.1007/978-3-319-63688-7_18

17. Emura, K., Seo, J.H., Youn, T.-Y.: Semi-generic transformation of revocable hierarchical identity-based encryption and its DBDH instantiation. IEICE Trans. 99-A(1), 83–91 (2016)

18. Gentry, C., Peikert, C., Vaikuntanathan, V.: Trapdoors for hard lattices and new cryptographic constructions. In: STOC 2008, pp. 197–206. ACM (2008)

19. Gentry, C., Silverberg, A.: Hierarchical ID-based cryptography. In: Zheng, Y. (ed.) ASIACRYPT 2002. LNCS, vol. 2501, pp. 548–566. Springer, Heidelberg (2002). https://doi.org/10.1007/3-540-36178-2_34

20. Ishida, Y., Shikata, J., Watanabe, Y.: CCA-secure revocable identity-based encryption schemes with decryption key exposure resistance. IJACT 3(3), 288–311 (2017)

21. Katsumata, S., Matsuda, T., Takayasu, A.: Lattice-based revocable (hierarchical) IBE with decryption key exposure resistance. In: Lin, D., Sako, K. (eds.) PKC 2019. LNCS, vol. 11443, pp. 441–471. Springer, Cham (2019). https://doi.org/10.1007/978-3-030-17259-6_15

22. Lee, K.: Revocable hierarchical identity-based encryption with adaptive security. IACR Cryptology ePrint Archive 2016:749 (2016)

23. Lee, K., Lee, D.H., Park, J.H.: Efficient revocable identity-based encryption via subset difference methods. Des. Codes Crypt. 85(1), 39–76 (2017)

24. Lee, K., Park, S.: Revocable hierarchical identity-based encryption with shorter private keys and update keys. Des. Codes Crypt. 86(10), 2407–2440 (2018)

25. Libert, B., Vergnaud, D.: Adaptive-ID secure revocable identity-based encryption. In: Fischlin, M. (ed.) CT-RSA 2009. LNCS, vol. 5473, pp. 1–15. Springer, Heidelberg (2009). https://doi.org/10.1007/978-3-642-00862-7_1

26. Ma, X., Lin, D.: A generic construction of revocable identity-based encryption. Cryptology ePrint Archive, Report 2019/299 (2019). https://eprint.iacr.org/2019/299

27. Mao, X., Lai, J., Chen, K., Weng, J., Mei, Q.: Efficient revocable identity-based encryption from multilinear maps. Secur. Commun. Netw. 8(18), 3511–3522 (2015)

28. Naor, D., Naor, M., Lotspiech, J.: Revocation and tracing schemes for stateless receivers. In: Kilian, J. (ed.) CRYPTO 2001. LNCS, vol. 2139, pp. 41–62. Springer, Heidelberg (2001). https://doi.org/10.1007/3-540-44647-8_3

29. Nguyen, K., Wang, H., Zhang, J.: Server-aided revocable identity-based encryption from lattices. In: Foresti, S., Persiano, G. (eds.) CANS 2016. LNCS, vol. 10052, pp. 107–123. Springer, Cham (2016). https://doi.org/10.1007/978-3-319-48965-0_7

30. Park, S., Lee, D.H., Lee, K.: Revocable hierarchical identity-based encryption from multilinear maps. CoRR, abs/1610.07948 (2016)

31. Park, S., Lee, K., Lee, D.H.: New constructions of revocable identity-based encryption from multilinear maps. IEEE Trans. Inf. Forensics Secur. 10(8), 1564–1577 (2015)

32. Qin, B., Deng, R.H., Li, Y., Liu, S.: Server-aided revocable identity-based encryption. In: Pernul, G., Ryan, P.Y.A., Weippl, E. (eds.) ESORICS 2015. LNCS, vol. 9326, pp. 286–304. Springer, Cham (2015). https://doi.org/10.1007/978-3-319-24174-6_15

33. Ryu, G., Lee, K., Park, S., Lee, D.H.: Unbounded hierarchical identity-based encryption with efficient revocation. In: Kim, H., Choi, D. (eds.) WISA 2015. LNCS, vol. 9503, pp. 122–133. Springer, Cham (2016). https://doi.org/10.1007/978-3-319-31875-2_11

34. Sahai, A., Waters, B.: Fuzzy identity-based encryption. In: Cramer, R. (ed.) EUROCRYPT 2005. LNCS, vol. 3494, pp. 457–473. Springer, Heidelberg (2005). https://doi.org/10.1007/11426639_27

35. Seo, J.H., Emura, K.: Revocable identity-based encryption revisited: security model and construction. In: Kurosawa, K., Hanaoka, G. (eds.) PKC 2013. LNCS, vol. 7778, pp. 216–234. Springer, Heidelberg (2013). https://doi.org/10.1007/978-3-642-36362-7_14

36. Seo, J.H., Emura, K.: Revocable hierarchical identity-based encryption via history-free approach. Theor. Comput. Sci. **615**, 45–60 (2016)

37. Shamir, A.: Identity-based cryptosystems and signature schemes. In: Blakley, G.R., Chaum, D. (eds.) CRYPTO 1984. LNCS, vol. 196, pp. 47–53. Springer, Heidelberg (1985). https://doi.org/10.1007/3-540-39568-7_5

38. Takayasu, A., Watanabe, Y.: Lattice-based revocable identity-based encryption with bounded decryption key exposure resistance. In: Pieprzyk, J., Suriadi, S. (eds.) ACISP 2017. LNCS, vol. 10342, pp. 184–204. Springer, Cham (2017). https://doi.org/10.1007/978-3-319-60055-0_10

39. Watanabe, Y., Emura, K., Seo, J.H.: New revocable IBE in prime-order groups: adaptively secure, decryption key exposure resistant, and with short public parameters. In: Handschuh, H. (ed.) CT-RSA 2017. LNCS, vol. 10159, pp. 432–449. Springer, Cham (2017). https://doi.org/10.1007/978-3-319-52153-4_25

40. Waters, B.: Efficient identity-based encryption without random oracles. In: Cramer, R. (ed.) EUROCRYPT 2005. LNCS, vol. 3494, pp. 114–127. Springer, Heidelberg (2005). https://doi.org/10.1007/11426639_7

41. Waters, B.: Dual system encryption: realizing fully secure IBE and HIBE under simple assumptions. In: Halevi, S. (ed.) CRYPTO 2009. LNCS, vol. 5677, pp. 619–636. Springer, Heidelberg (2009). https://doi.org/10.1007/978-3-642-03356-8_36

42. Yamada, S.: Asymptotically compact adaptively secure lattice IBEs and verifiable random functions via generalized partitioning techniques. In: Katz, J., Shacham, H. (eds.) CRYPTO 2017. LNCS, vol. 10403, pp. 161–193. Springer, Cham (2017). https://doi.org/10.1007/978-3-319-63697-9_6

43. Zhang, L., Yupu, H., Qing, W.: Adaptively secure identity-based broadcast encryption with constant size private keys and ciphertexts from the subgroups. Math. Comput. Modell. **55**(1–2), 12–18 (2012)

Certificateless Identity-Concealed Authenticated Encryption Under Multi-KGC

Chuang Li[1], Chunxiang Xu[1(✉)], Yunlei Zhao[2], Kefei Chen[3],
and Xiaojun Zhang[4]

[1] University of Electronic Science and Technology of China, Chengdu, China
LeeChuanglc@163.com, chxxu@uestc.edu.cn
[2] Fudan University, Shanghai, China
[3] Hangzhou Normal University, Hangzhou, China
[4] Southwest Petroleum University, Chengdu, China

Abstract. In the certificateless cryptography, users generate their partial private key and the Key Generation Centre (KGC) generates the other partial private key of users. In some certificateless application scenarios, a sender might want to send messages to a receiver which registers with another KGC. Unfortunately, no certificateless authenticated encryption scheme under multi-KGC has been put forward so far. In this work, we propose the first certificateless identity-concealed authenticated encryption scheme under multi-KGC. Our proposed scheme hides the public identity information of both sender and receiver from any third party. We build a security model for certificateless identity-concealed authenticated encryption scheme under multi-KGC. We prove that our proposed scheme is secure under the random oracle model. We also present a variant of our proposed scheme which supports bilateral identity-concealed authentication key exchange.

Keywords: Certificateless cryptography · Multi-centre scenario · Authenticated encryption · Identity concealment

1 Introduction

Authenticated encryption and zero-round trip time (0-RTT) has attracted wide attention since proposed. 0-RTT is the hot field in the design and analysis of cryptographic systems. Moreover, 0-RTT mode has been realised in QUIC connections in Google. In 1997, Zheng [19] proposed an authenticated encryption (namely signcryption) scheme. Signcryption is a cryptographic primitive that combines the functions of encryption and authentication in an efficient way. Zheng's scheme was proved secure by Baek et al. [3] in 2007. Thereafter, signcryption has attracted much focus and a lot of signcryption schemes have been put forward. But none of these schemes achieves concealment of the senders identity. In 2016, Zhao [18] proposed the first identity-concealed authenticated

© Springer Nature Switzerland AG 2020
Z. Liu and M. Yung (Eds.): Inscrypt 2019, LNCS 12020, pp. 397–415, 2020.
https://doi.org/10.1007/978-3-030-42921-8_23

encryption scheme based on certificate; he also proved the insider confidentiality and outsider unforgeability of his scheme under the random oracle model.

The concept of certificate-based encryption was proposed by Gentry in Eurocrypt 2003. In certificate-based encryption, the certification authority (CA) provides certificates for each user to bind its public key to its identity [13,15,17]. However, the certificate management in certificate-based cryptography is generally considered as a complex and costly task. To address this problem, identity-based encryption was introduced [7]. In identity-based encryption, a user's identity can be served as its public key and the public key generator (PKG) generates the user's private key. Once the PKG is corrupted, all users, who register with the PKG, can be easily compromised. To address this problem, certificateless cryptography was introduced [16].

Certificateless public key cryptography (CL-PKC), which was first proposed by Sattam et al. [1] in 2003, is a cryptography primitive where a user generates its partial private key and the Key Generation Centre (KGC) generates the rest part of the user's private key. Sattam et al. also present a specific certificateless public key encryption scheme and proofed its security in the random oracle model. Yang et al. [14] proposed a certificateless public key encryption scheme, which is secure against malicious KGC attacks, in the standard model in 2017.

In 2008, Barbosa et al. [4] introduced a certificateless signcryption scheme by adapting signcryption techniques to certificateless cryptology. But Barbosa et al.'s scheme didn't bind the sender's identity to the receiver's identity, which leads to a forgeability attack. Selvi et al. [10] provided an efficient certificateless signcryption scheme with no pairing operations, which cannot satisfy x-security. In 2010, Xie and Zhang [12] proposed a certificateless signcryption scheme which needs two pairing operations. Weng et al. [11] proposed a certificateless signcryption scheme which is secure under the standard model in 2011. Numerous certificateless signcryption schemes, and variants thereof, have been proposed over the past few years. But none of these schemes consider identity concealment and communication between separate KGCs. Chen [6] provides several authenticated key agreement protocols based on identity, which includes an authenticated key agreement protocol with separate trust authorities (TA). Unfortunately, no certificateless authenticated encryption scheme under multiple KGCs has been put forward so far.

Motivated by the above works, the main contributions of this paper are as follows.

- We introduce the first certificateless identity-concealed authenticated encryption (CL-ICAE, for short) scheme under multi-KGC. Our CL-ICAE under multi-KGC is a 0-RTT scheme that combines signcryption and identity concealment. Considering scenarios without signature, CL-ICAE under multi-KGC doesn't need an undeniable proof of the sender.
- We build two types of attack model under random oracle model and provide the specific security proof in each type of attack model, which indicates that our CL-ICAE scheme under multi-KGC achieves a number of security properties, including x-security and receiver deniability, etc.

- We provide the analysis of our scheme in terms of efficiency and security, we also give a comparison with three previous schemes.
- Finally, we propose a certificateless bilateral identity-concealed authentication key-exchange (CL-CAKE) scheme under multi-KGC, which combines the functions of certificateless signcryption and identity-concealed authentication key-exchange (CAKE).

2 Preliminaries

2.1 Hard Problems

We establish a BDH Parameter Generator and review hard problems including computation Diffie-Hellman (CDH) problem, bilinear Diffie-Hellman (BDH) problem, decision bilinear Diffie-Hellman (DBDH) problem and gap bilinear Diffie-Hellman (GBDH) problem [2,6].

BDH Parameter Generator: As described in [5], a BDH parameter generator IG takes as input the security parameter $\kappa > 0$, and outputs an additive cyclic group G_1, one generator of whom is P, a multiplicative cyclic group G_2 and pairing $e : G_1 \times G_1 \to G_2$. The order of G_1 and G_2 is prime q. We also randomly select elements a, b and c of Z_q^*.

CDH Problem: Input a tuple $(P, aP, bP) \in G_1^3$, compute abP.

CDH Assumption: There is no probabilistic algorithm in G_1 able to solve the CDH problem in polynomial time with non-negligible probability.

BDH Problem: Input $(P, aP, bP, cP) \in G_1^4$, compute $e(P, P)^{abc} \in G_2$.

DBDH Problem: Given a tuple $(P, aP, bP, cP, T) \in (G_1)^4 \times G_2$, outputs a bit $\sigma \in \{0, 1\}$ ($\sigma = 0$ if $T = e(P, P)^{abc}$; otherwise $\sigma = 1$).

GBDH Assumption: There is at least one probabilistic algorithm where DBDH problem can be solved in polynomial time and there is no probabilistic algorithm which can solve BDH problem within polynomial time with non-negligible probability.

2.2 Security Properties

A certificateless identity-concealed authenticated encryption scheme under multiple KGCs should possess the following security properties:

1. x-security: The confidentiality of message should not be compromised once ephemeral Diffie-Hellman exponents generated by running the scheme is leaked.
2. Forward security: If the adversary has compromised a user's long-term private key, it is acceptable that an adversary can impersonate this user, but the confidentiality of the previous messages sent by this user shouldn't be affected.

3. Identity concealment: We say that a CL-ICAE scheme under multi-KGC satisfies identity concealment when the probability for an adversary to compromise the public identity information, which is encrypted in the ciphertext sent between uncorrupted honest users, is negligible.
4. KGC-security: If the adversary has compromised the key generation centre (KGC), the confidentiality of the messages sent between uncorrupted honest users should not be affected.

In some application scenarios, a sender might want to avoid leaving an undeniable proof to the receiver. A CL-ICAE scheme under multi-KGC may also consider this and achieve deniability, which means a message could be denied by the sender because message receiver could also generate the same message.

2.3   AEAD

An authenticated encryption with associated data (AEAD) scheme [18] takes as input a message M and its public header information H and outputs a ciphertext C. In detail, we follow [9] for defining AEAD schemes and their security. An AEAD scheme is a three tuple $SE = (K_{se}, Enc, Dec)$. The probabilistic polynomial-time algorithm K_{se} samples from a non-empty and finite set $\mathcal{K}_{se}$. The encryption algorithm Enc takes as input $\mathcal{K}_{se} \times \{0,1\}^* \times \{0,1\}^*$ and outputs a string or the distinguished output $\bot$. The decryption algorithm Dec takes as input $\mathcal{K}_{se} \times \{0,1\}^* \times \{0,1\}^*$ and outputs a string or the distinguished output $\bot$. Figure 1 presents the security game of AEAD.

Suppose that A is an adversary. We define the probability that A wins the game to be $Adv_{SE}^{AEAD}(A) = |2 \cdot Pr[AEAD_{SE}^A \Rightarrow true] - 1|$. The SE scheme is AEAD-secure, if for any PPT adversary the advantage $Adv_{SE}^{AEAD}(A)$ is negligible. Besides, we could learn from [8] that after adaptively seeing ciphertext of key $K_1 \in \mathcal{K}_{se}$, message M and header information H, an efficient adversary cannot generate another valid ciphertext, whose plaintext is also M and H, encrypted by another independent key $K_2 \in \mathcal{K}_{se}$.

main $AEAD_{SE}^A$:	proc. $Enc(H, M_0, M_1)$:	proc. $Dec(H, C)$:
$K \leftarrow \mathcal{K}_{se}$	$C_0 \leftarrow Enc_K(H, M_0)$	If $\sigma = 1 \wedge C \notin \mathcal{C}$
$\sigma \leftarrow \{0,1\}$	$C_1 \leftarrow Enc_K(H, M_1)$	Ret $Dec_K(H, C)$
$\sigma' \leftarrow A^{Enc, Dec}$	If $C_0 = \bot$ or $C_1 = \bot$	Ret $\bot$
$Ret(\sigma' = \sigma)$	then Ret $\bot$	
	$C \overset{\cup}{\leftarrow} C_\sigma$; Ret C_σ	

Fig. 1. The security game of AEAD

3 Definition and Security Model

3.1 Definition of CL-ICAE Under Multi-KGC

In this paper, we focus on the strong security model for our scheme where there are multiple users and multiple KGCs. Our scheme is specified by five polynomial-time (PPT) algorithms: "Setup", "KGCKeyGen", "UserKeyGen", "CipherGen" and "Decryption and Validation (DecVal)". We assume that there are a total of n users and m key generation centres (KGC) in this case.

Setup: A PPT algorithm that takes as input a security parameter κ and outputs system parameters *params*, which will be used in the following run.

KGCKeyGen: A PPT algorithm that takes as input system parameters *params* and outputs a public-private key pair (P_{pub}, s) for each KGC.

UserKeyGen: A PPT algorithm that takes as input system parameters *params*, a public-private key pair (P_{pub}, s) of a KGC and user's identity information *id* and outputs a public-private key pair (pid, sid) for each user.

CipherGen: A PPT algorithm that takes as input a tuple $(H, M, id_s, sid_s, pid_r)$ where id_s is sender's identity, sid_s is sender's private key, pid_r is receiver's public key which includes receiver's identity id_r and public key pk_r, M is the message to be sent and H is the associated information of M, and outputs a ciphertext *Cipher* or a symbol $\perp$ indicating CipherGen failed.

DecVal: A deterministic polynomial-time algorithm that takes as input a ciphertext *Cipher*, receiver's public key pid_r and receiver's private key sid_r, and outputs (M, pid_s) or a symbol $\perp$ indicating DecVal failed.

3.2 Security Model of CL-ICAE Under Multi-KGC

Let n, m be the number of users and the number of KGCs in the system respectively, where n, m are polynomial in the security parameter κ. The key pairs of all the honest parties in the system are generated by the simulator according to the specified key generation algorithm. Denote by $HONEST/DISHONEST$ the set of public identity information of all the honest/dishonest users in the system. The adversary is able to request the following four oracles: HO oracle, UHO oracle, EXO oracle and Corrupt oracle.

HO oracle: For the query (H, M, id_s, id_r), HO returns ciphertext $id_r, Cipher = CipherGen(id_s, sk_s, id_r, H, M)$ if $id_s, id_r \in HONEST$; otherwise it returns $\perp$. HO stores the random number used to generate ciphertext, H, M, pid_s and pid_r into $\mathcal{ST}_C$, where pid_s and pid_r are the public keys of id_s and id_r respectively.

UHO oracle: For the query $(id_r, Cipher)$, UHO returns $(id_s, M) = DecVal(Cipher)$ if $id_r \in HONEST$; otherwise it returns $\perp$.

EXO oracle: For the query $(id_r, Cipher)$, EXO returns the corresponding random number stored in set $\mathcal{ST}_C$ if $id_r \in HONEST$ and *Cipher* is the output of an HO query; otherwise it returns $\perp$.

Corrupt oracle: For the query id_i, Corrupt returns id_i's private key if $id_i \in HONEST$, $id_i \neq id_s$ and $id_i \neq id_r$; otherwise it returns $\perp$. Note that the adversary can't request Corrupt queries of the target sender and the target reciever.

We consider two types of attacks for CL-ICAE scheme under Multi-KGC. The first attack, referred as Type-I attack, considers that the adversary cannot compromise the master key of the KGC but has access to the partial private key generated by any user. We name the adversary under Type-I attack model as Type-I adversary. The second attack, referred as Type-I attack, considers that the adversary is able to access the master key of the KGC, but cannot obtain the partial private key generated by any uncorrupted user. We also name the adversary under Type-II attack model as Type-II adversary. Both attacks need to satisfy outsider unforgeability and insider confidentiality which are defined below. We don't count in the case that the adversary cannot compromise either the master key of the KGC or partial private key generated by users, since our scheme is secure in this case if the above two types of attack model are secure in the random oracle model.

Outsider Unforgeability (OU). As described in [18], an outsider unforgeability adversary $\mathcal{A}^{OU}$ aims to forge a valid cipherptext sent between uncorrupted honest users. Note that the sender and the receiver may be the same. Before $\mathcal{A}^{OU}$ outputs the forgery, $\mathcal{A}^{OU}$ can query UHO oracle, EXO oracle and Corrupt oracle; however, $\mathcal{A}^{OU}$ is not allowed to query Corrupt(id_s) and Corrupt(id_r). $\mathcal{A}^{OU}$ is also allowed to query HO(id_s', id_r', H', M') as long as the output of HO(id_s', id_r', H', M') is different with the target output HO(id_s, id_r, H, M). We also allow the compromise of $\mathcal{ST}_C$ as in [18]. Finally, $\mathcal{A}^{OU}$ outputs ($id_r, Cipher$) as its forgery, where id_r is an uncorrupted user. A CL-ICAE scheme under Multi-KGC enjoys outsider unforgeability, if for any PPT adversary $\mathcal{A}^{OU}$, its advantage $Adv_{\mathcal{A}^{OU},\mathcal{ICAE}}$ on winning the game is negligible.

Insider Confidentiality (IC). A confidentiality adversary $\mathcal{A}^{IC}$ aims either to compromise the identity information, which is encrypted in the message, or to compromise the confidentiality of the message.

$\mathcal{A}^{IC}$ has a right to query HO oracle, UHO oracle, EXO oracle and Corrupt oracle except Corrupt(id_r), Corrupt(id_{s_1}) and Corrupt(id_{s_0}). First, $\mathcal{A}^{IC}$ sends two quadruples (M_0, H, id_{s_0}, id_r) and (M_1, H, id_{s_1}, id_r) where M_0, M_1 are equal-length and $id_{s_0}, id_{s_1}, id_r \in HONEST$ to the challenger. The challenger then chooses $\sigma \leftarrow \{0, 1\}$ randomly, generates the ciphertext $Cipher$ and sends $Cipher$ to $\mathcal{A}^{IC}$. After receiving the $Cipher$, $\mathcal{A}^{IC}$ could continue issuing HO, UHO and EXO queries except UHO($id_r, Cipher$) and EXO($Cipher$). And $\mathcal{A}^{IC}$ is allowed to issue Corrupt queries except Corrupt(id_r), Corrupt(id_{s_1}) and Corrupt(id_{s_0}).

Finally, $\mathcal{A}^{IC}$ outputs a bit σ'. $\mathcal{A}^{IC}$ wins the game if $\sigma' = \sigma$. We say that a CL-ICAE scheme under Multi-KGC achieves insider confidentiality, if for any PPT adversary $\mathcal{A}^{IC}$, its advantage $Adv_{\mathcal{A}^{IC},\mathcal{ICAE}}$ on winning the game is negligible.

4 Our Scheme

4.1 CL-ICAE Under Multi-KGC

We now present the detailed description of our Certificateless Identity-Concealed Authenticated Encryption (CL-ICAE) scheme under multi-KGC (see also in Fig. 2).

Setup. This algorithm takes security parameter κ as input and outputs system parameters $(G_1, G_2, e, \mathcal{K}, l, P, q, n, m)$. Among these parameters, we denote by G_1 an additive cyclic group whose generator is P, denote by G_2 a multiplicative cyclic. Denote by q the order of groups G_1, G_2. e is the bilinear mapping $e : G_1 \times G_1 \to G_2$. Denote by $\mathcal{K}$ the key space of symmetric keys. $n = F_1(\kappa)$ is the total number of users in κ for some polynomial function F_1. $m = F_2(\kappa)$ is the total number of KGCs in κ for some polynomial function F_2. $l = F_3(\kappa)$ is the number of bits needed by a symmetric key in $\mathcal{K}$ for some polynomial function F_3. We note that the CDH assumption and $GBDH$ assumption hold over groups G_1 and G_2. This algorithm then chooses two hash functions $h_1 : \{0,1\}^* \to G_1$, $h_2 : \{0,1\}^* \to Z_q$ and chooses a key derivation function $KDF : G_1 \times G_2 \times \{0,1\}^* \to \{0,1\}^l$. Then $params = (G_1, G_2, e, \mathcal{K}, l, P, q, n, h_1, h_2, KDF)$ are system parameters.

KGCKeyGen. Denote by KGC_t the identity of key generation center t where $1 \leq t \leq m$. KGC_t chooses master key $s_t \leftarrow Z_q^*$ randomly and generates its public key $P_{pubt} = s_t P$. For presentation simplicity, in this paper, there are two key generation centres KGC_1 and KGC_2 whose public-private key pairs are $(P_{pub1} = s_1 P, s_1)$ and $(P_{pub2} = s_2 P, s_2)$ respectively.

UserKeyGen. Denote by id_i the identity of user i ($1 \leq i \leq n$). User i registers with KGC_t and gets its partial private key $D_i = s_t Q_i = s_t h_1(id_i)$ from KGC_t. User i randomly selects $x_i \leftarrow Z_q^*$ as part of its private key. Then the public key of user i is $pid_i = (X_i = x_i P, id_i)$ and i's private key is $sid_i = (D_i, x_i)$. For presentation simplicity, in this paper, we assume that user A registers with KGC_1 and user B registers with KGC_2, $1 \leq A, B \leq n$.

CipherGen. Every time user A wants to send a message M with associated information H to user B, user A chooses a random number $r \in Z_q^*$ uniformly and computes $R = rP$. Then A computes $d = h_2(R, pid_A, pid_B, H, M)$, $R_s = dQ_A$, $\overline{R} = (dr + x_A)P$ and shared values $PS_1 = (dr + x_A)X_B$, $PS_2 = e(dD_A, X_B)e(Q_B, (dr + x_A)P_{pub2})$. A then derives key K from KDF function $K = KDF(PS_1, PS_2, R_s\|\overline{R}\|pid_B)$. After that, A generates $C = Enc_K(H, pid_A\|R\|M)$ and sends ciphertext $Cipher = (P_{pub1}, H, R_s, \overline{R}, C)$ to user B.

DecVal. On receiving ciphertext $Cipher = (P_{pub1}, H, R_s, \overline{R}, C)$, user B first computes $PS_1 = x_B \overline{R}$ and $PS_2 = e(R_s, x_B P_{pub1})e(D_B, \overline{R})$ and derives shared key K by computing $K = KDF(PS_1, PS_2, R_s\|\overline{R}\|pid_B)$. If $K \notin \mathcal{K}$ B aborts. User B decrypts C with K and gets (H', pid_A, R, M) by deriving its output. If $H' \neq H$ or pid_A is not valid, B aborts. B then computes $d = h_2(R, pid_A, pid_B, H, M)$. B aborts if $\overline{R} \neq dR + X_A$ or $R_s \neq dQ_A$. Finally, B accepts (pid_A, H, M, K).

$$\boxed{\begin{aligned} &UserA: Q_A = h_1(id_A) \\ &pid_A: X_A = x_A P, id_A \\ &sid_A: D_A = s_1 Q_A, x_A \end{aligned}}$$

$$\boxed{\begin{aligned} &UserB: Q_B = h_1(id_B) \\ &pid_B: X_B = x_B P, id_B \\ &sid_A: D_B = s_2 Q_B, x_B \end{aligned}}$$

$$r \leftarrow Z_q^*, R = rP$$
$$d = h_2(R, pid_A, pid_B, H, M)$$
$$R_s = dQ_A, \overline{R} = (dr + x_A)P$$
$$PS_1 = (dr + x_A)X_B$$
$$PS_2 = e(dD_A, X_B)e(Q_B, (dr + x_A)P_{pub2})$$
$$K = KDF(PS_1, PS_2, R_s\|\overline{R}\|pid_B)$$

$$\xrightarrow{P_{pub1}, H, R_s, \overline{R},\ C \leftarrow Enc_K(H, pid_A\|R\|M)}$$

$$PS_1 = x_B \overline{R}$$
$$PS_2 = e(R_s, x_B P_{pub1})e(D_B, \overline{R})$$
$$K = KDF(PS_1, PS_2, R_s\|\overline{R}\|pid_B)$$
$$(H, pid_A\|R\|M) = Dec_K(C)$$
$$d = h_2(R, pid_A, pid_B, H, M)$$
$$\overline{R} = dR + X_A, R_s = dQ_A$$

Accept if equations are established

Fig. 2. Protocol structure of our scheme

4.2   Correctness

Correctness of Shared Key. User A computes shared values PS_1 and PS_2 as follows:

$$\begin{aligned} PS_1 &= (dr + x_A)X_B &&= x_B(dr + x_A)P, \\ PS_2 &= e(dD_A, X_B)e(Q_B, (dr + x_A)P_{pub2}) \\ &= e(ds_1 Q_A, x_B P)e(Q_B, (dr + x_A)s_2 P) \\ &= e(Q_A, P)^{ds_1 x_B} e(Q_B, P)^{s_2(dr + x_A)}. \end{aligned}$$

User B computes shared values PS_1 and PS_2 as follows:

$$\begin{aligned} PS_1 &= x_B \overline{R} &&= x_B(dr + x_A)P, \\ PS_2 &= e(R_s, x_B P_{pub1})e(D_B, \overline{R}) \\ &= e(dQ_A, x_B s_1 P)e(s_2 Q_B, (dr + x_A)P) \\ &= e(Q_A, P)^{ds_1 x_B} e(Q_B, P)^{s_2(dr + x_A)}. \end{aligned}$$

Both user A and user B get the same PS_1 and PS_2. Both of them can compute $K = KDF(PS_1, PS_2, R_s\|\overline{R}\|pid_B)$. Moreover, user B can verify the correctness of shared key by checking whether the decrypted H' is equal to H which is included in cipher as plaintext.

Correctness of Ciphertext. User B can also verify the correctness of $\overline{R}$. For user A, $\overline{R}_1 = (dr + x_A)P$. After receiving the ciphertext and decryption, user B computes $\overline{R}_2 = dR + X_A = drP + x_A P = (dr + x_A)P = \overline{R}_1$. Then user B accepts the message when equations $\overline{R} = dR + X_A$ and $R_s = dQ_A$ holds.

5   Security Analysis

Consider an arbitrary adversary $\mathcal{A}$ and suppose that KDF and h_2 are modeled to be random oracles (RO). Now we provide security proofs under the random oracle model.

Theorem 1. The CL-ICAE scheme under multi-KGC presented in Fig. 2 achieves insider confidentiality under the GBDH assumption and AEAD security in the Type-I attack model.

Theorem 2. The CL-ICAE scheme under multi-KGC presented in Fig. 2 achieves outsider unforgeability under the CDH assumption and AEAD security in the Type-II attack model.

Theorem 3. The CL-ICAE scheme under multi-KGC presented in Fig. 2 achieves insider confidentiality under the CDH assumption and AEAD security in the Type-II attack model.

5.1   Proof of Theorem 1

Suppose that adversary $\mathcal{A}^{IC}$ can break insider confidentiality in the Type-I attack model with non-negligible probability ϵ_1. We now demonstrate that a challenger $\mathcal{C}$ can solve the hardness assumption of GBDH problem also with non-negligible probability ϵ_2. In this case, an adversary $\mathcal{A}^{IC}$ is able to access the partial private key generated by any user. Suppose that $\mathcal{A}^{IC}$ has not issued Corrupt(id_A) and Corrupt(id_B) queries.

Here, we also construct a challenger $\mathcal{C}$. $\mathcal{C}$ aims to solve the GBDH problem with non-negligible probability. $\mathcal{C}$ sets the public-private key pairs of all honest users except user A and user B in the system on its own, and sets partial private key x_A, x_B for user A and user B together with their public keys. Then $\mathcal{C}$ plays the role of all honest users except user A and user B. For presentation simplicity, we assume that senders register with KGC_1 whose public-private key pair is (P_{pub1}, s_1) and receivers register with KGC_2 whose public-private key pair is (P_{pub2}, s_2).

During the experiment, $\mathcal{A}^{IC}$ is allowed to issue HO, UHO, EXO queries except EXO query of the challenge ciphertext and Corrupt queries adaptively as long as the outputs of HO queries are not the same with $id_B, Cipher$. We now show that if $\mathcal{A}^{IC}$ can successfully break insider confidentiality of the ciphertext with non-negligible probability ϵ_1, $\mathcal{C}$ is able to solve the $GBDH$ problem with non-negligible probability ϵ_2.

During the attacking experiment, $\mathcal{C}$ executes as follows:

1. On receiving an HO(id_s, id_r, H, M) query, if $id_r \in DISHONEST$ or $id_s \in DISHONEST$, $\mathcal{C}$ returns "$\perp$". If $id_s \in HONEST$ and $id_s \neq id_A$, $\mathcal{C}$ returns ciphertext $Cipher$ by running **CipherGen** in Sect. 4 with the help of sid_s. If $id_r \in HONEST$ and $id_r \neq id_B$, $\mathcal{C}$ runs **CipherGen** as described in Sect. 4. $\mathcal{C}$ also computes $PS_2 = e(dQ_s, x_r P_{pub_1})e(D_r, (dr + x_s)P_{pub2})$ with

the help of sid_r. Then $\mathcal{C}$ returns ciphertext $Cipher$. If $id_s = id_A$ and $id_r = id_B$, $\mathcal{C}$ selects a random number r from Z_q^* and computes $R = rP$, $d = h_2(R, pid_A, pid_B, H, M)$, $R_s = dQ_A$, $\overline{R} = (dr + x_A)P$. S then sets $K \in \mathcal{K}$ randomly ensuring K is different from previous keys. $\mathcal{C}$ then computes $C = Enc_K(H, pid_A \| R \| M)$. Then $\mathcal{C}$ returns ciphertext $Cipher \leftarrow (P_{pub1}, H, R_s, \overline{R}, C)$ as the output of HO and stores the tuple $(R_s, \overline{R}, pid_B, K)$ into list $\mathcal{L}_{DBDH}$.

2. On receiving an $\mathsf{UHO}(id_r, Cipher = (P_{pub1}, H, R_s, \overline{R}, C))$ query, if $id_r \in DISHONEST$, $\mathcal{C}$ returns "$\perp$". If $id_r \in HONEST$ and $id_r \neq id_B$, $\mathcal{C}$ runs **DecVal** in Sect. 4 with the aid of sid_r. If $id_r = id_B$, $\mathcal{C}$ first checks whether $Cipher$ is output by HO with the help of K stored in list $\mathcal{L}_{DBDH}$. If $Cipher$ is output by HO, $\mathcal{C}$ returns (id_s, M) by decrypting the ciphertext $Cipher$. If $Cipher$ isn't output by HO, $\mathcal{C}$ computes $PS_1 = x_B \overline{R}$ and checks whether $PS_2/e(R_s, x_B P_{pub1}) = BDH(P_{pub2}, \overline{R}, Q_B)$ with the help of DBDH oracle for each KDF oracle query $KDF(PS_1, PS_2, R_s \| \overline{R} \| pid_B)$ with the same PS_1. If the equation holds, $\mathcal{C}$ gets K from $KDF(PS_1, PS_2, R_s \| \overline{R} \| pid_B)$, and decrypts C with K. $\mathcal{C}$ returns (id_s, M) to adversary $\mathcal{A}^{IC}$. If the equation doesn't hold, $\mathcal{C}$ returns $\perp$ to adversary $\mathcal{A}^{IC}$.

3. On receiving an $\mathsf{EXO}(id_r, Cipher)$ query, if $id_r \in DISHONEST$, $\mathcal{C}$ returns "$\perp$"; otherwise, $\mathcal{C}$ checks whether $Cipher$ is output by HO. If so, $\mathcal{C}$ returns the random number stored in set $\mathcal{ST}_C$ to $\mathcal{A}^{OU}$; otherwise, $\mathcal{C}$ returns "$\perp$".

4. On receiving a $\mathsf{Corrupt}(id_{Corrupt})$ query, if $id_{Corrupt} \in HONEST$, $id_{Corrupt} \neq id_A$ and $id_{Corrupt} \neq id_B$, then $\mathcal{C}$ returns $sid_{Corrupt}$; otherwise, $\mathcal{C}$ returns "$\perp$".

Denote by "`failure`" the event that $\mathcal{C}$ returns "$\perp$" while UHO does not. We now prove that the probability of "`failure`" event is negligible. A "`failure`" event occurs when adversary $\mathcal{A}^{IC}$ made a valid $\mathsf{UHO}(id_r, P_{pub1}, H, R_s, \overline{R}, C)$ query while $\mathcal{C}$ returns "$\perp$". That is, adversary $\mathcal{A}^{IC}$ generated a valid ciphertext $Cipher$ without knowing the corresponding PS_2.

We now consider $Cipher$ is the output of $\mathsf{HO}(id_s, id_B, H, M)$ where $id_s \in HONEST$ and (H, M) can be arbitrary. In this case, $PS_2 = e(dQ_s, x_B P_{pub1}) e(Q_B, (dr + x_s)P_{pub2})$. The target shared secrecy is $PS_{2(A,B)} = e(d'Q_A, x_B P_{pub1})e(Q_B, (d'r' + x_A)P_{pub2})$. We can see that $d' \neq d$ with overwhelming probability as $id_s \neq id_A$. If $r' = r$, $PS_2 = PS_{2(A,B)}$ with negligible probability because $id_s \neq id_A$ according to the unpredictability of hash function. If $d'r' = dr$, then $PS_2 \neq PS_{2(A,B)}$ with overwhelming probability as $id_s \neq id_A$. If $d'r' + x_A = dr + x_s$, $PS_2 \neq PS_{2(A,B)}$ since $d' \neq d$. If $d'r' + x_A \neq dr + x_s$, then $\overline{R} \neq \overline{R}_{(A,B)}$. In either way, $PS_2 \neq PS_{2(A,B)}$ with overwhelming probability. Then we can conclude that the shared-keys K and $K_{(A,A)}$ are independent of each other. UHO outputs $\perp$ with overwhelming probability by AEAD security. If $d' = d$ and $id_s = id_A$, HO chooses the shared-key K randomly from $\mathcal{K}$, which means that the probability of $K = K_{A,B}$ is negligible and the ciphertexts are different with overwhelming probability by AEAD security. In this case, UHO outputs "$\perp$" with overwhelming probability.

We then consider the possibility that ciphertext $Cipher$ is the output of $\mathsf{HO}(id_s, id_r, H, M)$ made by adversary $\mathcal{A}^{IC}$ for $id_r \neq id_B$. In this case, since $pid_r \neq pid_B$, the shared-keys K and $K_{A,B}$ are independent of each other through the KDF function. By the security of AEAD, UHO outputs "$\perp$" with overwhelming probability. This indicates that $Cipher$ is not the output of HO oracle. Adversary $\mathcal{A}^{IC}$ generates a valid $Cipher$ only when it successfully forges the symmetric key K corresponding to C. We then consider that $\mathcal{A}^{IC}$ generates a new valid symmetric key K' without KDF oracle, where UHO outputs "$\perp$" with overwhelming probability by AEAD security.

Therefore, it is negligible for a "**failure**" event to happen. That is, the simulation is indistinguishable from real attack experiment in the view of $\mathcal{A}^{IC}$. Then challenge experiment runs as follow.

First, $\mathcal{A}^{IC}$ sends two tuples (M_0, H, id_{s_0}, id_B) and (M_1, H, id_{s_1}, id_B), where M_0, M_1 are equal-length and $id_{s_0}, id_{s_1}, id_B \in HONEST$, to $\mathcal{C}$. $\mathcal{C}$ randomly chooses a bit $\sigma \leftarrow \{0,1\}$ and runs as follows.

$\mathcal{C}$ randomly chooses $r \leftarrow Z_q^*$ and computes $R = rP$, $d = h_2(R, pid_{s_\sigma}, pid_B, H, M_\sigma)$, $R_s = dQ_{s_\sigma}$ and $\overline{R} = (dr + x_{s_\sigma})P$. Then $\mathcal{C}$ checks whether $PS_2 = BDH(P_{pub_2}, \overline{R}, Q_B)$ has been queried in $KDF(PS_1, PS_2, R_s \| \overline{R} \| pid_B)$ with the help of DBDH oracle. If so, $\mathcal{C}$ aborts; otherwise, $\mathcal{C}$ randomly chooses $K \in \mathcal{K}$ and computes $C = Enc_K(H, pid_{s_\sigma} \| R \| M_\sigma)$. $\mathcal{C}$ returns $Cipher = (P_{pub1}, H, R_s, \overline{R}, C)$ to adversary $\mathcal{A}^{IC}$. $\mathcal{C}$ stores the tuple $(R_s, \overline{R}, pid_B, K)$ into list $\mathcal{L}_{DBDH}$.

On receiving a KDF query, $\mathcal{C}$ checks whether $PS_2 = BDH(P_{pub_2}, \overline{R}, Q_B)$ is valid with the aid of DBDH oracle. If so, $\mathcal{C}$ returns the corresponding K recorded in list $\mathcal{L}_{DBDH}$ and records the value of PS_2; otherwise $\mathcal{C}$ returns "$\perp$".

Note that $Cipher$ was not the output of HO oracle. r is chosen uniformly from Z_q^*, which indicates $d = h_2(R, pid_{s_\sigma}, pid_B, H, M_\sigma)$ is unpredictable and distributed uniformly over Z_q^*. Therefore, $\overline{R} = (dr + x_{s_\sigma})P$ and $R_s = dQ_{s_\sigma}$ are distributed uniformly over G_1 and perfectly blinds the sender's identity information. Then we can conclude $\mathcal{A}^{IC}$ wins the game in case that it generates a valid K corresponding to $Cipher$.

The goal of $\mathcal{A}^{IC}$ is to decide which quadruple is involved in the challenge ciphertext. We now consider the case adversary $\mathcal{A}^{IC}$ has non-negligible advantage ϵ_1 on outputting the right bit σ. According to the simulation, $\mathcal{A}^{IC}$ has made KDF query with non-negligible probability. $\mathcal{C}$ can get the valid $PS_2 = BDH(P_{pub_2}, \overline{R}, Q_B)$ from the KDF query $\mathcal{A}^{OU}$ made. Thus, $\mathcal{C}$ can solve $BDH(P_{pub_2}, \overline{R}, Q_B)$ with non-negligible probability, which violates the $GBDH$ assumption.

Consequently, adversary $\mathcal{A}^{IC}$ has negligible advantage on successfully outputting the right bit σ, our proposed scheme presented in Fig. 2 achieves insider confidentiality under the GBDH assumption and AEAD security in the Type-I attack model.

5.2   Proof of Theorem 2

We suppose adversary $\mathcal{A}^{OU}$ can break outsider unforgeability in the Type-II attack model with non-negligible probability ϵ_3. We now prove that a simulator $\mathcal{S}$ can solve the hardness assumption of CDH problem with non-negligible probability ϵ_4 by running the adversary $\mathcal{A}^{OU}$ as a subroutine.

In this attack model, adversary $\mathcal{A}^{OU}$ is allowed to access the master keys of all KGCs. Assume that adversary $\mathcal{A}^{OU}$ has not issued $\mathsf{Corrupt}(id_A)$ and $\mathsf{Corrupt}(id_B)$ queries. Suppose that adversary $\mathcal{A}^{OU}$ successfully forges a ciphertext $id_B, Cipher = (H, R_s, \overline{R}, C^*)$ from user A with non-negligible probability after issuing HO, UHO, EXO and Corrupt queries adaptively as long as the outputs of HO queries are not the same with $id_B, Cipher$.

Here, we construct a simulator $\mathcal{S}$ whose goal is to solve the CDH problem with non-negligible probability. $\mathcal{S}$ sets the public-private key pairs of all honest users except user A and user B in the system, and sets partial private key $D_A = s_1 Q_A, D_B = s_2 Q_B$ for user A and user B respectively together with their public key. Then $\mathcal{S}$ acts as all honest users except user A, B. We now show that if the adversary $\mathcal{A}^{OU}$ successfully forges the ciphertext, simulator $\mathcal{S}$ is able to solve a CDH problem, which violates the CDH assumption.

During $\mathcal{A}^{OU}$'s attacking experiment, $\mathcal{S}$ answers $\mathcal{A}^{OU}$'s queries as follows:

1. On receiving an $\mathsf{HO}(id_s, id_r, H, M)$ query, if $id_r \in DISHONEST$ or $id_s \in DISHONEST$, $\mathcal{S}$ returns "$\perp$". If $id_s \neq id_A$, $\mathcal{S}$ returns ciphertext $Cipher$ by running **CipherGen** with the help of sid_s. If $id_r \neq id_B$, $\mathcal{S}$ runs **CipherGen** as described in Sect. 4. $\mathcal{S}$ also computes $PS_1 = dr x_r P + x_r X_s$ with the help of sid_r. Then $\mathcal{S}$ returns ciphertext $Cipher$ to $\mathcal{A}^{OU}$. If $id_s = id_A$ and $id_r = id_B$, $\mathcal{S}$ randomly selects $r \in Z_q^*$ and computes $R = rP$, $d = h_2(R, pid_A, pid_B, H, M)$, $R_s = dQ_s$ and $\overline{R} = (dr + x_A)P$. $\mathcal{S}$ sets $K \in \mathcal{K}$ randomly ensuring K is different from previous keys. $\mathcal{S}$ then computes $C = Enc_K(H, pid_A \| R \| M)$. Finally $\mathcal{S}$ returns ciphertext $Cipher = (P_{pub1}, H, R_s, \overline{R}, C)$ as the output of HO and stores the tuple $(R_s, \overline{R}, pid_A, K)$ into list $\mathcal{L}_{DBDH}$.

   As long as the output of $\mathcal{S}$ is not "$\perp$", $\mathcal{S}$ stores the tuple (r, pid_A, pid_B, H, M) into set $\mathcal{ST}_C$ which is initiated to be empty.

2. On receiving an $\mathsf{UHO}(id_r, Cipher = (P_{pub1}, H, R_s, \overline{R}, C))$ query, if $id_r \in DISHONEST$, $\mathcal{S}$ returns "$\perp$". If $id_r \neq id_B$, $\mathcal{S}$ runs **DecVal** in Sect. 4 with sid_r and returns (id_s, M) to the adversary. If $id_r = id_B$, $\mathcal{S}$ first checks whether $Cipher$ was output by HO with the help of K stored in list $\mathcal{L}_{DBDH}$. If $Cipher$ was output by HO, $\mathcal{S}$ returns (id_s, M) by decrypting the ciphertext $Cipher$; otherwise, $\mathcal{S}$ checks whether $PS_1 = CDH(\overline{R}, X_B)$ by computing $e(PS_1, P) = e(\overline{R}, X_B)$ for each $KDF(PS_1, PS_2, R_s \| \overline{R} \| pid_B)$ query. If the equation holds, $\mathcal{S}$ derives K from the KDF function, decrypts C and returns (id_A, M) to $\mathcal{A}^{OU}$. If the equation doesn't hold, $\mathcal{S}$ returns $\perp$ to $\mathcal{A}^{OU}$.

3. On receiving an $\mathsf{EXO}(id_r, Cipher)$ query, if $id_r \in DISHONEST$, $\mathcal{S}$ returns "$\perp$"; otherwise, $\mathcal{S}$ checks whether $Cipher$ is output by HO. If $Cipher$ is output by HO, $\mathcal{S}$ returns the random number stored in set $\mathcal{ST}_C$ to $\mathcal{A}^{OU}$; otherwise, $\mathcal{S}$ returns "$\perp$".

4. On receiving a Corrupt($id_{Corrupt}$) query, if $id_{Corrupt} \in HONEST$, $id_{Corrupt} \neq id_A$ and $id_{Corrupt} \neq id_B$, $\mathcal{S}$ returns $sid_{Corrupt}$; otherwise, $\mathcal{S}$ returns "$\perp$".

Denote by "failure" the event where the output of $\mathcal{S}$ is different from the output in real attack experiment on receiving an UHO query. A "failure" event occurs when adversary $\mathcal{A}^{OU}$ made a valid UHO($id_r, Cipher$) query while simulator $\mathcal{S}$ returns "$\perp$". That is, adversary $\mathcal{A}^{OU}$ generated a valid ciphertext $Cipher$ without knowing the corresponding PS_1.

Consider that $Cipher$ is the output of HO(id_s, id_B, H, M) for arbitrary $id_s \in HONEST$ and arbitrary (H, M). In this case, $PS_1 = (dr + x_s)X_B$, the target $PS_{1(A,B)} = (d'r' + x_A)X_B$. We first assume $id_s \neq id_A$. If $d'r' = dr$ then $PS_2 \neq PS_{2(A,A)}$ since $id_s \neq id_A$. If $d'r' \neq dr$ then $\overline{R} \neq \overline{R}_{(A,B)}$ with overwhelming probability. In either way, the shared-keys generated by the KDF oracle are independent of each other with overwhelming probability. In this case, UHO outputs $\perp$ with overwhelming probability. If $id_s = id_A$, HO chooses the shared-key K randomly from $\mathcal{K}$, which indicates that the probability of $K = K_{A,B}$ is negligible and the ciphertexts are different with overwhelming probability by AEAD security. In this case, UHO outputs "$\perp$" with overwhelming probability.

We then consider the possibility that ciphertext $Cipher$ is the output of HO(id_s, id_r, H, M) made by adversary $\mathcal{A}^{OU}$ for $id_r \neq id_B$. In this case, since $pid_r \neq pid_B$, the shared-keys K and $K_{A,B}$ are independent of each other through the KDF function. UHO($id_A, Cipher$) outputs "$\perp$" with overwhelming probability. Then, we can conclude that $Cipher$ is not the output of HO oracle. Adversary $\mathcal{A}^{OU}$ generates a valid $Cipher$ only when it successfully forges the symmetric key K corresponding to C. We consider the case that $\mathcal{A}^{OU}$ generates a new valid symmetric key K' without KDF oracle. Then "failure" occurs with negligible probability by AEAD security.

Therefore, it is negligible for a "**failure**" event to happen. That is, the simulation is indistinguishable from real attack experiment in the view of $\mathcal{A}^{OU}$.

Consider that adversary $\mathcal{A}^{OU}$ has successfully forged a valid ciphertext $id_r^*, Cipher^* = (P_{pub1}, H^*, R_s^*, \overline{R}^*, C^*)$ where we consider $id_s^* = id_A$ and $id_r^* = id_B$. In this case, adversary $\mathcal{A}^{OU}$ must have made RO query $h_2(R^*, pid_A^*, pid_B^*, H, M) = d^*$ so that $\mathcal{A}^{OU}$ can computes $\overline{R}^* = d^*r^*P + X_A$ where r^* may be generated by $\mathcal{A}^{OU}$ itself; otherwise, decryption returns "$\perp$" with overwhelming probability. And $\mathcal{A}^{OU}$ must have made KDF query to get $K = KDF(PS_1, PS_2 = CDH(\overline{R}^*, X_B), R_s^* \| \overline{R}^* \| pid_B)$. $\mathcal{S}$ can get the valid $PS_2 = CDH(\overline{R}^*, X_B)$ from the KDF query. Thus, $\mathcal{S}$ can solve $CDH(\overline{R}^*, X_B)$ with non-negligible probability, which violates the CDH assumption.

Consequently, adversary $\mathcal{A}^{OU}$ has negligible probability to forge a valid ciphertext, our proposed scheme presented in Fig. 2 enjoys outsider unforgeability under the CDH assumption and AEAD security in the Type-II attack model.

5.3   Proof of Theorem 3

Suppose that adversary $\mathcal{A}^{IC}$ can break insider confidentiality in the Type-II attack model with non-negligible probability ϵ_5. We now demonstrate that a challenger $\mathcal{C}$ can solve the hardness assumption of CDH problem with non-negligible probability ϵ_6.

During $\mathcal{A}^{IC}$'s attacking experiment, $\mathcal{A}^{IC}$ is able to issue HO queries, UHO queries, EXO queries except EXO query of the challenge ciphertext and Corrupt queries except $\mathsf{Corrupt}(id_A)$. We construct a challenger $\mathcal{C}$ which initiates as simulator $\mathcal{S}$ as described in Sect. 5.2 and acts as all honest users except user A, B. $\mathcal{C}$ can also simulate the receiver id_B indistinguishably. $\mathcal{C}$'s goal is to solve CDH problem with non-negligible probability.

During the attack experiment, $\mathcal{A}^{IC}$ sends two quadruples (M_0, H, id_{s_0}, id_B) and (M_1, H, id_{s_1}, id_B) where M_0, M_1 are equal-length and $id_{s_0}, id_{s_1}, id_B \in HONEST$. Then $\mathcal{C}$ randomly chooses a bit $\sigma \leftarrow \{0,1\}$ and run as follows. $\mathcal{C}$ randomly chooses $r \leftarrow Z_q^*$ and computes $R = rP$, $d = h_2(R, pid_{s_\sigma}, pid_B, H, M_\sigma)$, $R_s = dQ_{s_\sigma}$ and $\overline{R} = (dr + x_{s_\sigma})P$. Then $\mathcal{C}$ checks whether $PS_1 = CDH(\overline{R}, X_B)$ has been queried in $KDF(PS_1, PS_2, R_s^* \| \overline{R}^* \| pid_B)$ with the same PS_2 by checking the validation of equation $e(PS_1, P) = e(\overline{R}, X_B)$. If so, $\mathcal{C}$ returns "failure". Otherwise, $\mathcal{C}$ randomly chooses $K \in \mathcal{K}$ and computes $C = Enc_K(H, pid_{s_\sigma} \| R \| M_\sigma)$. Finally, $\mathcal{C}$ returns $Cipher = (P_{pub1}, H, R_s, \overline{R}, C)$ to adversary $\mathcal{A}^{IC}$. $\mathcal{C}$ stores the tuple $(R_s, \overline{R}, pid_B, K)$ into a list $\mathcal{L}_{DBDH}$ that is maintained by $\mathcal{C}$.

On receiving a KDF query, $\mathcal{C}$ checks whether $e(PS_1, P) = e(\overline{R}, X_B)$ is valid. If so, $\mathcal{C}$ returns the corresponding K recorded in list $\mathcal{L}_{DBDH}$ and records the value of $PS_1 = CDH(\overline{R}, X_B)$; otherwise $\mathcal{C}$ returns "$\perp$".

Note that $Cipher$ is not the output of HO oracle. Since r is chosen uniformly from Z_q^*, which indicates $d = h_2(R, pid_{s_\sigma}, pid_B, H, M_\sigma)$ is unpredictable and distributed uniformly over Z_q^*. $R_s = dQ_{s_\sigma}$ and $\overline{R} = (dr + x_{s_\sigma})P$ are distributed uniformly over G_1. Then we can conclude $\mathcal{A}^{IC}$ wins the game only when it generates the symmetric K of $Cipher$.

Consider the case adversary $\mathcal{A}^{IC}$ has non-negligible advantage ϵ_5 on successfully outputting the right bit σ. According to Sect. 5.2, $\mathcal{A}^{IC}$ has made query $KDF(PS_1, , PS_2, R_s \| \overline{R} \| pid_B)$ with non-negligible probability. $\mathcal{C}$ can get the valid PS_1 from the KDF query. This indicates that $\mathcal{C}$ can solve $CDH(\overline{R}, X_B) = PS_1$ with non-negligible probability, which violates the CDH assumption.

Consequently, adversary $\mathcal{A}^{IC}$ has negligible advantage on outputting the right bit σ, our proposed scheme achieves insider confidentiality under the CDH assumption and AEAD security in the Type-II attack model.

6   Performance Analysis

Now we analyze the performance of our scheme in terms of efficiency and security. We give a comparison with an identity-based authenticated key-exchange protocol with separate trusted authentications (TAs) in [6] and two previous certificateless signcryption schemes under one KGC in [11] and [4] (see also in Table 1).

Now we introduce KGC-security, forward security, x-security, deniability and identity concealment of sender, which are 1,2,3,4 and 5 in the "security properties" column, respectively. All the security properties are defined in Sect. 2. In Table 1, a "$\sqrt{}$" means that the scheme satisfies this kind of security property, a "$\times$" means the scheme is not secure under this kind of security property, a "$\vee$" means the scheme is partially secure under this kind of security property.

Our CL-ICAE scheme under multi-KGC satisfies deniability since it does not provide any undeniable proof to the sender and the receiver. We also take KGC-security and forward security for the sender into consideration so that our proposed scheme satisfies all of them, which we can conclude from the security proof in Sect. 5. As for identity concealment, we can conclude from the attack experiment of insider confidentiality in Sect. 5 that an adversary cannot distinguish different senders of messages. It is also negligible for an adversary to identify the identity of the receiver without the receiver's private key. Thus, our proposed scheme also meets identity concealment. We can see from Sect. 5 that our CL-ICAE scheme under multi-KGC satisfies x-security under the Type-II attack model; unfortunately, we cannot achieve x-security under the Type-I attack model at present.

When considering the size of ciphertext, we denote by n_1 the bit-length of an element in G_1. Denote by n_q the bit-length of an element in Z_q. Denote by n_{id} the bit-length of a user's identity. We omit n_{id} in the "ciphertext size" column, because every scheme needs to include the sender's identity in its message. Denote by m the bit-length of the message being to become transformed in ciphertext. We don't count the length of associated information H, since H can be a packet header or an IP address which is included in every conversation.

In the "CipherGen" and "DecVal" columns, denote by the G_1 the number of double point operations in G_1. Denote by G_2 the number of exponentiations in G_2. And denote by e the number of pairing operations on elliptic curves. We don't count the point addition operations in G_1, point multiplication operations in G_2, hash operations, symmetric encryption and symmetric decryption, since they can be negligible on calculation when compared with the counted-in operations.

Since there is none authenticated scheme which can support identity concealment and signcryption simultaneously, we compare our scheme with two previous certificateless signcryption schemes in Table 1. We can conclude from Table 1 that our scheme has advantage in both security and computational overhead over the previous signcryption schemes in [4] and [11].

We also compare our scheme with a simple identity-based key exchange scheme under multiple TAs in [6]. Table 1 shows that the scheme in [6] cannot satisfy KGC-security, x-security and identity concealment of sender. Our scheme is as efficient as the identity-based scheme with multiple TAs in [6].

Table 1. Performance comparison

Scheme	Security properties					Ciphertext size	CipherGen			DecVal		
	1	2	3	4	5		G_1	G_2	e	G_1	G_2	e
[6]	×	√	×	√	×	–	1	1	2	1	1	2
[4]	√	√	×	×	×	$2n_1 + m$	4	1	1	1	0	5
[11]	√	√	√	×	×	$4n_1 + m$	3	1	0	0	0	5
Ours	√	√	√	√	√	$4n_1 + n_q + m$	6	1	2	4	1	2

$$UserA : Q_A = h_1(id_A)$$
$$pid_A : X_A = x_A P, id_A$$
$$sid_A : D_A = s_1 Q_A, x_A$$

$$UserB : Q_B = h_1(id_B)$$
$$pid_B : X_B = x_B P, id_B$$
$$sid_B : D_B = s_2 Q_B, x_B$$

$r \in Z_q^*, R_1 = rX_A, R_2 = rQ_A$

$$\xrightarrow{\quad R_1, R_2, P_{pub1} \quad}$$

$$y \in Z_q^*, Y = yP$$
$$d = h_2(Y, R_1, R_2, pid_B)$$
$$\overline{Y} = (dy + x_B)P$$
$$PS_1 = (x_B + dy)R_1$$
$$PS_2 = e(R_2, x_B P_{pub1})e(D_B, R_1)$$
$$K = KDF(PS_1, PS_2, pid_B \| \overline{Y})$$

$$\xleftarrow{\quad H, \overline{Y}, C \leftarrow Enc_K(H, pid_B \| Y) \quad}$$

$PS_1 = rx_A \overline{Y}, PS_2 = e(D_A, rX_B)e(Q_B, rx_A P_{pub2})$
$K = KDF(PS_1, PS_2, pid_B \| \overline{Y})$
$(H, pid_B \| Y) = Dec_K(C)$
$d = h_2(Y, R_1, R_2, pid_B)$
Accept if $\overline{Y} = dY + X_B$ is established
$C' = Enc_K(pid_A, r)$

$$\xrightarrow{\quad C' \quad}$$

$$(pid_A, r) = Dec_K(C')$$
$$\text{verify } R_1 = rX_A, R_2 = rQ_A$$

Fig. 3. Construction of certificateless CAKE under multi-KGC

7 Certificateless Identity-Concealed Authenticated Key Exchange Under Multi-KGC

Authentication key-exchange (AKE), especially bilateral authentication key-exchange, is always one of the hotest fields. An authentication key-exchange protocol generates a secret key, which is the core component in establishing a secure channel, between communicating parties. Participants of an authentication key-exchange protocol need to authenticate each other before achieving an agreement of a shared key, and each of them would have a contribution towards generating it. It is desirable in some scenarios where participants need to conceal their identity information from the third party. Identity-concealed AKE (CAKE) protocols based on certificate have been implemented in TLS 1.3. Therefore, it is valuable to construct a certificateless CAKE protocol. Now we present a variant of our proposed scheme which supports certificateless bilateral identity-concealed authenticated key-exchange (CL-CAKE) under multi-KGC (see also in Fig. 3).

As described in Sect. 4, the system parameters $params = (G_1, G_2, e, \mathcal{K}, l, P,$ $q, m, n, h_1, h_2)$ are generated. For presentation simplicity, there are two key generation centres KGC_1 and KGC_2 whose public-private key pairs are $(P_{pub1} = s_1 P, s_1)$ and $(P_{pub2} = s_2 P, s_2)$ respectively. We also assume that user A registers with KGC_1 and user B registers with KGC_2, $1 \leq A, B \leq n$.

Every time user A wants to execute key exchange protocol with user B, user A randomly chooses $r \leftarrow Z_q^*$, computes $R_1 = rX_A$, $R_2 = rQ_A$ and sends R_1, R_2, P_{pub1} to user B.

On receiving R_1, R_2, P_{pub1}, user B chooses $y \in Z_q^*$ randomly, and computes $Y = yP$, $d = h_2(Y, R_1, R_2, pid_B)$ and $\overline{Y} = (dy + x_B)P$. User B generates the shared secrecies $PS_1 = (x_B + dy)R_1$ and $PS_2 = e(R_2, x_B P_{pub1})e(D_B, R_1)$. User B obtains the shared key $K = KDF(PS_1, PS_2, pid_B \| \overline{Y})$. User B then computes $C = Enc_K(H, pid_B \| Y)$ and sends $Cipher = (H, \overline{Y}, C)$ to user A.

After receiving $Cipher = (H, \overline{Y}, C)$, user A first computes the shared secrecies $PS_1 = rx_A \overline{Y}$ and $PS_2 = e(D_A, rX_B)e(Q_B, rx_A P_{pub2})$ and derives the shared key from the equation $K = KDF(PS_1, PS_2, pid_B \| \overline{Y})$. If $K \notin \mathcal{K}$, user A aborts. User A decrypts C and derives H', pid_B, Y from its output. If $H' \neq H$, A aborts. A computes $d = h_2(Y, R_1, R_2, pid_B)$, and checks whether equation $\overline{Y} = dY + X_B$ is valid. If so, A authenticates the identity of B, accepts the message and sets the session key to be K; otherwise, A aborts. A then computes $C' = Enc_K(pid_A, r)$ and sends C' to B.

B computes $(pid_A, r) = Dec_K(C')$ with K after receiving C'. B then verifies the establishment of equations $R_1 = rX_A$ and $R_2 = rQ_A$. If established, B authenticates the identity of A, accepts the message and sets the session key to be K; otherwise, B aborts.

8   Conclusion

We have proposed the first 0-RTT certificateless identity-concealed authenticated encryption scheme under multi-KGC. We have built two attack models in random oracle where we proved our scheme secure in detail. Our scheme is as efficient as previous schemes and has more security properties. We also provided a variant of our certificateless identity-concealed authenticated encryption scheme under multi-KGC which supports bilateral identity-concealed authentication key exchange.

Acknowledgements. This work was supported by the National Natural Science Foundation of China under Grant 61872060, the National Key R&D program of China under Grant 2017YFB0802000, the National Natural Science Foundation of China under Grant 61370203, Sichuan Science and Technology Program under Grant 2019YFS0068 and the National Natural Science Foundation of China under Grant 61902327.

References

1. Al-Riyami, S.S., Paterson, K.G.: Certificateless public key cryptography. In: Laih, C.-S. (ed.) ASIACRYPT 2003. LNCS, vol. 2894, pp. 452–473. Springer, Heidelberg (2003). https://doi.org/10.1007/978-3-540-40061-5_29
2. Attrapadung, N., Furukawa, J., Gomi, T., Hanaoka, G., Imai, H., Zhang, R.: Efficient identity-based encryption with tight security reduction. In: Pointcheval, D., Mu, Y., Chen, K. (eds.) CANS 2006. LNCS, vol. 4301, pp. 19–36. Springer, Heidelberg (2006). https://doi.org/10.1007/11935070_2
3. Baek, J., Steinfeld, R., Zheng, Y.: Formal proofs for the security of signcryption. J. Cryptol. **20**(2), 203–235 (2007). https://doi.org/10.1007/s00145-007-0211-0
4. Barbosa, M., Farshim, P.: Certificateless signcryption. In: Proceedings of the 2008 ACM Symposium on Information, Computer and Communications Security, ASIACCS 2008, pp. 369–372 (2008). https://doi.org/10.1145/1368310.1368364
5. Boneh, D., Franklin, M.K.: Identity-based encryption from the Weil pairing. SIAM J. Comput. **32**(3), 586–615 (2003). https://doi.org/10.1137/S0097539701398521
6. Chen, L., Kudla, C.: Identity based authenticated key agreement protocols from pairings. In: 16th IEEE Computer Security Foundations Workshop (CSFW-16 2003), pp. 219–233 (2003). https://doi.org/10.1109/CSFW.2003.1212715
7. Liu, J., Lai, J., Huang, X.: Dual trapdoor identity-based encryption with keyword search. Soft. Comput. **21**(10), 2599–2607 (2017). https://doi.org/10.1007/s00500-015-1960-6
8. Paterson, K.G., Ristenpart, T., Shrimpton, T.: Tag size *does* matter: attacks and proofs for the TLS record protocol. In: Lee, D.H., Wang, X. (eds.) ASIACRYPT 2011. LNCS, vol. 7073, pp. 372–389. Springer, Heidelberg (2011). https://doi.org/10.1007/978-3-642-25385-0_20
9. Rogaway, P.: Authenticated-encryption with associated-data. In: Proceedings of the 9th ACM Conference on Computer and Communications Security, CCS 2002, pp. 98–107 (2002). https://doi.org/10.1145/586110.586125
10. Selvi, S.S.D., Vivek, S.S., Rangan, C.P.: Cryptanalysis of certificateless signcryption schemes and an efficient construction without pairing. In: Bao, F., Yung, M., Lin, D., Jing, J. (eds.) Inscrypt 2009. LNCS, vol. 6151, pp. 75–92. Springer, Heidelberg (2010). https://doi.org/10.1007/978-3-642-16342-5_6
11. Weng, J., Yao, G., Deng, R.H., Chen, M., Li, X.: Cryptanalysis of a certificateless signcryption scheme in the standard model. Inf. Sci. **181**(3), 661–667 (2011). https://doi.org/10.1016/j.ins.2010.09.037
12. Xie, W., Zhang, Z.: Efficient and provably secure certificateless signcryption from bilinear maps. In: Proceedings of the IEEE International Conference on Wireless Communications, Networking and Information Security, WCNIS 2010, pp. 558–562 (2010). https://doi.org/10.1109/WCINS.2010.5541841
13. Yang, W., Weng, J., Yang, A., Xie, C., Yang, Y.: Notes on a provably-secure certificate-based encryption against malicious CA attacks. Inf. Sci. **463–464**, 86–91 (2018). https://doi.org/10.1016/j.ins.2018.06.049
14. Yang, W., Weng, J., Zhang, F.: New certificateless public key encryption secure against malicious KGC attacks in the standard model. In: Qing, S., Mitchell, C., Chen, L., Liu, D. (eds.) ICICS 2017. LNCS, vol. 10631, pp. 236–247. Springer, Cham (2018). https://doi.org/10.1007/978-3-319-89500-0_21
15. Zhang, Y., Xu, C., Li, H., Yang, K., Zhou, J., Lin, X.: HealthDep: an efficient and secure deduplication scheme for cloud-assisted eHealth systems. IEEE Trans. Ind. Inform. **14**(9), 4101–4112 (2018). https://doi.org/10.1109/TII.2018.2832251

16. Zhang, Y., Xu, C., Lin, X., Shen, X.: Blockchain-based public integrity verification for cloud storage against procrastinating auditors. IEEE Trans. Cloud Comput. 1–15 (2019). https://doi.org/10.1109/TCC.2019.2908400
17. Zhang, Y., Xu, C., Ni, J., Li, H., Shen, X.: Blockchain-assisted public-key encryption with keyword search against keyword guessing attacks for cloud storage. IEEE Trans. Cloud Comput. 1–14 (2019). https://doi.org/10.1109/TCC.2019.2923222
18. Zhao, Y.: Identity-concealed authenticated encryption and key exchange. In: Proceedings of the 2016 ACM SIGSAC Conference on Computer and Communications Security, CCS 2016, pp. 1464–1479 (2016). https://doi.org/10.1145/2976749.2978350
19. Zheng, Y.: Digital signcryption or how to achieve cost(signature & encryption) $<<$ cost(signature) + cost(encryption). In: Kaliski, B.S. (ed.) Advances in Cryptology – CRYPTO 1997, CRYPTO 1997, vol. 1294, pp. 165–179. Springer, Heidelberg (1997). https://doi.org/10.1007/BFb0052234

Signatures

A Pairing-Less Identity-Based Blind Signature with Message Recovery Scheme for Cloud-Assisted Services

Mahender Kumar$^{(\boxtimes)}$ and Satish Chand

New Delhi, India

Abstract. The rapid growing big data enforces many organizations to shift their data and services like digital right management, e-payment, and e-voting systems to the cloud. In such cloud-assisted services, the blind signature scheme could be one of the cryptographic tools, which provides the integrity of data and user anonymity. It allows the user to ask the signer for signing on message without disclosing any information about the content to the signer. Since several blind signature schemes have been proposed, but due to the expensive computation and bandwidth cost, they are impractical for the cloud-assisted as well as Internet-based environment. In this paper, we propose a new provable secure identity-based blind signature scheme with message recovery (IDBS-MR) using the elliptic curve cryptography. The proposed IDBS-MR scheme does not transmit the message with the signature while the message is recovered during verification round; hence it has the least message-signature length. The security analysis shows that the proposed IDBS-MR scheme is secured against existential forgery attack under the adaptive chosen message and ID attacks (EF-ID-CMA) under the assumption of solving the ECDL problem, and random oracle model (ROM) and achieves blindness property. The performance analysis shows that our scheme is efficient as compared to related existing schemes.

Keywords: Blind signature · Identity based signature · User anonymity · Provable secure · Elliptic curve cryptography

1 Introduction

Due to the significant advantages of cloud computing technology such as resource pooling, utility-based pricing, on-demand self-service, and rapid elasticity, many service providers such as Amazon, Google, and Microsoft are outsourcing their huge data on cloud for processing, which could be difficult to process by the current technologies. Nowadays, many organizations, government, and banks are trying to offloads their data and services like digital right management, e-payment, and e-voting systems to the cloud [1]. However, these cloud-assisted

---

Supported by organization x.

Z. Liu and M. Yung (Eds.): Inscrypt 2019, LNCS 12020, pp. 419–434, 2020.
https://doi.org/10.1007/978-3-030-42921-8_24

services have several security challenges, for example, privacy-preserving of data, anonymity of data owner, public auditing of data integrity, and confidentiality of data. There have been discussed many cryptographic primitives to achieve such security challenges where the blind signature scheme has been gained a significant importance.

Blind signature in non-cloud environment was first introduced by the Chaum [1,2] for the electronic payment system. The blind signature scheme allows a user to ask the signer for the signature on his data item, in which the signer signs the data without identifying the actual content of the data. In an electronic payment system, blind signature protects the user's privacy for untraceable digital coin and overcomes the possibility of linkability, i.e., the user cannot make the multiple copies of the digital coin. Therefore, unlinkability and untraceability features of the blind signature scheme make it suitable for those internet-based as well as cloud-assisted services, where preserving the identity of data owner is a big problem. Since many conventional (non-ID based) blind signature schemes whose construction are based on the RSA, ECC, DSA, and ElGamal have been presented so far, e.g., [4–6], but they demand the recipient to lookup the sender's public key before verifying the signature. In such schemes, the trusted party known as the certifying authority (CA) manages the user's public keys by generating the digital certificate that binds the user's identity to his public key, which is managed in the pubic key infrastructure (PKI).

An alternative to traditional public key cryptosystem (PKC), Shamir [7] invented a novel identity-based cryptosystem (IBC) in 1984. It avoids to manage the digital certificates and hence, saves large amount of computation cost for the same. The state-of-art of the IBC was to use any binary string, e.g., name, e-mail address, and phone number as the public key of user, and the corresponding private key is generated by the trusted third party known as the private key generator (PKG). Zhang et al. [8,9] generalized the blind signature scheme to the identity-based blind signature scheme (IDBS) that alleviated the certificate management issue associated with the traditional (non-ID based) blind signature scheme. Since many ID-BS schemes have been discussed [8–23], some of them are found inefficient in terms of bandwidth as they gives large signature size.

The digital signature with message recovery (SMR) scheme produces the small message-signature size, where it restricts to send the message with signature while it is recovered on the recipient side during verification process. In this setting, the message is confidential until the verifier recovers it. So, SMR scheme provides confidentiality, integrity, and authenticity of data with small size signature, and hence it is worthy for low bandwidth medium. Zhang et al. [24] proposed the first signature with message recovery in the identity-based setting. The Identity-based blind signature scheme with message recovery (IDBS-MR) has been introduced by Han et al. [25] in 2005. Since many ID-based blind signature schemes with or without message recovery property have been presented, but they are designed on pairing. Thus, the existing pairing-based IDBS schemes [8–23] are found inefficient and do not suitable for implementing secure cloud-assisted services like e-commerce and e-voting systems in the Internet-based environment.

In this paper, we proposed a provable secure identity-based blind signature scheme with message recovery (IDBS-MR) using elliptic curve cryptosystem (ECC). Since the message is not included in the signature during communication and recovered during verification, the proposed IDBS-MR scheme has the least signature size as compared to other related schemes. Further, we formalize the existential forgery attack under the adaptive chosen message and ID attacks (EF-ID-CMA) and blindness security notion for the proposed IDBS-MR scheme. The security analysis shows that the proposed IDBS-MR scheme is secured against EF-ID-CMA under the assumption of solving the elliptic curve discrete logarithm (ECDLP) problem, and the random oracle model (ROM) and achieves blindness property. The performance analysis illustrates that our scheme performs better in term of computation cost with small signature size as compared to other related schemes. Thus, it is suitable for resource-limited devices with "cheap" communication cost.

Organization. The remainder of the paper is organized as follows. Section 2 gives the literature survey. Section 3 presents the preliminaries, brief discussion of our proposed IDBS-MR scheme and its security definition. The complete construction and its security proof of our proposed scheme are described in Sect. 4. Section 5 examines the comparison with other schemes. Finally, the conclusion is given in Sect. 6.

2 Related Work

Chaum [2,26] was the first to propose the blind signature scheme for the digital cash payment system, in 1983. Using the IBC technique, Zhang et al. [8] proposed the IDBS schemes based on the random oracle model (ROM) and computational Diffie-Hellman Problem (CDHP). The paper [9] improves the computation cost of the scheme [8] using elliptic curve cryptography, but later Huang et al. [10] show that the scheme [9] is not secured against the one more forger attack and rebuild a new ID-BS scheme using the bilinear pairing. In [11], Mao demonstrates that the schemes [8,10] do not achieve the unlinkability (which is one of the leading property of the blind signature). Gao et al. [13,14] proposed a new one-round ID-BS scheme whose security is achieved without ROS assumption; thus it reduces the security parameter size. In these settings [13,14], the signature is generated in one round of message exchange. In [15], Kumar et al. give a new IDBS scheme based on gap Diffie-Hellman (GDH) problem and ROM. He et al.'s IDBS scheme [16] avoids the expensive pairing operations.

Recently, Kumar et al. [17] present the IDBS scheme for implementing the provable secure electronic-voting system whose security is based on solving the ECDLP and CDHP. Dong et al. [18] address the key escrow problem associated with existing IDBS scheme and proposed an efficient certificateless blind signature scheme. The scheme [18] alleviates the computational cost and found to be secured against type-I and type-II adversaries attacks, given in [27]. Tian et al. [19] extend the IDBS to the identity based partial blind signature scheme (IDPBS), in which the user and signer are pre-negotiated on shared value. This scheme is found very suitable for the electronic-cash payment system. The use of IDPBS for implementing electronic-cash payment systems is given by Islam et al. [20]. Some other IDBS schemes for e-cash payment systems are given in [28,29]. Recently, Islam et al. [30] build a provable secure pairing-free certificate-less blind signature (CLBS) scheme that addresses the key escrow problem. The security of scheme [30] is based on the assumption of solving collusion attack algorithm with k-traitors (k-CAA) problem.

Another blind signature scheme is given by Galindo et al. [22] that uses the traditional (non-ID based) blind signature scheme and needs a digital certificate to verify the authenticity of signer's public key during verification. The scheme is inefficient because it produces the large signature size and demands high ver-ification cost. Xiao et al. [23] mitigate the extra operational cost which makes it efficient as it requires only two parameters exchange between the user and signer with less signature size as compared to [22]. An identity-based blind sig-nature scheme in message recovery setting is first proposed by Han et al. [25] in 2007. However, this scheme [25] is implemented using pairing on elliptic curves. Since then, very few IDBS-MR schemes have been offered, given in the literature [12,21,25,31–33]. Inspired on the design of Zhang et al. [8], Hassan et al. [12] in 2008 proposed a new IDBS-MR scheme which has least computation cost and signature size on comparing with Han et al. [25]. Also, Diao et al. [33] proposed a proxy blind signature with message recovery. In 2017, James et al. [31] pro-posed IDBS-MR scheme using pairing on elliptic curve. Recently, Verma et al. [21] present a new IDBS-MR scheme using pairing whose security is based on the assumption of ROM and the solving k-CAA problem.

From above discussed schemes, it has been noticed that the existing blind signature scheme with message recovery are designed on pairing on elliptic curves and hence due to high computation cost of pairing operation, they could not be suitable for the cloud-assisted services. The paper [29] shows that 128-bit key in ECC based system achieve the same security of 1024-bit key in RSA based system. Therefore, elliptic curve based operations (such as addition operation, the scalar multiplication operation, etc.) took less computation cost as compared to the pairing based operations. In this paper, we present a new identity-based blind signature scheme with message recovery without bilinear pairing.

3   System Architecture

3.1   System Model

The proposed network system consists of four entities: private key generator (PKG), service provider, user, and verifier, as shown in Fig. 1. The PKG regis-ters/authenticates the service provider and provides a private key (credential) against his identity ID. The service provider is an authority that signs on a mes-sage requested by the user without knowing any information about the original message. For instance, in an e-payment service, a service provider can be a bank that issues a coin to the customer (user), and in an e-voting system, it can be an election commission authority that issues a blind blank ballot to the voter (user) without knowing anything about his identity. In our system architecture, both PKG and service provider can use cloud computing and perform their computation performed on cloud. The main objective to use the cloud as a service provider is to offload the expensive computation on the cloud server and leave light computation on user side. The user can be a customer or voter that uses the lightweight device and services of the service provider.

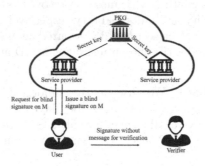

Fig. 1. Cloud assisted IDBS-MR System architecture

3.2   Design of Proposed IDBS-MR Scheme

Definition 1 *(Identity-Based Blind Signature with message recovery)*. The proposed IDBS-MR scheme consists of four randomized probabilistic polynomial-time (PPT) algorithms: setup, extract, blind signature, and verification. The scheme is performed amongst three entities: signer, user, and private key generator (PKG). In our proposed scheme, signer acts as the service provider, i.e., election commission authority or banking authority, and user acts as a voter (in e-voting system) or customer (in e-payment system).

1. *Setup*: Using security parameter, the PKG computes the master key and public parameters. PKG keeps the master key and publishes the public parameters.
2. *Extract*: For a given signer's identity, the PKG computes and provides the private key using its master key.
3. *Blind signature*: User delegate the signing process to the signer, as given by the following steps:
   (a) *Commitment*: For a secret number, the signer computes a public parameter, passes it to the user and keeps the secret number.
   (b) *Blinding*: On a given public parameter and message M, the user blinds the message using random secret numbers. The user then requests to the signer for the signature on the blinded message.
   (c) *Signature*: For each blinded message, the signer computes the blind signature using his private key and outputs it to the user.
   (d) *Unblinding*: User retrieves the blinded signature using his secret key and stores the original signature on the cloud.

4. *Verification*: User (verifier) fetch the signature and recovers the message. The verifier then verify the signature using the recovered message.

3.3   Security of Proposed IDBS-MR Scheme

To discuss the security of our proposed IDBS-MR schemes, we go through the definition of Zhang et al.'s identity-based blind signature scheme [8] and Tso et al.'s identity-based signature with message recovery scheme [37] where they discussed the unlinkability and unforgeability respectively. The proposed IDBS-MR scheme is considered to be secure if it is secured against existential forgeable attack (EF-ID-CMA) under the chosen message and ID attack and achieves the blindness property.

Definition 2 *EF-ID-CMA*: We discuss the unforgeability of our proposed IDBS-MR scheme through the following game playing between a forger F that acts as malicious user and challenger Ch that acts as the honest signer under adaptive chosen message and identity attack in the random oracle model (ROM).

Setup: The challenger Ch runs setup algorithm and computes the master key and public parameters. The Ch responds public parameter to F.

Oracles: F performs the following oracles.

– *Extract oracle*: For a given ID, forger F requests to run the extract algorithm. The Ch runs this oracle to compute the private key corresponding to an identity ID_i, where $1 \leq i \leq q_k$ and sends it to F. Besides, Ch saves the record in list L_{ext}, which is initially empty.
– *Blind signature oracle*: For a message $M_i \in \{0,1\}^{l_2}$ of its choice in an adaptive manner, forger F asks blind signature oracle to obtain the blind signature σ. The Ch executes the Blind signature oracle and responds the result to F and saves it in the list L_{BS}, which is initially empty.

Forgery: At the end, the forger F responds a signature σ^* on given message M^* with signer's identity ID^*. The forger F will win the game if it fulfills the following conditions.

– σ^* is the valid signature against M^* and ID^*.
– The blind signature oracle has not been queried on M^*.
– The extract oracle has not been queried on ID^*.

Under chosen message and identity attacks, the proposed IDBS-MR scheme is said to be existentially unforgeable, if any forger F has a negligible probability to succeed in the above game.

Definition 3 *Blindness.* Blindness security notion can be defined by the adversary Adv that acts as malicious signer and is engaged with two users U_0 and U_1 in the following game:

Setup: It computes the master key and public parameters and responds public parameter to Adv.

– For a given ID, Adv requests to run the extract algorithm. This oracle gives the private key corresponding to an identity ID_i, where $1 \le i \le q_k$ and sends it to Adv.
– For selective $b \in \{0, 1\}$, the U_0 and U_1 get two distinct message M_b and M_{1-b} respectively.
– U_0 and U_1 compute σ_b (signature on M_b) and σ_{1-b} (signature on M_{1-b} respectively and give it to Adv.

At the end, Adv predicts a bit $b' \in \{0, 1\}$ and wins the game if $b = b'$ holds with advantage.

$$|Pr[b = b']| \ge \frac{1}{2} + k^{-n} \tag{1}$$

The proposed IDBS-MR scheme is blind if Adv wins the above game with negligible advantage.

4 Proposed Identity-Based Blind Signature with Message Recovery Scheme

4.1 Abbreviations and Notations

Abbreviations and notations are given in Table 1.

Table 1. Notations and abbreviations used in our proposed IDBS-MR schemes.

Notations	Meaning
k	Security parameter
G_1, q, P	Groups on elliptic curve, its order and its generator
s_0, P_0	PKG's master key and public key
n_1, n_2	Random number known to signer
ID_S, A	Signer's unique identification and its public parameter
d_{IDS}	Signer's private key
g, h, i, j, k, l	Random number known to user
$M \in \{0, 1\}^{l2}$	Message of length $l2$
b_{M1}, b_{M2}	Blinded message
σ	Original signature on M
$absc(P)$	x coordinate of point P on elliptic curve
$\|$	Concatenation of two strings
$\overset{l}{_x}\|st\|$	First x bit of string st from left
$\|st\|_x^R$	First x bit of string st from right
$\oplus$	X-OR operation

4.2 Construction

Our proposed IDBS-MR scheme consists of four PPT algorithms: setup, extract, blind signature, and verify. These are defined as follow.

1. *Setup*: Given a security parameter k, the PKG assumes an additive group G_1 of order q, where q is large prime number of k-bit and P be its generator. Suppose three hash functions $H_1 : \{0,1\}^* \times G_1 \rightarrow Z_q$, $H_2 : G_1 \rightarrow Z_q$ and $H_3 : G_1 \rightarrow \{0,1\}^{|q|}$ and two functions $F_1 : \{0,1\}^{l_2} \rightarrow \{0,1\}^{l_1}$ and $F_2 : \{0,1\}^{l_1} \rightarrow \{0,1\}^{l_2}$, where l_1 and l_2 are two positive integers such that $l_1 + l_2 = |q|$. Suppose $absc(P)$ gives the x-coordinate of point P. The PKG chooses a random element $s_0 \in Z_q$ (its master key) and computes the public key $P_0 = s_0 P$. The PKG publishes the public parameter $param = \{G_1, q, P, P_0, H_1, H_2, F_1, F_2, l_1, l_2, k\}$, and keeps s_0 secret.
2. *Extract*: For given signer's identity IDS, param and its master key s_0, PKG chooses a random number $a \in Z_q$, computes the signer's private key $d_{IDS} = a + s_0 Q_{IDS}$, where $Q_{IDS} = H_1(A, IDS)$ and $A = aP$ and gives $<A, d_{IDS}>$ to the signer.
3. *Blind signature*: The signer and user perform the following steps to obtain a blind signature on message.
    - *Commitment*: The signer selects two random elements $n_1, n_2 \in Z_q$, computes $Q_1 = n_1 P$ and $Q_2 = n_2 P$, and sends them with its public parameter A to the user.
    - *Blinding*: For given received parameters $<Q_1, Q_2, A>$ and message $M \in \{0,1\}^{l_2}$, the user selects six elements $g, h, i, j, k, l \in Z_q$, such that $gcd(i,j) = 1$ and $ki + lj = gcd(i,j)$. For the selection of elements k and l, we use the Extended Euclidean algorithm. User then computes the parameters b_{M1} and b_{M2} given in Eqs. (2)–(8) and asks to the signer for signature on $<b_{M1}, b_{M2}>$.

$$R_1 = gQ_1 + iP, \; r_1 = absc(R_1) \tag{2}$$

$$R_2 = hQ_2 + jP, \; r_2 = absc(R_2) \tag{3}$$

$$r = r_1 r_2 \tag{4}$$

$$u = F_1(M) || F_2(F_1(M)) \oplus M \tag{5}$$

$$R = R_1 + R_2 + ru(A + Q_{ID} P_0) \tag{6}$$

$$b_{M1} = kg^{-1} i(H_2(R) - ru) \tag{7}$$

$$b_{M2} = lh^{-1} j(H_2(R) - ru) \tag{8}$$

    - *Signature*: On received parameters $<b_{M1}, b_{M2}>$ and its private key d_{IDS}, signer computes the blind signature $<s_1', s_2'>$ as given in Eqs. (9)–(10), and sends $<s_1', s_2'>$ to the user.

$$s_1' = (d_{IDS} b_{M1} - n_1) \tag{9}$$

$$s_2' = (d_{IDS} b_{M2} - n_2) \tag{10}$$

- *Unblinding*: On received parameters $<s_1', s_2'>$, user computes the original signature $<v, R>$ using his secret values, i.e., $<g, h, i, j>$ (given in Eqs. (11)–(14)). The user sends the signature $<v, R, A>$ to the verifier.

$$s_1 = (s_1'g - i) \tag{11}$$

$$s_2 = (s_2'h - j) \tag{12}$$

$$s = (s_1 + s_2) \tag{13}$$

$$v = u \oplus H_3(sP + R) \tag{14}$$

4. *Verify*: For given signature pair $<A, v, R>$, the user computes u and recovers M_0, given in Eqs. (15)–(16) and accepts the signature and message M_0 if and only if $_{l_1}^l|u| = F_1(M_0)$.

$$u = v \oplus H_3(H_2(R)(A + H_1(A, IDS)P_0)) \tag{15}$$

$$M_0 = F_2(_{l_1}^l|u|) \oplus |u|_{l2}^R \tag{16}$$

This competes the implementation of proposed IDBS-MR scheme.

5 System Analysis

5.1 Security Proof

Theorem 1 *(Correctness). Our proposed IDBS-MR scheme is correct.*

Proof. The consistency of proposed IDBS-MR scheme is verified as follows:
From Eq. (13), we have $s = (s_1 + s_2)$ then,

$$
\begin{aligned}
sP + R &= (s_1 + s_2)P + R \\
&= (s_1'g - i + s_2'h - j)P + R \\
&= ((d_{IDS}b_{M1} - n_1)g - i + (d_{IDS}b_{M2} - n_2)h - j)P + R \\
&= (d_{IDS}ki(H_2(R) - ru) - n_1g - i + d_{IDS}lj(H_2(R) - ru) - n_2h - j)P + R \\
&= d_{IDS}H_2(R)(ki + lj)P - (ki + lj)rud_{IDS}P - n_1gP - n_2hP - iP - jP + R \\
&= d_{IDS}H_2(R)P - (rud_{IDS}P + n_1gP + n_2hP + iP + jP) + R \\
&= (a + s_0Q_{ID})H_2(R)P - (ru(a + s_0Q_ID)P + gQ_1 + hQ_2 + iP + jP) + R \\
&= (A + Q_{ID}P_0)H_2(R) - R + R \\
&= (A + Q_{ID}P_0)H_2(R)
\end{aligned}
$$

This proves the consistency of the IDBS-MR scheme. Thus, $sP + R = (A + Q_{ID}P_0)H_1(R)$, and $u = v \oplus H_3(sP + R)$. Now, $u = F_1(M)\|F_2(F_1(M)) \oplus M$ and hence $_{l_1}^l|u| = F_1(M)$, $|u|_{l2}^R = M \oplus F_2(F_1(M))$ and check if $_{l_1}^l|u| = F_1(M)$. If this equality holds, verifier accepts the parameter $<A, v, R>$ as correct signature on message M.

Theorem 2 *(Un-forgeability). Suppose H_1 and H_2 are two random oracles model and a forger F wants to forge a signature on message M. Suppose forger F executes at most q_E extract oracles, q_B blind signature oracles, q_1 H_1 hash oracles, q_2 H_2 hash oracles, q_3 H_3 hash oracles runs at most t times with advantage at most k^{-n}. Under the assumption of ROM and intractable to solve the ECDLP, our proposed IDBS-MR Scheme is existentially unforgeable under adaptive chosen message and identity attacks. Forger $F(t, q_1, q_2, q_E, q_B, k^{-n})$ have the following advantage to breaks the proposed IDBS-MR scheme.*

$$|Pr[F(t, q_1, q_2 q_E, q_B, k^{-n})]| \geq \epsilon(1 - q_1/k)^{q_2 + q_E}$$

Proof. Due to the page limitation, authors could not provide the complete proof.

Theorem 3 *(Blindness). The proposed IDBS-MR scheme achieves the blindness property.*

Proof. Due to the page limitation, authors could not provide the complete proof.

5.2   Performance Analysis

In this section, we are comparing our proposed IDBS-MR scheme with existing related schemes [8,12,14,16–19,21,25,30] and [31] in terms of the computation and bandwidth cost. To discuss the computation cost of required cryptographic operations, we will follow the method given in [29,35–39]. We consider the Tate pairing defined over the Type-A curve of PBC library [40] with the 512-bit group, and embedding degree is 2, which is identical to the 1024-bit RSA security level. The Type-A super-singular elliptic curve $E/F_P : y^2 = x^2 + x$ built on two prime p and q, such that $|p| = 512$ bit, $q = 2^{159} + 2^{17} + 1$ is Solaris prime ($|q| = 160$ bit) satisfying $p + 1 = 12pq$. We consider super-singular curve over the binary field $F_{2^{271}}$ with the order of G_1 is 252 bit prime and G_2 is 1024 bit. Using compression technique [44], we consider $|G_1| = 34$ bytes, $|G_2| = 128$ bytes and $|Z_q| = 32$ bytes. Besides, we suppose the message size $|M| = 20$ bytes.

Table 2. Computational cost of required operations (in ms).

Notations	Operations	Computation cost (in ms)
T_M	Modular multiplication	0.23
T_{IN}	Modular inversion	2.67
T_A	Two elliptic curve points addition	0.03
T_{SM}	Elliptic curve scalar point multiplication	6.67
T_E	Exponentiation	4.83
T_{PM}	Pairing multiplication	6.67
T_H	Map-To-Point hash operation	6.67
T_P	Bilinear pairing	20.01

Implementation and Benchmarks. The implementation is considered to be run on Intel Pentium IV, 3 GHz CPU, 512 MB RAM and Microsoft Windows XP operating system [40]. We denote T_M as computations cost of modular multiplication, T_{IN} as computations cost of modular inversion, T_A as computations cost of two elliptic point addition, T_{SM} as computations cost of Scalar elliptic multiplication, T_E as computations cost of Exponentiation, T_H as computations cost of map-to-hash function and T_P as computations cost of bilinear pairing. It has been given in [35,36] that the computation cost of pairing operation is 20.01, and in [38], we have observed that $1T_P = 3T_{SM} = 87T_M$. From [42], we adopt the computation cost of modular exponentiation, T_E is approximately $240T_M$, and computation cost of map-to-hash function T_H is $29T_M$. Therefore, on similar system [40], the computation cost of modular exponentiation, T_E is $(T_P * 240)/87 = (20.01 * 240)/87 = 55.2$ ms. Table 2 shows the computation cost and notations of such operations run over the bilinear group.

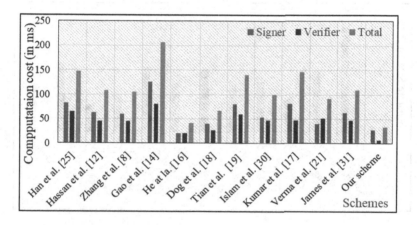

Fig. 2. Cloud assisted IDBS-MR System architecture

Computation Cost: We now compare the computation cost of blind signature and verification phases for our proposed IDBS-MR scheme and the corresponding phases of other schemes in the literature [8,12,14,16–19,21,25,30] and [31]. For examining computation cost, we avoid negligible computation cost operations such as hash function and modular addition. Using computation cost of different operations given in Table 2, we evaluate the computation of our proposed scheme with other related schemes, as summarized in Table 3. For blind signature algorithm, our proposed scheme needs $4T_{SM} + 2T_A + 7T_M = 4 * 6.67 + 2 * 0.23 + 7 * 0.03 = 27.35$ ms, while schemes [8,12,14,16–19,21,25,30] and [31] take 82.77 ms, 62.76 ms, 60.15 ms, 126.73 ms, 20.7 ms, 40.02 ms, 80.04 ms, 53.6 ms, 80.5 ms, 40.08 ms and 62.7 ms respectively, of computation time. Thus, blind signature phase of our proposed IDBS-MR scheme saves 67%, 56% 55%, 78%, 32%, 66%, 49%, 67%, 32% and 56% of corresponding phase of [8,12,14,17–19,21,25,30] and [31] respectively. For verification algorithm, our proposed

IDBS-MR scheme needs $1T_{SM} + 1T_A = 1 * 6.67 + 1 * 0.23 = 6.9\,\mathrm{ms}$, while schemes [8,12,14,16–19,21,25,30] and [31] take 64.86 ms, 44.85 ms, 44.85 ms, 80.04 ms, 20.04 ms, 26.68 ms, 60.03 ms, 46.7 ms, 46.7 ms, 51.5 ms and 46.7 ms respectively, of computation time. Therefore, verification phase of our proposed IDBS-MR scheme saves 89%, 85%, 85%, 91%, 66%, 74%, 88%, 85%, 85%, 87% and 85% of corresponding verify algorithm of [8,12,14,16–19,21,25,30] and [31] respectively. The total computation cost for our proposed scheme is 34.25 ms while schemes [8,12,14,16–19,21,25,30] and [31] are 147.6 ms, 107.6 ms, 105 ms, 206.77 ms, 40.74 ms, 66.70 ms, 140 ms, 100.3 ms, 147.2 ms, 91.58 ms and 109.4 ms respectively for blind signature and verification algorithms. Thus, our scheme saves 77%, 68%, 67%, 83%, 17%, 48%, 75%, 65%, 76%, 62% and 68% of total computation cost as compared to [8,12,14,16–19,21,25,30] and [31] respectively, as shown in Fig. 2.

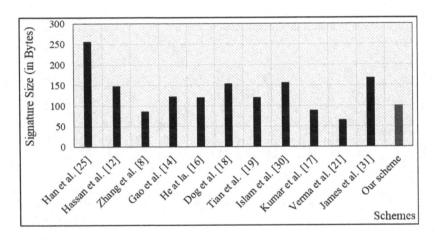

Fig. 3. Cloud assisted IDBS-MR System architecture

Bandwidth Size: Here, we compare the bandwidth cost of our proposed scheme with related schemes [8,12,14,16–19,21,25,30] and [31], shown in Table 4 and also Fig. 3. For evaluating the signature size, our proposed IDBS-MR scheme requires $|G_1| + 2|Z_q| = 98$ bytes, whereas schemes [8,12,14,16–19,21,25,30] and [31] need 256 bytes, 148 bytes, 86 bytes, 122 bytes, 120 bytes, 154 bytes, 120 bytes, 156 bytes, 88 bytes, 66 bytes and 168 bytes respectively. Here, we observe that our scheme saves around 62%, 34%, 20%, 18%, 36%, 18%, 37%, and 42% of [12,14,16,18,19,25,30], and [31] respectively, of signature size.

Security: The proposed scheme is constructed on the Random Oracle Model (ROM), and its security is equivalent to solve the elliptic curve discrete logarithm problem (ECDLP). Table 4 summarizes the security comparison of schemes with related schemes [8,12,14,16–19,21,25,30] and [31] where 1-mBDHIP denotes the one more bilinear Diffie-Hellman inversion problem, k-CAA3 denotes the

Table 3. Computational cost of required operations (in ms).

Schemes	Signer	Verifier	Total
Han et al. [25]	$2T_P + 6T_{SM} + 1T_{IN} + 2T_A(82.77)$	$3T_P + 1T_E(64.86)$	147.63
Hassan et al. [12]	$1T_P + 6T_{SM} + 1T_I N + 2T_A(62.76)$	$2T_P + 1T_E(44.85)$	107.61
Zhang et al. [8]	$1T_P + 6T_{SM} + 4T_A(60.15)$	$2T_P + 1T_E(44.85)$	105
Gao et al. [14]	$4T_P + 7T_{SM}(126.73)$	$4T_P(80.04)$	206.77
He et al. [16]	$3T_{SM} + 3T_M(20.7)$	$3T_{SM} + 1T_A(20.04)$	40.74
Dog et al. [18]	$6T_{SM}(40.02)$	$4T_{SM}(26.68)$	66.70
Tian et al. [19]	$2T_P + 6T_{SM}(80.04)$	$2T_P + 3T_{SM}(60.03)$	140.07
Islam et al. [30]	$1T_P + 5T_{SM} + 1T_M(53.6)$	$1T_P + 4T_{SM}(46.7)$	100.3
Kumar et al. [17]	$2T_P + 6T_{SM} + 2T_M(80.5)$	$2T_P + 1T_{SM} + 1T_A(46.77)$	147.2
Verma et al. [21]	$6T_{SM} + 2T_M(40.08)$	$2T_P + 1T_{SM} + 1E(51.5)$	91.58
James et al. [31]	$6T_{SM} + 1T_M + 1T_{IN}(62.7)$	$2T_P + 1T_{SM} + 1T_A(46.7)$	109.4
Our scheme	$4T_{SM} + 2T_A + 7T_M(27.35)$	$1T_{SM} + 1T_A(6.9)$	34.25

Table 4. Security comparison of our proposed IDBS-MR Scheme with other related schemes, where SA and MR represent as security assumption and message recovery respectively

Schemes	Cryptographic primitives	SA	MR	Signature size (in bytes)
Han et al. [25]	IBS & BS	IMWPP	Yes	$2|G_2|(256)$
Hassan et al. [12]	IBS & BS	BDHP	Yes	$|G_2| + |Z_q|(148)$
Zhang etal. [8]	IBS & BS	CDHP	No	$|G_1| + |Z_q| + |M|(86)$
Gao et al. [14]	IBS & BS	1-mBDHIP	No	$3|G_1| + |M|(122)$
He et al. [16]	IBS & BS	CDHP	No	$2|G_1| + |Z_q| + |M|(120)$
Dog et al. [18]	CLS & BS	ECDLP	No	$3|G_1| + |Z_q| + |M|(154)$
Tian et al. [19]	CLS & PBS	CDHP	No	$2|G_1| + |Z_q| + |M|(120)$
Islam et al. [30]	CLS & BS	k-CAA3	No	$4|G_1| + |M|(156)$
Kumar et al. [17]	IBS & BS	GDHP	No	$2|G_1| + |M|(88)$
Verma et al. [21]	IBS & BS	k-CAA	Yes	$|G_1| + |Z_q|(66)$
James et al. [31]	IBS & BS	ECDLP	No	$|G_2| + |Z_q| + |M|(168)$
Our scheme	IBS & BS	ECDLP	Yes	$|G_1| + 2|Z_q|(98)$

3 traitors collision attacks assumption, GDHP denotes the gap Diffie-Hellman Problem, PBS denotes the partial blind signature, IMWPP denotes Inversion of Modified Weil Pairings Problem and BDHP denotes Bilinear Diffie-Hellman Problem.

6   Conclusion

In this paper, we have presented a new identity-based blind signature scheme with message recovery (IDBS-MR) using the elliptic curve cryptography. The proposed IDBS-MR scheme gains the advantage of blind signature with message recovery in the identity-based setting. It avoids expensive cryptographic operations, for example, pairing and modular exponentiation operations and hence suitable for pairing-free environment. Considering the hypothesis of the ECDLP problem and ROM, the proposed IDBS-MR scheme is secured against existential forgery attack under adaptive chosen message and ID attack. The performance analysis demonstrated that our scheme performs better and gives the least signature size as compared to existing related schemes. Since proposed scheme has the least computation cost and comparable size of the signature, it would be suitable for cloud-assisted services where hiding user's identity is the primary concern. In the future, we will extend our work to improve the advantage of proposed IDBS-MR scheme for electronic-voting and electronic payment system, to obtain better efficiency and security.

References

1. Zhu, H., Tan, Y., Zhang, X., Zhu, L., Zhang, C., Zheng, J.: A round-optimal lattice-based blind signature scheme for cloud services. Future Gener. Comput. Syst. **73**, 106–114 (2017)
2. Chaum, D.: Blind signatures for untraceable payments. In: Chaum, D., Rivest, R.L., Sherman, A.T. (eds.) Advances in Cryptology, pp. 199–203. Springer, Boston (1983). https://doi.org/10.1007/978-1-4757-0602-4_18
3. Chaum, D.L.: Untraceable electronic mail, return addresses, and digital pseudonyms. Commun. ACM **24**(2), 84–90 (1981)
4. Camenisch, J.L., Piveteau, J.-M., Stadler, M.A.: Blind signatures based on the discrete logarithm problem. In: De Santis, A. (ed.) Workshop on the Theory and Application of of Cryptographic Techniques, pp. 428–432. Springer, Heidelberg (1994). https://doi.org/10.1007/BFb0053458
5. Horster, P., Michels, M., Petersen, H.: Comment: cryptanalysis of the blind signatures based on the discrete logarithm problem. Electron. Lett. **31**, 1827 (1995)
6. Lee, B., Boyd, C., Dawson, E., Kim, K., Yang, J., Yoo, S.: Secure key issuing in ID-based cryptography. In: Proceedings of the Second Workshop on Australasian Information Security, Data Mining and Web Intelligence, and Software Internationalisation, vol. 32, pp. 69–74 (2004)
7. Shamir, A.: Identity-based cryptosystems and signature schemes. In: Workshop on the Theory and Application of Cryptographic Techniques, pp. 47–53 (1984)
8. Zhang, F., Kim, K.: ID-based blind signature and ring signature from pairings. In: Zheng, Y. (ed.) ASIACRYPT 2002. LNCS, vol. 2501, pp. 533–547. Springer, Heidelberg (2002). https://doi.org/10.1007/3-540-36178-2_33
9. Zhang, F., Kim, K.: Efficient ID-based blind signature and proxy signature from bilinear pairings. In: Safavi-Naini, R., Seberry, J. (eds.) ACISP 2003. LNCS, vol. 2727, pp. 312–323. Springer, Heidelberg (2003). https://doi.org/10.1007/3-540-45067-X_27

10. Huang, Z., Chen, K., Wang, Y.: Efficient identity-based signatures and blind signatures. In: Desmedt, Y.G., Wang, H., Mu, Y., Li, Y. (eds.) CANS 2005. LNCS, vol. 3810, pp. 120–133. Springer, Heidelberg (2005). https://doi.org/10. 1007/11599371_11

11. Mao, J.: Linkability analysis of some blind signature schemes. In: Wang, Y., Cheung, Y., Liu, H. (eds.) CIS 2006. LNCS (LNAI), vol. 4456, pp. 556–566. Springer, Heidelberg (2007). https://doi.org/10.1007/978-3-540-74377-4_58

12. Elkamchouchi, H.M., Abouelseoud, Y.: A new blind identity-based signature scheme with message recovery. IACR Cryptol. ePrint Arch. **2008**, 38 (2008)

13. Gao, W., Wang, G., Wang, X., Li, F.: One-round ID-based blind signature scheme without ROS assumption. In: Galbraith, S.D., Paterson, K.G. (eds.) Pairing 2008. LNCS, vol. 5209, pp. 316–331. Springer, Heidelberg (2008). https://doi.org/10. 1007/978-3-540-85538-5_21

14. Gao, W., Wang, G., Wang, X., Li, F.: Round-optimal ID-based blind signature schemes without ROS assumption (2012)

15. Kumar, M., Katti, C.P., Saxena, P.C.: A new blind signature scheme using identity-based technique. Int. J. Control Theory Appl. **10**(15), 36–42 (2017)

16. He, D., Chen, J., Zhang, R.: An efficient identity-based blind signature scheme without bilinear pairings. Comput. Electr. Eng. **37**(4), 444–450 (2011)

17. Kumar, M., Katti, C.P., Saxena, P.C.: A secure anonymous E-voting system using identity-based blind signature scheme. In: Shyamasundar, R.K., Singh, V., Vaidya, J. (eds.) ICISS 2017. LNCS, vol. 10717, pp. 29–49. Springer, Cham (2017). https:// doi.org/10.1007/978-3-319-72598-7_3

18. Dong, G., Gao, F., Shi, W., Gong, P.: An efficient certificateless blind signature scheme without bilinear pairing. An. Acad. Bras. Cienc. **86**(2), 1003–1011 (2014)

19. Tian, X.-X., Li, H.-J., Xu, J.-P., Wang, Y.: A security enforcement ID-based partially blind signature scheme. In: 2009 International Conference on Web Information Systems and Mining, WISM 2009, pp. 488–492 (2009)

20. Islam, S.K.H., Amin, R., Biswas, G.P., Obaidat, M.S., Khan, M.K.: Provably secure pairing-free identity-based partially blind signature scheme and its application in online E-cash system. Arab. J. Sci. Eng. **41**, 1–14 (2016)

21. Verma, G.K., Singh, B.B.: Efficient identity-based blind message recovery signature scheme from pairings. IET Inf. Secur. **12**(2), 150–156 (2017)

22. Galindo, D., Herranz, J., Kiltz, E.: On the generic construction of identity-based signatures with additional properties. In: Lai, X., Chen, K. (eds.) ASIACRYPT 2006. LNCS, vol. 4284, pp. 178–193. Springer, Heidelberg (2006). https://doi.org/ 10.1007/11935230_12

23. Hu, X.-M., Huang, S.-T.: Secure identity-based blind signature scheme in the standard model. J. Inf. Sci. Eng. **26**(1), 215–230 (2010)

24. Zhang, F., Susilo, W., Mu, Y.: Identity-based partial message recovery signatures (or how to shorten ID-based signatures). In: Patrick, A.S., Yung, M. (eds.) FC 2005. LNCS, vol. 3570, pp. 45–56. Springer, Heidelberg (2005). https://doi.org/10. 1007/11507840_5

25. Han, S., Chang, E.: A pairing-based blind signature scheme with message recovery. Int. J. Inf. Technol. **2**(4), 187–192 (2005)

26. Zhang, L., Hu, Y., Tian, X., Yang, Y.: Novel identity-based blind signature for electronic voting system. In: 2010 Second International Workshop on Education Technology and Computer Science (ETCS), vol. 2, pp. 122–125 (2010)

27. Al-Riyami, S.S., Paterson, K.G.: Certificateless public key cryptography. In: Laih, C.-S. (ed.) ASIACRYPT 2003. LNCS, vol. 2894, pp. 452–473. Springer, Heidelberg (2003). https://doi.org/10.1007/978-3-540-40061-5_29

28. Kumar, M., Katti, C.P.: An efficient ID-based partially blind signature scheme and application in electronic-cash payment system. ACCENTS Trans. Inf. Secur. **2**(6), 36–42 (2016)

29. Kumar, M., Katti, C.P., Saxena, P.C.: An untraceable identity-based blind signature scheme without pairing for E-cash payment system. In: Kumar, N., Thakre, A. (eds.) UBICNET 2017. LNICST, vol. 218, pp. 67–78. Springer, Cham (2018). https://doi.org/10.1007/978-3-319-73423-1_7

30. Islam, S.K., Obaidat, M.S.: Design of provably secure and efficient certificateless blind signature scheme using bilinear pairing. Secur. Commun. Netw. **8**(18), 4319–4332 (2015)

31. James, S., Gowri, T., Babu, G.V., Reddy, P.V.: Identity-based blind signature scheme with message recovery. Int. J. Electr. Comput. Eng. **7**(5), 2088–8708 (2017)

32. James, S., Gayathri, N.B., Reddy, P.: Pairing free identity-based blind signature scheme with message recovery. Cryptography **2**(4), 29 (2018)

33. Diao, L., Gu, J., Yen, I.-L.: A new proxy blind signature scheme with message recovery. Inf. Technol. J. **12**(21), 6159 (2013)

34. Tso, R., Gu, C., Okamoto, T., Okamoto, E.: An efficient ID-based digital signature with message recovery based on pairing. IACR Cryptol. ePrint Arch. **2006**, 195 (2006)

35. Cao, X., Kou, W., Du, X.: A pairing-free identity-based authenticated key agreement protocol with minimal message exchanges. Inf. Sci. (Ny) **180**(15), 2895–2903 (2010)

36. Debiao, H., Jianhua, C., Jin, H.: An ID-based proxy signature schemes without bilinear pairings. Ann. Telecommun. Télécommun. **66**(11–12), 657–662 (2011)

37. Islam, S.K.H., Biswas, G.P.: A pairing-free identity-based authenticated group key agreement protocol for imbalanced mobile networks. Ann. Télécommun.-Ann. Telecommun. **67**(11–12), 547–558 (2012)

38. Barreto, P.S.L.M., Lynn, B., Scott, M.: On the selection of pairing-friendly groups. In: Matsui, M., Zuccherato, R.J. (eds.) SAC 2003. LNCS, vol. 3006, pp. 17–25. Springer, Heidelberg (2004). https://doi.org/10.1007/978-3-540-24654-1_2

39. Kumar, M., Chand, S.: ESKI-IBE: efficient and secure key issuing identity-based encryption with cloud privacy centers. Multimed. Tool Appl. **78**, 19753–19786 (2019)

40. Lynn, B.: The pairing-based cryptography (PBC) library (2010)

41. Shim, K.-A., Lee, Y.-R., Park, C.-M.: EIBAS: an efficient identity-based broadcast authentication scheme in wireless sensor networks. Ad Hoc Netw. **11**(1), 182–189 (2013)

42. Chung, Y.F., Huang, K.H., Lai, F., Chen, T.S.: ID-based digital signature scheme on the elliptic curve cryptosystem. Comput. Stand. Interfaces **29**(6), 601–604 (2007)

Group Signatures with Decentralized Tracing

Tingting Lu[1,2], Jiangtao Li[3,4](✉), Lei Zhang[1,2](✉), and Kwok-Yan Lam[5]

[1] Shanghai Key Laboratory of Trustworthy Computing, Software Engineering Institute, East China Normal University, Shanghai, China
leizhang@sei.ecnu.edu.cn
[2] State Key Laboratory of Cryptology, P.O. Box 5159, Beijing, China
[3] Shanghai Institute for Advanced Communication and Data Science, Shanghai, China
[4] School of Computer Engineering and Science, Shanghai University, Shanghai, China
[5] Nanyang Technological University, Singapore, Singapore

Abstract. Group signature is a useful cryptographic primitive that allows a message to be signed by a user on behalf of a group which is managed by some trusted authority, namely the group manager. However, group signature schemes typically place a disturbingly high level of trust on the group manager, which has become a major deployment issue in cyber applications where there is no centralized trust management. In this paper, we investigate mechanisms that aim to achieve a balance between anonymity and accountability in group signatures by decentralizing the operation of tracing the signer. We propose a practical group signature scheme with decentralized tracing. When comparing with a similar result by Benjumea *et al.* (FC 2008), our proposal has the advantage of a shorter signature size.

Keywords: Group signatures · Anonymity · Accountability · Decentralization · Signature size

1 Introduction

Group signature, introduced by Chaum and van Heyst [1], is a useful cryptographic primitive that allows a message to be signed by a user on behalf of a group which is managed by a trusted authority, namely the group manager. When a group signature is verified, it can be established that the signature was generated by a member in the group, but without revealing the identity of the particular member. At the same time, to achieve accountability, the group manager is given the capability of processing a group signature and revealing the identity of the signer (known as tracing the group signature). Since group signature schemes combine the features of anonymity and accountability, they have

J. Li—Work done while this author was at NTU.

Z. Liu and M. Yung (Eds.): Inscrypt 2019, LNCS 12020, pp. 435–442, 2020.
https://doi.org/10.1007/978-3-030-42921-8_25

promising applications in scenarios which require privacy-preserving authentications, such as Vehicular Ad-hoc Networks [2–4], and Cryptocurrencies [5]. However, group signature schemes typically place a disturbingly high level of trust on the group manager, which has become a major deployment issue in cyber applications where there is no centralized trust management.

The first step towards weakening trusted operations of the group manager was proposed by Kiayias and Yung [6]; Bellare, Shi and Zhang [7] who extended group signatures to dynamic cases. In dynamic group signatures, the group manager is separated into two authorities: the issuer and the opener. The former is responsible for issuing secret key for group members, while the latter is responsible for tracing the signature[1]. In this setting, a property called *non-frameability* is usually considered. This property requires that even if the issuer and opener collude with each other, they cannot frame an honest group member by forging 'his signature'. To achieve this goal, we need to force the opener to prove the correctness of the tracing process.

It is worth noting that, in dynamic group signatures, the opener remains a trusted authority who may otherwise violate users' privacy. On the other hand, if we discard the opener completely, the accountability feature of group signatures will be lost. In practical applications, it is desirable to find a good balance between anonymity and accountability.

1.1   Related Work

Since the introducing of group signatures, several variants have been proposed to address the conflicting requirements of anonymity and accountability of group signature schemes.

Weakening the Opener. Group signature with controlled linkability [8] is a variant of group signature which weakens the power of the opener. In these schemes, a linking authority is adopted instead of the opener. The linking authority can only tell if two signatures are generated by the same group member or not. Another related notion is named traceable group signature [9]. In addition to the property of tracing a signature, it also allows *user tracing* which enables the group manager to generate a tracing trapdoor corresponding to a member. The trapdoor can then be used to verify whether the signature is generated by this member. In both notions, however, a centralized trusted authority (i.e., linking authority or group manager) is still used.

Group signature with user-controlled linkability is usually considered in the context of Direct Anonymous Attestation [10] and anonymous credential [11]. In these schemes, the user can decide which of their signatures will be linkable when generating them. This method takes users' privacy in priority and hence loses efficient accountability. Recently, this concept is extended to support selective linkability [12]. In this scheme, the user does not need to specify which

---

[1] Sometimes known as opening the group signature. In the following, we will use the term trace and open alternately.

of his signatures will be linkable when generating them. When necessary, the group signatures will be sent to the (honest but curious) linking authority in a blinded form. This primitive is useful in authenticated data collecting. However, it assumes that the linking authority does not have direct access to the group signatures, this limits the applications of this primitive.

Decentralizing the Opener. Fair traceable (multi-)group signature proposed by Benjumea *et al.* [13] can be viewed as a decentralized version of traceable group signature. In a fair traceable (multi-)group signature scheme, new parties called fairness authorities are introduced who are used to open signatures and generate partial signature tracing trapdoors. Only the number of fairness authorities who agree to do the opening or revealing reaches a threshold t, then the t fairness authorities may open a signature or generate a valid tracing trapdoor.

In 2015, Blömer *et al.* [14] also proposed a group signature scheme with *distributed* traceability. In their work, they use the technique of threshold public key encryption [15] to distribute the power of the opener. The secret key for tracing is firstly generated at setup and later distributed among multiple openers. In this way, the signature will not be opened unless enough number of openers agree to do so. However, the secret value for tracing is still exposed to the authority who performs the setup. Besides, their scheme is constructed in the setting of static group signatures and hence is not secure against framing attacks.

1.2 Contribution

In this work, we invesigate the notion of group signatures with decentralized tracing and give a practical instantiation. The scheme is shown to be secure in the random oracle model. Especially, the group signature remains anonymous even if some of the openers are corrupted. When comparing with [13], our scheme is built over the q-Strong Diffie-Hellman (q-SDH) assumption while [13] is built over the strong RSA assumption[2]. For efficiency, our scheme has a much shorter signature size than the one in [13].

2 Preliminaries

2.1 Notations and Bilinear Maps

Notations. We use $a \leftarrow_R \mathbb{A}$ to denote the process of uniformly sampling an element from set $\mathbb{A}$ and assigning it to variable a. We also define the Lagrange coefficient $\Delta_{i,\mathbb{T}}(x) := \prod_{i \in \mathbb{T}, j \neq i} \frac{x-j}{i-j}$ for $i \in \mathbb{Z}_p$ and a set $\mathbb{T}$ of elements in $\mathbb{Z}_p$.

Bilinear Maps. A group generator PGGen is an algorithm which takes 1^λ as input and outputs a description $\mathcal{G} := (p, \mathbb{G}_1, \mathbb{G}_2, \mathbb{G}_T, e, g_1, g_2)$ of type 3 bilinear group. Here $\mathbb{G}_1, \mathbb{G}_2, \mathbb{G}_T$ are finite cyclic groups of prime order p and e is an admissible bilinear map. $g_1 \in \mathbb{G}_1$ and $g_2 \in \mathbb{G}_2$ are random generators of $\mathbb{G}_1$ and $\mathbb{G}_2$, and $g_T := e(g_1, g_2)$ will be a generator of group $\mathbb{G}_T$.

---

[2] Both schemes require the extra Decisional Composite Residuosity (DCR) and Decisional Diffie-Hellman (DDH) assumptions.

2.2 (Signature) Proof of Knowledge

We follow the notation introduced by Camenisch, Kiayias and Yung [16] to denote the zero-knowledge proofs of discrete logarithms and statements about them. For instance, $\mathrm{PK}\{(a,b,c) : y = g^a h^b \wedge y' = g^a h^c\}$ denotes a zero-knowledge proof of integers a, b, c (which are named witness) such that makes the equations $y = g^a h^b$ and $y' = g^a h^c$ hold. We use the notion $\mathrm{SPK}\{(a,b,c) : y = g^a h^b \wedge y' = g^a h^c\}(m)$ to denote a signature on message m with a proof of knowledge of the witnesses a, b, c that satisfies $y = g^a h^b$ and $y' = g^a h^c$.

A secure zero-knowledge proof scheme is usually required to satisfy completeness, simulation-soundness and zero-knowledge properties [16]. Besides, the proof of knowledge used in this work is also required to be extractable, i.e., there exist an extractor with oracle access to the prover can outputs the witness of a statement. If the extractor can extract the witness without rewinding, the proof is said to be online-extractable [17]. In the following, witnesses that are required to be online-extractable will be underlined.

3   A Group Signature with Decentralized Tracing

3.1   Description of the Scheme

- **Setup**$(1^\lambda, n, t)$: Run $\mathcal{G} := (p, \mathbb{G}_1, \mathbb{G}_2, \mathbb{G}_T, g_1, g_2, e) \leftarrow_{\mathrm{R}} \mathsf{PGGen}(1^\lambda)$ and generate $g, h, h_1, h_2 \leftarrow_{\mathrm{R}} \mathbb{G}_1$. Decide the group of openers $\{\mathcal{P}_1, \mathcal{P}_2, \ldots, \mathcal{P}_n\}$ and return the global system parameter $\mathsf{param} := (\mathcal{G}, g, h, h_1, h_2, \{\mathcal{P}_1, \mathcal{P}_2, \ldots, \mathcal{P}_n\})$. Besides, it initialize the state St by setting $St_{\mathsf{users}} := \emptyset$, $St_{\mathsf{trans}} := \epsilon$.
- **IKGen**$(1^\lambda, \mathsf{param})$: Generate $\mathsf{isk} := \gamma \leftarrow_{\mathrm{R}} \mathbb{Z}_p^*$, and compute $\mathsf{ipk} := g_2^\gamma$.
- **OKGen**: Each opener $\mathcal{P}_i$ performs $\mathsf{Gen}_i(1^\lambda, \mathsf{param}, n, t)$ as following:
  1. Choose a random polynomial $f_i(\xi) = c_{i,0} + c_{i,1}\xi + \cdots + c_{i,t-1}\xi^{t-1}$ and broadcast $C_{i,k} = g^{c_{i,k}}$ for $k \in \{0, 1, \ldots, t-1\}$ via the authenticated channel.
  2. Compute $s_{i,j} = f_i(j)$ for $j \in \{1, \ldots, n\}$ and send $s_{i,j}$ to $\mathcal{P}_j$ via secret and authenticated channel.

On receiving the shares $\{s_{1,j}, \ldots, s_{n,j}\}$, the opener $\mathcal{P}_j$ verifies the equation

$$g^{s_{i,j}} = \prod_{k=0}^{t-1} C_{i,k}^{j^k} \tag{1}$$

for all $i \in \{1, \ldots, n\}$. If there exists a share $s_{i,j}$ such that Eq. (1) does not holds, it publish the invalid share $s_{i,j}$ and aborts the protocol. Otherwise, it computes $s_{-,j} = \sum_{i=1}^n s_{i,j} \bmod p$, and sets its secret tracing key to be $\mathsf{osk}_j = s_{-,j}$. It also computes $S_{-,j} = g^{s_{-,j}}$ and publishes its public tracing key $\mathsf{opk}_j = (j, S_{-,j})$ via authenticated channel.

Finally, if no invalid share has been published by any openers, anyone who has a collection of $\{C_{i,0}\}_{i \in \{1,\ldots,n\}}$ and $\{\mathsf{opk}_j\}_{j \in \{1,\ldots,n\}}$ may select subsets

$\mathbb{T}^1, \mathbb{T}^2, \ldots, \mathbb{T}^w \subset \{1, \ldots, n\}$ such that (1) for all $\kappa \in \{1, \ldots, w\}$, $|\mathbb{T}^\kappa| = t$; and (2) $\bigcup_{\kappa \in \{1, \ldots, w\}} \mathbb{T}^\kappa = \{1, \ldots, n\}$. If $\prod_{i=0}^{n} C_{i,0} = \prod_{j \in \mathbb{T}^\kappa} (S_{-,j})^{\Delta_{j,\mathbb{T}^\kappa}(0)}$ holds for all $\kappa \in \{1, \ldots, w\}$, it computes $S := \prod_{i=0}^{n} C_{i,0}$ and sets $\mathsf{opk} := (S, \{\mathsf{opk}_j\}_{j \in \{1, \ldots, n\}})$; otherwise, it outputs a compliant and aborts. In default, we take opk, ipk and param as the input of all the rest algorithms or protocols.

- **Join**$^{(\mathcal{I}, \mathcal{U}_{uid})}$: The issuer $\mathcal{I}$ and the user $\mathcal{U}_{uid}$ runs the following interactive protocol $[\mathsf{J}_{\mathsf{user}}(1^\lambda), \mathsf{J}_{\mathsf{iss}}(1^\lambda, St, \mathsf{isk})]$:
  1. $\mathcal{U}_{uid}$ samples $y \leftarrow_{\mathsf{R}} \mathbb{Z}_p^*$ and computes $H = h_1^y$ as well as a proof $\pi_H \leftarrow_{\mathsf{R}} PK\{(y) : H = h_1^y\}$. It sends (uid, H, π_H) to the issuer $\mathcal{I}$ via authenticated channel.
  2. $\mathsf{J}_{\mathsf{iss}}$ verify that π_H is a valid proof with regard to H and param. If (1) $uid \in St_{\mathsf{users}}$; or (2) there exists an H in St_{trans}; or (3) the proof is not valid, it aborts the protocol. Otherwise, it selects $s, x \leftarrow_{\mathsf{R}} \mathbb{Z}_p^*$ and computes $A := (g_1 h_2^s H)^{\frac{1}{\gamma + x}}$. $\mathsf{J}_{\mathsf{iss}}$ sends the membership certificate $\mathsf{cert}_{uid} := (A, s, x)$ to $\mathcal{U}_{uid}$. Meanwhile, it stores $\mathsf{transcript}_{uid} = (H, \pi_H, \mathsf{cert}_{uid}, uid)$ in the state St_{trans} and updates $St_{\mathsf{users}} = St_{\mathsf{users}} \cup \{uid\}$.
  3. $\mathsf{J}_{\mathsf{user}}$ verify that $A \neq 1_{\mathbb{G}_1}$ and $e(A, g_2)^x e(A, \mathsf{ipk}) = e(g_1 h_1^y h_2^s, g_2)$. If the conditions are not satisfied, it aborts the protocol. Otherwise, it defines the membership certificate as $\mathsf{cert}_{uid} := (A, s, x)$ and the membership secret $\mathsf{sec}_{uid} := y$.
- **Sign**$(\mathsf{sec}_{uid}, \mathsf{cert}_{uid}, m)$: This algorithm is used for a group member to sign messages on behalf of the group. In detail, it performs the following:
  1. Select $b \leftarrow_{\mathsf{R}} \mathbb{Z}_p^*$, and compute $B_1 = g^b, B_2 = S^b h^y$ where S is published in the opk.
  2. Select $r_1, r_2 \leftarrow_{\mathsf{R}} \mathbb{Z}_p$, and compute $A' = A^{r_1}, \hat{A} = A'^{-x}(g_1 h_1^y h_2^s)^{r_1}, D = (g_1 h_1^y h_2^s)^{r_1} h_2^{-r_2}, r_3 = r_1^{-1}, s' = s - r_2 r_3$.
  3. Compute

$$\pi \leftarrow_{\mathsf{R}} SPK\{(b, x, y, r_2, r_3, s') : B_1 = g^b \wedge B_2 = S^b h^y$$
$$\wedge \hat{A} = A'^{-x} h_2^{r_2} D \wedge D^{r_3} h_2^{-s'} = g_1 h_1^y\}(m) \ (2)$$

  4. Return the finally signature $\sigma := (B_1, B_2, A', \hat{A}, D, \pi)$.
- **Verify**(σ, m): To verify the validation of the signature, it verifies $e(A', \mathsf{ipk}) = e(\hat{A}, g_2)$, and π is valid for $(B_1, B_2, A', \hat{A}, D)$ with regard to param, ipk and opk. If both conditions hold, it outputs 1, otherwise, it outputs 0.
- **OShare**$(\mathsf{osk}_i, \sigma, m)$: An opener $\mathcal{P}_i$ verifies the validation of the group signature σ. If $\mathsf{Verify}(m, \sigma) = 0$, it aborts. Otherwise, it computes $B_{-,i} = B_1^{s_{-,i}}$. Meanwhile, it generates a proof $\pi_{B_{-,i}} := PK\{s_{-,i} : B_{-,i} = B_1^{s_{-,i}} \wedge S_{-,i} = g^{s_{-,i}}\}$ where $S_{-,i}$ is part of opk_i. It returns the opening share $\mathsf{share}_i := (i, B_{-,i}, \pi_{B_{-,i}})$.
- **Open**$(m, \sigma, \mathbb{S}, St)$: Split $\mathbb{S}$ as $\{\mathsf{share}_1, \ldots, \mathsf{share}_n\}$ in which $\mathsf{share}_i = (i, B_{-,i}, \pi_{B_{-,i}})$ or $\mathsf{share}_i = \epsilon$. Select a set $\mathbb{T} \subset \{1, \ldots, n\}$ such that (1) $|\mathbb{T}| = t$; and (2) for all $i \in \mathbb{T}$, $\mathsf{share}_i \neq \epsilon$ and the proof $\pi_{B_{-,i}}$ is valid with regard to the param and opk. If there does not exist a set $\mathbb{T}$ satisfies above conditions, it returns $\perp$. Otherwise, it computes $\overline{H} = B_2 / \prod_{i \in \mathbb{T}} (B_{-,i})^{\Delta_{i,\mathbb{T}}(0)}$. If there exists a record $\mathsf{transcript}_{uid} = (H, \mathsf{cert}_{uid}, uid)$ in St_{trans} such that $H = \overline{H}$, it returns uid. Otherwise, it returns $\perp$.

3.2   Security Analysis

Our scheme achieves traceability, non-frameability and anonymity under the DDH, q-SDH and DCR assumptions [18] in the random oracle model. Especially, the anonymity guarantees that given a signature from one of two parties, it is not possible to tell from which of the two even if the adversary collude with some (no more than t) openers. Due to the space limitation, we refer the formal security definitions and security proofs to the full version of this paper.

3.3   Instantiation of the Proofs

To prove the knowledge of the discrete logarithms statements, we can use the Schnorr proofs [16]. Using Fiat-Shamir heuristics [19] we can make the proof non-interactive. With forking Lemma [20], these proofs can be made extractable in random oracle model by rewinding. For the witnesses that are required to be online-extractable, we can verifiably encrypt them to a public key which is defined in the common reference string (CRS). The verifiable encryption algorithm can be implemented using the instantiation by Camenisch and Shoup [21] which is secure under the Decisional Composite Residuosity (DCR) assumption.

4   Comparison and Extension

Comparison. When comparing with the fair traceable group signatures by Benjumea *et al.* [13], the scheme in [13] supports user tracing which is not supported in our scheme. However, our scheme is more suitable in some application scenarios where user tracing is not required (e.g., fair consensus [22]). In construction, our scheme is secure under the q-SDH assumption, while [13] is secure under the strong RSA assumption.

Table 1. Comparison of signature and member size

	Sign-size (bytes)		Member-size (bytes)	
	80-bits	128-bits	80-bits	128-bits
BCLY	1312	3904	1488	4428
This work	**245**	**389**	**1658**	**4802**

We also analyze the efficiency of our proposal and compares it with BCLY [13]. In Table 1, *sign-size* columns refer to the size of the group signatures. *Member-size* columns refer to the size of data that the issuer is required to keep for *each* member in the group. For both sizes, we consider 80-bits and 128-bits security respectively. The key sizes are derived from the ECRYPT 2 recommendations [23]. From the table, it is easy to see that the member size of our scheme is comparable with BCLY. However, the signature size of our scheme is much shorter than BCLY.

Extension. In this work, when considering the anonymity of the scheme, the adversary does not have access to the signing oracle. However, our scheme can be extended to satisfy the notion of full-anonymity where the signing queries are allowed. To achieve full-anonymity, the underlying encryption scheme is usually required to be CCA-secure. Meanwhile, a proof is required to prove the CCA-secure ciphertext encrypts the pseudonym (i.e., the element H in our scheme) honestly. This can be achieved using the technique by [17].

Acknowledgements. This work is supported by the National Key R&D Program of China (No.2017YFB0802000); by the National Natural Science Foundation of China (Nos. 61972159, 61572198); by the Fundamental Research Funds for the Central Universities; by the Research and Development Program in Key Areas of Guangdong Province (2018B010113001).

References

1. Chaum, D., van Heyst, E.: Group signatures. In: Davies, D.W. (ed.) EUROCRYPT 1991. LNCS, vol. 547, pp. 257–265. Springer, Heidelberg (1991). https://doi.org/10.1007/3-540-46416-6_22
2. Wu, Q., Domingo-Ferrer, J., González-Nicolás, Ú.: Balanced trustworthiness, safety, and privacy in vehicle-to-vehicle communications. IEEE Trans. Veh. Technol. **59**(2), 559–573 (2010)
3. Zhang, L., Wu, Q., Qin, B., Domingo-Ferrer, J., Liu, B.: Practical secure and privacy-preserving scheme for value-added applications in vanets. Comput. Commun. **71**, 50–60 (2015)
4. Zhang, L., Wu, Q., Solanas, A., Domingo-Ferrer, J.: A scalable robust authentication protocol for secure vehicular communications. IEEE Trans. Veh. Technol. **59**(4), 1606–1617 (2010)
5. Zhang, L., Li, H., Li, Y., Zhao, Y., Yu, Y.: An efficient linkable group signature for payer tracing in anonymous cryptocurrencies. CoRR, abs/1902.03420 (2019)
6. Kiayias, A., Yung, M.: Secure scalable group signature with dynamic joins and separable authorities. IJSN **1**(1/2), 24–45 (2006)
7. Bellare, M., Shi, H., Zhang, C.: Foundations of group signatures: the case of dynamic groups. In: Menezes, A. (ed.) CT-RSA 2005. LNCS, vol. 3376, pp. 136–153. Springer, Heidelberg (2005). https://doi.org/10.1007/978-3-540-30574-3_11
8. Slamanig, D., Spreitzer, R., Unterluggauer, T.: Adding controllable linkability to pairing-based group signatures for free. In: Chow, S.S.M., Camenisch, J., Hui, L.C.K., Yiu, S.M. (eds.) ISC 2014. LNCS, vol. 8783, pp. 388–400. Springer, Cham (2014). https://doi.org/10.1007/978-3-319-13257-0_23
9. Kiayias, A., Tsiounis, Y., Yung, M.: Traceable signatures. In: Cachin, C., Camenisch, J.L. (eds.) EUROCRYPT 2004. LNCS, vol. 3027, pp. 571–589. Springer, Heidelberg (2004). https://doi.org/10.1007/978-3-540-24676-3_34
10. Camenisch, J., Drijvers, M., Lehmann, A.: Anonymous attestation using the strong Diffie Hellman assumption revisited. In: Franz, M., Papadimitratos, P. (eds.) Trust 2016. LNCS, vol. 9824, pp. 1–20. Springer, Cham (2016). https://doi.org/10.1007/978-3-319-45572-3_1

11. Camenisch, J., Lysyanskaya, A.: An efficient system for non-transferable anonymous credentials with optional anonymity revocation. In: Pfitzmann, B. (ed.) EUROCRYPT 2001. LNCS, vol. 2045, pp. 93–118. Springer, Heidelberg (2001). https://doi.org/10.1007/3-540-44987-6_7

12. Garms, L., Lehmann, A.: Group signatures with selective linkability. In: Lin, D., Sako, K. (eds.) PKC 2019. LNCS, vol. 11442, pp. 190–220. Springer, Cham (2019). https://doi.org/10.1007/978-3-030-17253-4_7

13. Benjumea, V., Choi, S.G., Lopez, J., Yung, M.: Fair traceable multi-group signatures. In: Tsudik, G. (ed.) FC 2008. LNCS, vol. 5143, pp. 231–246. Springer, Heidelberg (2008). https://doi.org/10.1007/978-3-540-85230-8_21

14. Blömer, J., Juhnke, J., Löken, N.: Short group signatures with distributed traceability. In: Kotsireas, I.S., Rump, S.M., Yap, C.K. (eds.) MACIS 2015. LNCS, vol. 9582, pp. 166–180. Springer, Cham (2016). https://doi.org/10.1007/978-3-319-32859-1_14

15. Boneh, D., Boyen, X., Halevi, S.: Chosen ciphertext secure public key threshold encryption without random oracles. In: Pointcheval, D. (ed.) CT-RSA 2006. LNCS, vol. 3860, pp. 226–243. Springer, Heidelberg (2006). https://doi.org/10.1007/11605805_15

16. Camenisch, J., Kiayias, A., Yung, M.: On the portability of generalized schnorr proofs. In: Joux, A. (ed.) EUROCRYPT 2009. LNCS, vol. 5479, pp. 425–442. Springer, Heidelberg (2009). https://doi.org/10.1007/978-3-642-01001-9_25

17. Fischlin, M.: Communication-efficient non-interactive proofs of knowledge with online extractors. In: Shoup, V. (ed.) CRYPTO 2005. LNCS, vol. 3621, pp. 152–168. Springer, Heidelberg (2005). https://doi.org/10.1007/11535218_10

18. Boneh, D., Boyen, X.: Short signatures without random oracles and the SDH assumption in bilinear groups. J. Cryptol. **21**(2), 149–177 (2008)

19. Fiat, A., Shamir, A.: How to prove yourself: practical solutions to identification and signature problems. In: Odlyzko, A.M. (ed.) CRYPTO 1986. LNCS, vol. 263, pp. 186–194. Springer, Heidelberg (1987). https://doi.org/10.1007/3-540-47721-7_12

20. Pointcheval, D., Stern, J.: Security arguments for digital signatures and blind signatures. J. Cryptol. **13**(3), 361–396 (2000)

21. Camenisch, J., Shoup, V.: Practical verifiable encryption and decryption of discrete logarithms. In: Boneh, D. (ed.) CRYPTO 2003. LNCS, vol. 2729, pp. 126–144. Springer, Heidelberg (2003). https://doi.org/10.1007/978-3-540-45146-4_8

22. Asayag, A., et al.: A fair consensus protocol for transaction ordering. In: 2018 IEEE 26th International Conference on Network Protocols, ICNP 2018, Cambridge, UK, 25–27 September 2018, pp. 55–65 (2018)

23. ECRYPT-CSA: Algorithms, key size and protocols report 2018 (2018)

MQ Aggregate Signature Schemes with Exact Security Based on UOV Signature

Jiahui Chen[1], Jie Ling[1(✉)], Jianting Ning[2], Zhiniang Peng[3], and Yang Tan[4]

[1] School of Computer, Guangdong University of Technology, Guangzhou, China
csjhchen@gmail.com, jling@gdut.edu.cn
[2] School of Computing, National University of Singapore, Singapore, Singapore
jtning88@gmail.com
[3] Qihoo 360, Beijing, China
jiushigujiu@gmail.com
[4] Shenzhen Ringle.AI Technology Co. Ltd., Shenzhen, China
a7853z@qq.com

Abstract. Multivariate public key cryptography which relies on multivariate quadratic (MQ) problem is one of the main approaches to guarantee the security of communication in the post-quantum world. In this paper, we focus mainly on the yet unbroken (under proper parameter choice) Unbalanced Oil and Vinegar (UOV) scheme, and discuss the exact security of it. Then we propose a combined signature scheme which that (1) not only can reduce the public key size of the UOV signature scheme, and (2) but also can provide tighter security against chosen-message attack in the random oracle. On the other hand, we propose a novel aggregate signature scheme based on UOV signature scheme. Additionally, we give security proof for our aggregate signature scheme under the security of our proposed signature scheme.

Keywords: Multivariate cryptography · UOV signature scheme · Exact security · Aggregate signature

1 Introduction

Nowadays, the current major public-key cryptographic schemes are mainly based on the hardness of number theory such as integer factorization and discrete logarithm. Since according to the Shor's algorithm [1], these schemes will be broken in polynomial time after the emergence of quantum computers, which calls for doing research on the post-quantum cryptography [2].

According to the post quantum cryptography project submitted by the National Institute for Standards and Technology (NIST) [3], MPKC is popular for its efficiency in the post quantum cryptography aspect and signature schemes are promising. Also, multivariate signature schemes with special properties, such as proxy signature, ring signature and so on, are proposed. For example, Tang

© Springer Nature Switzerland AG 2020
Z. Liu and M. Yung (Eds.): Inscrypt 2019, LNCS 12020, pp. 443–451, 2020.
https://doi.org/10.1007/978-3-030-42921-8_26

et al. [4] proposed the first MPKC proxy signature scheme based on the problem of Isomorphisms of Polynomials (IP). Petzoldt et al. [5] proposed the first provable MPKC threshold ring signature scheme based on the result of [6]. Chen et al. [7] proposed the first online/offline signature based on UOV by utilizing the linear construction of the central map of UOV, so that the proposed scheme can be distributed in the wireless sensor networks. In addition, multivariate blind signature scheme by Petzoldt et al. [8] are proposed to enrich this area.

In this paper, we focus on this part, we firstly propose a combined signature scheme based on UOV signature, which can not only reduce the public key size of the UOV signature scheme but also can provide more tighter exact security proof. Thereafter, we propose a novel aggregate signature scheme based on the proposed signature scheme, which includes the stages of key generation, generation of signature, combination of signature and the verification of aggregate signature. We also give a strict security proof for our aggregate signature scheme under the security of our proposed signature scheme. We also give a toy example for our aggregate scheme. Finally, we propose parameters and comparisons for our proposed scheme.

The rest of the paper is organized as follows: In Sect. 2, we describe the schemes, the basic UOV signature scheme and the security models. In Sect. 3, we present our proposed signature scheme. Then the proposed aggregate signature scheme based on our signature scheme is described in Sect. 4. In Sect. 5, we present the analysis of our schemes. Finally we concludes the paper with a discussion in Sect. 6.

2   Preliminaries

2.1   Sequential Aggregate Signatures

Generally, a sequential aggregate signature scheme [10] $\mathcal{AS}$ is consisted with three algorithms :KeyGen, Sign, Verify:

- AggGen(1^λ): The algorithm inputs a security parameter 1^λ and outputs a signature key pair (sk, pk). In a sequential aggregation signature scheme, this algorithm is run by each user u_i and the corresponding key pair (sk_i, pk_i) is obtained.
- AggSign($m_i, sk_i, pk_1, ..., pk_{i-1}, \Sigma_{i-1}$): To generate a sequential aggregate signature, the algorithm is run by the user in this sequence using its secret key sk_i according to the message m_i. Then given the previous user's public key set $(pk_1, \ldots, pk_{i-1})$ and the previous aggregate signature Σ_{i-1}, the algorithm aggregates to generate an aggregate signature of Σ.
- AggVerify($(m_1, ..., m_k), \Sigma, (pk_1, \ldots, pk_k)$): Given $((m_1, \ldots, m_k), \Sigma, (pk_1, \ldots, pk_k))$, if Σ is valid, the algorithm outputs TRUE, otherwise it outputs FALSE.

2.2   UOV Signature Scheme

The UOV scheme [11] is a single field construction, it work solely in the polynomial ring $\mathbb{F}_q[X]$, where $X = \{x_1, ..., x_n\}$. Let $|V| = v$, $|O| = o$ and $v + o = n$. We randomly choose o quadratic polynomials $q_k(X) = q_k(x_1, ..., x_n)$ the polynomial ring $\mathbb{F}_q[X]$ by

$$q_k(X) = \sum_{i \in O, j \in V} \alpha_{ij}^{(k)} x_i x_j + \sum_{i,j \in V, i \leq j} \beta_{ij}^{(k)} x_i x_j + \sum_{i \in O \cup V} \gamma_i^{(k)} x_i + \eta^{(k)}, k = 1, ..., o,$$

(1)

To hide the structure of Q in the public key one concatenates it with an invertible affine map $T : F^n \rightarrow F^n$, then the public key of the UOV signature scheme is $P = Q \circ T$.

The key generation algorithm $\mathsf{UOVGen}(1^\lambda)$, takes 1^λ as input and outputs $pk = P$ and $sk = (T, Q)$.

Assume the document needs to be signed is $M = (y_1, y_2, ..., y_m)$, the signing algorithm $\mathsf{UOVSign}(M, T, Q))$ is as follows. Firstly, the user chooses the values of the v vinegar variables $V = (x_1, \ldots, x_v)$ at random, then it solves the equation: $M = Q(X, V)$, then it calculates $\sigma = T^{-1}(X, V)$ and get the signature σ.

Finally, the verification algorithm $\mathsf{UOVVerify}(\sigma, M, P)$ returns TRUE if $P(\sigma) = M$, otherwise returns FALSE.

2.3   Security Models

Exact Security Model for UOV Digital Signature. We quantify the security of UOV scheme as a uniform one-way function.

Definition 1. *We say that the UOV one-way function is $(t'(\lambda), \varepsilon'(\lambda)) - secure$ if there is no inverting algorithm that takes P, y as inputs and outputs a preimage x such that $P(x) = y$ at $t'(\lambda)$ processing time with probability at least $\varepsilon'(\lambda)$, where P is obtained by running $\mathsf{KeyGen}(1^\lambda)$ and y is randomly chosen from k^n. The standard asymptotic definition of security requests that the success probability of any PPT (probabilistic, polynomial time) algorithm is a negligible function of λ.*

Next, we quantify the exact security of UOV signature scheme. The exact security of the reduction which was used to prove the security of the full domain hash (FDH) signature scheme was first provides by Bellare and Rogaway [9] and analyzed in Theorem 1.

Similar to this work, we have

Definition 2. *We say that the UOV-based FDH signature scheme is $(t(\lambda), q_{sig}(\lambda), q_{hash}(\lambda), \varepsilon(\lambda)) - secure$ if there is no forger $\mathcal{A}$ who takes a public key pk generated via $(pk, \cdot) \leftarrow Gen(1^\lambda)$, after at most $q_{hash}(\lambda)$ queries to the random oracle, $q_{sig}(\lambda)$ signature queries, and $t(\lambda)$ processing time, then outputs a valid signature with probability at least $\varepsilon(\lambda)$.*

Security Model for Aggregated Signature. Similar to the work in [13], we formalize the sequential aggregation security under the selected message model in Definition 3.

Definition 3. *We say that a sequential aggregate signature scheme is* $(\varepsilon'', t'',$ $q'_{sig}, q'_{hash}) - secure$ *if there is no forger* $\mathcal{A}$ *can win in the above game and satisfies that:* $\mathcal{A}$ *runs in time at most* t''; $\mathcal{A}$ *makes at most* q'_{hash} *queries to the hash function and at most* q'_{sig} *queries to the aggregate signing oracle;* $AdvAggSig_A$ *is at least* ε''.

3   Our Proposed Signature Scheme

Our proposed signature scheme is consisted with three algorithms: Gen, Sig and Ver. The details are as follows.

The key generation algorithm Gen is described in Algorithm 1.

Algorithm 1. $\mathsf{Gen}(q, o, v, D\ )$

Input:
   q: the underlying field (i.e. $\mathbb{F}_q = GF(2^5)$);
   o,v: the number of Oil and Vinegar variables respectively;
   n: $n = v + o$;
   D: the number of non-trivial quadratic terms, $D = \frac{v \cdot (v+1)}{2} + o \cdot v$;
Output:
   (T, Q): the private key to sign the message;
   P: the public key corresponding to (T, Q);
 1: Choose a vector $\mathbf{b} = (b_0, ..., b_{D-1})$ at random.
 2: Choose an $n \times n$ invertible matrix T at random (given as a matrix $M_T = (t_{rs})_{r,s=1}^n$);
 3: Set the entries of the first D columns of P to $p_{ij} = b_{(j-i) \bmod D}$;
 4: Solve for $i = 0, ..., o - 1$ and $j = 0, ..., D - 1$ the linear systems given by $M' = Q \cdot A$ to get the non-zero coefficients of the quadratic terms of the central map Q, where the elements in A is

$$a_{kl}^{rs} = \begin{cases} t_{kr} \cdot t_{lr} (r = s) \\ t_{kr} \cdot t_{ls} + t_{ks} \cdot t_{lr} (r \neq s) \end{cases}$$

   and the elements in M' is p_{ij};
 5: Choose the coefficients of the linear and constant terms of the central map Q at random;
 6: Compute the remaining coefficients of the public polynomials by composing Q and T using the equation $P = Q \circ T$;
 7: **return** (Q, T, P);

Gen takes as inputs the underlying field, the number of Oil and Vinegar variables, and the number of non-zero quadratic terms, and returns the public/private key pairs. In fact in this part we use the strategy in [14]. We recommend to read more detail in [14].

In the signature generation part, we change the UOV signature into FDH-like signature scheme, so that we can make exact security proof. It firstly chooses a collision-resistant hash function $H : \{0,1\}^* \rightarrow \mathbb{F}_q^o$, and is described in Algorithm 2.

At last, the verification algorithm $\mathsf{Ver}(H, \sigma, m)$ returns 1 if $P(x) = H(m||r)$, otherwise it returns 0.

Algorithm 2. Sign(m, (T, Q))

Input:
   m: the message to sign;
   (T, Q): the private key to sign the message;
Output:
   σ: the signature on message m;
1: $x_v' \in_R \mathbb{F}_q^v$;
2: **repeat**
3: $l \in_R \mathbb{Z}$; $r \in_R \{0, 1\}^l$; $y \leftarrow H(m||r)$;
4: **until** $\{z_n | Q(z_n, x_v') = y\} \neq \emptyset$;
5: $x_n' \in_R \{z_n | Q(z_n, x_v') = y\}$;
6: $x \leftarrow T^{-1}(x_n', x_v')$;
7: **return** $\sigma = (x, r)$;

---

4   Our Proposed Sequential Aggregation Signature Scheme

In this section, we propose a novel sequential aggregation signature scheme based on our combined signature scheme. The main parts of this scheme are the key generation part, the aggregation signature generation part and the aggregation signature verification part.

4.1   Key Generation

Let $U = u_1, ..., u_k$ be the set of users. In the key generation algorithm of UOV-based sequential aggregation signature scheme, we assume each user u_i can generate a UOV key pair $((Q_i, T_i), P_i)$ through a given system parameter. Each user u_i then makes the public key P_i public and keeps the private key (Q_i, T_i). Also, we denote a split algorithm Split($*$) that splits arbitrary message with length $O + iV, i = 1, ..., k$ into $k + 1$ small messages, where the length of the first message is equal to the size of O, the length of the other parts is equal to the size of V.

4.2   Signature Generation

Let $\mathcal{H} : \mathbb{F}^* \rightarrow \mathbb{F}^o$ be a hash function that can hash any message into a message with length o. Suppose each user u_i has a message m_i to be signed. To generate a message to aggregate signature Σ according to the message $m_1, ..., m_k$, each user of the user set $u_1, ..., u_k$ runs Algorithm 3 separately. The resulting aggregate signature Σ is the output of user u_k.

4.3   Signature Verification

To verify the correctness of an aggregate signature Σ_i, we split Σ_i into two parts, the first part being the block Σ_{i_1}, which is a vector of o elements. The second part is $(\Sigma_{i_2}, ..., \Sigma_{1_2})$, which is a collection of vectors consisting of v elements. Thereafter, the signature verification part is similar to the verification of the normal UOV. The process is shown in Algorithm 4.

Algorithm 3. AggSign($m_i, sk_i = (T_i, Q_i), pk_1, ..., pk_{i-1}, \Sigma_{i-1}$)

Input:
    m_i: the messages that need to be signed;
    $sk_i = (T_i, Q_i)$: the private key of user i;
    $pk_1, ..., pk_{i-1}, \Sigma_{i-1}$: The previous public keys and aggregate signature
Output:
    Σ_i: the aggregate signature corresponding to $m_1, ..., m_i$;
1: if $i = 1$ then
2:    $\Sigma_{i-1_1} = 0^o$, $\Sigma_{i-1_2} = \emptyset$
3: else if AggVerify($pk_1, ..., pk_{i-1}, m_1, ..., m_{i-1}, \Sigma_{i-1}$)=TURE then
4:    $(\Sigma_{i-1_1}, \Sigma_{i-1_2}, ..., \Sigma_{1_2}) = \mathsf{Split}(\Sigma_{i-1})$
5: else
6:    return FALSE
7: end if
8: $D = H(m_1, ..., m_i)$
9: $\Sigma_i = \mathsf{UOVSign}((D + \Sigma_{i-1_1}), (T_i, Q_i))$
10: $(\Sigma'_{i_1}, \Sigma'_{i_2}) = \mathsf{Split}(\Sigma_i)$
11: $\Sigma_{i_1} = \Sigma'_{i_1}$
12: $\Sigma_{i_2} = (\Sigma'_{i_2} || \Sigma_{i-1_2} || ... || \Sigma_{1_2})$
13: $\Sigma_i = (\Sigma_{i_1} || \Sigma_{i_2})$
14: **return** Σ_i

Algorithm 4. AggVerify($pk_1, ..., pk_i, m, ..., m_i, \Sigma_i$)

Input:
    $pk_1, ..., pk_i, m, ..., m_i, \Sigma_i$: The public key, message, and aggregate signature corresponding to the previous i user respectively
Output:
    TRUE or FALSE: Determines whether the aggregate signature is valid;
1: $(\Sigma_{i_1}, \Sigma_{i_2}, ..., \Sigma_{1_2})=\mathsf{Split}(\Sigma_i)$
2: for $j = i$ to 1 do
3:    $D_j = H(m_1, ..., m_j)$
4:    $\Sigma_{j-1_1} = pk_j(\Sigma_{j_1}, \Sigma_{j_2}) - D_j$
5: end for
6: if $\Sigma_{0_1} = 0^o$
7: **return** TRUE
8: end if
9: else
10: **return** FALSE
11: end if

4.4 A Toy Example

We propose a toy example to further illustrate our scheme. Let $k = 3$, $q = 4, o = 2, v = 4$.

When $i = 1$ (the first sequence), the scheme will generate the first aggregate signature Σ_1. The scheme sets $\Sigma_{0_1} = 0^o$, $\Sigma_{0_2} = \emptyset$, assume $D = H(m_1) = \{1, 3\}$, we have $D + \Sigma_{0_1} = \{1,3\}$, then it will use this $D + \Sigma_{0_1}$ to submit a regular UOV signature $\sigma_1 = \mathsf{UOVSign}((D + \Sigma_{0_1}), sk_1) = \{3, 1, 3, 0, 0, 1\}$. Thereafter, the scheme sets $\Sigma_{1_1} = \{3, 1\}, \Sigma_{1_2} = \{3, 0, 0, 1\}$ and the first aggregate signature $\Sigma_1 = (\Sigma_{1_1}, \Sigma_{1_2}) = (\{3, 1\} || \{3, 0, 0, 1\})$, the scheme will go to the second aggregate signature process.

When $i = 2$ (the second sequence), the scheme will firstly call for a verifying algorithm of the aggregate scheme to verify the first aggregation signature, where it splits and gets $\Sigma_{1_1} = \{3, 1\}$ and $\Sigma_{1_2} = \{3, 0, 0, 1\}$, and computes $pk_1(\Sigma_{1_1}, \Sigma_{1_2}) = \{1, 3\}$, $D_1 = H(m_1) = \{1, 3\}$, we have

$\Sigma_{0_1} = pk_1(\Sigma_{1_1}, \Sigma_{1_2}) - D_1 = \{0, 0\}$, thus the verification is valid. Then the scheme will generate the second aggregate signature Σ_2. It first splits and gets $\Sigma_{1_1} = \{3, 1\}, \Sigma_{1_2} = \{3, 0, 0, 1\}$, assume $D_2 = H(m_1, m_2) = \{0, 2\}$, we have $D_2 + \Sigma_{1_1} = \{3, 3\}$, then we will use this $D_2 + \Sigma_{1_1}$ to submit a basic UOV signature $\sigma_2 = \mathsf{UOVSign}((D + \Sigma_{i_1}), sk_2) = \{0, 2, 0, 3, 1, 3\}$ and $(\Sigma'_{2_1}, \Sigma'_{2_2}) = (\{0, 2\}, \{0, 3, 1, 3\})$. Then the scheme set $\Sigma_{2_1} = \Sigma'_{2_1} = \{0, 2\}$ and $\Sigma_{2_2} = (\Sigma'_{2_2} || \Sigma_{1_2}) = \{0, 3, 1, 3\} || \{3, 0, 0, 1\}$. Then the second aggregate signature is $\Sigma_2 = (\Sigma_{2_1} || \Sigma_{2_2}) = (\{0, 2\} || \{0, 3, 1, 3\} || \{3, 0, 0, 1\})$, the scheme will go to the third aggregation signature process.

When $i = 3$ (the third sequence), the scheme will firstly call for a verifying algorithm of the aggregate scheme and find the verification valid. Then the scheme will generate the third aggregate signature Σ_3. It first splits and gets $\Sigma_{2_1} = \{0, 2\}, \Sigma_{2_2} = \{0, 3, 1, 3\}, \Sigma_{1_2} = \{3, 0, 0, 1\}$, assume $D = H(m_1, m_2, m_3) = \{3, 2\}$, we have $D + \Sigma_{2-1_1} = \{3, 0\}$, then we will use this $D + \Sigma_{2_1}$ to submit a signature $\sigma_3 = \mathsf{UOVSign}((D + \Sigma_{2_1}), sk_3) = \{2, 1, 3, 3, 1, 1\}$. Thereafter, the scheme sets $\Sigma_{3_1} = \{2, 1\}, \Sigma_{3_2} = \{3, 3, 1, 1\} || \{0, 3, 1, 3\} || \{3, 0, 0, 1\}$, then the aggregate signature process is finished and the final aggregate signature is $\Sigma_3 = (\Sigma_{3_1}, \Sigma_{3_2}) = (\{2, 1\} || \{3, 3, 1, 1\} || \{0, 3, 1, 3\} || \{3, 0, 0, 1\})$.

5   Analysis

Our signature scheme can reduce the size of public key of UOV, more details about this property we recommend to read [14].

Proposition 1. *The trapdoor function of our proposed scheme is as secure as the basic function of UOV under the current attack techniques.*

Due to page limitation, we omit the proof here.

Proposition 2. *If the function of our scheme is (t', ε') − secure, our signature scheme is $(\varepsilon, t, q_{sig}, q_{hash})$ − secure, where $\varepsilon(\lambda) \leq \frac{1}{(1 - \frac{1}{q_{sig}+1})^{q_{sig}+1}} \cdot q_{sig} \cdot \varepsilon'(\lambda)$ and $t(\lambda) \geq t'(\lambda) - (q_{hash} + q_{sig} + 1)(t_{UOV} + O(1))$, where t_{UOV} is the time to compute the UOV function.*

Due to page limitation, we omit the proof here.

Proposition 3. *If UOV signature scheme is $(\varepsilon, t, q_{sig}, q_{hash})$ − secure, then our aggregation signature scheme is $(\varepsilon'', t'', q'_{sig}, q'_{hash})$ − secure, where $\varepsilon''(\lambda) \leq 2(q'_{sig} + q'_{hash} + 1) \cdot \varepsilon(\lambda)$ and $t'' \leq t - (4kq'_{hash} + 4kq'_{sig} + 7k + 1)$.*

Due to page limitation, we omit the proof here.

Finally, for the compression ratio, it is not difficult to calculate the size of our aggregate signature scheme is $|\Sigma| = o + n \cdot v$. Thus the compression ratio is $\tau = 1 - \frac{\Sigma}{n \cdot \sigma} = 1 - \frac{o + n \cdot v}{n \cdot (o + v)}$.

6   Conclusions

In this paper, we propose a new signature scheme based on UOV signature, which is shown that our proposed signature scheme can reduce the public key size and have better exact security bound. In addition, we propose an aggregated signature scheme based on the UOV signature scheme and also give security proof under the security of our proposed signature scheme. Finally, we find that the aggregate signature compression rate obtained by our aggregated signature scheme be $1 - \frac{o + n \cdot v}{n \cdot (o + v)}$, indicating that our aggregate signature scheme is especially suitable for large-scale signature environments.

Acknowledgment. This work is supported by the Key Areas Research and Development Program of Guangdong Province (grant 2019B010139002), National Natural Science Foundation of China (grant 61902079) and the project of Guangzhou Science and Technology (grant 201902020006 & 201902020007).

References

1. Shor, P.W.: Polynomial-time algorithms for prime factorization and discrete logarithms on a quantum computer. SIAM J. Comput. **26**, 1484–1509 (1997)
2. Bernstein, D.J.: Introduction to post-quantum cryptography. In: Bernstein, D.J., Buchmann, J., Dahmen, E. (eds.) Post-quantum cryptography - PQCrypto 2009, LNCS, pp. 1–14. Springer, Heidelberg (2009). https://doi.org/10.1007/978-3-540-88702-7_1
3. NIST CSRC: Cryptographic technology group: submission requirements and evaluation criteria for the post-quantum cryptography standardization process (2016)
4. Tang, S., Xu, L.: Towards provably secure proxy signature scheme based on isomorphisms of polynomials. Future Gener. Comput. Syst. **30**, 91–97 (2014)
5. Petzoldt, A., Bulygin, S., Buchmann, J.: A multivariate based threshold ring signature scheme. Appl. Algebra Eng. Commun. Comput. **24**(3–4), 255–275 (2013)
6. Sakumoto, K., Shirai, T., Hiwatari, H.: On provable security of UOV and HFE signature schemes against chosen-message attack. In: Yang, B.-Y. (ed.) PQCrypto 2011. LNCS, vol. 7071, pp. 68–82. Springer, Heidelberg (2011). https://doi.org/10.1007/978-3-642-25405-5_5
7. Chen, J., Tang, S., He, D., Tan, Y.: Online/offline signature based on UOV in wireless sensor networks. Wirel. Netw. **23**(6), 1719–1730 (2017)
8. Petzoldt, A., Szepieniec, A., Mohamed, M.S.E.: A practical multivariate blind signature scheme. In: Kiayias, A. (ed.) FC 2017. LNCS, vol. 10322, pp. 437–454. Springer, Cham (2017). https://doi.org/10.1007/978-3-319-70972-7_25
9. Bellare, M., Rogaway, P.: The exact security of digital signatures-how to sign with RSA and Rabin. In: Maurer, U. (ed.) EUROCRYPT 1996. LNCS, vol. 1070, pp. 399–416. Springer, Heidelberg (1996). https://doi.org/10.1007/3-540-68339-9_34
10. Boneh, D., Gentry, C., Lynn, B., Shacham, H.: Aggregate and verifiably encrypted signatures from bilinear maps. In: Biham, E. (ed.) EUROCRYPT 2003. LNCS, vol. 2656, pp. 416–432. Springer, Heidelberg (2003). https://doi.org/10.1007/3-540-39200-9_26
11. Kipnis, A., Patarin, J., Goubin, L.: Unbalanced oil and vinegar signature schemes. In: Stern, J. (ed.) EUROCRYPT 1999. LNCS, vol. 1592, pp. 206–222. Springer, Heidelberg (1999). https://doi.org/10.1007/3-540-48910-X_15

12. Coron, J.-S.: On the exact security of Full Domain Hash. In: Bellare, M. (ed.) CRYPTO 2000. LNCS, vol. 1880, pp. 229–235. Springer, Heidelberg (2000). https://doi.org/10.1007/3-540-44598-6_14
13. Lysyanskaya, A., Micali, S., Reyzin, L., Shacham, H.: Sequential aggregate signatures from trapdoor permutations. In: Cachin, C., Camenisch, J.L. (eds.) EUROCRYPT 2004. LNCS, vol. 3027, pp. 74–90. Springer, Heidelberg (2004). https://doi.org/10.1007/978-3-540-24676-3_5
14. Petzoldt, A., Bulygin, S., Buchmann, J.: A multivariate signature scheme with a partially cyclic public key. In: Proceedings of SCC, pp. 229–235. Springer, Cham (2010)

Untraceability of Partial Blind and Blind Signature Schemes

Swati Rawal and Sahadeo Padhye[✉]

Department of Mathematics, Motilal Nehru National Institute of Technology
Allahabad, Prayagraj 211004, India
swati.rawal25@gmail.com, sahadeomathrsu@gmail.com

Abstract. Blind Signature is employed in privacy related protocols, where signer signs on a blinded message. It provides anonymity in various cryptographic applications such as electronic voting, digital cash system etc. Concerning the need for quantum resistant scheme, Ruckert and Tian et al. proposed the lattice based blind signature and partial blind signature schemes respectively. But, both the schemes left out one of the security requirement of a blind i.e. *Untraceability*, where the signer can't link the blinded signature with a valid message-signature pair even when it is revealed in public. In this article, we propose an attack on the untracebility property of both the schemes. The proposed attack opens the door for researchers to work on quantum resistant untraceable blind signature.

Keywords: Lattice cryptography · Digital signature · Blind signature · Partial blind signature

1 Introduction

Enhanced wireless sensor networks, IoT (Internet of Things) devices employed in e-cash systems and electronic voting is a crucial step towards smart city future. Moreover, with the development in big data, various organizations employ it in e-payments to cloud. In both the systems (e-payments and e-voting) blind signature plays an important role to protect user privacy and ensures the trustworthiness of big data in cloud.

Chaum [6], introduced the concept of blind signature in 1982, where the signer signs the document which is blinded by the user. Blind Signature become an important primitive in the application for e-voting, anonymous banking [12] and for oblivious transfer [7]. These applications will continue to have its importance in future as well.

Abe and Fujisaki [5] introduced the concept of partial blind signature in 1996 after pointing out the drawbacks of blind signature scheme while using it for e-payments. One particular drawback is that, as the signer's view is completely closed from the signatures, the signer has no control over the attributes except for those bound by the public key. For example, if a signer issues blind signatures

© Springer Nature Switzerland AG 2020
Z. Liu and M. Yung (Eds.): Inscrypt 2019, LNCS 12020, pp. 452–459, 2020.
https://doi.org/10.1007/978-3-030-42921-8_27

with validity of a week, then he has to change his public key per every week. This will seriously affect the availability and performance.

A partial blind signature allows the signer and user to come to agreement to explicitly include a shared information to the blind signature. For example, the signatory may attach the date of issue to his blind signature as a characteristic. If the signatory issues a large number of signatures in a day, including issue date will not violate anonymity. Accordingly, the properties of signatures can be fixed independently of the public key.

With the development in the technology, the current discrete logarithm and factoring based system are at threat from quantum computers. Still there are some assumptions that are conjunctured to be quantum safe. These protocols cover the *post-quantum* cryptography. Lattice based cryptography is one of them which works under the hardness of hard lattice problem. Constructing cryptographic protocols upon hard lattice problems has its benefits, unlike DLP and factoring, they withstand subexponential attacks and the best known algorithms [3] have an exponential complexity in the lattice dimension. Moreover, Ajtai [1] proved that lattice problems allows a worst-case to average-case reduction. Taking these as motivations, Ruckert [13] developed the first quantum safe blind signature, inspired from Lyubashevsky's ID scheme [9] combined with the Fiat-Shamir paradigm [8]. From Lyubashevsky's signature scheme [10] and Abe et al.'s construction [4], Tian et al. [14] developed the first quantum proof partial blind signature from lattice assumption. Both the schemes were proved to be one-more unforgeable and satisfy blindness property.

But a blind signature should also satisfy *Untraceability* property, which states that the signer should not be able to link a blinded signature with the valid message-signature pair, even when it is revealed in public. Hwang et al. [11] proposed the untraceable blind signature based on RSA. Afterwards, many untraceable blind signatures were proposed [15–18], but all are based on factoring or DLP.

In this article, we propose an attack on the traceability property of the above two blind and partial blind signature schemes. We first discuss some preliminaries about lattices. Then we describe the Tian et al.'s [14] partial blind signature scheme and discuss its untraceability property. Section 4 define the Ruckert's [13] blind signature scheme and the proposed attack. Last section concludes the paper with future direction.

2 Lattices: Background and Definition

Definition 1. *A Lattice $\mathcal{L}$ in $\mathbb{R}^m$ is an integer linear combination of vectors $b_1, b_2, \ldots, b_n$ in $\mathbb{R}^m$ where $n \leq m$,*

$$\mathcal{L}(\mathbf{B}) = \mathcal{L}(b_1, b_2, \ldots, b_n) = \{\Sigma_{i=1}^{n} \mathbf{x}_i b_i | \mathbf{x}_i \in \mathbb{Z}\} = \{\mathbf{B}^T \mathbf{x} | \mathbf{x} \in \mathbb{Z}^n\}$$

$\mathbf{B} = \{b_1, b_2, \ldots, b_n\}$ *is known as the basis of the lattice. The integers n and m represents the rank and dimension of the lattice. If $n = m$, then it is a full rank lattice.*

Definition 2 q-ary Lattice: [2] A Lattice $\mathcal{L}$ is known as q-ary lattice if $q\mathbb{Z}^n \subseteq \mathcal{L} \subseteq \mathbb{Z}^n$ holds for some integer q. For matrix $\mathbf{A} \in \mathbb{Z}_q^{n \times m}$, we can define two q-ary lattices of dimension m,

1. $\mathcal{L}^{\perp}(\mathbf{A}) = \{\mathbf{x} \in \mathbb{Z}^m | \mathbf{A}\mathbf{x} = 0 \mod q\}$
2. $\mathcal{L}_y^{\perp}(\mathbf{A}) = \{\mathbf{x} \in \mathbb{Z}^m | \mathbf{A}^T\mathbf{y} = \mathbf{x} \mod q \text{ for } y \in \mathbb{Z}^n\}$

2.1   Hard Computational Problems on Lattices

Now we define the *Hard-on average* problem introduced by Ajtai [1] known as *Shortest Integer Solution Problem*. Note that if not specified l_2- norm is considered.

Definition 3 *Shortest Integer Solution Problem* (SIS): For an integer q, a real β and a matrix $\mathbf{A} \in \mathbb{Z}_q^{n \times m}$, determine a non-zero integer vector $\mathbf{s} \in \mathbb{Z}^m$ such that $\mathbf{A}\mathbf{s} = 0 \mod q$ and $\|\mathbf{s}\| \leq \beta$.

Another variant of this problem, where inhomogeneous system is considered, is defined as below.

Definition 4 *Inhomogeneous   Shortest   Integer   Solution   Problem* (ISIS): For an integer q, a matrix $\mathbf{A} \in \mathbb{Z}_q^{n \times m}$, a syndrome $\mathbf{u} \in \mathbb{Z}_q^n$ and a real β, determine the non-zero integer vector $\mathbf{s} \in \mathbb{Z}^m$ such that $\mathbf{A}\mathbf{s} = \mathbf{u} \mod q$ and $\|\mathbf{s}\| \leq \beta$.

2.2   Discrete Gaussian over Lattices

Gaussian-like probability distributions plays an important role in lattice cryptography and are known as discrete gaussian. This section briefly discuss about them.

Definition 5 *Gaussian Function:* For $\sigma > 0$ a gaussian function $\rho : \mathbb{R}^n \longrightarrow \mathbb{R}^+$ centred at c is defined as

$$\rho_{\sigma,c}(x) = exp(-\pi\|x - c\|^2/\sigma^2), \forall x \in \mathbb{R}^n$$

Definition 6 *Discrete   Gaussian   Distribution:* For some $c \in \mathbb{R}^n$, $\sigma > 0$ and an n-dimensional lattice $\mathcal{L}$, discrete gaussian distribution can be defined as

$$D_{\mathcal{L},\sigma,c}(\mathbf{x}) = \frac{\rho_{\sigma,c}(\mathbf{x})}{\rho_{\sigma,c}(\mathcal{L})}, \forall \mathbf{x} \in \mathcal{L}$$

where, $\rho_{\sigma,c}(\mathcal{L}) = \sum_{\mathbf{y} \in \mathcal{L}} \rho_{\sigma,c}(\mathbf{y})$.

Note that σ and c are 1 and 0 respectively if omitted.

3 Tian et al.'s Partially Blind Signature Scheme over Lattices

Tian et al.'s [14] Partially Blind Signature Scheme over lattices works as follows

- $Setup(1^n)$: The polynomial time algorithm takes as input the security parameter and generates the parameters $(q, b, d, k, m, M, \sigma)$ according to Table 1 in [10]. Then it selects a matrix randomly $\mathbf{A} \leftarrow \mathbb{Z}_q^{n \times m}$ and two cryptographic hash functions $H : \{0,1\}^* \longrightarrow \{-1,0,1\}^k$ and $H' : \{0,1\}^* \longrightarrow \mathbb{Z}_q^{n \times m}$. Then finally returns the system parameters as $params = (q, b, d, k, m, M, \sigma, \mathbf{A}, H, H')$.
- $KeyGen(params)$: The algorithm takes system parameters $params$ as input and select $\mathbf{S} \leftarrow \{-d, \ldots, 0, \ldots, d\}^{m \times k}$ and computes $\mathbf{T} = \mathbf{AS} \mod q$. Then returns secret key as $\mathbf{S}$ and public keys as $(\mathbf{T})$.
- $SignGen(params, \mathbf{T}, \mathbf{S}, msg, info)$: To sign the message msg, the $User$ and the $Signer$ negotiate to agree on an information $info$ to be attached with the message. Then, interact as follows to obtain signature on msg
  - $Sign(Part1)$: On input $(params, \mathbf{T}, \mathbf{S}, info)$, signer randomly chooses $y \leftarrow D_\sigma^m$ and samples $(\epsilon_2^\star, z_2^\star) \in \{-1,0,1\}^k \times D_\sigma^m$ then computes
    - (i) $c_1 \leftarrow \mathbf{A}y \mod q$.
    - (ii) $c_2 \leftarrow \mathbf{A}z_2^\star - H'(info)\epsilon_2^\star \mod q$.

    $Signer$ sends the value (c_1, c_2) to the $User$.
  - $Blinding$: on input $(params, \mathbf{T}, msg, info)$ the $User$ first selects $\beta_1, \beta_2 \leftarrow \{-b+1, \ldots, 0, \ldots b-1\}^k$ and $\alpha_1, \alpha_2 \leftarrow D_\sigma^m$ randomly. Then he computes
    - (i) $c_1' \leftarrow c_1 + \mathbf{A}\alpha_1 - \mathbf{T}\beta_1 \mod q$,
    - (ii) $c_2' \leftarrow c_2 + \mathbf{A}\alpha_2 - H'(info)\beta_2 \mod q$,
    - (iii) $\epsilon \leftarrow H(c_1, c_2, H'(info), msg)$
    - (iv) $\epsilon^\star \leftarrow (\epsilon - \beta_1 - \beta_2) \mod 3$ where the set $\{-1,0,1\}^k$ is viewed as a representation of $\mathbb{Z}_3^k$.

    The $User$ then sends $\epsilon^\star$ to the signer.
  - $Signer(Part2)$: On receiving the value $\epsilon^\star$ signer computes
    - (i) $\epsilon_1^\star \leftarrow (\epsilon^\star - \epsilon_2^\star) \mod 3$,
    - (ii) $z_1^\star \leftarrow \mathbf{S}\epsilon_1^\star + y$ with probability $min(\frac{D_{\sigma^m}(z_1^\star)}{MD_{\mathbf{S}\epsilon_1^\star, \sigma^m}(z_1^\star)}, 1)$

    The $Signer$ sends the value $(z_1^\star, \epsilon_1^\star, z_2^\star, \epsilon_2^\star)$ to the $User$ with probability $min(\frac{D_{\sigma^m}(z_1^\star)}{MD_{\mathbf{S}\epsilon_1^\star, \sigma^m}(z_1^\star)}, 1)$. If nothing is sent, Restart.
  - $Unblinding$: On receiving $(z_1^\star, \epsilon_1^\star, z_2^\star, \epsilon_2^\star)$, $User$ unblinds it as follows
    - (i) $z_1 \leftarrow z_1^\star + \alpha_1$,
    - (ii) $z_2 \leftarrow z_2^\star + \alpha_2$,
    - (iii) $\epsilon_1 \leftarrow \epsilon_1^\star + \beta_1$,
    - (iv) $\epsilon_2 \leftarrow \epsilon_2^\star + \beta_2$

If $\|z_1\|, \|z_2\| \le 4\sigma\sqrt{m}$ and $\|\epsilon_1\|_1, \|\epsilon_2\|_1 \le b-2$ and

$$(\epsilon_1 + \epsilon_2) \mod 3 = H(\mathbf{A}z_1 - \mathbf{T}\epsilon_1, \mathbf{A}z_2 - H'(info)\epsilon_2, H'(info), msg) \quad (1)$$

then *User* returns the signature $sign = (z_1, z_2, \epsilon_1, \epsilon_2)$ for message msg and shared information $info$. Else, *User* stores it and later use it on a exception process of *Signer*. The following figure shows all interaction during the signature generation protocol.

Signer		Verifier
		$\beta_1, \beta_2 \leftarrow \{-b+1, \ldots, 0, \ldots b-1\}$
$y \leftarrow D_\sigma^m$		$\alpha_1, \alpha_2 \leftarrow D_\sigma^m$
$(\epsilon_2^\star, z_2^\star) \in \{-1, 0, 1\}^k \times D_\sigma^m$	(c_1, c_2)	$c_1' \leftarrow c_1 + \mathbf{A}\alpha_1 - \mathbf{T}\beta_1 \mod q$
$c_1 \leftarrow \mathbf{A}y \mod q$	$\longrightarrow$	$c_2' \leftarrow c_2 + \mathbf{A}\alpha_2 - H'(info)\beta_2 \mod q$
$c_2 \leftarrow \mathbf{A}z_2^\star - H'(info)\epsilon_2^\star \mod q$		$\epsilon \leftarrow H(c_1, c_2, H'(info), msg)$
		$\epsilon^\star \leftarrow (\epsilon - \beta_1 - \beta_2) \mod 3$
$\epsilon_1^\star \leftarrow (\epsilon^\star - \epsilon_2^\star) \mod 3$		
$z_1^\star \leftarrow \mathbf{S}\epsilon_1^\star + y$	$\epsilon^\star$	
with probability $min(\frac{D_\sigma^m(z_1^\star)}{MD_{\mathbf{S}\epsilon_1^\star, \sigma}^m(z_1^\star)}, 1)$	$\longleftarrow$	
	$(z_1^\star, \epsilon_1^\star, z_2^\star, \epsilon_2^\star)$	$z_1 \leftarrow z_1^\star + \alpha_1$
	$\longrightarrow$	$z_2 \leftarrow z_2^\star + \alpha_2$
		$\epsilon_1 \leftarrow \epsilon_1^\star + \beta_1$
		$\epsilon_2 \leftarrow \epsilon_2^\star + \beta_2$

- *Exception*: This protocol is independently set by the *Signer*. This maintains a local storage for unqualified signature and takes $(params, \mathbf{T}, (msg, info, sign))$ as input. If any message signature pair is not in local storage and if $\|z_1\|, \|z_2\| \le 4\sigma\sqrt{m}$ and $b-1 \le \|\epsilon_1\|, \|\epsilon_2\| \le b$ and (1) holds, the exception protocol starts the *SignGen* for a new signature with same shared information and stores the pair in local storage. Else the protocol stops.
- *Verify*: The algorithm takes $(params, \mathbf{T}, msg, info, sign)$ and checks the validity of signature in the same manner as the *User* does in the *Unbinding* protocol. This return 1 if it is a valid signature else return 0.

3.1 Attack on Traceability Property of Above Scheme

This section introduces an attack on the above partial blind signature that shows that the signature doesn't satisfy the **untraceability** property. If any adversarial signer, keeps a local storage for all the blinded messages that he has signed as requested by the *User*. The *Signer* then can link a valid signature $(z_1, z_2, \epsilon_1, \epsilon_2)$ to its signing protocol. The attack works as follows

- Signer keeps the record of his views i.e $c_1, c_2, \epsilon^\star, z_1^\star, z_2^\star, \epsilon_1^\star, \epsilon_2^\star$ for all the blinded messages he has signed.
- For a signature $(z_1, z_2, \epsilon_1, \epsilon_2)$ opened to public, the *Signer* can try his records he keeps to trace back to the signing procedure that generated this signature.
- Since, $z_1 = z_1^\star + \alpha_1$ and $z_2 = z_2^\star + \alpha_2$, thus the *Signer* can find,

$$\alpha_1' = z_1 - z_1^\star \text{ and}$$
$$\alpha_2' = z_2 - z_2^\star$$

- Similarly, since $\epsilon_1 = \epsilon_1^\star + \beta_1$ and $\epsilon_2 = \epsilon_2^\star + \beta_2$ then he can find

$$\beta_1' = \epsilon_1 - \epsilon_1^\star \text{ and}$$
$$\beta_2' = \epsilon_2 - \epsilon_2^\star$$

as $\epsilon_1, \epsilon_2 \in \{-b+2, \ldots 0, \ldots b-2\}^k$ and $\epsilon_1^\star, \epsilon_2^\star \in \{-1, 0, 1\}^k$ then clearly $\beta_1', \beta_2' \in \{-b+1, \ldots, 0, \ldots, b-1\}^k$ as required.

– Now, adversarial *Signer* can use these α_1', α_2', β_1' and β_2' to compute

$$c_1'' = c_1 + \mathbf{A}\alpha_1' + \mathbf{T}\beta_1' \mod q$$
$$c_2'' = c_2 + \mathbf{A}\alpha_2' - H'(info)\beta_2' \mod q$$
$$\epsilon' = H(c_1'', c_2'', H'(info), msg)$$

– Now, the *Signer* can compare this ϵ' with ϵ^* stored in the local storage. For which it is matched, it corresponds to the blinded message for the signature is generated.

Thus, any adversarial signer can easily attack the untraceability property in a limited number of trials of the signature, making it vulnerable whenever the signature is revealed in public.

4   Ruckert's Blind Signature Scheme and Attack on Its Traceability

Markus Ruckert [13] proposed the first blind signature over lattices, which is conjectured to be quantum safe. This section discusses the signature scheme and the proposed attack on the untracebility property.

The signature schemes consisting of a three tuple $(B.KeyGen, B.Sign, B.Verify)$ which works as follows:

– $B.KeyGen(1^n)$: Choose a secret key $\hat{s} \leftarrow D_s^m$, and $h \leftarrow \mathcal{H}(\mathbf{R}, M)$ a compression function. Let $\mathcal{C}(1^n) : \{0,1\}^* \times \{0,1\}^n \longrightarrow \{0,1\}^n$ be a commitment scheme. Chooses a function $com \leftarrow \mathcal{C}(1^n)$ and $H \leftarrow \mathcal{H}(1^n)$ which maps $\{0,1\}^* \leftarrow D_\epsilon \subset D$. Then, output the public key $\mathbf{S} \leftarrow h(\hat{s})$.
– $B.Sign$: To generate a signature on a message $M \in \{0,1\}^*$ this algorithm proceeds as follows:

Signer		Verifier
		$r \leftarrow \{0,1\}^n$
		$C \leftarrow com(M, r)$
$y \leftarrow D_y^m$	$\xrightarrow{\quad \mathbf{Y} \quad}$	$\alpha \leftarrow D_\alpha,\ \beta \leftarrow D_\beta$
$\mathbf{Y} \leftarrow h(\hat{y})$		$\epsilon \leftarrow H(\mathbf{Y} - \mathbf{S}\alpha - h(\beta), C)$
		$\epsilon^* \leftarrow \epsilon - \alpha$
		If $\epsilon^* \notin D_{\epsilon^*}$
		Restart with new α
$\hat{z}^* \leftarrow \hat{s}\epsilon^* + \mathbf{Y}$		
If $\hat{z}^* \notin G_*^m$	$\xleftarrow{\quad \epsilon^* \quad}$	
Trigger Restart		
		$\hat{z} = \hat{z}^* - \beta$
		If $\hat{z} \notin G^m$
	$\xrightarrow{\quad \hat{z}^* \quad}$	(Required Signature Space)
		Output $\leftarrow (C, \alpha, \beta, \epsilon)$
		Else
		Output $\leftarrow$ OK

If Output $\neq$ OK, then signer parse Output $= (C, \alpha, \beta, \epsilon)$ and verify $\epsilon^* + \alpha = \epsilon = H(\mathbf{Y} - \mathbf{S}\alpha - h(\beta), C)$ and $H(h(\hat{z}^* - \beta) - \mathbf{S}\epsilon, C) = \epsilon, \hat{z}^* - \beta \notin G^m$. If it holds then, signer "Trigger Restart".

Finally, verifier output $(M, r, \hat{z}, \epsilon)$ or $\perp$ if Output $\neq$ OK. Thus, the algorithm outputs the signature $(r, \hat{z}^*, \epsilon)$ on the given message M. Here, we should note that when restart is encountered then we only choose new α and when trigger restart is encountered then we execute with new r to make the new execution independent of the previous one. But, there is an exception at last, when the verifier again trigger restart then signer can stop the algorithm as the verifier despite having the valid signature call for a restart.

- $B.Verify$: This algorithm returns 1 if $\hat{z} \in G^m$ and $H(h(\hat{z}) - \mathbf{S}\epsilon, Com(M, r)) = \epsilon$, else return 0.

4.1   Attack on Traceability

Similar to the above attack, we attack the traceability of Ruckert's signature. The attack works as follows,

- Signer keeps the record of his views i.e $\epsilon^*, \hat{z}^*$ for all the blinded messages he has signed.
- For a signature $(M, r, \hat{z}, \epsilon)$ opened to public, the $Signer$ can try his records he keeps to trace back to the signing procedure that generated this signature.
- Since, $\hat{z} = \hat{z}^* - \beta$, thus the $Signer$ can find,

$$\beta' = \hat{z} - \hat{z}^*$$

- Similarly, since $\epsilon^* = \epsilon - \alpha$ then he can find

$$\alpha' = \epsilon^* - \epsilon$$

- Now, adversarial $Signer$ can use these α', β' to compute

$$\epsilon' = H(\mathbf{Y} - \mathbf{S}\alpha' - h(\beta'), C), \text{ where he can compute } C \leftarrow com(M, r).$$

- Now, the $Signer$ can compare this ϵ' with ϵ^* stored in the local storage. For which it is matched, it corresponds to the blinded message for the signature is generated.

Thus, any adversarial signer can easily attack the untraceability property in a limited number of trials of the signature, making it vulnerable whenever the signature is revealed in public.

5   Conclusion

The paper successfully prove that existing blind and partial blind signature schemes don't satisfy the untraceability property of a secure blind signature. We suggest to propose an Untraceable quantum safe blind signature scheme as future research direction of the paper.

References

1. Ajtai, M.: Generating hard instances of lattice problems (extended abstract). In: Proceedings of STOC 1996, pp. 99–108. ACM, New York (1996)
2. Ajtai, M.: Generating hard instances of the short basis problem. Proc. ICALP **1999**, 1–9 (1999)
3. Ajtai, M., Kumar, R., Sivakumar, D.: A sieve algorithm for the shortest lattice vector problem. In: STOC 2001, pp. 601–610. ACM, New York (2001)
4. Abe, M., Okamoto, T.: Provably secure partially blind signatures. In: Bellare, M. (ed.) CRYPTO 2000. LNCS, vol. 1880, pp. 271–286. Springer, Heidelberg (2000). https://doi.org/10.1007/3-540-44598-6_17
5. Abe, M., Fujisaki, E.: How to date blind signatures. In: Kim, K., Matsumoto, T. (eds.) ASIACRYPT 1996. LNCS, vol. 1163, pp. 244–251. Springer, Heidelberg (1996). https://doi.org/10.1007/BFb0034851
6. Chaum, D.: Blind signatures for untraceable payments. In: Chaum, D., Rivest, R., Sherman, A. (eds.) Proceedings of Advances in Cryptology, Crypto 1982. LNCS, pp. 199–203. Springer, New York (1982). https://doi.org/10.1007/978-3-540-72540-4_33
7. Camenisch, J., Neven, G., Shelat, A.: Simulatable adaptive oblivious transfer. In: Naor, M. (ed.) EUROCRYPT 2007. LNCS, vol. 4515, pp. 573–590. Springer, Heidelberg (2007). https://doi.org/10.1007/978-3-540-72540-4_33
8. Fiat, A., Shamir, A.: How to prove yourself: practical solutions to identification and signature problems. In: Odlyzko, A.M. (ed.) CRYPTO 1986. LNCS, vol. 263, pp. 186–194. Springer, Heidelberg (1987). https://doi.org/10.1007/3-540-47721-7_12
9. Lyubashevsky, V.: Lattice-based identification schemes secure under active attacks. In: Cramer, R. (ed.) PKC 2008. LNCS, vol. 4939, pp. 162–179. Springer, Heidelberg (2008). https://doi.org/10.1007/978-3-540-78440-1_10
10. Lyubashevsky, V.: Lattice signatures without trapdoors. In: Pointcheval, D., Johansson, T. (eds.) EUROCRYPT 2012. LNCS, vol. 7237, pp. 738–755. Springer, Heidelberg (2012). https://doi.org/10.1007/978-3-642-29011-4_43
11. Hwang, M.-S., Lee, C.-C., Lai, Y.-C.: An untraceable blind signature scheme based on the RSA cryptosystem. Technical report CYUT-IM-TR-2001-012, CYUT, September 2001
12. Rodrguez-Henrquez, F., Ortiz-Arroyo, D., Garca-Zamora, C.: Yet another improvement over the Mu–Varadharajan e-voting protocol. Comput. Stand. Interfaces **29**(4), 471–480 (2007)
13. Rückert, M.: Lattice-based blind signatures. In: Abe, M. (ed.) ASIACRYPT 2010. LNCS, vol. 6477, pp. 413–430. Springer, Heidelberg (2010). https://doi.org/10.1007/978-3-642-17373-8_24
14. Tian, H., Zhang, F., Wei, B.: A lattice based partially blind signature. Secur. Priv. **9**(12), 1820–1828 (2016)
15. Hwang, M.-S., Lee, C.-C., Lai, Y.-C.: Traceability on low-computation partially blind signatures for electronic cash. IEICE Trans. Fundam. Electron. Commun. Comput. Sci. **E85-A**, 1181–1182 (2002)
16. Hwang, M.-S., Lee, C.-C., Lai, Y.-C.: Traceability on RSA-based partially signature with low computation. Appl. Math. Comput. **145**, 465–468 (2002)
17. Hwang, M.-S., Lee, C.-C., Lai, Y.-C.: Traceability of Fan-Chen-Yeh blind signature scheme. Technical report CYUT-IM-TR-2001-009, CYUT, August 2001
18. Zuhua, S.: Improved user efficient blind signatures. Electron. Lett. **36**(16), 1372–1374 (2000)

Cryptanalysis

Improved Integral Attack on Generalized Feistel Cipher

Zhichao Xu[1], Hong Xu[1,2(✉)], and Xuejia Lai[2]

[1] Information Engineering University, Zhengzhou, China
xuzhichao4484@163.com, xuhong0504@163.com
[2] Shanghai Jiao Tong University, Shanghai, China
lai-xj@cs.sjtu.edu.cn

Abstract. Division property is a generalized integral property proposed by Todo in Eurocrypt 2015. Utilizing automated tools such as SAT and MILP, the complexity to search for integral distinguisher by division property was greatly reduced. Based on division property and automated tools, Derbez *et al.* obtained a 10-round integral distinguisher of RECTANGLE by considering the linear transformation of the input and output state bits of the cipher, which is one round longer than known integral distinguishers. In this paper, we further consider improved integral attack on block ciphers with Generalized Feistel Structure (GFS cipher) by considering the linear transformation of the S-boxes. Taking the 16-branch GFS cipher with 4-bit S-boxes as an example, using this improved method, we can increase the round of integral distinguishers by one round for many S-boxes. The result implies that ability to resist this improved integral attack should also be considered when designing corresponding GFS ciphers.

Keywords: Division property · SAT · Integral distinguisher ·
Generalized Feistel Structure

1 Introduction

Integral attack is one of the most important and efficient attacks on block ciphers, and the key point of an integral attack is to find long enough integral distinguishers. Division property is a new generalized integral property proposed by Todo [1] and the propagation rules of division property can be evaluated for basic operations such as Copy, XOR and S-box. With this method, new integral distinguishers have been found and improved integral attack have been presented on many block ciphers such as MISTY1, LBlock and TWINE [2,3]. In FSE 2016, Todo and Morii further introduced bit-based division property and successfully found the 14-round integral distinguisher of SIMON32 [4]. In CRYPTO 2016, Boura and Christina [5] introduced the concept of parity set to study division property. They utilized the parity set to exploit detailed properties of the S-box and linear layer of PRESENT, leading to improved integral distinguishers of PRESENT.

© Springer Nature Switzerland AG 2020
Z. Liu and M. Yung (Eds.): Inscrypt 2019, LNCS 12020, pp. 463–479, 2020.
https://doi.org/10.1007/978-3-030-42921-8_28

At ASIACRYPT 2016, Xiang *et al.* [6] characterized the propagation of bit-based division property of S-boxes and other basic operations by some inequalities, and constructed corresponding MILP model for automatic search of integral distinguishers. With MILP solver Gurobi, Xiang *et al.* found better integral distinguishers for several block ciphers including SIMON128, PRESENT and RECTANGLE. At ASIACRYPT 2017, Sun *et al.* [7] characterized the propagation of division property by some Boolean logical equations, and constructed corresponding SAT model for bit-based division property and SMT model for word-based division property. With some SAT and SMT solver, they found better integral distinguishers of block ciphers including SHACAL-2 and CLEFIA. Later in SAC 2018, Eskandari *et al.* [8] further provided a generalized search model for integral distinguisher of different kinds of block ciphers with SAT solver, and found many new or improved integral distinguishers including GIFT-128, LBlock and SM4, where detailed bit-based division property of S-boxes is considered as in MILP model.

Based on the division property and automated tools, longer integral distinguishers may be found for some block ciphers by considering the linear transformation of the input or output states of the block cipher. In this way, Derbez *et al.* [9] have presented an improved 10-round integral distinguisher of RECTANGLE with MILP model. Inspired by their work, we will further present improved method to search for integral distinguishers of block ciphers with Generalized Feistel Structure (GFS cipher) using SAT solver.

The Generalized Feistel Structure [10] is one of the basic structures of a block cipher. While basic Feistel ciphers divide a message into two sub-blocks, GFS cipher divides a message into m subblocks (branches) for some $m > 2$. Many block ciphers adopt generalized Feistel structure, such as CAST-256, CLEFIA, LBlock and TWINE. In 2010, Suzaki *et al.* [11] studied the diffusion property and security of GFS, and presented some optimal permutation layers of GFS when the number of branches is less than or equal to 16. For example, LBlock and TWINE are two 16-branch lightweight GFS ciphers with optimal permutation layers.

Our Contribution. In this paper, by considering the linear transformation of the S-boxes, we present an improved method to search for integral distinguishers of block ciphers with Generalized Feistel Structure (GFS cipher) using bit-based division property and SAT solver. Some examples are also provided for 16-branch GFS cipher with 4-bit S-boxes and optimal permutation layers as shown in [11]. The concrete results are summarized as follows:

– Let $\mathcal{F}$ be a GFS cipher, and $\mathcal{F}_L$ be a new GFS cipher obtained by substituting the S-box S with $S_L = L \circ S \circ L^{-1}$ for any invertible linear transformation L. It is shown that every integral distinguisher of $\mathcal{F}_L$, obtained by bit-based division property, corresponds to an integral distinguisher of $\mathcal{F}$. Using this method we may find some new integral distinguishers that can not be obtained by traditional bit-based division property. Particularly, when L is an identity transformation, $\mathcal{F}_L = \mathcal{F}$, so integral distinguishers which are obtained by traditional bit-based division property can also be obtained by our method.

– For 16-branch GFS cipher with 4-bit S-boxes and optimal permutation layers as shown in [11], a series of 64-bit GFS ciphers are constructed with different 4-bit S-boxes. The integral distinguishers of the constructed GFS cipher are searched for by traditional bit-based division property and improved method proposed in this paper respectively. The results shows that if the S-boxes of Serpent0, Serpent1, Serpent2, and Serpent17 [13] are used, for most of the constructed GFS ciphers, our method can find longer integral distinguishers than utilizing traditional bit-based division property.

Organization of the Paper. The rest of this paper is organized as follows: In Sect. 2, some notations, review of Generalized Feistel Structure, division property, and the corresponding SAT model are presented for searching of integral distinguishers with bit-based division property. In Sect. 3, our improved method is proposed to search for integral distinguishers of GFS ciphers. In Sect. 4, some examples of 16-branch GFS ciphers with 4-bit S-boxes are presented for which we can find longer integral distinguishers with our improved method. A short conclusion is presented in Sect. 5.

2 Preliminaries

2.1 Notations

Let $\mathbb{F}_2$ denote the finite field with only two elements and $\mathbb{F}_2^n$ denote the set of all n-bit string over $\mathbb{F}_2$. Let $\mathbb{Z}$ denote the integer ring, and $\mathbb{Z}^n$ denote the set of all vectors of length n whose coordinates are integers. For any $a \in \mathbb{F}_2^n$, let $a[i]$ denote the i-th bit of a, and the Hamming weight of a is calculated by $w(a) = \Sigma_{i=0}^{n-1} a[i]$. For any $\boldsymbol{a} = (a_0, a_1, ..., a_{m-1}) \in \mathbb{F}_2^{\ell_0} \times \mathbb{F}_2^{\ell_1} \times \cdots \times \mathbb{F}_2^{\ell_{m-1}}$, the vectorial Hamming weight of $\boldsymbol{a}$ is defined as $W(\boldsymbol{a}) = (w(a_0), w(a_1), ..., w(a_{m-1}))$ where $w(a_i)$ is the Hamming weight of a_i. Let $k = (k_0, k_1, ..., k_{m-1})$ and $k' = (k'_0, k'_1, ..., k'_{m-1})$ be two vectors in $\mathbb{Z}^m$. Define $k' \succeq k$ if $k'[i] \geq k[i]$ holds for all $i = 0, 1, ..., m - 1$, otherwise, $k' \not\succeq k$.

2.2 Generalized Feistel Structure (GFS)

Let m be an even integer. The Generalized Feistel structure with m branches is shown in Fig. 1. The round function R is a permutation over $(\mathbb{F}_2^n)^m$ defined as

$$R : (x_0, x_1, ..., x_{m-1}) \rightarrow (y_0, y_1, ..., y_{m-1}),$$

where $(y_0, y_1, ..., y_{m-1}) = \pi(x_0, F_0(x_0) \oplus x_1, ..., x_{m-2}, F_{(m-2)/2}(x_{m-2}) \oplus x_{m-1})$, $F_i : \mathbb{F}_2^n \rightarrow \mathbb{F}_2^n$ is a cryptographic keyed function which is called F-function, and $\pi : (\mathbb{F}_2^n)^m \rightarrow (\mathbb{F}_2^n)^m$ is a deterministic permutation. Here, we restrict π to be a block-wise permutation, i.e., a shuffle of m sub-blocks. An encryption transformation of a r-round GFS cipher is done by iterating the above round function for r rounds, where the input of the first round is the plaintext and the

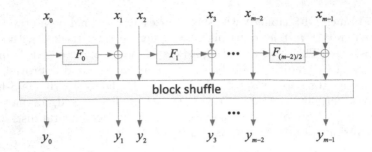

Fig. 1. The round function of the GFS with m branches

output of the r-round is the ciphertext. The permutation π in the last round is omitted to ensure the consistency of encryption and decryption.

Throughout the paper, when referring to the GFS cipher, m denotes the number of sub-blocks and n denotes the bit length of the sub-block. Thus a GFS cipher is always a mn-bit block cipher. For simplicity, we only consider the case when F-function is the composition of S-box function and key-XOR function, i.e., $F_i(x_i) = S(x_i \oplus k_{i/2})$ for $i = 0, 2, 4, ..., m-2$.

Table 1. Permutations of Type-II GFS and other GFS with best diffusion

Permutation	π
Type-II	[15,0,1,2,3,4,5,6,7,8,9,10,11,12,13,14]
No. 1	[1,2,9,4,15,6,5,8,13,10,7,14,11,12,3,0]
No. 2	[1,2,11,4,9,6,7,8,15,12,5,10,3,0,13,14]
No. 3	[1,2,11,4,9,6,15,8,5,12,7,10,3,0,13,14]
No. 4	[5,2,9,4,1,6,11,8,15,12,3,10,7,0,13,14]
No. 5	[5,2,9,4,11,6,15,8,3,12,1,10,7,0,13,14]
No. 6	[5,2,11,4,1,6,15,8,3,12,13,10,7,0,9,14]
No. 7	[1,2,11,4,3,6,7,8,15,12,5,14,9,0,13,10]
No. 8	[1,2,11,4,9,6,7,8,15,12,13,14,3,0,5,10]
No. 9	[1,2,11,4,9,6,15,8,5,12,7,14,3,0,13,10]
No. 10	[7,2,13,4,11,8,3,6,15,0,9,10,1,14,5,12]
No. 11	[7,2,13,4,11,8,9,6,15,0,3,10,5,14,1,12]
No. 12	[1,2,11,4,15,8,3,6,7,0,9,12,5,14,13,10]
No. 13	[5,2,11,6,13,8,15,0,3,4,9,12,1,14,7,10]

In [11], Suzaki *et al.* proposed some optimal permutation layers with best diffusion property against differential attacks. The instances found with 16 branches are shown in Table 1, where π indicates that the i-th sub-block is mapped to the $\pi[i]$-th sub-block. Take the second row for example, $\pi[0] = 15$ means that the

0-th sub-block is mapped to the 15-th sub-block. In this paper, we will further evaluate their ability against our improved integral attacks.

2.3 Review of Division Property

The division property proposed by Todo [1] in Eurocrypt 2015 is a generalized integral property, which can characterize the implicit properties between traditional ALL and BALANCE properties. We can first choose a set of plaintexts, whose division property follows initial division property. Then obtain the division property of the set for the $(i + 1)$-th round from the i-th round by the propagation rules, and determine the existence of integral distinguishers according to final division property.

In the following, we briefly review definition of division property, and propagation rules for some basic operations involved in GFS ciphers.

Definition 1 (Bit Product Function) [1]. *Assume $u \in \mathbb{F}_2^n$ and $x \in \mathbb{F}_2^n$. The Bit Product Function π_u is defined as:*

$$\pi_u(x) = \prod_{i=0}^{n-1} x[i]^{u[i]}.$$

For $u = (u_0, u_1, ..., u_{m-1}) \in \mathbb{F}_2^{\ell_0} \times \mathbb{F}_2^{\ell_1} \times \cdots \times \mathbb{F}_2^{\ell_{m-1}}$, let $x = (x_0, x_1, ..., x_{m-1}) \in \mathbb{F}_2^{\ell_0} \times \mathbb{F}_2^{\ell_1} \times \cdots \times \mathbb{F}_2^{\ell_{m-1}}$ be the input, the Bit Product Function π_u is defined as:

$$\pi_u(x) = \prod_{i=0}^{m-1} \pi_{u_i}(x_i).$$

Definition 2 (Division Property) [1]. *Let $\mathbb{X}$ be a multi-set whose elements take values from $\mathbb{F}_2^{\ell_0} \times \mathbb{F}_2^{\ell_1} \times \cdots \times \mathbb{F}_2^{\ell_{m-1}}$. When the multi-set $\mathbb{X}$ has the division property $\mathcal{D}_{\mathbb{K}}^{\ell_0, \ell_1, ..., \ell_{m-1}}$, where $\mathbb{K}$ denotes a set of m-dimensional vectors whose i-th element takes a value between 0 and ℓ_i, if fulfills the following conditions:*

$$\bigoplus_{x \in \mathbb{X}} \pi_u(x) = \begin{cases} unknown, & if \ there \ is \ k \in \mathbb{K} \ s.t. \ W(u) \succeq k, \\ 0, & otherwise. \end{cases}$$

Remark 1. Note that $\ell_0, \ell_1, ..., \ell_{m-1}$ are restricted to 1 when we consider **bit-based division property**. In this case, the division property of $\mathbb{X}$ is also denoted by $\mathcal{D}_{\mathbb{K}}^{1^m}$.

Propagation Rules for Division Property

Rule 1 (Key XOR) [1,5]. *Let f be a key XOR function, where the input x and the key k take values from $\mathbb{F}_2^n$, the output y is calculated as $y = x \oplus k$. Let $\mathbb{X}$ and $\mathbb{Y}$ be the input multi-set and output multi-set, respectively. Assuming that $\mathbb{X}$ has division property $\mathcal{D}_{\mathbb{K}}^{\ell_0, \ell_1, ..., \ell_{m-1}}$, then $\mathbb{Y}$ also has division property $\mathcal{D}_{\mathbb{K}}^{\ell_0, \ell_1, ..., \ell_{m-1}}$.*

Remark 2. Key XOR function can be neglected when considering the propagation of bit-based division property.

Rule 2 (Copy) [1,4]. *Let f be a copy function, where the input x takes value from $\mathbb{F}_2^n$ and the output is calculated as $(y_0, y_1) = (x, x)$. Let $\mathbb{X}$ and $\mathbb{Y}$ be the input and output multi-set, respectively. Assume that $\mathbb{X}$ has division property $\mathcal{D}_{\{k\}}^n$, then the division property of $\mathbb{Y}$ is $\mathcal{D}_{\mathbb{K}'}^{n,n}$, where*

$$\mathbb{K}' = \{(k - i, i) | 0 \leq i \leq k\}.$$

Rule 3 (XOR) [1,4]. *Let f be a XOR function, where the input (x_0, x_1) takes value from $\mathbb{F}_2^n \times \mathbb{F}_2^n$ and the output is calculated as $y = x_0 \oplus x_1$. Let $\mathbb{X}$ and $\mathbb{Y}$ be the input and output multi-set, respectively. Assume that $\mathbb{X}$ has division property $\mathcal{D}_{\mathbb{K}}^{n,n}$, the division property of $\mathbb{Y}$ is $\mathcal{D}_{\{k'\}}^n$, where*

$$k' = \min\{k_0 + k_1 | (k_0, k_1) \in \mathbb{K}\}.$$

For the propagation of division property for S-boxes, we use the bit-based division property as shown in [6].

Rule 4 (S-box) [6]. *Let f be a n-bit S-box function, where $x = (x_0, x_1, ..., x_{n-1})$ and $y = (y_0, y_1, ..., y_{n-1})$ be the input and the output, respectively, and y_i is expressed as a boolean function of $(x_0, x_1, ..., x_{n-1})$. The propagation of division property for S-box can be calculated as in Algorithm 1.*

Algorithm 1. Calculating division trails of an S-box

Input : The input division property of an n-bit S-box $\mathcal{D}_k^{1^n}$ where
$k = (k_0, k_1, ..., k_{n-1}) \in \mathbb{F}_2^n$

Output: A set $\mathbb{K}$ of vectors such that the output multi-set has division
property $\mathcal{D}_{\mathbb{K}}^{1^n}$

1 $\bar{\mathbb{S}} = \{\bar{k} | \bar{k} \succeq k\}$;
2 $F(X) = \{\pi_{\bar{k}}(x) | \bar{k} \in \bar{\mathbb{S}}\}$;
3 $\bar{\mathbb{K}} = \emptyset$;
4 **for** $u \in (\mathbb{F}_2)^n$ **do**
5 | **if** $\pi_u(y)$ *contains any monomial in* $F(X)$ **then**
6 | | $\bar{\mathbb{K}} = \bar{\mathbb{K}} \bigcup \{u\}$;
7 | **end**
8 **end**
9 $\mathbb{K} = SizeReduce(\bar{\mathbb{K}})$;
10 return $\mathbb{K}$;

Remark 3. If $k' \succeq k$, then k' is redundant and can be removed from $\mathbb{K}$. The formula $\mathbb{K} = SizeReduce(\bar{\mathbb{K}})$ in Algorithm 1 means removing all redundant vectors in $\mathbb{K}$.

Definition 3 (Division Trail). *Let f be the round function of block cipher. Assume that the input multi-set has division property $\mathcal{D}_{\{k\}}^{\ell_0,\ell_1,\ldots,\ell_{m-1}}$, and the internal state after i rounds has division property $\mathcal{D}_{\mathbb{K}_i}^{\ell_0,\ell_1,\ldots,\ell_{m-1}}$. Thus we have the following chain of division propagations:*

$$\{k\} \triangleq \mathbb{K}_0 \xrightarrow{f} \mathbb{K}_1 \xrightarrow{f} \mathbb{K}_2 \xrightarrow{f} \cdots \xrightarrow{f} \mathbb{K}_r$$

Moreover, for any vector $k_i^* \in \mathbb{K}_i (0 \leq i \leq r)$, there must exist a vector $k_{i-1}^* \in \mathbb{K}_{i-1}$ such that k_{i-1}^* can propagate to k_i^* by propagation rules.

Proposition 1 (Integral Property) [1,6]. *Assume that multi-set $\mathbb{X}$ has the bit-based division property $\mathcal{D}_{\mathbb{K}}^{1^n}$. If there is a unit vector $e_i \notin \mathbb{K}$, then the i-th bit of multi-set $\mathbb{X}$ is balanced.*

2.4   SAT Model for Searching of Integral Distinguishers

In computer science, the Boolean Satisfiability Problem (SAT) [12] is the problem of determining if there exists an interpretation that satisfies a given Boolean formula. In other words, it discusses whether the variables involved in a given Boolean formula can be consistently replaced by the value True or False so that the formula is evaluated to be True. If this is the case, the formula is called **satisfiable**.

By modeling the propagation of bit-based division property by certain Boolean logical equations, the searching for integral distinguishers can be transformed into the problem of solving the SAT model. By calling the CryptoMiniSat[1] solver, the corresponding integral distinguishers can be found.

Model 1 (Bit-based Copy) [7]. *Let $(a) \xrightarrow{Copy} (b_0, b_1)$ be a division trail of Copy function, then the following logical equations are sufficient to depict the propagation of bit-based division property of Copy function:*

$$\begin{cases} \overline{b_0} \vee \overline{b_1} = 1 \\ a \vee b_0 \vee \overline{b_1} = 1 \\ a \vee \overline{b_0} \vee b_1 = 1 \\ \overline{a} \vee b_0 \vee b_1 = 1 \end{cases}$$

Model 2 (Bit-based XOR) [7]. *Let $(a_0, a_1) \xrightarrow{XOR} (b)$ be a division trail of XOR function, then the following logical equations are sufficient to depict the propagation of bit-based division property of XOR function:*

$$\begin{cases} \overline{a_0} \vee \overline{a_1} = 1 \\ a_0 \vee a_1 \vee \overline{b} = 1 \\ a_0 \vee \overline{a_1} \vee b = 1 \\ \overline{a_0} \vee a_1 \vee b = 1 \end{cases}$$

---

[1] https://github.com/msoos/cryptominisat.

Similar as in [6] and [8], we can also characterize detailed bit-based division property of S-box with SAT model as follows:

Model 3 (S-box). *Let* $(a_0, a_1, ..., a_{n-1}) \xrightarrow{S-box} (b_0, b_1, ..., b_{n-1})$ *be a division trail of S-box function. Assume that multi-set* $\{(x_0^i, x_1^i, ..., x_{n-1}^i, y_0^i, y_1^i, ...\ y_{n-1}^i)|0 \leq i \leq t-1\}$ *consists of all the vectors that don't appear in the division trail. the following logical equations are sufficient to depict the propagation of bit-based division property of S-box function:*

$$
\begin{cases}
(a_0 \oplus x_0^0) \vee \cdots \vee (a_{n-1} \oplus x_{n-1}^0) \vee (b_0 \oplus y_0^0) \vee \cdots \vee (b_{n-1} \oplus y_{n-1}^0) = 1 \\
(a_0 \oplus x_0^1) \vee \cdots \vee (a_{n-1} \oplus x_{n-1}^1) \vee (b_0 \oplus y_0^1) \vee \cdots \vee (b_{n-1} \oplus y_{n-1}^1) = 1 \\
\qquad\qquad\qquad\qquad\qquad \vdots \\
(a_0 \oplus x_0^{t-1}) \vee \cdots \vee (a_{n-1} \oplus x_{n-1}^{t-1}) \vee (b_0 \oplus y_0^{t-1}) \vee \cdots \vee (b_{n-1} \oplus y_{n-1}^{t-1}) = 1
\end{cases}
$$

Let $a^0 = (a_0^0, a_1^0, ..., a_{mn-1}^0) \rightarrow \cdots \rightarrow a^r = (a_0^r, a_1^r, ..., a_{mn-1}^r)$ be an r-round division trail. When searching for integral distinguishers, we first construct a set of logical equations to characterize the division trail for the i-th round encryption

$$
a^{i-1} = (a_0^{i-1}, a_1^{i-1}, ..., a_{mn-1}^{i-1}) \rightarrow a^i = (a_0^i, a_1^i, ..., a_{mn-1}^i)
$$

by Model 1, Model 2 and Model 3, then iterated the equations for r times to characterize the division trail for r rounds. The concrete process to search for integral distinguishers is presented in Algorithm 2, and the initial division property and stopping rule are given as follows.

Initial Division Property and Stopping Rule. It is known that when the weight of initial division a^0 is higher, longer integral distinguishers may be obtained, so we need only to test the situation $a^0 = in_j$, where the j-th bit of in_j is 0, while the remaining bits are 1. By Proposition 1, the division property after r rounds can be set to unit vectors e_k, where the k-th bit of e_k is 1, while the remaining bits are 0. Then we call CryptoMiniSat solver to solve the SAT problem. If there exists some $j \in \{0, 1, ..., mn - 1\}$ such that for any $k \in \{0, 1, ..., mn - 1\}$, the SAT problem is satisfiable, then the output division property contains all unit vectors, and the corresponding multi-set, *i.e.*, the outputs of the r-th round, does not have any integral property, and the propagation should stop and an $(r - 1)$-round distinguisher is obtained. Otherwise, if there is at least one index k, such that the SAT problem is not satisfiable for the k-th unit vector e_k, then we can proceed to the $(r + 1)$-th round and evaluate the division property in a similar way.

3   Improved Method to Search for Integral Distinguishers of GFS Ciphers

In this section, we will propose an improved method to search for integral distinguishers based on division property with SAT solver.

3.1   New Form of Integral Distinguishers

Definition 4 (Linear equivalent GFS cipher). *Let $\mathcal{F}$ be a GFS cipher whose round function R is given as*

$$R : (x_0, x_1, ..., x_{k-1})$$
$$\rightarrow \pi(x_0, S(x_0 \oplus k_0) \oplus x_1, ..., x_{m-2}, S(x_{m-2} \oplus k_{(m-2)/2}) \oplus x_{m-1}) \quad (1)$$

Define a new GFS cipher $\mathcal{F}_L$ whose round function R_L is given as:

$$R_L : (x_0, x_1, ..., x_{k-1})$$
$$\rightarrow \pi(x_0, S'(x_0 \oplus k_0') \oplus x_1, ..., x_{m-2}, S'(x_{m-2} \oplus k_{(m-2)/2}') \oplus x_{m-1}) \quad (2)$$

where $S' = L \circ S \circ L^{-1}, k_j' = L(k_j)$, L is an invertible linear transformation over $\mathbb{F}_2^n$, and $\circ$ is the composition function. Then the new GFS cipher $\mathcal{F}_L$ is called the linear equivalent GFS cipher of $\mathcal{F}$ with respect to the linear transformation L.

There is a connection between R and R_L about the input and output by the definition of linear equivalent GFS cipher.

Lemma 1 (Relationship between Round Function). *Let L be an invertible linear transformation over $\mathbb{F}_2^n$, and $\mathcal{F}_L$ be the linear equivalent GFS cipher of $\mathcal{F}$ with respect to L. Denote by R and R_L the round function of $\mathcal{F}$ and $\mathcal{F}_L$, respectively. Assume that $x = (x_0, x_1, ..., x_{m-1})$ and $y = (y_0, y_1, ..., y_{m-1})$ are the input and output of round function R, respectively, where $x_i, y_i \in \mathbb{F}_2^n$. Let $x_L = (L(x_0), L(x_1), ..., L(x_{m-1}))$ be the input of round function R_L, then $y_L = (L(y_0), L(y_1), ..., L(y_{m-1}))$ is the output of round function R_L.*

Recursively, from Lemma 1 we can easily obtain the following conclusion.

Theorem 1 (Relationship between Ciphers). *Let L be a invertible linear transformation over $\mathbb{F}_2^n$, and $\mathcal{F}_L$ be the linear equivalent GFS cipher of $\mathcal{F}$ with respect to L. Assume that $x = (x_0, x_1, ..., x_{m-1})$ and $y = (y_0, y_1, ..., y_{m-1})$ are the input and the output of the GFS cipher $\mathcal{F}$ over r round respectively, where $x_i, y_i \in \mathbb{F}_2^n$. Let $x_L = (L(x_0), L(x_1), ..., L(x_{m-1}))$ be the input of the GFS cipher $\mathcal{F}_L$ over r rounds, then $y_L = (L(y_0), L(y_1), ..., L(y_{m-1}))$ is the output of the GFS cipher $\mathcal{F}_L$ over r rounds.*

Let L be an invertible linear transformation over $\mathbb{F}_2^n$. Then $\mathcal{F}$ is the linear equivalent GFS cipher of $\mathcal{F}_L$ with respect to L^{-1}. If there is an integral distinguisher of $\mathcal{F}_L$, where the plaintext and ciphertext set are denoted by $\mathbb{X}_L$ and $\mathbb{Y}_L$ respectively, and $\mathbb{Y}_L$ has balanced bits, then there is also an integral distinguisher of $\mathcal{F}$ too, whose plaintext set is

$$\mathbb{X} = \{(L^{-1}(x_0')), (L^{-1}(x_1')), ..., (L^{-1}(x_{m-1}')))|(x_0', x_1', ..., x_{m-1}') \in \mathbb{X}_L\},$$

and the ciphertext set is

$$\mathbb{Y} = \{(L^{-1}(y_0')), (L^{-1}(y_1')), ..., (L^{-1}(y_{m-1}')))|(y_0', y_1', ..., y_{m-1}') \in \mathbb{Y}_L\}.$$

Ciphertext set $\mathbb{Y}$ may not have balanced bit, but a linear transformation of $\mathbb{Y}$, i.e., $\mathbb{Y}_L$, has balanced bits.

In this paper, the F-function is of the form $F(x) = S(x \oplus k)$. From remark 2 we know that the integral distinguisher found with bit-based division property is independent of the key in that case. Thus we need only to consider the transformation of S-boxes when constructing $\mathcal{F}_L$, that is, we need only to replace the S-box S of $\mathcal{F}$ by $L \circ S \circ L^{-1}$, while making no change to the key.

If a r-round integral distinguisher of $\mathcal{F}_L$ is found by bit-based division property with plaintexts set $\mathbb{X}_L$, and the j-th bit of corresponding ciphertexts set $\mathbb{Y}_L$ is balanced, then we can get a r-round integral distinguisher of $\mathcal{F}$ with the plaintexts set

$$\mathbb{X} = \{(L^{-1}(x_0'), L^{-1}(x_1'), ..., L^{-1}(x_{m-1}')) | (x_0', x_1', ..., x_{m-1}') \in \mathbb{X}_L\}, \qquad (3)$$

and the corresponding ciphertexts set is denoted by $\mathbb{Y}$. Denote

$$\mathbb{Y}' = \{(L(y_0), L(y_1), ..., L(y_{m-1})) | (y_0, y_1, ..., y_{m-1}) \in \mathbb{Y}\}.$$

Then the j-th bit of $\mathbb{Y}'$ is balanced.

From above we know that even if we cannot find a r-round integral distinguisher for the GFS cipher $\mathcal{F}$ with traditional searching method based on bit-based division property, we may find some linear transformation L such that a r-round integral distinguisher can be found for the linear equivalent cipher $\mathcal{F}_L$ of $\mathcal{F}$. That is, even if there exists no balanced bits in the ciphertext set $\mathbb{Y}$ of r-round encryption of $\mathcal{F}$ for all kinds of plaintexts set choosed by traditional searching method, there still may exist some balanced bits when considering the linear transformation L of the ciphertexts set $\mathbb{Y}$ for certain plaintexts set $\mathbb{X}$ as shown in equation (3). Hence longer integral properties can be obtained with this improved method. In the following we will show how to find the linear transformation efficiently and present some examples such that the improved searching method works.

3.2   Algorithm Optimization

There are $\prod_{i=0}^{n-1}(2^n - 2^i)$ invertible linear transformations defined over $\mathbb{F}_2^n$. If we generate a new linear equivalent GFS cipher $\mathcal{F}_L$ for each invertible linear transformation L, and search for its integral distinguishers, there will be too many experiments to be done. Therefore, it is necessary to remove some redundant invertible linear transformation and pick out these useful linear transformations before searching for integral distinguishers.

Remove Redundant Invertible Linear Transformations. Permutation is a special kind of invertible linear transformations, which only change the position of bits. For a n-bit permutation P, it can be shown as follows that the round of the longest integral distinguishers that can be found with bit-based division property are the same for $\mathcal{F}_L$ and $\mathcal{F}_{P \circ L}$.

For a GFS cipher, only the function Copy, XOR and S-box are performed when the propagation of bit-based division property is considered. For the round function R of $\mathcal{F}$, if there is a division trail $k \xrightarrow{R} k'$, where $k = (k_0, k_1, ..., k_{m-1}) \in (\mathbb{F}_2^n)^m, k' = (k'_0, k'_1, ..., k'_{m-1}) \in (\mathbb{F}_2^n)^m$, then for the round function R_P of $\mathcal{F}_P$, there is also a division trail $k_P \xrightarrow{R_P} k'_P$, where $k_P = (P(k_0), P(k_1), ..., P(k_{m-1})), k'_P = (P(k'_0), P(k'_1), ..., P(k'_{m-1}))$. If a r-round integral distinguisher of cipher $\mathcal{F}$ is obtained by bit-based division property, then a r-round integral distinguisher of cipher $\mathcal{F}_P$ can also be obtained by bit-based division property.

Definition 5 (Permutation Equivalent). *Denote by Ω_n the set of all invertible linear transformations over $\mathbb{F}_2^n$, and Ψ_n the set of all permutations over $\mathbb{F}_2^n$. For any linear transformations $L \in \Omega_n$ and $P \in \Psi_n$, if $L' = P \circ L$, then L' is called **Permutation Equivalent** with L. Moreover, for any linear transformation $L \in \Omega_n$, the set $\Omega_n^L = \{P^* \circ L | P^* \in \Psi_n\}$ is called a **Permutation Equivalence class** of L.*

Let $\mathcal{F}$ be a GFS cipher, and $\mathcal{F}_L$ and $\mathcal{F}_{P \circ L}$ be the linear equivalent GFS cipher of $\mathcal{F}$ with respect to L and $P \circ L$, respectively. It is obvious that $\mathcal{F}_{P \circ L}$ is also the linear equivalent GFS cipher of $\mathcal{F}_L$ with respect to P. If a r-round integral distinguisher of cipher $\mathcal{F}_L$ is found by bit-based division property, then a r-round integral distinguisher of cipher $\mathcal{F}_{P \circ L}$ can also be found by bit-based division property, that is, the linear transformation L and $P \circ L$ have the same effect with our method. Thus we need only to consider all permutation inequivalent linear transformations.

Denote by Ω all permutation inequivalent linear transformations over $\mathbb{F}_2^n$, then $|\Omega| = \frac{|\Omega_n|}{|\Omega_n^L|}$. The number of all invertible linear transformations Ω_n over $\mathbb{F}_2^n$ is equal to the number of all $n \times n$ invertible matrices over $\mathbb{F}_2$, and the number of all permutation equivalent linear transformations of L is equal to the number of all n-bit permutations, so we have

$$|\Omega| = \frac{|\Omega_n|}{|\Omega_n^L|} = \frac{\prod_{i=0}^{n-1}(2^n - 2^i)}{n!}.$$

Particularly if $n = 4$, then $|\Omega_4| = 20160$, and $|\Omega| = 840$, which is far less than 20160.

From above discussion we need only to exhaust all permutation inequivalent linear transformations L when searching for integral distinguishers of $\mathcal{F}_L$. Once a r-round distinguisher of $\mathcal{F}_L$ is obtained, a r-round distinguisher of $\mathcal{F}$ can be obtained accordingly. The concrete improved method to search for integral distinguishers of a GFS cipher is presented in Algorithm 2.

Choose Better Invertible Linear Transformation. From above we know that even if the length of the S-box is 4, there are still 840 permutation inequivalent invertible linear transformations need to be tested. To further improve the efficiency of the search, we will make some filtering and select some fine linear transformations from Ω instead of traversing all linear transformations. The linear transformation L is selected according to whether the corresponding new S-box $S_L = L \circ S \circ L^{-1}$ achieves fine propagation of bit-based division property.

In [5], Boura et al. utilized the propagation of bit-based division property of S-box to increase the round of integral distinguisher of PRESENT, where the following two properties were utilized:

(1) For $k' \in \mathbb{F}_2^n$, denote $\mathbb{K} = \{k \in \mathbb{F}_2^4 | \text{there is a division trail } k \xrightarrow{S-box} k'\}$. Then when $k' = (0,0,0,1)$, $\mathbb{K}$ contains less elements and does not contain any element of weight 3.

(2) For $k \in \mathbb{F}_2^n$, denote $\mathbb{K}' = \{k' \in \mathbb{F}_2^4 | \text{there is a division trail } k \xrightarrow{S-box} k'\}$. Then when $k = (1,0,1,1)$, $\mathbb{K}'$ contains less elements and does not contain any element of weight 1. Similar conditions can be used to filter the linear transformations. For all division trails $k \xrightarrow{S_L} k'$ of S-box function, when k' is fixed, it is expected that the weight of k is as low as possible and such division trails $k \xrightarrow{S_L} k'$ are as few as possible. Similarly, when k is fixed, it is expected that the weight of k' is as high as possible and such division trails $k \xrightarrow{S_L} k'$ are as few as possible. In these cases, the bit-based division property is less likely to propagate to unit vectors over several rounds, and longer integral distinguishers are likely to be obtained.

However, there may not exist S-boxes such that the above conditions hold for all fixed k or k'. So we use weaker conditions instead. It is required that there exist some k' with $w(k') = 1$ such that for all division trails $k \xrightarrow{S_L} k'$, the weight of k is as low as possible and such division trails $k \xrightarrow{S_L} k'$ are as few as possible, or there exist some k with $w(k) = n - 1$ such that for all division trails $k \xrightarrow{S_L} k'$, the weight of k' is as high as possible and such division trails $k \xrightarrow{S_L} k'$ are as few as possible.

According to the above analysis, we can filter linear transformations from Ω as follows:

(1) For all invertible linear transformations L in Ω, construct a new S-box $S_L = L \circ S \circ L^{-1}$ and call Algorithm 1 to search for the division trail of S_L. For any fixed element k' of weight 1 in $\mathbb{F}_2^n$, denote

$$\mathbb{K}(S_L, k') = \{k | \text{there is a division trail } k \xrightarrow{S_L} k'\}.$$

For any invertible linear transformation L in Ω, save all linear transformations L satisfying that there exists some k' of weight 1 such that $\mathbb{K}(S_L, k')$ contains the least number of vectors of weight $n - 1$, and denote the remaining set by Ω_{n-1}^O. Then for any invertible linear transformation L in Ω_{n-1}^O, save all linear transformations L satisfying that there exists some k' of weight 1 such that $\mathbb{K}(S_L, k')$ contains the least number of vectors of weight $n - 2$, and denote the remaining set by Ω_{n-2}^O, $\cdots$, Continuously, denote

Algorithm 2. Improved algorithm to search for integral distinguishers of a GFS cipher

---

Input : A GFS cipher $\mathcal{F}$, length n of the S-box

Output: round r of the integral distinguisher, invertible linear transformation L over $\mathbb{F}_2^n$, initial bit-based division property $\mathcal{D}_{\{k\}}^{1^{mn}}$ and the set $Bset$ of balanced bits

---

1 $set0 = \{L|L$ is an invertible linear transformation over $\mathbb{F}_2^n\}$;
2 $\Psi = \{P|P$ is a permutation over $\mathbb{F}_2^n\}$;
3 $\Omega = \emptyset$;
4 $r = 0$;
6 **while** $set0 \neq \emptyset$ **do**
7 $\quad$ Select an invertible linear transformation L from $set0$, and generate a new set: $set1 = \{P \circ L|P \in \Psi\}$;
8 $\quad$ $set0 = set0 \setminus set1$;
9 $\quad$ $\Omega = \Omega \cup \{L\}$;
10 **end**
11 **for** $L \in \Omega$ **do**
12 $\quad$ Replace the S-box S in the GFS cipher $\mathcal{F}$ with $S_L = L \circ S \circ L^{-1}$, and obtain a new GFS cipher $\mathcal{F}_L$;
13 $\quad$ Construct SAT model of $\mathcal{F}_L$ by bit-based division property and search for the integral distinguishers, and obtain the longest round r_L of the integral distinguishers, an initial division property $\mathcal{D}_{\{k\}}^{1^{mn}}$ and corresponding balanced bits set $Bset$;
14 $\quad$ **if** $r_L > r$ **then**
15 $\quad\quad$ $r = r_L$;
16 $\quad\quad$ $Distinguisher = (r, L, k, Bset)$;
17 $\quad$ **end**
18 **end**
19 **Return** $Distinguisher$;

---

by Ω_1^O the set of all linear transformations L in Ω_2^O satisfying that there exists some k' of weight 1 such that $\mathbb{K}(S_L, k')$ contains the least number of vectors of weight 1.

(2) For all invertible linear transformations L in Ω, construct a new S-box $S_L = L \circ S \circ L^{-1}$ and call Algorithm 1 to search for the division trail of S_L. For any fixed element k of weight $n-1$ in $\mathbb{F}_2^n$, denote

$$\mathbb{K}'(S_L, k) = \{k'|\text{there is a division trail } k \xrightarrow{S_L} k'\}.$$

For any invertible linear transformation L in Ω, save all linear transformations L satisfying that there exists some k of weight $n-1$ in $\mathbb{F}_2^n$ such that $\mathbb{K}'(S_L, k)$ containing the least vectors of weight 1, and denote the remaining set by Ω_1^I. For any invertible linear transformation L in Ω_1^I, save all linear transformations L satisfying that there exists some k of weight $n-1$ in $\mathbb{F}_2^n$ such that $\mathbb{K}'(S_L, k)$ containing the least vectors of weight 2, and denote the remaining set by $\Omega_2^I, \cdots$, Continuously, denote by Ω_{n-1}^I the set of all linear transformations L in Ω_{n-2}^I

satisfying that there exists some k of weight $n - 1$ such that $\mathbb{K}'(S_L, k)$ contains the least number of vectors of weight $n - 1$.

The final linear transformations can be selected from $\Omega_1^O \bigcup \Omega_{n-1}^I$. Taking the 4-bit S-box Serpent0 used in Serpent as an example, Ω, Ω_3^O, Ω_2^O and Ω_1^O have 840, 224, 24 and 12 transformations respectively, and Ω, Ω_1^I, Ω_2^I and Ω_3^I have 840, 224, 24 and 12 transformations respectively, so there are totally 24 invertible linear transformations satisfying conditions (1) or (2).

To verify the efficiency of our improved method, we first searched for the integral distinguishers of LBlock and TWINE, but no longer integral distinguishers can be found with our method. As a result, we further construct other instances of GFS ciphers. For example, when the Serpent0 S-box [13] and the No.2 permutation as shown in Table 1 are used, longer integral distinguishers can be found. In this case, when the linear transformations are chosen from Ω, there are 224 in 840 transformations that can lead to longer distinguishers. When the linear transformations are chosen from $\Omega_3^O \bigcup \Omega_1^I$, there are 224 in 400 transformations that can lead to longer distinguishers. When the linear transformations are chosen from $\Omega_2^O \bigcup \Omega_2^I$, there are 40 in 48 transformations that can lead to longer distinguishers. When the linear transformations are chosen from $\Omega_1^O \bigcup \Omega_3^I$, there are 20 in 24 transformations that can lead to longer distinguishers. It is easier to obtain a longer distinguisher using transformations from $\Omega_1^O \bigcup \Omega_3^I$.

For any fixed S-box, if the identity transformation I_n does not belong to $\Omega_1^O \bigcup \Omega_{n-1}^I$, then according to the criteria of (1) and (2), we think that it may be easier to search for longer integral distinguishers of $\mathcal{F}_L$ than $\mathcal{F}$ by traditional bit-based division property. In this case, we call the S-box **distinguishable**.

For 4-bit S-boxes, we found that the S-boxes used in LBlock and TWINE are not distinguishable, but some S-boxes used in Serpent, Midori [14] and Spongent [15] *etc.* are distinguishable. For these distinguishable S-boxes, we may obtain longer integral distinguishers of $\mathcal{F}_L$, and longer integral distinguishers of $\mathcal{F}$ may also be found with our improved method as shown in Algorithm 2. Some examples are given in next section.

4   Experimental Results

In order to verify the validity of our improved method, we construct a series of 64-bit GFS ciphers with 16-branch and 4-bit distinguishable S-boxes. The constructed GFS ciphers use the permutation layers of Type-II GFS and the optimal permutation layers as shown in Table 1 and [11]. Improved integral distinguishers can be found for some S-boxes used in Serpent, Midori and Spongent. The round of the longest integral distinguishers that can be found by different methods are listed in Table 2, where the third column indexed by 'Integral' indicates the round of the longest integral distinguisher obtained in [11], the fourth column indexed by 'DP' indicates the round of the longest integral distinguisher obtained by traditional bit-based division property, and the last column indexed by '$newDP$' indicates the round of the longest integral distinguisher obtained by our improved searching method.

The experimental results in Table 2 show that if Serpent0, Serpent1, Serpent2 and Serpent17 are selected as S-boxes in a GFS cipher with 16-branch, for most of the constructed ciphers, our method can find longer integral distinguisher than by traditional bit-based division property. For simplicity, in our experiments we only use one invertible linear transformation L in $\Omega_1^O \bigcup \Omega_{n-1}^I$ to construct linear equivalent GFS cipher F_L and search for its integral distinguishers. If more invertible linear transformations L are used, more improved results may be obtained.

Table 2. Improved integral distinguishers for some GFS ciphers

Permutation	S-box used in the GFS cipher	Integral	DP	$newDP$
type-II	Serpent0, Serpent1, Serpent2, Serpent17	32	33	34
type-II	Midori Sb_0	32	34	35
No. 2	Serpent0, Serpent1, Serpent2, Serpent17	15	17	18
No. 3	Serpent0, Serpent1, Serpent2, Serpent17	15	17	18
No. 4	Serpent0, Serpent1, Serpent2, Serpent17	15	17	18
No. 5	Serpent0, Serpent1, Serpent2, Serpent17	15	16	17
No. 6	Serpent0, Serpent1, Serpent2, Serpent17	15	17	18
No. 7	Spongent S-box, Midori Sb_0	15	17	18
No. 8	Serpent0, Serpent1, Serpent2, Serpent17, Midori Sb_0	15	17	18
No. 9	Midori Sb_0	16	17	18
No. 10	Serpent0, Serpent1, Serpent2, Serpent17	15	16	17
No. 10	Spongent S-box	15	17	18
No. 12	Serpent2, Spongent S-box, Midori Sb_0	16	17	18
No. 13	Serpent0, Serpent1, Serpent2, Serpent17	15	17	18

5 Conclusions

Division property is an important integral property used recently to search for integral distinguishers of block ciphers. Let $\mathcal{F}$ be a GFS cipher, and $\mathcal{F}_L$ be a new GFS cipher obtained by substituting the S-box S with $S_L = L \circ S \circ L^{-1}$ for some invertible linear transformation L. It is shown that the integral distinguisher of $\mathcal{F}$ can be transformed into the integral distinguisher of $\mathcal{F}_L$, and vice versa. Thus we can first try to find some longer integral distinguishers of $\mathcal{F}_L$ than that of $\mathcal{F}$ for some L utilizing basic search method with bit-based division property, and then derive the corresponding integral distinguishers of $\mathcal{F}$ accordingly. Experiments are also given for some 16-branch GFS ciphers to show the efficiency of our improved search method. This result implies that ability to resist our improved integral attack should also be considered when designing corresponding GFS ciphers.

Acknowledgements. We thank the anonymous reviewers for their careful reading of our paper and helpful comments. This research was supported by the National Natural Science Foundation of China (Nos. U1536101, 61521003) and the National cryptography Development Fund of China (Nos. MMJJ20180204, MMJJ20170103).

References

1. Todo, Y.: Structural evaluation by generalized integral property. In: Oswald, E., Fischlin, M. (eds.) EUROCRYPT 2015. LNCS, vol. 9056, pp. 287–314. Springer, Heidelberg (2015). https://doi.org/10.1007/978-3-662-46800-5_12
2. Zhang, H., Wu, W.: Structural evaluation for generalized Feistel structures and applications to LBlock and TWINE. In: Biryukov, A., Goyal, V. (eds.) INDOCRYPT 2015. LNCS, vol. 9462, pp. 218–237. Springer, Cham (2015). https://doi.org/10.1007/978-3-319-26617-6_12
3. Todo, Y.: Integral cryptanalysis on full MISTY1. In: Gennaro, R., Robshaw, M. (eds.) CRYPTO 2015. LNCS, vol. 9215, pp. 413–432. Springer, Heidelberg (2015). https://doi.org/10.1007/978-3-662-47989-6_20
4. Todo, Y., Morii, M.: Bit-based division property and application to SIMON family. In: Peyrin, T. (ed.) FSE 2016. LNCS, vol. 9783, pp. 357–377. Springer, Heidelberg (2016). https://doi.org/10.1007/978-3-662-52993-5_18
5. Boura, C., Canteaut, A.: Another view of the division property. In: Robshaw, M., Katz, J. (eds.) CRYPTO 2016. LNCS, vol. 9814, pp. 654–682. Springer, Heidelberg (2016). https://doi.org/10.1007/978-3-662-53018-4_24
6. Xiang, Z., Zhang, W., Bao, Z., Lin, D.: Applying MILP method to searching integral distinguishers based on division property for 6 lightweight block ciphers. In: Cheon, J.H., Takagi, T. (eds.) ASIACRYPT 2016. LNCS, vol. 10031, pp. 648–678. Springer, Heidelberg (2016). https://doi.org/10.1007/978-3-662-53887-6_24
7. Sun, L., Wang, W., Wang, M.: Automatic search of bit-based division property for ARX ciphers and word-based division property. In: Takagi, T., Peyrin, T. (eds.) ASIACRYPT 2017. LNCS, vol. 10624, pp. 128–157. Springer, Cham (2017). https://doi.org/10.1007/978-3-319-70694-8_5
8. Eskandari, Z., Kidmose, A.B., Kölbl, S., Tiessen, T.: Finding integral distinguishers with ease. In: Cid, C., Jacobson, M.J. (eds.) SAC 2018. LNCS, vol. 11349, pp. 115–138. Springer, Heidelberg (2019). https://doi.org/10.1007/978-3-030-10970-7_6
9. Derbez, P., Fouque, P.-A., Lambin, B.: Linearly equivalent S-boxes and the Division Property. Cryptology ePrint Archive, 2019/097 (2019)
10. Nyberg, K.: Generalized Feistel networks. In: Kim, K., Matsumoto, T. (eds.) ASIACRYPT 1996. LNCS, vol. 1163, pp. 91–104. Springer, Heidelberg (1996). https://doi.org/10.1007/BFb0034838
11. Suzaki, T., Minematsu, K.: Improving the generalized Feistel. In: Hong, S., Iwata, T. (eds.) FSE 2010. LNCS, vol. 6147, pp. 19–39. Springer, Heidelberg (2010). https://doi.org/10.1007/978-3-642-13858-4_2
12. Cook, S.A.: The complexity of theorem-proving procedures. In: STOC 1971, pp. 151–158. ACM (1971)
13. Biham, E., Anderson, R., Knudsen, L.: Serpent: a new block cipher proposal. In: Vaudenay, S. (ed.) FSE 1998. LNCS, vol. 1372, pp. 222–238. Springer, Heidelberg (1998). https://doi.org/10.1007/3-540-69710-1_15

14. Banik, S., et al.: Midori: a block cipher for low energy. In: Iwata, T., Cheon, J.H. (eds.) ASIACRYPT 2015. LNCS, vol. 9453, pp. 411–436. Springer, Heidelberg (2015). https://doi.org/10.1007/978-3-662-48800-3_17
15. Bogdanov, A., Knežević, M., Leander, G., Toz, D., Varıcı, K., Verbauwhede, I.: SPONGENT: a lightweight hash function. In: Preneel, B., Takagi, T. (eds.) CHES 2011. LNCS, vol. 6917, pp. 312–325. Springer, Heidelberg (2011). https://doi.org/10.1007/978-3-642-23951-9_21

Enhanced Differential Cache Attacks on SM4 with Algebraic Analysis and Error-Tolerance

Xiaoxuan Lou[1,2], Fan Zhang[2,3,4(✉)], Guorui Xu[3], Ziyuan Liang[1,3,4], Xinjie Zhao[5], Shize Guo[5], and Kui Ren[3,4]

[1] Department of Eletronic Engineering,
College of Information Science and Electronic Engineering,
Zhejiang University, Hangzhou 310027, China
[2] State Key Laboratory of Cryptology, P.O. Box 5159, Beijing 100878, China
[3] School of Cyber Science and Technology,
College of Computer Science and Technology, Zhejiang University,
Hangzhou 310027, China
fanzhang@zju.edu.cn
[4] Alibaba-Zhejiang University Joint Institute of Frontier Technologies,
Zhejiang University, Hangzhou 310027, China
[5] The Institute of North Electronic Equipment, Beijing 100878, China

Abstract. Block ciphers with Feistel structures are vulnerable to a specific type of cache attacks named differential cache attacks. The attacks leverage side-channel leakages from cache and differential property of cipher component to reveal the master key of cipher. In this paper, we combine the algebraic analysis to enhance the attacks, and propose a novel method named *Algebraic Differential Cache Attack (ADCA)*. By converting both cipher and cache leakages to algebraic equations, ADCA can reveal the cipher key automatically with the help of the SAT solver, which allows the analysis on much deeper rounds and makes a considerable reduction in attack complexity. When it is applied to the block cipher SM4, 10 plaintexts are enough to reveal the master key in 8-rounds analysis, while the traditional differential cache attack needs 20 ones. Finally, to eliminate the impact from noise, an error-tolerant method is proposed to deduce cache events from the leakage traces. It vastly enhances the robustness of attack, and makes the attack more practical. The experimental results show that the error-tolerant ADCA can correctly reveal the master key even when the uncertainty rate of cache events reaches to 60%.

Keywords: SM4 · Side channel attacks · Differential cache attacks · Algebraic analysis · Error-tolerance

1 Introduction

Cache attacks are a class of side-channel attacks that monitor the leakages from cache to extract the cipher key. [15] first proposed such attacks theoretically, and

© Springer Nature Switzerland AG 2020
Z. Liu and M. Yung (Eds.): Inscrypt 2019, LNCS 12020, pp. 480–496, 2020.
https://doi.org/10.1007/978-3-030-42921-8_29

discussed the feasibility of revealing the master key of DES with captured cache leakages. Then [20] followed the idea and demonstrated the first practical cache attack. After that, a number of cache attacks involving different techniques have been presented. Depending on the side-channel leakages used, cache attacks can be divided into three classes: time-driven [3,20], access-driven [12,14] and trace-driven [5,17]. These attacks pose a significant threat to various ciphers, including AES, CLEFIA, Camellia, and the target of this paper, SM4. As the standard commercial block cipher in China, SM4 [2] (formerly known as SMS4) has a typical unbalanced Feistel structure. In recent years, with the wide application of SM4, multiple general cryptography libraries start to support the cipher, like the latest OpenSSL 1.1.1 [1]. Since it was released in 2006, SM4 has been subjected to extensive researches. Numerous works were arisen to evaluate the reliability and security of the cipher, which roughly contain two primary categories: cache attacks and algebraic analysis.

Cache attacks are usually the first choices to analyze the block cipher like SM4. [4] carried out an effective cache attack on SM4, showing that 5000 power traces are enough to recover the master key. [22] used access-driven cache attack to analyze the first four rounds of encryption in the SM4, and revealed the cipher key within 80 plaintext samples. Among the cache attacks on SM4, there is a specific class named *Differential Cache Attack (DCA)*. In [17], trace-driven attacks were first combined with differential analysis, where the differential properties of S-Boxes are used to recover the key of CLEFIA in less than 2^{14} traces. This novel attack is the so-called *Differential Cache Attack*, which is further improved in [18] and also applied to Camellia in [16]. DCA is very suited to ciphers with Feistel structures, like the SM4. [13] proposed a differential cache attack on SM4, it used 2^{10} plaintexts to recover the master key of SM4 from the power traces for the 64-byte cache line.

Besides the cache attacks, algebraic analysis is also an available way to appraise the cipher. Some previous works targeted on the algorithm structure of SM4 to reveal partial cipher key, like 14-round square attack [23], 17-round impossible differential analysis [6], 22-round differential analysis [21] and 23-round linear analysis [7]. Beyond that, [10] described SM4 cipher as systems of quadratic equations over $GF(2)$ and $GF(2^8)$, and also estimated the complexities of XL algorithm for solving the two equations systems. And [8] performed algebraic analysis on 5-round SM4 leveraging the Gröbner basis and Minisat solver. With the algebraic analysis, the attacker can effectively decrease the search space of master key, and finally reveal it with simple brute force.

In this paper, we propose an enhanced differential cache attack on SM4, which combines with algebraic analysis and adopts an error-tolerant method to deduce cache events. It releases the analyst from sophisticated analysis and improves the robustness of attack. To thoroughly evaluate the resistance of SM4 against such attack, we first present a traditional DCA method to reveal the master key of SM4. Experiments show that it requires 20 plaintexts when both cache hits and cache misses are analyzed. However, such traditional method is sophisticated and limited by the depth of analysis rounds. To enhance the attack, we combine it with algebraic analysis, proposing a novel attack named *Algebraic Differential Cache Attack (ADCA)*. Such attack derives the algebraic equations of both cipher algorithm and cache leakages, then sets them up as the system of equations, which is further solved by the SAT solver automatically. The outputted solution would contain the master key so that the attacker can extract it. Since the new attack only requires the transformation of algebraic equations, and leaves the complicated analysis to the SAT solver, it is much simpler and more generic than previous DCA methods. Based on the results of experiments, ADCA can reveal the key of SM4 with only 10 plaintext by analyzing the first 8 rounds. Finally, in order to make the attack more practical, we introduce an error-tolerant method to deduce cache hit/miss events from the captured side-channel traces. With two stated thresholds, only the events whose leakage values locate in the range would be analyzed, and the others would be marked as uncertain and be discarded. It effectively prevents the impact of noise and improves the robustness of attacks. The enhanced ADCA can reveal the key when the uncertainty rate of deduced cache events is less than 60%.

The contributions of the paper are as follows:

- We give a security analysis of SM4 against *Differential Cache Attack (DCA)*, and present a practical DCA method that uses 20 plaintexts to reveal the master key of SM4.
- We combine algebraic analysis with DCA to give a novel attack named *Algebraic Differential Cache Attack (ADCA)*, illustrating the process of constructing equations of cipher algorithm and cache events.
- We demonstrate a practical ADCA on SM4, which extract the master key of SM4 with analyzing first 8 rounds and only 10 plaintexts. It greatly reduces the attack complexity and bypasses the sophisticated analysis.
- We propose an error-tolerant enhancement to improve the robustness of ADCA, eliminating the influence from uncertain cache events caused by noise.

The rest of this paper is organized as follows: Sect. 2 introduces the SM4 cipher and specifies the differential cache attack model. Section 3 demonstrates the details of proposed DCA and shows the results of attack experiments. Then in Sect. 4, the attack model of ADCA and relevant theoretical basis are introduced. Section 5 describes the detailed implementation process of such novel attack, while Sect. 6 evaluates its performance. Section 7 discusses the error-tolerant enhancement and Sect. 8 concludes the paper.

2 Preliminaries

2.1 Notation

For the sake of legible expression, notations used in this paper are listed first. Throughout the paper, MK denotes the master key of SM4, $(X_i, X_{i+1}, X_{i+2}, X_{i+3})$ are four intermediate variables inputted to the round i $(0 \leq i < 32)$, and (Y_0, Y_1, Y_2, Y_3) denote the final ciphertexts. rk_i is the round key generated from MK and used for i-th round. Let q_j denote the j-th S-Box lookup in the execution of SM4, λ denote the number of table lookups considered in the attack, $0 \leq j < \lambda$. The lookup index of q_j is denoted as l_j. Suppose the size of cache line is 2^μ bytes, and that of S-Box is 2^δ bytes. As a result, the S-Box occupies $2^{\delta-\mu}$ cache lines, and the higher $b = \delta - \mu$ bits of lookup index l_j identify which cache line contains the access target. Let $\langle l_j \rangle$ denote the most significant b bits leaked from the cache accesses in the attack.

2.2 SM4 Cipher

SM4 has a 32-rounds iterative Feistel structure, as shown in Fig. 1. The cipher adopts a 128-bits master key, which further generates 32-bits round keys for each round. Equation (1) depicts the encryption process of SM4:

$$
\begin{aligned}
X_{i+4} &= F(X_i, X_{i+1}, X_{i+2}, X_{i+3}, rk_i) \\
&= X_i \oplus T(X_{i+1} \oplus X_{i+2} \oplus X_{i+3} \oplus rk_i)
\end{aligned}
\tag{1}
$$

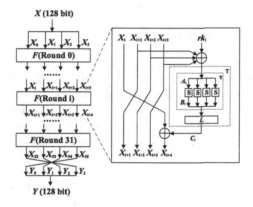

Fig. 1. The structure of SM4 cipher.

where T is a function composed of the nonlinear part τ and the linear part L, i.e., $T(.) = L(\tau(.))$. The nonlinear conversion τ is achieved with four table lookups on the 8×8 S-Box, whose inputs are $A_i = (a_{i,0}, a_{i,1}, a_{i,2}, a_{i,3})$ and outputs are $B_i = (b_{i,0}, b_{i,1}, b_{i,2}, b_{i,3})$. Each pair of $a_{i,t}$ and $b_{i,t}$ corresponds to t-th S-Box lookup in round i, $0 \leq t < 4$. For the following linear conversion L, it takes B_i as input and outputs $C_i = (c_{i,0}, c_{i,1}, c_{i,2}, c_{i,3})$ like shown in Eq. (2). As the result of function T, C_i further XORs with X_i to generate X_{i+4}.

$$
C_i = L(B_i) = B_i \oplus (B_i \lll 2) \oplus (B_i \lll 10) \oplus (B_i \lll 18) \oplus (B_i \lll 24)
\tag{2}
$$

2.3   Differential Cache Attacks

Following the explanation of differential cache attacks in [17], we introduce how to perform such attack and propose the attack model, as shown in Fig. 2. Suppose the cache has been flushed before the encryption, and there are λ S-Box lookups being analyzed in the attack. For a certain lookup q_j among them, to figure out its index l_j, we let U_j denote a set of public variables (plaintexts) and V_j denote a set of secret variables (round keys), then introduce the function $f(.)$ that computes the l_j from U_j and V_j. Recall that $\langle l_j \rangle$ $(0 \le j < \lambda)$ denotes the most significant b bits of l_j, which indicate the index of accessed cache line. Hence, the relationship between different $\langle l_j \rangle$ can be deduced from the cache hit/miss sequences, which also provides constrains to help the revealing of secret variable V_j.

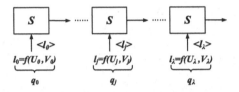

Fig. 2. Differential cache attack model.

Assume the cache has been flushed beforehand, so the first lookup q_0 would cause a cache miss. Then we take the second S-Box lookup q_1 for example to discuss. The memory access in the q_1 can be either cache hit or cache miss, the former indicates q_1 accesses the same cache line with q_0, i.e., $\langle l_0 \rangle = \langle l_1 \rangle$, so that Eq. (3) can be derived. The latter means the target data is absent in the cache, so q_1 would load it and there is Eq. (4).

$$\langle l_0 \rangle = \langle l_1 \rangle \implies \langle f(U_0, V_0) \rangle_b = \langle f(U_1, V_1) \rangle_b \tag{3}$$

$$\langle l_0 \rangle \neq \langle l_1 \rangle \implies \langle f(U_0, V_0) \rangle_b \neq \langle f(U_1, V_1) \rangle_b \tag{4}$$

In this way, the cache access events are transformed to the equations about U_j and V_j. To recover the key, multiple plaintext samples are sent to the cipher, and then differential equations between them are constructed. For instance, assume the input plaintexts X and X' both cause a cache hit in q_1, so they both meet Eq. (3), which further derives the differential equation as below:

$$\langle f(U_0, V_0) \oplus f(U_0', V_0) \rangle_b = \langle f(U_1, V_1) \oplus f(U_1', V_1) \rangle_b \tag{5}$$

Because of the feature of Feistel structure, V_1 in Eq. (5) generally can be eliminated, only leaving the V_0 unknown. And based on the property of the S-Box, the value of V_0 can be uniquely recovered with a certain number of plaintext samples. Hence, with the differential cache attack, the adversary can leverage a number of plaintext pairs to reduce the search space of secret variables and finally reveal the correct key.

3   Differential Cache Attack on SM4

In this section, we first present a traditional differential cache attack on the SM4. The attack is improved from [11] and analyzes the first four rounds of cipher to reveal the master key MK. The work lays a foundation for the design of subsequent enhanced attack method.

For the first round of SM4, it needs to perform four S-Box lookups whose inputs, namely lookup indexes, are denoted as $a_{0,t}$, $(0 \le t < 4)$. Each $a_{0,t}$ is computed as: $a_{0,t} = X_{1,t} \oplus X_{2,t} \oplus X_{3,t} \oplus rk_{0,t}$, where $X_{i,t}$ and $rk_{i,t}$ denote the t-th block (each block is 8-bit) of variables X_i and rk_i. As mentioned above, since q_0 always be a cache miss, the analysis starts from q_1. If q_1 results in a cache hit, there should be $\langle l_0 \rangle = \langle l_1 \rangle$ (i.e., $\langle a_{0,0} \rangle = \langle a_{0,1} \rangle$), and Eq. (6) is derived. The equation offers the possible values of $\langle rk_{0,0} \oplus rk_{0,1} \rangle$.

$$
\langle a_{0,0} \rangle = \langle a_{0,1} \rangle \quad \Longrightarrow \quad \langle rk_{0,0} \oplus rk_{0,1} \rangle =
$$
$$
\langle X_{1,0} \oplus X_{2,0} \oplus X_{3,0} \oplus X_{1,1} \oplus X_{2,1} \oplus X_{3,1} \rangle \tag{6}
$$

On the contrary, if q_1 causes a cache miss, the equation would give the impossible values of $\langle rk_{0,0} \oplus rk_{0,1} \rangle$. Similarly, for the following lookups, depending on their cache accessing state, the attacker can extract possible values and discard impossible values of corresponding round keys. As a result, after the analysis of the first round, the values of $\langle rk_{0,0} \oplus rk_{0,1} \rangle$, $\langle rk_{0,0} \oplus rk_{0,2} \rangle$ and $\langle rk_{0,0} \oplus rk_{0,3} \rangle$ can be recovered. With the same way to analyze deeper rounds, finally the first three round keys rk_0, rk_1, rk_2 and partial bits of rk_3 can be recovered. The remaining unknown bits, lower $(8 - b)$ bits in each $rk_{3,t}$, can be revealed with brute force, whose search space is 2^{32-4b}. Finally the master key can be recovered from these revealed round keys based on key scheduling.

The attack method has been applied to a SM4 cipher implemented on the 32-bit ARM microprocessor NXP LPC2124, whose cache line has 16 bytes [9]. The S-Box used in the SM4 cipher is of size 256 bytes. Hence, the number of bits for indexing the cache lines is $b = 4$. The electromagnetic radiation of microprocessor is captured by the EMK near-field probe on the oscilloscope, which is further used to depict the leakage traces. To evaluate the efficiency of the attack, we focus on the relation between the search space of round keys and the number of plaintext samples, depicting the variation tendency of such relation. For the first round, as shown in Fig. 3(a), the increasing analyzed plaintexts cause the search space of rk_0 to decrease rapidly. By analyzing both cache hits and cache misses, we find that 30 plaintexts are enough to reduce the search space from 2^{32} to 2^{20}, while only considering cache miss needs 35 plaintexts. The second round has analogous variation trend with the first round, like illustrated in Fig. 3(b). The search space of round keys (rk_0 and rk_1) decreases from 2^{64} to 2^{16} with the increasing of analyzed plaintexts. As for the following rounds, e.g., the third round and the fourth round, the relation between such two factors are pretty much similar, guaranteeing the reduction of round keys' search space with the increase of analyzed plaintexts.

After the analysis of the first four rounds, we have revealed whole rk_0, rk_1, rk_2 and partial rk_3, so that the search space of them is reduced from 2^{128} to 2^{16}, as depicted in Fig. 3(c). It requires 20 plaintext samples when both cache hit and miss are analyzed, remaining 16 bits in the rk_3 unknown, which are easy to be solved with the brute force. Finally, according to the key schedule algorithm of SM4, the master key is calculated from the revealed (rk_0, rk_1, rk_2, rk_3).

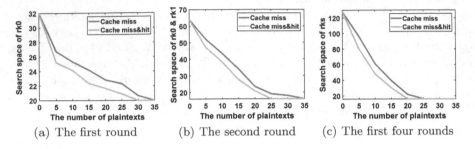

(a) The first round   (b) The second round   (c) The first four rounds

Fig. 3. Relation between the search space of round keys and the number of plaintexts.

4   Algebraic Differential Cache Attack

4.1   The Defects of DCA

Even above *Differential Cache Attack* method can recover the master key of SM4 effectively, there are still some exposed defects, making it less practical in the real scenarios. Firstly, the analysis is so complicated that generally requires analyst to own sophisticated knowledge, and the complexity would grow exponentially with the increase of analysis rounds, the overlarge search space remained from previous rounds would also cause the current round too complex to analyze. Secondly, the traditional DCA follows the *divide and conquer* strategy to recover the round keys block by block, which does not fully utilize the correlation between the algorithm structure and the round keys.

4.2   Attack Model

In this section we enhance the differential cache attack with the algebraic analysis and propose a novel attack named *Algebraic Differential Cache Attack* (ADCA). The attack model of ADCA is shown in Fig. 4, which contains three phases: (S1) Construct algebraic equations of the cipher; (S2) Deduce cache hit/miss sequences from the captured leakage traces then construct algebraic equations for these cache events; (S3) Use the SAT solver, which is commonly adopted in algebraic analysis, to solve the system of equations consisting of equations derived from (S1) and (S2), finally recover the master key. We will discuss these three phases in detail below.

Construct Algebraic Equations of Cipher. In essence, revealing the cipher key is equivalent to finding the solution that satisfies the algebraic equations of

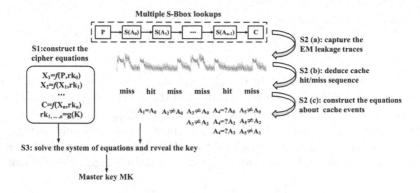

Fig. 4. The attack model of ADCA.

cipher. Hence, we need to first construct the algebraic equations of the cipher, which describe the algorithm with the plaintext X, the ciphertext Y, the round key rk and the master key MK. The detailed process of constructing equations of SM4 will be shown in Sect. 5.1.

Construct Algebraic Equations of Cache Events. However, only the cipher equations are not enough to reveal the master key. It is necessary to introduce additional information, like cache access sequence, to provide more constraints for analysis. Hence, the cache events deduced from captured leakage traces are transformed to algebraic equations, which can be seen as the kernel of ADCA. Such phase includes three steps, i.e., S2(a) to S2(c) in Fig. 4. First, multiple SM4 encryptions with different plaintexts are carried out, and at the same time, the electromagnetic radiation during each encryption process is also monitored. Then the cache events are deduced based on the captured traces, which are further used to construct the algebraic equations. The detailed process of constructing cache event equations is shown below.

Follow the notations defined in the Sect. 2.1, for the j-th lookup q_j, the most significant b bits of its index l_j, i.e., $\langle l_j \rangle$, can be revealed from the cache access, as long as q_j hits a certain cache line. Assume there have been r cache misses before the analyzed lookup q_j, and the set of lookup indexes of these cache misses is denoted as $S_M = \{l_{m1}, l_{m2}, \ldots, l_{mr}\}$. If q_j results in a cache hit, it means the lookup accesses one of the cache lines that have been loaded before, so that the index l_j must have the same most significant b bits with one of elements in the S_M. Hence, similar with the analysis in the traditional DCA, we can get the set of possible values of $\langle l_j \rangle$, denoting as set $L_j = \{\langle l_{m1} \rangle, \langle l_{m2} \rangle, \ldots, \langle l_{mr} \rangle\}$.

In order to improve the efficiency of comparing the values of $\langle l_j \rangle$ and $\langle l_{mt} \rangle$, one element in the L_j $(1 \leq t \leq r)$, each $\langle l_{mt} \rangle$ is substituted with a b-bits variable, which is denoted as $D_t = \langle l_{mt} \rangle = d_t^1 d_t^2 \ldots d_t^b$. Besides that, b single-bit variables denoted as $e_t^k (1 \leq k \leq b)$, and one single-bit variable c_t are also introduced, whose values are:

$$e_t^k = \neg(l_j^k \oplus d_t^k), \quad c_t = \prod_{k=1}^{b} e_t^k \tag{7}$$

where e_t^k shows if the k-th bit in the $\langle l_j \rangle$ and $\langle l_{mt} \rangle$ are equal, and c_t indicates whether all b bits of the $\langle l_j \rangle$ are equal to that of $\langle l_{mt} \rangle$. If $l_j^k = d_t^k$, there is $e_t^k = 1$; otherwise $e_t^k = 0$. As for the c_t, it has $c_t = 1$ if $\langle l_j \rangle = \langle l_{mt} \rangle$, or else $c_t = 0$.

As a result, if q_j causes a cache hit, there must be one and only one $\langle l_{mt} \rangle = \langle l_j \rangle$ in the set L_j, which is equivalent to only having one $c_t = 1$ in the set $C = \{c_1, c_2, ..., c_r\}$. Such feature can be used to construct algebraic equations as below:

$$\prod_{c_t \in C_2} c_t = 0, \quad \prod_{c_t \in C} (c_t \oplus 1) = 0 \tag{8}$$

where C_2 is a two-element subset of set C. Then, we introduce two important parameters, the number of introduced variables (V) and the number of constructed equations (EQ). In this case, their values can be computed as:

$$V = (b+1) \times r, \quad EQ = 1 + (b+1) \times r + \frac{r \times (r-1)}{2} \tag{9}$$

where V includes e_t^k and c_t and EQ contains Eqs. (7) and (8).

In contrast, if q_j results in a cache miss, we can get the set of impossible values of $\langle l_j \rangle$, denoted as set $\overline{L}_j = \{\langle l_{m1} \rangle, \langle l_{m2} \rangle, ..., \langle l_{mr} \rangle\}$. We also introduce variables e_t^k and c_t to describe the comparison between elements in the $\overline{L}_j$ and $\langle l_j \rangle$. The analysis method is the same as the above. As the $\langle l_j \rangle$ is not equal to any $\langle l_{mt} \rangle$ in the $\overline{L}_j$, so that every $c_t = 0$, the algebraic equations can be constructed as below:

$$\prod_{c_t \in C} (c_t \oplus 1) = 1 \tag{10}$$

And the two introduced parameters V and EQ can be calculated as:

$$V = (b+1) \times r, \quad EQ = 1 + (b+1) \times r \tag{11}$$

Solve the System of Equations. After constructing the algebraic equations of both cipher and cache events, we can combine them as the system of equations and then solve it to recover the master key. There are multiple typical methods for solving the algebraic equations, include linearization method [10], Gröbner basis [8] and some SAT solvers like zChaff, Minisat and CryptoMinisat [19]. This paper adopts CryptoMinisat to solve the algebraic equations.

5   The Implementation of ADCA

5.1   Construct Algebraic Equations of SM4 Cipher

As the kernel nonlinear component of cipher, the S-Box is usually the focus of constructing cipher equations. For the SM4, the input size m and output size

Table 1. Descriptions of used variables

Variables	Descriptions
$rk_{i,s}$	The s-th bit in the i-th round key rk_i
$A_{i,s}$	The s-th bit in the input A_i to S-Boxes
$B_{i,s}$	The s-th bit in the output B_i from S-Boxes
$C_{i,s}$	The s-th bit in the output C_i of round function T
$X_{i,s}$	The s-th bit in the intermediate variable X_i

n of S-Box are both 8 bits, i.e., $m = n = 8$. To illustrate better, we first sort out the variables that would be used for constructing equations and list them in Table 1 ($0 \le i < 32, 0 \le s < 32$).

Then we can construct the algebraic equations of SM4 algorithm as below:

$$X_{i+1,s} \oplus X_{i+2,s} \oplus X_{i+3,s} \oplus rk_{i,s} \oplus A_{i,s} = 0$$
$$B_i \oplus \tau[A_i] = 0$$
$$C_{i,s} \oplus L(B_i)_s = 0 \tag{12}$$
$$C_{i,s} \oplus X_{i,s} \oplus X_{i+4,s} = 0$$

Based on Eq. (12), for the 32-round encryption of the SM4, there are 4352 equations on $GF(2)$, including 1024 nonlinear equations and 3328 linear equations, which contain 5248 variables. As for the key schedule algorithm, with the same analysis method, it derives 4096 equations consisting of 1024 nonlinear ones and 3072 linear ones, with 4224 introduced variables. In summary, there are totally 8448 equations with 9472 variables constructed for the whole process of SM4. However, in the real attack experiments, actually it only needs to construct parts of them since analysis on the first few rounds is enough to reveal the master key.

5.2   Transform Cache Events to Algebraic Equations

To solve above cipher equations, whose solution contains the master key, more constraints are introduced by transforming cache events to algebraic equations. Figure 5 gives three samples of captured cache event sequences, each sequence covers the first 8 rounds (a total of 32 S-Box lookups) of the encryption. The black blocks in the figure denote cache misses while the white blocks denote cache hits. The x-axis indicates the ID of S-Box lookup, y-axis indicates the ID of sample. From the figure, we can know that after the fourth round (i.e., the 16-th S-Box lookup), the frequency of cache hits significantly increases, as almost S-Box lines have been loaded.

We take the sample S_1 in Fig. 5 as an example to explain how to construct algebraic equations for cache events. The initial analysis is similar to the traditional DCA, like the eighth S-Box lookup q_7 in S_1 causes a cache miss, it can get the set of the impossible values of $\langle l_7 \rangle$: $\overline{L_7} = \{\langle l_0 \rangle, \langle l_1 \rangle, \langle l_3 \rangle, \langle l_6 \rangle\}$. Then based

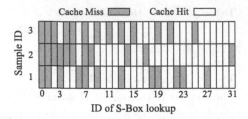

Fig. 5. Samples of cache event sequences.

on the Eq. (11), 20 new variables would be introduced to construct 21 algebraic equations. As for the ninth lookup q_8, which causes a cache hit, the set of the possible values of $\langle l_8 \rangle$ can be obtained: $L_8 = \{\langle l_0 \rangle, \langle l_1 \rangle, \langle l_3 \rangle, \langle l_6 \rangle, \langle l_7 \rangle\}$. And based on the Eq. (9), there would be 25 introduced variables and 36 constructed algebraic equations.

Now consider the general case of constructing algebraic equations for cache events. Suppose N_c is the number of cache lines that the entire S-Box occupies, N_j is the number of cache lines that have been accessed before the j-th S-Box lookup q_j, and P_j is the probability of that q_j results in a cache hit. Assume N_c cache lines are accessed with equal probability in each S-Box lookup, then for a certain cache line, the probability of it has never been accessed before q_j is $((N_c - 1)/N_c)^j$. After that the values of N_j and P_j can be computed as below:

$$N_j = N_c \times \left(1 - (\frac{N_c - 1}{N_c})^j \right), \quad P_j = \frac{N_j}{N_c} = 1 - (\frac{N_c - 1}{N_c})^j \qquad (13)$$

As the N_j essentially denotes the number of cache misses before q_j (each cache miss would occupy a new cache line), it means that the variable r in the Eqs. (9) and (11) can be substituted with N_j. Hence, for the j-th lookup, the number of introduced variables (V_j) and constructed equations (EQ_j) can be indicated as:

$$V_j = (b + 1) \times N_j$$
$$EQ_j = 1 + (b + 1) \times N_j + P_j \times \frac{N_j \times (N_j - 1)}{2} \qquad (14)$$

Following the increase of analysis rounds or namely j, the overheads for both constructing cipher equations and cache event equations become larger. Figure 6 depicts the ratio of the overhead between constructing cache event equations and cipher equations, providing a better view on their variation trend. The blue curve illustrates the overhead ratio of introduced equation of two constructions, while the red curve indicates the overhead ratio of variables. From the figure, the ratio of equation overhead is about 1 in the 8-th round, which means the number of constructed equations for cipher and cache events are nearly equal. After the 8-th round, with the increase of analyzed rounds, the equation overhead increases rapidly while the search space of secret keys reduces slightly. As the attack requires a reasonable compromise between the analysis rounds and the overhead, it seems that analyzing the first 8 rounds is a good choice.

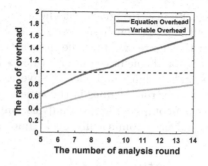

Fig. 6. The overhead of equations and variables. (Color figure online)

5.3 Recover the Master Key

In this paper, we leverage the SAT solver CryptMinisat to solve the system of equations, whose solution can be further used for extracting the master key. The solver CryptMinisat takes CNFs (Conjunctive Normal Forms) as its input, so that above constructed algebraic equations need to be converted to the equivalent CNFs. However, since the CryptMinisat can convert linear equations to CNFs automatically, the analyst actually doesn't need to consider this step. For the cipher equations, each S-Box substitution can be converted to 254 CNFs. After taking the key schedule algorithm into account, each round would generate 1336 CNFs. The cache event equations are also converted to CNFs and sent to the solver together. Then the solver is launched to solve the system of equations automatically [19], which effectively release the analyst from complex analysis. Finally, the master key is extracted from the solved solution.

6 Experimental Evaluation

6.1 Setup

The attack platform for the ADCA experiments is the same to that in Sect. 3, where has $N_c = 16$ and $b = 4$. We assume that side-channel leakages can be captured effectively, and the corresponding cache hit/miss sequences can also be deduced correctly. Then the solving of the system of equations is achieved by the CryptMinisat (version 2.9.4) running on a normal PC (CPU: Intel Core i7-7700 @ 3.60 GHz, Memory: 16G).

6.2 Attack Time

First the time required for a successful attack is studied, i.e., the time of solving the system of equations with CryptMinisat. Note that the attacks exceed 24 h are considered as failed. Based on the depiction in Fig. 6, to effectively reveal the master key without introducing too much overhead, analyzing the first 8 rounds is an appropriate choice. Figure 7(a) gives the distribution of attack time of 20 experiments, which all analyze the first 8 rounds of SM4 with 10 different plaintext samples. From the figure, we find the attack time almost distributes exponentially, most attacks can be achieved in 12 h (4.32×10^4 s) and nearly 30% of them can be succeeded in less than one hour. The average attack time is about 4.79 h that is affected by the extreme values in the time sequence. Longer attack time is the price of removing complex manual analysis, but as all the computing can be completed by the solver automatically, such time cost is tolerable.

6.3   Influence Factors on Attack Time

After illustrating the approximate distribution of attack time, we further explore the influence factors on attack time. The first is the number of analysis rounds, denoting as R. Empirically, the bigger R would result in shorter attack time, since it offers more constraints to the system of equations. However, it also introduces larger overhead of equations and variables, which makes the target equations more complex. Figure 7(b) shows the variation tendency of attack time with the increase of analysis rounds R, and the sample size of plaintexts is fixed as 20. For each R, 5 experiments are performed to get the corresponding average attack time. The trend indicates that with the fixed number of plaintexts, the increase of R can reduce the attack time, but once R exceeds a certain range (e.g., $R = 7$), the attack time increases rapidly with R. The second parameter is the number of plaintext samples, denoting as S. Similar to the R, the increase of S gives more constraints but also larger overhead. As a result, S has the same influence to the variation of attack time, in a certain range the increasing S makes the attack time decrease, but beyond the range the attack time increases fast. To further illustrate the influence from S to the attack, we discuss the relation between the attack success rate and the plaintext sample size in the following.

6.4   Attack Success Rate

A successful attack means the SAT solver is able to solve the system of equations in a given time (less than 24 h), so the success rate of ADCA is essentially equivalent to the probability of solving the solution in the required time. Figure 7(c) depicts the success rates of the attacks that all take the first 5 rounds for analysis but utilize different size of plaintext samples. The success rate is calculated from 10 repetitive experiments. As the figure shows, the success rate does not always increase with the sample size, when the sample size larger than a certain threshold, the overhead of introduced equations becomes so large that it gets much harder for the solver to solve these equations. Since the solver cannot get the solution in the limited time, it makes the attack success rate decrease rapidly.

Based on above results, in order to conduct a successful algebraic different cache attack, we should choose appropriate analysis rounds R and sample size S, besides we also need to consider the trade-off between these two parameters. In the actual experiment, when the analysis rounds $R = 8$ and the sample size

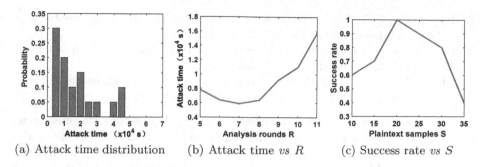

(a) Attack time distribution   (b) Attack time *vs* R (c) Success rate *vs* S

Fig. 7. Results of experiment evaluation.

$S = 10$, the attack can obtain the best result, whose attack time is short and success rate is high.

7 Error-Tolerant Enhancement

In above attack experiments, it assumes that all the deduced cache events are correct, so that we can directly construct algebraic equations of them to solve the key. However, in practice, the cache events deduced from side-channel leakage traces are always contain more or less misjudgments. There are two main reasons: the noise that fluctuates the accurate leakage traces and the improper threshold that mislead the inference. As such error cache events would compromise the analysis or even make the attack failed, it is necessary to propose an error-tolerant method to improve the robustness and practicality of ADCA.

7.1 Error-Tolerant Method

Since errors in cache events are essentially misjudgments of captured side-channel leakages, our error-tolerant method focuses on the interpretation of leakage traces. In general, the noise of instruments and environment is the white noise, which changes the values of monitored leakages in a certain range. To deal with such attached noise, a flexible threshold range is adopted to decide the type of cache events, i.e., cache hit or miss. It can efficiently filter most of the noise and make sure the correctness of deduced events. Besides that, since the judgment of cache events depends on a range rather than an accurate value, it also reduces the sophisticated works for choosing a strict threshold.

The error-tolerant method is designed to enhance the ADCA. First, two thresholds V_M and V_H are set, the former is the lowest peak value that can be deduced as cache miss, and the latter is the highest peak value that can be seem as cache hit. Let V_j denote the peak value in the leakage trace that corresponds to the j-th S-Box lookup q_j. After that, the cache events can be judged from the captured traces as following:

1. if $V_j \leq V_H$, q_j is considered as a cache hit, then constructing equations of cache events based on the Eqs. (7) and (8).
2. if $V_j \geq V_M$, q_j is considered as a cache miss, then constructing equations of cache events based on the Eqs. (7) and (10).
3. if $V_H \leq V_j \leq V_M$, it is difficult to confirm whether q_j is a cache hit or cache miss, so mark it as the uncertain event and leave it alone.

For the cache events whose V_j satisfies $V_H \leq V_j \leq V_M$, as they are ambiguous, the best solution is ignoring them. Although dropping them would result in the information loss of analysis, it is still better than introducing errors. And the choice of V_M and V_H must be careful, it should balance between the information loss and introduced errors. In general, first a number of experiments should be performed on the current platform to determine the base line between cache hit and cache miss. Then, combining the results in the captured leakage traces, the values of V_M and V_H are chosen by shifting up or down the base line.

In order to better explain the proposed error-tolerant method, the uncertainty ratio e is introduced to describes the proportion of uncertain cache events in the population. The parameter e can be denoted as: $e = \frac{N_E}{N_A}$, where N_E is the number of uncertain cache events, and N_A is the number of all cache events. The higher e generally means the larger noise in the experiments and the harder it is to obtain the correct key. Besides, it should be noted that the choice of V_M and V_H also make a great influence to the value of e.

7.2   Evaluation

The setup for evaluating the error-tolerant attack is the same as that shown in Sect. 6, and the attack analyzes the first 8 rounds of encryption. As we cannot manipulate the noise of instruments and environment as will, the values of V_M and V_H are adjusted to achieve changing the uncertainty rate e, which has the same effect as the variation of noise. Then the efficiency of attacks under different e is evaluated. Figure 8 depicts the average sample size of plaintexts required for revealing the key under different uncertainty ratio e. The curve in the figure indicates that the required sample size increases exponentially with the e, and such

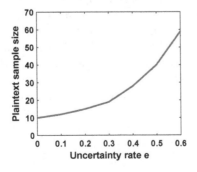

Fig. 8. Required plaintext sample size for attacks with different error ratio e

observation is in line with our expectations. Our error-tolerant attack method is able to reveal the key with 59 plaintext samples when the uncertainty rate e is 60%, and while e is less than 30% the method can recover the master key of SM4 within 20 input samples.

8 Conclusions

This paper enhances the traditional differential cache attack with algebraic analysis and error-tolerance, proposing an error-tolerant algebraic differential cache attack method. With applying on the block cipher SM4, it shows that the new attack makes a great reduction in the attack complexity and bypass the sophisticated manual analysis effectively. Only 10 plaintexts with the analysis on the first 8 rounds are enough to recover the master key of SM4, and the analysis is automatically finished by the SAT solver. The proposed error-tolerant method further improves the robustness and practicality of the attack, which allows to reveal the cipher key successfully when the uncertainty rate is less than 60%. Such work provides the reference for following physical security evaluation on other typical block ciphers, such as ARIA and Camellia.

Acknowledgments. This work was supported in part by Alibaba-Zhejiang University Joint Institute of Frontier Technologies, by Zhejiang Key R&D Plan (Grant No. 2019C03133), by Major Scientific Research Project of Zhejiang Lab (Grant No. 2018FD0ZX01), by Open Fund of State Key Laboratory of Cryptology (Grant No. MMKFKT201805), by National Natural Science Foundation of China (Grant No. 61772236), by Young Elite Scientists Sponsorship Program by CAST (Grant No. 17-JCJQ-QT-045), by National Natural Science Foundation of China (Grants No. 61772236, 61972348) and by Research Institute of Cyberspace Governance in Zhejiang University.

References

1. OpenSSL 1.1.1 source code. https://www.openssl.org/source/old/1.1.1/
2. The SM4 block cipher algorithm and its modes of operations (2019). https://tools.ietf.org/id/draft-crypto-sm4-00.html
3. Acıiçmez, O., Schindler, W., Koç, Ç.K.: Cache based remote timing attack on the AES. In: Cryptographers' Track at the RSA Conference, pp. 271–286 (2007)
4. Bai, X., Guo, L., Xu, Y., Li, Z.: Research on differential power analysis attack on SMS4 algorithm. J. Chin. Comput. Syst. **3**, 541–544 (2009)
5. Bertoni, G., Zaccaria, V., Breveglieri, L., Monchiero, M., Palermo, G.: AES power attack based on induced cache miss and countermeasure. In: International Conference on Information Technology: Coding and Computing (ITCC 2005)-Volume II, vol. 1, pp. 586–591 (2005)
6. Chen, J., Hu, Y., Zhang, Y.: Impossible differential attack on the 17-round block cipher SMS4. J. Xidian Univ. **3**, 455–488 (2008)
7. Cho, J.Y., Nyberg, K.: Improved linear cryptanalysis of SMS4 block cipher. In: Symmetric Key Encryption Workshop, pp. 1–14 (2011)

8. Erickson, J., Ding, J., Christensen, C.: Algebraic cryptanalysis of SMS4: Gröbner basis attack and sat attack compared. In: Lee, D., Hong, S. (eds.) ICISC 2009. LNCS, vol. 5984, pp. 73–86. Springer, Heidelberg (2010). https://doi.org/10.1007/978-3-642-14423-3_6

9. Gallais, J.F., Kizhvatov, I.: Error-tolerance in trace-driven cache collision attacks. In: International Workshop on Constructive Side-Channel Analysis and Secure Design, COSADE, pp. 222–232 (2011)

10. Ji, W., Hu, L., Ou, H.: Algebraic attack to SMS4 and the comparison with AES. In: 2009 Fifth International Conference on Information Assurance and Security, vol. 1, pp. 662–665 (2009)

11. Lou, X., Zhang, F., Huang, J., Zhao, X., Liu, H.: Research on trace driven cache analysis on SM4. J. Cryptologic Res. 5(4), 430–441 (2018)

12. Neve, M., Seifert, J.P.: Advances on access-driven cache attacks on AES. In: Biham, E., Youssef, A.M. (eds.) Selected Areas in Cryptography, SAC 2006. Lecture Notes in Computer Science, vol. 4356, pp. 147–162. Springer, Heidelberg (2007). https://doi.org/10.1007/978-3-540-74462-7_11

13. Nguyen, P.H., Rebeiro, C., Mukhopadhyay, D., Wang, H.: Improved differential cache attacks on SMS4. In: Kutyłowski, M., Yung, M. (eds.) Inscrypt 2012. LNCS, vol. 7763, pp. 29–45. Springer, Heidelberg (2013). https://doi.org/10.1007/978-3-642-38519-3_3

14. Osvik, D.A., Shamir, A., Tromer, E.: Cache attacks and countermeasures: the case of AES. In: Pointcheval, D. (ed.) CT-RSA 2006. LNCS, vol. 3860, pp. 1–20. Springer, Heidelberg (2006). https://doi.org/10.1007/11605805_1

15. Page, D.: Theoretical use of cache memory as a cryptanalytic side-channel. IACR Cryptology ePrint Archive 2002/169 (2002)

16. Poddar, R., Datta, A., Rebeiro, C.: A cache trace attack on CAMELLIA. In: Joye, M., Mukhopadhyay, D., Tunstall, M. (eds.) Security Aspects in Information Technology. InfoSecHiComNet 2011. Lecture Notes in Computer Science, vol. 7011, pp. 144–156. Springer, Heidelberg (2011). https://doi.org/10.1007/978-3-642-24586-2_13

17. Rebeiro, C., Mukhopadhyay, D.: Cryptanalysis of CLEFIA using differential methods with cache trace patterns. In: Kiayias, A. (ed.) CT-RSA 2011. LNCS, vol. 6558, pp. 89–103. Springer, Heidelberg (2011). https://doi.org/10.1007/978-3-642-19074-2_7

18. Rebeiro, C., Poddar, R., Datta, A., Mukhopadhyay, D.: An enhanced differential cache attack on CLEFIA for large cache lines. In: Bernstein, D.J., Chatterjee, S. (eds.) INDOCRYPT 2011. LNCS, vol. 7107, pp. 58–75. Springer, Heidelberg (2011). https://doi.org/10.1007/978-3-642-25578-6_6

19. Soos, M., Nohl, K., Castelluccia, C.: Extending SAT solvers to cryptographic problems. In: Kullmann, O. (ed.) SAT 2009. LNCS, vol. 5584, pp. 244–257. Springer, Heidelberg (2009). https://doi.org/10.1007/978-3-642-02777-2_24

20. Tsunoo, Y., Saito, T., Suzaki, T., Shigeri, M., Miyauchi, H.: Cryptanalysis of DES implemented on computers with cache. In: Walter, C.D., Koç, Ç.K., Paar, C. (eds.) CHES 2003. LNCS, vol. 2779, pp. 62–76. Springer, Heidelberg (2003). https://doi.org/10.1007/978-3-540-45238-6_6

21. Zhang, M., Liu, J., Wang, X.: Differential attack on 22-round SMS4 block cipher. Acta Scientiarum Naturalium Univ. Sunyatseni 2, 43–47 (2010)

22. Zhao, X., Wang, T., Zheng, Y.: Cache timing attack on SMS4. J. Commun. 6, 89–98 (2010)

23. Zhong, M., Hu, Y., Chen, J.: Square attack on the 14-round block cipher SMS4. J. Xidian Univ. 1, 105–109 (2008)

Authentication

Round-Efficient Anonymous Password-Authenticated Key Exchange Protocol in the Standard Model

Qihui Zhang[1], Wenfen Liu[2(✉)], Kang Yang[3], Xuexian Hu[1], and Ying Mei[4]

[1] PLA SSF Information Engineering University, Zhengzhou 450001, China
[2] Guilin University of Electronic Technology, Guilin 541004, China
liuwenfen@guet.edu.cn
[3] State Key Laboratory of Cryptology, Beijing 100878, China
[4] Automobile NCO School, Army Military Transportation University, Bengbu 233000, China

Abstract. Anonymous password-authenticated key exchange (APAKE) protocols allow for authenticating legitimate users via low-entropy passwords while keeping their actual identities private. They are important cryptographic primitives for privacy protection, which have attracted much attention recently and have been standardized in the international standard ISO/IEC 20009-4. However, most of the existing APAKE schemes (especially including all the APAKE schemes in the storage-extra setting) are developed in the random oracle model. In this paper, we present the first storage-extra APAKE protocol in the standard model by combing the technique of algebraic MAC with oblivious designated-verifier non-interactive zero-knowledge (DVNIZK) proof. Toward our aim, we first give out a new construction of the oblivious DVNIZK proof system, which is compatible with a new class of algebraic MAC schemes. As a consequence, our APAKE protocol needs only 2 flows of messages in the authentication phase, which is very efficient in terms of rounds. Moreover, we show that this protocol enjoys stronger security guarantees while achieves considerably computational performance.

1 Introduction

Among numerous mechanisms for user authentication, passwords are definitely the most commonly used method of accessing modern computer networks and information systems [1]. Password authentication, usually integrated with key exchange simultaneously, has been proven to enjoy many advantages. For example, it can be easily operated and deployed as it only requires users to remember low-entropy passwords [2]; it is naturally compatible with various authentication means such as smart cards and biometric templates because passwords are convenient to obtain [3]. As a consequence, much attention has been paid on the fundamental security of passwords [4], the theoretical analyses and designing techniques of password authenticated key exchange (PAKE) protocols [5], as well as the standardization of password authentication schemes [6].

© Springer Nature Switzerland AG 2020
Z. Liu and M. Yung (Eds.): Inscrypt 2019, LNCS 12020, pp. 499–516, 2020.
https://doi.org/10.1007/978-3-030-42921-8_30

Anonymous Password Authenticated Key Exchange. Along with the increased awareness of security and privacy, there is an urgent need for strengthening the widely deployed PAKE protocols with additional anonymity property [7]. To be specific, it is desirable to authenticate legitimate users via low-entropy passwords while keeping their actual identities private to outside adversaries and even to the server.

To address this need, Viet et al. [8] proposed the first anonymous password authenticated key exchange (APAKE) protocol, through neatly blending an oblivious transfer (OT) protocol into a traditional two-party PAKE scheme. Since then, many research results have been put forward on the construction of more secure and more efficient APAKE protocols, either in password-only setting [9–12] or in the storage-extra setting [13–16]. Furthermore, the international organization for standardization (ISO) has developed and published the international standard ISO/IEC 20009-4 [17], which standardizes both the above two types of APAKE protocols.

For password-only APAKE protocols [8,11,12], a password is the only long-term secret that a user needs. They are very convenient from a user's point of view, but enjoy poor scalability since the computational complexity is in linear proportion to the number N of possible users [13]. As an innovative solution, APAKE protocols in the storage-extra setting were proposed by Yang et al. [13,14], and further improved by Zhang et al. [15] and Shin et al. [16], in which each user obtains a credential from the server, protects it by her password and stores the password-wrapped credential on some public storage (e.g., a public directory or an ipad). Then, in the authentication phase, the user recovers the credential via using her password and shows the possession of a valid credential to the server in an anonymous way, usually relying on some appropriate zero-knowledge proof systems. Notably, the computational cost needed by the server in the storage-extra setting is independent of the number of registered users, thus breaking the lower bound $\mathcal{O}(N)$ in the password-only setting.

However, we note that most of the existing APAKE protocols are developed in the random oracle model. Specifically, only few of APAKE protocols in the password-only setting [12,18] and, to the best of our knowledge, no APAKE protocols in the storage-extra setting have been proven secure in the standard model. Note that the random oracle model is only an ideal abstraction for the cryptographic hash functions, and there exists no random oracle definition that a public PPT algorithm can hope to satisfy [19]. Therefore, it is urgent to design storage-extra APAKE protocols in the standard model.

Storage-Extra APAKE in the Standard Model. Although we might be able to adapt classic storage-extra APAKE protocols to provide security in the standard model by adopting zero-knowledge proof schemes in the standard model (and without pairing-based assumptions). This approach will inherently increase the round number of the resulting APAKE protocols, since it is well known that one zero-knowledge proof typically requires at least three moves in this scenario.

The situation seems to be changed with the introduction of designated-verifier non-interactive zero-knowledge (DVNIZK) proof systems by Chaidos et al. [20], which could provide proof of knowledge for a wide variety of algebraic statements related with some public words. One may wish to construct storage-extra APAKE protocols in standard model by starting from the efficient APAKE protocol [15] in the random oracle model based on algebraic message authentication codes (MACs) [21], and simply replacing the underlying zero-knowledge proof systems by some kind of DVNIZK proof schemes. Nevertheless, it is shown by Couteau et al.'s work [22] that constructing DVNIZK proof schemes compatible with algebraic MACs is not as simple as we first thought, because that the secret MAC keys have been re-used in the verification of the DVNIZK proofs. The solution developed by Couteau et al. consists of not only introducing additional random masks (i.e., $t_i \cdot G$ in Sect. 5.2 of [22]), but also requiring the underlying algebraic MAC scheme to satisfy a stronger (and cumbersome) notion of unforgeability called extended unforgeability.

Our Contributions. In this paper, we present a new storage-extra APAKE protocol in the standard model by further exploiting the construction of DVNIZK proof system compatible with algebraic MACs. Our main contributions can be summarized as follows:

- We give out a new construction of the oblivious DVNIZK proof scheme compatible with a new class of algebraic MAC schemes. Recall that Couteau et al. constructed oblivious DVNIZK proofs only for the algebraic MAC scheme abstracted from MAC_{GGM}, which is one of the two MAC schemes presented in [23]. We present an oblivious DVNIZK proof system for a class of algebraic MAC schemes generalized from MAC_{wBB}, which is based on the weak Boneh-Boyen signature [24].
- We avoid the requirement of the cumbersome security notion of extended unforgeability for the algebraic MAC scheme, which is quite hard to be verified and brings additional difficulties to the security proof. Note that the main reason for such a complicated definition is that the secret MAC key has been reused in the verification process of the DVNIZK proof. We overcome this obstacle by simulating verification oracles of the DVNIZK proof through the outputs of the MAC scheme instead of the MAC key.
- We present the first storage-extra APAKE protocol in the standard model without pairing-based assumptions, based on algebraic MACs and oblivious DVNIZK proofs. Beyond proving possession of a credential on a single value of identity, our construction can support credentials certifying many attributes at once and thus could handle more complex access policies such as expiration dates and access rights. Our APAKE protocol needs only 2 flows of messages during the authentication phase, which is very efficient in terms of round efficiency.

Organization. In Sect. 2, we briefly recall the necessary preliminaries. In Sect. 3, our construction of an oblivious DVNIZK proof system for a new class of algebraic MAC scheme is presented. Then, a new storage-extra APAKE protocol in the standard model is proposed in Sect. 4.

2   Preliminaries

In this section, we review the main cryptographic primitives needed in our construction. Throughout this paper, λ denotes the security parameter.

2.1   Algebraic Message Authentication Codes

A message authentication code (MAC) is defined by the following four PPT algorithms $M = (M.Setup, M.KeyGen, M.Mac, M.Verify)$ with an associated tag space $\mathcal{T}$, such that

- $M.Setup(1^\lambda)$ sets up the public parameters pp of the MAC, which will be implicitly (or explicitly) passed as an argument to the algorithms below.
- $M.KeyGen(\text{pp})$ is a key generation algorithm which takes as input the public parameters pp, outputs a secret key sk and public issuer parameters ipp;
- $M.Mac(sk, m)$ is a MAC algorithm which takes as input the key sk and a message m, generates an authentication tag σ on the message;
- $M.Verify(sk, m, \sigma)$ is the verification algorithm which takes as input the key sk, a message m and a tag σ, outputs $b = 1$ when σ is a valid tag with respect to sk and m and outputs $b = 0$ otherwise.

We will need MAC schemes that are existentially unforgeable under chosen message and verification attacks (UF-CMVA).

Definition 1 (UF-CMVA Security). *A MAC scheme M is* UF-CMVA *secure if for any PPT adversary $\mathcal{A}$ which has access to the public issuer parameters* ipp *as well as the MAC and verification oracles, it holds that*

$$\Pr\left[\begin{array}{l} Q \leftarrow \emptyset, \text{pp} \leftarrow M.Setup(1^\lambda), \\ (sk, \text{ipp}) \leftarrow M.KeyGen(\text{pp}), : \\ (m, \sigma) \leftarrow \mathcal{A}^{\mathcal{O}_{sk}(\cdot)}(\text{pp}, \text{ipp}) \end{array} \begin{array}{l} M.Verify(sk, m, \sigma) = 1, \\ \wedge\ m \notin Q \end{array}\right] \leq negl(\lambda),$$

where the oracle $\mathcal{O}_{sk}(\cdot)$ treats the MAC and verification queries as follows: $\mathcal{O}.Mac(m)$ *outputs $M.Mac(sk, m)$ and sets $Q \leftarrow Q \cup \{m\}$;* $\mathcal{O}.Verify(m, \sigma)$ *outputs $M.Verify(sk, m, \sigma)$.*

For our purpose, we additionally require the MAC scheme to satisfy pseudorandomness property, which means that, as long as the MAC key is kept secret, no PPT adversary could distinguish a valid MAC tag from a random one. Based on the definitions of pseudorandom functions (PRFs) and weak pseudorandomness [15], we define the pseudorandomness property as follows.

Definition 2 (Pseudorandomness). *A MAC scheme M is said to satisfy pseudorandomness property, if for any PPT adversary $\mathcal{A}$, it holds that*

$$\Pr\left[\begin{array}{l} \text{pp} \leftarrow M.Setup(1^\lambda), \\ (sk, \text{ipp}) \leftarrow M.KeyGen(\text{pp}), \\ (m^*, \text{st}) \leftarrow \mathcal{A}^{\mathcal{O}.Mac(\cdot)}(\text{ipp}), \quad : b' = b \\ \sigma_0 = M.Mac(sk, m^*), \sigma_1 \leftarrow \mathcal{T}, \\ b \leftarrow \{0, 1\}, b' = \mathcal{A}^{\mathcal{O}.Mac(\cdot)}(y_b, \text{st}) \end{array}\right] \leq \frac{1}{2} + negl(\lambda).$$

Algebraic MACs are a special kind of MACs that consist of only group operations instead of block ciphers or hash functions, thus easily suitable for efficient zero-knowledge proof of statements related to these MAC tags. In [23], Chase et al. proposed the first two algebraic MACs with efficient protocols for proof of knowledge, which are based on generic group model (GGM) and decisional Diffie-Hellman (DDH) assumption respectively. Since then, several improved algebraic MAC schemes have been put forward [15,25,26].

In this paper, we will use the algebraic MAC scheme MAC_{wBB} proposed in [26], which is based on the weak Boneh-Boyen signature [24]. Denote by β a positive integer and $\mathbf{m} = (m_1, m_2, \cdots, m_\beta)$ a vector of message. Let $GGen(1^\lambda)$ be an efficient algorithm which generates a multiplicative group $\mathbb{G}$ of order p and a generator g of this group. The scheme consists of the following algorithms.

- $M.Setup(1^\lambda)$ outputs $\mathbf{pp} = (\mathbb{G}, g, p) \leftarrow GGen(1^\lambda)$;
- $M.KeyGen(\mathbf{pp})$ chooses randomly $\beta + 1$ elements $x_i \leftarrow \mathbb{Z}_p^*$, computes $X_i = g^{x_i}$ for every $i \in \{0, 1, \cdots, \beta\}$. Then, the secret key is $sk = (x_0, x_1, \cdots, x_\beta)$ and the public issuer parameter is $\mathbf{ipp} = (X_0, X_1, \cdots, X_\beta)$;
- $M.Mac(sk, \mathbf{m})$ takes as input the key $sk = (x_0, x_1, \cdots, x_\beta)$ and a vector of messages $\mathbf{m} = (m_1, m_2, \cdots, m_\beta)$, computes $\sigma = g^{1/(x_0 + \sum_{j=1}^{\beta} x_j \cdot m_j)}$ and $\sigma_j = \sigma^{x_j}$ for $j = 1, 2, \cdots, \beta^1$, and sets the MAC tag as $\Sigma = (\sigma, \sigma_1, \cdots, \sigma_\beta)$;
- $M.Verify(sk, \mathbf{m}, (\sigma, \sigma_1, \cdots, \sigma_\beta))$ is the verification algorithm, which outputs $b = 1$ iff $\sigma = g^{1/(x_0 + \sum_{j=1}^{\beta} x_j \cdot m_j)}$ and $\sigma_j = \sigma^{x_j}$ for $j = 1, 2, \cdots, \beta$.

With respect to the security, it has been proven by Camenisch et al. [26] that this algebraic MAC scheme is UF-CMVA under the SCDHI assumption, which is a computational variation of the SDDHI assumption [27]. Moreover, we can easily prove that under the SDDHI assumption this algebraic MAC scheme satisfies the pseudorandomness property.

Theorem 1. *If the SDDHI and SCDHI assumptions hold in group $\mathbb{G}$, then the algebraic MAC scheme MAC_{wBB} satisfies the pseudorandomness property.*

2.2 Additively Homomorphic Encryption Schemes

A public key encryption scheme is defined as a triple of PPT algorithms $\mathcal{E} = (\mathcal{E}.KeyGen, \mathcal{E}.Enc, \mathcal{E}.Dec)$ with an associated message space $\mathbb{Z}_N$ and a random space $\mathbb{Z}_R$, such that

- $\mathcal{E}.KeyGen(1^\lambda)$ takes as input the security parameter 1^λ and outputs a pair of encryption and decryption keys (ek, dk);
- $\mathcal{E}.Enc(ek, m; r)$ takes as input a public encryption key ek, a message $m \in \mathbb{Z}_N$ and a random value $r \in \mathbb{Z}_R$, and outputs a ciphertext c;
- $\mathcal{E}.Dec(dk, c)$ takes as input a decryption key dk and a ciphertext c, and outputs a message m or $\perp$.

---

[1] As pointed out by Camenisch et al. [26], the auxiliary information σ_j are not required for the MAC verification, but they are useful to improve the efficiency of credential presentation, and additionally remove the requirement of extended unforgeability.

The IND-CPA security for a public key encryption scheme is defined as follows.

Definition 3 (IND-CPA Security). *A public key encryption scheme $\mathcal{E}$ is IND-CPA secure, if for any PPT adversary $\mathcal{A}$, it holds that*

$$\Pr\left[\begin{array}{l} (ek, dk) \leftarrow \mathcal{E}.KeyGen(1^\lambda), \\ (m_0, m_1, \mathrm{st}) \leftarrow \mathcal{A}(ek), b \leftarrow \{0,1\}, \\ r \leftarrow \mathbb{Z}_R, c \leftarrow \mathcal{E}.Enc(ek, m_b; r), b' = \mathcal{A}(\mathrm{st}, c) \end{array} : b' = b\right] \leq \frac{1}{2} + negl(\lambda).$$

In this paper, we focus on public key encryption schemes that are additively homomorphic for both the message and the random value. We say that an encryption scheme is *strongly additive*, if there exists an efficient operation $\oplus$ such that for any key pair $(ek, dk) \leftarrow \mathcal{E}.KeyGen(1^\lambda)$, any two ciphertexts $c_i = \mathcal{E}.Enc(ek, m_i; r_i)$ of messages $m_i \in \mathbb{Z}_N$ under the randomness $r_i \in \mathbb{Z}_R$ for $i \in \{1, 2\}$, it holds that $c_1 \oplus c_2 = \mathcal{E}.Enc(ek, m_1 + m_2 \mod N; r_1 + r_2 \mod R)$. For an integer $\rho \in \mathbb{Z}$, we denote by $\rho \odot c$ the ciphetext $\mathcal{E}.Enc(ek, \rho m \mod N; \rho r \mod R)$, which can be efficiently computed using the formula of the form $\mathcal{E}.Enc(ek, m; r) \oplus \cdots \oplus \mathcal{E}.Enc(ek, m; r)$. Moreover, given two ciphertexts c, c', we denote by $c \ominus c'$ the operation $c \oplus ((-1) \odot c')$.

A strongly additive encryption scheme $\mathcal{E}$ is further said to be *DVNIZK-friendly*, if $gcd(N, R) = 1$ and for any $(ek, dk) \leftarrow \mathcal{E}.KeyGen(1^\lambda)$, the value $\mathcal{E}.Enc(ek, m; 0)$ is efficiently decodable to get the plaintext $m \mod N$. For DVNIZK-friendly encryption scheme over groups $\mathbb{Z}_N$ of composite order of the form $N = pq$, we can resort to a slight variation [20, 28] of the well-known Paillier encryption scheme [29]; For groups $\mathbb{Z}_N$ of prime order $N = p$, we could instantiate it with the Castagnos-Laguillaumie encryption scheme [30].

Note that the above encryption/decryption algorithms and scalar product could be extended to vectors in a natural way. For example, given vectors $\mathbf{m} = (m_1, m_2, \cdots, m_\beta)$ and $\mathbf{r} = (r_1, r_2, \cdots, r_\beta)$ of the length $\beta \geq 1$, we could view $\mathcal{E}.Enc(ek, \mathbf{m}; \mathbf{r})$ as the vector $(\mathcal{E}.Enc(ek, m_i; r_i))_{i=1}^{\beta}$. Given $\rho = (\rho_1, \rho_2, \cdots, \rho_\beta)$ and $c = \mathcal{E}.Enc(ek, m; r)$, we let $\rho \odot c$ denote the vector $(\mathcal{E}.Enc(ek, \rho_i m; \rho_i r))_{i=1}^{\beta}$.

2.3 Designated-Verifier Non-interactive Zero-Knowledge Proof

A designated-verifier non-interactive zero-knowledge (DVNIZK) proof system [20] for a family of languages $\{\mathfrak{L}_{\mathrm{crs}}\}$ consists of four algorithms $\Pi = (\Pi.Setup, \Pi.KeyGen, \Pi.Prove, \Pi.Verify)$. The setup algorithm $\Pi.Setup(1^\lambda)$ outputs a common reference string crs; The algorithm $\Pi.KeyGen(\mathrm{crs})$ outputs a public proving key pk and a secret verification key vk; The proving algorithm $\Pi.Prove(pk, x, w)$ takes as input the proving key pk, a word x and a witness w for the statement $x \in \mathfrak{L}_{\mathrm{crs}}$, generates a proof π; The verification algorithm $\Pi.Verify(pk, vk, x, \pi)$ outputs $b \in \{0, 1\}$ indicating either accept or reject.

However, when taking an algebraic MAC tag with respect to a user's identity as her credential, the original definition of DVNIZK proof system cannot be directly used to prove knowledge of the identity. The main difficulty is that the MAC verification cannot be carried out by the user while she does not know the secret MAC key. To tackle this problem, Couteau et al. [22] introduced a new primitive called oblivious DVNIZK proof system, which can be used to prove knowledge of a witness w corresponding to a secret relation $R(sk, w, x) = 1$ with sk unknown to the prover.

In this paper, we will focus on secret relations $\{R_{crs}(sk, \cdot, \cdot)\}$ and languages $\{\mathcal{L}_{crs}\}$ that are defined by algebraic MAC schemes. Given a MAC scheme M with secret MAC key sk, we will simply set sk as the secret relation key, and take a MAC message and tag pair as a witness and word pair, in the sense that $R_{crs}(sk, w, x) = 1$ and $x \in \mathcal{L}_{crs}$ if and only if $M.Verify(sk, w, x) = 1$.

Definition 4 (Oblivious DVNIZK Proof [22]). *An oblivious DVNIZK proof system for a family of languages related with secret relations $\{R_{crs}\}$ is defined by the following algorithms $\Pi = (\Pi.Setup, \Pi.RelSetup, \Pi.KeyGen, \Pi.Prove, \Pi.Verify)$, such that*

- *$\Pi.Setup(1^\lambda)$ takes as input the security parameter 1^λ, outputs a common reference string* crs *and a trapdoor* td;
- *$\Pi.RelSetup(\text{crs})$ generates a secret key sk for the secret relation, together with some public issuer parameters* ipp;
- *$\Pi.KeyGen(\text{crs})$ outputs a key pair (pk, vk), consisting of a public proving key pk and a secret verification key vk;*
- *$\Pi.Prove(\text{crs}, \text{ipp}, pk, (x_p, x_s), w)$ takes as input the parameters* crs, ipp, *the proving key pk, a word $x = (x_p, x_s) \in \mathcal{L}_{crs}$ consisting of a public subword x_p and a secret subword x_s, and a witness for the relation $R_{crs}(sk, w, x) = 1$, then outputs a proof π;*
- *$\Pi.Verify(\text{crs}, \text{ipp}, pk, vk, sk, x_p, \pi)$ is the verification algorithm which verifies whether a proof π is valid with respect to the relation $R_{crs}(sk, w, x) = 1$. It outputs $b = 1$ if the proof is valid and $b = 0$ otherwise.*

We say that an oblivious DVNIZK proof system is secure, if it satisfies completeness, knowledge extractability (which is a strengthening of soundness) and oblivious zero-knowledge properties defined as follows.

Definition 5 (Completeness). *An oblivious DVNIZK proof system Π satisfies completeness property, if for all parameters $(\text{crs}, \text{td}) \leftarrow \Pi.Setup(1^\lambda)$, $(sk, \text{ipp}) \leftarrow \Pi.RelSetup(\text{crs})$, $(pk, vk) \leftarrow \Pi.KeyGen(\text{crs})$, and every proof $\pi \leftarrow \Pi.Prove(\text{crs}, \text{ipp}, pk, (x_p, x_s), w)$, it holds that $\Pi.Verify(\text{crs}, \text{ipp}, pk, vk, sk, x_p, \pi) = 1$.*

Definition 6 (Knowledge Extractability). *An oblivious DVNIZK proof system Π for secret relations $\{R_{crs}\}$ defined by an algebraic MAC M is said to satisfy knowledge extractability property, if for every PPT adversary $\mathcal{A}$, there exists an efficient extracting algorithm Ext such that*

$$\Pr \left[\begin{array}{l} (\text{crs}, \text{td}) \leftarrow \Pi.Setup(1^\lambda), \\ (sk, \text{ipp}) \leftarrow \Pi.RelSetup(\text{crs}), \\ (pk, vk) \leftarrow \Pi.KeyGen(\text{crs}), \\ (\pi, x_p) \leftarrow \mathcal{A}^{O_{M.Mac}, O_{\Pi.Ver}}(\text{crs}, \text{ipp}, pk) \\ (x_s, w) \leftarrow Ext(\text{crs}, \text{ipp}, pk, x_p, \pi, \text{td}) \end{array} \right. : \left. \begin{array}{l} R_{crs}(sk, w, (x_p, x_s)) = 0, \\ \Pi.Verify(\text{crs}, \text{ipp}, pk, \\ vk, sk, x_p, \pi) = 1 \end{array} \right] \leq negl(\lambda),$$

where the oracle $O_{M.Mac}(\cdot)$ denotes $M.Mac(sk, \cdot)$, and the oracle $O_{\Pi.Ver}(\cdot, \cdot)$ denotes $\Pi.Verify(\mathbf{crs}, \mathbf{ipp}, pk, vk, sk, \cdot, \cdot)$. In addition, it is required that the oracle $O_{\Pi.Ver}(\cdot, \cdot)$ should be efficiently simulated, when the secret key sk is replaced by oracle access to $M.Verify(sk, \cdot, \cdot)$.

Definition 7 (Oblivious Zero Knowledge). *An oblivious DVNIZK proof system Π for secret relations $\{R_{\mathrm{crs}}\}$ defined by an algebraic MAC M is said to satisfy oblivious zero knowledge property, if for every PPT adversary $\mathcal{A}$, there exists an efficient algorithm Sim such that*

$$\left| \Pr\left[\begin{array}{l} (\mathbf{crs}, \mathbf{td}) \leftarrow \Pi.Setup(1^\lambda), \\ (pk, vk) \leftarrow \Pi.KeyGen(\mathbf{crs}), \\ (x, w, sk, \mathbf{ipp}, \mathbf{st}) \leftarrow \mathcal{A}(\mathbf{crs}, pk, vk) \\ \pi \leftarrow \Pi.Prove(\mathbf{crs}, \mathbf{ipp}, pk, x, w) \end{array} : \begin{array}{l} R_{\mathrm{crs}}(sk, w, x) = 1, \\ \wedge \mathcal{A}(\mathbf{st}, \pi) = 1 \end{array} \right] \right.$$

$$\left. - \Pr\left[\begin{array}{l} (\mathbf{crs}, \mathbf{td}) \leftarrow \Pi.Setup(1^\lambda), \\ (pk, vk) \leftarrow \Pi.KeyGen(\mathbf{crs}), \\ (x, w, sk, \mathbf{ipp}, \mathbf{st}) \leftarrow \mathcal{A}(\mathbf{crs}, pk, vk) \\ \pi \leftarrow Sim(\mathbf{crs}, \mathbf{ipp}, pk, x_p, vk, sk) \end{array} : \begin{array}{l} R_{\mathrm{crs}}(sk, w, x) = 1, \\ \wedge \mathcal{A}(\mathbf{st}, \pi) = 1 \end{array} \right] \right| \leq negl(\lambda),$$

where $x = (x_p, x_s)$ consists of a public subword x_p and a secret subword x_s.

3   A New Construction of Oblivious DVNIZK Proof

In this section, we introduce a new construction of oblivious DVNIZK proof system for languages related to the algebraic MAC scheme MAC_{wBB} presented in Sect. 2.1, and prove the security properties of our construction.

3.1   The Construction of Oblivious DVNIZK Proof

We will take an algebraic MAC tag on a user's attributes as a credential for this user, which is treated in a similar way as in [22,23]. Nevertheless, the specific property of the algebraic MAC scheme MAC_{wBB} based on weak Bonel-Boyen signature (see definition in Sect. 2.1) will allow us to build a more efficient oblivious DVNIZK proof system than before. Recall that, when the algebraic MAC scheme MAC_{wBB} is considered, a MAC tag on a vector of attributes $\mathbf{m} = (m_1, m_2, \cdots, m_\beta)$ under the secret key $sk = (x_0, x_1, \cdots, x_\beta)$ is of the form $\Sigma = (\sigma, \sigma_1, \cdots, \sigma_\beta)$, where $\sigma = g^{1/(x_0 + \sum_{j=1}^\beta x_j \cdot m_j)}$. It can be rewritten as $\sigma^{-\sum_{j=1}^\beta x_j \cdot m_j} \cdot g = \sigma^{x_0}$, where the first part $\sigma^{-\sum_{j=1}^\beta x_j \cdot m_j} \cdot g$ has exponents linear in both attributes $\mathbf{m} = (m_1, m_2, \cdots, m_\beta)$ and secret keys $(x_1, x_2, \cdots, x_\beta)$. This property would be preserved even after some re-randomize technique has been applied on the credential σ. For example, when it is re-randomized as $T = \sigma^a$ for a random a, it still holds that $T^{-\sum_{j=1}^\beta x_j \cdot m_j} \cdot g^a = T^{x_0}$.

Based on the above observation, we are now ready to present our construction of oblivious DVNIZK proof system for secret relations defined by the algebraic MAC scheme MAC_{wBB}. Given the algebraic MAC scheme MAC_{wBB} denoted by $MAC_{\mathsf{wBB}} = (M.Setup, M.KeyGen, M.Mac, M.Verify)$ and a DVNIZK-friendly encryption scheme $\mathcal{E} = (\mathcal{E}.KeyGen, \mathcal{E}.Enc, \mathcal{E}.Dec)$ with message space $\mathbb{Z}_N$ of prime order $N = p$, the concrete steps of the oblivious DVNIZK proof system Π are as follows.

- $\Pi.Setup(1^\lambda)$ takes as input the security parameter 1^λ, computes $(ek, dk) \leftarrow \mathcal{E}.KeyGen(1^\lambda)$ and $\mathtt{pp} = (\mathbb{G}, g, p) \leftarrow M.Setup(1^\lambda)$, sets the common reference string as $\mathtt{crs} = (ek, \mathtt{pp})$ and the trapdoor as $\mathtt{td} = dk$. Without loss of generality, we assume that the public key ek also determines the message space $\mathbb{Z}_N$, the random source $\mathbb{Z}_R$ and a public bound B on R;
- $\Pi.RelSetup(\mathtt{crs})$ is essentially the key generation algorithm of the underlying MAC scheme MAC_{wBB}. It chooses randomly $\beta + 1$ elements $x_i \leftarrow \mathbb{Z}_p^*$ and computes $X_i = g^{x_i}$ for every $i \in \{0, 1, \cdots, \beta\}$. Then, the secret key is $sk = (x_0, x_1, \cdots, x_\beta)$ and the public issuer parameter is $\mathtt{ipp} = (X_0, X_1, \cdots, X_\beta)$;
- $\Pi.KeyGen(\mathtt{crs})$ chooses at random a value $e \leftarrow \mathbb{Z}_l$ where $l = 2^\lambda \cdot N \cdot B$, then sets the secret verification key as $vk = e$ and the public proving key as $pk = \mathcal{E}.Enc(ek, 0; e)$;
- $\Pi.Prove(\mathtt{crs}, \mathtt{ipp}, pk, (x_p, x_s), w)$ takes as input the parameters $\mathtt{crs}, \mathtt{ipp}$, the proving key pk, a credential $x = (x_p = \perp, x_s = \sigma)$ and a vector of attributes $w = (m_1, m_2, \cdots, m_\beta)$, selects a random value $a \leftarrow \mathbb{Z}_N$ and computes $T = \sigma^a$. It then chooses at random $a' \leftarrow \mathbb{Z}_N$, $m'_j \leftarrow \mathbb{Z}_N$ for $j = 1, 2, \cdots, \beta$, and computes $T' = \Pi_{j=1}^\beta \sigma_j^{-a \cdot m'_j} \cdot g^{a'}$. Next, it chooses a random vector $\mathbf{r} = (r_0, r_1, \cdots, r_\beta) \leftarrow \mathbb{Z}_R^{\beta+1}$, sets $\overline{\mathbf{m}} = (a, m_1, m_2, \cdots, m_\beta)$ and $\overline{\mathbf{m}}' = (a', m'_1, m'_2, \cdots, m'_\beta)$, and computes $\mathbf{X} = \mathcal{E}.Enc(ek, \overline{\mathbf{m}}; \mathbf{r})$ and $\mathbf{X}' = \mathcal{E}.Enc(ek, \overline{\mathbf{m}}'; \mathbf{0}) \ominus (\mathbf{r} \odot pk)$. At last, the proving algorithm outputs a proof $\pi = (T, T', \mathbf{X}, \mathbf{X}')$.
- $\Pi.Verify(\mathtt{crs}, \mathtt{ipp}, pk, vk, sk, x_p = \perp, \pi)$ verifies the proof π as follows. It first parses π as $\pi = (T, T', \mathbf{X}, \mathbf{X}')$, computes $\mathbf{X}' \oplus (e \odot \mathbf{X})$ and checks that the values in this vector are decodable, then decodes them to a vector $\mathbf{d} = (d_0, d_1, \cdots, d_\beta)$. Next, it checks that $T \neq 1$ and

$$(T^{x_0})^e \cdot T' = T^{-\sum_{j=1}^\beta x_j \cdot d_j} \cdot y^{d_0}. \tag{1}$$

Finally, it outputs $b = 1$ if π can be parsed correctly, $\mathbf{X}' \oplus (e \odot \mathbf{X})$ is decodable and the above equation holds; otherwise, it outputs $b = 0$.

3.2   Security Analysis

In this section, we show that our oblivious DVNIZK proof system satisfies completeness, knowledge extractability and oblivious zero-knowledge properties.

Theorem 2. *If the underlying encryption scheme $\mathcal{E}$ is DVNIZK-friendly, then the oblivious DVNIZK proof system Π satisfies the completeness property.*

Proof. Firstly, if a proof $\pi = (T, T', \mathbf{X}, \mathbf{X}')$ is generated honestly, one can easily deduce that

$$\mathbf{X}' \oplus (e \odot \mathbf{X}) = (\mathcal{E}.Enc(ek, \overline{\mathbf{m}}'; 0) \ominus (\mathbf{r} \odot pk)) \oplus (e \odot \mathcal{E}.Enc(ek, \overline{\mathbf{m}}; \mathbf{r}))$$
$$= \mathcal{E}.Enc(ek, \overline{\mathbf{m}}'; -e \cdot \mathbf{r}) \oplus \mathcal{E}.Enc(ek, e \cdot \overline{\mathbf{m}}; e \cdot \mathbf{r})$$
$$= \mathcal{E}.Enc(ek, \overline{\mathbf{m}}' + e \cdot \overline{\mathbf{m}}; 0),$$

which is decodable according to the definition of DVNIZK-friendly encryption schemes. Moreover, we can obtain that $\mathbf{d} = \overline{\mathbf{m}}' + e \cdot \overline{\mathbf{m}} \mod N$, yielding that $d_0 = a' + e \cdot a \mod N$ and $d_j = m'_j + e \cdot m_j \mod N$ for all $j = 1, 2, \cdots, \beta$. Therefore, by combining with the equation $T^{-\sum_{j=1}^{\beta} m_j \cdot x_j} \cdot g^a = T^{x_0}$, we have

$$(T^{x_0})^e \cdot T' = \left(T^{-\sum_{j=1}^{\beta} x_j \cdot m_j} \cdot g^a \right)^e \cdot \left(\Pi_{j=1}^{\beta} \sigma_j^{-a \cdot m'_j} \cdot g^{a'} \right)$$
$$= \left(T^{-\sum_{j=1}^{\beta} x_j \cdot m_j} \cdot g^a \right)^e \cdot \left(T^{-\sum_{j=1}^{\beta} x_j \cdot m'_j} \cdot g^{a'} \right)$$
$$= T^{-\sum_{j=1}^{\beta} x_j \cdot (m'_j + e \cdot m_j)} \cdot g^{a' + e \cdot a}$$
$$= T^{-\sum_{j=1}^{\beta} x_j \cdot d_j} \cdot g^{d_0}.$$

Theorem 3. *If the underlying encryption scheme $\mathcal{E}$ is DVNIZK-friendly, and the algebraic MAC scheme MAC_{wBB} is* UF-CMVA *secure, then the oblivious DVNIZK proof system Π satisfies the knowledge extractability property.*

Proof. Our proof starts with the construction of an extracting algorithm Ext. Given a proof $\pi = (T, T', \{T'_j\}_{j=1}^{\beta}, \mathbf{X}, \mathbf{X}')$ and the trapdoor $\mathtt{td} = dk$, the algorithm Ext computes $\overline{\mathbf{m}} = (a, m_1, m_2, \cdots, m_\beta) = \mathcal{E}.Dec(dk, \mathbf{X})$, sets $\sigma = T^{1/a}$ and then outputs $(x_s = \sigma, w = (m_1, m_2, \cdots, m_\beta))$.

We next turn to estimate the probability of the event $R_{\mathtt{crs}}(sk, w, (x_p, x_s)) = 0 \wedge \Pi.Verify(\mathtt{crs}, \mathtt{ipp}, pk, vk, sk, x_p, \pi) = 1$. Recall that we only focus on secret relations that are defined by algebraic MAC schemes in the sense that $R(sk, w, x) = 1 \Leftrightarrow M.Verify(sk, w, x) = 1$. It is then sufficient to show that the oracle $O_{\Pi.Ver}(\cdot, \cdot) = \Pi.Verify(\mathtt{crs}, \mathtt{ipp}, pk, vk, sk, \cdot, \cdot)$ can be efficiently simulated, with sk replaced by oracle access to $M.Verify(sk, \cdot, \cdot)$.

We denote by $O_{SimVer}(\cdot, \cdot) = SimVerify(\mathtt{crs}, \mathtt{ipp}, pk, vk, dk, \cdot, \cdot)$ the simulated verification algorithm with access to the oracle $M.Verify(sk, \cdot, \cdot)$, and proceed as follows. Assuming that $(\mathtt{crs}, \mathtt{td} = dk), (sk, \mathtt{ipp}), (pk, vk)$ are generated as before and $(\mathtt{crs}, \mathtt{ipp}, pk, vk, dk)$ are provided to $SimVerify$ as input. Then, for each query $(x_p = \perp, \pi)$ asked by the adversary $\mathcal{A}$, we can decrypt the ciphertexts $\mathbf{X}, \mathbf{X}'$ to vectors $\overline{\mathbf{m}} = (a, m_1, m_2, \cdots, m_\beta) \leftarrow \mathcal{E}.Dec(dk, \mathbf{X})$, $\overline{\mathbf{m}}' = (a', m'_1, m'_2, \cdots, m'_\beta) \leftarrow \mathcal{E}.Dec(dk, \mathbf{X}')$. Finally, we compute $\sigma = T^{1/a}$, and check that all the following equations are true:

$$-e \odot (\mathbf{X} \ominus \mathcal{E}.Enc(ek, \overline{\mathbf{m}}; 0)) = \mathbf{X}' \ominus \mathcal{E}.Enc(ek, \overline{\mathbf{m}}'; 0), \tag{2}$$

$$M.Verify(sk, (m_1, m_2, \cdots, m_\beta), \sigma) = 1, \tag{3}$$

$$T' = T^{-\sum_{j=1}^{\beta} x_j \cdot m'_j} \cdot g^{a'}. \tag{4}$$

If all the checks succeeded, $SimVerify$ outputs 1; otherwise, it outputs 0.

Here we remark that, under the conditions $\sigma = T^{1/a}$ and $M.Verify(sk, (m_1, m_2, \cdots, m_\beta), \sigma) = 1$, the check Eq. (4) could in fact be calculated without the knowledge of the secret key $sk = (x_0, x_1, \cdots, x_\beta)$. Alternatively, we can ask to the MAC oracle to get $(\sigma, \sigma_1, \cdots, \sigma_\beta) = M.Mac(sk, (m_1, m_2, \cdots, m_\beta))$ and then check that

$$T' = \Pi_{j=1}^{\beta} \sigma_j^{-a \cdot m'_j} \cdot g^{a'}. \tag{5}$$

This property is very attractive for the context of DVNIZK proof, since it enables us to avoid resorting to a stronger notion of unforgeability (called extended unforgeability [22]) for the underlying algebraic MAC schemes.

In the following, we will prove that the simulated oracle $O_{SimVer}(\cdot, \cdot)$ is indistinguishable from the real oracle $O_{\Pi.Ver}(\cdot, \cdot)$. First, we show that, given a query π, if $O_{SimVer}(\bot, \pi) = 1$, then $O_{\Pi.Ver}(\bot, \pi) = 1$. Recall that $\overline{\mathbf{m}} \leftarrow \mathcal{E}.Dec(dk, \mathbf{X})$ and $\overline{\mathbf{m}}' \leftarrow \mathcal{E}.Dec(dk, \mathbf{X}')$, it follows immediately that the Eq. (2) implies $\mathbf{X}, \mathbf{X}'$ are of the form $\mathbf{X} = \mathcal{E}.Enc(ek, \overline{\mathbf{m}}; \mathbf{r})$ and $\mathbf{X}' = \mathcal{E}.Enc(ek, \overline{\mathbf{m}}'; -e \cdot \mathbf{r})$ for some random vector $\mathbf{r}$. Henceforth, the vector $\mathbf{X}' \oplus (e \odot \mathbf{X})$ is decodable, and the decoded vector is $\mathbf{d} = \overline{\mathbf{m}}' + e \cdot \overline{\mathbf{m}}$. On the other hand, if the Eq. (3) is satisfied, it yields that $\sigma = g^{1/(x_0 + \sum_{j=1}^{\beta} x_j \cdot m_j)}$, which in turn implies that $T^{-\sum_{j=1}^{\beta} x_j \cdot m_j} \cdot g^a = T^{x_0}$. Combining these facts with Eq. (4), we can easily get the equation $(T^{x_0})^e \cdot (\Pi_{j=1}^{\beta}(T'_j)^{-x_j} \cdot T') = T^{-\sum_{j=1}^{\beta} x_j \cdot d_j} \cdot g^{d_0}$. This indicates that $O_{\Pi.Ver}(\bot, \pi) = 1$.

Next, we prove that, if $O_{\Pi.Ver}(\bot, \pi) = 1$, then $O_{SimVer}(\bot, \pi) = 1$. Assume that $\mathbf{X} = \mathcal{E}.Enc(ek, \overline{\mathbf{m}}; \mathbf{r})$ and $\mathbf{X}' = \mathcal{E}.Enc(ek, \overline{\mathbf{m}}'; \mathbf{r}')$ for some random vectors $\mathbf{r}$ and $\mathbf{r}'$. We would easily deduce from the fact $\mathbf{X}' \oplus (e \odot \mathbf{X})$ is decodable that $\mathbf{r}' = -e \cdot \mathbf{r}$, which thus yields that the Eq. (2) is satisfied. Furthermore, to obtain a contradiction, we now suppose that Eq. (1) holds, while the Eqs. (3) or (4) is rejected. Note that the Eq. (1) can be rewritten as

$$\left(T^{x_0}/T^{-\sum_{j=1}^{\beta} x_j \cdot m_j} \cdot g^a\right)^e = T^{-\sum_{j=1}^{\beta} x_j \cdot m'_j} \cdot g^{a'}/T'. \tag{6}$$

If the Eq. (3) does not hold, we get $T^{x_0}/T^{-\sum_{j=1}^{\beta} x_j \cdot m_j} \cdot g^a \neq 1$; if (4) does not hold, we have $T^{-\sum_{j=1}^{\beta} x_j \cdot m'_j} \cdot g^{a'}/T' \neq 1$. Since e is randomly chosen from some sufficiently large space, it holds with overwhelming probability that $e \neq 0 \mod N$. Hence, we can conclude that $T^{x_0}/T^{-\sum_{j=1}^{\beta} x_j \cdot m_j} \cdot g^a \neq 1$ and $T^{-\sum_{j=1}^{\beta} x_j \cdot m'_j} \cdot g^{a'}/T' \neq 1$ will happen simultaneously. Using a similar technique as in [20], we can then get from Eq. (6) the value $e \mod N$, which is supposed to be statistically hidden.

Now, since the simulated oracle $O_{SimVer}(\cdot, \cdot)$ is indistinguishable from the real oracle $O_{\Pi.Ver}(\cdot, \cdot)$, and the valid of secret relation has essentially been checked through Eq. (3), we conclude that the event $R(sk, w, (x_p, x_s)) = 0 \wedge \Pi.Verify(\mathtt{crs}, \mathtt{ipp}, pk, vk, sk, x_p, \pi) = 1$ happens with only negligible probability. This completes the proof.

Theorem 4. *If the underlying encryption scheme $\mathcal{E}$ is* IND-CPA *secure, then the oblivious DVNIZK proof system Π is obliviously zero-knowledge.*

Proof. The proof will be divided into two steps: constructing a simulator and proving the indistinguishability. We first construct a simulator $Sim(\mathtt{crs}, \mathtt{ipp}, pk, x_p, vk, sk)$ which producing simulated zero-knowledge proof π as follows. It first selects randomly $T \leftarrow \mathbb{G}$ and $\mathbf{d} = (d_0, d_1, \cdots, d_\beta) \leftarrow \mathbb{Z}_N^{\beta+1}$, and computes

$$T' = T^{-\sum_{j=1}^{\beta} x_j \cdot d_j} \cdot g^{d_0} / (T^{x_0})^e. \tag{7}$$

The simulator then chooses at random $\overline{\mathbf{m}} = (a, m_1, m_2, \cdots, m_\beta) \leftarrow \mathbb{Z}_N^{\beta+1}$, $\overline{\mathbf{m}}' = (a', m_1', m_2', \cdots, m_\beta') \leftarrow \mathbb{Z}_N^{\beta+1}$ and $\mathbf{r} = (r_0, r_1, \cdots, r_\beta) \leftarrow \mathbb{Z}_R^{\beta+1}$, and computes

$$\mathbf{X} = \mathcal{E}.Enc(ek, \overline{\mathbf{m}}; \mathbf{r}), \tag{8}$$
$$\mathbf{X}' = \mathcal{E}.Enc(ek, \mathbf{d} - e \cdot \overline{\mathbf{m}}; -e \cdot \mathbf{r}). \tag{9}$$

We now show that, given an adversary $\mathcal{A}$ against the indistinguishability of $\Pi.Prove$ and Sim, we can construct an adversary $\mathcal{A}_S$ against the IND-CPA security of S. The IND-CPA adversary $\mathcal{A}_S$ first obtains $(x = (x_p = \perp, x_s = \sigma), w = (m_1, m_2, \cdots, m_\beta))$ from the adversary $\mathcal{A}$, then it chooses randomly $a \leftarrow \mathbb{Z}_N$, sets $\overline{\mathbf{m}} = (a, m_1, m_2, \cdots, m_\beta)$ and $T = \sigma^a$, picks at random $\widetilde{\mathbf{m}} = (\tilde{a}, \tilde{m}_1, \tilde{m}_2, \cdots, \tilde{m}_\beta) \leftarrow \mathbb{Z}_N^{\beta+1}$, and sends the $(\overline{\mathbf{m}}, \widetilde{\mathbf{m}})$ to the IND-CPA challenger to get back a challenging ciphertext $\mathbf{X}$. Next, it selects randomly $\mathbf{d} = (d_0, d_1, \cdots, d_\beta) \leftarrow \mathbb{Z}_N^{\beta+1}$, computes $\mathbf{X}' = \mathcal{E}.Enc(ek, \mathbf{d}; \mathbf{0}) \ominus (e \cdot \mathbf{X})$, and sets T' as in Eq. (7). Finally, the adversary $\mathcal{A}_S$ sends $\pi^* = (T, T', \mathbf{X}, \mathbf{X}')$ to the adversary $\mathcal{A}$, and takes the bit $b \in \{0, 1\}$ outputted by $\mathcal{A}$ as its own output.

While the relation $R_{\mathtt{crs}}(sk, w, x) = 1$ holds, it is easy to check that, if the challenging ciphertext $\mathbf{X} = \mathcal{E}.Enc(ek, \overline{\mathbf{m}}; \mathbf{r})$, then the proof π^* is distributed identical to a proof in the real game; if $\mathbf{X} = \mathcal{E}.Enc(ek, \widetilde{\mathbf{m}}; \mathbf{r})$, then the proof π^* is distributed exactly as that is produced by the simulator. Therefore, if the adversary $\mathcal{A}$ has non-negligible probability in distinguishing $\Pi.Prove$ and Sim, then the adversary $\mathcal{A}_S$ will win the IND-CPA game with non-negligible probability. $\qquad \square$

4   A New Storage-Extra APAKE Protocol

In this section, we first describe the construction of our new storage-extra APAKE protocol. Then, the design rationale and detailed comparisons of our protocols, in terms of both efficiency and security, are presented.

4.1   The Construction of the APAKE Protocol

Assume that $MAC_{\mathtt{wBB}} = (M.Setup, M.KeyGen, M.Mac, M.Verify)$ is the algebraic MAC scheme presented in Sect. 2.1, $\mathcal{E} = (\mathcal{E}.KeyGen, \mathcal{E}.Enc, \mathcal{E}.Dec)$ is a DVNIZK-friendly homomorphic encryption scheme as defined in Sect. 2.2, and $\Pi = (\Pi.Setup, \Pi.RelSetup, \Pi.KeyGen, \Pi.Prove, \Pi.Verify)$ is the oblivious DVNIZK proof scheme introduced in Sect. 3.1. We also use a traditional MAC scheme $\mathtt{M} = (\mathtt{KeyGen}, \mathtt{Mac}, \mathtt{Verify})$ and a traditional signature scheme $S = (S.KeyGen, S.Sign, S.Verify)$.

For each user $U \in \mathbf{U}$, denote by $\mathbf{m} = (m_1, m_2, \cdots, m_\beta)$ the vector of attributes and by pw the password held by this user. The construction of the APAKE protocol consists of the following steps.

Setup. In the setup phase, we first run $\Pi.Setup(1^\lambda)$ to obtain $\mathtt{crs} = (ek, \mathtt{pp}) = (ek, (\mathbb{G}, g, p))$ and the trapdoor $\mathtt{td} = dk$, run $\Pi.KeyGen(\mathtt{crs})$ to generate a secret relation key $sk = (x_0, x_1, \cdots, x_\beta)$ and $\mathtt{ipp} = (X_0, X_1, \cdots, X_\beta)$, run $S.KeyGen(1^\lambda)$ to get a signing key SK and the related signature verification key VK. Then, we select a random element $h \leftarrow \mathbb{G}$, set the common reference string of the APAKE protocol as $(\mathtt{crs}, \mathtt{ipp}, VK, h)$, and provide to the server with the secret keys (sk, SK).

Registration. In this phase, each user registers to the server to prepare for subsequent anonymous authentication. The registration phase is assumed to be executed over secure channels. To begin with, each user sends her attributes[2] $\mathbf{m} = (m_1, m_2, \cdots, m_\beta)$ to the server. Upon receiving this registration request, the server generates a MAC tag $\Sigma = (\sigma, \sigma_1, \cdots, \sigma_\beta) \leftarrow M.Mac(sk, \mathbf{m})$ and sends it to the user as its credential[3]. When the credential Σ is received, the client encrypts it with her password pw to obtain a password-wrapped credential $[\Sigma]_{pw}$, and puts it on some (publicly) extra-storage.

Authentication. To login the server, a user interacts with the server as follows.

1. At the beginning, the server runs $\Pi.KeyGen(\mathtt{crs})$ to generate a proof verification key $vk = e$ and the corresponding proving key $pk = \mathcal{E}.Enc(ek, 0; e)$, picks at random $\gamma \leftarrow \mathbb{Z}_p$ and computes $Y = h^\gamma$, $\sigma_S = S.Sign(SK, (pk, Y))$. Then, the server sends to the client the message (pk, Y, σ_S).

2. Upon receiving the message (pk, Y, σ_S) from the server, the client first checks the validity of the signature σ_S. Next, she fetches back the password-wrapped credential $[\Sigma]_{pw}$ and decrypts it with her password pw to recover the credential $\Sigma = (\sigma, \sigma_1, \cdots, \sigma_\beta)$. Then, the user generates a DVNIZK proof $\pi \leftarrow \Pi.Prove(\mathtt{crs}, \mathtt{ipp}, pk, (x_p, x_s), w)$, where $x = (x_p = \perp, x_s = \sigma)$ and $w = (m_1, m_2, \cdots, m_\beta)$. The user also chooses randomly $\xi \leftarrow \mathbb{Z}_p$, computes $X = h^\xi$, $tk_U^{(1)} = Y^\xi$, $tk_U^{(2)} = \Pi_{j=1}^\beta \sigma_j^{-a \cdot m_j} \cdot g^a$ and $\sigma_U = \mathtt{Mac}(tk_U^{(2)}, \sigma_S || X || \pi)$. Finally, the user sends (X, π, σ_U) to the server, and computes the session key as $K_U = tk_U^{(1)} \cdot tk_U^{(2)}$.

3. When the server receives (X, π, σ_U), it ensures that $T \neq 1$, computes $tk_S^{(1)} = X^\gamma$, $tk_S^{(2)} = T^{x_0}$, checks that $\sigma_U = \mathtt{Mac}(tk_S^{(2)}, \sigma_S || X || \pi)$, verifies the DVNIZK

---

[2] Beyond a single value of identity, here we consider a vector of attributes, which could handle more complex access policies such as expiration dates and access rights.

[3] Together with the credential Σ, the server perhaps, if needed, sends a zero-knowledge proof proving that this MAC tag is honestly generated. The ZK proof could be either a NIZK proof secure in the random oracle model, or a DVNIZK proof secure in the standard model where the proving key is sent to the server along with the attributes.

proof π, and aborts if any of these checks is failed. If all checks are valid, the server computes the session key as $K_S = tk_S^{(1)} \cdot tk_S^{(2)}$.

4.2 Design Rationale

The core of our construction is a DVNIZK proof π to prove that the algebraic MAC tag σ held by the user is valid, without compromising the privacy of this credential and the user's attributes. The privacy protection property is guaranteed by the zero-knowledge property of the underlying DVNIZK proof scheme; and the soundness property of the DVNIZK proof system ensures that, the user in communication is a legitimate member with a valid algebraic MAC tag as her credential.

Based on these observations, we could even obtain a one-pass variant of the above protocol for anonymous entity authentication, through sending only one flow of message consisting of the DVNIZK proof π to the server. The resulting protocol guarantees privacy-preserving non-interactive authentication, as expected by [20]. However, as a one-pass protocol, it is inherently open to replay attacks [31]. Although it is well-known that replay attacks can be prevented by maintaining synchronized state (via counters or timestamps) between the sender and receiver, we emphasize that synchronized timestamps are actually quite tedious in practical applications.

In order to prevent replay attacks and to establish a secure session key for subsequent use, we alternatively choose to have the server send an additional message (pk, Y, σ_S) to the client. In this message, the server generates and sends a fresh proving key pk for every session, which guarantees that the DVNIZK proof π is newly generated as well. Moreover, with the extra flow of message, we can embed in this protocol of a Diffie-Hellman tuple (X, Y), which offers forward security for both participants.

4.3 Comparisons with Existing Storage-Extra APAKE Protocols

In the following, we compare our storage-extra APAKE protocol with similar anonymous authentication protocols, in terms of both security and efficiency.

Security Comparisons. First, recall that our main purpose is to design a storage-extra APAKE protocol secure in the standard model, instead of in the random oracle model. As indicated in Table 1, our storage-extra APAKE protocol is the only one with proven security in the standard model, while all the existing protocols [14–16] are analyzed in the random oracle model. However, the random oracle model is arguably "unnatural" and differs from real-world constructions significantly [19]. We thus have reasons to believe that an APAKE protocol with provable security in the standard model would provide a stronger guarantee of security than those only proven secure in the random oracle model. In addition, our protocol not only satisfies the same mutual authentication property as the existed protocols, but also permits more flexibility in terms of identity type, as our protocol allows users to prove a vector of personal attributes rather than a single value of identity.

Efficiency Comparisons. With respect to efficiency, we compare our protocol with the existing storage-extra APAKE protocols in terms of rounds, communication and computational cost. The details are illustrated in Table 2. We stress that our protocol requires only two flows of messages during the authentication phase, which is very efficient for a protocol with explicitly mutual authentication. Although our protocol is less efficient, which is similar to those protocols with provable security in the standard model, than its counterpart proven secure in the random oracle, it is still considerably efficient. In particular, when the length of attributes is set to $\beta = 1$, we get a protocol that is even more efficient than Yang et al.'s scheme [14], which is right the storage-extra APAKE protocol contained in the standard ISO/IEC 20009-4 [17].

Table 1. Security comparisons among storage-extra APAKE protocols

Protocols	Model	Mutu-Auth	Identity-Type
Yang et al.'s [14]	Random oracle	Yes	Single value
Zhang et al.'s [15]	Random oracle	Yes	Single value
Shin et al.'s [16]	Random oracle	Yes	Single value
Our protocol	Standard model	Yes	Attribute vector

Legend: Mutu-Auth represents explicitly mutual authentication, Identity-Type denotes the type of user's identity which the protocol supports.

Table 2. Efficiency comparisons among storage-extra APAKE protocols

Protocols	Rounds	Comm.	Computational cost	
			User side	Server side
Yang et al.'s [14]	3	$7\|\mathbb{G}_1\| + \|\mathbb{G}_T\|$ $+6\|p\|$	$9E_{\mathbb{G}_1} + 1E_{\mathbb{G}_1}^2$ $+1E_{\mathbb{G}_T}^5 + 2P$	$E_{\mathbb{G}_1} + 3E_{\mathbb{G}_1}^2$ $+1E_{\mathbb{G}_T}^6 + 4P$
Zhang et al.'s [15]	2	$4\|\mathbb{G}\| + 4\|p\|$	$3E_{\mathbb{G}} + 2E_{\mathbb{G}}^2$	$3E_{\mathbb{G}} + 1E_{\mathbb{G}}^2$
Shin et al.'s [16]	3	$3\|\mathbb{G}\| + 2\|\mathcal{H}\|$	$5E_{\mathbb{G}}$	$3E_{\mathbb{G}}$
Our protocol	2	$10\|\mathbb{G}\| + 1\|\mathcal{T}\|$	$3E_{\mathbb{G}} + 2E_{\mathbb{G}}^{\beta+1}$ $+2\beta Enc$	$(\beta + 3)E_{\mathbb{G}}$ $+2E_{\mathbb{G}}^2$

Legend: $\|\mathbb{G}_1\|$ denotes the bit size of an element from the group $\mathbb{G}_1$, $\|p\|$ represents the size of an element from $\mathbb{Z}_p$, $\|\mathcal{H}\|$ and $\|\mathcal{T}\|$ denote the size of an output of a hash function and a MAC scheme, respectively; $E_{\mathbb{G}}$ represents one exponentiation in $\mathbb{G}$, $E_{\mathbb{G}}^n$ denotes a multi-exponentiation of n values in $\mathbb{G}$, P represents a bilinear pairing operation, Enc denotes a homomorphic encryption operation.

4.4 Security Analysis of the APAKE Protocol

By utilizing a security model for storage-extra APAKE protocol formalized by Zhang et al. in [15], we could prove that the APAKE protocol presented above guarantees AKE security of session keys and achieves user anonymity with respect to the honest-but-curious server. However, the detailed security model and rigorous proofs are omitted here due to the page limit. We refer the reader to our full paper for more details.

5 Conclusions

In this paper, we first give out a new construction of the oblivious DVNIZK proof system compatible with a new class of algebraic MAC schemes, which avoids the requirement of the cumbersome security notion called extended unforgeability. Then, we present a new APAKE protocol in the standard model by combing the technique of algebraic MAC with oblivious designated-verifier non-interactive zero-knowledge (DVNIZK) proof. Comparisons show that our protocol enjoys stronger security guarantees as well as achieves considerably communication and computation performance.

Acknowledgments. Qihui Zhang and Wenfen Liu are supported by the National Nature Science Foundation of China (Grant Nos. 61862011, 61872449), and Guangxi Natural Science Foundation (Grant No. 2018GXNSFAA138116) and the Guangxi Key Laboratory of Cryptography and Information Security (Grant No. GCIS201704). Kang Yang is supported by the National Key Research and Development Program of China (Grant No. 2018YFB0804105), and the National Natural Science Foundation of China (Grant Nos. 61932019, 61802021).

References

1. Wang, D., Zhang, Z., Wang, P., Yan, J., Huang, X.: Targeted online password guessing: an underestimated threat. In: ACM CCS 2016, pp. 1242–1254. ACM (2016)
2. Bellovin, S., Merritt, M.: Encrypted key exchange: password-based protocols secure against dictionary attacks. In: IEEE Computer Society Symposium on Research in Security and Privacy, pp. 72–84 (1992)
3. Jiang, Q., Qian, Y., Ma, J., Ma, X., Cheng, Q., Wei, F.: User centric three-factor authentication protocol for cloud-assisted wearable devices. Int. J. Commun. Syst. **32**(6), e3900 (2019)
4. Wang, D., Cheng, H., Wang, P., Huang, X., Jian, G.: Zipf's law in passwords. IEEE Trans. Inf. Forensics Secur. **12**(11), 2776–2791 (2017)
5. Abdalla, M.: Password-based authenticated key exchange: an overview. In: Chow, S.S.M., Liu, J.K., Hui, L.C.K., Yiu, S.M. (eds.) ProvSec 2014. LNCS, vol. 8782, pp. 1–9. Springer, Cham (2014). https://doi.org/10.1007/978-3-319-12475-9_1
6. Schmidt, J.: Requirements for password-authenticated key agreement (PAKE) schemes. RFC 8125 (2017)
7. Lindell, Y.: Anonymous authentication. J. Priv. Confid. **2**(2), 35–63 (2007)

8. Viet, D.Q., Yamamura, A., Tanaka, H.: Anonymous password-based authenticated key exchange. In: Maitra, S., Veni Madhavan, C.E., Venkatesan, R. (eds.) INDOCRYPT 2005. LNCS, vol. 3797, pp. 244–257. Springer, Heidelberg (2005). https://doi.org/10.1007/11596219_20
9. Shin, S.H., Kobara, K., Imai, H.: A secure threshold anonymous password-authenticated key exchange protocol. In: Miyaji, A., Kikuchi, H., Rannenberg, K. (eds.) IWSEC 2007. LNCS, vol. 4752, pp. 444–458. Springer, Heidelberg (2007). https://doi.org/10.1007/978-3-540-75651-4_30
10. Shin, S.H., Kobara, K., Imai, H.: Very-efficient anonymous password-authenticated key exchange and its extensions. In: Bras-Amorós, M., Høholdt, T. (eds.) AAECC 2009. LNCS, vol. 5527, pp. 149–158. Springer, Heidelberg (2009). https://doi.org/10.1007/978-3-642-02181-7_16
11. Yang, J., Zhang, Z.: A new anonymous password-based authenticated key exchange protocol. In: Chowdhury, D.R., Rijmen, V., Das, A. (eds.) INDOCRYPT 2008. LNCS, vol. 5365, pp. 200–212. Springer, Heidelberg (2008). https://doi.org/10.1007/978-3-540-89754-5_16
12. Zhang, Q., Chaudhary, P., Kumari, S., Kong, Z., Liu, W.: Verifier-based anonymous password-authenticated key exchange protocol in the standard model. Math. Biosci. Eng. 16(5), 3623–3640 (2019)
13. Yang, Y., Zhou, J., Weng, J., Bao, F.: A new approach for anonymous password authentication. In: the 25th Annual Computer Security Applications Conference, pp. 199–208, December 2009
14. Yang, Y., Zhou, J., Wong, J.W., Bao, F.: Towards practical anonymous password authentication. In: the 26th Annual Computer Security Applications Conference, pp. 59–68. ACM (2010)
15. Zhang, Z., Yang, K., Hu, X., Wang, Y.: Practical anonymous password authentication and TLS with anonymous client authentication. In: ACM CCS 2016, pp. 1179–1191. ACM (2016)
16. Shin, S., Kobara, K.: Simple anonymous password-based authenticated key exchange (SAPAKE), reconsidered. IEICE Trans. Fundam. Electron. Commun. Comput. Sci. 100(2), 639–652 (2017)
17. ISO/IEC 20009-4: Information technology - security techniques - anonymous entity authentication - part 4: Mechanisms based on weak secrets. Standard (2019). https://www.iso.org/standard/64288.html
18. Hu, X., Zhang, J., Zhang, Z., Liu, F.: Anonymous password authenticated key exchange protocol in the standard model. Wirel. Pers. Commun. 96(1), 1451–1474 (2017)
19. Leurent, G., Nguyen, P.Q.: How risky is the random-oracle model? In: Halevi, S. (ed.) CRYPTO 2009. LNCS, vol. 5677, pp. 445–464. Springer, Heidelberg (2009). https://doi.org/10.1007/978-3-642-03356-8_26
20. Chaidos, P., Couteau, G.: Efficient designated-verifier non-interactive zero-knowledge proofs of knowledge. In: Nielsen, J.B., Rijmen, V. (eds.) EUROCRYPT 2018. LNCS, vol. 10822, pp. 193–221. Springer, Cham (2018). https://doi.org/10.1007/978-3-319-78372-7_7
21. Dodis, Y., Kiltz, E., Pietrzak, K., Wichs, D.: Message authentication, revisited. In: Pointcheval, D., Johansson, T. (eds.) EUROCRYPT 2012. LNCS, vol. 7237, pp. 355–374. Springer, Heidelberg (2012). https://doi.org/10.1007/978-3-642-29011-4_22
22. Couteau, G., Reichle, M.: Non-interactive keyed-verification anonymous credentials. In: Lin, D., Sako, K. (eds.) PKC 2019. LNCS, vol. 11442, pp. 66–96. Springer, Cham (2019). https://doi.org/10.1007/978-3-030-17253-4_3

23. Chase, M., Meiklejohn, S., Zaverucha, G.: Algebraic MACs and keyed-verification anonymous credentials. In: ACM CCS 2014, pp. 1205–1216. ACM (2014)
24. Boneh, D., Boyen, X.: Short signatures without random oracles and the SDH assumption in bilinear groups. J. Cryptol. **21**(2), 149–177 (2008)
25. Barki, A., Brunet, S., Desmoulins, N., Traoré, J.: Improved algebraic MACs and practical keyed-verification anonymous credentials. In: Avanzi, R., Heys, H. (eds.) SAC 2016. LNCS, vol. 10532, pp. 360–380. Springer, Cham (2017). https://doi.org/10.1007/978-3-319-69453-5_20
26. Camenisch, J., Drijvers, M., Dzurenda, P., Hajny, J.: Fast keyed-verification anonymous credentials on standard smart cards. In: Dhillon, G., Karlsson, F., Hedström, K., Zúquete, A. (eds.) SEC 2019. IAICT, vol. 562, pp. 286–298. Springer, Cham (2019). https://doi.org/10.1007/978-3-030-22312-0_20
27. Camenisch, J., Hohenberger, S., Kohlweiss, M., Lysyanskaya, A., Meyerovich, M.: How to win the clonewars: efficient periodic n-times anonymous authentication. In: ACM CCS 2006, pp. 201–210. ACM (2006)
28. Damgård, I., Jurik, M., Nielsen, J.B.: A generalization of Paillier's public-key system with applications to electronic voting. Int. J. Inf. Secur. **9**(6), 371–385 (2010)
29. Paillier, P.: Public-key cryptosystems based on composite degree residuosity classes. In: Stern, J. (ed.) EUROCRYPT 1999. LNCS, vol. 1592, pp. 223–238. Springer, Heidelberg (1999). https://doi.org/10.1007/3-540-48910-X_16
30. Castagnos, G., Laguillaumie, F.: Linearly homomorphic encryption from DDH. In: Nyberg, K. (ed.) CT-RSA 2015. LNCS, vol. 9048, pp. 487–505. Springer, Cham (2015). https://doi.org/10.1007/978-3-319-16715-2_26
31. Halevi, S., Krawczyk, H.: One-pass HMQV and asymmetric key-wrapping. In: Catalano, D., Fazio, N., Gennaro, R., Nicolosi, A. (eds.) PKC 2011. LNCS, vol. 6571, pp. 317–334. Springer, Heidelberg (2011). https://doi.org/10.1007/978-3-642-19379-8_20

Strong Authenticity with Leakage Under Weak and Falsifiable Physical Assumptions

Francesco Berti[1]([✉]), Chun Guo[1,2], Olivier Pereira[1], Thomas Peters[1], and François-Xavier Standaert[1]

[1] ICTEAM/ELEN/Crypto Group, UCLouvain,
1348 Louvain-la-Neuve, Belgium
francesco.berti@uclouvain.be

[2] School of Cyber Science and Technology and Key Laboratory of Cryptologic Technology and Information Security, Ministry of Education,
Shandong University, Jinan, China

Abstract. Authenticity can be compromised by information leaked via side-channels (e.g., power consumption). Examples of attacks include direct key recoveries and attacks against the tag verification which may lead to forgeries. At FSE 2018, Berti et al. described two authenticated encryption schemes which provide authenticity assuming a *leak-free implementation* of a Tweakable Block Cipher (TBC). Precisely, security is guaranteed even if all the intermediate computations of the target implementation are leaked in full but the TBC long-term key. Yet, while a leak-free implementation reasonably models strongly protected implementations of a TBC, it remains an idealized physical assumption that may be too demanding in many cases, in particular if hardware engineers mitigate the leakage to a good extent but (due to performance constraints) do not reach leak-freeness. In this paper, we get rid of this important limitation by introducing the notion of *Strong Unpredictability with Leakage* for BC's and TBC's. It captures the hardness for an adversary to provide a fresh and valid input/output pair for a (T)BC, even having oracle access to the (T)BC, its inverse and their leakages. This definition is game-based and may be verified/falsified by laboratories. Based on it, we then provide two Message Authentication Codes (MAC) which are secure if the (T)BC on which they rely are implemented in a way that maintains a sufficient unpredictability. Thus, we improve the theoretical foundations of leakage-resilient MAC and extend them towards engineering constraints that are easier to achieve in practice. (The full version of this paper is available on ePrint [8].)

1 Introduction

Message Authentication Codes (MAC) are widely used to authenticate data. Efficient MAC are usually constructed from conceptually simpler symmetric primitives such as (tweakable) block ciphers (e.g., CBC [5]) and hash functions (e.g.,

© Springer Nature Switzerland AG 2020
Z. Liu and M. Yung (Eds.): Inscrypt 2019, LNCS 12020, pp. 517–532, 2020.
https://doi.org/10.1007/978-3-030-42921-8_31

HMAC [4,5]), and enjoy reliable "provable security guarantees", i.e., security reductions to the underlying primitives.

Side-channel attacks, since introduced in the 1990s [22,23], have now been recognized as one of the main real-world security threats (e.g., see [2, chapter 1.2]). In response, various implementation-level countermeasures have been proposed and even formally proved effective. However, they typically induce significant overheads. As a complementary, the methodology of *leakage-resilience* was proposed [15] and followed by many (see [21] for a survey). Schemes proved leakage-resilient enjoy security even if a moderate amount of sensitive information is leaked via side-channels. Consequently, their implementations could leverage less protected circuits and thus reduce the overall overheads.

It is not a surprise that with leakages, classical MAC such as CBC and HMAC are not secure at all, even if leakages only contain the input/output values of the underlying functions (see, e.g., [13]). This means their implementations have to be heavily protected when used in sensitive settings such as the IoT, which may be hard to achieve given application cost constraints. Therefore, exploring the construction of leakage-resilient MAC is a natural direction, which was initiated in [9,19,25,26] and later improved in [3,7,10] to achieve security in the presence of *both tag generation and verification leakages.*[1] We remark that the premises used in these works are significantly different. For example, [3,25] leveraged bilinear maps in the generic group model to ease secret-sharing/masking-based implementations of their MAC, while [7,9,10,26] model a heavily protected (tweakable) block cipher (for example, using high-order masking [16,20]) as leak-free and focus on making the other mode-level leakages harmless.

From the efficiency viewpoint, sticking with simple symmetric primitives is naturally desirable.[2] Yet, a drawback of the aforementioned papers [7,9,10,26] is the use of leak-free cipher model. Despite it is theoretically possible to reach very high security levels with masking (approaching black box security [16,20]), it implies (very) high overheads that may not be acceptable in practice. Besides, the leak-free assumption (that is, nothing is leaked about the key used and the outputs remain pseudorandom) cannot be accompanied by any well-defined security game—somewhat resembling the random oracle model.

Our Contribution. The goal of this paper is to bridge the above theory gap (i.e., seeking for some well-defined leakage assumptions on the block cipher that allows the leakage-resilient MAC security reductions) while also enabling more modular security guarantees that may degrade gracefully when the physical assumption is respected only to some extent. Our answer to this challenge is *Strong Unpredictability in the presence of Leakages* for a (T)BC, henceforth abbreviated as SUL2. In detail, it captures the hardness of providing a fresh input/output pair for the (T)BC even having access to its leaking oracle and leaking inverse oracle (following the notations of [18], the variant without leaking inverse oracle would

---

[1] Note that some MACs were parts of authenticated encryption (AE) proposals.
[2] The MAC of [3,25] consumes ≈ 4s to generate a tag on a 32-bit ARM.

be SUL1). It can be viewed as a natural extension of the unpredictable block cipher assumption introduced by Dodis and Steinberger [13,14].

With this new assumption, we revisit existing (tweakable) block cipher-based leakage-resilient MAC. We first consider the simplest Hash-then-BC scheme $\tau = F_k(H(m))$, the leakage security of which was analyzed by Berti et al. [9,10]. While the security reduction seems straightforward, Berti et al. [10] changed the verification process of $\mathsf{Vrfy}_k(m, \tau)$ from "If $\tau = F_k^*(H(m))$, then return 1" to "If $H(m) = F_k^{*,-1}(\tau)$, then return 1" (i.e., leveraging the inverse $F_k^{*,-1}$ to avoid leaking sensitive information).[3] As a result, they achieve better mode-level leakage-resilience using leak-free block ciphers. We show that the SUL2 assumption for F^* is actually sufficient to obtain similar guarantees, further assuming an ideal hash H.[4] We then revisit the recently proposed Hash-then-TBC scheme [7], which was also used in the NIST AE submission Spook [6]. In detail, its tag generation is $\mathsf{Tag}_k(m) = \tau = F_k^*(h_1, h_2)$, where h_2 is the tweak of F^* and $h_1 \| h_2 = H(m)$ (i.e., the $2n$-bit output of H is divided into two halves, h_1 and h_2), while for verification $\mathsf{Vrfy}_k(m, \tau)$ we compute $\tilde{h}_1 = F_k^{*,-1}(\tau, h_2)$ and compare it with h_1, from $h_1 \| h_2 = H(m)$. We show that using a $2n$-bit hash, we can achieve the beyond-birthday-bound security for this Hash-then-TBC construction.

Both schemes are natural, extremely simple and should be easy to implement for practical uses. We expect the block cipher based construction (next: HBC) to be slightly more efficient than the tweakable version (next: HTBC) as a secure TBC typically consumes more rounds than a secure BC. However, we also note that HBC admits forgery attacks with lower data complexity (simply utilizing a hash collision), while HTBC solves this problem by doubling the size of the hash and using a TBC (that has a larger input size) to absorb the digest.

In summary, our results improve the theory foundations for existing efficient (tweakable) block cipher-based leakage-resilient MAC. We believe the SUL2 assumption could find more applications in future leakage-resilient analyses. In practice, unpredictability is widely believed to be more relaxed than PRP [13].[5] Thus it potentially enables using *reduced-round* (tweakable) BCs for MAC. As the heavily protected ciphers are much more costly than the hash functions (that do not need protection), they are expected to be the performance bottleneck, and reducing the number of rounds may significantly improve the overall performance (e.g., in terms of latency and energy consumption).

Related Work. The idea of basing MAC security on unpredictable ciphers is not new, dating back to [1] and witnessing recent achievements [13,14,28]. In fact, as argued in [13], it is natural to consider reducing the unpredictability of the "bigger" MAC to the unpredictability of the "smaller" ciphers.

---

[3] F^* means that the BC F is implemented in a leak-free way.

[4] This idealized assumption is used for simplifying our analyzes, since our focus is on the leak-free blocks. We leave its relaxation as an interesting open problem.

[5] Indeed, Unpr can be based on weaker complexity assumptions [12].

2 Background

Notations. A $(q_1, ..., q_d, t)$-adversary A against Π is an algorithm A having oracle access to $\mathcal{O}_1, ..., \mathcal{O}_d$, making at most q_i queries to oracle $\mathcal{O}_i$, running in time bounded by t, and outputting a finite string of bits. The leakage function due to the implementation of an algorithm Algo is denoted L_{Algo}. This function might be non deterministic. A leaking query to Algo is denoted LAlgo and results in running both Algo and L_{Algo} on the same input.

The set of binary strings of length n is denoted by $\{0, 1\}^n$, while the set of all finite strings by $\{0, 1\}^*$. Given two strings, x and y, we let $x \| y$ denote the concatenation of these two strings. Given a non-empty set $\mathcal{X}$, we let $x \xleftarrow{\$} \mathcal{X}$ denote the draw of an element x from $\mathcal{X}$ uniformly at random. The *view* of a game consists of all queries made by the adversary to his oracles, the oracles' answers, and the final output of the adversary, recorded in order of appearance. A value is *fresh* at some point in the view if it was never recorded earlier.

2.1 Cryptographic Primitives

Tweakable Block Ciphers. A *tweakable block cipher* [24] (TBC) is a function $F : \mathcal{K} \times \mathcal{TW} \times \mathcal{X} \longmapsto \mathcal{Z}$, where $\mathcal{K}$ (*resp.* $\mathcal{TW}$) is the key space (*resp.* the tweak space), and such that for any key $k \in \mathcal{K}$ and any tweak $tw \in \mathcal{TW}$, the function $F_k^{tw} : \mathcal{X} \mapsto \mathcal{Z}; x \mapsto F_k^{tw}(x) := F_k(tw, x) := F(k, tw, x)$ is a permutation. We denote the inverse of this function by $F_{k,tw}^{-1} := F_k^{-1}(tw, \cdot)$. A Block Cipher (BC) is a TBC with an empty tweak space: the only tweak is the "empty string".

Message Authentication Codes with Leakage. A *message authentication code* (MAC) is a couple of algorithms (Tag, Vrfy), Tag $: \mathcal{K} \times \mathcal{M} \longmapsto \mathcal{T}$ and Vrfy $: \mathcal{K} \times \mathcal{M} \times \mathcal{T} \longmapsto \{0, 1\}$, where $\mathcal{K}$, $\mathcal{M}$ and $\mathcal{T}$ are respectively called the key space, the message space and the tag space, and such that for any key $k \in \mathcal{K}$ and any message $m \in \mathcal{M}$, $1 \leftarrow \mathsf{Vrfy}_k(m, \mathsf{Tag}_k(m))$.

Definition 1. *A* MAC $=$ (Tag, Vrfy) *is* (q_T, q_V, t, ϵ) *strongly existentially unforgeable against chosen-message and verification attacks, or* (q_T, q_V, t, ϵ)-suf-vcma, *if for all* (q_T, q_V, t)-*adversary* A, *we have*

$$\Pr[\mathsf{FORGE}_{\mathsf{A,MAC}}^{\mathsf{suf\text{-}vcma}} = 1] \leq \epsilon$$

where the $\mathsf{FORGE}^{\mathsf{suf\text{-}vcma}}$ *experiment is defined in Table 1.*

To model the ability of an adversary to get leakage on tag generation and verification, we extend the $\mathsf{FORGE}^{\mathsf{suf\text{-}vcma}}$ experiment by allowing the oracles to additionally return the evaluation of L_{Tag} and L_{Vrfy}, where $L = (L_{\mathsf{Tag}}, L_{\mathsf{Vrfy}})$ is the leakage function pair due to an implementation of the MAC. Given an adversary A, we write A^L to specify that the adversary knows the implementation and that it can learn the leakage for chosen keys, which models any leakage learning phase on other devices with the same implementation.

Table 1. The FORGE$^{\text{suf-vcma}}$ experiment.

Table 1. The FORGE$^{\text{suf-vcma}}$ experiment.

FORGE$^{\text{suf-vcma}}_{\text{MAC,A}}$ experiment	
Initialization:	Oracle Tag(m):
$\quad k \xleftarrow{\$} \mathcal{K}$	$\quad \tau \leftarrow \text{Tag}_k(m)$
$\quad \mathcal{S} \leftarrow \emptyset$	$\quad \mathcal{S} \leftarrow \mathcal{S} \cup \{(m, \tau)\}$
	$\quad$ Return τ
Finalization:	
$\quad (m, \tau) \leftarrow \mathsf{A}^{\text{Tag}(\cdot),\text{Vrfy}(\cdot,\cdot)}$	Oracle Vrfy(m, τ):
$\quad$ If $(m, \tau) \in \mathcal{S}$ Return 0	$\quad$ Return $\text{Vrfy}_k(m, \tau)$
$\quad$ Return $\text{Vrfy}_k(m, \tau)$	

Definition 2. *A* MAC $=$ (Tag, Vrfy), *whose implementation has leakage function* L $=$ (L$_{\text{Tag}}$, L$_{\text{Vrfy}}$) *is* $(q_T, q_V, q_L, t, \epsilon)$ *strongly existentially unforgeable against chosen message and verification attacks with leakage in tag-generation and verification, or* $(q_T, q_V, q_L, t, \epsilon)$*-suf-L2, if for any* (q_T, q_V, q_L, t)*-adversary* A, *we have*

$$\Pr[\text{FORGE-L2}^{\text{suf-vcma}}_{\text{A,MAC,L}} = 1] \le \epsilon,$$

where the FORGE-L2$^{\text{suf-vcma}}$ *experiment is defined in Table 2, and where* A^{L} *makes at most* q_L *queries to* L.

Table 2. The FORGE-L2$^{\text{suf-vcma}}$ experiment.

FORGE-L2$^{\text{suf-vcma}}_{\text{MAC,A}}$ experiment	
Initialization:	Oracle LTag(m):
$\quad k \xleftarrow{\$} \mathcal{K}$	$\quad \tau \leftarrow \text{Tag}_k(m),\ \ell_{\text{m}} \leftarrow \text{L}_{\text{Tag}}(k, m)$
$\quad \mathcal{S} \leftarrow \emptyset$	$\quad \mathcal{S} \leftarrow \mathcal{S} \cup \{(m, \tau)\}$
	$\quad$ Return (τ, ℓ_{m})
Finalization:	
$\quad (m, \tau) \leftarrow \mathsf{A}^{\text{LTag}(\cdot),\text{LVrfy}(\cdot,\cdot),\text{L}}$	Oracle LVrfy(m, τ):
$\quad$ If $(m, \tau) \in \mathcal{S}$, return 0	$\quad \ell_{\text{v}} \leftarrow \text{L}_{\text{Vrfy}}(k, m, \tau)$
$\quad$ Return $\text{Vrfy}_k(m, \tau)$	$\quad$ Return $(\text{Vrfy}_k(m, \tau), \ell_{\text{v}})$

Note that the L2 notation is for leakage during both tag generation and verification (the variant without tag verification leakage would use L1, following [18]).

Unbounded Leakage. Our new security analysis of the MACs relies on one of the weakest assumptions about the leakage: additionally to their own leakage functions, all the cryptographic tools of a scheme (hash function, TBC ...) fully leak all their I/Os except the key. A proof under this assumption is called a proof in the unbounded leakage model.

3   Unpredictability of Leaking TBC

Dodis and Steinberger [13] introduced the definition of *unpredictability with leakage* for BC. At a high level, the definition says it is unfeasible to produce a valid input-output couple of the BC even if we got the leakage besides of the outcome of the computation of the BC on chosen inputs. We extend this notion by granting the adversary with the inverse oracle of the BC and its leakage. To save some place, we directly describe this notion for TBCs. We get the corresponding notion for BCs by removing all the tweaks in the definition below.

We denote by $L = (L_{Eval}, L_{Inv})$ the leakage function pair associated to an implementation of the TBC, where $L_{Eval}(k, tw, x)$ (*resp.* $L_{Inv}(k, tw, z)$) is the leakage resulting from the computation of $F_k(tw, x)$ (*resp.* $F_k^{-1}(tw, z)$). We also allow the adversary A to profile the leakages and write A^L as before, like in [26].

Definition 3. *A tweakable block cipher* $F : \mathcal{K} \times \mathcal{TW} \times \mathcal{X} \longmapsto \mathcal{Z}$ *with leakage function pair* $L = (L_{Eval}, L_{Inv})$ *is* $(q_E, q_I, q_L, t, \epsilon)$ *strongly unpredictable with leakage in evaluation and inversion, or* $(q_E, q_I, q_L, t, \epsilon)$-*SUL2, if for any* (q_E, q_V, q_L, t)-*adversary* A, *we have*

$$\Pr[\text{SUL2}_{A,F,L} \Rightarrow 1] \leq \epsilon,$$

where the SUL2 *experiment is defined in Table 3, and where* A^L *makes at most* q_L *(offline) queries to* L.

Table 3. Strong unpredictability with leakage in evaluation and inversion experiment.

SUL2$_{A,F,L}$ experiment	
Initialization:	**Oracle LEval(tw, x):**
$k \xleftarrow{\$} \mathcal{K}$	$z = F_k(tw, x)$
$\mathcal{L} \leftarrow \emptyset$	$\ell_e = L_{Eval}(k, tw, x)$
	$\mathcal{L} \leftarrow \mathcal{L} \cup \{(x, tw, z)\}$
Finalization:	Return (z, ℓ_e)
$(x, tw, z) \leftarrow A^{LEval(\cdot, \cdot), LInv(\cdot, \cdot), L}$	
If $(x, tw, z) \in \mathcal{L}$	**Oracle LInv(tw, z):**
Return 0	$x = F_k^{-1}(tw, z)$
If $z == F_k(tw, x)$	$\ell_i = L_{Inv}(k, tw, z)$
Return 1	$\mathcal{L} \leftarrow \mathcal{L} \cup \{(x, tw, z)\}$
Return 0	Return (x, ℓ_i)

4   First Leakage-Resilient MAC: HBC

We now revisit one of the most common designs to build a MAC from a hash function H and a block cipher F. This MAC is the well-known hash-then-BC scheme, named here HBC, except that we analyze it in a leakage setting and through the lens of the unpredictability of F. As we want to show the security of HBC even when F leaks its inputs and outputs in full, we just have to tweak the usual verification algorithm by using the inversion of the BC to avoid leaking valid tags just by processing invalid pairs (m, τ). As mentioned in introduction, our analysis models H as a random oracle for simplicity and since our focus is on the leak-free blocks. Yet, it does not suggest any reason why an ideal object would be needed, and its relaxation is an interesting open problem.

4.1   HBC Description

Let $\mathcal{M} = \{0,1\}^*$ and $\mathcal{X} = \mathcal{Z} = \{0,1\}^n$. Considering a hash function $H : \mathcal{M} \mapsto \mathcal{X}$ and a block cipher $F : \mathcal{K} \times \mathcal{X} \mapsto \mathcal{Z}$, we build $HBC = (\text{Tag}, \text{Vrfy})$:

Tag$_k(m)$: compute $h = H(m)$, then compute and output $\tau = F_k(h)$.
Vrfy$_k(m, \tau)$: compute $h = H(m)$ and $\tilde{h} = F_k^{-1}(\tau)$, then output 1 if $h = h'$, and
    0 otherwise.

We highlight that Tag only evaluates F while Vrfy only computes its inverse. This feature is at the core of the argument showing that unbounded leakages do not decrease the unforgeability of this hash-then-BC design. This idea was already used for the authentication part of the AE modes DTE2, EDT and FEMALE [10,18]. We illustrate HBC in Fig. 1.

4.2   Security of HBC

In the unbounded leakage model, the adversary receives all the ephemeral values computed during the tag generation and the verification. Only the key of the BC, which is the key of the MAC, remains hidden as implicitly defined by the leakage function pair of its implementation $L = (L_{\text{Eval}}, L_{\text{Inv}})$. More precisely, the unbounded leakage function pair $L^* = (L^*_{\text{Tag}}, L^*_{\text{Vrfy}})$ of HBC is thus:

$L^*_{\text{Tag}}(k, m)$: return $h = H(m)$ and $L_{\text{Eval}}(k, h)$;
$L^*_{\text{Vrfy}}(k, m, \tau)$: return $h = H(m)$ and $\tilde{h} = F_k^{-1}(\tau)$ as well as $L_{\text{Inv}}(k, \tau)$.

Despite H is a public function, we explicitly include its outputs in the leakage. It can be considered as redundant but, as we rely on a random oracle to prove the security of HBC, we prefer making them fully available to avoid any confusion.

Theorem 1. *Let* $F : \mathcal{K} \times \{0,1\}^n \longrightarrow \{0,1\}^n$ *be a* $(q_T, q_V, q_L, t, \epsilon_{\text{SUL2}})$-*strongly unpredictable block cipher in the presence of leakage, and* $H : \mathcal{S} \times \{0,1\}^* \longrightarrow \{0,1\}^n$ *be a hash function modeled as a random oracle that is queried at most* q_H

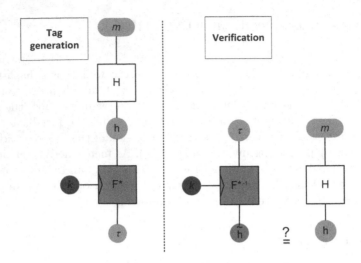

Fig. 1. The leakage resilient MAC HBC. Leakage reveals the orange value. (Color figure online)

times, then, HBC *is a* $(q_T, q_V, q_L, t, \epsilon)$-*strongly unforgeable MAC in the unbounded leakage setting, with* $L^* = (L^*_{Tag}, L^*_{Vrfy})$ *defined above, where*

$$\epsilon \leq (q_H + q_V + 1)(q_V + 1)\epsilon_{SUL2} + 2(q_H + q_T + q_V + 1)^2/2^n,$$

and $t_H(q_H + q_T + q_V + 1) + (q_T + q_L - q)t_F + (q_V + q)t_{F^{-1}} \leq t$ *for any* $q \leq q_L$, *and where we assume that all the* H-*query involved in the* q_L *queries are already among the* q_H *queries.*

Idea of the Proof. Assuming that an adversary A succeeds in the FORGE-L2$^{suf\text{-}vcma}_{A,HBC,L^*}$ experiment by making a total of q_T leaking tag queries and q_V leaking verification queries, let (m, τ) be the forgery, i.e., the couple returned by A in the finalization phase. To bound this winning probability, we partition this event into sub events: (1) The tag τ appears in the answer to a leaking tag query (and thus, as an input of F_k); (2) The tag τ never appears in the answer to a leaking tag query (and thus, τ can only be involved with the block cipher as an input of F_k^{-1}) and: (a) m appears as an input of H before $F_k^{-1}(\tau)$ was ever computed in the experiment; (b) τ appears as an input of F_k^{-1} before $H(m)$ was ever computed in the experiment. We cover all the cases since when both m and τ are fresh in a verification query, we always compute (or ask the computation of) $H(m)$ first so that we can say that m appears "before" (the computation of F_k^{-1} on input) τ, and since we view the last verification in the finalization as the $(q_V + 1)$-th verification query.

The goal of the proof is to show that the collision resistance of H ensures that winning in case 1 is negligible, the unpredictability of F ensures that winning in case 2a is negligible and that the collision resistance again along with the uniform distribution of the outputs of H ensures that winning in case 2b is negligible as well, since up to collisions it comes to compute a preimage.

In case 1, there is a tag query on m' which defines $\tau = F_k(H(m'))$. Since (m, τ) is a forgery we have $F_k(H(m)) = \tau$ with $m \neq m'$. Then, m and m' produce a collision as F_k is a permutation: $H(m) = F_k^{-1}(\tau) = H(m')$.

In case 2a, we assume that F is SUL2-secure. Since m appears before τ, as a challenger we have to use the value $h = H(m)$ and we "wait" for the good tag in a verification query to win the SUL2 game. But, we do not have to consider the message for which A makes a tag query. However, we cannot know in advance what will be the right tag and we cannot wait until the finalization of the unforgeability experiment because even if A's output (m, τ) is the right pairs, τ may have been already used in a previous verification query. If so, the challenger should have already made a leaking inverse query of the block cipher with input τ to get $\tilde{h} = F_k^{-1}(\tau)$ and $\ell_i \leftarrow LInv(k, m)$ to simulate $LVrfy(m, \tau)$, and it could no more win the game against F with τ. Therefore, for all possible m involved in a H-query or a verification query, we have to guess what will be the right τ in verification. Then, we need to consider all the possible such pairs and we thus have to make at most $(q_H + q_V + 1)(q_V + 1)$ reductions.

In case 2b, the reduction can generate the key k itself and then evaluate F and its inverse by itself. The first time τ appears, we define the H-target $\tilde{h} = F_k^{-1}(\tau)$. If this value $\tilde{h}$ appears earlier it can only be as a result of the computation of $H(m')$ in any type of query for some $m' \neq m$ as m still does not appear by assumption and F_k is a permutation. But then, since (m, τ) is valid we find a collision because $H(m) = \tilde{h} = H(m')$. So, we can now assume that $\tilde{h}$ is fresh. Therefore, the validity of (m, τ) means that m is a preimage of $\tilde{h}$, as $H(m) = F_k^{-1}(\tau)$, while $H(m)$ is random. In the proof below, we start by removing all the collision on H to avoid relying on the collision resistance too many times and to deal with it once and for all.

Proof. To prove the theorem, we use a sequence of games. Given an adversary A, we start with Game 0 which is the $FORGE\text{-}L2_{A,HBC,L^*}^{suf\text{-}vcma}$ experiment and we end with a game where all the leaking verification queries deem the given input pair (m_i, τ_i) invalid, including the last verification at the finalization which is the $(q_V + 1)$-th verification query by convention.

Game 0. This game is depicted in Table 2. Let E_0 be the event that the adversary A^{L^*} wins this game, that is, the output of the experiment is 1.

Game 1. We introduce a failure event F_1 with respect to Game 0, where F_1 occurs if among the at most $(q_H + q_T + q_V + 1)$ hash computations there is at least one collision. In Game 1, if F_1 occurs we abort the game and return 0. We let E_1 be the event that the adversary A^L wins this game.

Bounding $|\Pr[E_0] - \Pr[E_1]|$. Since Game 0 and Game 1 are identical as long as F_1 does not occur, we have

$$|\Pr[E_0] - \Pr[E_1]| \leq \Pr[F_1] \leq (q_H + q_T + q_V + 1)^2/2^n.$$

Note: from now on, A wins if τ never appears in a leaking tag query. Moreover, $\tilde{h} = F_k^{-1}(\tau)$ is fresh when τ appears in a leaking verification query for the first time if m was never used as input of H at that time. (See above.)

Game 2. We modify the winning condition of the previous game. In the finalization, once A outputs (m, τ) we say that A does not win and return 0 if A fails as before or if m appears as an input of H before the first apparition of τ during a leaking verification query. If we call F_2 the event that makes the adversary winning in Game 1 but loosing in Game 2, we have $|\Pr[E_2] - \Pr[E_1]| \leq \Pr[F_2]$, where E_2 is the event that A wins in this game.

Bounding $\Pr[F_2]$. If we call V_i the event that (m, τ) appears for the first time in the i-th leaking verification query (m^i, τ^i), we just have to bound $\Pr[F_2 \wedge V_i]$, for all $i = 1$ to $q_V + 1$. By considering all the input-output pairs defined by H before the i-th leaking verification query, except those defined during a leaking tag query, we can build straightforwards reduction from the SUL2-security of F. We thus have, $\Pr[F_2 \wedge V_i] \leq (q_H + q_V + 1)\epsilon_{\mathsf{SUL2}}$ and finally

$$\Pr[F_2] = \sum_{i=1}^{q_V+1} \Pr[F_2 \wedge V_i] \leq (q_H + q_V + 1)(q_V + 1)\epsilon_{\mathsf{SUL2}}.$$

Note: in Game 2, the adversary wins only if τ appears before m and τ first appears in a leaking verification query while $\tilde{h} = F_k^{-1}(\tau)$ is not yet a defined output of H.

Game 3. In this we follow the specification of $\mathsf{FORGE\text{-}L2}_{\mathsf{A,HBC,L^*}}^{\mathsf{suf\text{-}vcma}}$ except that we always output 0 at the end of the game.

Bounding $|\Pr[E_3] - \Pr[E_2]| = \Pr[E_2]$. From the last note, we know that $\tilde{h} = F_k^{-1}(\tau)$ is not yet a defined output of H. Since any fresh H-query result in a uniform output which is independent of the view at that time, $\Pr[H(m) = \tilde{h}] = (q_H + q_T + q_V + 1)/2^n$, and then $\Pr[E_2] \leq (q_H + q_T + q_V + 1)/2^n$

To summarize, we have

$$\Pr[E_0] \leq (q_H + q_V + 1)(q_V + 1)\epsilon_{\mathsf{SUL2}} + \frac{2(q_H + q_T + q_V + 1)^2}{2^n}$$

as desired.   □

5   Second Leakage-Resilient MAC: HTBC

The design of our second construction is very similar to that of HBC. The main difference in HTBC is that the hash function has a double output length. A TBC replaces the BC to use the tweak as a support for the additional part of the digest. The primary goal of this modification is to get a better bound, even in the unbounded leakage setting. However, we analyze this design under the perspective of the unpredictability of the TBC for the first time.

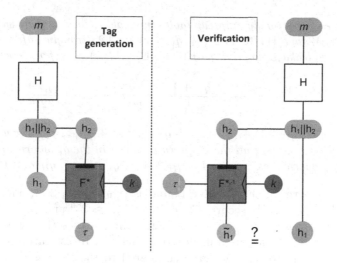

Fig. 2. The leakage resilient HBC-scheme.

5.1 HTBC Description

Let $\mathcal{M} = \{0,1\}^*$ and $\mathcal{TW} = \mathcal{X} = \mathcal{Z} = \{0,1\}^n$. Considering a hash function $H : \mathcal{M} \mapsto \mathcal{X} \times \mathcal{TW} = \{0,1\}^{2n}$ and a tweakable block cipher $F : \mathcal{K} \times \mathcal{TW} \times \mathcal{X} \mapsto \mathcal{Z}$, we build $\mathsf{HTBC} = (\mathsf{Tag}, \mathsf{Vrfy})$:

$\mathsf{Tag}_k(m)$: first compute $h_1 \| h_2 = H(m)$ and $\tau = F_k(h_2, h_1)$ and output τ.
$\mathsf{Vrfy}_k(m, \tau)$: first compute $h_1 \| h_2 = H(m)$ and $\tilde{h}_1 = F^{-1}_{k,h_2}(\tau)$, then output 1 if $h_1 = \tilde{h}_1$, and 0 otherwise.

We stress again that Tag only evaluates F while Vrfy only computes its inverse. HTBC was proposed as the authenticator of TEDT [7] (also adopted in [6,17]), with the motivation to break the birthday security barrier in the Hash-then-Block-cipher HBC. As the hash digest has been increased to $2n$ bits, the standard hash collision-based attack turns unfeasible. We illustrate HTBC in Fig. 2.

5.2 Security of HTBC

The unbounded leakage function pair $\mathsf{L}^* = (\mathsf{L}^*_{\mathsf{Tag}}, \mathsf{L}^*_{\mathsf{Vrfy}})$ of HTBC is defined as

$\mathsf{L}^*_{\mathsf{Tag}}(k, m)$: return $h_1 \| h_2 = H(m)$ and $\mathsf{L}_{\mathsf{Eval}}(k, h_2, h_1)$;
$\mathsf{L}^*_{\mathsf{Vrfy}}(k, m, \tau)$: return $h_1 \| h_2 = H(m)$ and $\tilde{h}_1 = F^{-1}_{k,h_2}(\tau)$ as well as $\mathsf{L}_{\mathsf{Inv}}(k, h_2, \tau)$.

As we rely on the random oracle model to prove the security of HTBC, we include the digests in the leakage to capture the fact that H is actually a public function.

Theorem 2. *Let* $H : \{0,1\}^* \longmapsto \{0,1\}^n \times \{0,1\}^n$ *be a hash function modeled as a random oracle, and* $F^* : \mathcal{K} \times \{0,1\}^n \times \{0,1\}^n \longmapsto \{0,1\}^n$ *be a*

$(q_T, q_V, q_L, t, \epsilon_{\mathsf{SUL2}})$-*strongly unpredictable tweakable block cipher with leakage* $\mathsf{L} = (\mathsf{L_{Eval}}, \mathsf{L_{Inv}})$, *then* HTBC *is a* (q_T, q_V, t, ϵ)-suf-L2 *strongly unforgeable* MAC *with unbounded leakage function pair* $\mathsf{L}^* = (\mathsf{L^*_{Tag}}, \mathsf{L^*_{Vrfy}})$ *as defined above, where*

$$\epsilon \le \frac{(q_H + q_T + q_V)^2}{2^{2n}} + \frac{(q_V + 1)}{\epsilon_{\mathsf{SUL2}}^{-1}} + \frac{q_H^2 q_V}{2^n \cdot \epsilon_{\mathsf{SUL2}}^{-1}} + \frac{q_V(q_H + q_V)}{2^{2n}},$$

and $t_H(q_H + q_T + q_V + 1) + (q_T + q_L - q)t_{\mathsf{F}} + (q_V + q)t_{\mathsf{F}^{-1}} \le t$ *for any* $q \le q_L$, *and where we assume that all the* H-*query involved in the* q_L *queries are already among the* q_H *queries, as long as* $4 \le q_H + q_T + q_V$, $4q_V \le q_H$ *and* $10q_H \le 2^n$.

The leading term in the security bound is $\epsilon_{\mathsf{SUL2}} \cdot q_H^2 q_V 2^{-n}$. This time, for $n = 128$ and $\epsilon_{\mathsf{SUL2}} \approx 2^{-96}$, security holds up to $q_H \approx 2^{80}$ and $q_V = 2^{64}$. As for Theorem 1, we are not aware of a realistic matching attack (i.e., if a reasonable hash function and TBC are used in the construction). Investigating whether the additional $q_H 2^{-n}$ factor that we gain compared to the BC-based construction can get closer to 2^{-n} is an interesting open problem.

The structure of the proof for HTBC is different from that of HBC. The main reason is that the collision resistance of H does not cover all the winning cases when the adversary's τ of the forgery appears in an LTag query. Indeed, we might have $\mathsf{H}(m) = h_1 \| h_2 \ne h_1' \| h_2' = \mathsf{H}(m')$ such that $\mathsf{F}_k(h_2, h_1) = \tau = \mathsf{F}_k(h_2', h_1')$ with m' in an LTag query. That is because F_{k,h_2} and $\mathsf{F}_{k,h_2'}$ can be seen as two different permutations given that $h_2 \ne h_2'$: an output τ defines many possible tweak-input pairs. As we will see the distribution and the freshness of (h_2, τ) will play an important role in the proof.

Idea of the Proof. Let (m, τ) be a forgery and write $\mathsf{H}(m) = h_1 \| h_2$. If no triple of the form $(\star, h_2, \tau)$ appears during the computation of all the evaluations and inversions of F, (h_1, h_2, τ) is a valid fresh triple for F which breaks the unpredictability of the TBC. However, if it is not the case, a triple $(\star, h_2, \tau)$ appears either in the evaluation of F during an LTag query or only in the inversion of F in an LVrfy query. In the former case, as the answer to an LTag query is necessarily valid, the triple $(\star, h_2, \tau)$ must actually be $(\mathsf{F}_k^{-1}(h_2, \tau), h_2, \tau)$, i.e. (h_1, h_2, τ). Of course, if the adversary has made an LTag query on m, it cannot win. If the adversary is successful, it means that it managed to request the computation of a hash value which collides on $\mathsf{H}(m)$, which only occurs with a beyond-birthday probability in $n = |k| = |\tau|$. We can thus focus on the latter case where a triple $(\star, h_2, \tau)$ only appears when answering an LVrfy query, i.e. in an inversion of F.

We split the remaining winning conditions into: (1) m appears as an input of H before ever computing a TBC inversion on input (h_2, τ) when answering a leaking verification query; (2) m appears strictly after the first computation of a TBC inversion on input (h_2, τ) when answering a leaking verification query; no matter whether τ appears first in an LTag answer or in an LVrfy query. We note that we no more need to consider the H computation in the LTag queries as we already dealt with H-collisions. In a nutshell, the first case means the adversary chooses τ depending on the view of the hash value $h_1 \| h_2$ and hence it relates to the unpredictability of F. In the second case, the target $h_1\|h_2$ is fixed in the leaking verification query while the output of $H(m)$ remains uniformly random and independent of the view at that time. By convention, if m and τ first appear for the first time together in an LVrfy query, we first compute $H(m)$ so that we always consider that m appears "before" τ. In addition, we consider the forgery as the $(q_V + 1)$-th LVrfy query.

In case 1, $H(m) = h_1\|h_2$ appears before the computation of a TBC triple $(\star, h_2, \tau)$ which will first be run when answering a leaking verification query. We want to build an adversary B against F which ends by sending (h_1, h_2, τ). To make B successful, we have to prevent B from making an LInv query on input (h_2, τ) earlier, since otherwise (h_1, h_2, τ) is not a winning triple at the end. Such a query can happen only if A manages to make an LVrfy query on some (m', τ) such that $H(m') = h_1'\|h_2'$ with $h_2' = h_2$. Of course, this happens if $m = m'$ and, indeed, A can win if (m, τ) appears in an LVrfy query before the $(q_V + 1)$-th one. This explains the term $\epsilon_{\mathsf{SUL2}}(q_V + 1)$ of the security bound. However, it can also happen if $m' \neq m$. Then, $h_1' \neq h_1$ and (m', τ) is necessarily invalid but we cannot simulate the leaking verification query if we would like to win against F. Fortunately, if the first time (h_2, τ) appears in an LVrfy query is with $m' \neq m$, we know that m appeared in a hash computation earlier for the first time (and it cannot be in an LTag query). To sum up, we cannot build a single B but by considering all the hash computations in the H queries and the LVrfy queries to combine with all the tags in the LVrfy queries, we have at most $(q_H + q_V)q_V$ reductions to build to cover all the possibilities. Fortunately, we only have to consider the messages m' with $H(m') = h_1'\|h_2'$ such that h_2' appears in a subsequent LVrfy query. Furthermore, we can see when this happens before having to invert the TBC with tweak h_2'. The full proof will show that the probability of multi-collision on the h_2'-value involved in the i-th LVrfy query will decrease the probability by a factor of roughly $q_H/2^n$, which gives us a beyond birthday term eventually.

In case 2, the adversary outputs a forgery (m, τ) while (h_2, τ) appears in a leaking verification query before the first computation of $H(m)$. Here, we simply pick the key of the TBC to simulate the forgery experiment. If (h_2, τ) already appears in an LVrfy query the valid triple $(\tilde{h}_1, h_2, \tau)$ is already fixed in the answer to that query (necessarily invalid). Therefore $H(m)$ which is still uniformly random and independent of the view at that time will have to match the target $(\tilde{h}_1, h_2)$. This match thus happens with probability $1/2^{2n}$ for each future hash evaluation in a H-query or in a next LVrfy query. Of course we do not know what will be the right (h_2, τ) until the adversary output its forgery in the finalization phase. So, if (h_2^i, τ^i) denotes the input of the inversion of F in the i-th leaking verification query, we actually defines q_V targets $(\tilde{h}_1^i, h_2^i, \tau^i)$, since $i < q_V + 1$ here. Therefore, the probability that this case occurs is upper-bounded by $q_V(q_H + q_V)/2^{2n}$.

The proof is given in the full version of the paper [8].

6   Conclusion and Open Problems

We revisit the security proofs of MACs based on the "Hash-then-(T)BC" construction, an approach that has often been adopted in the context of leakage-resilient cryptography. While previous works have been modeling the (T)BC as a leak-free component, we only require that the (T)BC remains unpredictable in the presence of leakage, an assumption that has the major advantage of being easy to test on any implementation. We show that unpredictability with leakage is a suitable assumption for the analysis of the leakage-resilience of two standard MAC constructions, a result that has a direct impact on several recent constructions of AE modes of operation that are based on this approach. Apart from making security proofs more satisfactory, relying on unpredictability of the (T)BC rather than on its pseudorandomness prompts for investigating whether block cipher implementations that only seek to offer unpredictability with leakage could also require less rounds and, as a result, deliver better efficiency and cheaper protection against side-channel attacks.

As discussed in the paper, our bounds may not be tight due to some additional computations that are required in our reductions that actual adversaries may not need. Investigating whether these bounds can be improved is therefore an interesting challenge. Besides, for simplicity we model our hash function as an ideal random object (but do not require any form of progammability or other conveniences that come with the random oracle model). This fits well with many applications, for instance when the hash function is based on a sponge that is also traditionally modeled as an ideal permutation. Still, our analysis does not suggest any reason why an ideal object would be needed, and it would therefore be interesting to investigate whether and how this assumption could be relaxed.

As a final note, we conjecture that strong unpredictability with leakage may also be sufficient to prove confidentiality under ideal oracle (e.g., cipher, permutation) assumptions, assorted with oracle-free leakage functions, as introduced in [27] for block ciphers and recently used for the analysis of sponge-based designs [11,17]. Indeed, in such models the leakage about a key is useless as long as it does not lead to a full key-recovery. But as a result, the interpretation of this unpredictability assumption in terms of quantitative security degradation (e.g., in the situation where an implementation is not leak-free but has high enough unpredictability with leakage) is also more delicate: the ideal objects transform an unpredictable value into something that is indistinguishable from random, hence possibly hiding the level of security degradation caused by the leakage.

Acknowledgments. Thomas Peters and François-Xavier Standaert are respectively post-doctoral researcher and senior research associate of the Belgian Fund for Scientific Research (F.R.S.-FNRS). This work has been funded in parts by the European Union through the ERC project SWORD (724725) and the Walloon Region FEDER USERMedia project 501907-379156. Chun Guo was partly supported by the Program of Qilu Young Scholars of Shandong University.

References

1. An, J.H., Bellare, M.: Constructing VIL-MACs from FIL-MACs: message authentication under weakened assumptions. In: Wiener, M. (ed.) CRYPTO 1999. LNCS, vol. 1666, pp. 252–269. Springer, Heidelberg (1999). https://doi.org/10.1007/3-540-48405-1_16
2. Aumasson, J.-P., et al.: CHAE: challenges in authenticated encryption. ECRYPT-CSA D1.1, Revision 1.05 (March 2017). https://chae.cr.yp.to/whitepaper.html
3. Barwell, G., Martin, D.P., Oswald, E., Stam, M.: Authenticated encryption in the face of protocol and side channel leakage. In: Takagi, T., Peyrin, T. (eds.) ASIACRYPT 2017. LNCS, vol. 10624, pp. 693–723. Springer, Cham (2017). https://doi.org/10.1007/978-3-319-70694-8_24
4. Bellare, M., Canetti, R., Krawczyk, H.: Keying hash functions for message authentication. In: Koblitz, N. (ed.) CRYPTO 1996. LNCS, vol. 1109, pp. 1–15. Springer, Heidelberg (1996). https://doi.org/10.1007/3-540-68697-5_1
5. Bellare, M., Kilian, J., Rogaway, P.: The security of the cipher block chaining message authentication code. J. Comput. Syst. Sci. **61**(3), 362–399 (2000)
6. Bellizia, D., et al.: Spook: sponge-based leakage-resilient authenticated encryption with a masked tweakable block cipher. Submission to NIST Lightweight Cryptography (2019). https://www.spook.dev/
7. Berti, F., Guo, C., Pereira, O., Peters, T., Standaert, F.-X.: TEDT, a leakage-resilient AEAD mode for high (physical) security applications. IACR Cryptology ePrint Archive, 2019:137 (2019)
8. Berti, F., Guo, C., Pereira, O., Peters, T., Standaert, F.-X.: Strong authenticity with leakage under weak and falsifiable physical assumptions. Cryptology ePrint Archive, Report 2019/1413 (2019). https://eprint.iacr.org/2019/1413. Full version of this paper
9. Berti, F., Koeune, F., Pereira, O., Peters, T., Standaert, F.-X.: Ciphertext integrity with misuse and leakage: definition and efficient constructions with symmetric primitives. In: AsiaCCS, pp. 37–50. ACM (2018)
10. Berti, F., Pereira, O., Peters, T., Standaert, F.-X.: On leakage-resilient authenticated encryption with decryption leakages. IACR Trans. Symmetric Cryptol. **2017**(3), 271–293 (2017)
11. Dobraunig, C., Mennink, B.: Leakage resilience of the duplex construction. In: Galbraith, S.D., Moriai, S. (eds.) ASIACRYPT 2019. LNCS, vol. 11923, pp. 225–255. Springer, Cham (2019). https://doi.org/10.1007/978-3-030-34618-8_8
12. Dodis, Y., Kiltz, E., Pietrzak, K., Wichs, D.: Message authentication, revisited. In: Pointcheval, D., Johansson, T. (eds.) EUROCRYPT 2012. LNCS, vol. 7237, pp. 355–374. Springer, Heidelberg (2012). https://doi.org/10.1007/978-3-642-29011-4_22
13. Dodis, Y., Steinberger, J.: Message authentication codes from unpredictable block ciphers. In: Halevi, S. (ed.) CRYPTO 2009. LNCS, vol. 5677, pp. 267–285. Springer, Heidelberg (2009). https://doi.org/10.1007/978-3-642-03356-8_16
14. Dodis, Y., Steinberger, J.: Domain extension for MACs beyond the birthday barrier. In: Paterson, K.G. (ed.) EUROCRYPT 2011. LNCS, vol. 6632, pp. 323–342. Springer, Heidelberg (2011). https://doi.org/10.1007/978-3-642-20465-4_19
15. Dziembowski, S., Pietrzak, K.: Leakage-resilient cryptography. In: FOCS, pp. 293–302. IEEE Computer Society (2008)
16. Goudarzi, D., Rivain, M.: How fast can higher-order masking be in software? In: Coron, J.-S., Nielsen, J.B. (eds.) EUROCRYPT 2017. LNCS, vol. 10210, pp. 567–597. Springer, Cham (2017). https://doi.org/10.1007/978-3-319-56620-7_20

17. Guo, C., Pereira, O., Peters, T., Standaert, F.-X.: Towards low-energy leakage-resistant authenticated encryption from the duplex sponge construction. IACR Cryptology ePrint Archive, 2019:193 (2019)

18. Guo, C., Pereira, O., Peters, T., Standaert, F.-X.: Authenticated encryption with nonce misuse and physical leakage: definitions, separation results and first construction. In: Schwabe, P., Thériault, N. (eds.) LATINCRYPT 2019. LNCS, vol. 11774, pp. 150–172. Springer, Cham (2019). https://doi.org/10.1007/978-3-030-30530-7_8

19. Hazay, C., López-Alt, A., Wee, H., Wichs, D.: Leakage-resilient cryptography from minimal assumptions. In: Johansson, T., Nguyen, P.Q. (eds.) EUROCRYPT 2013. LNCS, vol. 7881, pp. 160–176. Springer, Heidelberg (2013). https://doi.org/10.1007/978-3-642-38348-9_10

20. Journault, A., Standaert, F.-X.: Very high order masking: efficient implementation and security evaluation. In: Fischer, W., Homma, N. (eds.) CHES 2017. LNCS, vol. 10529, pp. 623–643. Springer, Cham (2017). https://doi.org/10.1007/978-3-319-66787-4_30

21. Kalai, Y.T., Reyzin, L.: A survey of leakage-resilient cryptography. IACR Cryptology ePrint Archive, 2019:302 (2019)

22. Kocher, P.C.: Timing Attacks on implementations of Diffie-Hellman, RSA, DSS, and other systems. In: Koblitz, N. (ed.) CRYPTO 1996. LNCS, vol. 1109, pp. 104–113. Springer, Heidelberg (1996). https://doi.org/10.1007/3-540-68697-5_9

23. Kocher, P., Jaffe, J., Jun, B.: Differential power analysis. In: Wiener, M. (ed.) CRYPTO 1999. LNCS, vol. 1666, pp. 388–397. Springer, Heidelberg (1999). https://doi.org/10.1007/3-540-48405-1_25

24. Liskov, M., Rivest, R.L., Wagner, D.: Tweakable block ciphers. In: Yung, M. (ed.) CRYPTO 2002. LNCS, vol. 2442, pp. 31–46. Springer, Heidelberg (2002). https://doi.org/10.1007/3-540-45708-9_3

25. Martin, D.P., Oswald, E., Stam, M., Wójcik, M.: A leakage resilient MAC. In: Groth, J. (ed.) IMACC 2015. LNCS, vol. 9496, pp. 295–310. Springer, Cham (2015). https://doi.org/10.1007/978-3-319-27239-9_18

26. Pereira, O., Standaert, F.-X., Vivek, S.: Leakage-resilient authentication and encryption from symmetric cryptographic primitives. In: ACM Conference on Computer and Communications Security, pp. 96–108. ACM (2015)

27. Yu, Y., Standaert, F.-X., Pereira, O., Yung, M.: Practical leakage-resilient pseudorandom generators. In: ACM Conference on Computer and Communications Security, pp. 141–151. ACM (2010)

28. Zhang, L., Wu, W., Wang, P., Zhang, L., Wu, S., Liang, B.: Constructing rate-1 MACs from related-key unpredictable block ciphers: PGV model revisited. In: Hong, S., Iwata, T. (eds.) FSE 2010. LNCS, vol. 6147, pp. 250–269. Springer, Heidelberg (2010). https://doi.org/10.1007/978-3-642-13858-4_14

Mathematical Foundations

Improving ECDLP Computation in Characteristic 2

Fangguo Zhang[1,2]($\boxtimes$), Zhijie Liu[1,2], Ping Wang[3], and Haibo Tian[1,2]

[1] School of Data and Computer Science, Sun Yat-sen University,
Guangzhou 510006, China
`isszhfg@mail.sysu.edu.cn`
[2] Guangdong Key Laboratory of Information Security,
Guangzhou 510006, China
[3] College of Electronics and Information Engineering, Shenzhen University,
Shenzhen 518060, China

Abstract. Pollard rho and its parallelized variants are at present known as the best generic algorithms for computing discrete logarithms in groups of elliptic curves over finite fields. The $r + h$-mixed walk, one of the variant parallelized rho method in characteristic 2, is expected to have r times point addition operations and h times point halving operations. We observe that by reducing the randomness but increasing the ratio of h/r, the overall efficiency for parallelized rho method can be improved. Hence, we try to find the best ratio to get the best overall efficiency for parallelized rho method. And then, we provide an optimal configuration with the best overall efficiency for the parallelized rho method. Our experiments show that the optimal configuration can improve the overall efficiency of ECC2-79 by about 36%. Further, we give algorithms to improve the efficiency of basic operations in $\mathbb{F}_{2^{131}}$ and estimate that the optimal configuration can improve the overall efficiency of ECC2-131 by about 39%.

Keywords: Parallelized rho method · Elliptic curves · Discrete logarithm · Point halving

1 Introduction

Public-key cryptography based on elliptic curves over finite fields was introduced by Koblitz [15] and Miller [16] in 1985. Since then, elliptic curves over finite fields have been used to implement many cryptographic systems and protocols, such as the Diffie-Hellman key agreement scheme [2,7], the elliptic curve variant of the Digital Signature Algorithm [1,17], etc. In elliptic curve cryptography (ECC), the major security consideration is the intractability of the *elliptic curve discrete logarithm problem* (ECDLP).

Let $\mathcal{E}$ be an elliptic curve defined over a finite field $\mathbb{F}_q$. Let $P \in \mathcal{E}$ be a point of prime order n, and let $\langle P \rangle$ be the prime order subgroup of $\mathcal{E}$ generated by P.

© Springer Nature Switzerland AG 2020
Z. Liu and M. Yung (Eds.): Inscrypt 2019, LNCS 12020, pp. 535–550, 2020.
https://doi.org/10.1007/978-3-030-42921-8_32

If $Q \in \langle P \rangle$, then $Q = kP$ for some integer k, $0 \leq k < n$. The problem of finding k, given P, Q, and the parameters of $\mathcal{E}$, is known as the ECDLP.

Up to date, Pollard rho method [18] is the most efficient general algorithm to solve the ECDLP. The pollard rho method works for any cyclic groups and does not make use of any additional structure present in elliptic curve groups. The rho method is a randomized algorithm for computing discrete logarithms based on the Birthday Paradox. More precisely, an iteration function $F : G \to G$ is used to define a pseudo-random sequence Y_i by $Y_{i+1} = F(Y_i)$ for $i = 0, 1, 2, ...$, with some starting value Y_0. The sequence $Y_0, Y_1, Y_2, ...$ represents a walk in the group G. Because the order of the group is finite, the sequence will ultimately reach an element that has occurred before. This is called a *collision* or a *match*.

A distinguished point is one that has some easily checked property such as having a fixed number of leading zero bits. During the pseudo-random walk, distinguished points are stored. Collision can be detected when a distinguished point is encountered twice. Van Oorschot and Viener [24] showed that the modified Pollard rho method which makes use of the distinguished point technique can be parallelized with linear speedup.

The iteration function $F : G \to G$ is a random mapping. In the sense that for any $Y_i \in G$, the function F maps Y_i to each element in G with the same probability $\frac{1}{|G|}$. However, in practice the iteration function $F : G \to G$ is not a truly random mapping, which always results in more iteration requirements. Furthermore, an efficient pseudo random walk for parallel rho method is very important. Here, "efficient" means that the cost of obtaining a new point should require essentially no more than one group operation, and use only constant or polynomial storage in total.

Pollard rho method employs an iterating function of a random walk to produce a sequence of random terms. Most computations use pseudorandom walks where each step is an addition. But walks that include doubling operations can be useful in practice, and more resilient to short cycles. Teske [22] studied two types of random walk: r-adding walk and $(r + q)$-mixed walk (where q is the number of point doubling operations in the iterating function).

Erik Knudsen [13] and Richard Schroeppel [19] independently proposed a new method for scalar multiplication of elliptic curves over binary fields. The idea is to replace all point doublings in double-and-add methods with a potentially faster operation called point halving. Knudsen [13] presented some rough analysis which suggests that scalar multiplication with halvings could be 39% faster than scalar multiplication with doublings ([20] claims a 50% improvement). Bessalov [4] firstly used the idea of halving (he called division of points by two) to ECDLP, however, there was no detailed analysis for his approach. Furthermore, Zhang and Wang [25] proposed a new iteration function ($r + h$-mixed walks, h is the number of point halving operations in the iterating function) for the rho method by exploiting the fact that point halving is more efficient than point addition for elliptic curves over binary fields.

In 1997, Certicom [5] introduced ECC challenges to increase industry acceptance of ECC. The challenges with fields of size less than 100 bits were proposed as exercise and were solved quickly. For the challenges with fields of size more than 100 bits, there are two Levels: Level I, comprising 109-bit and 131-bit challenges; and Level II, comprising 163-bit, 191-bit, 239-bit and 359-bit challenges. There are three kinds of curves for each k-bits challenges: ECCp-k denotes a randomly selected elliptic curve over a prime field; ECC2-k denotes a randomly selected elliptic curve over a characteristic 2 finite field F_{2^m}, where m is prime; and ECC2K-k denotes a Koblitz curve. Untill now, ECC2K-108 [10], ECC2-109, ECCp-109 were solved. The next larger Certicom challenge is ECC2K-130, and further is ECC2-131. Many efforts [3] have been made in the ECC2K-130, but it is still open.

Our Contribution. Experimentally, we show that different curves with the same ratios h/r yield similar performances in $r+h$-mixed walks. Then, we analyze the relationship between the randomness and the ratio in $r + h$-mixed walks. We discover that the overall efficiency for parallelized rho method can be promoted by reducing the randomness but increasing the ratio in $r + h$-mixed walks. Our goal is to provide an optimal configuration with the best overall efficiency by finding the best ratio of h/r. With the theoretical efficiency of point halving, we show that the configuration can make parallelized rho method for binary field about 18.3% more efficient than before (under the assumption that one inverse is equal to eight multiplications). Usually, the overall efficiency for parallelized rho method is up to the practical cost of point halving and point addition. The more efficient the point halving is, the faster the method will be. As a concept verification, we select an optimal configuration to compute ECDLP over ECC2-79 and show that the optimal configuration can improve the overall efficiency of ECC2-79 by about 36%. With the optimization of the basic operations in $\mathbb{F}_{2^{131}}$, we deduce that the optimal configuration can improve the overall efficiency of ECC2-131 by about 39%.

Organization: The rest of this paper is organized as follows. We recall the elliptic curve over finite field with characteristic 2 and the Pollard rho method and its parallelized variant with distinguished point in Sect. 2. In Sect. 3, we analyze the relationship between the ratio of point halving, point addition and the randomness in $r + h$-mixed walks. We discuss our experimental data in detail and apply it in ECC2-79. In Sect. 4, we improve basic operations in $\mathbb{F}_{2^{131}}$ and apply our idea in ECC2-131. The conclusion of this paper is placed in Sect. 5.

2   Preliminaries

In this section, we recall the Pollard rho method for ECDLP computations and its parallelized variant with the distinguished point method. Also, we give the definitions needed throughout the paper.

2.1   ECC and ECDLP

Let $\mathbb{F}_q$ be a finite field of q elements. An elliptic curve $\mathcal{E}$ over $\mathbb{F}_q$ is a cubic curve defined by Weierstrass equation:

$$\mathcal{E} : \; y^2 + a_1 xy + a_3 y = x^3 + a_2 x^2 + a_4 x + a_6 \; (a_i \in \mathbb{F}_q).$$

The set of $\mathbb{F}_q$-rational points of $\mathcal{E}$ is defined as,

$$\mathcal{E}(\mathbb{F}_q) := \{(x, y) \in \mathbb{F}_q \times \mathbb{F}_q : y^2 + a_1 xy + a_3 y = x^3 + a_2 x^2 + a_4 x + a_6\} \cup \{\mathcal{O}\},$$

where $\mathcal{O}$ is the point at infinity. Equipped with the so-called "chord-and-tangent" rule, $\mathcal{E}(\mathbb{F}_q)$ becomes an Abelian group [21].

In this paper, we consider the elliptic curve over finite field with characteristic 2. Note that if the characteristic of the finite field is 2, the Weierstrass equation of an elliptic curve $\mathcal{E}$ can be transformed into a short but isomorphic one,

$$y^2 + xy = x^3 + ax^2 + b,$$

where $a, b \in \mathbb{F}_{2^m}, b \neq 0$.

Let n be a prime integer which is coprime to q. Let GenG be an elliptic curve group generation algorithm. Taking as input a security parameter 1^κ, GenG outputs q which defines a finite field $\mathbb{F}_q$, an Elliptic Curve $\mathcal{E}$ over $\mathbb{F}_q$, and a point $P \in \mathcal{E}(\mathbb{F}_q)$ of order n. Denote by $\langle P \rangle$ the group of order n generated by P. If $Q \in \langle P \rangle$, it must holds that $Q = sP$ for some integer s, $0 \leq s < n$, which is called the logarithm of Q to the base P and denoted by $\log_P Q$. The problem of finding s, given P, Q and the parameters of $\mathcal{E}$, is known as the Elliptic Curve Discrete Logarithm Problem (ECDLP).

2.2   Point Halving

For an elliptic curve $\mathcal{E}$ over finite field with characteristic 2, let $H = (x_1, y_1) \in \mathcal{E}$ be a point with $x_1 \neq 0$. Then $Q = 2H = (x_2, y_2)$ can be computed as follows:

$$x_2 = \lambda^2 + \lambda + a, \; y_2 = x_1^2 + (\lambda + 1)x_2, \; \lambda = x_1 + \frac{y_1}{x_1}.$$

Point halving is the reverse operation of point doubling: given $Q = (x_2, y_2)$, compute $H \triangleq \frac{1}{2}Q = (x_1, y_1)$ such that $Q = 2H$. One can compute point halving as follows: solve $\lambda^2 + \lambda = x_2 + a$ for λ, and $x_1^2 = y_2 + (\lambda + 1)x_2$ for x_1, and finally compute $y_1 = x_1^2 + \lambda x_1$. More precisely, we summarize the above steps in the following Algorithm 1.

Further, one can generalize Algorithm 1 to the case of curve $\mathcal{E}$ with $\mathrm{Tr}(a) = 0$, that is $|\mathcal{E}(\mathbb{F}_{2^m})| = 2^k n$ with $k > 1$ and n is odd [13]. Fong et al. [8] provided a careful analysis of the actual efficiency of point halving for elliptic curves over binary fields with polynomial basis, such as the NIST-recommended random binary curves over $\mathbb{F}_{2^m}$ [9]. We summarize the results as follows. Let M, S and I denote the cost of field multiplication, squaring and inversion respectively. Then

---

Algorithm 1. Point halving

Input: λ-representation (x_2, λ_Q) or affine representation (x_2, y_2) of $Q \in \langle P \rangle$.
Output: λ-representation (x_1, λ_P) of $H = (x_1, y_1) \in \langle P \rangle$, where $Q = 2H$.
1: compute λ such that $\lambda^2 + \lambda = x_2 + a$.
2: If the input is in λ-representation, then $t = x_2(x_2 + \lambda_Q + \lambda)$; else $t = y_2 + x_2\lambda$.
3: **if** $\mathrm{Tr}(t) = 0$ **then**
4:     $\lambda_P \leftarrow \lambda$, $x_1 \leftarrow \sqrt{t + x_2}$.
5: **else**
6:     $\lambda_P \leftarrow \lambda + 1$, $x_1 \leftarrow \sqrt{t}$.
7: **end if**
8: Return (x_1, λ_P).

---

experimentally, the cost of solving the quadratic equation is approximately in the range $\frac{1}{2}M$ to $\frac{2}{3}M$, and the cost of computing square roots in $\mathbb{F}_{2^m}$ is expected to be in the range $\frac{1}{8}M$ to $\frac{1}{2}M$. As a result, the cost of a point halving with λ-representation is roughly in the range of $[\frac{13}{8}M, \frac{13}{6}M]$. While point addition and doubling in affine coordinates need approximately the same costs: $I + 2M + S$. A careful analysis of the software implementation of multiplication and inversion in $\mathbb{F}_{2^m}$ is necessary for a fair comparison of halving and addition. Extensive experiments from [8] suggest that a realistic estimate of the ratio I/M of inversion to multiplication cost is 8 (or higher). Thus the cost of point addition or doubling in affine coordinates is generally larger than $10M$.

2.3   ECDLP Using Parallelized Pollard Rho and Halving

Pollard [18] proposed an elegant generic algorithm for the discrete logarithms based on the Birthday Paradox and called it the rho method, which is an improvement over the well-known "baby-step giant-step" algorithm, attributed to Shanks [6]. Pollard rho method works by first defining a sequence of elements that will be periodically recurrent, then looking for a *match* in the sequence. The *match* will lead to a solution of the discrete logarithm problem with high probability. The two key ideas involved are the iteration function for generating the sequence and the cycle-finding algorithm for detecting a *match*.

According to the $r + q$-mixed walks of Teske [22], let r and q be integers and then $M_1, \ldots, M_r \in G$. Let $v : G \rightarrow 1, \ldots, r + q$ be a hash function. A walk (Y_i) in the finite group G such that $Y_{i+1} = F(Y_i)$ for some iterating function $F : G \rightarrow G$ is called $r + q$-*mixed* if F is of the form

$$Y_{i+1} = F(Y_i) = \begin{cases} Y_i + M_{v(Y_i)} & v(Y_i) \in \{1, \cdots, r\}, \\ 2Y_i & v(Y_i) \in \{r+1, \cdots, r+q\}. \end{cases}$$

One advantage of the point halving is that it is more efficient than point doubling for elliptic curve over binary fields. Zhang and Wang [25] introduced point halving into the random walk to speed up the iteration for the rho method.

Let P be a point of prime order n on an elliptic curve $\mathcal{E}$ over binary field, and let G be the subgroup of $\mathcal{E}$ generated by P. For any $Q \in G$, to compute k such that $Q = kP$, we generate $2r$ random numbers,

$$m_j, n_j \in \{0, 1, \cdots, n-1\}, \text{ for } j = 1, 2, \cdots, r.$$

Then we precompute r multipliers $M_1, M_2, \cdots, M_r$ where,

$$M_j = m_j P + n_j Q, \text{ for } j = 1, 2, \cdots, r.$$

Define a hash function,

$$v : G \rightarrow \{1, 2, \cdots, r + h\}.$$

The iteration function $F : G \rightarrow G$ is called $r + h$-mixed walks if F defined as,

$$Y_{i+1} = F(Y_i) = \begin{cases} Y_i + M_{v(Y_i)} & v(Y_i) \in \{1, \cdots, r\} \\ \frac{1}{2} Y_i & v(Y_i) \in \{r+1, \cdots, r+h\} \end{cases}$$

Let the initial value $Y_0 = a_0 P + b_0 Q$ where a_0 and b_0 are two random numbers in $[0, n-1]$. Then each Y_i has the form $a_i P + b_i Q$, and the sequence (a_i) (and similarly for (b_i)) can be computed as follows,

$$a_{i+1} = \begin{cases} a_i + m_{v(Y_i)} & (\text{mod } n) & v(Y_i) \in \{1, \cdots, r\} \\ \frac{1}{2} a_i & (\text{mod } n) & a_i \text{ is even and } v(Y_i) \in \{r+1, \cdots, r+h\} \\ \frac{1}{2}(a_i + n) & (\text{mod } n) & a_i \text{ is odd and } v(Y_i) \in \{r+1, \cdots, r+h\} \end{cases}$$

Correspondingly, once finding a *match* (Y_i, Y_j), we have the following equation:

$$a_i P + b_i Q = a_j P + b_j Q$$

Then, if $\gcd(b_i - b_j, n) = 1$, we have $k = (a_j - a_i)(b_i - b_j)^{-1} \bmod n$.

On the other hand, to find the collision in the pseudo-random walks, it always need storage. In order to minimize the storage requirements, a collision detection algorithm can be applied with a small penalty in the running time. The idea of the distinguished point method is to search for a *match* not among all terms of the sequence, but only among a small subset of terms that satisfy a certain distinguishing property. It works as follows: One defines a set D, a subset of G, that consists of group elements that satisfy a certain distinguishing property. During the pseudo-random walks, points that satisfy the distinguishing property are stored. The collision can be detected when a distinguished point is encountered twice.

Van Oorschot and Viener [24] showed that the expected speedup of the direct parallelization of the Pollard rho method, using m processors, is only a factor of $\sqrt{m}$. This is a very inefficient usage of parallelization. They provided a modified version of Pollard rho method that make use of the distinguished point technique can be parallelized with linear speedup. That is, the expected running time of the modified version, using m processors, is roughly $\sqrt{\pi |G|/2}/m$ group operations.

In the modified version, to perform a parallel collision search each processor proceeds as follows. Select a random starting point $Y_0 \in G$ and produce the trail of points $Y_{i+1} = F(Y_i)$, for $i = 0, 1, 2, \ldots$, until a distinguished point Y_d is reached based on some easily testable distinguishing property. Then, store Y_d and start producing a new trail from a new random starting point Y_0. Finally, one can find the collision among these stored distinguished points to solve the ECDLP.

3   Improving Parallelized Pollard Rho with an Optimal Configuration

In this section, we show that different curves with the same ratios h/r yield similar performances in $r + h$-mixed walks. Further, we consider the relationship between the randomness and the ratio in $r + h$-mixed walks. The "randomness" can be treated as a sum that is total number of solving ECDLP. The more random it is, the fewer walks it takes. We discover that the overall efficiency for parallelized rho method can be improved by reducing randomness but increasing the ratio.

Furthermore, we try to find the best ratio h/r to improve the overall efficiency for parallelized rho method. And then, we offer an optimal configuration with the best overall efficiency for parallelized rho method. Under the theoretical efficiency of point halving, the overall efficiency of parallelized rho method of binary field can be improved by about 18.30% by using the optimal configuration. And our experiments show that the optimal configuration can improve the overall efficiency of ECC2-79 by about 36%.

3.1   Getting an Optimal Configuration

Computing (Y_i, a_i, b_i) repeatedly, we try to find a match (Y_i, Y_j) for some $j \neq i$ with the $r + h$-mixed walks. According to [23], Teske showed that $r + q$-mixed walks with $r \geq 16$ and $q/r \approx 1/4$ yielded a performance that was similar to a random walk performance, while the performance got worse if the ratio got much larger than 1. Experimentally, the $r + h$-mixed walks have a similar randomness to $r + q$-mixed walks. As the ratio of h/r is increased, the performance will get worse, that means the walks is needed more until a match is found.

Let Nols be an average number of iterations performed until a match is found under the $r + h$-mixed walks. The experimental statistical average value of the randomness can be defined as:

$$L_{r,h} = \frac{\text{Nols}}{\sqrt{|G|}}.$$

Let A be an average time spent of point addition and H be an average time spent of point halving. The total time spent of finding a match or reaching the first collision can be calculated as:

$$T'(A, H, r, h) = \frac{A \cdot r + H \cdot h}{r + h} \cdot \text{Nols}.$$

Let λ be a cost ratio of time spent of point addition and point halving, that is $\lambda = \frac{A}{H}$. More generally, the overall efficiency of finding a match can be calculated as:

$$T(r, h, \lambda) = \frac{r \cdot \lambda + h}{r + h} \cdot L_{r,h}.$$

Teske [23] tried to find the best randomness to improve parallelized rho method with $r + q$-mixed walks. Compared with the goal of Teske, our aim is to find a minimum total time spent of finding a match to accelerate the speed of parallelized rho method. In the case of a random walk, the density function [11] belongs to a certain Weibull distribution, such distributions are extensively studied in reliability engineering. Thus, we can use the reliability engineering method to choose the size of the sample space carefully. And Teske suggested that if we worked with a sample space of size 1000, the average values may differ up to 5%, while choosing size with 10000 produces fairly constant average values. This opinion can be used as a guideline for our later experiments.

To judge the performance of $r + h$-mixed walks, we conduct experiments with dozens of different elliptic curve subgroups of prime order over $\mathbb{F}_{2^{41}}$ and $\mathbb{F}_{2^{57}}$, respectively. For each elliptic curve, we randomly generate a point P and fix a integer k, $0 \leq k < n$, where n is a order of P. After that, we calculate the point Q by $Q = kP$. We structure the instances of ECDLP with the point pair (P, Q) for each elliptic curve to find the fixed integer k.

We choose several combinations of r and h for each instance of ECDLP. With the thousand times solved the ECDLP, we count the average $L_{r,h}$. Note that, in our experiments, the minimum number of subset of group G is 32. Here, we make sure $r \geq 16$ when the ratio h/r is 1, as shown in Table 1. And next, taking the implementation efficiency of the iteration function into consideration, we select 64, 128 and 256 as the numbers of subsets, respectively. Furthermore, we can get more details about the relationship between the randomness with the ratio, as shown in Tables 2, 3 and 4.

Table 1. The average $L_{r,h}$ whit 32 subsets of group G

r+h (#subset)	r (#addings)	h (#halvings)	Average $L_{r,h}$ of $\mathbb{F}_{2^{41}}$	Average $L_{r,h}$ of $\mathbb{F}_{2^{57}}$	Average $L_{r,h}$
32	16	16	1.4958	1.4244	1.4601
	8	24	1.9190	1.9433	1.9312
	6	26	2.1091	2.1500	2.1295
	4	28	2.6254	2.6623	2.6439
	2	30	3.6989	3.7155	3.7072
	1	31	5.1782	5.1372	5.1577

According to our experimental results, with the same ratios and the same number of subsets, there is an interesting phenomenon. Different elliptic curve

Table 2. The average $L_{r,h}$ whit 64 subsets of group G

r+h (#subset)	r (#addings)	h (#halvings)	Average $L_{r,h}$ of $\mathbb{F}_{2^{41}}$	Average $L_{r,h}$ of $\mathbb{F}_{2^{57}}$	Average $L_{r,h}$
64	32	32	1.4856	1.4100	1.4478
	16	48	1.8655	1.8632	1.8644
	8	56	2.6280	2.5501	2.5890
	6	58	2.9908	2.9240	2.9574
	5	59	3.2596	3.1933	3.2264
	4	60	3.6693	3.5374	3.6033
	2	62	5.0605	4.8527	4.9566
	1	63	7.0727	7.2036	7.1381

Table 3. The average $L_{r,h}$ whit 128 subsets of group G

r+h (#subset)	r (#addings)	h (#halvings)	Average $L_{r,h}$ of $\mathbb{F}_{2^{41}}$	Average $L_{r,h}$ of $\mathbb{F}_{2^{57}}$	Average $L_{r,h}$
128	64	64	1.4718	1.4028	1.4373
	43	85	1.6285	1.6677	1.6481
	32	96	1.9071	1.8794	1.8933
	21	107	2.2507	2.1703	2.2105
	16	112	2.6329	2.6080	2.6204
	8	120	3.6251	3.6493	3.6372
	4	124	5.0127	4.9852	4.9989
	2	126	7.1445	7.3946	7.2696
	1	127	9.9285	9.9537	9.9411

Table 4. The average $L_{r,h}$ whit 256 subsets of group G

r+h (#subset)	r (#addings)	h (#halvings)	Average $L_{r,h}$ of $\mathbb{F}_{2^{41}}$	Average $L_{r,h}$ of $\mathbb{F}_{2^{57}}$	Average $L_{r,h}$
256	128	128	1.4201	1.3941	1.4071
	64	192	1.9278	1.9215	1.9246
	32	224	2.5516	2.5768	2.5642
	18	238	3.4033	3.2808	3.3420
	16	240	3.5853	3.5826	3.5840
	13	243	3.8557	3.9467	3.9012
	8	248	5.1596	5.0083	5.0839
	4	252	6.9975	7.2173	7.1074
	2	254	10.3106	10.1010	10.2058
	1	255	14.3612	14.3776	14.3694

subgroups of prime order obtain the similar performances in $r + h$-mixed walks. For example, in 32 subsets of group G, when $h/r = 1$, $L_{r,h}$ in $\mathbb{F}_{2^{41}}$ and $\mathbb{F}_{2^{57}}$ both are approximate 1.46 and when $h/r = 3$, they are approximate 1.93. For the same instances of the ECDLP, if the scale of subsets of group be fixed, the iteration function will have an analogous route to search a collision. So, different elliptic curve subgroups of prime order with the same ratios get very similar results in the case of same instances of the ECDLP.

Moreover, the group G will be divided more finely, if the number of subsets are increased. For example, we can get a ratio 59/5 in 64 instead of in 32 subsets. Although the group G can be divided more carefully by increasing the size of subsets, the benefit is not obvious. Considering the implementation efficiency of the iteration function F in $r+h$-mixed walks and the benefit, the largest partition of group is 256 subsets which are enough in our experiments. On this basis, we get optimal configurations with the minimum overall efficiency for parallelized rho method by computing the experimental results in above table, that is $T(r, h, \lambda) = Min\{\frac{r \cdot \lambda + h}{r+h} \cdot L_{r,h}\}$, as shown in Table 5.

Table 5. The optimal configuration in $r+h$-mixed walks

Cost ratio λ	Optimal configuration r:h	Minimum $T(r, h, \lambda)$	Minimum $T(\frac{r+h}{2}, \frac{r+h}{2}, \lambda)$
1	128:128	1.4071	1.4071
2	128:128	2.1107	2.1107
3	43:85	2.7554	2.8746
4	16:48	3.2627	3.5179
5	21:107	3.6612	4.2215
6	21:107	4.0238	4.9251
7	21:107	4.3865	5.6286
8	21:107	4.7492	6.3322
9	21:107	5.1118	7.0358
10	21:107	5.3881	7.7394
11	21:107	5.6620	8.4430
12	18:238	5.9269	9.1466
13	18:238	6.1619	9.8502

In theory, the cost of point addition in affine coordinates is $I + 2M + S$ in $\mathbb{F}_{2^m}$. Assuming that the practical estimate of the ratio I/M of inversion to multiplication cost is 8, then the cost of point addition in affine coordinates is generally larger than $10M$. The cost of point halving is about $\frac{13}{8}M$. Further, the cost ratio λ is at least 6. With our experimental data in Table 5, we get the minimum overall efficiency for parallelized rho method $T(21, 107, 6) = 4.0238$. Namely, the optimal configuration is $21+107$ subsets, where the number of point addition and point halving is 21 and 107, respectively. Compared with the total overall efficiency of original $r + h$-mixed walks $T(64, 64, 6) = 4.9251$, the optimal configuration can improve the overall efficiency of parallelized rho method by about $\frac{4.9251 - 4.0238}{4.9251} * 100\% \approx 18.30\%$.

3.2 Testing in ECC2-79 with an Optimal Configuration

Usually, the actual cost ratio λ determines the overall speed improved for parallelized rho method. The more efficient the point halving is, the faster the method will be. Besides, the practical cost of point halving and point addition generally has a gap with the theoretical value. Hence, To illustrate our thought more clearly, we give a practical example ECC2-79.

The challenge curve ECC2-79 is the elliptic curve over $\mathbb{F}_{2^{79}}$ with

$$a = 4A2E38A8F66D7F4C385F, b = 2C0BB31C6BECC03D68A7.$$

The group order is $\sharp E(\mathbb{F}_{2^{79}}) = 2n$, where

$$n = 302231454903954479142443,$$

is a 79-bit prime number.

The challenge is given with respect to a polynomial-basis representation of $\mathbb{F}_{2^{79}} = \mathbb{F}_2[z]/f(z)$ with $f(z) = z^{79} + z^9 + 1$. The field elements are naturally given as bit strings with respect to this basis; the Certicom challenge represents them as hexadecimal numbers, padded with 0's on the left, by grouping four bits into one hexadecimal number. The base point P and the challenge point Q have coordinates:

$$P_x = 30CB127B63E42792F10F, \; P_y = 547B2C88266BB04F713B,$$

$$Q_x = 00202A9F035014497325, \; Q_y = 5175A64859552F97C129.$$

We represent a 79-bit polynomial with a 128-bit vectors in our computing platform. The number of cpu cycle counts of point addition and point halving are 1823 and 103, respectively (all cpu cycle counts were obtained on one core of an Intel Core i7-782x(Skylake-X) at 3.60 GHZ, running Ubuntu 18.04 LTS). So, the cost ratio λ is about 18. Further, the optimal configuration is $13 + 243$ subsets and the minimum overall efficiency for parallelized rho method is $T(13, 243, 18) = 7.2691$. Compared with the overall efficiency of original $r + h$-mixed $T(128, 128, 18) = 13.3681$, our optimal configuration can improve the overall efficiency of ECC2-79 by about $\frac{13.3681 - 7.2691}{13.3681} * 100\% \approx 45.62\%$.

To truly reflect the increased efficiency of the optimal configuration, we compute the ECC2-79 and count the average time in our workstation. The statistical results of our experiments in Table 6 reveal that the actual value $\frac{22137640 - 14073260}{22137640} * 100\% \approx 36.43\%$ has a deviation with theoretical value 45.62%. In practice, each iteration requires additional evaluation, e.g., computing a_i, computing b_i, etc. As the ratio of h/r be increased, more iterations are required. Thus, the time consumed by the additional calculations cannot be ignored. This is why our experimental results differ from the theoretical ones. In this config-uration with $13 + 243$ subsets, experimentally, the deviation is about 9%. The optimal configuration can still improve the overall efficiency for parallelized rho method, although there is a deviation with the increase of the number of itera-tions.

Table 6. The average time in $\mathbb{F}_{2^{79}}$ until a match is found with 16 threads

Cost ratio λ	Optimal configuration r : h	Average time
18	128 : 128	22137640 ms
	13 : 243	14073260 ms

4   Apply to Break ECC2-131

The challenge curve ECC2-131 is the elliptic curve over $\mathbb{F}_{2^{131}}$ with

$$a = 07EBCB7EECC296A1C4A1A14F2C9E44352E,$$

$$b = 00610B0A57C73649AD0093BDD622A61D81.$$

The group order is $\sharp E(\mathbb{F}_{2^{131}}) = 2n$, where

$$n = 1361129467683753853898082827025389846147$$

is a 130-bit prime number.

The challenge is given with respect to a polynomial-basis representation of $\mathbb{F}_{2^{131}} = \mathbb{F}_2[z]/f(z)$ with $f(z) = z^{131} + z^{13} + z^2 + z + 1$. Field elements are naturally given as bit strings with respect to this basis; the Certicom challenge represents them as hexadecimal numbers, padded with 0's on the left, by grouping four bits into one hexadecimal number. The base point P and the challenge point Q have coordinates:

$$P_x = 00439CBC8DC73AA981030D5BC57B331663,$$

$$P_y = 014904C07D4F25A16C2DE036D60B762BD4,$$

$$Q_x = 0602339C5DB0E9C694AC8908528C51C440,$$

$$Q_y = 04F7B99169FA1A0F2737813742B1588CB8.$$

The ECC2-131 challenge is more complicated than ECC2K-130. In this paper, we focus on ECC2-131. First of all, we improve the basic operations in $\mathbb{F}_{2^{131}}$ and provide an optimal configuration for ECDLP in ECC2-131. We show that our configuration can improve the overall efficiency of ECC2-131 by about 39%.

4.1 Multiplication and Squaring in $\mathbb{F}_{2^{131}}$

To make the algorithms more efficient for software implementation, we use the implementation platform which has a 64-bit architecture to design the bits. The bits of a 64-bit architecture are numbered from 0 to 63, with the rightmost bit of the architecture designated as bit 0. The elements of $\mathbb{F}_{2^{131}}$ are the binary polynomials of degree at most 130. A field element $a(z) = a_{130}z^{130} + \cdots + a_2z^2 + a_1z + a_0$ is associated with the binary vector $a = (a_{130}, \ldots, a_2, a_1, a_0)$ of length 131. In software, we store a in an array of three 64-bit architectures: $a = (a[2], a[1], a[0])$, where the rightmost bit of $a[0]$ is a_0, and the leftmost 61 bits of $a[2]$ are unused and always set to 0.

It is well-known that the modern cpu has intrinsic functions which allow two 128-bit architectures to do bitwise operations. So in our implementation, we use two 64-bit architectures to make up a 128-bit architectures. Which means that we use an array of two 128-bit architectures to store the field elements a in software, just like $a = (A[1], A[0])$. The rightmost bit of $A[0]$ is a_0, and the leftmost 125 bits of $A[1]$ are unused and always set to 0.

Most modern cpus have PCLMULQDQ instruction which is the most interesting for fast multiplication of two binary polynomials represented by two 64-bits. The multiplication of two polynomials with degree $d \leq 64$ can be performed by a single instruction. According to the instruction, we use the Karatsuba-Ofman algorithm [14, section 4.3.3] to find the minimum number of the scalar multiplication operations and squaring operations.

4.2 Solving the Quadratic Equation in $\mathbb{F}_{2^{131}}$

The basic algorithm of solving the quadratic equation is described in [8]. Here, we propose a more efficient way to implement the algorithm by introducing a constant matrix in $\mathbb{F}_{2^{131}}$. Let's review the proposed algorithm in Algorithm 2. Here, the half-trace $H : \mathbb{F}_{2^m} \to \mathbb{F}_{2^m}$ be defined as

$$H(c) = \sum_{i=0}^{(m-1)/2} c^{2^{2i}}. \ c \in F_{2^m}, m \text{ is odd.}$$

We introduce the $PEXTU64$ instruction [12] to improve the efficiency of the step 5 in Algorithm 2. This instruction can extract bits from unsigned 64-bit integer at the corresponding bit locations specified by mask to contiguous low bits in destination and the remaining upper bits in destination are set to zero. In addition, we precompute the sum value $\sum_{i=1}^{(m-1)/2} c_{2i-1}H(z^{2i-1})$. And then, we store them into a constant matrix HF. As soon as we get c_{odd}, we will get the sum with looking up the constant matrix immediately. The detail is shown in Algorithm 3.

4.3 Getting an Optimal Configuration in ECC2-131

To evaluate the performance, the algorithms are implemented in C++ language. All cpu cycle counts were obtained on one core of an Intel Core i7-782x(Skylake-

---

Algorithm 2. Solve $z^2 + z = c$ in $\mathbb{F}_{2^m}$

Input: $c = \sum_{i=0}^{m-1} c_i z^i \in F_{2^m}$ with $Tr(c) = 0$.
Output: A solution s of $z^2 + z = c$.
1: Precompute $H(z^i)$ for odd i, $0 \le i \le m - 2$.
2: $s \leftarrow 0$.
3: **for** $i = \frac{m-1}{2}$ **to** 1 **do**
4:    **if** $c_{2i} = 1$ **then**
5:       $c \leftarrow c + z^i, s \leftarrow s + z^i$.
6:    **end if**
7: **end for**
8: $s \leftarrow s + \sum_{i=1}^{(m-1)/2} c_{2i-1} H(z^{2i-1})$.
9: **return** s..

Algorithm 3. Solve $z^2 + z = c$ in $\mathbb{F}_{2^{131}}$

Input: $c = (C[1], C[0]) = \{(0, c[2]), (c[1], c[0])\} = (0, \cdots, 0, c_{130}, \cdots, c_0)$.
Output: $r = (R[1], R[0])$ where R is a solution of $z^2 + z = c$.
1: Precompute $\sum_{i=1}^{64} c_{2i-1} H(z^{2i-1})$ store into a constant matrix HF and $H(z^{129})$.
2: $\Omega = [0x5555555500000000, 0x55550000, 0x5500, 0x50, 0x4]$.
3: $S = (s[1], s[0])$, $T = (t[1], t[0])$.
4: $t[1] = PEXTU64(c[2], 0x5)$.
5: $c[1] = c[1] \oplus t[1]$, $s[1] = s[1] \oplus t[1]$.
6: $t[0] = PEXTU64(c[1], 0x5555555555555555) \lll 32$.
7: $c[0] = c[0] \oplus t[0]$, $s[0] = s[0] \oplus t[0]$.
8: **for all** $k \in \Omega$ and $j = 16$ **do**
9:    $t[0] = PEXTU64(c[0], k) \lll j$.
10:    $c[0] = c[0] \oplus t[0]$, $s[0] = s[0] \oplus t[0]$.
11:    $j = j/2$
12: **end for**
13: **if** $c_{129} = 1$ **then**
14:    $r = H(z^{129})$.
15: **else**
16:    $r = 0$.
17: **end if**
18: $t[1] = PEXTU64(c[1], 0xaaaaaaaaaaaaaaaa) \lll 32$.
19: $t[0] = PEXTU64(c[0], 0xaaaaaaaaaaaaaaaa) \oplus t[1]$.
20: **return** $r = r + HF[t[0]]$.

X) at 3.60 GHZ, running Ubuntu 18.04 LTS. Table 7 presents the number of cpu cycles of algorithms in ECC2-131.

With the number of cpu cycle counts in Table 7, we get the cost ratio λ is about 14. Further, the optimal configuration is $18+238$ subsets and the minimum overall efficiency is $T(18, 238, 14) = 6.3969$. Compared with the original $r + h$-mixed walks that the total overall efficiency is $T(128, 128, 14) = 10.5537$, our optimal configuration is expected to bring about $\frac{10.5537-6.3969}{10.5537} * 100\% \approx 39.39\%$ time gain.

Table 7. Cpu cycle counts of algorithms in ECC2-131.

Operations	Cycle counts
Squaring	23
Multiplication	29
Square root	38
Solve the quadratic equation	40
Inversion	3167
Point halving	232
Point adding	3229

5 Conclusion

In $r + h$-mixed walks, different curves with the same ratios h/r have similar performances with the same instance of the ECDLP. Therefore, we consider the relationship between the randomness and the ratio in $r + h$-mixed walks to improve parallelized rho method. The overall efficiency for parallelized rho method can be improved by reducing the randomness but increasing the ratio in $r + h$-mixed walks. We provide an optimal configuration by finding the best ratio.

We show that the configuration can improve the overall efficiency of parallelized rho method by 18.30% under the theoretical efficiency of point halving. The speedup for parallelized rho method is usually up to the practical cost of point halving and point addition. If the point halving is more efficient than point addition, the method can get higher acceleration. In practice, our experiments show that the optimal configuration can improve the overall efficiency of ECC2-79 by about 36%. With the optimization of the basic operations in $\mathbb{F}_{2^{131}}$, we deduce that the optimal configuration can improve the overall efficiency of ECC2-131 by about 39%.

Acknowledgement. This work is supported by the National Key R&D Program of China (No. 2017 YFB0802500), the National Natural Science Foundation of China (No. 61672550, No. 61972429), the Natural Science Foundation of Guangdong Province of China (No. 2016A030310027, No. 2018A0303130133) and Shenzhen Technology Plan (No. JCYJ20170818144026871, JCYJ20170818140234295).

References

1. ANSI X9.62-199x: Public Key Cryptography for the Financial Services Industry: The Elliptic Curve Digital Signature Algorithm (ECDSA), 13 January 1998
2. ANSI X9.63-199x: Public Key Cryptography for the Financial Services Industry: Elliptic Curve Key Agreement and Transport Protocols, 5 October 1997
3. Bailey, D.V., Batina, L., et al.: Breaking ECC2K-130. Cryptology ePrint Archive, Report 2009/541 (2009)

 4. Bessalov, A.V.: A method of solution of the problem of taking the discrete logarithm on an elliptic curve by division of points by two. Cybern. Syst. Anal. **37**(6), 820–823 (2001)
 5. Certicom: Certicom ECC Challenge (2009). https://www.certicom.com/content/dam/certicom/images/pdfs/challenge-2009.pdf
 6. Cohen, H.: A Course in Computational Algebraic Number Theory, vol. 139. Springer, Heidelberg (1993). https://doi.org/10.1007/978-3-662-02945-9
 7. Diffie, W., Hellman, M.: New directions in cryptography. IEEE Trans. Inf. Theory **22**(6), 644–654 (1976)
 8. Fong, K., Hankerson, D., et al.: Field inversion and point halving revisited. IEEE Trans. Comput. **53**(8), 1047–1059 (2004)
 9. Gallagher, P.: Digital signature standard. Federal Information Processing Standards Publication, February 2013:186–3
10. Harley, R.: Elliptic curve discrete logarithms project. http://pauillac.inria.fr/~harley/ecdl/
11. Harris, B.: Probability distribution related to random mappings. Ann. Math. Statist. **31**, 1045–1062 (1960)
12. Intel: Intel intrinsics guide. http://software.intel.com/sites/landingpage/IntrinsicsGuide/
13. Knudsen, E.W.: Elliptic scalar multiplication using point halving. In: Lam, K.-Y., Okamoto, E., Xing, C. (eds.) ASIACRYPT 1999. LNCS, vol. 1716, pp. 135–149. Springer, Heidelberg (1999). https://doi.org/10.1007/978-3-540-48000-6_12
14. Knuth, D.E.: Seminumerical Algorithms, the Art of Computer Programming. Addison-Wesley, Boston (1997)
15. Koblitz, N.: Elliptic curve cryptosystems. Math. Comput. **48**(177), 203–209 (1987)
16. Miller, V.S.: Use of elliptic curves in cryptography. In: Williams, H.C. (ed.) CRYPTO 1985. LNCS, vol. 218, pp. 417–426. Springer, Heidelberg (1986). https://doi.org/10.1007/3-540-39799-X_31
17. FIPS, PUB: Digital Signature Standard, Federal Information Processing Standards Publication 186. US Department of Commerce, National Institute of Standards and Technology (NIST), National Technical Information Service. Springfield, Virginia (1994)
18. Pollard, J.: Monte Carlo methods for index computation mod p. Math. Comput. **32**(143), 918–924 (1978)
19. Schroeppel, R.: Elliptic curve point halving wins big. In: The 2nd Midwest Arithmetical Geometry in Cryptography Workshop, Urbana, Illinois, November 2000
20. Schroeppel, R.: Elliptic curve point ambiguity resolution apparatus and method. U.S. Patent 7,200,225, 3 Apr 2007
21. Silverman, J.H.: The Arithmetic of Elliptic Curves. GTM, vol. 106. Springer, New York (2009). https://doi.org/10.1007/978-0-387-09494-6
22. Teske, E.: Speeding up Pollard's rho method for computing discrete logarithms. In: Buhler, J.P. (ed.) ANTS 1998. LNCS, vol. 1423, pp. 541–554. Springer, Heidelberg (1998). https://doi.org/10.1007/BFb0054891
23. Teske, E.: On random walks for Pollard's rho method. Math. Comput. **70**(234), 809–825 (2001)
24. Van Oorschot, P., Wiener, M.: Parallel collision search with cryptanalytic applications. J. Cryptol. **12**(1), 1–28 (1999)
25. Zhang, F., Wang, P.: Speeding up elliptic curve discrete logarithm computations with point halving. Des. Codes Cryptogr. **67**(2), 197–208 (2013)

Linear Complexity of New q-ary Generalized Cyclotomic Sequences of Period $2p^n$

Vladimir Edemskiy$^{(\boxtimes)}$ and Nikita Sokolovskii

Novgorod State University, Veliky Novgorod, Russia
vladimir.edemsky@novsu.ru, sokolovskiy.nikita@gmail.com

Abstract. In this paper, we construct new q-ary generalized cyclotomic sequences of length $2p^n$. We study the linear complexity of these sequences over the finite field of order q and show that they have high linear complexity when $n \geq 2$. These sequences are constructed by new generalized cyclotomic classes presented by Zeng et al.

Keywords: Linear complexity · q-ary sequences · Cyclotomy · Finite field

1 Introduction

Pseudo-random sequences are widely used in many fields, for example in cryptography. Linear complexity (L) is a very important merit factor for measuring unpredictability of pseudo-random sequences, which are often used as key stream sequences in stream ciphers. This is defined as the length of the shortest linear feedback shift register that can generate the sequence [10].

One of the methods for constructing sequences with high linear complexity is to use cyclotomic and generalized cyclotomic classes. There are a lot of papers devoted to studying the linear complexity of cyclotomic sequences and generalized cyclotomic sequences. In particular, in recent years there has been some research on generalized cyclotomic binary and non-binary sequences of period p^n [1,2,4,13,15] (see also references therein), where p is an odd prime. Binary sequences considered in [19] were defined from generalized cyclotomic classes modulo $2p^m$ for an integer $m \geq 1$. Later the results from [19] were generalized in [5,9].

New generalized cyclotomic classes were presented by Zeng et al. in [18]. Using them Xiao et al. presented a new family of cyclotomic binary sequences of period p^n [14]. The linear complexity of these sequences was studied in [6, 14,16]. Recently, in [11] Ouyang et al. presented two new classes of generalized cyclotomic binary sequences of period $2p^m$ and computed their linear complexity.

V. Edemskiy and N. Sokolovskii were supported by RFBR-NSFC according to the research project No. 19-51-53003.

Z. Liu and M. Yung (Eds.): Inscrypt 2019, LNCS 12020, pp. 551–559, 2020.
https://doi.org/10.1007/978-3-030-42921-8_33

They used new generalized cyclotomic classes and the method from [6]. These results were generalized in [7].

As noted in [16] we have a link between new cyclotomic classes and Euler quotient. We mention here that Du et al. defined a class of d-ary sequence using the Euler quotient, which can be regarded as a generalization of the binary case, and then analyze the linear complexity of the proposed sequence [3]. Very recently, Ye et al. published a paper devoted to studying the linear complexity of d-ary sequence using the Euler quotient with a period p^n [17].

In this paper, we generalize the construction from [6,11] and we present q-ary generalized cyclotomic sequences of period $2p^n$. We study the linear complexity of these sequences over a finite field of q elements and show that these sequences have high linear complexity when $n \geq 2$. Thus, it can be said that this article develops the results presented in [3,6,11,17].

2   Preliminaries

Throughout this paper, we will denote by $\mathbb{Z}_N$ the ring of integers modulo N for a positive integer N, and by $\mathbb{Z}_N^*$ the multiplicative group of $\mathbb{Z}_N$. We need some preliminary notation and results before we begin.

Let $s^\infty = (s_0, s_1, s_2, \dots)$ be a q-ary sequence of period N and $S(x) = s_0 + s_1 x + \cdots + s_{N-1} x^{N-1}$. By Blahut's theorem the linear complexity of s^∞ can be given by

$$L = N - \left| \left\{ i \in \mathbb{Z}_N \mid S(\alpha^i) = 0 \right\} \right|, \tag{1}$$

where α is a primitive N-th root of unity in an extension field of $\mathbb{F}_q$, $\gcd(N, q) = 1$.

Let p be an odd prime and $p = ef + 1$, where e, f are positive integers. Let g be a primitive root modulo p^n. It is well known [8] that an odd number from g or $g + p^n$ is also a primitive root modulo $2p^j$ for each integer $j \geq 1$. Hence, we can assume that g is an odd number. Below we recall the definitions of generalized cyclotomic classes introduced in [18] and [11].

Let n be a positive integer. For $j = 1, 2, \cdots, n$, denote $d_j = p^{j-1}f$ and define

$$D_i^{(p^j)} = \left\{ g^{i+t \cdot d_j} \pmod{p^j} \mid 0 \leq t < e \right\}, 0 \leq i < d_j \text{ and}$$

$$D_i^{(2p^j)} = \left\{ g^{i+t \cdot d_j} \pmod{2p^j} \mid 0 \leq t < e \right\}, \quad 0 \leq i < d_j.$$

By definitions we see that $\left\{ D_0^{(p^j)}, D_1^{(p^j)}, \dots, D_{d_j-1}^{(p^j)} \right\}$ and $\left\{ D_0^{(2p^j)}, D_1^{(2p^j)}, \dots, D_{d_j-1}^{(2p^j)} \right\}$ form partitions of $\mathbb{Z}_{p^j}^*$ and $\mathbb{Z}_{2p^j}^*$ for each integer $j \geq 1$, respectively.

Let q be an odd prime and $q \mid f$ and let b be an integer with $0 \leq b < p^{n-1}f$. Denote $d_j/q = p^{j-1}f/q$ by h_j and define the following sets for $k = 0, 1, \dots, q-1$

$$C_k^{(2p^j)} = \bigcup_{i=kh_j}^{(k+1)h_j-1} \left(D_{(i+b) \pmod{d_j}}^{(2p^j)} \cup 2D_{(i+b) \pmod{d_j}}^{(2p^j)} \right), \text{ and } \mathscr{C}_k^{(2p^n)} = \bigcup_{j=1}^{n} p^{n-j} C_k^{(2p^j)}.$$

It is clear that $\mathbb{Z}_{2p^n} = \mathscr{C}_0^{(2p^n)} \cup \cdots \cup \mathscr{C}_{q-1}^{(2p^n)} \cup \{0\} \cup \{p^n\}$ and $|\mathscr{C}_j^{(p^n)}| = 2(p^n-1)/q$.

A family of almost balanced q-ary sequences $s^\infty = (s_0, s_1, s_2, \dots)$ of period $2p^n$ can thus be defined as

$$s_i = \begin{cases} k, & \text{if } i \ (\text{mod } 2p^n) \in \mathscr{C}_k^{(p^n)}, \\ y, & \text{if } i \ (\text{mod } 2p^n) = 0, \\ z, & \text{if } i \ (\text{mod } 2p^n) = p^n, \end{cases} \qquad (2)$$

where $y, z \in \mathbb{F}_q, y \pm z \neq 0$.

In this paper we will study the linear complexity of these sequences over $\mathbb{F}_q$, $q > 2$.

3   Linear Complexity of Generalized Cyclotomic Sequences

This section will investigate the linear complexity of s^∞ defined in (2) for some integers f such that $q|f$. We will limit ourselves here with p such that $q^{p-1} \not\equiv 1$ (mod p^2). By [12] $p : q^{p-1} \equiv 1$ (mod p^2) is not frequent. If $2^{p-1} \equiv 1$ (mod p^2) then p is called Wieferich prime. The main result in this paper is given as follows.

Theorem 1. Let $p = ef + 1$ be an odd prime with $q^{p-1} \not\equiv 1$ (mod p^2), $2^{p-1} \not\equiv 1$ (mod p^2) and q divides f. Let s^∞ be a generalized cyclotomic q-ary sequence of period $2p^n$ defined in (2). Then the linear complexity of s^∞ over $\mathbb{F}_q$ is given by

$$L = 2p^n - r \cdot \text{ord}_p(q), \quad 0 \leq r \leq \frac{(q+1)(p-1)}{q \, \text{ord}_p(q)}.$$

Furthermore, $0 \leq r \leq \frac{(p-1)}{\text{ord}_p(q)}$ for $v|\frac{f}{q}$ or $v = 2$, $v \neq f$, where $v = \gcd\left(\frac{p-1}{\text{ord}_p(q)}, f\right)$ and $\text{ord}_p(q)$ denote the order of q modulo p.

We will first give some subsidiary statements, and then investigate the linear complexity of s^∞ defined in (2).

Let $S(x) = s_0 + s_1 x + \cdots + s_{2p^n-1} x^{2p^n-1}$ for the generalized cyclotomic sequences s^∞ defined in (2). Then,

$$S(x) = \sum_{l=0}^{q-1} l \sum_{j=1}^{n} \sum_{i=lh_j}^{(l+1)h_j-1} \left(\sum_{\substack{t \in D_{i+b}^{(2p^j)} \ (\text{mod } d_j)}} x^{p^{n-j}t} + \sum_{\substack{t \in 2D_{i+b}^{(2p^j)} \ (\text{mod } d_j)}} x^{p^{n-j}t} \right) + y + zx^{p^n}.$$

$$(3)$$

For convenience of presentation, we define polynomials

$$E_i^{(p^j)}(x) = \sum_{\substack{t \in D_{i+b}^{(p^j)} \ (\text{mod } d_j)}} x^t, \quad 1 \leq j \leq n, 0 \leq i < d_j, \qquad (4)$$

and

$$G_k^{(p^j)}(x) = \sum_{l=0}^{q-1} l \sum_{i=lh_j}^{lh_j+h_j-1} E_{i+k \pmod{d_j}}^{(p^j)}(x), \quad 0 \le k < d_j,$$

$$F_k^{(p^m)}(x) = \sum_{j=1}^{m} (G_{k+\mathrm{ind}_g^{(p^j)}2}^{(p^j)}(x^{p^{m-j}}) - G_k^{(p^j)}(x^{p^{m-j}})) + y - z, \quad m = 1, 2, \cdots, n.$$

$$H_k^{(p^m)}(x) = \sum_{j=1}^{m} (G_k^{(p^j)}(x^{p^{m-j}}) + G_{k+\mathrm{ind}_g^{(p^j)}2}^{(p^j)}(x^{p^{m-j}})) + y + z.$$

$$(5)$$

Notice that the subscripts i in $E_i^{(p^j)}$, $G_i^{(p^j)}(x)$, $F_i^{(p^j)}(x)$ and $H_i^{(p^j)}(x)$ are all taken modulo the order d_j. In the rest of this paper the modulo operation will be omitted when no confusion can arise.

Let $\overline{\mathbb{F}}_q$ be an algebraic closure of $\mathbb{F}_q$ and $\beta_n \in \overline{\mathbb{F}}_q$ be a primitive p^n-th root of unity. Denote $\beta_j = \beta_n^{p^{n-j}}$, and $\alpha_j = -\beta_j, j = 1, 2 \ldots, n-1$. Then β_j, α_j are primitive p^j-th root and $2p^j$-th root of unity in an extension of the field $\mathbb{F}_q$, respectively.

Lemma 1. *For $S(x), F_n^{(p^j)}(x)$ and $H_n^{(p^j)}(x)$ defined as in (3), (5) we have*

(i) $S(\alpha_n^a) = F_n^{(p^j)}(\beta_n^a)$ *for $a \equiv 1 \pmod{2}$; and*
(ii) $S(\alpha_n^a) = H_n^{(p^j)}(\beta_n^a)$ *for $a \equiv 0 \pmod{2}$, where $\alpha_n = -\beta_n$, β_n is a p^n-th primitive root of unity and $a \in \mathbb{N}$.*

The statements of this lemma follows from (3)–(5).

By (1) and Lemma 1 the linear complexity of s^∞ in (2) can thus be given by

$$L = 2p^n - \left| \{ i \in \mathbb{Z}_{p^n} \mid F_b^{(p^n)}(\beta_n^i) = 0 \} \right| - \left| \{ i \in \mathbb{Z}_{p^n} \mid H_b^{(p^n)}(\beta_n^i) = 0 \} \right|. \quad (6)$$

It is clear from (3)–(5) that the properties of $F_b^{(p^n)}(x)$ and $H_b^{(p^n)}(x)$ depend on the properties of the polynomials $E_i^{(p^j)}(x)$ and $G_i^{(p^j)}(x)$ for $1 \le j \le n$ and $0 \le i < d_j$. Some basic properties of these polynomials are given in the following lemma.

Lemma 2. *Let $\beta_j = \beta_n^{p^{n-j}}$, $1 \le j \le n$, be a p^j-th primitive root of unity. Given any element $a \in D_k^{(p^j)}$, we have*

(i) $E_i^{(p^j)}(\beta_j^{p^l a}) = E_{i+k}^{(p^{j-l})}(\beta_{j-l})$ *and* $G_i^{(p^j)}(\beta_j^{p^l a}) = G_{i+k}^{(p^{j-l})}(\beta_{j-l})$ *for $0 \le l < j$; and*
(ii) $E_i^{(p^j)}(\beta_j^{p^l a}) = e \pmod{q}$ *and* $G_i^{(p^j)}(\alpha_j^{p^l a}) = 0$ *for $l \ge j$.*

The proof of this lemma is similar to the proof of Lemma 6 from [6].

The following proposition characterizes some properties of $F_i^{(p^m)}(x)$ and $H_i^{(p^m)}(x)$.

Proposition 1. *For any $a \in D_k^{(p^j)}$, we have*

(i) $F_i^{(p^m)}(\beta_m^{p^l a}) = F_{i+k}^{(p^{m-l})}(\beta_{m-l})$ *and* $H_i^{(p^m)}(\beta_m^{p^l a}) = H_{i+k}^{(p^{m-l})}(\beta_{m-l})$ *for* $0 \leq l < m$; *and*

(ii) $\sum_{j=1}^{m} G_k^{(p^j)}(\beta_j) + 1 = \sum_{j=1}^{m} G_{k+h_m}^{(p^j)}(\beta_j)$, *where* $h_m = d_m/q = p^{m-1}f/q$; *and*

(iii) $F_{i+h_m}^{(p^m)}(\beta_m^a) = F_i^{(p^m)}(\beta_m^a)$; *and*

(iv) $H_{i+h_m}^{(p^m)}(\beta_m^a) = H_i^{(p^m)}(\beta_m^a) + 2$.

Proof. (i) The first statement of this lemma follows from the definition in (5) and Lemma 2.

(ii) By definition we see that

$$\sum_{j=1}^{m} G_k^{(p^j)}(\beta_j^a) = \sum_{j=1}^{m} \sum_{u=0}^{q-1} u \sum_{i=uh_j}^{uh_j+h_j-1} E_{i+k}^{(p^j)}(\beta_j^a).$$

Since $h_m \equiv h_j \pmod{d_j}$, it follows that

$$\sum_{j=1}^{m} G_{k+h_m}^{(p^j)}(\beta_j) + \sum_{j=1}^{m} \sum_{u=0}^{q-1} \sum_{i=uh_j}^{uh_j+h_j-1} E_{i+k+h_j}^{(p^j)}(\beta_j^a) = \sum_{j=1}^{m} G_k^{(p^j)}(\beta_j).$$

The desired result thus follows.

(iii) Since by (5) $F_k^{(p^m)}(\beta_m^a) = \sum_{j=1}^{m} \left(G_{k+\text{ind}_g^{(p^j)}2}^{(p^j)}(\beta_j^a) - G_k^{(p^j)}(\beta_j^a) \right) + y - z$, $m = 1, 2, \cdots, n$, it follows from (ii) that $F_{i+h_m}^{(p^m)}(\beta_m^a) = F_i^{(p^m)}(\beta_m^a)$

(iv) This statement can be proved the same way as (iii).   □

Corollary 1. $\sum_{j=1}^{m} G_{i+kh_m}^{(p^j)}(\beta_j) = \sum_{j=1}^{m} G_i^{(p^j)}(\beta_j) + k$ *and* $H_{i+kh_m}^{(p^m)}(\beta_m^a) = H_i^{(p^m)}(\beta_m^a) + 2k$ *for* $k = 1, 2, q-1$.

Corollary 2. *Let* $\text{ind}_g^{(p^m)}2 = hp^{m-1}f/q$ *for* $h \in \mathbb{N}$. *Then* $F_i^{(p^m)}(\beta_m) = h + y - z$.

Remark 1. If $2^{p-1} \not\equiv 1 \pmod{p^2}$, i.e., p is non-Wieferich prime then $\text{ind}_g^{(p^m)}2 \not\equiv 0 \pmod{p^{m-1}}$ for any $m > 1$ [6].

We now examine the value of $F_b^{(p^n)}(\beta_n^i)$ and $H_b^{(p^n)}(\beta_n^i)$.

Proposition 2. *Let* q: $q^{p-1} \not\equiv 1 \pmod{p^2}$ *and* $2^{p-1} \not\equiv 1 \pmod{p^2}$. *Then* $F_b^{(p^n)}(\alpha_n^i) \neq 0$ *and* $H_b^{(p^n)}(\alpha_n^i) \neq 0$ *for* i: $i \not\equiv 0 \pmod{p^{n-1}}$.

Proof. (i) We will show $F_b^{(p^n)}(\beta_n^i) \neq 0$ by contradiction. Without loss of generality, by Proposition 1 (i) we can assume $F_0^{(p^m)}(\beta_m) = 0$ for $m > 1$.

By Proposition 1 (iii) we have $F_{d_m/q}^{(p^m)}(\beta_m) = 0$. Suppose $q \equiv g^u \pmod{p^m}$ for some integer u. It is clear that $u \not\equiv 0 \pmod{p}$. Let $u_1 \equiv u \pmod{d_m}$ and

$v = \gcd(u_1, d_m)$. Since the subscript of $F_i^{(p^m)}(x)$ is taken modulo d_m, it is easily seen as in [6] that

$$0 = F_{d_m/q}^{(p^m)}(\beta_m) = F_{d_m/q+iv}^{(p^m)}(\beta_m), \quad i = 1, \cdots, d_m/v - 1.$$

Hence, $F_{f/q}^{(p^m)}(\beta_m) = 0$ and $F_0^{(p^m)}(\beta_m) - F_{f/q}^{(p^m)}(\beta_m) = 0$.

For the convenience we denote $\mathrm{ind}_g^{(p^m)} 2$ by T_m and let

$$\xi = -G_0^{(p^m)}(\beta_m) + G_{T_m}^{(p^m)}(\beta_m) + G_{f/q}^{(p^m)}(\beta_m) - G_{f/q+T_m}^{(p^m)}(\beta_m).$$

Then

$$\xi = -\sum_{j=1}^{m-1} \left(-G_0^{(p^j)}(\beta_j) + G_{T_j}^{(p^j)}(\beta_j) + G_{f/q}^{(p^j)}(\beta_j) - G_{f/q+T_j}^{(p^j)}(\beta_j) \right) \in \mathbb{F}_q(\beta_{m-1}).$$

On the other hand, by eliminating the overlapping terms in $G_0^{(p^m)}(\beta_m)$, $G_{T_m}^{(p^m)}(\beta_m)$, $G_{f/q}^{(p^m)}(\beta_m)$ and $G_{f/q+T_m}^{(p^m)}(\beta_m)$ we obtain

$$\xi = -\sum_{t \in \mathscr{D}} \beta_m^t + \sum_{t \in \mathscr{C}} \beta_m^t,$$

where $\mathscr{D} = D_0^{(p^m)} \cup \cdots \cup D_{f/q-1}^{(p^m)} \cup \cdots \cup D_{(q-1)d_m/q}^{(p^m)} \cup \cdots \cup D_{(q-1)d_m/q+f/q-1}^{(p^m)}$ and $\mathscr{C} = D_{T_m}^{(p^m)} \cup \cdots \cup D_{f/q-1+T_m}^{(p^m)} \cup \cdots \cup D_{(q-1)d_m/q+T_m}^{(p^m)} \cup \cdots \cup D_{(q-1)d_m/q+f/q-1+T_m}^{(p^m)}$.

We have $D_{ld_m/q+t}^{(p^m)} \pmod{p} = D_{lf/q+t \pmod{f}}^{(p)}$. Hence $\mathscr{D} \pmod{p} = \mathscr{C} \pmod{p} = \mathbb{Z}_p^*$ Thus, by letting $t \pmod{p} = \bar{t}$ for any $t \in \mathscr{D} \cup \mathscr{C}$ we have

$$\xi = \sum_{t \in \mathscr{C}} \beta_m^t - \sum_{l \in \mathscr{D}} \beta_m^l = \sum_{t \in \mathscr{C}} \beta_{m-1}^{(t-\bar{t})/p} \beta_m^{\bar{t}} - \sum_{l \in \mathscr{D}} \beta_{m-1}^{(l-\bar{l})/p} \beta_m^{\bar{l}} = \sum_{i=1}^{p-1} c_i \beta_m^i,$$

and $c_i \in \mathbb{F}_q(\beta_{m-1})$.

Here we need to consider two cases.

(i) Suppose to exist i such that $c_i \neq 0$. It means that β_m is a root of the polynomial $f(x) = \sum_{i=1}^{p-1} c_i x^i - \xi$ over $\mathbb{F}_q(\beta_{m-1})$. This implies $[\mathbb{F}_q(\beta_m) : \mathbb{F}_q(\beta_{m-1})] < p$, as in [6] we will have a contradiction in this case.

(ii) Let $c_i = 0$ for $i = 1, 2, \ldots, p-1$. In this case for any $t \in \mathscr{C}$ there exists $l \in \mathscr{D}$ such that $l \equiv t \pmod{p}$ and $\beta_{m-1}^{(t-\bar{t})/p} = \beta_{m-1}^{(l-\bar{l})/p}$. Hence $t \equiv l \pmod{p^m}$. Since $|\mathscr{C}| = |\mathscr{D}| = p-1$, it follows that $\mathscr{C} = \mathscr{D}$. For $\mathrm{ind}_g^{(p^m)} 2 \not\equiv 0 \pmod{p^{m-1} f/q}$ this is impossible.

The statement $H_b^{(p^n)}(\beta_n^i) \neq 0$ we can proof the same way as above. $\square$

By Proposition 2, we only need to study the values of $F_b^{(p)}(\beta_1^a)$ and $H_b^{(p)}(\beta_1^a)$ for any $a \in \mathbb{Z}_p^*$. The following lemma examines the value of $H_i^{(p)}(\beta_1)$ according to the relation between f and $\mathrm{ord}_p(q)$.

Lemma 3. *Let $p = ef + 1$ be an odd prime, q divides f and $v = \gcd(\frac{p-1}{\mathrm{ord}_p(q)}, f)$. Then,*

(i) $\left| \left\{ k \in \mathbb{Z}_f \mid H_k^{(p)}(\beta_1) = 0 \right\} \right| \leq f/q$ *and* $\left| \left\{ k \in \mathbb{Z}_f \mid H_k^{(p)}(\beta_1) = 0 \right\} \right| = f/q$ *if $v = f$;*

(ii) $\left| \left\{ k \in \mathbb{Z}_f \mid H_k^{(p)}(\beta_1) = 0 \right\} \right| = 0$ *if $v \mid \frac{f}{q}$, or $v = 2$ and $f \neq v$.*

Proof. (i) By Corollary 1 we have $H_{k+lf/q}^{(p)}(\beta_1) = H_k^{(p)}(\beta_1) + 2l$ for $l = 1, \ldots, q-1$

Thus, if $H_k^{(p)}(\beta_1) = 0$ then $H_{k+lf/q}^{(p)}(\beta_1) \neq 0$ for $l = 1, \ldots, q-1$ and we obtain the first part of statement (i).

Further, suppose $v = f$; then $q \in D_0^{(p)}$ and $H_k^{(p)}(\beta_1) \in \mathbb{F}_q$ for any k. In this case we see that just one of numbers $H_{k+lf/q}^{(p)}(\beta_1)$, $l = 0, 1, \ldots, q-1$ is equal to zero.

(ii) The proof of this statement is similar to the proof of Proposition 3 from [6]. $\qquad \square$

Proof of Theorem 1. By (6) the linear complexity of s^∞ is given by

$$L = 2p^n - \left| \{ i \in \mathbb{Z}_{p^n} \mid F_b^{(p^n)}(\beta_n^i) = 0 \} \right| - \left| \{ i \in \mathbb{Z}_{p^n} \mid H_b^{(p^n)}(\beta_n^i) = 0 \} \right|.$$

By Proposition 2 $F_b^{(p^n)}(\beta_n^i) \neq 0$, $H_b^{(p^n)}(\beta_n^i \neq 0)$ when i belongs to $\mathbb{Z}_{p^n} \setminus p^{n-1}\mathbb{Z}_p$. From definition we have $F_b^{(p^n)}(0) = y - z \neq 0$ and $H_b^{(p^n)}(0) = y + z \neq 0$.

Further, if $F_0^{(p)}(\beta_1) = 0$ then $0 = \left(F_0^{(p)}(\beta_1) \right)^q = F_{\mathrm{ind}_g q}^{(p)}(\beta_1)$ and so on. Hence, $|\{a : F_0^{(p)}(\beta_1^a) = 0, a = 1, 2, \ldots, p-1\}| = r \cdot \mathrm{ord}_p(q) - 1$, $0 \leq r \leq \frac{p-1}{\mathrm{ord}_p(q)}$. By Lemma 3 $|\{a : H_0^{(p)}(\beta_1^a) = 0, a = 1, 2, \ldots, p-1\}| = r \cdot \mathrm{ord}_p(q) - 1$, $0 \leq r \leq \frac{p-1}{q \cdot \mathrm{ord}_p(q)}$. So, we immediately obtain the desired result from two last formulae and (6).

4   Remarks

In this section, we will look at a couple of special cases and make a few comments on the variants that are not considered in Theorem 1.

Lemma 4. *If $\mathrm{ind}_g^{(p^m)} 2 = hp^{m-1}f/q$ for $h \in \mathbb{N}$ then*

$$|\{a : F_b^{(p^m)}(\beta_m^a) = 0, a \in \mathbb{Z}_{p^m}\}| = \begin{cases} p^m - 1, & \text{if } h + y - z \equiv 0 \pmod{q}, \\ 0, & \text{if } h + y - z \not\equiv 0 \pmod{q}. \end{cases}$$

The statement of this lemma follows from Corollary 2.

Hence, the linear complexity of s^∞ depends on $\text{ind}_g^{(p^m)} 2$ for Wieferich primes. So, if W is the maximum degree such that $2^{p-1} \equiv 1 \pmod{p^{W-1}}$ and $n \le W$ then L can be less than a half of period for $h + y - z \equiv 0 \pmod{q}$. It is worth noting that s^∞ will have high linear complexity for $h + y - z \not\equiv 0 \pmod{q}$, but in this case the 1-error linear complexity $L_1(s^\infty) \le p^m + 1$. So, it is better not to use these sequences in cryptography.

Note that in a general case the estimate of r in Theorem 1 is a difficult task. The value r depends on $p, q, \text{ind}_g^{(p)} 2$ and $\text{ind}_g^{(p)} q$. We will illustrate it by a simple example.

Let $q = f$. By Corollaries 1, 2 and the proof of Lemma 4 we see that

$$F_i^{(p)}(\beta_1^a) = \text{ind}_g^{(p)} 2 + y - z \quad \text{and} \quad H_i^{(p)}(\beta_1^a) = 2G_i^{(p)}(\beta_1^a) + \text{ind}_g^{(p)} 2 + y + z$$

for $a \in \mathbb{Z}_p^*$. So, by Proposition 2 we obtain for non-Wieferich primes p that

$$L = \begin{cases} 2p^n - (q+1)(p-1)/q, & \text{if } \text{ind}_g^{(p)} 2 + y - z \equiv 0 (\text{mod } q) \text{ and } q \in D_0^{(p)}, \\ 2p^n - p + 1, & \text{if } \text{ind}_g^{(p)} 2 + y - z \equiv 0 (\text{mod } q) \text{ and } q \notin D_0^{(p)}, \\ 2p^n - (p-1)/q, & \text{if } \text{ind}_g^{(p)} 2 + y - z \not\equiv 0 (\text{mod } q) \text{ and } q \in D_0^{(p)}, \\ 2p^n, & \text{otherwise.} \end{cases}$$

We will have even more options for L when $f/q \ge 2$.

Finally, suppose that $q^{p-1} \equiv 1 \pmod{p_0^m}$ and $q^{p-1} \not\equiv 1 \pmod{p_0^m}$ for $m_0 > 1$. In this case Proposition 2 will be true for $n > m_0$ and the linear complexity of s^∞ over $\mathbb{F}_q$ will be high when $n > m_0$ and p is an non-Wieferich prime.

5 Conclusion

We presented new q-ary generalized cyclotomic sequences of length $2p^n$ and studied the linear complexity of these sequences over the finite field of order q. We showed that they have high linear complexity when $n \ge 2$. These sequences are constructed by new generalized cyclotomic classes presented by Zeng et al. We generalized the results about new binary cyclotomic sequences of Ouyang et al. and the results of Ye et al. obtained earlier.

References

1. Ding, C., Helleseth, T.: New generalized cyclotomy and its applications. Finite Fields Appl. **4**(2), 140–166 (1998)
2. Du, X., Chen, Z.: A generalization of the Hall's sextic residue sequences. Inf. Sci. **222**, 784–794 (2013)
3. Du, X.N., Wu, C.H., Wei, W.Y.: An extension of binary threshold sequence from Fermat quotient. Adv. Math. Commun. **10**(4), 743–752 (2016)
4. Edemskiy, V.: About computation of the linear complexity of generalized cyclotomic sequences with period p^{n+1}. Des. Codes Cryptograph. **61**(3), 251–260 (2011)

5. Edemskiy, V., Antonova, O.: The linear complexity of generalized cyclotomic sequences with period $2p^n$. AAECC **25**(3), 213–223 (2014)
6. Edemskiy, V., Li, C., Zeng, X., Helleseth, T.: The linear complexity of generalized cyclotomic binary sequences of period p^n. Des. Codes Cryptograph. **87**(5), 1183–1197 (2019)
7. Edemskiy, V., Wu, C.: On the linear complexity of binary sequences derived from generalized cyclotomic classes modulo $2^n p^m$. WSEAS Trans. Math. **18**, 197–202 (2019)
8. Ireland, K., Rosen, M.: A Classical Introduction to Modern Number Theory. Graduate Texts in Mathematics. Springer, Heidelberg (1990). https://doi.org/10.1007/978-1-4757-2103-4
9. Ke, P., Zhang, J., Zhang, S.: On the linear complexity and the autocorrelation of generalized cyclotomic binary sequences of length $2p^m$. Des. Codes Cryptograph. **67**(3), 325–339 (2013)
10. Lidl, R., Niederreiter, H.: Finite Fields. Encyclopedia of Mathematics and Its Applications, vol. 20. Addison-Wesley, Boston (1983)
11. Ouyang, Y., Xie, X.: Linear complexity of generalized cyclotomic sequences of period $2p^m$. Des. Codes Crypt. **87**, 2585–2596 (2019). https://doi.org/10.1007/s10623-019-00638-5
12. Montgomery, P.L.: New solutions of $a^{p-1} \equiv 1 (mod\ p^2)$. Math. Comput. **61**(203), 361–363 (1993). Special Issue Dedicated to Derrick Henry Lehmer
13. Wu, C., Chen, Z., Du, X.: The linear complexity of q-ary generalized cyclotomic sequences of period p^m. J. Wuhan Univ. **59**(2), 129–136 (2013)
14. Xiao, Z., Zeng, X., Li, C., Helleseth, T.: New generalized cyclotomic binary sequences of period p^2. Des. Codes Cryptograph. **86**(7), 1483–1497 (2018)
15. Yan, T., Li, S., Xiao, G.: On the linear complexity of generalized cyclotomic sequences with the period p^m. Appl. Math. Lett. **21**(2), 187–193 (2008)
16. Ye, Z., Ke, P., Wu, C.: A further study of the linear complexity of new binary cyclotomic sequence of length p^n. AAECC (2018). https://doi.org/10.1007/s00200-018-0368-9
17. Ye, Z., Ke, P., Chen, Z.: Linear complexity of d-ary sequence derived from euler quotients over $GF(q)$. Chin. J. Electron. **28**(3), 529–534 (2019)
18. Zeng, X., Cai, H., Tang, X., Yang, Y.: Optimal frequency hopping sequences of odd length. IEEE Trans. Inf. Theor. **59**(5), 3237–3248 (2013)
19. Zhang, J.W., Zhao, C.A., Ma, X.: Linear complexity of generalized cyclotomic binary sequences of length $2p^m$. AAECC **21**, 93–108 (2010)

Author Index

Printed in the United States
By Bookmasters